College Football "Bowl Games of the 21st Century"
{Part II – 2011-2020}

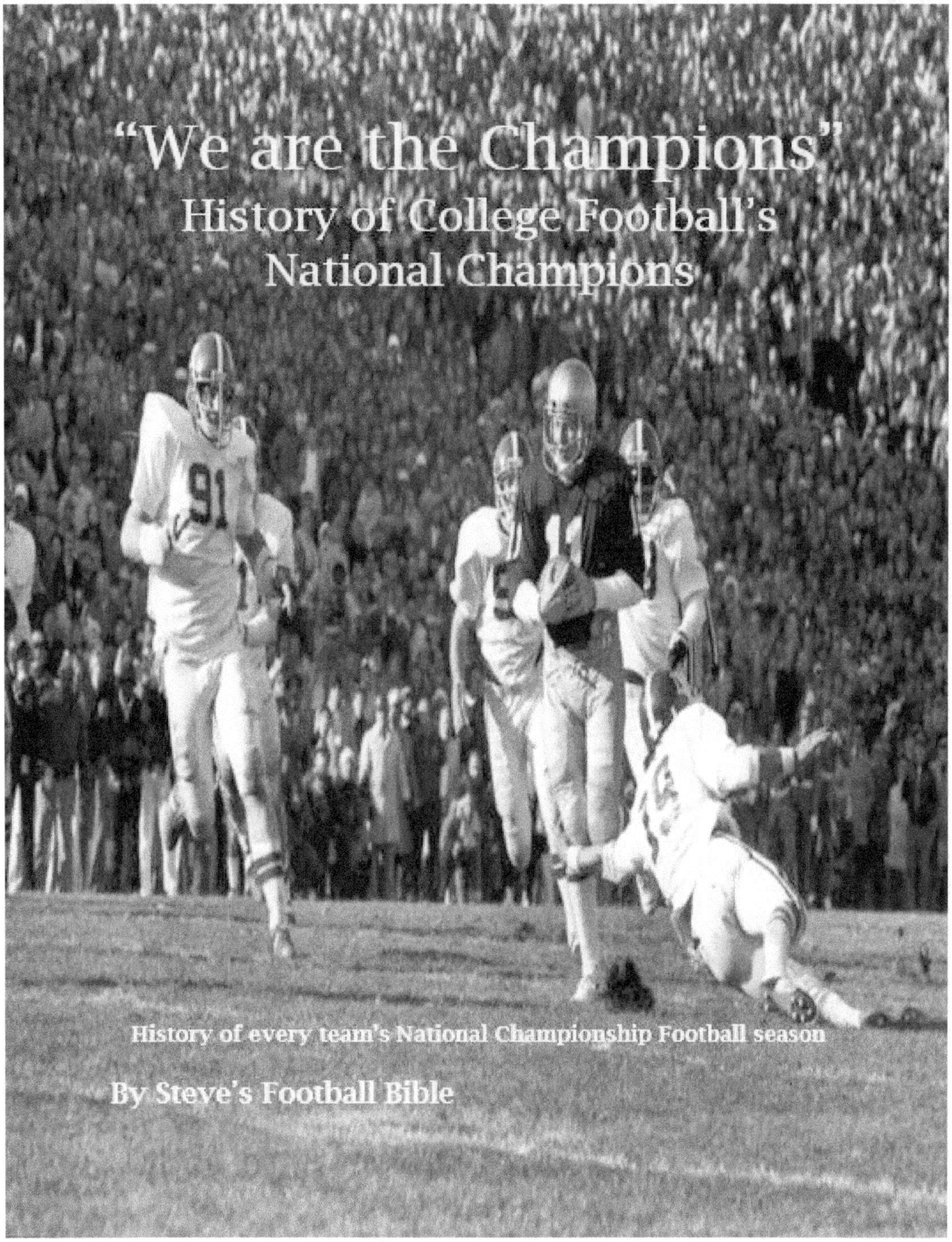

Text Copyright © 2022 by Steve's Football Bible, LLC
All Rights Reserved

Information in this book is for educational and entertainment purposes.

Information in this book was derived from numerous news services and college media guides available on the internet, including, but not limited to, Wikipedia, Arizona Daily Star, Associated Press, Bentley Historical Society, USA Today, Bleacher Report, SB Nation, "Sugar Bowl Classic: A history by Marty Mulé", Cotton Bowl Classic web site, Sun Bowl Classic web site, Orange Bowl Classic web site, Tournament of Roses web site, Washington Times, Los Angeles Times, New York Times, Philadelphia Inquirer, Washington Post, Boston Globe, NBC Sports, CBS Sportsline, Deseret News, ESPN, Black Shoes Diaries, ABC Sports Online, BCS Football.com, Sportsline USA, Chicago Tribune, Milwaukee Sentinel-Journal, UPI, Fort Worth Star-Telegram, Orlando Sentinel, Las Vegas Sun, Daily Press, San Jose Mercury News, Raycom Media, CollegeFootballPoll.com, SportsDayDFW.com, WVUIlustrated.com, GatorZone.com, Garnet and Gold, ECUPirates.com, HuskerMax.com, Lions Den, GoldenEagles.net, GoDucks.com, CU at the game, NUSports.com, Reuters News Service.

The following Colleges and Universities media guides and/or websites: Alabama, Appalachian State, Arizona, Arkansas State, Army, Auburn, Baylor, Boise State, Bowling Green, BYU, California, Central Michigan, Cincinnati, Colorado, Colorado State, Duke, East Carolina, Florida, Florida State, Fresno State, Georgia, Georgia State, Georgia Tech, Hawaii, Houston, Illinois, Indiana, Indiana, Iowa, Iowa State, Kansas State, LSU, Louisiville, Marshall, Maryland, Memphis, Miami, Michigan State, Middle Tennessee, Minnesota, Mississippi, Mississippi State, Missouri, Navy, Nebraska, North Carolina A&T, North Carolina, NC State, Northern Illinois, Northwestern, Notre Dame, Ohio, Ohio State, Oklahoma, Oklahoma State, Oregon, Oregon State, Penn State, Pittsburgh, Purdue, San Diego State, Southern Miss, SMU, South Carolina, South Florida, Stanford, Syracuse, Tennessee, TCU, Texas A&M, Toledo, Troy, Tulsa, UCLA, UNLV, Utah, Utah State, Villanova, Virginia, Virginia Tech, Wake Forest, Washington.

ISBN: 9-781393709-93-0

Introduction

My love of College Football began in 1966. As a 7 year old kid I remember watching the Notre Dame-Michigan State "Game of the Century". Next, I remember the 1967 USC-UCLA game and O.J. Simpson weaving through the UCLA defense for the winning touchdown with 6 minutes left in the game. I remember the 1968 Rose Bowl, Indiana vs USC. Who was this Indiana team that went to the Rose Bowl over my beloved Minnesota Golden Gopher's? I attended my first college football game in 1971. Michigan vs Minnesota at Memorial Stadium on the Campus of the University of Minnesota. My Aunt Roberta took me. I was hooked after that. The Golden Gophers were defeated that day 35-7 by the Wolverines. George Honza of the Golden Gophers scored the only touchdown that day on a pass from Craig Curry. Ironically, I met Mr. Honza in January of 2017 while officiating a basketball game.

Growing up in a rural farming town (Alden) in southern Minnesota, as a youth I spent a lot of my Saturday's in the fall watching ABC Sports College game of the week. I don't think I missed many Michigan-Ohio State games followed by the USC-UCLA game in the afternoon every third Saturday in November. The 1971 Nebraska-Oklahoma game stands out as one of the more memorable games I watched as a kid. Every New Year's Day I spent watching all the Bowl games. Cotton and Sugar Bowl at noon, followed by the Rose Bowl in the afternoon, finishing up with the Orange Bowl in the evening. The only day of New Year's Day Bowl games I missed was in January 1978, when I was in the Army, while traveling back to Ft. McClellan, Alabama to start my A.I.T., after being on Christmas leave.

This book is for all the College Football fans, casual or diehard, historians or those who just plain love the College game. I hope everyone enjoys.

Steve Fulton

Contents

Introduction iii
Chapter 1 – 2011-2015 1
    2011 Outback Bowl 1
    2011 Gator Bowl 2
    2011 Capital One Bowl 3
    2011 TicketCity Bowl 4
    2011 Rose Bowl 5
    2011 Fiesta Bowl 7
    2011 Orange Bowl 8
    2011 Sugar Bowl 9
    2011 GoDaddy.com Bowl 10
    2011 Cotton Bowl Classic 11
    2011 BBVA Compass Bowl 12
    2011 Kraft Fight Hunger Bowl 13
    2011 BCS Championship Game 14
    2011 New Orleans Bowl 15
    2011 Famous Idaho Potato Bowl 16
    2011 New Mexico Bowl 17
    2011 Beef 'O' Brady's Bowl 18
    2011 Poinsettia Bowl 19
    2011 Maaco Bowl 20
    2011 Hawai'i Bowl 21
    2011 Independence Bowl 22
    2011 Belk Bowl 23
    2011 Little Caesars Pizza Bowl 23
    2011 Military Bowl 24
    2011 Holiday Bowl 25
    2011 Champs Sports Bowl 26
    2011 Alamo Bowl 27
    2011 Armed Forces Bowl 28
    2011 Music City Bowl 29
    2011 Pinstripe Bowl 30
    2011 Insight Bowl 31
    2011 Liberty Bowl 31
    2011 Sun Bowl 32
    2011 Meineke Car Care Bowl of Texas 33
    2011 Kraft Fight Hunger Bowl 34
    2011 Chick-Fil-A Peach Bowl 35
    2012 Outback Bowl 36
    2012 Gator Bowl 37
    2012 TicketCity Bowl 38

2012 Capital One Bowl	39
2012 Rose Bowl	40
2012 Fiesta Bowl	41
2012 Sugar Bowl	42
2012 Orange Bowl	44
2012 Cotton Bowl Classic	45
2012 BBVA Compass Bowl	46
2012 GoDaddy.com Bowl	47
2012 BCS Championship Game	47
2012 New Mexico Bowl	48
2012 Famous Idaho Potato Bowl	49
2012 Poinsettia Bowl	50
2012 Beef 'O' Brady's Bowl	51
2012 Maaco Bowl	52
2012 New Orleans Bowl	53
2012 Hawai'i Bowl	54
2012 Little Caesars Pizza Bowl	55
2012 Military Bowl	56
2012 Belk Bowl	57
2012 Holiday Bowl	58
2012 Russell Athletic Bowl	59
2012 Independence Bowl	60
2012 Meineke Car Care Bowl of Texas	60
2012 Armed Forces Bowl	61
2012 Kraft Fight Hunger Bowl	62
2012 Pinstripe Bowl	63
2012 Buffalo Wild Wings Bowl	65
2012 Alamo Bowl	65
2012 Music City Bowl	66
2012 Liberty Bowl	67
2012 Sun Bowl	67
2012 Chick-Fil-A Peach Bowl	68
2013 Gator Bowl	69
2013 Heart of Dallas Bowl	71
2013 Outback Bowl	72
2013 Capital One Bowl	73
2013 Rose Bowl	74
2013 Orange Bowl	75
2013 Sugar Bowl	76
2013 Fiesta Bowl	77
2013 Cotton Bowl Classic	78
2013 BBVA Compass Bowl	79

2013 GoDaddy.com Bowl 80
2013 BCS Championship Game 81
2013 New Orleans Bowl 82
2013 Famous Idaho Potato Bowl 83
2013 New Mexico Bowl 84
2013 Las Vegas Bowl 85
2013 Beef 'O' Brady's Bowl 86
2013 Hawai'i Bowl 87
2013 Little Caesars Pizza Bowl 88
2013 Poinsettia Bowl 88
2013 Military Bowl 89
2013 Fight Hunger Bowl 90
2013 Texas Bowl 91
2013 Belk Bowl 92
2013 Buffalo Wild Wings Bowl 93
2013 Russell Athletic Bowl 94
2013 Pinstripe Bowl 95
2013 Armed Forces Bowl 96
2013 Music City Bowl 97
2013 Holiday Bowl 98
2013 Alamo Bowl 98
2013 Liberty Bowl 100
2013 Independence Bowl 100
2013 Sun Bowl 101
2013 Chick-Fil-A Peach Bowl 102
2014 Gator Bowl 103
2014 Heart of Dallas Bowl 104
2014 Outback Bowl 105
2014 Capital One Bowl 106
2014 Rose Bowl 107
2014 Fiesta Bowl (January) 108
2014 Sugar Bowl 109
2014 Cotton Bowl Classic 110
2014 Orange Bowl 111
2014 BBVA Compass Bowl 112
2014 GoDaddy Bowl 113
2014 BCS Championship Game 114
2014 New Orleans Bowl 116
2014 New Mexico Bowl 116
2014 Famous Idaho Potato Bowl 117
2014 Las Vegas Bowl 117
2014 Camellia Bowl 118

2014 Miami Beach Bowl	119
2014 Boca Raton Bowl	120
2014 Poinsettia Bowl	121
2014 Bahamas Bowl	122
2014 Hawai'i Bowl	123
2014 Heart of Dallas Bowl	124
2014 Quick Lane Bowl	125
2014 St. Petersburg Bowl	125
2014 Military Bowl	126
2014 Sun Bowl	127
2014 Independence Bowl	128
2014 Pinstripe Bowl	129
2014 Holiday Bowl	130
2014 Liberty Bowl	131
2014 Russell Athletic Bowl	132
2014 Texas Bowl	133
2014 Music City Bowl	133
2014 Belk Bowl	134
2014 Foster Farms Bowl	135
2014 Chick-Fil-A Peach Bowl	136
2014 Fiesta Bowl (December)	137
2014 Orange Bowl	138
2015 Outback Bowl	139
2015 Cotton Bowl Classic (January)	140
2015 Buffalo Wild Wings Citrus Bowl	141
2015 Rose Bowl (CFP National Semifinal)	142
2015 Sugar Bowl (CFP National Semifinal)	143
2015 Armed Forces Bowl	145
2015 Gator Bowl	146
2015 Alamo Bowl	147
2015 Cactus Bowl	148
2015 Birmingham Bowl	149
2015 GoDaddy Bowl	150
2015 CFP Championship Game	151
2015 Air Force Reserve Celebration Bowl	152
2015 New Mexico Bowl	153
2015 Las Vegas Bowl	154
2015 Camellia Bowl	155
2015 AutoNation Cure Bowl	156
2015 New Orleans Bowl	157
2015 Miami Beach Bowl	158
2015 Famous Idaho Potato Bowl	159

2015 Boca Raton Bowl ... 160
2015 Poinsettia Bowl ... 160
2015 GoDaddy Bowl ... 161
2015 Bahamas Bowl ... 162
2015 Hawai'i Bowl ... 163
2015 St. Petersburg Bowl ... 164
2015 Sun Bowl ... 164
2015 Heart of Dallas Bowl ... 165
2015 Pinstripe Bowl ... 166
2015 Independence Bowl ... 167
2015 Foster Farms Bowl ... 168
2015 Military Bowl ... 168
2015 Quick Lane Bowl ... 169
2015 Armed Forces Bowl ... 170
2015 Russell Athletic Bowl ... 171
2015 Arizona Bowl ... 172
2015 Texas Bowl ... 173
2015 Birmingham Bowl ... 174
2015 Belk Bowl ... 175
2015 Music City Bowl ... 176
2015 Holiday Bowl ... 177
2015 Chick-Fil-A Peach Bowl ... 177
2015 Orange Bowl (CFP National Semifinal) ... 178
2015 Cotton Bowl Classic (December) (CFP National Semifinal) ... 180

Chapter 2 – 2016-2020 ... 182

2016 Outback Bowl ... 182
2016 Buffalo Wild Wings Citrus Bowl ... 182
2016 Fiesta Bowl ... 183
2016 Rose Bowl ... 184
2016 Sugar Bowl ... 186
2016 Gator Bowl ... 187
2016 Liberty Bowl (January) ... 187
2016 Alamo Bowl ... 188
2016 Cactus Bowl ... 190
2016 CFP Championship Game ... 191
2016 Air Force Reserve Celebration Bowl ... 192
2016 New Mexico Bowl ... 193
2016 LAS VEGAS BOWL ... 194
2016 CAMELLIA BOWL ... 194
2016 AutoNation CURE BOWL ... 195
2016 NEW ORLEANS BOWL ... 196
2016 MIAMI BEACH BOWL ... 196

2016 BOCA RATON BOWL	197
2016 POINSETTIA BOWL	198
2016 FAMOUS IDAHO POTATO BOWL	199
2016 ARMED FORCES BOWL	200
2016 BAHAMAS BOWL	201
2016 DOLLAR GENERAL BOWL	202
2016 HAWAII BOWL	202
2016 ST. PETERSBURG BOWL	203
2016 QUICK LANE BOWL	204
2016 INDEPENDENCE BOWL	205
2016 HEART OF DALLAS BOWL	205
2016 MILITARY BOWL	206
2016 HOLIDAY BOWL	207
2016 CACTUS BOWL	208
2016 PINSTRIPE BOWL	208
2016 RUSSELL ATHLETIC BOWL	209
2016 FOSTER FARMS BOWL	210
2016 TEXAS BOWL	211
2016 BIRMINGHAM BOWL	211
2016 BELK BOWL	212
2016 ALAMO BOWL	213
2016 LIBERTY BOWL	214
2016 SUN BOWL	214
2016 MUSIC CITY BOWL	216
2016 ARIZONA BOWL	216
2016 ORANGE BOWL	217
2016 BUFFALO WILD WINGS CITRUS BOWL	218
2016 TAXSLAYER BOWL (GATOR BOWL)	219
2016 Chick-Fil-A Peach Bowl (National Semifinal)	220
2016 Fiesta Bowl (National Semifinal)	221
2017 OUTBACK BOWL	221
2017 COTTON BOWL CLASSIC	222
2017 ROSE BOWL	223
2017 SUGAR BOWL	224
2017 CFP NATIONAL CHAMPIONSHIP	225
2017 Air Force Reserve Celebration Bowl	226
2017 NEW ORLEANS BOWL	227
2017 AUTO NATION CURE BOWL	228
2017 LAS VEGAS BOWL	229
2017 NEW MEXICO BOWL	229
2017 CAMELLIA BOWL	231
2017 BOCA RATON BOWL	232

2017 FRISCO BOWL	232
2017 GASPARILLA BOWL	233
2017 BAHAMAS BOWL	234
2017 FAMOUS IDAHO POTATO BOWL	235
2017 BIRMINGHAM BOWL	235
2017 ARMED FORCES BOWL	236
2017 DOLLAR GENERAL BOWL	237
2017 HAWAII BOWL	238
2017 HEART OF DALLAS BOWL	239
2017 QUICK LANE BOWL	240
2017 CACTUS BOWL	241
2017 INDEPENDENCE BOWL	242
2017 PINSTRIPE BOWL	242
2017 FOSTER FARMS BOWL	243
2017 TEXAS BOWL	244
2017 MILITARY BOWL	245
2017 CAMPING WORLD BOWL	245
2017 ALAMO BOWL	246
2017 HOLIDAY BOWL	247
2017 BELK BOWL	248
2017 SUN BOWL	249
2017 MUSIC CITY BOWL	249
2017 ARIZONA BOWL	250
2017 COTTON BOWL	251
2017 GATOR BOWL	252
2017 LIBERTY BOWL	253
2017 FIESTA BOWL	253
2017 ORANGE BOWL	255
2018 OUTBACK BOWL	256
2018 CHICK-FIL-A PEACH BOWL	256
2018 CITRUS BOWL	257
2018 ROSE BOWL (National Semifinal)	259
2018 SUGAR BOWL (National Semifinal)	260
2018 CFP CHAMPIONSHIP GAME	261
2018 Air Force Reserve Celebration Bowl	262
2018 NEW MEXICO BOWL	263
2018 AUTO NATION CURE BOWL	264
2018 LAS VEGAS BOWL	265
2018 CAMELLIA BOWL	265
2018 NEW ORLEANS BOWL	266
2018 BOCA RATON BOWL	267
2018 FRISCO BOWL	267

2018 GASPARILLA BOWL	268
2018 BAHAMAS BOWL	269
2018 FAMOUS IDAHO POTATO BOWL	270
2018 BIRMINGHAM BOWL	270
2018 ARMED FORCES BOWL	271
2018 DOLLAR GENERAL BOWL	272
2018 HAWAII BOWL	273
2018 FIRST RESPONDERS BOWL	274
2018 QUICK LANE BOWL	274
2018 CHEEZ-IT BOWL	275
2018 INDEPENDENCE BOWL	276
2018 PINSTRIPE BOWL	277
2018 TEXAS BOWL	277
2018 MUSIC CITY BOWL	278
2018 CAMPING WORLD BOWL	279
2018 ALAMO BOWL	280
2018 CHICK-FIL-A PEACH BOWL	281
2018 BELK BOWL	282
2018 ARIZONA BOWL	283
2018 ORANGE BOWL (NATIIONAL SEMIFINAL)	284
2018 COTTON BOWL (NATIONAL SEMIFINAL)	285
2018 MILITARY BOWL	286
2018 SUN BOWL	287
2018 REDBOX BOWL	288
2018 LIBERTY BOWL	288
2018 HOLIDAY BOWL	290
2018 GATOR BOWL	291
2019 OUTBACK BOWL	291
2019 CITRUS BOWL	292
2019 FIESTA BOWL	293
2019 ROSE BOWL	294
2019 SUGAR BOWL	296
2019 CFP CHAMPIONSHIP GAME	297
2019 BAHAMAS BOWL	298
2019 FRISCO BOWL	299
2019 AIR FORCE RESERVE CELEBRATION BOWL	300
2019 NEW MEXICO BOWL	301
2019 AUTO NATION CURE BOWL	302
2019 BOCA RATON BOWL	303
2019 CAMELLIA BOWL	303
2019 LAS VEGAS BOWL	304
2019 NEW ORLEANS BOWL	305

2019 GASPARILLA BOWL	306
2019 HAWAII BOWL	307
2019 INDEPENDENCE BOWL	308
2019 QUICK LANE BOWL	308
2019 MILITARY BOWL	309
2019 PINSTRIPE BOWL	310
2019 TEXAS BOWL	311
2019 HOLIDAY BOWL	312
2019 CHEEZ-IT BOWL	313
2019 CAMPING WORLD BOWL	313
2019 COTTON BOWL	314
2019 CHICK-FIL-A PEACH BOWL (NATIONAL SEMIFINAL)	315
2019 FIESTA BOWL (NATIONAL SEMIFINAL)	316
2019 FIRST RESPONDER BOWL	318
2019 MUSIC CITY BOWL	318
2019 REDBOX BOWL	319
2019 ORANGE BOWL	320
2019 BELK BOWL	321
2019 SUN BOWL	322
2019 LIBERTY BOWL	322
2019 ARIZONA BOWL	323
2019 ALAMO BOWL	324
2020 CITRUS BOWL	325
2020 OUTBACK BOWL	325
2020 ROSE BOWL	326
2020 SUGAR BOWL	327
2020 BIRMINGHAM BOWL	328
2020 TAXSLAYER GATOR BOWL	329
2020 FAMOUS IDAHO POTATO BOWL	330
2020 ARMED FORCES BOWL	330
2020 LENDING TREE BOWL	331
2020 CFP CHAMPIONSHIP GAME	332

Chapter 1 – 2011-2015

2011 Outback Bowl

The 2011 Outback Bowl, the 25th edition of the bowl game, matched the Florida Gators of the SEC against the Penn State Nittany Lions of the Big Ten, at the Raymond James Stadium in Tampa, Florida. The game was played on January 1, 2011 and was telecast on ABC. The Florida Gators won with a final score of 37-24.

Game Notes - This was the third time that the two squads have met in school history. Florida currently leads the matchup 3–0. Both prior meetings were also in bowl games, the 1962 Gator Bowl and the 1998 Citrus Bowl. The game drew a national television rating of 7.1, the fourth highest among all 2010/2011 Bowl Games.

2011 Outback Bowl	Line	1	-	2	-	3	-	4	-	Final
Florida	(-7.0)	0	-	14	-	6	-	17	-	37
Penn State	(48.0)	7	-	10	-	7	-	0	-	24

Scoring Summary
Penn State - Moye 5 yard pass from McGloin (Wagner kick)
Florida - Hines 16 yard run (Henry kick)
Florida - McCray 27 yard blocked punt return (Henry kick)
Penn State - Zordich 1 yard run (Wagner kick)
Penn State - Wagner 20 yard field goal
Florida - Henry 30-yard field goal
Penn State - McGloin 2 yard run (Wagner kick)
Florida - Henry 47 yard field goal
Florida - Gillislee 1 yard run (Henry kick)
Florida - Henry 20 yard field goal
Florida - Black 80 yard interception return (Henry kick)

Associated Press Outback Bowl Game Summary - Joe Paterno and Urban Meyer met at midfield for a postgame handshake and hug, the 84-year-old Penn State coach looking forward to next season, the 46-year-old Florida coach heading toward some time away from the game. Meyer closed out a highly successful six-year run that included a pair of national championships by leading the Gators back from a second-half deficit to beat JoePa's Nittany Lions 37-24 in the Outback Bowl on Saturday. Omarius Hines and Mike Gillislee ran for touchdowns, Chas Henry kicked three second-half field goals, and Ahmad Black sealed the win with an 80-yard interception return TD to help Florida (8-5) send Meyer out with a smile of his own. Meyer said he was stepping away from coaching because of health concerns and to spend more time with his family. As for Paterno, he -- and his wife and Penn State officials -- spent the week leading up to the game repeatedly shooting down rumors that the Outback Bowl could be his last. All week long, Meyer paid tribute to Paterno, the all-time bowl wins leader with 24. He continued to talk about admiration for the Hall of Famer during his postgame news conference. Paterno expects to be back for a 46th season with Penn State (7-6). At one point, he called the speculation about his future -- including reports that he might be in poor health and had been hospitalized -- "ridiculous." He reiterated Friday that he has no plans to retire. Paterno hoped the Nittany Lions' record 37th bowl trip under him would set a nice tone for next season. The six losses are the most Penn State's had since going 4-7 in 2004, and the legendary coach is confident the team is headed in the right direction. Senior receiver Brett Brackett said none of the Nittany Lions brought up the subject of Paterno's future after the game. Meyer initially resigned in December 2009 only to change his mind the following day, returning for what turned out to be a disappointing year for a program he guided to national championships two of the past four seasons. He sent shockwaves through college football again on Dec. 8 when he stepped down again. There have been indications that he could be headed for a broadcasting job. The Gators already have hired former Texas head coach-in-waiting Will Muschamp as Meyer's replacement. He'll inherit a talented team that on Saturday continued to make the type of mistakes that contributed to their worst record in six seasons under Meyer, who won Southeastern Conference championships and national titles in 2006 and 2008. Meyer improved to 5-1 in bowl games with Florida, and he was especially to end with a win to avoid finishing with a two-game slide. The Gators lost their regular season finale 31-7 at archrival Florida State. John Brantley threw an interception on Florida's first play from scrimmage, Andre Debose mishandled a kickoff leading to the Gators starting their second possessions from their own 6 and Trey Burton -- one of three Quarterbacks Meyer used -- cost his team when he fumbled into the end zone after a short run to the Penn State 1. Matt McGloin turned Brantley's interception into a 5-yard TD pass to Derek Moye for a 7-0 Nittany Lions lead. Cornerback D' Anton Lynn recovered Burton's fumble for a touchback that helped Penn State stay ahead until Florida's Hines scored on a 16-yard end around set up by an interception -- the Gators' second off McGloin. Lerentee McCray returned a blocked punt 27 yards for a touchdown that gave Florida a brief 14-7 lead. McGloin's 44-

yard completion to Moye positioned Penn State for Michael Zordich's 1-yard TD run, and the Nittany Lions took advantage of a short punt to go up 17-14 at the half on Collin Wagner's 20-yard field goal. Henry kicked field goals of 30, 47 and 20 yards, the latter giving Florida a 30-24 lead midway through the fourth quarter. Penn State led 24-17 after McGloin scored on a 2-yard run set up when Henry, who's also Florida's punter, was stopped short of a first down on a fake punt play. The Nittany Lions Quarterback threw five interceptions after only being picked off four times in 174 passing attempts during the regular season. He finished 17 of 41 for 211 yards and one touchdown. Florida's fourth interception -- Black's second of the day -- stopped a potential game-winning drive after McGloin marched the Nittany Lions to the Gators 26 with under two minutes to go. Black cut in front of intended receiver Kevin Haplea and headed up the sideline in front of Penn State bench. After the safety reached the end zone, Meyer received a Gatorade bath and Florida faithful among the announced crowd of 60,574 began chanting "Urban Meyer, Urban Meyer."

2011 Gator Bowl

The 2011 Gator Bowl game was played between the Michigan Wolverines of the Big Ten and Mississippi State Bulldogs of the SEC, and was played on January 1, 2011 at EverBank Field in Jacksonville, Florida. It was the sixty sixth edition of the bowl game and was broadcast by ESPN2. It was the first time these two teams have ever met. After the game started close, Mississippi State ultimately pulled away and routed Michigan 52-14. It was the most points ever scored by one team in the Gator Bowl, and the worst loss Michigan has ever suffered in any bowl game in its long history. Rich Rodriguez was fired by Michigan after the game, marking the beginning of the "Brady Hoke Era," as Hoke would be named Rodriguez's replacement as Michigan head coach. Konica Minolta ended its sponsorship after the 2010 Gator Bowl game. On December 14, 2010, the Gator Bowl Association announced that Progressive Insurance would become the title sponsor for the 2011 Gator Bowl.

2011 Gator Bowl	Line	1	-	2	-	3	-	4	-	Final
#21 Mississippi State	(-5.0)	10	-	21	-	14	-	7	-	52
Michigan	(60.0)	14	-	0	-	0	-	0	-	14

Scoring Summary
Michigan - Roundtree 10 yard pass from Robinson (Gibbons kick)
Mississippi State - Clark 4 yard pass from Relf (Depasquale kick)
Mississippi State - Depasquale 42 yard Field goal
Michigan - Odoms 27 yard pass from Robinson (Gibbons kick)
Mississippi State - Ballard 2 yard run (Depasquale kick)
Mississippi State - Relf 1 yard run (Depasquale kick)
Mississippi State - Sanders 15 yard pass from Relf (Depasquale kick)
Mississippi State - Ballard 1 yard run (Depasquale kick)
Mississippi State - Ballard 7 yard run (Depasquale kick)
Mississippi State - Carr 31 yard pass from Relf (Depasquale kick)

2011 GATOR BOWL SUMMARY {U-M Athletic Department Press Release} - The University of Michigan football team was unable to climb out from a first-half deficit at the 2011 Gator Bowl on New Year's Day, falling 52-14 to No. 21 Mississippi State at Everbank Field. The Wolverines were unable to even their all-time bowl record and finish the campaign with a 7-6 record. Sophomore Quarterback Denard Robinson gained 313 yards of total offense. He carried the ball 11 times for 59 yards and completed 27-of-41 passes for 254 yards with two touchdowns and one interception. Junior wide receiver Darryl Stonum and junior/sophomore Roy Roundtree led the receiving effort. Roundtree had a game-high nine catches for 53 yards with one touchdown, while Stonum hauled in seven passes for a team-best 59 yards. The Wolverines were led defensively by junior/sophomore Kenny Demens, who had 11 tackles on the day. Junior linebacker J.B. Fitzgerald recorded a game-high two tackles for loss, including his first career sack for a loss of 19 yards. Michigan took the opening kickoff and marched 78 yards in 10 plays to take a 7-0 lead on a 10-yard pass from Robinson to Roundtree. Robinson had two huge runs during the drive, a run of 24 yards into Bulldogs territory and a 22-yard scamper to the 11-yard line. He completed all three passes for 27 yards on the drive. Sophomore running back Vincent Smith added four carries for nine yards. Mississippi State answered on its opening possession on a four-yard pass from Chris Relf to receiver Arceto Clark on third-and-goal. After holding the Wolverines on their second possession, the Bulldogs grabbed the lead, 10-7, on a 42-yard field goal by Derek Depasquale with 2:23 remaining in the first quarter. Mississippi State received great field position at U-M's 29-yard line after blocking a punt by freshman Will Hagerup. The Wolverines took the ensuing kickoff and regained the lead, 14-10, on a 27-yard touchdown pass to junior Martavious Odoms with 34 second left in the first quarter. The five-play drive covered 72 yards in 100 seconds. Robinson completed all four passes for 72 yards, with each of the four completions coming to a different receiver. The Bulldogs continued the scoring affair with a two-yard TD run by running back Vick

Ballard to grab a 17-10 lead. Nine of their 10 plays on the scoring drive were on the ground, the only pass being a 29-yard toss from Relf to Clark that set up a first-and-goal at U-M's five-yard line. Relf carried for three yards on the very next play and Ballard scored on second down. Mississippi State received possession in Michigan territory for the second time on the day as Robinson's third-down pass intended for senior/junior wide receiver Junior Hemingway was intercepted on a diving catch by Jonathan Banks. The Bulldogs took over at Michigan's 43-yard line and converted a fourth-down and two third-down plays, including the one-yard scoring run over right end by Relf. The Bulldogs' scoring drive covered 43 yards in 12 plays and increased their lead to 24-14 at 6:35 of the second quarter. The Wolverines took the ensuing kickoff and moved to the Bulldogs' 31-yard line but were unable to convert a fourth down play relinquishing possession. Robinson tossed a 36-yard pass to junior tight end Kevin Koger to move the ball to MSU's 42-yard line on the initial play of the series. Robinson added a 10-yard run to gain another first down before the series stalled on four consecutive plays. Mississippi State took a 31-14 lead with 25 seconds left in the first half as Relf completed a 15-yard touchdown pass to Ricco Sanders. The 11-play, 68-yard drive consumed 3:01. The defense forced the Bulldogs into their first punt on the opening series of the second half. Hemingway gave U-M excellent field position as he returned the punt 33 yards to the Bulldogs' 23-yard line. Michigan was unable to gain a first down and could not gain any points as redshirt freshman kicker Brendan Gibbons pushed a 35-yard field goal attempt wide left. Mississippi State increased its lead to 38-14 as Vick Ballard scored on a one yard run over left tackle on a fourth down play. The 14-play, 80-yard drive covered 5:27, with Ballard carrying six times for 26 yards. Relf completed both passes for 11 and 12 yards and added a two-yard run. For the third straight series, Michigan moved into scoring position but came up empty as Robinson's fourth-down pass fell incomplete in the right corner of the end zone. The pass intended for Hemingway was batted down by cornerback Johnathan Banks. Mississippi State increased its lead to 45-14 on a seven-yard touchdown run by Vick Ballard with 10 seconds remaining in the third quarter. It was Ballard's third rushing score of the game. The Bulldogs hit an 81-yard inside screen to LaDarius Perkin to the seven-yard line. Ballard scored on the very next play. Following a turnover on downs, Relf tossed a 31-yard touchdown pass to receiver Michael Carr on a fourth-and-10 play to close the scoring at 52-14.

2011 Capital One Bowl

The 2011 Capital One Bowl was the sixty-fifth edition of the bowl game, and was played at the Citrus Bowl in Orlando, Florida. The game was played on January 1, 2011 and matched the Alabama Crimson Tide from the Southeastern Conference (SEC) with the Michigan State Spartans from the Big Ten Conference.

Alabama - The defending National Champions Alabama Crimson Tide entered the game with a 9–3 record. The Tide were led by All-American wide receiver Julio Jones who set school records in catches with 75 and yards with 1,084 this season.

Michigan State - Michigan State was one of the surprises of the 2010 season and narrowly missed out on a BCS Bowl berth. The 11–1 Spartans won a share of the Big Ten Championship for the first time in 20 years. State was led by tailback Edwin Baker, who ranked third in the Big Ten with 1,187 yards rushing.

2011 Capital One Bowl	Line	1	-	2	-	3	-	4	-	Final
#15 Alabama	(-10.0)	7	-	21	-	14	-	7	-	49
#7 Michigan State	(52.0)	0	-	0	-	0	-	7	-	7

Scoring Summary
Alabama - Ingram 1 yard run (Shelley kick)
Alabama - Richardson 8 yard run (Shelley kick)
Alabama - Ingram 6 yard run (Shelley kick)
Alabama - Jones 35 yard run (Shelley kick)
Alabama - Maze 37 yard pass from McElroy (Shelley kick)
Alabama - Lacy 12 yard run (Shelley kick)
Alabama - Lacy 62 yard run (Shelley kick)
Michigan State - Fowler 49 yard pass from Nichol (Conroy kick)

Alabama Media Guide Capital One Bowl Game Summary - Mark Ingram ran for two scores to break the school record for career touchdowns, and the 15th-ranked Alabama Crimson Tide rolled past No. 7 Michigan State 49-7 in the most lopsided Capital One Bowl in the game's history. The 2009 Heisman Trophy winner had 59 yards rushing on 12 carries and a 30-yard reception against the team he rooted for as a kid. Greg McElroy threw for 220 yards and one touchdown, and the game got so out of hand that the Crimson Tide (10-3) pulled most of their starters early in the third quarter. Ingram also moved past Shaun Alexander's mark (41) with 42 career touchdowns. The margin of victory topped East Texas State's 33-0 victory over Tennessee Tech in the 1953 game, then known as the Tangerine Bowl. The bowl dates to 1947. The Crimson Tide found the end zone on their first five possessions, held the Spartans (11-2) to 171 total yards and sacked Kirk Cousins four times in their most dominant performance all season. Cousins had 120 yards passing, threw one interception and was under pressure all game. Edwin Baker was held to 14 yards rushing for a Spartans team that felt snubbed by the BCS after sharing the Big Ten title. Instead, they were bullied and bruised by a team that knows the big stage well. Alabama (10-3) took the opening kickoff 79 yards on 13 plays and Ingram scored on a 1-yard run to the right side. The Tide never looked back. Ingram, the 2009 Heisman Trophy winner, had 59 yards on 12 carries. He sat most of the second half. Michigan State (11-2) took its opening drive and looked to have something going, but Quarterback Kirk Cousins was intercepted by Alabama's Robert Lester. A short time later, Richardson scored on an 8-yard run to help the Tide grab a 14-0 lead. The Spartans again looked to have something going in the second quarter, driving to Alabama's 7-yard line, but linebacker Courtney Upshaw hit Cousins from the blindside, forcing a fumble that stalled another Michigan State drive. Upshaw finished with five total tackles, two sacks, and three tackles for loss. He was voted the game's most valuable player. On the following drive, Alabama drove 80 yards on seven plays and scored when Ingram burst through on the left side for a 6-yard touchdown to put the Tide up by three scores. The touchdown was Ingram's 42nd career rushing touchdown, making him the school's all-time leader, passing Shaun Alexander. McElroy, playing his final game for Alabama, was nearly flawless. The fifth-year senior was 13-of-17 for 220 yards and even made a block that sprung Julio Jones on a 35-yard reverse for a touchdown. McElroy was replaced by backup A.J. McCarron at the 9:05 mark in the third quarter. The Spartans, which had the third-best rushing attack in the Big Ten, managed only 48 yards on the ground. It was the second fewest yards allowed on the ground by an Alabama team since 1962. Edwin Baker, the Big Ten's third-leading rusher, was held to 14 yards on 12 carries. Alabama outgained Michigan State 546-171 in total yards. Alabama rushed for 275 yards on 44 attempts, a 6.2 average. Cousins was under pressure most of the day. The junior was sacked four times and the last one, by Alabama linebacker Alex Watkins, forced him to the sidelines. He was replaced by redshirt freshman Andrew Maxwell, who didn't fare much better. Maxwell was sacked twice and was replaced by Keith Nichol in the fourth quarter. Nichol connected with wideout Bennie Fowler for a 49-yard touchdown pass with 5:45 left to avoid the shutout.

2011 TicketCity Bowl

The 2011 TicketCity Bowl was played at Cotton Bowl in Dallas, Texas. The game was played on January 1, 2011 and was telecast on ESPNU. This game replaced the Cotton Bowl Classic, which moved from its long-time home to Cowboys Stadium in nearby Arlington in 2010 and pitted the Northwestern Wildcats from the Big Ten Conference against the Texas Tech Red Raiders from the Big 12 Conference. The game was originally labeled "The Dallas Football Classic," but on November 8, 2010, a deal was announced for TicketCity to become the title sponsor of the bowl.

2011 TicketCity Bowl	Line	1	-	2	-	3	-	4	-	Final
Northwestern	(61.0)	0	-	6	-	18	-	14	-	38
Texas Tech	(-9.0)	10	-	14	-	14	-	7	-	45

Scoring Summary
Texas Tech - Williams 24 yard Field goal
Texas Tech - Zouszalik 13 yard pass from Potts (Williams kick)
Northwestern - Colter 1 yard run (Pass failed)
Texas Tech - Potts 1 yard run (Williams kick)
Texas Tech - Leong 6 yard pass from Potts (Williams kick)
Northwestern - Demos 18 yard Field goal
Texas Tech - Stephans 86 yard run (Williams kick)
Northwestern - Colter 1 yard run (Rooks pass from Colter)
Texas Tech - Swindall 6 yard pass from Potts (Williams kick)
Northwestern - Watkins 4 yard run (Demos kick)
Northwestern - Fields 18 yard pass from Watkins (Demos kick)
Texas Tech - Leong 11 yard pass from Potts (Williams kick)
Northwestern - Mabin 39 yard interception return (Demos kick)

Associated Press Ticket City Bowl Game Summary - Tommy Tuberville knew better. The last two onside kicks he called this season were returned for touchdowns. The most recent came in this very stadium. The thing is, he just couldn't help himself. Leading Northwestern by three touchdowns late in the third quarter, the Texas Tech coach tried it again -- and it backfired again, setting up an exciting finish in the inaugural TicketCity Bowl. The Wildcats rallied to get within a touchdown twice in the fourth quarter and were driving for a tie or win when the Red Raiders intercepted a heave on the final play, preserving a 45-38 victory and allowing Tuberville to joke about his risky move. Taylor Potts threw for 369 yards and four touchdowns and scored another on a trick play, and Eric Stephens ran 86 yards for a TD to help Tech close its first post-Mike Leach season at a solid 8-5. The Red Raiders got off to a herky-jerky start under

Tuberville, going 2-2, 3-3 and 4-4. But they won three of their last four. Tuberville also became just the fifth coach to win a bowl game at three schools, having also done it at Auburn and Ole Miss. Northwestern (7-6) lost its eighth straight bowl game, extending a drought that dates to 1949. Coming close after being down by 22 points wasn't much solace because the Wildcats were close the last two postseasons, dropping both in overtime. The consolation prize is coach Pat Fitzgerald is now counting on the guys who've endured three straight crushing bowl losses to come out hungry as seniors next fall. He challenged them with a fiery opening statement to his postgame news conference that's certain to be replayed all offseason. Freshmen Quarterbacks Evan Watkins and Kain Colter led Northwestern's second-half rally with three straight touchdown drives and Jordan Mabin, part of that junior class, returned an interception 39 yards for a touchdown with 5:37 left. The Wildcats' defense kept the Red Raiders from running out the clock, but Watkins had only 24 seconds and no timeouts to go 75 yards. LaRon Moore caught the final throw, ending a game that featured 927 yards of total offense and 53 points scored in the second half. The game was played at the Cotton Bowl, site of more bowl games than any stadium but the Rose Bowl in Pasadena, Calif. The building was empty last bowl season because the namesake game moved to Cowboys Stadium. Attendance was announced as 40,121, well under half of capacity; the actual crowd was several thousand less. Not even a game sponsored by a ticket-seller could lure folks other than fans of both schools to an 11 a.m. kickoff on a windy New Year's morning with temperatures in the 30s. Potts was 43 of 56 for 369 yards. He ran twice for 19 yards, 13 coming when he threw a screen to Austin Zouzalik on the right side of the field and Zouzalik threw it back to him. Potts scored easily behind a convoy of blockers. The throwback was ruled a lateral, so it went down as a rushing play. Stephens' big play was the second-longest in a bowl game at this stadium, topped only by the 95-yarder in the 1954 Cotton Bowl that was awarded when Alabama's Tommy Lewis came off the bench to tackle Rice's Dickie Maegle. He ran 14 times for 128 yards and contributed to the dramatic finish by failing to get the first downs needed for Tech to run out the clock. The Wildcats surprised the Red Raiders with an in-game switch to an option offense. They ran for 229 yards, their most since 2008. Colter led the way with 105 yards and two touchdowns. Watkins, a redshirt freshman who took over when Dan Persa tore an Achilles' tendon in mid-November, was 10 of 21 for 76 yards and a touchdown. He also ran for 13 yards and a touchdown. Midway through the fourth quarter, Northwestern safety Hunter Bates -- son of former Dallas Cowboys standout Bill Bates -- broke a leg and had to be carted off the field. Northwestern scored its most points of the season against a Tech defense run by line coach Sam McElroy. He took over following the departure of coordinator James Willis earlier this week. His unit was solid in the first half, then gave up scores on the first four drives it faced in the second half.

2011 Rose Bowl

The 2011 Rose Bowl was the 97th edition of the annual bowl game played on January 1, 2011, as part of the 2010 NCAA Division I FBS football season. Played in Pasadena, California, the TCU Horned Frogs of the Mountain West Conference defeated the Wisconsin Badgers of the Big Ten Conference by a score of 21-19. The Pasadena Tournament of Roses Association was the organizer of the game. This game marked the first time a team from a non-Automatic Qualifying Conference won the Rose Bowl since the 1934 game when Columbia beat Stanford, 7-0. The offensive MVP named was TCU senior QB Andy Dalton. The defensive MVP named was TCU junior LB Tank Carder. The Rose Bowl Game, themed Building Dreams, Friendships, & Memories, was a contractual sell-out, with 64,500 tickets allocated to the participating teams and conferences. Ticket prices for all seats in the Rose Bowl are listed at $145.

Wisconsin Badgers - Bret Bielema's squad brought in a solid defense that had allowed just 7 rushing touchdowns this season. On the other side of the ball, Wisconsin had 3 running backs with at least 13 touchdowns (John Clay, Montee Ball, and James White) and had the top rushing attack in the Big Ten. Wisconsin QB Scott Tolzien, who led the nation in completion percentage (by completing 74.3% of his passes), played his final game as a Badger. This was the seventh Rose Bowl appearance for Wisconsin and their first since the 2000 Rose Bowl. It was the ninth consecutive bowl game appearance for Wisconsin. Head coach Bret Bielema also played on the 1990 Iowa Hawkeyes football team that went to the 1991 Rose Bowl.

TCU Horned Frogs - The Horned Frogs finished the regular season with a perfect 12-0 record, winning eight conference games and the Mountain West Conference title. The game not only marked their first trip to Pasadena but the first by a team from the conference to play in a New Year's Day bowl game. The Frogs had completed their second consecutive perfect regular season and were making their sixth consecutive bowl appearance. The Rose Bowl was their second consecutive BCS bowl game and the fourth appearance by a Mountain West conference member. TCU came into the game with the nation's #1 ranked defense. The Frogs were led by senior Quarterback Andy Dalton, who completed 194 of 293 passes for 2,638 yards for 26 touchdowns, and tailback Ed Wesley, who carried 162 times for 1,065 yards and scored 11 touchdowns. TCU became the fifth team outside of the conference partnership to play in the Rose Bowl game since the formation of the BCS.

2011 Rose Bowl	Line	1	-	2	-	3	-	4	-	Final
#4 Wisconsin	(37.0)	10	-	3	-	0	-	6	-	19
#3 TCU	(-3.0)	14	-	0	-	7	-	0	-	21

Scoring Summary
Wisconsin - Welch 30 yard Field goal
TCU - Johnson 23 yard pass from Dalton (Evans kick)
Wisconsin - Clay 1 yard run (Welch kick)
TCU - Dalton 4 yard run (Evans kick)
Wisconsin - Welch 37 yard Field goal
TCU - Shivers 1 yard run (Evans kick)
Wisconsin - Ball 4 yard run (Pass failed)

Associated Press Rose Bowl Game Summary - When Tank Carder leaped with perfect timing and swatted Wisconsin's final pass to the turf, the TCU linebacker felt as if he got a boost from every player at every school that never even imagined playing in the Rose Bowl. Sure, these unbeaten Horned Frogs realized they couldn't win the national title. They still celebrated their perfection on the hallowed Pasadena turf in the name of all the little guys outside the monolithic powers of major college football. Andy Dalton threw a touchdown pass and ran for a score, Carder batted down a 2-point conversion pass attempt with 2 minutes to play, and third-ranked TCU hung on to beat Wisconsin 21-19 on Saturday. Bart Johnson caught an early TD pass and recovered a late onside kick for the Mountain West champion Horned Frogs (13-0), who followed up their second straight unbeaten regular season with their first BCS victory. TCU is the first school from a non-automatic qualifying conference to play in the Rose Bowl since the advent of the BCS, and the Frogs were right at home. Either Auburn or Oregon will win the national title after they meet in the BCS championship game in nine days. These ferocious Frogs still proved they can play with anybody on college football's biggest stages. TCU lost last year's Fiesta Bowl to Boise State by a touchdown, but that's still the only loss of the past two seasons for the improbable power built deep in the heart of football-crazy Texas by Coach Gary Patterson. The non-AQ schools improved to 5-2 in BCS bowls with the Frogs' triumph -- 4-1 vs. the leagues with automatic bids. Fans can debate where TCU's win in Pasadena ranks with Boise State's thrilling one-point win over Oklahoma in the 2007 Fiesta Bowl or Utah's upset of Alabama in the 2009 Sugar Bowl, but the Frogs will always be the first back-to-back BCS busters -- even after they head to the Big East in 2012. Montee Ball rushed for 132 yards and a late score for the Big Ten co-champion Badgers (11-2), whose loss capped a nightmare New Year's Day for their conference. The Big Ten went 0-5 in bowl games Saturday, and the Badgers fell just short of a late rally when Carder made a defensive play that will live forever in TCU lore. Luke Shivers' 1-yard TD run put TCU ahead 21-13 early in the third quarter, but neither team scored again until Wisconsin mounted a 77-yard drive in the waning minutes. Ball rushed for a 4-yard score with 2 minutes to play, and the Frogs expected the Badgers to run for the conversion behind their dominant line. But Wisconsin came out in a spread, and Carder was blocked in a blitz attempt at the line -- and he still batted down Scott Tolzien's throw. Jacob Pedersen was open in the end zone, but the ball never got close to the Wisconsin tight end. Johnson easily grabbed Wisconsin's onside kick, and TCU rushed for a final first down to kill the clock. Patterson stopped his players from dumping a Gatorade bucket on him before time ran out, lecturing them with a smile on his face. When the final seconds ticked off, the Frogs ran about the field in a frenzy, eventually collecting near the TCU band and the quarter of the Rose Bowl stands filled with purple-clad fans. And eventually the Frogs doused their coach, too. Dalton went 15 for 23 and rushed for a first-quarter score, winning the game's offensive MVP award. But the defense deserved the credit for hanging on when TCU couldn't score in the game's final 26 minutes. TCU's defense led the nation in several categories this season, but critics said the Frogs hadn't faced the likes of Wisconsin's fearsome offensive line. The Badgers were dominant at times, particularly in a frenetic first quarter that featured 24 combined points, but TCU hung on against Wisconsin's attack with guts, third-down stops -- and plenty of Carder. With a litany of big plays that included a de-cleating sack of Tolzien to kill a third-quarter drive, Carder was the leader all game -- and the hero on Wisconsin's final snap. Tolzien went 12 of 21 for 159 yards for the Badgers, and John Clay rushed for a first-quarter score. Wisconsin outgained the Frogs 385-301 and held the ball for all but three plays in the second quarter, but twice settled for field goals by Philip Welch, who also missed a 39-yard field goal attempt before halftime. Most of the Frogs stayed on the field after the trophy presentation to soak in another minute of the biggest achievement for TCU football since the national championship season in 1938 -- the only other unbeaten campaign for the school that produced Davey O'Brien, "Slingin' Sammy" Baugh and LaDainian Tomlinson. While O'Brien won the Heisman Trophy in 1938, Dalton has his own unbeaten season -- and his third bowl MVP award.

2011 Fiesta Bowl

The 2011 Tostitos Fiesta Bowl was played between the Connecticut Huskies (UConn), co-champions of the Big East Conference, and the Oklahoma Sooners, champions of the Big 12 Conference, at University of Phoenix Stadium in Glendale, Arizona, on January 1, 2011. The game, the 40th contest in Fiesta Bowl history. Oklahoma was selected to participate in the Fiesta Bowl after an 11–2 regular season that culminated with a 23-20 win over Nebraska in the 2010 Big 12 Championship Game. Facing the Sooners were the Connecticut Huskies with a regular season record of 8–4; they earned the Big East's BCS berth by defeating fellow co-champions Pittsburgh and West Virginia in consecutive regular season games. Pregame coverage focused on Oklahoma's struggles in past BCS games dating back to the 2004 Sugar Bowl as well as Connecticut's difficulties in selling their designated ticket allotment from the Fiesta Bowl. The Sooners scored on their first two possessions and held a 14–0 lead at the end of the first quarter. The Huskies responded with an interception returned for a touchdown early in the second quarter; after an exchange of field goals the halftime score was 20–10 in favor of Oklahoma. In the second half, Oklahoma pulled away with multiple passing and interception-return touchdowns. While Connecticut responded with a 95-yard kickoff return for a touchdown, they failed to score a touchdown on offense at any point during the game. Oklahoma Quarterback Landry Jones was named the game's most valuable player on offense and defensive back Jamell Fleming was named the defensive most valuable player. Jones had a school bowl record of 429 passing yards; he completed three passes for touchdowns. Within 24 hours following the game Connecticut suffered two notable defections: running back Jordan Todman announced that he was leaving school early to enter the 2011 NFL Draft and head coach Randy Edsall was hired as the new head coach at the University of Maryland. In the wake of the 2011 contest, the Fiesta Bowl released an internal report stating that several members illegally gave campaign contributions and were reimbursed for it.

2011 Fiesta Bowl	Line	1	-	2	-	3	-	4	-	Final
#25 Connecticut	(54.0)	0	-	10	-	10	-	0	-	20
#9 Oklahoma	(-17.0)	14	-	6	-	14	-	14	-	48

Scoring Summary
Oklahoma - Hanna 8 yard pass from Jones (Stevens kick)
Oklahoma - Murray 3 yard run (Stevens kick)
Connecticut - Gratz 46 yard interception return (Teggart kick)
Oklahoma - Stevens 41 yard field goal
Oklahoma - Stevens 24 yard field goal
Connecticut - Teggart 37 yard field goal
Oklahoma - Kenney 59 yard pass from Jones (Stevens kick)
Oklahoma - Fleming 55 yard interception return (Stevens kick)
Connecticut - Frey 95 yard kickoff return (Teggart kick)
Connecticut - Teggart 38 yard field goal
Oklahoma - Broyles 5 yard pass from Jones (Stevens kick)
Oklahoma - Jefferson 22 yard interception return (Stevens kick)

Associated Press Fiesta Bowl Game Summary - Watching film of their two previous, disastrous trips to the Fiesta Bowl back at the team hotel, Oklahoma's players didn't cringe, didn't get that here-we-go-again feeling. The Sooners got mad and took it out on Connecticut, finally ending that BCS losing streak. Landry Jones and Ryan Broyles had record-setting games, Oklahoma's defense scored two touchdowns while holding UConn's offense without one, and the ninth-ranked Sooners ended their five-game BCS bowl losing streak with a 48-20 victory over Connecticut in the Fiesta Bowl on Saturday night. Oklahoma (12-2) carried plenty of BCS baggage after losing three straight title games and two Fiesta Bowls. The Sooners avoided the setback six pack behind Jones, Broyles and a dominating defense. Showing he's emerged from the shadow of Heisman Trophy winner Sam Bradford; Jones threw for a school bowl-record 429 yards -- breaking his own record of 418 in last season's Sun Bowl -- and three touchdowns on 34-of-49 passing. Broyles, OU's All-America receiver, set a team record with 170 yards receiving, matched another with 13 catches and had the put-it-out of reach touchdown, a tiptoeing 5-yarder midway through the fourth quarter. Jamell Fleming and Tony Jefferson each returned interceptions for scores and the defense made UConn scrap for everything it got, giving the Sooners their first Fiesta Bowl victory since beating Wyoming in 1976. Connecticut (8-5), despite the final score, didn't embarrass itself in the program's first BCS bowl. The hopeful Huskies steadied themselves after an initial barrage from Oklahoma and avoided a complete New Year's Day desert disaster behind hard-nosed running by Jordan Todman and a handful of big plays. Todman, who declared for the NFL draft after the game, had 121 yards on 32 carries and Robbie Frey returned a kickoff 95 yards for a touchdown, helping UConn provide at least a glimmer of hope that it's not just a basketball school anymore. Oklahoma had been down this road before. The Sooners played in the 2007 and 2008 Fiesta Bowls, so they know the town, the stadium, the routine. They also know disappointment. In both games, Oklahoma came into the desert favorites and left embarrassed; first to trick-playing, BCS-busting Boise State, then in lopsided fashion to West Virginia. To shake up their mojo, the Sooners switched hotels, practice sites, everything possible to keep from getting that here-we-go-again Fiesta feeling. It worked. Oklahoma followed a businesslike week with a similar approach in the game, jumping out to a 14-0 lead and withstanding a few mid-game mistakes to pull away for its first BCS bowl win in eight years. This was all new to the Huskies. An FBS program for just nine years, UConn was in its fourth straight bowl, getting the Bowl Championship Series nod after winning the final five games and earning the tiebreaker as co-Big East champions. But everything about this trip was bigger, from the airport greeting to the shine of the national spotlight. More than that, though, the Huskies had to worry about Oklahoma's speed-you-up offense. Edsall said OU has so many talented players, it was like the little boy trying to put his fingers in all the holes in the dike. The Sooners also play fast, snapping off more plays than any team in the country while averaging over 478 yards and 36 points per game. UConn tried a variety of speed-up tactics in practice to simulate Oklahoma's pace, but the real test was going to come in the first few series, when the Sooners pressed the gas and the Huskies tried to keep up. They couldn't. With former Quarterback Josh Heupel calling plays for the first time, Oklahoma hit UConn with a Manny Pacquiao-esque round of punches in its opening drive for an 8-yard touchdown from Jones to James Hanna. Next drive: boom, boom, boom, DeMarco Murray scores on a he's-bottled-up, no-he-isn't 3-yard TD run. Then, finally, UConn got something right. Jones, after completing his first 12 passes, led a receiver too much and cornerback Dwayne Gratz picked it off, racing in 46 yards for a touchdown. The Huskies had life. UConn's offense got a spark after that behind Zach Frazer and the defense held Oklahoma to a pair of field goals by Jimmy Stevens, leaving the Huskies at a manageable 20-10 halftime deficit. The Sooners looked ready to run away with it to start the third, getting a 59-yard touchdown pass from Jones to Cameron Kenney (seven catches, 154 yards) and Fleming's 55-yard interception return 1:11 later after a pass deflected off receiver Michael Smith's hands. Trailing 34-10, the Huskies still wouldn't go away. Frey returned the ensuing kickoff 95 yards for a touchdown, Dave Teggart hit his second field goal from 38 yards and Lawrence Wilson stripped Broyles when he appeared to be headed for a punt return touchdown. UConn got another big play when Jerome Junior broke up a pass on a fake field goal early in the fourth quarter, but that was it. Broyles hauled in his sideline touchdown pass midway through the quarter and Jefferson turned a bobbled pass into a 22-yard touchdown, giving the Sooners their long-awaited win. In recognition for his performance during the game, Oklahoma Quarterback Landry Jones was named the game's offensive most valuable player. Jones passed for a school bowl record of 429 yards which included three touchdown passes. On defense, Oklahoma's Jamell Fleming was awarded the defensive most valuable player. Fleming had intercepted a pass and returned it for a 55-yard touchdown.

2011 Orange Bowl

The 2011 Discover Orange Bowl was played between the Virginia Tech Hokies and the Stanford Cardinal on Monday, January 3, 2011, at Sun Life Stadium in Miami Gardens, Florida. The game, the 77th edition of the Orange Bowl, was televised on ESPN and the broadcast was seen by an estimated 8.23 million viewers. Virginia Tech was selected to participate in the Orange Bowl after an 11–2 regular season that culminated with a 44–33 win in the 2010 ACC Championship Game. Stanford was picked as the other half of the matchup following an 11–1 campaign that included the school's best-ever regular-season record. That performance earned the Cardinal a No. 4 ranking in the BCS Poll and the automatic bid to a BCS game that accompanies a top-4 ranking of a second school in a conference other than the champion.

2011 Orange Bowl	Line	1	-	2	-	3	-	4	-	Final
#5 Stanford	(-3.5)	7	-	6	-	13	-	14	-	40
#12 Virginia Tech	(59.5)	2	-	10	-	0	-	0	-	12

Scoring Summary
Stanford - Stewart 60 yard run (Whitaker kick)
Virginia Tech - Safety - Hall tackled in end zone
Virginia Tech - Wilson 11 yard pass from Taylor (Hazley kick)
Stanford - Ertz 25 yard pass from Luck (kick failed)
Virginia Tech - Hazley 37 yard Field goal
Stanford - Marecic 1 yard run (Whitaker kick)
Stanford - Fleener 41 yard pass from Luck (Whitaker kick)
Stanford - Fleener 58 yard pass from Luck (Whitaker kick)
Stanford - Fleener 38 yard pass from Luck (Whitaker kick)

Associated Press Orange Bowl Game Summary - John Elway flashed his familiar grin and Jim Harbaugh gave a jubilant shout from the sideline as Andrew Luck sprinted up the field to join a celebration in the end zone. Nearly a quarter remained in the Orange Bowl, but the Stanford Cardinal (No. 4 BCS, No.

5 AP) were on the way to their first bowl victory in 14 years. And it was a blowout. Now, the biggest question that remains about the Cardinal is whether their star Quarterback and coach are coming back. Luck, the Heisman Trophy runner-up, threw for 287 yards and four touchdowns Monday night to lead Stanford past Virginia Tech (No. 13 BCS, No. 12 AP), 40-12. The sophomore turned in a performance reminiscent of Elway, the former Stanford Quarterback who is expected to become the Denver Broncos' chief football executive this week. Elway served as honorary captain, and ex-Stanford QB Jim Plunkett also was on hand to lend support. When the game ended, two Stanford players lifted Harbaugh on their shoulders, and he raised an arm in triumph. The Cardinal (12-1) likely will end the season ranked in the top 5 for the first time since the unbeaten 1940 team finished No. 2. Their success comes only four years after they went 1-11 and hired Harbaugh as coach to lead a turnaround. Virginia Tech (11-3), playing in a bowl game for the 18th consecutive year, fell to 1-27 against top-5 teams. Stanford threw a completion for a bizarre safety and blew two extra points but overcame those mistakes with six plays gaining more than 30 yards. Two came in succession on a two-play, 97-yard "drive," and the Cardinal outscored Tech 27-0 in the second half. Tight end Coby Fleener caught scoring passes of 41, 58 and 38 yards from Luck, all in the final 21 minutes. Zach Ertz had a 25-yard TD reception, Jeremy Stewart scored on a 60-yard run and Stepfan Taylor added a 56-yard run. Fullback-linebacker Owen Marecic scored on a 1-yard run and had a sack. Luck went 18 for 23 and was chosen the most valuable player. Fleener had six catches for 173 yards for the Cardinal, who outgained Tech 534-288. The game might have been the last at Stanford for Harbaugh and Luck. Harbaugh is expected to be courted by NFL teams and perhaps alma mater Michigan after leading the Cardinal to a school-record win total. Luck is projected as the likely first pick in the draft if he turns pro this year. During the trophy ceremony, Stanford fans chanted, "One more year." Stanford began to pull away by going the length of the field in 29 seconds in the third quarter. After Delano Howell made an interception at the 3 to snuff a Tech threat, Taylor busted loose and reached Hokies territory. On the next play, Luck threw deep to Fleener for a 26-12 lead. Luck also threw for a safety that cut Stanford's lead to 7-2. His pass was batted backward by Antoine Hopkins to 303-pound offensive tackle Derek Hall, who caught the ball rather than knocking it down and was tackled in the end zone. The Hokies' offense had trouble scoring. Tyrod Taylor threw for 222 yards but was held to 22 yards rushing, and Tech twice came away empty after driving inside the Stanford 35. Taylor's scrambling skills helped the Hokies score their only touchdown. On third-and-goal he rolled left, retreated, spun 180 degrees near the Stanford bench and threw to David Wilson for an 11-yard score. After the play, Taylor asked Harbaugh if he had stepped on the sideline. Harbaugh told him he hadn't. Taylor moved the Hokies 60 yards in the final 47 seconds of the first half to set up a 37-yard field goal by Chris Hasley, but they netted only 109 yards in the second half.

2011 Sugar Bowl

The 2011 Allstate Sugar Bowl was part of the Bowl Championship Series (BCS) for the 2010 NCAA Division I FBS football season and was the 77th Sugar Bowl. The contest took place on January 4, 2011, in the Louisiana Superdome in New Orleans, Louisiana.

The Sugar Bowl Committee overlooked the #4 Stanford Cardinal and selected as its participants the #6 Ohio State Buckeyes from the Big Ten Conference and the #8 Arkansas Razorbacks from the Southeastern Conference. Ohio State Quarterback Terrelle Pryor was named the game's Most Valuable Player.

Notes - The Buckeyes came into the game 0–9 against SEC schools in bowl games all-time. Furthermore, Ohio State had not beaten a Southeastern Conference opponent since 1988, when it defeated Louisiana State in a regular-season game by a score of 36–33 (coincidentally, the Tigers were OSU's opponents in their last bowl game against an SEC team prior to the 2011 Sugar Bowl, which was also the last time OSU played in a bowl game in New Orleans).

2011 Sugar Bowl	Line	1	-	2	-	3	-	4	-	Final
#6 Ohio State	(-3.5)	14	-	14	-	3	-	0	-	31
#8 Arkansas	(57.5)	7	-	3	-	11	-	5	-	26

Scoring Summary
Ohio State - Sanzenbacher recovered fumble in end zone (Barclay kick)
Arkansas - Adams 17 yard pass from Mallett (Hocker kick)
Ohio State - Herron 9 yard run (Barclay kick)
Ohio State - Sanzenbacher 15 yard pass from Pryor (Barclay kick)
Ohio State - Posey 43 yard pass from Pryor (Barclay kick)
Arkansas - Hocker 20 yard field goal
Arkansas - Hocker 46 yard field goal
Ohio State - Barclay 46 yard field goal
Arkansas - Wright 22 yard pass from Mallett (Mallett pass to Williams)
Arkansas - Safety - Herron tackled in end zone by Bequette
Arkansas - Hocker 47 yard Field goal

Sugar Bowl Recap by Sugar Bowl historian Marty Mulé
The game - and the Quarterbacks - lived up to all expectations, though the 77th Sugar Bowl was partitioned into 30-minute segments and coming within 58 seconds of being remembered as an instant classic. In the first half Ohio State, and Pryor, dominated Arkansas like no other opponent did all season (and remember, the Hogs' two losses came from national champion Auburn and defending national champ Alabama), opening a 28-7 lead until four seconds before intermission. In the second half the Razorbacks, and Ryan, had their way with the Buckeyes, closing to within five points of pulling off one of the most spectacular finishes in Sugar Bowl history. Pryor got the Buckeyes off to a roaring start, passing for 203 yards and two touchdowns, and rushing for 52 more as Ohio State took complete control of the game. In a demonstration of how well things were unfolding for Ohio State, the Buckeyes scored on their first possession, going 74 yards in eight plays and getting OSU's first points when Pryor took off on a 34-yard run, then when the Hogs' Thomas Tramain forced a fumble, lost the ball at the 3. The ball bounced into the end zone where receiver Dane Sanzenbacher fell on it. Meanwhile, Ryan was putting the ball right on his wide-outs fingertips - where many were dropped, despite constant hounding by Heyward, whose daddy once played for the New Orleans Saints. Ryan did tie things up with a 17-yard pass to Joe Adams on the Hogs' second series. The Buckeyes went on a tear, scoring 21 unanswered points on: a one-yard run by Herron after a seven-play, 68-yard drive; a 15-yard pass from Pryor to Sanzenbacher; and a 43-yard pass from Pryor to Posey with 1:59 to play in the half. Arkansas used the remaining time well, driving from its 10 to the OSU 3 where Zach Hocker kicked a field goal to send the teams to the dressing room with a 28-10 score. The Razorbacks really looked cooked. Not so fast, my friend. In the last 30 minutes, Arkansas cut Ohio State's point production from four touchdowns to one field goal, which also allowed the Hogs to get back on track offensively. Hocker and OSU's Devin Barclay traded field goals of 46 yards. Then Mallett found Jarious Wright for a 22-yard touchdown pass. The Hogs added a two-point conversion from Ryan to D.J. Williams to cut the lead to 31-21. There was 11:52 to play, but the game was now definitely on! Arkansas' defense then made it even more interesting. After a Dylan Breeding punt inside the 5-yard line, the Hogs' Jake Bequette tackled Danny Herron in the end zone for a safety that put the Razorbacks within hailing distance at 31-23. When Arkansas got the ball after the safety, Hocker kicked another field goal from 47 yards out to make the difference 31-26 - one touchdown away from victory - with 8:55 remaining. Time was vital now, and twice in their next two possessions the Buckeyes were able to kill more of the clock because of Pryor's running skills. On third-and-five at the OSU 19, Pryor ran out of the shotgun for nine yards for the first; Later, in the same series, on third-and-15 at the OSU 23, Pryor slipped through tacklers at right end for a first down at the 37, though he seriously injured his foot on the run. After having to give up possession, the Bucks got the ball again with 4:33 to go. Trying to drain more time off the clock, on second-and-nine and third-and-one, the hobbled Pryor made eight and one yards, again elongating Ohio State's possession time before the Hogs finally forced a punt. However, that's when the window of opportunity grew wider. Arkansas' Colton Nash came through the middle of the Buckeyes' line to block the kick. But instead of scooping up the ball and running it in from the 18, which seemed entirely possible, the Hogs fell on it. Arkansas' final chance started with a dropped pass (the last of six by Arkansas receivers) senior tight end D.J. Williams. It was one of six passes dropped by Razorback receivers. On the next play Mallett made one of his few mistakes. Baited by coverage, Ryan let loose a pass that Solomon Thomas cut in front of, going down to the Superdome turf with the ball cradled in his arms with 58 seconds to play. That ended any chance of a stirring finish. As it turned out, each one of the previously suspended Buckeyes made significant contributions to the victory. Herron gained 93 yards and scored a touchdown; Posey caught three passes for 70 yards and a touchdown; Smith helped open the holes as OSU amassed 446 yards of offense. And Pryor passed for 221 yards and rushed for 115 yards, many on those crucial third down plays. Mallett didn't do badly either, throwing for 277 yards and two touchdowns. But, without doubt, Pryor was the MVP of the Sugar Bowl. Of course, in a technical sense, Ohio State didn't finally beat an SEC team. The Sugar Bowl was one of the victories from the 2010 season the Buckeyes later vacated due to NCAA-related issues.

2011 GoDaddy.com Bowl

The 2011 GoDaddy.com Bowl, the twelfth edition of the bowl game, was played at Ladd-Peebles Stadium in Mobile, Alabama on January 6, 2011. The game was telecast on ESPN and matched Miami from the MAC versus Middle Tennessee from the Sun Belt. Previously, the bowl game was known as the GMAC Bowl.

2011 GoDaddy.com Bowl	Line	1	-	2	-	3	-	4	-	Final
Middle Tennessee	(Pk)	14	-	0	-	7	-	0	-	21
Miami-Ohio	(48.5)	7	-	7	-	14	-	7	-	35

Scoring Summary
Middle Tennessee - Tanner 18 yard run (Gendreau kick)
Miami-Ohio - Merriweather 3 yard run (Cook kick)
Middle Tennessee - Dasher 51 yard run (Gendreau kick)
Miami-Ohio - Merriweather 3 yard run (Cook kick)
Miami-Ohio - Nunley 52 yard interception return (Cook kick)
Middle Tennessee - Tanner 54 yard run (Gendreau kick)
Miami-Ohio - Givens 17 yard pass from Boucher (Cook kick)
Miami-Ohio - Harwell 5 yard pass from Boucher (Cook kick)

Associated Press GoDaddy.com Bowl Game Summary - Not even an interim coach and a freshman Quarterback could keep Miami of Ohio from the best turnaround season in college football history. Austin Boucher threw for 289 yards and two touchdowns in his fourth career start and the RedHawks capped a historic season with a 35-21 win Thursday night over Middle Tennessee in the GoDaddy.com Bowl. The RedHawks (10-4) are the first team in Football Bowl Subdivision history to win 10 games one season after losing 10. Miami finished a dismal 1-11 in 2009 but recovered to win the Mid-American Conference title and finish this season on a six-game winning streak. MTSU (6-7) won three games in a row to become bowl eligible but was hurt by five turnovers. Miami's Dayonne Nunley was responsible for two of them, recovering a fumble and returning an interception 52 yards for a touchdown. Thomas Merriweather rushed for 100 yards and two touchdowns. MTSU's Dwight Dasher threw four interceptions -- all in the second half. It was a sweet ending for the RedHawks, especially considering there was plenty of adversity along the way. Miami played its first bowl since 2004 without Coach Mike Haywood, who accepted the head coaching job at Pittsburgh in December. Haywood has since been fired from Pitt after being arrested on a felony domestic violence charge. On Monday, a magistrate entered a not guilty plea for Haywood on the felony charge. The RedHawks also lost starting Quarterback Zac Dysert to a lacerated spleen in November, but Boucher kept the offense going. The redshirt freshman wasn't perfect, throwing two interceptions, but completed 22 of 35 passes, including several clutch throws to keep drives alive. Thomas Merriweather rushed for 100 yards and two touchdowns. Nick Harwell caught seven passes for 86 yards and a touchdown. Miami outgained MTSU, 416-370. MTSU's Dasher was stellar in the first half, accounting for 158 total yards, including a 49-yard touchdown run late in the first quarter that gave the Blue Raiders a short-lived 14-7 lead. But the senior struggled in the second half, throwing four interceptions. He finished with 162 passing yards, 90 rushing yards and a touchdown while Phillip Tanner rushed for 87 yards and two touchdowns. Miami took the lead for good late in the third quarter, when Boucher hit Chris Givens for a 17-yard touchdown pass, pushing the score to 28-21. The RedHawks put the game out of reach in the fourth quarter with Boucher's 5-yard touchdown pass to Nick Harwell.

2011 Cotton Bowl Classic

The 2011 AT&T Cotton Bowl Classic was the 75th edition of the annual bowl game. The game featured the LSU Tigers of the Southeastern Conference who defeated the Texas A&M Aggies of the Big 12 Conference by a score of 41-24. The game was held at Cowboys Stadium in Arlington, Texas. This was the second time it was held in Cowboys Stadium. The game was broadcast by Fox.

Teams - The meeting between the Tigers and the Aggies was the 50th all-time between the teams, but the first since the 1995 season. LSU and Texas A&M met every year from 1986 through 1995 before the series was discontinued. It was the second time LSU and Texas A&M squared off in a bowl game, the first being the 1944 Orange Bowl.

2011 Cotton Bowl Classic	Line	1	-	2	-	3	-	4	-	Final
#11 LSU	(-1.5)	7	-	21	-	7	-	6	-	41
#18 Texas A&M	(49.0)	10	-	7	-	0	-	7	-	24

Scoring Summary
Texas A&M - Nwachukwu 6 yard pass from Tannehill (Bullock kick)
Texas A&M - Bullock 39 yard field goal
LSU - Toliver 42 yard pass from Jefferson (Jasper kick)
LSU - Jefferson 1 yard run (Jasper kick)
Texas A&M - Nwachukwu 14 yard pass from Gray (Bullock kick)
LSU - Ridley 17 yard run (Jasper kick)
LSU - Toliver 2 yard pass from Jefferson (Jasper kick)
LSU - Toliver 41 yard pass from Jefferson (Jasper kick)
Texas A&M - McNeal 4 yard pass from Tannehill (Bullock kick)
LSU - Jasper 50 yard field goal
LSU - Jasper 26 yard field goal

Cotton Bowl Classic Game Summary - In the first primetime game in Classic history, it was LSU who stole the show in a 41-24 win over the Texas A&M Aggies. LSU (11-2) won its third AT&T Cotton Bowl in the last four tries, while Texas A&M (9-4) snapped a six-game winning streak and saw its overall record in the Classic drop to 4-8. On the night of the Classic's 75th anniversary, where former Syracuse great Jim Brown and 20 other Hall of Fame players and coaches were honored, it was the Tigers' Quarterback, Jordan Jefferson who joined the likes of other memorable performances in the tradition rich bowl. Jefferson's receiver, Terrance Tolliver, tied a Cotton Bowl record with three touchdown receptions and earned the Sanford Trophy presented to the game's most outstanding offensive player. The Tigers featured two 100-yard rushers with Stevan Ridley and Spencer Ware. LSU became the second team in Cotton Bowl history to boast two 100-yard rushers and a 100-yard receiver in the same game joining Arkansas in the 1990 Classic. While the LSU offense was busy setting records, the Tigers' defense rebounded from a slow start to stymie the Texas A&M offensive attack as the game progressed. The LSU defense forced four A&M turnovers including three interceptions and one fumble. Freshman cornerback Tyrann Mathieu led the Tigers' defensive charge earning eight tackles, a sack, an interception, two forced fumble and a fumble return. He stripped Texas A&M wide receiver Hutson Prioleau and appeared to return the loose ball 37 yards for a touchdown, before a penalty brought the play back. LSU maintained possession, however, and the Tigers ran out the clock to clinch the win. For his defensive efforts, Mathieu earned the McKnight Trophy as the outstanding defensive player of the game. Although the Tigers came out victorious, it was not without a hard fought effort put up by Texas A&M. Texas A&M Quarterback Ryan Tannehill completed 22-of-35 passes for 204 yards and two touchdowns, but also was intercepted three times and sacked twice. Aggies' running back Cyrus Gray earned 100 yards on 20 carries, while wide receiver Jeff Fuller had seven receptions netting 83 yards. Thanks to a stunning kickoff return by Coryell Judie, the Aggies took the first quarter by storm an amassed 10-0 lead, but with the power offense displayed by the Tigers, the Aggies didn't stand a chance. LSU Quarterback Jordan Jefferson assisted in leading the Tiger charge, connecting with receiver Terrance Toliver three times for three scores throughout the rest of the game. By the end of the first quarter, the Tigers led 28-17 from scores by Ridley and Toliver. The 45 combined points scored by both teams in the first half tied the Classic record matching the 2009 Ole Miss-Texas Tech and the 1985 Houston-Boston College games. LSU wasted little time revving back up the offense after the halftime break. In the third quarter, after another touchdown reception, Toliver tied USC's Keyshawn Johnson for the Cotton Bowl record of three touchdown receptions in a game. LSU kept a 35-17 lead heading into the final quarter of play. The Aggies' offense was on the march to begin the fourth quarter going 73 yards on 13 plays to the end zone. On third and goal at the four yard-line, Tannehill spotted Kenric McNeal for a four-yard touchdown pass and Randy Bullock converted on the extra point; A&M cut into the LSU lead at 35-24 with 10:04 to play. But, on the following LSU drive of 19 yards in seven plays, Jasper tied a Cotton Bowl record by nailing a 50-yard field goal. He joined Alabama's Greg Gantt (1973) and Miami's Carlos Huerta (1991) on the record-breaking field goal list. Jasper was called on again on the Tigers' next offensive possession, hitting a 26-yard field goal with 3:04 remaining. A fumble recovery by LSU's Mathieu on the next play from scrimmage ended Texas A&M's drive and clinched the victory for the Tigers, 41-24.

2011 BBVA Compass Bowl

The 2011 BBVA Compass Bowl (formerly known as the Papajohns.com Bowl and the Birmingham Bowl) was between teams from the Big East Conference and from the SEC played at Legion Field in Birmingham, Alabama on January 8, 2011. ESPN provided television coverage. The game was initially renamed "The Birmingham Bowl" after previous title sponsor PapaJohns.com decided not to renew their sponsorship of the game.

2011 BBVA Compass Bowl	Line	1	-	2	-	3	-	4	-	Final
Pittsburgh	(-3.5)	0	-	13	-	7	-	7	-	27
Kentucky	(52.0)	3	-	0	-	7	-	0	-	10

Scoring Summary
Kentucky - McIntosh 50 yard Field goal
Pittsburgh - Hutchins 21 yard Field goal
Pittsburgh - Hutchins 33 yard Field goal
Pittsburgh - Sunseri 1 yard run (Hutchins kick)
Pittsburgh - DeCicco 13 yard pass from Sunseri (Hutchins kick)
Kentucky - Allen 1 yard run (McIntosh kick)
Pittsburgh - Lewis 2 yard run (Hutchins kick)

Associated Press BBVA Compass Bowl Game Summary - Pittsburgh players dumped the cooler full of sports drink on Phil Bennett. They hoped Dave Wannstedt, watching on TV in Naples, Fla., also felt an affectionate chill. Pittsburgh scored touchdowns off two mistakes by Kentucky's punting team and the Panthers, playing for their former coach, beat the Wildcats 27-10 in the BBVA Compass Bowl on Saturday. Pittsburgh players dedicated the win to Wannstedt, who was forced to resign following a disappointing regular season. Bennett, the defensive coordinator, was the acting head coach in his final game with Pittsburgh. Bennett was hired Friday as Baylor's defensive coordinator. Pitt hired Miami of Ohio coach Mike Haywood to replace Wannstedt, but Haywood was fired less than three weeks later after he was jailed in Indiana on a domestic violence charge. The school has yet to hire another head coach. Pittsburgh's players were not overwhelmed by the turmoil. Andrew Taglianetti blocked a punt to set up Pittsburgh's first touchdown late in the first half. An incomplete pass on Kentucky's fake punt early in the second half set up Tino Sunseri's 13-yard touchdown pass to Brock DeCicco. Sunseri also ran for a touchdown. The Panthers (8-5) protected the lead with their running game. Dion Lewis ran for 105 yards and a touchdown, and Ray Graham added 90 yards rushing as the Panthers outgained Kentucky 261-104 on the ground. Sunseri completed 9 of 19 passes for 96 yards and a touchdown. Kentucky (6-7), playing without suspended Quarterback Mike Hartline, fell far below its average of 33 points per game. Morgan Newton making his first start since his 2009 freshman season, was 21 of 36 passing for 211 yards. Pitt led 20-3 before the Wildcats' only touchdown, a 1-yard run by Moncell Allen late in the third quarter. The Panthers answered with a long drive and 2-yard touchdown run by Lewis. Randall Cobb set the Southeastern Conference's single-season record for all-purpose yards, but the versatile junior couldn't help the Wildcats overcome their special team's mistakes. Pittsburgh led 6-3 on two field goals by Dan Hutchins before Taglianetti blocked Ryan Tydlacka's punt late in the first half. Tydlacka appeared to take an extra step before attempting a rugby style punt. Pitt's Kolby Gray recovered at the Kentucky 10, setting up Sunseri's 1-yard scoring run for a 13-3 lead with only 34 seconds remaining in the half. Kentucky's first possession of the second half ended with another key mistake by its punting team. Matt Roark took the snap on the apparent punt, but he didn't have time to make his planned pass. He was ruled down on the Kentucky 35 before throwing an incomplete pass. Following a 21-yard run by Graham, Sunseri's touchdown pass to DeCicco gave the Panthers a 20-3 lead. Craig McIntosh gave Kentucky a 3-0 lead with a 50-yard field goal, matching the longest of the sophomore's career, in the first quarter. The kick also was the longest in the five-year history of the bowl. McIntosh missed from 41 yards in the fourth quarter. There were offsetting personal fouls when players traded punches in the second quarter. Tempers flared when Pittsburgh was called for a false start and a Kentucky player hit Sunseri as officials attempted to stop the play. Pittsburgh's Jason Pinkston responded with a shove to set off the brawl. Coaches from each team were successful in keeping players on the sidelines. Cobb passed former Arkansas running back Darren McFadden's 2007 SEC record of 2,310 all-purpose yards. Cobb entered the game 119 yards behind McFadden's mark. Cobb, who had three carries for 23 yards and five catches for 62 yards, added 119 yards on returns for 204 all-purpose yards. The junior said he'll decide on entering the NFL draft within a week.

2011 Kraft Fight Hunger Bowl

The 2011 Kraft Fight Hunger Bowl game was the 9th edition of the annual bowl game known previously as the Emerald Bowl. It was played at AT&T Park in San Francisco, California on January 9, 2011 between the Nevada Wolf Pack and the Boston College Eagles. ESPN television broadcast the game with Kraft as the title sponsor. This marked the first time in the bowl's history that the game was not played in December; the game was played the night before the BCS National Championship Game.

2011 Kraft Fight Hunger Bowl	Line	1	-	2	-	3	-	4	-	Final
Nevada	(-7.5)	14	-	3	-	3	-	0	-	20
Boston College	(55.0)	7	-	0	-	3	-	3	-	13

Scoring Summary
Boston College - Williams 30 yard run (Freese kick)
Nevada - Matthews 27 yard pass from Kaepernick (Martinez kick)
Nevada - Matthews 72 yard punt return (Martinez kick)
Nevada - Martinez 32 yard Field goal
Boston College - Freese 22 yard Field goal
Nevada - Martinez 27 yard Field goal
Boston College - Freese 32 yard Field goal

Associated Press Kraft Fight Hunger Bowl Game Summary - Nevada rode Colin Kaepernick and a high-powered offense to its most successful season since joining the top division of college football. With Kaepernick and the Wolf Pack's potent running game bottled up most of the night, it was the defense and special teams that delivered. Rishard Matthews caught a touchdown pass and returned a punt for another score, and Nevada (No. 15 BCS, No. 13 AP) used its best defensive game of the season to beat Boston College 20-13 in the Kraft Fight Hunger Bowl on Sunday night. Kaepernick threw for 192 yards and a touchdown for the Wolf Pack (13-1), who snapped a four-game bowl losing streak by tying a school record for wins in a season, set when it played in what used to be Division I-AA. The win was appropriately sealed by Khalid Wooten's interception on the final drive of the game for the Eagles (7-6). The final win was unlike almost all the others as Nevada had a season-low in points and finished more than 200 yards shy of its season average. But the Wolf Pack got their first punt return for a touchdown in nine years and gave up a season-low 185 yards. The game matched BC's top-ranked rushing defense against Nevada's high-powered pistol attack that was third in the nation in rushing. The defense won that battle, holding the Wolf Pack to a season-low 114 yards on the ground, including just 22 for Kaepernick. Freshman Chase Rettig completed 14 of 34 passes for 121 yards and two interceptions. Boston College played without leading rusher Montel Harris, who got hurt stretching before the game. The teams traded field goals in the third quarter, giving Nevada a 20-10 lead. Boston College was unable to capitalize on an interception that Luke Kuechly returned to the Wolf Pack 6. But two runs netted just a yard and Rettig threw an incompletion, forcing the kick. After Nevada's field goal late in the third, Rettig's was intercepted by Marlon Johnson on a deflected ball that gave Nevada possession at the BC 41. Vai Taua fumbled the ball right back but once again the Eagles were unable to take advantage. Helped by a pair of pass interference penalties, BC got a 32-yard field goal from Nate Freese with 3:52 to play to make it 20-13. The Eagles got the ball back at their 10 with 3:06 to go and got a 32-yard pass from Rettig to Chris Pantale on their first play. Two plays later, Wooten intercepted a pass to send thousands of Nevada fans home happy. The Wolf Pack sold about 15,500 tickets, surpassing California and Navy for the most in the nine-year history of this game. The attendance of 41,063 was the second largest for the bowl. It included one streaker, who ran on the field in the fourth quarter, causing a brief delay. After an early fumble by Kaepernick led to a 30-yard touchdown run by Andre Williams, Matthews provided the Nevada fans plenty to cheer about in the first half. First, Matthews got behind the defense as Kaepernick scrambled to his left. Kaepernick then flicked a pass toward the end zone for an easy 27-yard score that tied the game for Nevada. The Wolf Pack then held the Eagles to a three-and-out and Matthews returned the punt 72 yards to make it 14-7. That was Nevada's first punt return for a score since Oct. 13, 2001. Nevada added a 32-yard field goal by Anthony Martinez to take a 10-point lead at the half. The game was sponsored by Kraft, which is using the bowl to promote its efforts to fight hunger in the United States. Instead of a coin for the opening toss, officials tossed an Oreo cookie that was chocolate on one side and vanilla on the other.

2011 BCS Championship Game

The 2011 Tostitos BCS National Championship Game was to determine the national champion of the 2010 NCAA Division I Football Bowl Subdivision (FBS) season. The finale of the 2010-2011 Bowl Championship Series was played at the University of Phoenix Stadium, the host facility of the Fiesta Bowl in Glendale, Arizona on January 10, 2011. The Auburn Tigers from the Southeastern Conference faced the Oregon Ducks of the Pacific-10 Conference for the National Championship. A 19-yard field goal by Wes Byrum, as time expired, won the game for the Tigers, with the final score 22-19. The game was the first BCS National Championship Game not televised on network television, instead being aired on ESPN and simulcast on ESPN3, and recorded a 16.1 rating, the highest overnight rating on record for a cable television program, topping the previous high of 14.4, set by Patriots/Saints on ESPN in 2009. This marked the second time that the National Championship under the BCS system was played in Arizona. It was also the first time that the BCS National Championship was streamed to a video game console, specifically the Xbox 360.

Teams - Finishing No. 1 and No. 2 in the final BCS ranking respectively, the Auburn Tigers from the Southeastern Conference faced the Oregon Ducks of the Pacific-10 Conference for the National Championship. Both teams finished the regular season undefeated. The coaches' poll had Auburn as the No. 1 team in the country, with Oregon as No. 2.

Oregon Ducks - The Ducks led the conference in scoring offense (592 points, 49.3 average), rushing offense (42 touchdowns, 303.8 yards per game), rushing defense (11 touchdowns, 117.6 yards per game), and total offense (71 touchdowns, 537.5 yards per game). Oregon was wearing the Nike new Pro Combat uniforms, their 13th uniform combination worn this season.

Auburn Tigers - The Tigers completed the season on top of the conference in scoring offense (42.7 points per game), rushing offense (287.2 yards per game) and total offense (497.7 yards per game). Auburn also led the conference in pass efficiency (174 of 261 passes, 6 interceptions, 66.7%, 29 touchdowns), third-down conversions (77 of 145, 53.1%) and first downs (316 or 24.3 per game).

2011 BCS Championship	Line	1	-	2	-	3	-	4	-	Final
#2 Oregon	(74.0)	0	-	11	-	0	-	8	-	19
#1 Auburn	(-2.5)	0	-	16	-	3	-	3	-	22

Scoring Summary
Oregon - Beard 26 yard field goal
Auburn - Burns 35 yard pass from Newton (Byrum kick)
Oregon - James 8 yard pass from Thomas (Beard run)
Auburn - Safety - James tackled in end zone by Blanc
Auburn - Blake 30 yard pass from Newton (Byrum kick)
Auburn - Byrum 28 yard field goal
Oregon - James 2 yard pass from Thomas (Maehl pass from Thomas)
Auburn - Byrum 19 yard field goal

Auburn Media Guide BCS Championship Game Summary - Wes Byrum kicked the sixth and biggest game-winning field goal of his career on the last play of the game from 19 yards to give No. 1 Auburn a 22-19 victory over Oregon in the BCS National Championship Game. It was Auburn's second national title in history and ninth comeback win in 14 games during the 2010 season. After Oregon had tied the score at 19 with a touchdown and two point conversion with 2:33 to go, the biggest drive in Auburn history began at its own 25-yard line. After a 15-yard pass from Cam Newton to Emory Blake, Michael Dyer, who was named the Offensive Player of the Game after rushing for 143 yards on 22 carries, looked to be tackled after a short gain, but was never down while laying on top of an Oregon defender, and he bounced up to complete a 37-yard run to the Oregon 23. After short gains by Dyer and Newton, Dyer followed with a 16-yard gain up the middle to the 1 with 10 seconds remaining. One play later, Byrum provided the final heroics. Oregon scored on the second play of the second quarter on a 26-yard field goal by Rob Beard for the first points of the game. On Auburn's next possession, Newton threw a 35-yard touchdown pass to Kodi Burns for a 7-3 Auburn lead. Oregon responded after taking over at the Duck 7 as Thomas threw an 81-yard pass on first down to Meahl, then found James on an 8-yard TD pass. A 2-point conversion run by kicker Rob Beard on a fake gave Oregon an 11-7 lead. The Tigers then drove to the Oregon 1, but Newton's fourth-down pass to Eric Smith fell incomplete. On first down, Mike Blanc tackled James in the end zone for a safety to draw the Tigers to within 11-9 with 3:26 left in the half. After Oregon kicked off following the safety, Auburn quickly covered 66 yards in six plays, capped by a Newton to Blake 30-yard touchdown pass to give the Tigers a 16-11 lead at the half. On the opening drive of the second half, Wes Byrum kicked a 28-yard field goal to give Auburn a 19-11 lead. Oregon then reached a first-and goal on the Auburn 3, but the Tigers held the Ducks for four plays, capped by a stop on fourth and goal from the 1 as Mike McNeil and Nick Fairley hit Kenjon Barner just shy of the goal line. Fairley was named the Defensive Player of the Game after recording five tackles, including three for losses and one sack, while also forcing a fumble. Auburn ran a season high and BCS Championship Game record 85 plays. The Tigers outgained the Ducks 519 yards to 449 as Newton was 20-of-34 for 265 yards and two touchdowns. He also rushed for 64 yards on 22 carries.

Notes - Seven BCS Championship game records were broken or tied, including the longest pass play when Darron Thomas passed to Jeff Maehl for 81 yards, the most team passing yards (374, Oregon), and most 2-point conversions (2). The combined passing yardage of the two teams (639 yards) were also the most in the games. Auburn's 85 total plays were a new record, exceeding the record set at the January 4, 2006 game between Texas and USC with 82 plays.

2011 New Orleans Bowl

The 2011 R+L Carriers New Orleans Bowl took place on December 17, 2011, at the Mercedes-Benz Superdome in New Orleans, Louisiana. The 11th edition of the game featured the Louisiana–Lafayette Ragin' Cajuns from the Sun Belt Conference (Sun Belt), and the San Diego State Aztecs from the Mountain West Conference. The game was telecast on ESPN and ESPN 3D. In 2015, the NCAA vacated Louisiana–Lafayette's New Orleans Bowl win due to major violations including ACT exam fraud and payments to recruits.

2011 New Orleans Bowl	Line	1	-	2	-	3	-	4	-	Final
San Diego State	(-4.5)	3	-	0	-	14	-	13	-	30
Louisiana-Lafayette	(59.0)	6	-	7	-	6	-	13	-	32

Scoring Summary
San Diego State - Perez 27 yard Field goal
UL-Lafayette - Gautier 18 yard pass from Lawson (Kick blocked)
UL-Lafayette - Surgent 87 yard punt return (Baer kick)
UL-Lafayette - Gautier 20 yard pass from Green (Kick blocked)
San Diego State - Lindley 16 yard pass from Lockett (Perez kick)
San Diego State - Lindley 16 yard pass from Lockett (Perez kick)
UL-Lafayette - Gautier 11 yard pass from Lawson (Baer kick)
San Diego State - Muema 5 yard run (Perez kick)
UL-Lafayette - Baer 22 yard Field goal
San Diego State - Lindley 12 yard pass from Lockett (Pass failed)
UL-Lafayette - Baer 50 yard Field goal

Associated Press New Orleans Bowl Game Summary - Blaine Gautier's record-setting passing and a long clutch kick by Brett Baer gave Louisiana-Lafayette fans the kind of thrills they haven't had since Jake Delhomme was playing for the Ragin' Cajuns. Gautier passed for 470 yards and three scores, and Baer kicked a 50-yard field goal as time ran out, lifting Louisiana-Lafayette to 32-30 victory over San Diego State in the R+L Carriers New Orleans Bowl on Saturday night. Before the kick had even sailed through the uprights, Baer was off and running in celebration and briefly jumped into the first row of the Superdome stands before teammates caught up with him and lifted the kicker onto their shoulders. Playing in their first bowl game as a Division I FBS team, the Ragin Cajuns (9-4) led most of the way but fell behind 30-29 when Aztecs Quarterback Ryan Lindley connected with Colin Lockett on a 12-yard touchdown strike with 35 seconds to go. Gautier drove Louisiana-Lafayette 44 yards to the Aztecs 38 to set up what was initially a 55-yard attempt, but a pre-snap penalty on SDSU (8-5) for trying to bait the Cajuns into a false start moved the winning kick 5 yards closer. Gautier finished with 2,958 yards passing and 23 TDs on the season, breaking Delhomme's single-season school records. Delhomme held those records since 1996, when he passed for 2,901 yards and 20 TDs. Gautier's passing total also shattered the New Orleans Bowl record for yards passing, set a season ago when Troy's Corey Robinson passed for 387. Gautier threw two touchdown passes to Javone Lawson, from 18 and 11 yards out, and had a 20-yard scoring strike to Ladarius Green. Darryl Surgent returned a punt 87 yards for a score, slicing through SDSU's punt coverage with a quick cut to his right and a sprint back to the left. The receiver finished with 283 all-purpose yards. The Ragin' Cajuns had not appeared in a bowl of any kind since playing in the Grantland Rice Bowl 41 years ago. Thousands of red-clad, bowl-starved fans followed the Ragin' Cajuns to New Orleans and helped set a New Orleans Bowl attendance record of 42,841. Lawson, who grew up in suburban New Orleans, made nine catches for 193 yards, including a 52-yard catch and run that set up Green's TD. Green caught five passes for 121 yards. Until his final kick, Baer thought he might have cost his team the game by missing two extra-point tries. Lindley was 28 of 49 for 413 yards and three touchdowns. The Aztecs needed every bit of that as their offensive star, running back Ronnie Hillman, was largely bottled up and finished with 55 yards, well below his average of 138 yards. Lindley found Lockett for a pair of 16-yard scoring passes in the third quarter, when the Aztecs trimmed a 19-3 deficit to 19-17. Lockett's second TD capped a seven-play, 99-yard drive. The Ragin' Cajuns responded with a 14-play, 78-yard drive that included three third-down conversions and Lawson's second TD. Adam Muema's 5-yard touchdown run up the middle pulled SDSU back to 26-24 with 5:40 left, but the Cajuns marched right back down the field and were in position to put the game away. Surgent made a one-handed catch while reaching around behind defensive back Leon McFadden, even as McFadden was interfering with him. He then broke free of McFadden for a 56-yard gain to the SDSU 20. Lawson then pulled down a catch between two defenders while being interfered with, giving the Cajuns a first down on the 3. But Louisiana-Lafayette was forced to settle for Baer's 22-yard field goal, setting up the wild finish. The Aztecs were left to regret missed opportunities, including a 36-yard field goal attempt that Abeladro Perez hooked wide right with just more than 10 minutes to go. They had a first-and-goal on the 4 on their opening drive, only to go backward and settle for Perez's 27-yard field goal. Early in the second quarter, SDSU appeared to have a successful short passing play set up on fourth-and 1 from the Louisiana-Lafayette 6, but Dylan Denso could not keep his feet as a he made the catch and landed inches short of the first-down marker.

Controversy - Prior to a 55-yard field goal attempt by the UL-Lafayette Cajuns with four seconds to go, an official called a five-yard "illegal stemming" penalty against the SDSU Aztecs to set up the Cajuns' 50-yard game-winning field goal. Following the game, Aztecs coach Rocky Long said it was a "phantom call," claiming that no one was moving on the Aztec's side. The replays clearly show the Aztec defender was not moving.

2011 Famous Idaho Potato Bowl

The 2011 Famous Idaho Potato Bowl, the 15th edition of the game, was held on December 17, 2011 at Bronco Stadium on the campus of Boise State University in Boise, Idaho. This was the first year the game was known as the Famous Idaho Potato Bowl. The game was known as the Humanitarian Bowl in 2010.

2011 Famous Idaho Potato Bowl	Line	1	-	2	-	3	-	4	-	Final
Ohio	(60.0)	0	-	7	-	10	-	7	-	24
Utah State	(-1.5)	9	-	0	-	14	-	0	-	23

Scoring Summary
Utah State - Team safety
Utah State - Lloyd 3 yard pass from Kennedy (Thompson kick)
Ohio - Roback 26 yard pass from Tettleton (Weller kick)
Utah State - Smith 63 yard run (Thompson kick)

Ohio - Weller 32 yard Field goal
Utah State - Smith 11 yard run (Thompson kick)
Ohio - Brazill 44 yard pass from Tettleton (Weller kick)
Ohio - Tettleton 1 yard run (Weller kick)

Associated Press Famous Idaho Potato Bowl Game Summary - Tyler Tettleton's late heroics helped Ohio erase decades of misery in the postseason. The sophomore calmly led a 61-yard drive in the final 2:02 and scored on a 1-yard keeper with 13 seconds left to give Ohio its first bowl victory, 24-23 over Utah State on Saturday in the Famous Idaho Potato Bowl. Ohio had been winless in five bowl appearances, including setbacks the last two seasons. But Tettleton changed all that, going 3 of 4 passing in the final drive, including a 14-yard completion to LaVon Brazill on fourth down to give Ohio a first down inside the 1 with 37 seconds left. After getting stuffed on his first attempt to punch the ball in, Tettleton rolled right on the next play and outran two defenders to cap the comeback and set a new course for Ohio's postseason future. The victory also gave Ohio its first 10-win season since 1968 and helped blunt the bitterness of letting Northern Illinois rally from a 20-point deficit in the Mid-American Conference title game two weeks ago. Tettleton, the son of former major league catcher Mickey Tettleton, was effective throughout the game and kept the Bobcats close enough with his legs and arm. Tettleton was 19 of 26 passing for 220 yards and two touchdowns and rushed 16 times for 31 yards. He was only sacked twice and spread his completions around to seven receivers and the Bobcats had 345 total yards on offense. For Utah State, the loss was a heartbreaker. The Aggies dominated the first half and extended their lead to 23-10 in the third quarter behind a bruising rushing attack that kept Tettleton off the field and rolled up 345 yards. The Aggies came into the game with the nation's sixth-best rushing attack, averaging 277 yards per game. Michael Smith rushed for a career-best 157 yards and two touchdowns on 12 carries, including a 63-yard scoring run early in the third quarter that put Utah State up 16-10. Smith scored later in the third on an 11-yard run up the middle, giving the Aggies (7-6) a 13-point lead. Robert Turbin added 101 yards on 20 carries, and Kerwynn Williams had 69 yards on nine carries. But Utah State, which finished second in the Western Athletic Conference and was making its first bowl appearance since 1997, failed to close the deal and paid a price for missing two scoring chances early in the game. On their first possession, the Aggies (7-6) drove to the 1, but Turbin was stopped short of the goal line on fourth down. The Aggies missed another chance late in the second quarter when a 39-yard field-goal attempt by Josh Thompson sailed wide right. Still, head coach Gary Andersen, whose team closed the season with five straight wins to earn the school's first bowl invitation since 1997, believes there is plenty to feel good about and even more to build upon. The Aggies had a chance to ice the game when they took possession at their own 7 with 4:23 to go. But Ohio's defense stopped the Aggies on three straight running plays to force a punt. On the winning drive, Tettleton scrambled for 14 yards and completed passes of 19, 7 and 14 yards to Brazill. The last reception was initially ruled a touchdown, but a review concluded he was down before the end zone, giving Ohio a first down inside the 1 and setting up Tettleton's big play. Brazill, who was voted MVP for the game, led the Bobcats with eight catches for 108 yards, including a 44-yard touchdown pass from Tettleton that pulled Ohio to 23-17 with 3:45 left in the third quarter. The Aggies had just two possessions in the fourth quarter, but managed just two first downs, putting the onus on a defense that had let leads slip away in the last minute in games against Auburn and Brigham Young.

2011 New Mexico Bowl

The 2011 New Mexico Bowl was held on December 17, 2011 at University Stadium on the campus of the University of New Mexico in Albuquerque, New Mexico. The game, which was telecast on ESPN, featured the Wyoming Cowboys from the Mountain West Conference versus the Temple Owls from the Mid-American Conference. Temple made its first trip to the New Mexico Bowl, becoming the first team from the MAC to appear in the game. The Owls made just their fourth bowl appearance in school history, and their second in the last three years. Wyoming appeared in its second New Mexico Bowl. The Cowboys were 35–28 victors over Fresno State in the 2009 New Mexico Bowl. The two schools have only previously played each other on one occasion. Wyoming won the 1990 matchup in Laramie, Wyoming by a score of 38–23.

2011 New Mexico Bowl	Line	1	-	2	-	3	-	4	-	Final
Temple	(-7.0)	7	-	21	-	3	-	6	-	37
Wyoming	(50.5)	0	-	7	-	0	-	8	-	15

Scoring Summary
Temple - Pierce 1 yard run (McManus kick)
Temple - Pierce 1 yard run (McManus kick)
Temple - Brown 1 yard run (McManus kick)
Wyoming - Doctson 21 yard pass from Smith (Sullivan kick)
Temple - Streater 61 yard pass from Coyer (McManus kick)
Temple - McManus 34 yard Field goal
Temple - McManus 37 yard Field goal
Temple - McManus 34 yard Field goal
Wyoming - Sutton 14 yard pass from Smith (Smith run)

Associated Press New Mexico Bowl Game Summary - Temple came out swinging against Wyoming, jumping to a 21-0 lead in the first half of the Gildan New Mexico Bowl on Saturday. But when Wyoming freshman Brett Smith threw a 21-yard touchdown pass to Josh Doctson with 37 seconds remaining in the first half, Temple Quarterback Chris Coyer feared that Wyoming found a spark. Then, moments later, Coyer responded with 61-yarder to Rod Streater to give the Owls a 28-7 lead. It was never close again. Bernard Pierce ran for two early touchdowns and Coyer threw for 169 yards and the touchdown to help Temple overwhelm Wyoming 37-15 in the New Mexico Bowl -- the first bowl game of the season. The Owls (9-4) had three interceptions -- tying a New Mexico Bowl record -- enroute to the second bowl victory in school history. The first interception came at the start of the second quarter when Temple's Kee-arye Griffin picked off Smith's pass to setting up Matt Brown's 1-yard touchdown run that gave the Owls a 21-0 lead. The last one came late in the game to Temple's Kevin Kroboth, resulting in a field goal. The New Mexico Bowl was Temple's second bowl game in three years, but that 2009 game -- a 30-21 loss to UCLA in the EagleBank Bowl in Washington -- was the Owls' first bowl in 30 years. The Mid-American Conference East runner-up did not get a bowl invite last year despite going 8-4. Coyer, who also rushed for 71 yards, was selected the game's offensive MVP. Meanwhile, Smith was held to just 127 yards by a greedy Owls defensive line that prevented the Cowboys from getting anything started. The loss dropped the Cowboys (8-5) to 6-7 in bowl games. It was a disappointed effort by Wyoming after the Cowboys won the 2009 New Mexico Bowl in double overtime, beating Fresno State 35-28.

2011 Beef 'O' Brady's Bowl

The 2011 Beef O'Brady's Bowl St. Petersburg, the fourth edition of the game, was held on December 20, 2011 at Tropicana Field in St. Petersburg, Florida, and telecast on ESPN. Marshall defeated Florida International 20–10 for their 7th victory of the season. The final standings are Marshall 7–6 and Florida International 8–5.

2011 Beef 'O' Brady's Bowl	Line	1	-	2	-	3	-	4	-	Final
Florida International	(-4.0)	7	-	3	-	0	-	0	-	10
Marshall	(48.5)	3	-	7	-	0	-	10	-	20

Scoring Summary
Marshall - Warner 37 yard Field goal
Florida International - Hilton 2 yard run (Griffin kick)
Florida International - Griffin 46 yard Field goal
Marshall - Dobson 31 yard pass from Cato (Warner kick)
Marshall - Warner 39 yard Field goal
Marshall - Dobson 35 yard pass from Cato (Warner kick)

Associated Press Beef 'O' Brady's Bowl Game Summary - Marshall's Rakeem Cato was back in the state of Florida, so it wasn't surprising that the freshman Quarterback felt so comfortable and confident that he pushed coach Doc Holliday to give him a chance to seal the Beef 'O' Brady's Bowl. Cato threw for 226 yards and two touchdowns to pace a 20-10 victory over Florida International on Tuesday night. Cato threw TD passes of 31 and 35 yards to Aaron Dobson, the latter putting the game away in the closing seconds. Warner's 39-yard field goal set up by a blocked punt snapped a 10-10 with 5:16 remaining. Marshall (7-6) overcame a slow start to win five of its last seven games and avoid a losing record in its second season under Holliday. FIU (8-5) was denied a school-record ninth victory and there is speculation that Coach Mario Cristobal may be a leading candidate to fill a job opening at Pittsburgh. The coach has not commented on reports that he may have met with Pitt already. Athletic director Pete Garcia was interviewed by ESPN during the network's telecast of the game, which drew an announced crowd of 20,072 at Tropicana Field. Cato, a freshman from Miami who is one of 28 players on Marshall's roster recruited from the state of Florida, completed 27 of 39 passes and was intercepted once. Dobson had seven receptions for 81 yards, including a TD catch that wiped out a 10-3 FIU lead just before halftime. All-purpose threat T.Y. Hilton scored on a 2-yard run for FIU, which also got a 46-yard field goal from Jack Griffin. Hilton had eight catches for 88 yards, ran for 22 yards on three carries and returned two kickoffs for 36 yards, but Quarterback Wesley Carroll had difficulty getting the ball to him in open space in the second half. Carroll was 19 of 29 passing for 150 yards. Marshall struggled early against a tough schedule, losing in September to West Virginia, Ohio and Virginia Tech before regrouping late win four of six down the stretch to become bowl eligible and finish second behind Southern Mississippi in the Conference USA East Division standings. FIU is a relative newcomer to the Football Bowl Subdivision. The Panthers launched their program in 2002, joined the Sun Belt Conference in 2005 and have made steady progress in five seasons under Cristobal, who led the school to its first Sun Belt championship a year ago. Hilton has been a big part of that success, setting FIU and Sun Belt records for career receiving and all-purpose yards. The senior from Miami caught a TD pass and scored on an 89-yard kickoff return to help the Panthers beat Toledo in last year's Little Caesars Bowl, and FIU showcased his versatility early against Marshall. The 5-foot-10, 185-pound receiver took a handoff on FIU's first play from scrimmage and ran for 20 yards before fumbling 5 yards backward. He had a 17-yard reception on the next play, then later in the opening quarter gained 14 yards on a catch-and-run to the Marshall 2. Hilton scored his first rushing touchdown of the season on the next play, giving the Panthers a 7-3 lead. Marshall answered Jack Griffin's 46-yard field goal that put FIU up 10-3 with a six-play, 55-yard drive that Cato finished with his 31-yard TD pass to Dobson to make it 10-10 with 23 seconds left in the first half. Neither team was able to generate much offense in the third and fourth quarters. Zach Dunston blocked a punt to set up Warner's go-ahead field goal, and Cato began the clinching drive from his own 40 after FIU fumbled.

2011 Poinsettia Bowl

The 2011 San Diego County Credit Union Poinsettia Bowl, the seventh edition of the game, was held on December 21, 2011 at Snapdragon Stadium in San Diego, California. The game was televised on ESPN and featured the Louisiana Tech Bulldogs from the Western Athletic Conference (WAC) versus the TCU Horned Frogs from the Mountain West Conference.

2011 Poinsettia Bowl	Line	1	-	2	-	3	-	4	-	Final
TCU	(-10.0)	0	-	10	-	7	-	14	-	31
Louisiana Tech	(56.0)	3	-	7	-	14	-	0	-	24

Scoring Summary
Louisiana Tech - Nelson 23 yard Field goal
TCU - Evans 25 yard Field goal
Louisiana Tech - Patton 2 yard pass from Cameron (Nelson kick)
TCU - Wesley 7 yard run (Evans kick)
TCU - Tucker 1 yard run (Evans kick)
Louisiana Tech - Lee 2 yard run (Nelson kick)
Louisiana Tech - White 61 yard run from Cameron (Nelson kick)
TCU - Shivers 1 yard run (Evans kick)
TCU - Dawson 42 yard pass from Pachall (Evans kick)

Associated Press Poinsettia Bowl Game Summary - Casey Pachall and the TCU Horned Frogs are headed to the Big 12 Conference on an eight-game winning streak. Pachall highlighted a record-setting game with a 42-yard touchdown pass to Skye Dawson with 4:26 left to lift TCU to a 31-24 victory against Louisiana Tech in the San Diego County Credit Union Poinsettia Bowl on Wednesday night. It was the eighth straight victory for Mountain West Conference champion TCU (11-2), which moves to the Big 12 next year. It was the third time this season TCU overcame a fourth-quarter deficit to win, including a 36-35 victory at Boise State on Nov. 12, the Broncos' only loss. Pachall was 15 of 29 for 206 yards. He set school single-season records with 228 completions, 2,921 yards and a completion percentage of 66.5, breaking marks previously held by Andy Dalton. On the winning play, the sophomore took the snap in the shotgun and Dawson ran past safety Chad Boyd to pull in the long pass. Pachall said he changed the play when he saw a blitz coming. The Horned Frogs, who beat Wisconsin in the Rose Bowl last season, had hoped to make it to a BCS bowl for the third straight season. TCU tied the game at 24 on Luke Shivers' 1-yard run with 7:49 left that capped an 18-play, 72-yard drive that consumed 9 minutes, 21 seconds. A replay review took away one yard on a completion from Pachall to Matthew Tucker to bring up a fourth-and-1 from the Bulldogs' 9-yard line. Tucker gained six yards for the first down. On third-and-goal from the 8, a pass interference call against the Bulldogs in the end zone gave TCU a first down on the 2. Shivers scored two plays later. The Bulldogs had to punt on their next drive and TCU scored the go-ahead touchdown six plays later. Louisiana Tech seemed to have the momentum after turning two TCU turnovers into scores in the third quarter to take a 24-17 lead. TCU's Brandon Carter fumbled a punt that was recovered on the 12, setting up Hunter Lee's 2-yard run that tied the game at 17. Quinn Giles intercepted a pass from Pachall on the Louisiana Tech 39-yard line. Three plays later, Myles White made a sensational one-handed, over-the-shoulder catch of a 61-yard pass from Colby Cameron for a touchdown and a 24-17 lead. White reached up for the ball with his right hand and pulled it in. The teams traded field goals in the first half before Quinton

Patton pulled in a 2-yard TD pass from Cameron. The play originally was ruled an incompletion but was overturned after video review. Patton got one foot inbounds before tumbling out of the side of the end zone. Late in the first half, TCU cornerback Greg McCoy jumped a route, intercepted Cameron and returned it 25 yards to the Bulldogs' 25. Four plays later, Ed Wesley ran 7 yards up the gut to tie the game at 10. TCU had 190 yards rushing.

2011 Maaco Bowl

The 2011 Maaco Bowl Las Vegas, the 20th edition of the game, was held on December 22, 2011 at Sam Boyd Stadium in Whitney, Nevada. The game, broadcast on ESPN, featured the Boise State Broncos from the Mountain West Conference versus the Arizona State Sun Devils from the Pac-12 Conference.

2011 Maaco Bowl	Line	1	-	2	-	3	-	4	-	Final
Arizona State	(66.5)	0	-	3	-	7	-	14	-	24
#8 Boise State	(-14.0)	14	-	14	-	7	-	21	-	56

Scoring Summary
Boise State - Martin 100 yard kickoff return (Frisina kick)
Boise State - Shoemaker 14 yard pass from Moore (Frisina kick)
Boise State - Miller 2 yard pass from Moore (Frisina kick)
Arizona State - Garouette 32 yard Field goal
Boise State - Efaw 5 yard pass from Miller (Frisina kick)
Arizona State - Ross 98 yard kickoff return (Garouette kick)
Boise State - Taylor 100 yard interception return (Frisina kick)
Boise State - Harper 4 yard run (Frisina kick)
Boise State - Stanaway 26 yard fumble recovery (Frisina kick)
Arizona State - Robinson 21 yard pass from Osweiler (Garouette kick)
Boise State - Martin 2 yard run (Frisina kick)
Arizona State - Bell 30 yard pass from Osweiler (Garouette kick)

Associated Press Maaco Bowl Game Summary - The MAACO Bowl Las Vegas might not have been the capper Boise State Quarterback Kellen Moore wanted for his college career, but the NCAA's winningest passer got to end his run the way he wanted -- with one more win. He threw for 293 yards and two touchdowns, though he also had two interceptions and lost a fumble. The turnovers won't matter as fans in Idaho remember their greatest star, whose set school records for passing yards, touchdowns, completions and total offense, and finished fifth all-time among NCAA Quarterbacks for passing yards while racking up 50 total wins. Boise State (12-1) was able to rest easy from the game's start. Doug Martin returned the opening kickoff 100 yards for a touchdown, giving Boise State a lead 14 seconds into the game. Martin rushed for 151 yards and another touchdown and was voted the game's MVP. Arizona State (6-7) never seriously threatened the Broncos (12-1), even though Moore had three turnovers and allowed a 97-yard kickoff return for a touchdown by the Sun Devils to start the second half. Boise State finished seventh in the BCS standings but wasn't invited to one of its big-money bowl games. The Mountain West and Pac 12 conferences each received $1.1 million for the MAACO Bowl. Arizona State missed on several opportunities to make the game closer, wasting a bowl-record 241-yard receiving effort by Gerell Robinson, who caught a touchdown in the fourth quarter after the Broncos had already scored 49 points. Moore -- the NCAA's winningest player at the position -- played well enough in his last college game to keep his team scoring, despite some missteps. Martin finished with 301 all-purpose yards, breaking a bowl record set in 1997 by Air Force's Pat Johnson. His touchdown return also set a record for the longest kickoff return in MAACO Bowl history. It was the first time the opening kickoff had been returned for a score in any bowl game since Ted Ginn Jr. did it in the 2007 BCS title game. Boise State finished with a bowl record in points scored by a single team, and the teams combined for the highest scoring game in the bowl's 20-year history. The costliest mistake for Arizona State came in the third quarter, as the Sun Devils tried to capitalize on a fumble by Moore -- his third turnover of the game. The Sun Devils drove 49 yards to Boise State's 1-yard line, but Quarterback Brock Osweiler's fourth-down pass was intercepted by Jamar Taylor, who returned it for a touchdown to make the score 35-10. Moments before the play, Arizona State coach Dennis Erickson tried to call a timeout as his team was late to the line of scrimmage, but his attempts weren't acknowledged by the referees. Osweiler, threw for 395 yards with two touchdowns in defeat. Osweiler said his team had some confusion before the play, with the wrong players on the field and a delay in communicating what they wanted to do. The Broncos led 28-3 at halftime with Martin's kick return, Moore's passing touchdowns and another by wide receiver Matt Miller on a trick play in the second quarter. Arizona State didn't score after its first interception and failed to pick off a lofty, poorly aimed toss from Moore's brother, receiver Kirby Moore that hit a Sun Devils defender in the chest during a trick play. Boise State scored its fourth touchdown later in the drive.

2011 Hawai'i Bowl

The 2011 Sheraton Hawaii Bowl, the 10th edition of the game, was held on December 24, 2011 at Aloha Stadium in Honolulu, Hawai'i. The game, which telecast on ESPN, featured the Nevada Wolf Pack from the Western Athletic Conference (WAC) versus the Southern Miss Golden Eagles from Conference USA.

2011 Hawaii Bowl	Line	1	-	2	-	3	-	4	-	Final
Nevada	(63.5)	0	-	14	-	3	-	0	-	17
#22 Southern Miss	(-7.5)	0	-	17	-	0	-	7	-	24

Scoring Summary
Southern Miss - Becton-Martin blocked punt return (Hrapmann kick)
Nevada - Mark 5 yard run (Hardison kick)
Nevada - Mark 45 yard run (Hardison kick)
Southern Miss - Hrapmann 45 yard Field goal
Southern Miss - Lampley 2 yard pass from Davis (Hrapmann kick)
Nevada - Hardison 37 yard Field goal
Southern Miss - Bolden 4 yard pass from Davis (Hrapmann kick)

Associated Press Hawaii Bowl Game Summary - Austin Davis made the plays when it counted to send Southern Mississippi coach Larry Fedora out a winner. Davis threw two touchdowns, including a 4-yarder late in the game, and Southern Miss (No. 21 BCS, No. 22 AP) earned a school-record 12th victory by holding off Nevada 24-17 in the Sheraton Hawaii Bowl on Saturday night. Davis overcame a shaky game for the Conference USA-champion Golden Eagles (12-2), and the defense in the second half managed to shut down Nevada's potent pistol attack led by Lampford Mark. Davis was off most of the night but made it count on the game-winning drive. On third-and-goal, he scrambled right and found Kelvin Bolden for the 4-yard score, capping a seven-play, 68-yard drive. He had just 59 yard passing at halftime and finished 18 of 41 for 165 yards. On the winning drive, Davis was 3 of 4 for 66 yards, including a 43-yard completion to Dominique Sullivan down the right sideline and a 19-yarder to a crossing William Spight. Sullivan had five catches for 75 yards. With Davis held in check, the Golden Eagles relied on their defense, stopping Mark on fourth-and-1 at midfield with 3:56 left. Mark had 183 yards rushing for the Wolf Pack (7-6) but was held to just 21 yards in the second half. Nevada was without its top receiver, Rishard Matthews, who has 91 receptions for 1,364 yards and eight TDs. The game featured a Hawaii Bowl-record 17 punts, and the 41 combined points was the fewest in bowl history. Cody Fajardo was 8 of 19 for 60 yards for Nevada. He also was held to just 14 yards rushing on nine carries before being replaced by Tyler Lantrip. The Golden Eagles got another big win after capturing their fifth C-USA title by upsetting previously unbeaten Houston 49-28 in the conference championship game. This was the first 10-win season for Southern Miss since 1988. Nevada tied the game 17-all late in the third quarter on a 37-yard field goal by Allen Hardison, taking advantage of a miscue by Southern Miss. Tracey Lampley waved for a fair catch on a punt and was run into by teammate Alex Smith. The ball bounced off Lampley's left leg and Nevada's Brandon Marshall recovered on the Southern Miss 14, leading to the field goal. Just as Nevada seemed to take control of the game, Southern Miss scored 10 points in the final 1½ minutes of the first half to take a 17-14 lead into the break. Mark's 45-yard run gave the Wolf Pack a 14-7 lead with about 5 minutes left in the half, and Nevada took the ball right back on the ensuing kickoff. Lorenzo Devers returned the kickoff 61 yards and appeared to be heading for a touchdown. After shedding the kicker, Devers was stripped from behind by Khalid Wooten and Thaddeus Brown returned it 16 yards to the Nevada 36. But the team from Reno gambled and ended up turning it over on downs on its own 45 when Mark was stopped short on fourth-and-1. That led to a 48-yard field goal by Danny Hrappman with 1:21 left in the half. On the kickoff, Wooten fumbled, and Southern Mississippi's Emmanuel Johnson recovered at the Nevada 24. Seven plays later, Davis threw a 2-yard pass to Lampley in the back of the end zone for the go-ahead score. A brief scuffle broke out between some of the players after the catch, but no one was ejected. With both teams struggling to get going, special teams got the Golden Eagles on the scoreboard from a blocked punt by Tim Green early in the second quarter. Green burst through the middle and leaped in the air, getting his hand on the ball as he flipped over a blocker. Tray Becton-Martin then dropped on the ball in the end zone, giving the Golden Eagles a 7-0 lead. Becton-Martin is the 25th different player to score for the Golden Eagles this year, which leads the nation. Nevada answered with a 5-yard touchdown run by Mark, who had a 25-yard scamper to begin the 81-yard drive. Mark had 41 yards rushing on the drive, giving him 112 yards and his sixth-straight game with 100 or more. Both teams blew good scoring opportunities in the first quarter. Mark burst up the middle for 43 yards and was chased down from behind by Presley, getting Nevada inside the red zone. But Fajardo's pass on third down was tipped and intercepted in the end zone by Jacorius Cotton.

2011 Independence Bowl

The 2011 AdvoCare V100 Independence Bowl, the 36th edition of the game, was held on December 26, 2011 at Independence Stadium in Shreveport, Louisiana. The game, telecast on ESPN2, featured the Missouri Tigers from the Big 12 Conference versus the North Carolina Tar Heels from the Atlantic Coast Conference.

2011 Independence Bowl	Line	1	-	2	-	3	-	4	-	Final
Missouri	(-5.0)	14	-	17	-	7	-	3	-	41
North Carolina	(52.5)	7	-	3	-	7	-	7	-	24

Scoring Summary
North Carolina - Jones 22 yard pass from Renner (Moore kick)
Missouri - Kemp 40 yard pass from Moe (Barrow kick)
Missouri - Franklin 2 yard run (Barrow kick)
Missouri - Barrow 31 yard Field goal
Missouri - Jackson 8 yard pass from Franklin (Barrow kick)
Missouri - Lawrence 9 yard run (Barrow kick)
North Carolina - Moore 21 yard Field goal
North Carolina - Boyd 44 yard pass from Renner (Moore kick)
Missouri - Franklin 2 yard run (Barrow kick)
Missouri - Barrow 26 yard Field goal
North Carolina - Highsmith 17 yard pass from Renner (Moore kick)

Associated Press Independence Bowl Game Summary - James Franklin's hard running and timely passing led Missouri to an easy win in its final game as a member of the Big 12. It also gives the Tigers plenty of hope heading into their new home in the Southeastern Conference. Franklin ran for two touchdowns and threw for another, and the Tigers easily beat North Carolina 41-24 in the Independence Bowl on Monday night. Missouri (8-5) ends the season on a four-game winning streak for the first time since 1965. The Tigers will join the SEC next fall and showed one reason they should be a factor immediately: The 6-foot-2, 225-pound Franklin, a sophomore who generally did as he pleased in both the running and passing games. Missouri coach Gary Pinkel said Franklin has just started to realize his potential. Franklin, named the game's offensive Most Valuable Player, rushed for 142 yards and threw for 132 despite less than ideal conditions in the cold and rain at Independence Stadium. He led the Tigers to 31 first-half points -- an Independence Bowl record. For North Carolina (7-6), a season that started with a promising 5-1 record ends with a lopsided loss. The Tar Heels lost five of their final seven under interim coach Everett Withers, who leaves to become defensive coordinator at Ohio State under Urban Meyer. North Carolina had the Atlantic Coast Conference's second-best rushing defense, giving up just 106.2 yards per game. But the Tigers found plenty of running room with Franklin and Kendial Lawrence, repeatedly gashing the Tar Heels for big gains. Lawrence rushed for 108 yards and a touchdown as the Tigers racked up 337 yards on the ground. North Carolina's poor defense wasted a productive game by Quarterback Bryn Renner, who threw for 317 yards, three touchdowns and an interception. But Renner couldn't offset the Tar Heels' anemic running game, which produced just 36 yards. Freshman running back Giovani Bernard rushed for 31 yards -- more than 70 yards less than his season average. Withers said he didn't think the program's upcoming coaching change had any bearing on the outcome. The Tar Heels hired Southern Mississippi's Larry Fedora last week. Missouri's mascot -- Truman the Tiger -- shattered most of the original Independence Bowl trophy before the game started in a pre-game accident. The Tigers were more than happy to claim the replacement. Pinkel didn't shy away from the importance of the game, saying the result would be "a trivia question after I'm long gone." North Carolina scored first, with Renner hitting Dwight Jones for a 22-yard touchdown pass with 12:12 left in the first quarter. That would be the high point for the Tar Heels. Missouri responded with a 40-yard touchdown pass from receiver T.J. Moe to Wes Kemp after a lateral from Franklin. Moe hadn't thrown a touchdown pass since his days as a high school Quarterback in suburban St. Louis, and it was just his second complete pass of the season. The Tigers scored again on Franklin's 2-yard run to take a 14-7 lead late in the first quarter. The touchdown was set up by Franklin's 16-yard pass to L'Damian Washington that put the Tigers at the 2-yard line. Washington grew up in Shreveport, just a few miles from Independence Stadium. And Missouri just kept piling on. The Tigers scored two touchdowns and a field goal during the second quarter to take a 31-10 halftime lead. North Carolina had a glimmer of hope late in the third when Jheranie Boyd caught a 44-yard touchdown pass from Renner to pull the Tar Heels to 34-17, but Missouri responded minutes later with Franklin's second touchdown run and the rout continued.

2011 Belk Bowl

The 2011 Belk Bowl, the 10th edition of the game, was held on December 27, 2011 at Bank of America Stadium in Charlotte, North Carolina. The game was telecast on ESPN and featured the NC State Wolfpack from the Atlantic Coast Conference and the Louisville Cardinals from the Big East Conference. Previously known as the Meineke Car Care Bowl in 2010, the 2011 contest was the first under its new name and sponsorship agreement with Belk, the Charlotte-based department store chain. Louisville-NC State is expected to become a yearly game as in 2014 Louisville will join the ACC and is expected to replace Maryland in the Atlantic Division (where NC State plays).

2011 Belk Bowl	Line	1	-	2	-	3	-	4	-	Final
Louisville	(44.5)	7	-	3	-	7	-	7	-	24
NC State	(-1.0)	7	-	14	-	10	-	0	-	31

Scoring Summary
NC State - Graham 6 yard pass from Glennon (Sade kick)
Louisville - Bridgewater 8 yard run (Philpott kick)
Louisville - Philpott 32 yard Field goal
NC State - Palmer 35 yard pass from Glennon (Sade kick)
NC State - Graham 68 yard pass from Glennon (Sade kick)
NC State - Sade 34 yard Field goal
NC State - Amerson 65 yard interception return (Sade kick)
Louisville - Nord 2 pass from Bridgewater (Philpott kick)
Louisville - Bellamy 2 yard pass from Bridgewater (Philpott kick)

Associated Press Belk Bowl Game Summary - North Carolina State coach Tom O'Brien took a lot of heat when he decided to part ways with star Quarterback Russell Wilson and go with unproven junior Mike Glennon as his starter. It all worked out on Tuesday night in the Belk Bowl, with Glennon throwing for 264 yards and three touchdowns to lead N.C. State over Louisville 31-24 -- and earn MVP honors in the process. So, O'Brien feels vindicated, right? Well, not so much. O'Brien ran his record to 8-2 in bowl games. Glennon threw two of his touchdown passes to senior receiver T.J. Graham, who made the most of his final game at N.C. State with seven catches for 116 yards, including a 65-yard score on a nifty catch-and-run. He threw another to Tobais Palmer, who made what Glennon called "the best catch I've seen all year" when Palmer completely turned his body around in midair and managed to catch it and keep running to the end zone for a 35-yard score. Glennon finished the season with 31 touchdown passes. N.C. State (8-5) also got a huge effort from its defense, which came in leading the country in interceptions. David Amerson, the nation's individual leader in interceptions, had two of the Wolfpack's three picks on Louisville freshman Quarterback Teddy Bridgewater. He returned one 65 yards for a touchdown to put the Wolfpack up by 21 midway through the third quarter and later sealed the win with a pick on a final fourth-and-23 heave by Bridgewater with 41 seconds left. Amerson finished the season with 13 interceptions, a new Atlantic Coast Conference record. Bridgewater had an up and down night, throwing for 274 yards and two touchdowns and running for another. But the three picks hurt. Down 21, Louisville coach Charlie Strong used a fake punt and recovered an onside kick to get back in the game after falling behind by 21. Bridgewater threw 2-yard touchdown passes to tight end Nate Nord and wide receiver Josh Bellamy to close the gap to 31-24 with 3:55 left in the game. The Cardinals had one last chance to send the game into overtime after stopping N.C. State on fourth-and-2. However, on a third-and-12, Dontae Johnson sacked Bridgewater for an 11-yard loss to set up Amerson's clinching interception. O'Brien was worried about his young special teams unit coming into the game and his worst fears were realized early in the game when freshman punter Will Baumann mishandled a low snap from center and was swarmed under at the 5-yard line. The Cardinals cashed in three plays later on an 8-yard touchdown run by Bridgewater to tie the game. After Louisville went ahead 10-7, Glennon bounced back from an early interception by completing five straight passes for 80 yards, capped by a 35-yard touchdown to Palmer, who made a nice adjustment with the ball in midair to haul in the pass. Then came the play of the game as Graham caught a pass over the middle from Glennon and broke two tackles enroute to a 68-yard touchdown reception giving the Wolfpack a 21-10 lead at the break.

2011 Little Caesars Pizza Bowl

The 2011 Little Caesars Pizza Bowl, the 15th edition of the game, was held on December 27, 2011 at Ford Field in Detroit, Michigan. The game, which was telecast on ESPN, featured the Western Michigan Broncos from the Mid-American Conference versus the Purdue Boilermakers from the Big Ten Conference. The 2011 Little Caesars Pizza Bowl was the third ever football meeting between the two universities. Purdue led the all-time series 2–0 coming into the game.

2011 Little Caesars Pizza Bowl	Line	1	-	2	-	3	-	4	-	Final
Western Michigan	(61.0)	8	-	7	-	10	-	7	-	32
Purdue	(-2.5)	7	-	20	-	7	-	3	-	37

Scoring Summary
Western Michigan - White 49 yard pass from Carder (Potter kick)
Purdue - Pegram 1 yard pass from Marve (Wiggs kick)
Purdue - Wiggs 49 yard Field goal
Western Michigan - Schaffer 1 yard pass from Carder (Potter kick)
Purdue - Mostert 99 yard kickoff return (Wiggs kick)
Purdue - Pegram 1 yard run (Wiggs kick)
Purdue - Wiggs 19 yard Field goal
Western Michigan - Potter 21 yard Field goal
Purdue - Bush 33 yard pass from Terbush (Wiggs kick)
Western Michigan - Drake 1 yard run (Potter kick)
Purdue - Wiggs 26 yard Field goal
Western Michigan - Ravenell 5 yard pass from Carder (Potter kick)

Little Caesars Pizza Bowl Game summary - Taking advantage of a Purdue fumble, the Broncos scored first on a 49-yard flea flicker to go up 8–0 after making a two-point conversion. Purdue responded by with its own touchdown to cut the deficit to 8–7 at the end of the first quarter. The Boilermakers then recovered an onside kick to keep the ball in their possession. Purdue was unable to capitalize on the onside kick, fumbling the ball at WMU's 14-yard line. On the next drive, however, WMU threw an interception, which led to a Purdue field goal. On the next drive, WMU scored on a one-yard touchdown pass to Josh Schaffer to take the lead 15–10. On the ensuing kickoff, though, Purdue's Raheem Mostert returned the kickoff 99-yards for a touchdown, making it 17–15 Purdue. The Boilermakers then recovered their second onside kick of the game on the kickoff. This time, the Boilermakers were able to capitalize, going up 24–15 on a Reggie Pegram rushing touchdown. After the Broncos turned the ball over on downs, the Boilermakers added to their lead on a 19-yard Carson Wiggs field goal to make it 27–15 at the end of the first half. In the third quarter, the Broncos were able to cut the deficit 27–18 on a 21-yard John Potter field goal. Purdue then added to their lead on a 33-yard passing touchdown to make it 34–18. On the next Broncos drive, Quarterback Alex Carder's pass was intercepted by Purdue's Gerald Gooden at Purdue's six-yard line. However, Gooden fumbled the ball on the return, giving the ball back to the Broncos at the Purdue 29-yard line. Continuing the drive, the Broncos scored on a one-yard Tevin Drake rushing touchdown make it 34–25 going into the fourth quarter. In the fourth quarter, the Boilermakers added to their lead on a 26-yard Carson Wiggs field goal to make it 37–25. On the next drive, WMU turned the ball over on an interception. The Broncos were able to get the ball back after forcing Purdue to punt. On the next Broncos drive on a fourth-and-10 play at Purdue's 12-yard line, Carder fumbled the ball after being sacked. Purdue's Ryan Russell recovered the ball but fumbled on the return, giving the ball back to the Broncos. Continuing the drive, the Broncos cut the lead 37–32 on a five-yard touchdown pass to Caleb Ravenell. After forcing Purdue to punt, the Broncos had one last chance to win the game. However, Carder fumbled the ball, giving the ball to the Boilermakers. The Boilermakers were then able to run the clock out to seal a victory. With the loss, WMU fell 0–5 all time in bowl games.

2011 Military Bowl

The 2011 Military Bowl Presented by Northrop Grumman, the fourth edition of the game, was held on December 28, 2011 at Robert F. Kennedy Memorial Stadium in Washington, D.C.

2011 Military Bowl	Line	1	-	2	-	3	-	4	-	Final
Toledo	(-3.5)	21	-	7	-	7	-	7	-	42
Air Force	(70.0)	14	-	14	-	7	-	6	-	41

Scoring Summary
Toledo - Reedy 17 yard pass from Owens (Casano kick)
Toledo - Thomas 41 yard run (Casano kick)
Air Force - Jefferson 22 yard run (Herrington kick)
Toledo - Page 87 yard kickoff return (Casano kick)
Air Force - DeWitt 3 yard run (Herrington kick)
Air Force - Clark 1 yard run (Herrington kick)
Toledo - Reedy 49 yard pass from Owens (Casano kick)
Air Force - Warzeka 37 yard pass from Jefferson (Herrington kick)
Toledo - Robinson 37 yard interception return (Casano kick)
Air Force - DeWitt 2 yard run (Herrington kick)
Toledo - Reedy 33 yard pass from Owens (Casano kick)
Air Force - Kauth 33 yard pass from Jefferson (Run failed)

Associated Press Military Bowl Game Summary - Even the youngest head coach in the country knows not to expect the conventional from Air Force. After all, the Falcons had already scored three fourth-down touchdowns, including the one that had just tied the Military Bowl Presented by Northrop Grumman with 52 seconds to play. So, 32-year-old Matt Campbell, leading Toledo for the first time, wasn't surprised when Air Force lined up to kick the extra point and then ran a fake, going for two to win the game instead of sending it to overtime. The Rockets were ready. Holder David Baska got bottled up trying to run the option. The ball squirted toward kicker Parker Herrington, who chased it until it went out of bounds in the end zone, and Toledo started celebrating its 42-41 victory Wednesday night at RFK Stadium. Toledo succeeded in taking a one-point lead with a 2-point conversion near the end of last year's Little Caesars Pizza Bowl, but the Rockets lost the game to Florida International on a field goal on the game's final play. This time, the wild ending to a wild game went their way in the school's first bowl win since 2005. Bernard Reedy's third touchdown of the game -- a 37-yard catch, spin and run on a pass from Terrance Owens -- gave Toledo a 42-35 lead with 5:01 remaining and put the Rockets (9-4) over the 40-point mark for a sixth straight game. Reedy, had a career-high 126 yards receiving on four catches and was named the game's MVP. The game matched two of the top 25 scoring teams in the country, and they wasted little time living up to their reputations. It was Mid-American Conference member Toledo's spread offense against Mountain West Air Force's triple option, and the idea of a huddle seemed a quaint, antiquated concept. Back and forth they went. A kickoff return for 87 yards. A pitch around the left end for 60. Touchdown passes for 49 and 37 yards. A pair of botched onside kicks. And that was just the first half. Toledo's Adonis Thomas finished with 108 yards on 22 carries. Paul Hornung Award finalist Eric Page caught 13 passes for 59 yards, but his biggest play was an 87-yard kickoff return in the first half. Owens, getting most of the work at Quarterback, completed 19 of 24 passes for 210 yards and three touchdowns. Owens got the nod over Austin Dantin, who started the first 10 games of the season before sitting out the last two with a concussion. Tim Jefferson, the first Quarterback in service academy history to lead his team to four consecutive bowl games, completed 13 of 22 passes for 159 yards with two touchdowns and one interception for Air Force (7-6). Jonathan Warzeka had a career-best 60-yard run to set up one touchdown, and his 37-yard reception on fourth-and-3 tied the game 28-all heading into halftime. There was even room for a defensive score: Toledo safety Jermaine Robinson's 37-yard interception runback after he corralled a tipped pass deep in the secondary. But it all came down to a gutsy decision on a 2-point conversion. It appeared that Baska tried to pitch the ball to Herrington, but Air Force coach Troy Calhoun said the ball just popped out. Either way, the coach wasn't about to second-guess himself.

2011 Holiday Bowl

The 2011 Bridgepoint Education Holiday Bowl, the 34th edition of the game, was played between the Texas Longhorns of the Big 12 Conference and the California Golden Bears of the Pac-12 Conference (Pac-12), on December 28, 2011 at Qualcomm Stadium in San Diego, California. The game ended in a 21-10 victory for Texas.

2011 Holiday Bowl	Line	1	-	2	-	3	-	4	-	Final
California	(47.5)	3	-	0	-	7	-	0	-	10
Texas	(-3.5)	0	-	7	-	7	-	7	-	21

Scoring Summary
California - Tavecchio 49 yard Field goal
Texas - Ash 4 yard pass from Shipley (Tucker kick)
California - Sofele 6 yard run (Tavecchio kick)
Texas - Goodwin 47 yard pass from Ash (Tucker kick)
Texas - Johnson 4 yard run (Tucker kick)

Associated Press Holiday Bowl Game Summary - The next time Texas coach Mack Brown sees Joey Harrington; the memory shouldn't be quite so painful. David Ash added his name to the list of Quarterbacks who've caught a touchdown pass in the Holiday Bowl and he also threw for one score to lead Texas to a 21-10 victory against California on Wednesday night. Ash caught a 4-yard pass from wide receiver Jaxon Shipley in the second quarter to join BYU's Steve Young, Texas A&M's Bucky Richardson and Oregon's Harrington as Quarterbacks who've caught touchdown passes in the Bridgepoint Education Holiday Bowl. The Longhorns had the ball first-and-goal when Ash handed off to running back Malcolm Brown who then handed off to Shipley as if the Longhorns were going to run a reverse. Ash slipped into the end zone and caught Shipley's pass to give Texas a 7-3 lead. Shipley has thrown three touchdown passes this season, all while lining up at wide receiver. Brown joked on Tuesday how much it still bugged him that Harrington caught a TD pass in the Ducks' 35-30 win against Texas in the 2000 Holiday Bowl. The Oregon offensive coordinator then was Jeff Tedford, who has been Cal's coach since 2002. Harrington now works for the Longhorn Network. Brown credited the play to co-offensive coordinator Bryan Harsin, who previously had coached and played at Boise State. Ash had another impressive play in the third quarter when he threw a 47-yard touchdown pass to Marquise Goodwin, who made a nice over-the-shoulder catch in full stride. That gave the Longhorns a 14-10 lead. The Longhorns (8-5) were even more impressive on defense, getting five takeaways and sacking Cal's Zach Maynard six times, both season highs. The Golden Bears (7-6) are winless in five games against the Longhorns, dating to 1959. Texas put it away on Cody Johnson's 4-yard touchdown run on the first play of the fourth quarter, which was set up when Maynard was sacked and fumbled, which was recovered by Chris Whaley at the Cal 44. Goodwin ran for 37 yards and Johnson had a 3-yard gain before his touchdown run. Cal briefly took the lead at 10-7 after Isi Sofele's 6-yard run to cap the opening drive of the second half. Ash's long TD pass to Goodwin came four plays into the next Texas drive.

Game notes - This was Cal's second bowl loss in a row, going back to the 2009 Poinsettia Bowl, and Texas' second straight Holiday Bowl victory, following a win in 2007 over Arizona State. Cal is 1–3 in its bowl trips to San Diego. Texas' record against Cal improved to 5–0.

2011 Champs Sports Bowl

The 2011 Champs Sports Bowl, the 22nd edition of the game, was held on December 29, 2011 at the Citrus Bowl in Orlando, Florida. The game, which was telecast on ESPN and ESPN 3D. It was FSU's second Champs Bowl, and Notre Dame's first. Notre Dame was invited through an option in the Big East tie-in. The game sold out on December 7, marking the Champs Sports Bowl's first ever sellout.

Teams - The two teams met for the seventh time since 1981. The Seminoles lead the all-time series 5–2, including a 2–0 bowl record against the Fighting Irish. The other bowl meeting was the Orange Bowl following the 1995 season. The teams also had a 1994 regular season meeting in Orlando, a year after the teams met in South Bend ranked #1 and #2 in the nation. Beginning in 2014, Notre Dame will play Florida State at least once every three years as part of the Irish's agreement to play five ACC football schools each year, as in 2013, Notre Dame became a non-football member of the ACC, maintaining its football independence.

2011 Champs Sports Bowl	Line	1	-	2	-	3	-	4	-	Final
Florida State	(-3.0)	0	-	0	-	3	-	15	-	18
Notre Dame	(46.5)	7	-	0	-	7	-	0	-	14

Scoring Summary
Notre Dame - Motta 29 yard fumble return (Ruffer kick)
Notre Dame - Floyd 5 yard pass from Rees (Ruffer kick)
Florida State - Hopkins 42 yard Field goal
Florida State - Reed 18 yard pass from Manuel (Pass failed)
Florida State - Greene 15 yard pass from Manuel (Pass failed)
Florida State - Hopkins 29 yard Field goal

Associated Press Champs Sports Bowl Game Summary - The day before his team took the field for its Champs Sports Bowl matchup with Notre Dame, Florida State coach Jimbo Fisher acknowledged that he had higher hopes for his team than how they ended up in 2011. Loaded with talent and expectations in the preseason, the Seminoles (No. 25 AP) squandered early season opportunities against ranked foes and fizzled again late in the year to end any path back to the Bowl Championship Series. Thursday night's 18-14 win over Notre Dame in front of a sellout crowd at Florida's Citrus Bowl might not have been the national stage FSU expected to be on this season, but how it won the game could be proof it is finally making progress. The Seminoles rallied from a 14-point second-half deficit and used a pair of touchdown passes by EJ Manuel and two field goals from Dustin Hopkins to earn their fourth straight bowl win and second under Fisher. FSU receiver Rashad Greene, who caught one of Manuel's touchdown passes, was selected the game's MVP. The Seminoles finished the game with 290 yards, including going 3 for 14 on third down, and got an efficient night from Manuel. He played behind a young offensive line but was 20 for 31 passing for 249 yards. Injuries forced the Seminoles to start four freshmen on their line and they gave up five sacks, but their defense picked off Notre Dame Quarterbacks Tommy Rees and Andrew Hendrix three times and also had four sacks. Notre Dame shuffled between Rees and Hendrix throughout the game, but both struggled. They were a combined 19 for 35 and 187 yards passing. FSU scored on all four of its red zone chances. The Irish also were without their biggest offensive weapon late, with receiver Michael Floyd being forced to the sideline following a third quarter touchdown catch with what coach Brian Kelly described afterward was an "upper body injury." He returned to the game but was a non-factor. Junior linebacker Manti Te'o, who led Notre Dame with 13 tackles and got in on a sack Thursday, said fatigue was not a factor in the Irish not being able to maintain pressure on Manuel in the fourth quarter. After some stagnant offense on both sides in the first half, FSU trailed 14-0 early in the third quarter before finding some momentum through the air. The Seminoles closed the gap to 14-9 with an 18-yard touchdown pass from Manuel to Bert Reed to open the fourth quarter but failed on their 2-point conversion attempt. They took the lead just 1:32 later after Nigel Bradham intercepted a Hendrix pass inside the Notre Dame 20 to set up an 18-yard touchdown catch by Greene to make it 15-14 with just over 13 minutes to play following another failed 2-point try. The Seminoles added their second field goal of the game a series later. Notre Dame punted on its next possession but pinned FSU inside its own 5 and forced a quick three-and-out. A poor punt by the Seminoles and a facemask penalty on the return gave the Irish the ball on the FSU 28 with 3:56 to play, but Rees was picked off in the end zone with 2:48 left and FSU was able run out most of the remaining time. Notre Dame took a 14-0 lead on its opening drive of the second half by capping a nine-play, 62-yard drive with a 5-yard touchdown pass from Rees to Floyd. Floyd fought Seminoles cornerback Greg Reid for the ball on to play, juggling it multiple times before finally getting his hands around it. Reid stayed down on the turf after the play and left the game with concussion symptoms. FSU bounced right back with a 77-yard kickoff return by Lamarcus Joyner, but Notre Dame's fifth sack of the night on Manuel helped force the Seminoles to settle for a 42-yard field goal by Hopkins. Safety Terrance Brooks, who had a late interception to help seal the win, said belief in themselves is the biggest thing they will carry into next season.

2011 Alamo Bowl

The 2011 Valero Alamo Bowl, the 19th edition of the game, was held on December 29, 2011 at the Alamodome in San Antonio, Texas. The game, which was telecast on ESPN, featured the Baylor Bears, led by Heisman Trophy winner Robert Griffin III, from the Big 12 Conference versus the Washington Huskies from the Pac-12 Conference. With a total combined score of 123 points, the game is currently the second highest-scoring regulation bowl game in college football history.

2011 Alamo Bowl	Line	1	-	2	-	3	-	4	-	Final
Washington	(79.0)	7	-	28	-	14	-	7	-	56
#15 Baylor	(-9.5)	21	-	3	-	29	-	14	-	67

Scoring Summary
Baylor - Wright 11 Yard Pass from Griffin III (Jones Kick)
Washington - Price 5 Yard Run (Folk Kick)
Baylor - Salubi 36 Yard Run (Jones Kick)
Baylor - Griffin III 24 Yard Run (Jones Kick)
Washington - Johnson 12 Yard Pass from Price (Folk Kick)
Washington - Aguilar 1 Yard Pass from Price (Folk Kick)
Washington - Price 15 Yard Run (Folk Kick)
Washington - Polk 56 Yard Run (Folk Kick)
Baylor - Jones 42 Yard Field goal
Washington - Kearse 80 Yard Pass from Price (Folk Kick)
Baylor - Salubi 7 Yard Run (Jones Kick)
Baylor - Ganaway 89 Yard Run (Monk pass from Griffin III)
Washington - Aguilar 13 Yard Pass from Price (Folk Kick)
Baylor - Ganaway 1 Yard Run (Jones Kick)
Baylor - Ganaway 1 Yard Run (Jones Kick)
Washington - Price 8 Yard Run (Folk Kick)
Baylor - Ganaway 4 Yard Run (Jones Kick)
Baylor - Ganaway 43 Yard Run (Jones Kick)

Game summary - Baylor scored first on an 11-yard touchdown pass to Kendall Wright. Washington responded with a 5-yard Keith Price touchdown run to tie the game 7-7. The Bears were able to score two more rushing touchdowns from Jarred Salubi and Robert Griffin III to go up 21-7 at the end of the 1st quarter. In the 2nd quarter, Washington cut the deficit 21-14 on a 12-yard touchdown pass to James Johnson. After forcing Baylor to punt, the Huskies tied the game 21-21 on a 1-yard touchdown pass to Devin Aguilar. On the ensuing drive, Baylor's Robert Griffin III fumbled the ball at Washington's 43-yard line. Taking advantage of the fumble, Washington took the lead 28-21 on a 15-yard touchdown run from Keith Price. After Baylor turned the ball over on downs, Washington took a 35-21 lead with only 1 play on a 56-yard touchdown run from Chris Polk. Baylor was able to cut the deficit 35-24 at the end of the half on a 42-yard field goal. Washington received the ball in the 3rd quarter. The Huskies quickly took a 42-24 lead on an 80-yard touchdown pass to Jermaine Kearse. Baylor responded with a Jarred Salubi touchdown run to make it 42-31. Baylor's defense was then able to force Washington to punt. However, Washington's defense responded by forcing a three and out. On the ensuing punt, Washington's Kasen Williams returned the punt 46 yard to Baylor's 17-yard line. However, on the next play, Washington's Chris Polk fumbled the ball, giving Baylor the ball back at the Baylor's 11-yard line. Baylor quickly cut the deficit 42-39 on an 89-yard Terrance Ganaway touchdown run (Baylor's went for a two-point conversion and succeeded). Washington answered with a 13-yard Devin Aguilar touchdown reception to make it 49-39. On the next drive, Baylor once again made it a 3-point game on a 1-yard touchdown run by Terrance Ganaway. After Washington's Eric Folk missed a 43-yard field goal, Baylor took a 53-49 lead on another touchdown run from Terrance Ganaway. Washington retook the lead 56-53 in the 4th quarter on a 13-play, 76-yard drive that took 6 minutes, 18 seconds that was capped off by an 8-yard touchdown run from Keith Price. Baylor, however, retook the lead again 60-56 on a 4-yard touchdown run from Terrance Ganaway. Baylor's defense was able to force Washington to turn the ball over on downs with 3:20 left in regulation. The Bears then scored again on a 43-yard touchdown run from Ganaway to go up 67-56. After Washington fumbled the ensuing kickoff, Baylor was able to run out the clock to preserve the victory.

Records - Several records were set in the 2011 Alamo Bowl. The 123 combined points were the most scored in regulation in a bowl game. The game also had 1,397 combined yards of offense and 17 touchdowns, both bowl game records. Baylor's 67 points were the most scored in bowl history. However, the record stood for just six days, when the West Virginia Mountaineers defeated the Clemson Tigers 70-33 in the 2012 Orange Bowl. The Huskies allowed a school record 777 yards of total offense in the 2011 Alamo Bowl. Because of the Huskies' defensive performance, defensive coordinator Nick Holt was fired, as were defensive assistants Mike Cox (linebackers), and Jeff Mills (safeties) on December 31. With the win, Baylor secured their first 10-win season since 1980. Baylor also won its first bowl game since 1992.

2011 Armed Forces Bowl

The 2011 Bell Helicopter Armed Forces Bowl, the ninth edition of the game held on December 30, 2011 at Gerald J. Ford Stadium on the campus of SMU in University Park, Texas. The game, telecast on ESPN, featured Tulsa versus BYU. BYU won the game by a score of 24–21. This is the second and last year that the bowl was held at Gerald J. Ford Stadium. In 2012, the bowl will return to Amon G. Carter Stadium on the campus of TCU after the completion of a renovation on the stadium.

2011 Armed Forces Bowl	Line	1	-	2	-	3	-	4	-	Final
BYU	(58.0)	3	-	7	-	7	-	7	-	24
Tulsa	(-1.0)	7	-	7	-	0	-	7	-	21

Scoring Summary
Tulsa - Johnson 8 yard pass from Kinne (Fitzpatrick kick)
BYU - Sorensen 35 yard Field goal
Tulsa - Sears 14 yard pass from Kinne (Fitzpatrick kick)
BYU - Hoffman 17 yard pass from Nelson (Sorensen kick)
BYU - Hoffman 30 yard pass from Nelson (Sorensen kick)
Tulsa - Burnham 30 yard pass from Kinne (Fitzpatrick kick)
BYU - Hoffman 2 yard pass from Nelson (Sorensen kick)

Associated Press Armed Forces Bowl Game Summary - Riley Nelson hurriedly led BYU to the line with a call from the sideline to spike the ball and stop the clock. Instead, Nelson faked the spike and then threw his third touchdown pass to Cody Hoffman with 11 seconds left to give the Cougars a 24-21 victory over Tulsa on Friday in the Bell Helicopter Armed Forces Bowl and another 10-win season. The Cougars (10-3) wrapped up their season of independence by winning 10 games for the fifth time in Mendenhall's seven years. They won nine of their past 10 games after consecutive losses in September. BYU needed 12 plays to go 48 yards on its last drive. Nelson converted a fourth-and-9 with a 14-yard scramble and later ran 8 yards on third-and-5. Out of timeouts at the 2 with the clock still running, Nelson decided to go with a play that the Cougars hadn't practiced in about two months. And one he remembered seeing Dan Marino pull off when he was watching the NFL as a kid. Tulsa defensive back Dexter McCoil, who had two interceptions and a third nullified by a penalty. Hoffman stood upright on the far right side waiting for the snap, then took a few steps into the end zone and turned around to make his third TD catch of the game. Hoffman had eight catches for 122 yards. During the recent frenzy of conference realignment, BYU opted to become a football independent this season after its departure from the Mountain West. There are no immediate plans to get back in another league. G.J. Kinne threw three TD passes for Tulsa (8-5), including a 30-yarder to Bryan Burnham with 10:42 left for a 21-17 lead. Tulsa, who's other four losses this season came against top-10 teams, failed to take advantage when BYU was penalized for running into the punter on fourth down from the 10 with about 6 minutes left. But the Golden Hurricane punted the ball away four plays later, setting up the winning drive for the Cougars. Hoffman got his first TD just before halftime after an impressive block gave Nelson time to throw the ball. Nelson was scrambling to his left to avoid pressure and threw back toward the middle of the field after 305-pound offensive tackle Matt Reynolds, who had lost his helmet on the play, retreated for a crushing block that flattened pursuing 275-pound defensive end Cory Dorris. Hoffman made the catch, then lunged forward with the ball in his outstretched hand for the 17-yard score that cut Tulsa's lead to 14-10. Long snapper Reed Hornung set up that score with a hustle play on special teams. The 249-pound Hornung scampered down the field to hit J.D. Ratliff at the end of a 41-yard punt, forcing a fumble that was recovered by BYU's David Foote. Kinne, whose 81 career TD passes fell two short of the school record, was 17 for 31 for 214 yards. The Golden Hurricane were held to a season-low 272 total yards and lost their second consecutive game after a seven-game winning streak. Tulsa had won three consecutive bowl games since losing 25-13 to Utah in the Armed Forces Bowl five years ago. Nelson, who became the starting Quarterback after leading a comeback win at Utah State three months ago, finished 17 of 40 for 250 yards with two interceptions. He was also sacked three times and hit many other times. The Cougars went in front for the first time on Hoffman's 30-yard TD catch with 1:41 left in the third quarter. Hoffman helped set up his score when he reached up in traffic for a 20-yard catch on third-and-10 earlier in the nine-play, 71-yard drive. Tulsa's Kevin Fitzpatrick was wide right on a 46-yard field goal attempt earlier in the period. The Golden Hurricane had gone from first down at the BYU 14 to fourth-and-25 after linebacker Kyle Van Noy tackled running back Ja'Terian Douglas for a 6-yard loss, then sacked Kinne on the next play. Tulsa opened the game with an 11-play, 76-yard drive. Kinne finished it in style, scrambling to the left to avoid defenders before hitting Ricky Johnson in the back of the end zone for a 5-yard touchdown. Kinne also threw a 14-yard pass to Clay Sears for a 14-3 lead in the second quarter. Kinne set up the score with a 55-yard pass to Burnham. The Armed Forces Bowl plans to return to the TCU campus next year for its 10th annual game. The Fort Worth-based bowl was played from 2003-09 at Amon G. Carter Stadium, which has been undergoing a $164 million renovation that will be completed before the 2012 season.

2011 Music City Bowl

The 2011 Franklin American Mortgage Music City Bowl, the 14th edition of the game, was held on December 30, 2011 at LP Field in Nashville, Tennessee. The game, which was telecast on ESPN, featured the Wake Forest Demon Deacons from the Atlantic Coast Conference versus the Mississippi State Bulldogs from the Southeastern Conference. Mississippi State won, 23–17, securing its fifth bowl win in a row and its second in two seasons.

2011 Music City Bowl	Line	1	-	2	-	3	-	4	-	Final
Wake Forest	(48.0)	7	-	0	-	7	-	3	-	17
Mississippi State	(-6.5)	7	-	9	-	0	-	7	-	23

Scoring Summary
Wake Forest - Pendergrass 14 yard run (Newman kick)
Mississippi State - Ballard 60 yard run (DePasquale kick)
Mississippi State - Clark 31 yard pass from Relf (DePasquale kick)
Mississippi State - DePasquale 33 yard Field goal
Wake Forest - Bohanon 1 yard run (Newman kick)
Mississippi State - Ballard 72 yard run (DePasquale kick)
Wake Forest - Newman 46 yard Field goal

Associated Press Music City Bowl Game Summary - Playing in the Southeastern Conference dimmed Mississippi State's high expectations this year. With the two longest touchdown runs in the programs bowl history, senior Vick Ballard gave the Bulldogs plenty to celebrate in capping the season. The game's MVP ran for a career-high 180 yards, including TD runs of 60 and 72 yards, to lead Mississippi State over Wake Forest 23-17 Friday night in the Franklin American Mortgage Music City Bowl -- the Bulldogs' fifth straight bowl victory and second consecutive under coach Dan Mullen. Those high expectations were hurt by losses to SEC teams either ranked at the time or going into bowl season. Now the Bulldogs (7-6) have won consecutive bowls for only the second time and first since 1999-2000. Two of the Bulldogs' losses came to LSU and Alabama, who will play in the BCS national title game on Jan. 9. Mullen said this win will propel the Bulldogs into the offseason, and their quest remains winning an SEC title. Mississippi State overcame four turnovers thanks to Ballard's long TD runs and six sacks -- its highest total since piling up seven in a win over Florida in 2000. Wake Forest (6-7) snapped a two-game bowl winning streak. The Demon Deacons of the Atlantic Coast Conference now have lost both bowls against the SEC and finish the season having lost five of their past six games. Chris Relf started for the Bulldogs and played the whole game with Tyler Russell limited by a sprained knee. Relf ran for 64 yards and threw for 129 yards and a TD with two interceptions. Mullen said Russell would have played if something happened to Relf. The Demon Deacons, who held the ball for more than 35 minutes, tried to rally. They converted two fourth downs before Brandon Maye sacked Tanner Price for the sixth time, forcing Wake Forest to kick a 46-yard field goal to pull within 23-17 with 3:27 left. Wake Forest forced Mississippi State to punt, getting the ball back with 2:15 to go. But Price threw incomplete on three straight passes, the last to Terrence Davis on fourth-and-7 with 1:40 left. That had Bulldogs fans clanking their cowbells and chanting "S-E-C, S-E-C" as Mississippi State ran out the clock. Ballard came just shy of Walter Packer's school-record of 183 yards rushing in the 1974 Sun Bowl against North Carolina. The senior more than compensated for a first-quarter fumble that led to Wake Forest's first TD and only lead with his 60-yard TD. Mississippi State scored 16 straight points after that to take control, and the Bulldogs' 16-7 lead at halftime would have been bigger if not for three turnovers in the first half, including an interception in the end zone with a second left. Bud Noel intercepted a Relf pass at the Wake Forest 1 in the second half. The Demon Deacons opened the second half by driving 64 yards before Tommy Bohanon ran in a TD from a yard out to pull Wake Forest within 16-14. But Mississippi State sacked Tanner Price four times in the third quarter alone and harassed him into plenty of throws that hit the ground before reaching receivers. Relf scooped up a low snap in the shotgun and got the ball to Ballard, who ran through the middle of the line and outraced the Demon Deacons for a 72-yard TD with 12:53 left. That put the Bulldogs up 23-14 and gave Ballard 179 yards on 11 carries. His first TD came three plays after Wake Forest turned one of his fumbles into a 14-yard TD by Brandon Pendergrass. Wake Forest nose guard Nikita Whitlock said he thought they did a good job stopping Ballard most of the game and blamed missed assignments, including some by himself, for the TDs. "They took it to the house on us a couple times," Whitlock said. Fletcher Cox had a sack and also blocked a 33-yard field goal grabbed out of the air by teammate Johnathan Banks. That set up the Bulldogs' go-ahead drive as Relf broke loose for his longest run this season of 27 yards. Relf then dropped back and hit Arceto Clark with a 31-yard TD pass and a 13-7 lead with 12:41 left in the second quarter.

2011 Pinstripe Bowl

The 2011 New Era Pinstripe Bowl, the second edition of the game, was held on December 30, 2011 at Yankee Stadium in the Bronx, New York.

2011 Pinstripe Bowl	Line	1	-	2	-	3	-	4	-	Final
Rutgers	(-2.0)	0	-	17	-	0	-	10	-	27
Iowa State	(44.5)	6	-	0	-	0	-	7	-	13

Scoring Summary
Iowa State - Guyer 40 yard Field goal
Iowa State - Guyer 45 yard Field goal
Rutgers - Jamison 1 yard run (Te kick)
Rutgers - Te 21 yard Field goal
Rutgers - Jamison 21 yard Field goal (Te kick)
Rutgers - Te 29 yard Field goal
Iowa State - Woody 20 yard run (Guyer kick)
Rutgers - Coleman 86 yard pass from Dodd (Te kick)

Associated Press Pinstripe Bowl Game Summary - Rutgers coach Greg Schiano was handed the big glass trophy his Scarlet Knights earned by beating Iowa State in the Pinstripe Bowl on Friday and had just one thing to say. "Hey Big E! Hey Big E!" Schiano shouted into the microphone as he stood at midfield at Yankee Stadium and pointed toward the press box. "This one's for you, buddy." Eric LeGrand, bound to a wheelchair more than a year after being paralyzed making a tackle during a game, is still very much a part of Rutgers football. The former defensive end was shown on the huge video scoreboard while Schiano spoke, and he busted out a wide grin. He then went to the locker room and celebrated a 27-13 victory with his former teammates. He said he even did a little shoulder dancing. On the field, it was a couple of redshirt freshmen who lit it up for the Scarlet Knights. Brandon Coleman hauled in an 86-yard touchdown pass in the fourth quarter after Iowa State had trimmed the lead to 20-13, and Jawan Jamison ran for 131 yards and two scores on 27 carries. The Scarlet Knights (9-4) ran their bowl winning streak to five and improved to 2-0 this season at Yankee Stadium, where they beat Army last month. Rutgers, which played in one bowl game before 2005, is 5-1 in the postseason under Schiano. The Cyclones (6-7) finished the season on a three-game losing streak, their last win coming on Nov. 18 in Ames, Iowa, when they pulled off the biggest upset of the season against Oklahoma State. That night Jared Barnett threw for 376 yards. In this game, Steele Jantz, who started the first six games, relieved Barnett in the second quarter and helped pull the Cyclones within 20-13 in the fourth on Jeff Woody's 20-yard touchdown run with 10:00 left. After an exchange of punts left Rutgers deep in its own end, Chas Dodd went deep to Coleman. The 6-foot-6 Coleman went over 5-7 cornerback Jeremy Reeves, then outran the corner to the end zone to make it 27-13 with 5:47 left. It was Coleman's only catch, but it turned out to be the play of the game. Rutgers grabbed a 7-6 lead early in the second quarter when Jamison powered through a tackler and scored on fourth-and-goal from the 1. On the next possession, Iowa State couldn't handle one of Rutgers' many blitzes, and Greene and Wayne Warren swarmed and stripped Barnett. Scott Vallone scooped up the fumble and returned it 12 yards to the Iowa State 4. The Cyclones managed to hold Rutgers to San San Te's 21-yard field goal. Jantz replaced Barnett on the next Iowa State series. The Cyclones' defense didn't hold up as well on Rutgers' next possession. The Scarlet Knights marched 66 yards, 49 on the ground, and Jamison juked his way into the end zone from 12 yards out to make 17-6. Justin Francis finished Rutgers' strong second half by blocking Zach Guyer's 44-yard field goal attempt with 57 seconds left. Iowa State jumped out to a 6-0 lead in the first quarter, with Guyer kicking field goals of 40 and 46 yards on the Cyclones' first two possessions. Inaccurate throws by Barnett were key to stalling each drive. The redshirt freshman was 2 for 7 before giving way to Jantz, who was 15 for 31 for 197 yards and ran for 36 yards. The Scarlet Knights missed the postseason last year for the first time since 2004 but rebounded this season to challenge for the Big East title behind a defense that came in ranked 14th in the nation. Greene led the charge Friday with 13 tackles, three for losses, before being carted off in the fourth quarter with an ankle injury. The junior was on crutches after the game and said he thinks he'll be OK in the long run.

2011 Insight Bowl

The 2011 Insight Bowl, the 23rd edition of the game, was held on December 30, 2011 at Sun Devil Stadium in Tempe, Arizona. The game was telecast on ESPN. The Iowa Hawkeyes of the Big Ten Conference faced the Oklahoma Sooners of the Big 12 Conference. Oklahoma won by a score of 31–14. The game was briefly suspended with 2:24 remaining in the fourth quarter when one of ESPN's skycams crashed onto the field, nearly hitting Iowa wide receiver Marvin McNutt, Jr. The incident has since gone viral on YouTube.

2011 Insight Bowl	Line	1	-	2	-	3	-	4	-	Final
Iowa	(57.5)	0	-	0	-	0	-	14	-	14
#19 Oklahoma	(-14.0)	7	-	7	-	7	-	10	-	31

Scoring Summary
Oklahoma - Bell 4 yard run (Hunnicutt kick)
Oklahoma - Bell 4 yard run (Hunnicutt kick)
Oklahoma - Ratterree 3 yard pass from Jones (Hunnicutt kick)
Iowa - Fiedorowicz 5 yard pass from Vandenberg (Meyer kick)
Iowa - Canzeri 9 yard pass from Vandenberg (Meyer kick)
Oklahoma - Hunnicutt 35 yard Field goal
Oklahoma - Bell 21 yard run (Hunnicutt kick)

Iowa Media Guide Insight Bowl Game Recap - Iowa rallied in the second half, closing to within a touchdown with 6:56 remaining, but 14th-ranked Oklahoma controlled the ball over the second half of the final period in recording a 31-14 win at the 2011 Insight Bowl. The Hawkeyes are now 14-11-1 in 26 bowl appearances. Oklahoma built a 21-0 advantage before Iowa got its offense going in the second half. Iowa used a 16-play drive that consumed 7:50, scoring on a 5-yard pass from QB James Vandenberg to TE C.J. Fiedorowicz on the second play of the final quarter. After holding Oklahoma to three plays on consecutive possessions, the Iowa offense drove 78 yards in 12 plays, cutting the deficit to 21-14 on a 9-yard pass from Vandenberg to RB Jordan Canzeri. Oklahoma was able to drive to the Iowa 21 before adding a field goal with 2:33 remaining for a 24-14 advantage. After Iowa failed on a fourth down attempt, the Sooners added a final touchdown in the closing minute of play. Oklahoma took a 7-0 lead in the first period, covering 12 yards in two plays following a pass interception. Oklahoma's only extended offensive drive of the second quarter covered 66 yards in 13 plays as the Sooners led 14-0 at halftime. Iowa's defense held the Sooners to just 89 yards total offense in the 1st half. Oklahoma, which entered the game ranked fourth in the nation in total offense, was held to 275 yards total offense, its lowest output of the season. Vandenberg completed 23-44 passes for 216 yards and two scores, with one interception. Canzeri led Iowa's ground attack with 58 yards on 22 carries and he added six pass receptions for 28 yards and a touchdown. WR Marvin McNutt, Jr. recorded four receptions for 46 yards. He tied Iowa's single-season reception record with 82 catches in 13 games. The Iowa defense was led by senior LB Tyler Nielsen with eight tackles, while LB Christian Kirksey added seven. Senior DT Mike Daniels recorded three tackles for loss and two QB sacks among his five tackles and senior DE Broderick Binns recorded Iowa's only pass interception.

2011 Liberty Bowl

The 2011 AutoZone Liberty Bowl, the 53rd edition of the game, was held on December 31, 2011 at Liberty Bowl Memorial Stadium in Memphis, Tennessee. The game, which was telecast on ABC, featured the Cincinnati Bearcats, Big East co-champions, versus the Vanderbilt Commodores of the SEC. It was the first Liberty Bowl game to be aired by ABC since 1980.

Teams - After finishing the 2011 season with six wins and six losses, the Vanderbilt Commodores ended in fourth place in the Southeastern Conference (SEC) East Division. They were chosen as the SEC representative to the Liberty Bowl. The Commodores' roster included junior-year Quarterback Jordan Rodgers, the younger brother of Green Bay Packers' Super Bowl-winning Quarterback Aaron Rodgers. The Cincinnati Bearcats ended the regular season with nine wins and three losses and were co-champions of the Big East Conference. Cincinnati was chosen as part of the alternate Big East tie-in with the Liberty Bowl in place of the Conference USA champions. The Bearcats' squad included Ralph Abernathy IV, grandson of civil rights leader Ralph Abernathy. In the 2011 season, both teams had beaten Connecticut. Vanderbilt won 24-21 at home in the second game of their season. Cincinnati won 35-27 at home in their final regular-season game. Both teams also lost to Tennessee. Vanderbilt dropped their second-to-last game on the road to the Volunteers by a score of 21-27. Cincinnati's loss was also in Knoxville by a score of 23-45 in the second game of their season.

2011 Liberty Bowl	Line	1	-	2	-	3	-	4	-	Final
Cincinnati	(49.0)	0	-	14	-	0	-	17	-	31
Vanderbilt	(-1.5)	7	-	0	-	7	-	10	-	24

Scoring Summary
Vanderbilt - Stacy 7 yard run (Fowler kick)
Cincinnati - Winn 69 yard run (Miliano kick)
Cincinnati - McClung 8 yard pass from Collaros (Miliano kick)
Vanderbilt - Seymour 5 yard run (Fowler kick)
Cincinnati - Miliano 44 yard field goal
Vanderbilt - Boyd 68 yard pass from Smith (Fowler kick)
Cincinnati - Abernathy 90 yard kickoff return (Miliano kick)
Cincinnati - Pead 12 yard run (Miliano kick)
Vanderbilt - Fowler 35 yard field goal

Cincinnati Media Guide Liberty Bowl Game Summary - University of Cincinnati Head Coach Butch Jones rang the bell on the AutoZone Liberty Bowl trophy, eager to get the Bearcats' party started. And he knew just the place to celebrate in Memphis. Isaiah Pead ran for 149 yards and a touchdown, and Ralph David Abernathy IV's 90-yard kickoff return early in the fourth quarter put Cincinnati ahead to stay as the Bearcats edged Vanderbilt 31-24 on Saturday. The Bearcats (10-3) capped the season with their third straight victory by snapping a two-game skid in bowl games. It was their first bowl win since downing Southern Miss in the 2007 PapaJohns.com Bowl. They also notched their fourth 10-win season in the past five years, bouncing back from 4-8 in 2010 during Jones' first season. But the 2011 BIG EAST Conference co-champs had to work to put away Vanderbilt (6-7), a team that tied for fourth in the Southeastern Conference's East Division, despite forcing three turnovers and coming up with two sacks. The Commodores led 21-17 when Abernathy became the first Cincinnati player to return a kickoff for a TD in the program's 13 bowl appearances. Abernathy is the grandson of the civil rights leader who was in Memphis with Martin Luther King when he was assassinated in 1968 at the Lorraine Motel, a few miles away from the Liberty Bowl Memorial Stadium. Vanderbilt cornerback Casey Hayward called the return a dagger, and Jones called it very fitting for the Abernathy family. Vandy's Archibald Barnes blocked Tony Miliano's 39-yard field goal with 3:58 left, giving the Commodores the ball with plenty of time to go ahead. Nick Temple picked off Larry Smith's pass with 3:15 remaining, and Pead sealed the victory with a 12-yard TD run with 1:52 left. Pead was the game's MVP, and the senior finally got to celebrate a bowl win. Vanderbilt kicked a 35-yard field goal with 35 seconds left, but the Bearcats D.J. Woods (Strongsville, Ohio/Strongsville) recovered the onside kick to kneel down for the victory. George Winn also scored on a 69-yard TD run when he replaced Pead, while the BIG EAST Offensive Player of the Year got his helmet fix. Jones credited equipment manager Todd McMinn as an unsung hero with Winn scoring on the longest run of his career. Zach Collaros (Steubenville, Ohio/Steubenville) completed one of the more remarkable comebacks in college football, starting under center 47 days following surgery to correct a broken right ankle on Nov. 14. Collaros threw a touchdown pass and was 12 of 29 for 80 yards passing, moving around well. Pead was just happy to have Collaros back. The Bearcats led 14-7 at halftime and couldn't take advantage of two Vanderbilt turnovers in the third quarter. J.K. Schaffer (Cincinnati, Ohio/LaSalle) was UC's defensive MVP, finishing with nine tackles, including one for a loss and a sack.

2011 Sun Bowl

The 2011 Hyundai Sun Bowl, the 78th edition of the game, was held on December 31, 2011 at Sun Bowl Stadium in El Paso, Texas. The game, which was telecast on CBS, featured a team from the Atlantic Coast Conference, Georgia Tech Yellow Jackets versus the Utah Utes in their first year of membership in the Pac-12 Conference. The Utah Utes won the game 30–27. The game was broadcast on the radio nationally by Sports USA Radio with Eli Gold and Doug Plank calling the action.

2011 Sun Bowl	Line	1	-	2	-	3	-	4	-	OT	-	Final
Georgia Tech	(-2.5)	0	-	7	-	0	-	17	-	3	-	27
Utah	(50.0)	7	-	3	-	0	-	14	-	6	-	30

Scoring Summary
Utah - Asiata 1 yard pass from Hays (Petersen kick)
Georgia Tech - Lyons 36 yard run (Moore kick)
Utah - Petersen 25 yard field goal
Georgia Tech - Moore 32 yard field goal
Georgia Tech - Hill 31 yard pass from Washington (Moore kick)
Georgia Tech - Nealy 74 yard interception return (Moore kick)
Utah - Moeai 3 yard pass from Hays (Petersen kick)
Utah - Christopher 28 yard pass from Hays (Petersen kick)
Georgia Tech - Moore 34 yard field goal
Utah - White 8 yard run

Official Sun Bowl Game Recap - John White IV secured the overtime win for the Utes with an eight-yard run on third and goal. The win marked the ninth time in the past thirteen Sun Bowl games that the final score has been decided by 3 points or less and the first overtime game in bowl history. Utah had the early momentum as they took a 10-7 halftime lead with a 25-yard Coleman Petersen field goal, with 15 seconds remaining in the first half. This lead would prove to be short lived when Georgia Tech came out firing in the third quarter, scoring on three separate occasions, tallying 17 points to take a 24-10 edge. The fourth quarter was where Utah, led by Quarterback Jon Hays, managed to fight their way back into the game with a pair of touchdown tosses. Hays hit Kendrick Moeai for a three-yard score with almost 7:00 to play to cut Tech's lead to seven. With only 1:32 left to play, on fourth-and-14, Hays found DeVonte Christopher in the corner of the end zone to lock up the score at 24 apiece. However, Georgia Tech used the time it had left to march the field and set up David Scully for a 48-yard field goal that would have won the game with time expiring, but the attempt failed. After winning the coin toss, Utah deferred possession in overtime, putting Tech out on offense first. After a quick three and out, they settled for a field goal from 34 yards, and Justin Moore nailed the kick to put Tech up by 3. Utah, with the help of Hays and White IV, drove down to the three yard line only to have a false start penalty bring them back five yards. The very next play proved to be the game winner for the Utes, as White IV took it in for the victory. Hays finished with 193 yard passing with three touchdowns and one interception. White led the rushing attack with 115 yards on 26 carries and one touchdown. The Yellow Jackets had a strong performance from Quarterback Tevin Washington as he completed 11 of 15 passes for 137 yards and one touchdown. Defensively, Tech had a huge play from Quayshawn Johnson, as he had an interception return of 74 yards for a touchdown. For Georgia Tech, it was the Jackets' seventh-straight bowl loss, and they remain winless in the postseason under Coach Paul Johnson. The win put Utah 6-1 in postseason play under Coach Kyle Whittingham. He is 7-1 all-time in bowl games as a member of the Utah coaching staff.

2011 Meineke Car Care Bowl of Texas

The 2011 Meineke Car Care Bowl of Texas, the sixth edition of the game, was held on December 31, 2011 at Reliant Stadium in Houston, Texas. This was the first year the game was known as the Meineke Car Care Bowl of Texas. The game was previously known as the Texas Bowl in 2010 and is not to be confused with the previous Meineke Car Care Bowl held in North Carolina which is now called the Belk Bowl.

2011 Meineke Car Care Bowl	Line	1	-	2	-	3	-	4	-	Final
Texas A&M	(-10.0)	3	-	17	-	10	-	3	-	33
Northwestern	(69.0)	0	-	7	-	0	-	15	-	22

Scoring Summary
Texas A&M - Bullock 25 yard Field goal
Northwestern - Mark 2 yard run (Budzien kick)
Texas A&M - Malena 1 yard run (Bullock kick)
Texas A&M - Fuller 26 yard pass from Tannehill (Bullock kick)
Texas A&M - Bullock 40 yard Field goal
Texas A&M - Malena 19 yard run (Bullock kick)
Texas A&M - Bullock 47 yard Field goal
Northwestern - Kolter 1 yard run (Fields pass from Ebert)
Northwestern - Riley 2 yard pass from Kolter (Budzien kick)
Texas A&M - Bullock 31 yard Field goal

Associated Press Meineke Car Care Bowl of Texas Game Summary - After everything Texas A&M had been through in the last month, interim coach Tim DeRuyter worried how the Aggies would respond in the Meineke Car Care Bowl. It didn't take long for DeRuyter to see that his team was going to be just fine. Ryan Tannehill threw for 329 yards and a touchdown and Ben Malena ran for two more scores to lead Texas A&M to a 33-22 win over Northwestern on Saturday. Northwestern led 7-3 early in the second quarter before A&M reeled off 27 straight points to take a decisive lead and then fight off a late rally to capture its first bowl victory since 2001. Texas A&M (7-6) broke a five-game bowl losing streak in a win the team dedicated to fired coach Mike Sherman and offensive lineman Joseph Villavisencio, who was killed in a car accident last week. A&M won a bowl for the first time since a 28-9 victory over TCU after the 2001 season. That also came in Houston, when this game was called the Galleryfurniture.com bowl and played next door at the Astrodome. Tannehill said all the adversity simply gave them extra motivation. Malena ran for 77 yards, filling in ably for Cyrus Gray, who missed his second straight game with a stress fracture in his left shoulder. Northwestern (6-7) hasn't won a bowl game since the 1949 Rose Bowl, a span of nine losses. Dan Persa, who finished with 213 yards passing, was disappointed he couldn't help the team break its bowl win drought. Persa set an NCAA record for career completion percentage (73.6) by going 25-of-37 to end his career 460-of-633. He entered the game needing 19 attempts to meet the minimum standards to qualify for the record. The Aggies were up 30-7 before Brian Peters intercepted Tannehill early in the fourth quarter and the Wildcats took advantage of that mistake when Kain Colter scored on a 1-yard run for Northwestern's first points since early in the second quarter. The 2-point conversion left A&M ahead 30-15. Colter found Tim Riley in the corner of the end zone for on a 2-yard touchdown pass to get Northwestern within 30-22 with less than six minutes remaining. A&M responded with a clock-eating drive capped by a 31-yard field goal to secure the win. Senior Jeff Fuller, who has had a disappointing and injury-plagued year, had a key third down catch for 29 yards on that drive and finished with a season-high 119 yards receiving. DeRuyter was with the team for his last game before leaving to become Fresno State's coach. The Aggies hired former Houston coach Kevin Sumlin earlier this month to replace Sherman, but he wasn't involved in bowl preparations. Texas A&M wore helmet decals honoring Villavisencio, who died Dec. 22. The black and white decal, which says 'Joey V.,' had his No. 67 and the Texas A&M logo. There was a moment of silence for Villavisencio before the game and fellow offensive lineman Danny Baker wore his number and greeted his father before the game. Texas A&M erased a 7-3 second quarter deficit thanks to touchdowns by Malena and Fuller and a field goal by Randy Bullock to lead 20-7 at halftime. Malena's second touchdown came on a 19-yard run early in the third quarter that made it 27-7. Another field goal by Bullock, this one from 47 yards, pushed A&M's advantage to 30-7. The Wildcats alternated Quarterbacks for much of the day with Persa leading the more traditional offense and Colter directing the wildcat offense. But neither player could generate much offense while often under heavy pressure from the Aggies, who finished with eight sacks. Northwestern coach Pat Fitzgerald said the loud, heavily A&M crowd made things difficult for his offense. Texas A&M's offense got rolling in the second quarter when Tannehill found Ryan Swope, who was a high school running back, on a short pass that he took 37 yards to the 1. Swope tight-roped the sideline and avoided a half dozen tacklers before he was brought down. Malena scored a play later to put A&M on top 10-7. Northwestern took a 7-3 lead in the second quarter when Venric Mark scored 2-yard option run. Mark provided another highlight for the Wildcats on a nifty 47-yard punt return where he spun away from a pair of tacklers before hurdling another one before being pushed out of bounds in the second half.

2011 Kraft Fight Hunger Bowl

The 2011 Kraft Fight Hunger Bowl, the 10th edition of the game, was held on December 31, 2011 at AT&T Park in San Francisco, California. The game, which was telecast on ESPN, featured the UCLA Bruins (6–7) versus the Illinois Fighting Illini (6–6). The Bruins, with a losing record, were granted a waiver to play in a bowl game by the NCAA after the Pac-12 conference did not have enough eligible teams to fill its bowl commitments. Both teams fired their head coach this season after .500 records. Mike Johnson, who replaced Rick Neuheisel, is the interim coach for UCLA. The Fighting Illini were led by interim coach Vic Koenning while their newly hired head coach Tim Beckman, who replaced Ron Zook, was on the sidelines. UCLA lost the matchup and subsequently finished the season with a losing record (6–8).

2011 Kraft Fight Hunger Bowl	Line	1	-	2	-	3	-	4	-	Final
Illinois	(-3.0)	0	-	3	-	7	-	10	-	20
UCLA	(46.5)	0	-	7	-	0	-	7	-	14

Scoring Summary
UCLA - Embree 16 yard pass from Prince (Gonzales kick)
Illinois - Dimke 36 yard Field goal
Illinois - Hawthorne 39 yard interception return (Dimke kick)
Illinois - Dimke 37 yard Field goal
Illinois - Jenkins 60 yard pass from Scheelhaase (Dimke kick)
UCLA - Rosario 38 yard pass from Prince (Gonzales kick)

Associated Press Kraft Fight Hunger Bowl Game Summary - Waiting 12 weeks between wins was hard enough for Illinois. Terry Hawthorne and a stingy defense made sure the Illini didn't have to wait an entire offseason as well. Hawthorne returned an interception 39 yards for Illinois' first touchdown late in the third quarter and the Illini snapped a six-game losing streak by beating UCLA 20-14 in the Kraft Fight

Hunger Bowl. Nathan Scheelhaase added a 60-yard touchdown pass to A.J. Jenkins midway through the fourth quarter to seal the first victory for Illinois (7-6) since beating Indiana on Oct. 8. It also gave the Illini bowl wins in back-to-back seasons for the first time in school history. The players celebrated it by dumping Gatorade on interim coach Vic Koenning during a postgame celebration. The game between two six-win teams who have already fired their head coaches matched the underwhelming expectations as there was little excitement before Hawthorne's third-quarter touchdown that gave Illinois its first lead. UCLA (6-8) was held to 18 yards rushing in its third straight loss. Kevin Prince threw two TD passes, including one in the closing minute to Nelson Rosario after the game had been decided. It was an earlier pass by Prince that proved decisive. Three plays after Derek Dimke missed a 37-yard field goal for Illinois, Prince dropped back and threw to his left looking for Shaquelle Evans. Hawthorne read the play perfectly and stepped in front of the throw for the interception and had a clear path to the end zone for the score that gave the Illini a 10-7 lead. Dimke added a 37-yard field goal early in the fourth quarter and Scheelhaase and Jenkins combined on their big play to make it 20-7 with 5:36 to go. Scheelhaase finished 18 for 30 for 139 yards with 110 yards rushing to lead the Illinois offense. Prince completed just 14 for 29 for 201 yards and the Bruins were held to a season-low in rushing, well below their 190.7 yard per game average, by the stout Illini front. The matchup between Big Ten and Pac-12 teams on New Year's weekend at a picturesque setting in California conjures up memories of Rose Bowls past. But this game was played on San Francisco's waterfront instead of with the San Gabriel Mountains in the background in Pasadena and was between two teams that had little to celebrate this season. Both teams fired their coaches after disappointing regular seasons with Ron Zook getting let go by Illinois after losing six straight games to end the season and Rick Neuheisel getting run out at UCLA after a 50-0 loss to rival Southern California in the regular season finale. Neuheisel coached the Bruins when they lost the Pac-12 title game at Oregon, leaving them as the first team to go to a bowl with a losing record since North Texas in 2001. With their head coaches gone and new coaches Tim Beckman at Illinois and Jim Mora at UCLA not set to take over until January, interim coaches Koenning and Mike Johnson ran the Illini and Bruins respectively. There was so much turmoil that Koenning did not know if his offensive assistants would take part in the game until seeing interim offensive coordinator Jeff Brohm at breakfast before the game. The Illini opened up the playbook in the first half but still trailed 7-3 at the break. They called a throwback pass to Scheelhaase, a reverse, a fake field goal and went for it on fourth-and-1 from their own territory. UCLA stuffed Donovonn Young for a loss on that run from the Illinois 45, setting up Prince's 16-yard TD pass to Taylor Embree for the first score of the game. The game, which is sponsored by Kraft, generated three meals for local food banks for each of the 29,878 tickets sold. Officials used an Oreo cookie for the opening coin toss.

2011 Chick-Fil-A Peach Bowl

The 2011 Chick-fil-A Bowl, the 44th edition of the game, was held on December 31, 2011 at the Georgia Dome in Atlanta, Georgia. The game, which was telecast on ESPN and ESPN 3D, featured the Virginia Cavaliers from the Atlantic Coast Conference versus the Auburn Tigers from the Southeastern Conference. Auburn's star Running Back Michael Dyer was suspended for this game which would also be Auburn Offense Coordinator Gus Malzahn's last game as he would be taking a job as the Head Coach at Arkansas State.

2011 Chick-Fil-A Peach Bowl	Line	1	-	2	-	3	-	4	-	Final
Auburn	(-3.0)	7	-	21	-	12	-	3	-	43
Virginia	(49.0)	7	-	10	-	7	-	0	-	24

Scoring Summary
Virginia - Burd 27 yard pass from Rocco (Randolph kick)
Auburn - Frazier 3 yard run (Parkey kick)
Virginia - Burd 6 yard pass from Rocco (Randolph kick)
Auburn - McCalebb 3 yard run (Parkey kick)
Auburn - Frazier 1 yard run (Parkey kick)
Auburn - McCalebb 25 yard pass from Trotter (Parkey kick)
Virginia - Randolph 24 yard field goal
Auburn - Mason 22 yard run (Parkey kick)
Virginia - Parks 1 yard run (Randolph kick)
Auburn - TEAM Safety
Auburn - Parkey 45 yard field goal
Auburn - Parkey 37 yard field goal

Auburn Media Guide Peach Bowl Game Summary - Offensive MVP Onterio McCalebb rushed for a season-high 109 yards and had 180 all-purpose yards, Emory Blake caught six passes for a career-high tying 108 yards and Barrett Trotter came off the bench to throw for 175 yards and one touchdown to lead Auburn to a 43-24 victory over Virginia in the Chick-fil-A Bowl in the Georgia Dome on Dec. 31. Trotter completed

11-of-18 passes after he and Kiehl Frazier came in for injured starter Clint Moseley in the first quarter. Frazier had 16 carries for 55 yards and became the ninth Tiger to score two touchdowns in a bowl game. Tre Mason gained 64 yards on nine carries and had his first career rushing touchdown. Auburn used a big second quarter as it scored 21 consecutive points to take control of the game, 28-14. After Virginia took a 14-7 lead, Auburn quickly answered as McCalebb ran it in from three yards out on third down to tie it 14-14 with 10:33 left in the half. Then, Parkey successfully recovered his onside kick at the Auburn 41 as the Tigers went on to take the lead for good, 21-14, on Frazier's 1-yard third down rush with 8:44 left. Trotter completed a 50-yard pass to Blake to the Virginia 5. Auburn's 14 consecutive points came on 11 plays and 144 yards in 4:08. On the ensuing possession, Chris Davis snuffed out a Virginia fake field goal after Eltoro Freeman broke up a Cavalier pass in the end zone the play before. Auburn scored a touchdown on its third-straight possession as Trotter completed a 29-yard touchdown pass to McCalebb with 59 seconds left in the half to give Auburn a 28-14 lead. Virginia scored first, but walk-on Garrett Harper stepped up to help the Tigers even the score on the next possession. Harper blocked the first punt of his career as Auburn took over on the Virginia 15. The Tigers tied it 7-7 as Frazier scored on a 3-yard touchdown run up the middle with 4:02 left in the opening quarter. McCalebb set it up with a 12-yard run the play before. Mason scored his first career rushing touchdown to open the third quarter with a 22-yarder to put Auburn up 35-17 almost four minutes in. Virginia scored with 6:20 left in the third, cutting the lead to 35-24, but the Cavaliers would come no closer. Steven Clark pinned Virginia at its own 6-yard line and the Tigers defense held the Cavs to three and out as Gabe Wright made his first career sack at the 1-yard line. Then, Angelo Blackson blocked UVa's punt out of the end zone for a safety and a 37-24 lead with 1:57 remaining in the third. It's the first time Auburn had blocked two punts in the same game since 2003 vs. Louisiana-Monroe. Quan Bray took the ensuing kickoff and returned it 57 yards to the Virginia 15. Parkey nailed a 45-yard field goal after a personal foul and false start penalty to make it 40-24 with 47 seconds to go in the third. Parkey drilled his second field goal of the game, a 37-yarder, to give Auburn a 43-24 lead with 8:09 remaining.

2012 Outback Bowl

The 2012 Outback Bowl, the 26th edition of the game, was held on January 2, 2012, at the Raymond James Stadium in Tampa, Florida. The game, which was telecast to a national audience on ABC, featured the Georgia Bulldogs from the Southeastern Conference versus the Michigan State Spartans from the Big Ten Conference. The Michigan State Spartans won 33–30 in the third overtime period.

2012 Outback Bowl	Line	1	2	3	4	OT	2OT	3OT	Final
#12 Michigan State	(50.0)	0	0	14	13	0	3	3	33
#18 Georgia	(-3.0)	2	14	0	11	0	3	0	30

Scoring Summary
Georgia - Safety - Martin tackled in end zone
Georgia - King 80 Yard Pass from Murray (Walsh kick)
Georgia - Boykin 92 Yard Punt Return (Walsh kick)
Michigan State - Bell 8 Yard Run (Linthicum pass from Cousins)
Michigan State - Dennard 38 Yard Interception Return (Pass failed)
Georgia - Walsh 32 yard Field goal
Michigan State - Nichol 7 Yard Pass from Cousins (Pass failed)
Georgia - Boykin 13 Yard Pass from Murray (Mitchell pass from Murray)
Michigan State - Bell 1 Yard Run (Conroy Kick)
Georgia - Walsh 48 yard Field goal
Michigan State - Conroy 35 yard Field goal
Michigan State - Conroy 28 yard Field goal

Game summary - The Bulldogs scored first when Brandon Boykin tackled Keshawn Martin in the end zone for a safety. On the ensuing drive, the Bulldogs drove to MSU's 5-yard line. However, on a 4th-and-1 play at the 5-yard line, UGA's Ken Malcome was stopped for a 1-yard loss, turning the ball over to MSU. The rest of the 1st quarter remained scoreless. In the 2nd quarter, UGA scored on an 80-yard touchdown pass to Tavarres King to go up 9-0. On the ensuing drive, the Bulldog defense forced the Spartans to punt. UGA's Brandon Boykin preceded to return the punt 92 yards to go up 16-0 at the end of the half. The Spartans finally got on board in the 3rd quarter on an 8-yard Le'Veon Bell touchdown run to cut the deficit 16-8 after a two-point conversion. MSU closed the gap even further when Darqueze Dennard intercepted Aaron Murray 38 yards for a touchdown. The two-point conversion attempt failed, making it 16-14 going into the 4th quarter. Taking advantage of an interception, Georgia extended their lead 19-14 in the 4th quarter on a 32-yard field goal from Blair Walsh. The Spartans retook the lead on a 7-yard touchdown pass to Keith Nichol to make it 20-19 after a failed two-point conversion. Georgia responded with a 13-yard touchdown pass to Brandon Boykin to go up 27-20 after making a two-point conversion. On the ensuing drive, Jonathan Jenkins intercepted Kirk Cousins with only 3:56 left in regulation. However, Georgia was unable to run out the game clock and punted the ball away. With 85-yards to go, no timeouts and only 1 minute and 55 seconds left in regulation, Michigan State was able to tie the game 27-27 on a 1-yard touchdown run from Le'Veon Bell with only 14 seconds left in the game, forcing overtime. Michigan State was on offense first in the 1st overtime period. The Spartan's offensive possession end when Kirk Cousins' pass was intercepted by Bacarri Rambo. UGA's Blair Walsh, however, missed a game winning 42-yard field, forcing a 2nd overtime period. Michigan State and Georgia both traded field goals to go into the 3rd overtime period tied 30-30. In the 3rd overtime period, MSU's Dan Conroy kicked a 28-yard field goal to go ahead 33-30. Georgia attempted to force a 4th overtime on a 47-yard field goal attempt from Blair Walsh. However, Walsh's kick was blocked, sealing the victory for Michigan State. Georgia cornerback Brandon Boykin was named game MVP for scoring on offense, defense and special teams. Several Outback Bowl records were broken in the 2012 game, including longest punt return for a touchdown (Boykin's 92-yard punt return) and receiving touchdown (Tavarres King's 80-yard touchdown reception)

2012 Gator Bowl

The 2012 TaxSlayer.com Gator Bowl, the 67th edition of the game, was held on January 2, 2012 at EverBank Field in Jacksonville, Florida. TaxSlayer.com was named the corporate title sponsor on September 1, 2011. The game was a rematch of the 2007 BCS National Championship Game, where Florida emerged victorious. Florida's head coach for the 2007 game, Urban Meyer, was named head coach at Ohio State in November 2011 and took over the Buckeye football program in the 2012 season.

2012 Gator Bowl	Line	1	-	2	-	3	-	4	-	Final
Florida	(-2.0)	7	-	7	-	7	-	3	-	24
Ohio State	(44.0)	0	-	10	-	0	-	7	-	17

Scoring Summary
Florida – Thompson 17 yard pass from Brantley (Sturgis kick)
Ohio State - Posey 5 yard pass from Miller (Basil kick)
Florida – Debose 99 yard kickoff return (Sturgis kick)
Ohio State - Basil 47 yard field goal
Florida – Stewart 14 yard blocked punt return (Sturgis kick)
Florida – Sturgis 17 yard field goal
Ohio State – Hall 11 yard pass from Miller (Basil kick)

Associated Press Gator Bowl Game Recap - Florida's Jaye Howard timed the snap perfectly, blew through two defenders and violently slammed Ohio State Quarterback Braxton Miller to the ground. Urban Meyer's future team got a good look at his former team, and the Buckeyes learned just how fast the Gators can be. Florida's defense and special teams came up big in the TaxSlayer.com Gator Bowl, recording six sacks and scoring twice as the Gators beat Ohio State 24-17 on Monday. Andre Debose returned a kickoff 99 yards -- the longest scoring play in bowl history -- and Chris Rainey blocked a punt that was returned for a touchdown. The speedsters helped the Gators (7-6) avoid their first losing season since 1979 and pick up some much-needed momentum after losing six of their previous eight games. Ohio State (6-7) dropped four straight to finish below .500 for the first time since 1988 and lost seven games for the first time since 1897. The Buckeyes can take solace in knowing that Meyer, who officially takes over for interim coach Luke Fickell at Ohio State this week, will make it a priority to improve special teams. Meyer did that in his six seasons in Gainesville, and Rainey and Debose were two of his most prized recruits. Ohio State fell to 0-10 in bowl games against teams from the Southeastern Conference. Yes, the Buckeyes beat Arkansas in the Sugar Bowl last year. But that victory was vacated as part of NCAA sanctions. The latest loss had everything to do with Florida's speed. The Gators dominated the defensive line of scrimmage. They had a season-high six sacks, harassing Braxton Miller on nearly every passing play. Howard and Sharrif Floyd were disruptive all afternoon. Florida had similar success the last time it played Ohio State. The Gators were dominant on defense in a 41-14 win in the 2007 Bowl Championship Series national title game in Glendale, Ariz. Meyer was coaching Florida that night. Debose and Rainey proved to be the difference in the much-hyped rematch that centered on Meyer. Just after Ohio State tied the game at 7 on Miller's 5-yard pass to DeVier Posey in the second quarter, Debose took the kickoff, made one cut to the outside and went untouched for his third career kickoff return for a touchdown. The Buckeyes never got close enough to even swipe at him, let alone make the tackle. Florida was up 14-10 at halftime and essentially put the game out of reach on the opening possession of the third. Rainey came off the left end and blocked Ben Buchanan's punt. Seldom-used linebacker Graham Stewart scooped it up at the 14-yard line and scored the first touchdown of his career. It was Rainey's sixth blocked punt of his career, breaking the school and SEC record. Rainey also ran for 71 yards on a warm and sunny day in Jacksonville. John Brantley completed 12 of 16 passes for 132 yards, with a touchdown and an interception. He had a 17-yard strike to Deonte Thompson in the first. Ohio State wasn't nearly as effective. Miller completed 18 of 23 passes for 162 yards and two touchdowns. He also ran 15 times for 20 yards. He completed an 11-yard TD pass to Jordan Hall with 57 seconds remaining. The Buckeyes failed to recover an onside kick, and Florida ran out the clock for its sixth bowl victory in the last seven years, including four in a row. Players doused Muschamp with ice water in the final seconds, but the coach later made it clear his team still has strides to make to get back to national prominence.

2012 TicketCity Bowl

The 2012 TicketCity Bowl, the second edition of the game, was held on January 2, 2012 at the Cotton Bowl in Dallas, Texas. The game, which was telecast on ESPNU, featured the Houston Cougars from Conference USA versus the Penn State Nittany Lions from the Big Ten Conference. The Houston Cougars won 30–14. The 2012 TicketCity Bowl marked the head coaching debut of Tony Levine, and the last college game of Quarterback Case Keenum.

2012 TicketCity Bowl	Line	1	-	2	-	3	-	4	-	Final
#24 Penn State	(56.5)	0	-	7	-	7	-	0	-	14
#20 Houston	(-7.0)	17	-	7	-	3	-	3	-	30

Scoring Summary
Houston - Edwards 40 yard pass from Keenum (Hogan kick)
Houston - Hogan 35 yard Field goal
Houston - Johnson 8 yard pass from Keenum (Hogan kick)
Penn State - Green 6 yard run (Fera kick)
Houston - Edwards 75 yard pass from Keenum (Hogan kick)
Houston - Hogan 38 yard Field goal
Penn State - Brown 69 yard pass from Bolden (Fera kick)
Houston - Hogan 22 yard Field goal

Associated Press TicketCity Bowl Game Summary - Pacing the Penn State sideline just the way his dad did for 46 seasons, Jay Paterno couldn't help but wonder what JoePa might be doing back home in Happy Valley. A 30-14 loss to Houston at the TicketCity Bowl on Monday ended a tumultuous season for a program shrouded with uncertainty following the firing of a Hall of Fame coach in the aftermath of a child sex-abuse scandal that shook college sports. The 24th-ranked Nittany Lions were picked apart by Case Keenum and the 20th-ranked Cougars. He threw for 532 yards and three touchdowns, a dispiriting finish for a defense that was allowing 162 yards passing per game. Keenum threw for more than double that by halftime. Now, Houston (13-1) gets to relish in the satisfaction of extending its school record for victories in a season. Penn State must push forward still without a permanent head coach. Longtime defensive coordinator Tom Bradley, who was appointed the interim coach after Paterno's dismissal, is a candidate in a search that overshadowed the game itself.   Keenum burned the Nittany Lions' veteran secondary with touchdown passes of 40 and 75 yards to build a 24-7 lead by halftime. It was the school's first bowl game without Paterno as head coach since the 1962 Gator Bowl, a 17-7 loss to Florida. Paterno was fired Nov. 9 by school trustees amid mounting criticism that school leaders should have done more to prevent the shocking abuse allegations against retired assistant Jerry Sandusky. He is awaiting trial after pleading not guilty last month. Bradley's enormous task: guide players besieged by the resulting media scrutiny. Bypassed by more prominent bowls, some Nittany Lions (9-4) debated whether to travel to Dallas at all, then vowed they were over getting jilted and focused on stopping Houston. Turned out Linebacker U got trampled over by Keenum and Houston's high-octane offense. Start with receiver Patrick Edwards, who burned safety Malcolm Willis for a 40-yard touchdown pass from Keenum down the left sideline for a 7-0 lead just 1:52 into the game that often resembled a one-sided track meet. Keenum hit Justin Johnson for an 8-yard TD pass with 2:35 left for a 17-0 lead. Houston coach Tony Levine, leading the Cougars for the first time since replacing Kevin Sumlin, was impressed. Already the NCAA career leader coming into the game for passing yardage and touchdown passes, Keenum added another record to his impressive resume. His 227 first quarter passing yards set the record for most passing yards in one quarter in any bowl game, breaking the mark previously held by Louisville's Browning Nagle (223 yards) against Alabama in the first quarter of the 1991 Fiesta Bowl, according to TicketCity Bowl officials. Penn State All-American defensive tackle Devon Still, already slowed by turf toe, couldn't keep up with Keenum's quick release and Houston's no-huddle attack. The Cougars exploited Penn State's bend-but-don't -break defense across the middle, including Edwards 75-yard touchdown reception up the seam from a scrambling Keenum for a 24-7 lead by halftime. Keenum finished 45 of 69 passing -- two fewer attempts than the number of offensive plays Penn State ran all afternoon. Down by 20 midway through the third quarter, cornerback Stephon Morris tried to keep his fellow defenders motivated on the bench with high-fives. The struggling offense without injured starting Quarterback Matt McGloin provided a glimmer of hope after Rob Bolden connected with Justin Brown for a 69-yard touchdown pass to cut the lead to 27-14 at 2:38 of the third quarter.   Penn State's defense adjusted to hold the Cougars to just two field goals in the second half, but the early deficit proved too much to overcome, and Bolden threw three second-half interceptions -- two by safety Nick Saenz. With 12 minutes left in the fourth quarter, Penn State had already given up 552 yards of total offense to Houston, the most allowed by the Nittany Lions all season. This wasn't the lasting impression Bradley wanted to leave on the Penn State committee searching for Paterno's replacement. The outgoing Bradley, who is popular with players, is among the candidates who have been interviewed. Acting athletic director David Joyner has said he hopes to have a new coach in place to give him a few weeks to recruit before Feb. 1, when high school seniors can announce their college choices. Bolden finished 7 of 26 passing for 137 yards, while Stephfon Green ran for 63 yards on 15 carries including a 6-yard scoring run on a direct snap in the second quarter. It was one of the few times the Cougars' D got tricked. After getting upset 49-28 by Southern Mississippi in the Conference USA title game to lose a chance to play in the BCS, Houston ended the season with an impressive win over a power conference team. Edwards finished with 10 catches and 228 yards for two touchdowns, while Johnson had 12 catches for 148 yards at the 92,000-seat Cotton Bowl. The stands were about half-full on a sunny afternoon that ended with Houston's red-clad fans celebrating and chanting "Houston."

2012 Capital One Bowl

The 2012 Capital One Bowl, the 66th edition of the game, was held on January 2, 2012 at the Citrus Bowl in Orlando, Florida. The game, which was telecast on ESPN, featured the #10 South Carolina Gamecocks from the Southeastern Conference versus the #21 Nebraska Cornhuskers from the Big Ten Conference.

2012 Capital One Bowl	Line	1	-	2	-	3	-	4	-	Final
#21 Nebraska	(46.0)	13	-	0	-	0	-	0	-	13
#10 South Carolina	(-2.5)	9	-	7	-	0	-	14	-	30

Scoring Summary
Nebraska - Bell 30 yard pass from Martinez (Kick blocked)
South Carolina - Gilmore PAT return
South Carolina - Shaw 1 yard run (Wooten kick)
Nebraska - Ameer 1 yard run (Maher kick)
South Carolina - Jeffery 51 yard pass from Shaw (Wooten kick)
South Carolina - Miles 9 yard pass from Shaw (Wooten kick)
South Carolina - Miles 3 yard run (Wooten kick)

South Carolina Media Guide Capital One Bowl Game Recap - No. 10 South Carolina wrapped up one of the most successful seasons in school history with a 30-13 victory over No. 21 Nebraska in the Capital One Bowl. With the win, Carolina finishes the season 11-2, becoming the first team in school history to reach 11 wins. Junior receiver Alshon Jeffery played a key role in leading South Carolina to its record-setting win and made a little history of his own. Jeffery finished the day with four receptions for 148 yards and a touchdown on his way to earning bowl MVP honors. Gamecock Quarterback Connor Shaw had a stellar end to his sophomore campaign, completing 11-of-17 passes for 230 yards and two touchdowns. He added 42 yards and one touchdown on the ground. Junior running back Kenny Miles finished with 67 yards and a touchdown on 15 carries and had two receptions for 13 yards and a score. The Gamecock defense delivered another solid performance, holding Nebraska to 253 yards of total offense with just 64 yards allowed in the second half. Carolina tied a season-high with six sacks on the day, including two from freshman Jadeveon Clowney and 1.5 from senior Melvin Ingram. Junior D.J. Swearinger and senior Antonio Allen led the way with seven tackles apiece. The Cornhuskers (9-4) struck first. On Nebraska's third play from scrimmage, Quarterback Taylor Martinez found Kenny Bell for a 30-yard touchdown strike. However, Travian Robertson blocked the extra point and Stephon Gilmore returned it for two points to make it a 6-2 game. Bruce Ellington gave Carolina excellent field position on the ensuing possession with a 45-yard kickoff return. A 24-yard run by Miles set up the Gamecocks deep in Nebraska territory. Shaw capped the drive on fourth and goal by punching it in from a yard out, giving Carolina a 9-6 advantage. Nebraska answered with an eight-play, 60-yard scoring drive, aided by a Carolina drive-extending penalty, to regain the lead. Ameer Abdullah finished off the drive with a 1-yard touchdown run to give the Cornhuskers a 13-9 lead. Both teams missed golden opportunities to score in the second quarter. Nebraska lost a fumble in the red zone, then Carolina came up empty after a 78- yard pass to Jeffery set them up with a first-and-goal situation. Stephon Gilmore gave the Gamecocks one more chance to score before halftime by intercepting a Martinez pass at the Gamecock 26. With seven seconds until intermission from the Carolina 49, Shaw rolled right and heaved it downfield where Jeffery leaped over a defender, came down with the ball and dove into the end zone for a 16-13 lead heading into the locker room. The Gamecocks pushed their lead to 23-13 early in the fourth quarter with a five-play, 41-yard scoring drive. Shaw hooked up with Ace Sanders for a 23- yard pass play on third and 18 to move the ball to the Nebraska 11. Two plays later, Shaw found a wide-open Miles for a 9-yard touchdown pass. Miles added a 3-yard touchdown run with 3:05 left for the final score.

2012 Rose Bowl

The 2012 Rose Bowl, the 98th edition of the annual game, was played on Monday, January 2, 2012 at the Rose Bowl stadium in Pasadena, California. The Oregon Ducks of the Pac-12 Conference beat the Wisconsin Badgers of the Big Ten Conference, 45–38, for their first Rose Bowl win in 95 years. The Pasadena Tournament of Roses Association was the organizer of the game and dedicated the game in honor of all wounded military personnel, who tossed the game coin by their representative Grand Marshal J.R. Martinez. The Rose Bowl Game, themed Just Imagine …, was a contractual sell-out, with 64,500 tickets allocated to the participating teams and conferences. The remaining tickets went to the Tournament of Roses members, sponsors, City of Pasadena residents, and the general public.

Oregon - The Ducks were led by LaMichael James in scoring with 19 touchdowns and 114 points in 11 games. Oregon was ranked 3rd in the nation in points scored (46.2 points per game) and 5th in rushing yards (295.7). Coming into the game, Oregon had held opponents to 23.6 points per game and allowed 243.5 yards in pass defense and 137.5 yards per game in rush defense. Combining the rushing yardage with the passing offense of 219.5 yards per game, the Ducks had a total offense of 515.2 yards per game.

Wisconsin - Wisconsin, winning 11 games and losing 2 during the season, had the best offense in the Big Ten, scoring 80 touchdowns, 7 field goals for a total of 580 points. Wisconsin was ranked 4th in the nation in scoring (44.6 points per game) and 10th in rushing yards (237.4). The Badgers had limited opponents to just 17 points per game, 155 yards in passing and 138 yards in rushing. The team had passed for 229.5 yards per game for a total offense of 466.9 yards in total offense.

2012 Rose Bowl	Line	1	-	2	-	3	-	4	-	Final
#9 Wisconsin	(72.0)	14	-	14	-	10	-	0	-	38
#6 Oregon	(-5.5)	14	-	14	-	7	-	10	-	45

Scoring Summary
Wisconsin – Abbrederis 38 yard Pass from Wilson (Welch Kick)
Oregon – James 1 yard Run (Maldonado Kick)
Wisconsin – Wilson 4 yard Run (Welch Kick)
Oregon – Thomas 91 yard Run (Maldonado Kick)
Wisconsin – Ball 3 yard Run (Welch Kick)
Oregon – Barner 54 yard Pass from Thomas (Maldonado Kick)
Wisconsin – Nzegwu 33 yard Fumble Return (Welch Kick)
Oregon – Tuinei 3 yard Pass from Thomas (Maldonado Kick)
Oregon – Thomas 64 yard Run (Maldonado Kick)
Wisconsin – Welch 29 yard Field goal
Wisconsin – Toon 18 yard Pass from Wilson (Welch Kick)
Oregon – Tuinei 11 yard Pass from Thomas (Maldonado Kick)
Oregon – Maldonado 30 yard Field goal

Records
- Most Points scored in 1st Half of Rose Bowl (Both teams): 56 points
- Longest Rushing TD in Rose Bowl: 91 yards by De'Anthony Thomas (Oregon)
- Most Points scored in regulation in Rose Bowl (Both teams): 83 points
- Most Rushing TD over 60 yards in Rose Bowl: 2 TDs De'Anthony Thomas (Oregon)

Associated Press Rose Bowl Game Summary - The Oregon Ducks had waited 95 years to win another Rose Bowl presented by Vizio, and the last few seconds stretched for an eternity. The players in mirrored helmets held each other back on the sideline, waiting on tiptoes for video review to confirm Wisconsin was out of time. The call went Oregon's way. The Ducks stormed the hallowed field. The most futuristic team in college football had buried another bit of history, and that revolutionary offense finally has a shiny trophy that will look right at home among those eye-catching uniforms. Darron Thomas passed for three touchdowns, De'Anthony Thomas scored on runs of 91 and 64 yards, and the Ducks (No. 5 BCS, No. 6 AP) earned their first bowl victory under coach Chip Kelly, holding off the Badgers 45-38 Monday night in the highest-scoring Rose Bowl ever played. The last time Oregon won the Rose Bowl, beating Penn 14-0 in 1917, the players wore leather helmets, not those shiny numbers that exemplify every innovation the Ducks have created during Kelly's three-year tenure. Oregon (12-2) showed off that creativity with 621 total yards -- second-most in Rose Bowl history -- against the tough Badgers, playing at its usual frantic pace until the final whistle. Lavasier Tuinei caught eight passes for 158 yards and two TDs for the Ducks, who had no postseason success to show for Kelly's otherwise wildly successful three-year tenure until this landmark offensive performance. Maybe so, but it's unlikely anybody from Oregon will forget how this one ended. With two long passes, Russell Wilson moved the Badgers to the Oregon 25, but with 2 seconds left and no timeouts. After waiting for the ball to be set, he spiked it to set up a last-ditch heave to the end zone, but the clock hit zeroes while he did it. The Ducks were winners after video review, holding Wisconsin scoreless in the fourth quarter. The Ducks don't doubt it: The 98th Rose Bowl was that kind of game. The Granddaddy of Them All had never seen this many points, beating the record 80 scored by Washington and Iowa in 1991. Montee Ball rushed for 122 of his 164 yards in the first half for the Badgers (11-3), who lost the Rose Bowl for the second straight year despite managing 508 yards of their own. Ball tied Barry Sanders' FBS record with his 39th touchdown of the season, but the Heisman Trophy finalist was held to three carries for no yards in the fourth quarter. Wisconsin had two drives to tie it after Oregon kicked a field goal with 6:50 to play, but Jared Abbrederis fumbled near the Oregon sideline after making a long catch. The ball plopped onto the turf without even bouncing, and Oregon's Michael Clay jumped on it with 4:06 left. That video review went the Ducks' way, too. The Ducks and Badgers produced the highest-scoring first quarter (14-14) and first half (28-28) in Rose Bowl history, eventually surpassing the 80 scored in Washington's 46-34 win over Iowa in 1991. Oregon's yardage fell just short of USC's 633 yards against Illinois in 2008. Sure, Baylor's 67-56 win over Washington in the Valero Alamo Bowl last Thursday might have packed bigger sheer numbers. But Wisconsin and Oregon commanded a much bigger stage -- and the Ducks unleashed every bit of their formidable offensive power. Tuinei was named the Ducks' offensive player of the game, but their flashiest star in those futuristic helmets was De'Anthony Thomas, the freshman from Los Angeles who showed off his electrifying athleticism on the longest scoring run in Rose Bowl history in the second quarter, going 91 yards up the middle. He added a 64-yard scoring run in the opening minute of the second half as Oregon won the matchup of the last two losers of the Rose Bowl. Wisconsin lost 21-19 to TCU last season, and the Ducks lost to Ohio State two years ago before losing the BCS title game last year. LaMichael James rushed for 159 yards and an early TD in his likely college finale for the Ducks, and Kenjon Barner caught a TD pass from Darron Thomas. Nick Toon caught a TD pass for Wisconsin, and defensive end Louis Nzegwu returned a fumble 33 yards for a score in the second quarter. Both teams won their respective conferences' first-ever league title games to earn this trip to Pasadena. Although the Ducks' drought was generations longer, Wisconsin hasn't won in Pasadena since Jan. 1, 2000, when Ron Dayne led the Badgers to back-to-back Rose Bowl titles. Oregon quickly debunked the theory that teams with extra time to prepare for the Ducks' inventive offense have a better chance to stop it. The Ducks were 1-4 in bowl games and season openers under Kelly until they carved up Wisconsin with the second-biggest yardage performance in Rose Bowl history. Wisconsin set the tone from its opening drive, going 77 yards in seven plays for Abbrederis' wide-open 38-yard TD catch just 3:12 in. De'Anthony Thomas ended the record-breaking first quarter by bursting through the Wisconsin line and sprinting down the Oregon sideline for a 91-yard score, surpassing Tyrone Wheatley's bowl-record 88-yard run in 1993 and capping the second-longest scoring drive in Rose Bowl history at 95 yards with Oregon's longest run all season. Wisconsin opened the second quarter with Ball's record-tying TD, but Darron Thomas found Barner open down the seam for a 54-yard score on Oregon's next play. Both defenses then got a brief chance to shine: The Ducks stopped Wisconsin on fourth down inside the Oregon 20, but blitzing Wisconsin linebacker Mike Taylor forced Darron Thomas' fumble moments later, and Nzegwu scooped and scored. Oregon calmly answered with Tuinei's 3-yard TD catch with 30 seconds left. The teams' 56 combined points in the first half surpassed the record 45 scored by Wisconsin and UCLA in 1999. De'Anthony Thomas' 64-yard TD run put Oregon ahead for the first time, but the Badgers swung ahead with Wilson's 18-yard TD pass to Toon. After the Quarterbacks traded interceptions, Darron Thomas found Tuinei for his second score just 25 seconds into the fourth quarter, putting the Ducks ahead to stay. Game notes: The game-time temperature was 82 degrees, making it the warmest bowl game in Wisconsin history. ... It was also the highest-scoring bowl game in Wisconsin history, and the Badgers tied the school bowl record with 38 points. ... Oregon is 2-4 in the Rose Bowl. ... Oregon LB Kiko Alonso was the defensive player of the game with an interception and 1½ sacks.

2012 Fiesta Bowl

The 2012 Tostitos Fiesta Bowl was played at University of Phoenix Stadium in Glendale, Arizona. The Oklahoma State Cowboys, champions of the Big 12 Conference, played the Stanford Cardinal, an at-large selection from the Pac-12 conference. Oklahoma State won the game, 41–38, in overtime. Originally this game was scheduled for January 5 pending resolution of the 2011 NFL lockout and a possible Monday Night Football game on January 2. However, with the resolution of the lockout, the game was moved to the spot following the 2012 Rose Bowl. The game aired on ESPN.

Oklahoma State - Big 12 champion Oklahoma State made their first ever trip to a BCS bowl game. Oklahoma State ranked second in passing offense (386.25 yards per game), scoring offense (49.33 points), and turnover margin (1.67) during the season, and turnovers (42). The Cowboy offense featured the combination of Quarterback Brandon Weeden and wide receiver Justin Blackmon, both of whom were taken in the 2012 NFL Draft. Weeden in 12 games, completed 379 of 522 passes for 4,328 yards while Blackmon caught 113 passes for 1,336 yards. Oklahoma State was not selected for the National Championship game, after being upset in the previous weeks.

Stanford - Stanford has a 5–7 record against the Big 12 Conference teams (1–0 Kansas; 1–0 Missouri; 1–4 Oklahoma; 2–2 Texas; 0–1 Texas A&M). Stanford played in the 2009 Sun Bowl and lost to Oklahoma 31–27. Prior to its loss to Oregon on November 12, the Cardinal were winners of its first nine games of the season and 17 in a row. The team ranked second in the conference and 22nd nationally in rushing offense (207.92 yards per game), led by All-American Quarterback Andrew Luck, who was the first player selected in the 2012 NFL Draft.

2012 Fiesta Bowl	Line	1	-	2	-	3	-	4	-	OT	-	Final
#4 Stanford	(74.0)	7	-	14	-	7	-	10	-	0	-	38
#3 Oklahoma State	(-4.0)	0	-	21	-	3	-	14	-	3	-	41

Scoring Summary
Stanford – Montgomery 53 yard pass from Luck (Williamson kick)
Stanford – Stewart 24 yard run (Williamson kick)
Oklahoma State – Blackmon 43 yard pass from Weeden. (Sharp kick)
Oklahoma State – Blackmon 67 yard pass from Weeden. (Sharp kick)
Stanford – Taylor 4 yard run (Williamson kick)
Oklahoma State – Weeden 2 yard run (Sharp kick)
Stanford – Ertz 16 yard pass from Luck (Williamson kick)
Oklahoma State – Sharp 19 yard field goal
Stanford – Williamson 30 yard field goal
Oklahoma State – Blackmon 17 yard pass from Weeden (Sharp kick)
Stanford – Taylor 1 yard run (Williamson kick)
Oklahoma State – Randle 4 yard run. (Sharp kick)
Oklahoma State – Sharp 22 yard field goal

Fiesta Bowl Game Summary - Like two heavyweight boxers, BCS no. 4 Stanford and BCS no. 3 Oklahoma State, boasting two of the nation's most prolific offenses, traded punches into overtime before the Cowboys captured the 2012 Fiesta Bowl trophy with a 41–38 victory on Quinn Sharp's 22-yard field goal. Enroute to the first 12-win season in school history, Oklahoma State was forced to stage repeated comebacks in the face of a withering Stanford offense that amassed 590 total yards (nearly 200 more than OSU) to take leads of 14–0, 21–14, 28–21, 31-24 and 38–31. The Cowboys never led until their game-winning field goal and their normally balanced offense produced only 13 rushing yards on 15 carries. After Stanford opened the scoring with a first-quarter touchdown pass by all-American Quarterback Andrew Luck, the anticipated offensive fireworks began in the second quarter when the two powerhouses tallied five touchdowns in a span of six possessions. Luck, the 2011 Maxwell Award and Walter Camp Award recipient as the nation's player of the year and a two-time Heisman Trophy runner-up, completed 27 of 31 passes for 347 yards and two touchdowns. His OSU counterpart, Brandon Weeden, was equally impressive, connecting on 29 of 42 tosses for 399 yards and three touchdowns. It marked the first time in Fiesta Bowl history both Quarterbacks eclipsed 300 yards passing while setting the two-team record for total passing yards (746). Justin Blackmon, Oklahoma State's two-time Biletnikoff Award winner as the nation's best receiver, caught all three Weeden touchdown throws (43, 67, 17 yards) to equal the Fiesta Bowl record. Blackmon's second and third six-point receptions tied the game at 14–14 and 31–31, respectively. It was the sixth time in OSU's 13 games and 12th time overall Blackmon caught two or more touchdown passes and marked the 19th time in his 38-game college career he exceeded 100 receiving yards. The 67-yard scoring strike was OSU's longest pass play of the season. OSU running back Joseph Randle tied the see-saw contest for the final time at 38–38 on a four-yard run with 1:51 remaining in the fourth quarter. Knotted at 38–38 in the late going, two errant Stanford field-goal attempts — the first (35 yards) on the final play of regulation, the second (43 yards) to cap the Cardinal's only overtime possession — gave OSU life. The Cowboys seized the moment following the latter when Weeden completed a 24-yard pass to Colton Chelf to Stanford's one-yard line. After Weeden centered the ball on the next snap with a kneel-down, Sharp punched his chip-shot 22-yard game-winning field goal through the uprights to end the third overtime game in Fiesta Bowl history.

2012 Sugar Bowl

The 2012 Allstate Sugar Bowl was the 78th edition of the Sugar Bowl. It featured the Michigan Wolverines and the Virginia Tech Hokies on Tuesday, January 3, 2012, at the Mercedes-Benz Superdome in New Orleans, Louisiana. The game ended with 23–20 Michigan victory in overtime. Michigan represented the Big Ten Conference (Big Ten) as the at-large team from the conference, while Virginia Tech represented the

Atlantic Coast Conference (ACC) as its at-large team. The game was televised on ESPN. This was the first Sugar Bowl since 2000, as well as only the sixth since World War II and the tenth overall, not to feature a Southeastern Conference (SEC) team. Michigan was offered a berth after it finished the season with a 10–2 record—its highest win total since the 2006 season—that ended with a 40–34 win against arch-rival Ohio State. Virginia Tech was offered a berth after it finished its season 11–2, which culminated in a 38–10 loss in the 2011 ACC Championship Game to Clemson. In recognition of his performance, Michigan's Junior Hemingway was named the game's most valuable player.

2012 Sugar Bowl	Line	1	-	2	-	3	-	4	-	OT	-	Final
#13 Michigan	(-2.5)	0	-	10	-	7	-	3	-	3	-	23
#17 Virginia Tech	(51.0)	3	-	3	-	3	-	11	-	0	-	20

Scoring Summary
Virginia Tech - Myer 37 yard field goal
Virginia Tech - Myer 43 yard field goal
Michigan - Hemingway 45 yard pass from Robinson (Gibbons kick)
Michigan - Gibbons 24 yard field goal
Michigan - Hemingway 18 yard pass from Robinson (Gibbons kick)
Virginia Tech - Myer 36 yard field goal
Virginia Tech - Thomas 1 yard run (Davis pass from Thomas)
Michigan - Gibbons 39 yard field goal
Virginia Tech - Myers 25 yard field goal
Michigan - Gibbons 37 yard field goal

Sugar Bowl Recap by Sugar Bowl historian Marty Mulé

Brandon Gibbon was lost in pleasant thoughts. He was thinking of pretty girls on the beach. With the score knotted at 20, the Michigan place-kicker was 37 yards away from the first overtime victory in the Sugar Bowl's 78-year history, though naturally opponent Virginia Tech had called time-out to "ice" him, and he was taking Coach Brady Hoke's advice for such situations: "Enjoy the moment. Settle down. Enjoy life. Think of pretty girls on the beach." His fantasies couldn't have been better than his boot, which went straight through the goal posts. In stark contrast to his kicking miseries the season before, this was Gibbons' third field goal in three attempts - obviously a major factor in the Wolverines prevailing 23-20. It was a night of stories about kickers during a postseason of the kicking game failing to lift teams. Georgia lost to Michigan State in the Outback Bowl when a Bulldog place-kicker missed in triple overtime, and Wisconsin lost the Rose Bowl trying in vain to spike the ball for a field-goal attempt against Oregon. Across the Mercedes-Benz Superdome sidelines, Gibbons' counterpart, Justin Myer, was in agony. Without him, Virginia Tech wouldn't have been close on the scoreboard. And amazingly, he was an expected contributor. The senior, who had never kicked a field goal as a collegian, going 0-for-2 in his limited role, was pressed into emergency service for the Sugar Bowl. The Hokies' first-string place-kicker was suspended after a run-in with the law shortly after the team's selection to the game. Then the backup was sent home after breaking curfew once the Hokies got to New Orleans. Myer simply stepped up and connected on his first four college field goals from 37, 48, 39 and 25 yards away. The story of this night, though, faded on his fifth attempt. In overtime, with a chance to put Tech ahead, Myer hooked his kick, giving Gibbons his chance at the game-winner. For a game that stirred such an uproar when the pairing was made, Michigan-Virginia Tech was an interesting matchup. The Hokies played with a chip on their collective shoulder, determined to show they belonged in a major bowl. Virginia Tech had almost double the Wolverines' offensive output, 377 yards to 184, and 22 first downs to Michigan's 12. But the game will probably be remembered as much for Tech's misfortune, miscues and misjudgments, all of which sealed its fate in losing a close game against an opponent it dominated. The defeat was typified by the series of overtime events that led to Myers' miss and Gibbons' game-winner. On third down of the Hokies' overtime possession, senior flanker Danny Coale appeared to make a diving catch in the end zone. Replay overturned the play, indicating Coale did not have possession when he landed. There were other turns that did in the Hokies. After taking a 6-0 lead on a couple of Myer field goals, the Hokies appeared on their way to adding to their lead. However, they failed to execute what could have been a touchdown play changing the game's momentum significantly. On fourth-and-1 from the Wolverines' 4, Tech tried a sneak by Logan Thomas. In 24 previous such situations this season, a run by Thomas succeeded 23 times. This time he didn't. The Hokies' line failed to get a push and Thomas was stopped six inches short. That still left the Wolverines 96 yards from the opposite goal line. But they covered it with help from the Hokies. A roughing the kicker penalty kept the drive alive. Denard Robinson, from the Hokies' 45, lobbed a pass toward Hemingway near the 20. Tech defender Eddie Whitley went for the ball instead of the man and missed and hit a teammate. All Hemingway had to do was catch it and scoot untouched into the end zone. Suddenly, after Gibbons' PAT, Virginia Tech was behind 7-6 with 49 seconds left in the half. What's that saying about whatever can go wrong will go wrong? That's exactly what happened to Virginia Tech. Hokie Tony Gregory fumbled when hit on the kickoff, and Delonte Hollowell recovered for Michigan on the 26. Three plays later, after a dropped pass in the end zone by Roy Roundtree, the Wolverines lined up for a 30-yard field goal. Instead, holder Drew Dileo, from Baton Rouge, threw for Hemingway near the 10. Tech's Kyle Fuller deflected the ball, but it went into the arms of snapper Jareth Glanda for a first down at the 8 with eight seconds to play. A swing pass from Robinson to Vincent Smith was stopped at the 1 with two seconds to play, but Gibbons returned to the field, knocking home the "gimme" field goal to make the score 10-6 at the break. Early in the third quarter, Elliot Mealer snared an interception and returned it to the Tech 36 for the Wolverines. A crucial play, as it turned out. Robinson hit Hemingway for an 18-yard touchdown to put the Wolverines in what seemed like complete control, 17-6. That second touchdown catch also lined Hemingway up for game MVP honors, despite those being his only grabs of the evening. Despite the hard luck and the deficit, the Hokies rallied to make a game - an interesting game - of it. Virginia Tech rallied to tie it at 17 with a touchdown, two-point conversion and another Myer field goal. But then, they made a fatal miscalculation. On fourth-and-1 from the Michigan 48, Beamer elected to use Coale on a fake punt. He didn't have a chance and was brought down by Jake Ryan for a 7-yard loss. From there, the Wolverines moved to the 22 where Gibbons' field goal made the score 20-17 with 4:08 remaining. That was just enough time for the plucky Hokies to win it, going to the Michigan 8 - where Tech jumped. A Logan Thomas to Jarrett Boykin pass only got the ball back to the 8, forcing the field goal with two seconds to go - and the overtime. After Myer's miss, it was up to Gibbons to make his third try of the night. In the lowest offensive output for a winning team since Georgia's 127 total yards against Notre Dame in the 1981 Sugar Bowl, Robinson was 9-of-21 for 117 yards and two touchdowns. While the Hokies contained the star Quarterback, they just couldn't contain Gibbons high kicks, the main difference for just the fifth Michigan team to win as many as 11 games. Meanwhile Myers sat red-eyed in the Tech locker room, feeling he cost his team a victory even though he was the only Hokie to consistently dent the scoreboard.

2012 Orange Bowl

The 2012 Discover Orange Bowl was played on Wednesday, January 4, 2012, at Sun Life Stadium in Miami Gardens, Florida. West Virginia tied or broke eight separate team and individual bowl game records, while the combined 69 points West Virginia and Clemson scored in the first half set another new record.

Teams - This was Clemson's fourth appearance in the Orange Bowl, while it marked the first time WVU had been invited. Both teams averaged at least 33 points and over 440 yards per game.

2012 Orange Bowl	Line	1	-	2	-	3	-	4	-	Final
#22 West Virginia	(61.0)	14	-	35	-	14	-	7	-	70
#13 Clemson	(-3.0)	17	-	3	-	6	-	7	-	33

Scoring Summary
Clemson - Ellington 68 yard run (Catanzaro kick)
West Virginia - Alston 4 yard run (Bitancurt kick)
Clemson - Watkins 27 yard pass from Boyd (Catanzaro kick)
West Virginia - Austin 8 yard pass from Smith (Bitancurt kick)
Clemson - Catanzaro 42 yard field goal
West Virginia - Austin 27 yard pass from Smith (Bitancurt kick)
West Virginia - Cook 99 yard fumble recovery (Bitancurt kick)
Clemson - Catanzaro 43 yard field goal
West Virginia - Smith 7 yard run (Bitancurt kick)
West Virginia -: Austin 3 yard pass from Smith (Bitancurt kick)
West Virginia - Alston 1 yard run (Bitancurt kick)
West Virginia - Bailey 6 yard pass from Smith (Bitancurt kick)
West Virginia - Austin 37 yard pass from Smith (Bitancurt kick)
Clemson - Hopkins 28 yard pass from Boyd (Pass failed)
West Virginia - Milhouse 7 yard pass from Smith (Bitancurt kick)
Clemson - McDowell 4 yard run (Catanzaro kick)

Orange Bowl Game Summary - WVU Wins Record-Setting Orange Bowl—The West Virginia Mountaineers rode a record-breaking offensive performance by Quarterback Geno Smith, who grew up in the shadow of Sun Life Stadium, to defeat the Clemson Tigers 70-33 in the 2012 Discover Orange Bowl. The Mountaineers' 70 points set an all-time bowl record while Smith's six touchdown passes and Tavon Austin's four touchdown receptions both set Orange Bowl records and tied all-time bowl records. Smith, a veteran of the Orange Bowl Youth Football Alliance, threw for 407 yards and broke Tom Brady's Orange Bowl record for most passing yards in a game. In addition to his six passing touchdowns, Smith added a rushing touchdown. Despite the offensive fireworks, the game turned on a defensive play when with Clemson only a yard away from a game-leading touchdown, Darwin Cook recovered a fumble and took it 99 yards for a touchdown to extend West Virginia's second quarter lead to 28-17. West Virginia closed the second quarter on a 21-0 run over the final two-plus minutes, scoring three of its five second quarter touchdowns in the final minutes of the first half. The ACC Champion Tigers were led by Quarterback Tajh Boyd who threw for 250 yards and two touchdowns. Running back Andre Ellington rushed for a game-high 116 yards and one touchdown.

Records - Team touchdowns: West Virginia's ten touchdowns tied the record. **Combined points in a half:** The 69 points between West Virginia and Clemson at halftime set a record. **Total points:** West Virginia's 70 points broke the record set 1 week earlier by Baylor in the 2011 Alamo Bowl. **Points in a quarter:** West Virginia's 35 points in the second quarter set a record. **Points in a half:** West Virginia's 49 points in the first half set a record. The previous record was 45, held by Colorado at the 1999 Insight.com Bowl and Oklahoma State at the 1988 Holiday Bowl. **Individual passing touchdowns:** Geno Smith's six touchdowns tied Chuck Long's record in the 1984 Freedom Bowl. **Individual total touchdowns:** Smith also rushed for a touchdown, giving him seven overall, which tied another record. **Individual total points:** Smith's seven touchdowns scored 42 points, also tying a record. **Individual receiving touchdowns:** Tavon Austin's four touchdown receptions, becoming the fourth player to do so in a bowl game.

2012 Cotton Bowl Classic

The 2012 AT&T Cotton Bowl Classic, the 76th edition of the game, was held on January 6, 2012 at Cowboys Stadium in Arlington, Texas. The game, which was telecast on FOX, featured the Kansas State Wildcats from the Big XII Conference versus the Arkansas Razorbacks from the SEC Conference. Arkansas won the game 29–16, which was their first win over Kansas State since 1967. This was only the second time in the BCS era that a non-BCS bowl had two teams with higher BCS rankings playing than teams in a BCS bowl (the first being the 2008 Poinsettia Bowl). The 2012 Sugar Bowl, and 2012 Orange Bowl had teams with lower BCS rankings squaring off. As of the 2013 season, this is the most recent bowl game involving an SEC team that was not played within the conference footprint, as Texas A&M did not join the SEC until 2012.

2012 Cotton Bowl Classic	Line	1	-	2	-	3	-	4	-	Final
#11 Kansas State	(63.0)	0	-	9	-	7	-	0	-	16
#7 Arkansas	(-8.0)	3	-	16	-	7	-	3	-	29

Scoring Summary
Arkansas – Hocker 26 yard field goal
Arkansas – Adams 51 yard punt return (Hocker kick)
Arkansas – Hocker 22-yard field goal
Arkansas – Wright 45 yard pass from Wilson (Kick blocked)
Kansas State – Malone 2-point defensive conversion
Kansas State – McDonald 4 yard pass from Klein (Cantele kick)
Kansas State – Klein 6 yard run (Cantele kick)
Arkansas – Hamilton 9 yard pass from Wilson (Hocker kick)
Arkansas – Hocker 30-yard field goal

Cotton Bowl Classic Game Summary - It wasn't pretty, but a potent offense and tenacious defensive play gave Arkansas a 29-16 victory over Kansas State in the 76th AT&T Cotton Bowl Classic. Despite the lack of offensive fireworks early on, All-SEC Quarterback Tyler Wilson was efficient in the pocket, passing for 216 yards and two touchdowns. The second was a 9-yarder to Cobi Hamilton with four minutes in the third quarter after Kansas State (10-3) scored 16 straight points. However, it was the defense – led by senior defensive end Jake Bequette- that ultimately propelled the Razorbacks (11-2) to a school record tying 11th victory. The unit harassed Kansas State Quarterback Collin Klein all night and sacked the Big-12 All Purpose Player of the Year six times. Joe Adams gave Arkansas a commanding 10-0 lead early in the second quarter with his fourth punt return for a touchdown this season. The Razorbacks scored a non-offensive touchdown in six out of their last seven games this year. The Cotton Bowl was the only non-BCS game with both teams in the top 15 of the Bowl Championship Series standings. It was also the only bowl featuring the SEC vs. the Big 12, but it was apparent which conference flexed their muscles. Kansas State failed to match its school record 11th win and has now lost its last four bowl games. After a 45-yard touchdown strike from Wilson to Jarius Wright that put Arkansas up 19-0, Raphael Guidry blocked the extra point and Nigel Malone returned it 98 yards for two points. It was the first blocked extra point in Cotton Bowl history. Klein continued the momentum with a 3-yard touchdown pass to tight end Andre McDonald just before halftime. But the offensive sputtered in the second half, and the Wildcats failed to score in the fourth quarter. Klein only mustered 41 yards on the ground but scored on a 6-yard touchdown run that got the Wildcats to 19-16.

That tied the single-season FBS record for most rushing touchdowns by a Quarterback. Jerico Nelson helped Arkansas cap off a dominant defensive performance by picking off Klein in the game's final minute. The Razorbacks are now 4-0 in Cowboys Stadium. Arkansas also improved their overall Cotton Bowl record to 4-7-1 after losing in its last two appearances.

2012 BBVA Compass Bowl

The 2012 BBVA Compass Bowl, the sixth edition of the game, was held on January 7, 2012, at Legion Field in Birmingham, Alabama. The game, which was telecast on ESPN. This was Pittsburgh's second consecutive appearance in the game, and just as in the previous contest the Panthers were led by an interim head coach, Keith Patterson, after Todd Graham resigned on December 13, 2011. Pittsburgh and SMU met for the first time in 29 years. The SEC conference did not have enough bowl-eligible teams this season and the SMU football team was selected by the organizers to play in the bowl. Pittsburgh and SMU had met five times previously, the last time at the 1983 Cotton Bowl on New Year's Day, when the Mustangs won 7–3.

2012 BBVA Compass Bowl	Line	1	-	2	-	3	-	4	-	Final
SMU	(47.5)	21	-	0	-	7	-	0	-	28
Pittsburgh	(-3.5)	0	-	3	-	3	-	0	-	6

Scoring Summary
SMU - Johnson 50 yard pass from McDermott (Hover kick)
SMU - McDermott 1 yard run (Hover kick)
SMU - Wimbley 2 yard run (Hover kick)
Pittsburgh - Harper 32 yard Field goal
SMU - Wimbley 1 yard run (Hover kick)
Pittsburgh - Harper 34 yard Field goal

Associated Press BBVA Compass Bowl Game Summary - SMU has not lost this season when it scores first or puts up at least 21 points. The Mustangs were quick to check off both benchmarks to give Coach June Jones his 100th collegiate win. SMU put up three first-quarter touchdowns, including scoring runs and passes by J.J. McDermott, to beat Pittsburgh 28-6 Saturday in the BBVA Compass Bowl. Rishaad Wimbley ran for two scores for SMU (8-5), which tied a school record by playing in its third straight bowl under Jones. Before Jones' arrival in in 2008, SMU had played in the postseason since beating Notre Dame in the 1984 Aloha Bowl. McDermott completed 16 of 26 passes for 239 yards and a touchdown, to Darius Johnson early in the first. Pittsburgh (6-7) was held without a first down and fell behind 21-0 in the first quarter. Kevin Harper kicked field goals of 32 and 34 yards. The Panthers were coached by defensive coordinator Keith Patterson, who took over after Todd Graham left to coach at Arizona State. It was Patterson last game before he starts his new job as the defensive coordinator at Arkansas State. Pittsburgh's newly hired coach, former Wisconsin offensive coordinator Paul Chryst, flew into Birmingham on Saturday and watched the game from the press box level. Chryst visited with Pitt alumni and fans before the game. He said he wanted to maintain a respectful distance from the team until the game ended, signaling the start of his era. McDermott beat Pitt's blitz when lobbed a 50-yard touchdown pass to Johnson for the Mustangs' first touchdown. Johnson had seven catches for 120 yards and was named the game's MVP. The 50-yard catch was the longest in the six-year history of the bowl. After McDermott's 1-yard run capped an eight-play drive to push the lead to 14-0, Ja'Gared Davis hit Pitt Quarterback Tino Sunseri, forcing a fumble that was recovered by Taylor Reed at the Panthers' 27. McDermott's 19-yard pass to Cole Beasley set up Wimbley's 2-yard touchdown run. Wimbley added a 1-yard touchdown run in the third quarter. Pitt was making its second straight appearance in the bowl after beating Kentucky in last year's game. A series of key plays went against Pitt in the second quarter. Following the field goal, Pitt recovered an onside kick, but the officials said there was an inadvertent whistle before the ball was recovered. Pitt fans booed as the officials said another kickoff was necessary. With SMU still leading 21-3 later in the quarter, Pitt drove from its 16 to a first and goal at the Mustangs' 10. On third down from the 5, Sunseri's pass bounced off tailback Isaac Bennett. The deflection was caught by SMU linebacker Stephon Sanders for an interception. The half ended with Pitt again coming away with no points at the end of a long drive. Harper's 47-yard field goal attempt hit the left upright to end a 14-play drive. Jones said SMU running back Jared Williams suffered a probable broken left leg in the fourth quarter. Williams' left leg was placed in a brace before he was placed on a stretcher. Williams led the Mustangs with 11 carries for 40 yards before the injury. Sunseri was 19 of 28 passing for 183 yards with an interception. Attendance was 29,726.

2012 GoDaddy.com Bowl

The 2012 GoDaddy.com Bowl was the thirteenth of the annual games now known as theGoDaddy.com Bowl, it took place on January 8, 2012, at Ladd Peebles Stadium in Mobile, Alabama. The Northern Illinois Huskies from the Mid-American Conference (MAC) defeated the Arkansas State Red Wolves from the Sun Belt Conference, 38–20. The first quarter saw the Red Wolves build up a 13–0 lead, but then the Huskies scored 31 unanswered points to put the game away in the second half.

2012 GoDaddy.com Bowl	Line	1	-	2	-	3	-	4	-	Final
Arkansas State	(-1.5)	13	-	0	-	0	-	7	-	20
Northern Illinois	(65.0)	7	-	14	-	7	-	10	-	38

Scoring Summary
Arkansas State - Davis 32 yard Field goal
Arkansas State - Davis 36 yard Field goal
Arkansas State - Aplin 2 yard run (Davis kick)
Northern Illinois - Ashford 9 yard pass from Harnish (Sims kick)
Northern Illinois - Lynch 3 yard run (Sims kick)
Northern Illinois - Womble 1 yard run (Sims kick)
Northern Illinois - Moore 43 yard pass from Harnish (Sims kick)
Northern Illinois - Sims 22 yard Field goal
Arkansas State - Stockemer 16 yard pass from Aplin (Davis kick)
Northern Illinois - Durante 36 yard interception return (Sims kick)

Chicago Tribune GoDaddy.com Bowl Game Summary - The Mid-American Conference acquitted itself quite well in the 2011 postseason, winning four of five, including Sunday night's 38-20 Northern Illinois victory over Arkansas State in the GoDaddy.com Bowl. The Huskies won their ninth straight game under first-year head coach Dave Doeren, finishing the season with an 11-3 record and their first MAC championship in 28 years. Arkansas State (10-3), winners of the Sun Belt Conference, had its nine-game winning streak snapped. Temple beat Wyoming in the New Mexico Bowl; Ohio topped Utah State in the Famous Idaho Potato Bowl; and Toledo edged Air Force in the Military Bowl. The only MAC loss was in the Little Caesars Pizza Bowl, where Purdue toppled Western Michigan. Chandler Harnish completed 18 of 36 passes for 270 yards, one touchdown and one interception for NIU. Martel Moore caught eight passes for 223 yards and one TD, and Perez Ashford had seven catches for 74 yards and one TD. Harnish was named the game's Most Valuable Player, while Moore was the Offensive player of the game and Dechane Durante was named Defensive Player of the game. Moore's receiving was the third-most in a game in school history. After falling behind 13-0, NIU drove to the Red Wolves' 15-yard line and lined up for an apparent field-goal attempt. But the Huskies faked the attempt as holder Ryan Neir flipped the ball to fullback Pat McAvoy, who gained 4 yards for the first down NIU scored a touchdown with 1 minute left in the first quarter on a 9–yard pass from Harnish to Ashford. Harnish aggravated a left ankle injury with 12:10 left in the second quarter. He was hit after delivering a pass to Ashford, who ran 33 yards after the catch. Jordan Lynch took over for Harnish, who had to be helped off the field. Mathew Sims missed a 33-yard field goal at the end of the drive with 10:05 left in the half. Lynch scored on a 3-yard run with 4:49 left in the half. Sims' extra point gave NIU a 14-13 advantage. Lynch was masterful on the seven-play, 78-yard drive, completing a 41-yard pass to Moore and a 16-yarder to Ashford. With 3:02 left in the half, Harnish returned to the lineup. The Huskies recovered an Arkansas State fumble following a Neir punt. Dominique Ware recovered the fumble by Rod Hall. NIU was forced to punt again, but a roughing-the-kicker penalty gave NIU the ball at the Red Wolves' 25. The Huskies drove to the 1, and on fourth down, 247-pound running back Jamal Womble bulldozed his way into the end zone on the final play of the first half to make it 21-13 NIU. Arkansas State and NIU exchanged interceptions on their first possessions of the third quarter. Harnish took advantage with a 43-yard TD pass to Moore on a play-action fake. With 13:30 left in the third, NIU led 28-13. Following a 22-yard field goal by Sims, Ryan Aplin (30 of 57 for 351 yards) passed to Taylor Stockemer for a 17-yard TD with 11:12 left to make it 31-20. NIU safety Durante had a 36-yard pick-six with 8:19 left to give the Huskies a 38-20 lead.

2012 BCS Championship Game

The 2012 Allstate BCS National Championship Game was between the Alabama Crimson Tide and the LSU Tigers and determined the national champion of the 2011 NCAA Division I FBS football season on Monday, January 9, 2012, at the Mercedes-Benz Superdome in New Orleans, Louisiana. Alabama beat LSU 21–0 to win their 14th national championship, marking the first shutout in a national championship game since the 1992 Orange Bowl and the first ever shutout in a BCS bowl game. The game had the third-lowest TV rating, 14.01, in the 14-year history of the BCS National Championship game. It was LSU's first loss in a bowl played in New Orleans (which has a proximity to the LSU campus in Baton Rouge) since the 1987 Sugar Bowl.

Teams - LSU was selected to participate in the BCS National Championship Game after a 13–0 regular season that culminated with a 42–10 win over the University of Georgia in the 2011 SEC Championship Game. Alabama was picked as the other half of the match-up following an 11–1 campaign, with their only loss coming against LSU in overtime during the regular season. Over the following weeks, a series of upsets resulted in the Crimson Tide receiving a No. 2 ranking in the final BCS Rankings to qualify for the championship game. The selection of Alabama was controversial, and decried by writers such as Rick Reilly, and by fans who claimed other opponents, most prominently the Oklahoma State Cowboys (who finished second in most of the computer rankings), were more deserving of a spot in the game. The controversy lent support to the ever-increasing call for a college football playoff and clear SEC bias, specifically about Alabama. This game was the first time in the 14-year history of the BCS that the National Championship Game featured two teams from the same conference, let alone the same division (like what happened in the 2011 NCAA Division I Baseball Tournament six months prior, featuring two teams from the SEC, although that match-up came about through a playoff). This was also the first time that the BCS National Championship Game was a rematch from a regular season game, although the 1996 season's Bowl Alliance National Championship game was also a rematch, when Florida defeated Florida State 52–20 for the national title in the 1997 Sugar Bowl. As a result of the matchup, the SEC's streak of producing the BCS champion was assured of extending to six straight seasons.

2012 BCS Championship	Line	1	-	2	-	3	-	4	-	Final
#2 Alabama	(-1.5)	3	-	6	-	6	-	6	-	21
#1 LSU	(40.0)	0	-	0	-	0	-	0	-	0

Scoring Summary
Alabama – Shelley 23 yard Field goal
Alabama – Shelley 34 yard Field goal
Alabama – Shelley 41 yard Field goal
Alabama – Shelley 35 yard Field goal
Alabama – Shelley 44 yard Field goal
Alabama – Richardson 34 yard run (Kick failed)

Alabama Media Guide BCS Championship Game Summary - A staunch defensive effort, combined with a record-setting night from kicker Jeremy Shelley, propelled the University of Alabama football team to its 14th national championship with a 21-0 victory over LSU in the 2012 BCS National Championship Game at the Mercedes-Benz Superdome The Crimson Tide's defense held LSU to just 92 total yards and five first downs as Defensive Player of the Game Courtney Upshaw and Jerrell Harris each had seven tackles. As a unit, the defense had 11 tackles for loss, four sacks and an interception. Fifteen of UA's 21 points came from the leg of kicker Jeremy Shelley, who converted on a bowl-record five field goals from 23, 34, 41, 35 and a career-long 44 yards. The defense provided the offense with excellent field position all evening and Quarterback AJ McCarron did a masterful job under center completing 23-of-34 passes for 234 yards to earn Offensive Player of the Game honors. Thanks to Shelley, the Tide carried a 15-0 lead into the final quarter when LSU mounted its first legitimate charge after being held to just 55 yards in the previous three quarters. Upon crossing midfield for the first time all game, the drive stalled and left the Tigers facing 4th and 18 to gain on the UA 40. The Tide defense came through again as Dont'a Hightower sacked LSU's Jordan Jefferson and knocked the ball loose at the 50-yard line. Nick Gentry fell on the fumble to end the drive and set the UA offense up at midfield with 6:15 left in the contest. Four plays later, Trent Richardson raced 34 yards for the first touchdown of the game and the Heisman Trophy semifinalist finished with 96 yards on 20 carries and 107 all-purpose yards. Alabama put up the first points of the game when Shelley capped off a five-play, 20-yard drive with a 23-yard field goal with five minutes left in the first quarter. Shelley would come up big for the Tide on two more occasions in the first half, connecting from 34 and 41 yards to give Alabama a 9-0 lead at the break. Alabama held LSU to one first down throughout the first half, while collecting 13 of its own. The Tide also collected 156 total yards compared to the Tigers' 26 total yards in the first 30 minutes.

2012 New Mexico Bowl

The 2012 Gildan New Mexico Bowl was held on December 15, 2012, at University Stadium in Albuquerque, New Mexico. The seventh edition of the New Mexico Bowl was televised on ESPN. It featured the Nevada Wolf Pack, who represented the Mountain West Conference in their first year as a member, against the Arizona Wildcats, who represented the Pac-12 Conference. The Wolf Pack accepted their invitation with a 7–4 record in their first eleven games of the season, while the Wildcats accepted their invitation after finishing the regular season at 7–5. The bowl was the first of 35 played in the 2012–13 bowl game season. Coming into the game, both teams had sound offenses and were led by their respective running backs, sophomore Ka'Deem Carey for Arizona and senior Stefphon Jefferson for Nevada, who ranked number one and number two respectively in total rushing yards during the regular season. Arizona and Nevada ranked third and fourth respectively in total offense. Both teams' defenses were ranked towards the bottom of college football. Consequently, the game was widely expected to be high scoring. Despite losing the game, Nevada possessed the ball nearly twice as long and gained twice as many rushing yards as Arizona. Arizona Quarterback Matt Scott was named the game's offensive most valuable player (MVP), and teammate Marquis Flowers, a linebacker, was named the game's defensive MVP.

2012 New Mexico Bowl	Line	1	-	2	-	3	-	4	-	Final
Nevada	(79.0)	21	-	10	-	14	-	3	-	48
Arizona	(-8.5)	7	-	21	-	0	-	21	-	49

Scoring Summary
Nevada - Jefferson 16 yard run (Hardison kick)
Nevada - Sudfield 17 yard pass from Fajardo (Hardison kick)
Nevada - Sudfield 28 yard pass from Fajardo (Hardison kick)
Arizona - Carey 21 yard run (Bonano kick)
Arizona - Scott 1 yard run (Bonano kick)
Arizona - Carey 1 yard run (Bonano kick)
Nevada - Jefferson 14 yard run (Hardison kick)
Arizona - Carey 9 yard run (Bonano kick)
Nevada - Hardison 27 yard Field goal
Nevada - Turner 33 yard pass from Fajardo (Hardison kick)
Nevada - Fajardo 1 yard run (Hardison kick)
Arizona - Hill 64 yard pass from Scott (Bonano kick)
Nevada - Hardison 25 yard Field goal
Arizona - Hill 2 yard pass from Scott (Bonano kick)
Arizona - Slavin 2 yard pass from Scott (Bonano kick)

Associated Press New Mexico Bowl Game Summary - Matt Scott watched helplessly as Nevada kicked a field goal to pad its lead. The Arizona Quarterback had already thrown two interceptions, and now needed two quick scores and some luck -- in a hurry, too -- to somehow win the Gildan New Mexico Bowl. Scott even admitted he didn't have "positive" thoughts before returning to the field. But in the final 46 seconds, Scott threw two short touchdown passes and college football's postseason started with a wild one as Arizona rallied past Nevada 49-48 Saturday. Overcoming a slow start and three big turnovers, Arizona (8-5) recovered an onside kick in the last minute, setting up Scott's 2-yard toss to Tyler Slavin with 19 seconds left for the winning score. Arizona trailed 21-0 in the first quarter and was down 45-28 entering the final period. Scott threw for 382 yards and marched his team back into the game despite those two earlier interceptions. The nation's rushing leader, Ka'Deem Carey, gained 172 yards for the Wildcats but fell short of becoming only the 16th running back in NCAA history to reach 2,000 yards in a season. Arizona receiver Austin Hill caught eight passes for 175 yards and two touchdowns. The teams combined for 1,237 total yards. Cody Fajardo threw for three touchdowns and ran for another score to lead the Wolf Pack (7-6). He had 256 yards passing and 140 yards rushing and controlled most of the game, completing 22-of-32 throws. Stefphon Jefferson, the nation's second-leading rusher, ran for 180 yards for Nevada and seemed unstoppable as the Wolf Pack took a big lead and held on to it for most of the game. But after forcing Nevada to kick a field goal with 1:48 left that made it 48-35, Scott drove the Wildcats down 75 yards in about a minute. Arizona then recovered an onside kick and Scott marched his team into the end zone after three plays and 51 yards. Nevada coach Chris Ault said the team pass defense just didn't make a play when it was needed. Ault said a late injury to Fajardo also hurt Nevada's running game in the last six or so minutes of the game. Rodriguez, who took a year off from coaching after a disappointing stint at Michigan, is now 3-5 in bowl game appearances. He called his New Mexico Bowl win among his best career wins as a coach.

2012 Famous Idaho Potato Bowl

The 2012 Famous Idaho Potato Bowl was held on December 15, 2012 at Bronco Stadium in Boise, Idaho in the United States. The sixteenth edition of the Famous Idaho Potato Bowl was televised on ESPN. The Rockets accepted their invitation after earning a 9–2 record in the regular season, while the Aggies accepted theirs after earning a 10–2 record. Utah State won the game 41–15.

2012 Famous Idaho Potato Bowl	Line	1	-	2	-	3	-	4	-	Final
Toledo	(58.5)	3	-	3	-	0	-	9	-	15
Utah State	(-10.5)	7	-	3	-	3	-	28	-	41

Scoring Summary
Toledo - Detmer 37 yard Field goal
Utah State - Keeton 65 yard run (Diaz kick)
Toledo - Detmer 37 yard Field goal
Utah State - Diaz 27 yard Field goal
Utah State - Diaz 44 yard Field goal
Toledo - Detmer 29 yard Field goal
Utah State - Williams 63 yard run (Diaz kick)
Utah State - Williams 5 yard run (Diaz kick)
Utah State - Williams 25 yard run (Diaz kick)
Toledo - Reedy 87 yard kickoff return (Kick failed)
Utah State - Hill 24 yard run (Diaz kick)

Associated Press Famous Idaho Potato Bowl Game Summary - Utah State running back Kerwynn Williams was having a quiet day when things took a turn for the worse in the fourth quarter when he fumbled deep in his own territory. As it has all season, the Aggies' defense did its job, holding Toledo to a field goal that cut the lead to 13-9 with 7:28 to go. Then Williams atoned for his mistake -- in a big way. On the next possession, Williams broke through the defense and raced 63 yards for a touchdown. On the next two possessions, the senior was unstoppable, ripping off a 56-yard run and scoring TDs on runs of 5 and 25 yards, all within a span of less than 4 minutes to lift No. 18 Utah State to a 41-15 victory over Toledo in the Famous Idaho Potato Bowl on Saturday. Williams' fourth-quarter spree fueled a 28-point Aggies scoring burst that turned a close game into a blowout. Williams finished with a career-best 235 yards rushing on 18 carries, with 182 of those yards coming on six carries in the fourth quarter and was voted MVP. Williams' heroics also capped the most successful season in the history of Utah State football. The Aggies finished 11-2, won the Western Athletic Conference title outright and won a bowl game for the first time since 1993. Utah State also will likely finish ranked for the first time since 1961. The Aggies, bolstered all year by one of the best defenses in FBS, rolled up 582 yards total on offense. Quarterback Chuckie Keeton was 21-of-31 passing for 229 yards and 92 yards rushing, including a 62-yard dash that put Utah State up 7-3 in the first quarter. The defense also turned in another impressive performance. Toledo (9-4) was able to move the ball at times and made five trips inside the red zone. But penalties, miscues and an inability to execute on critical plays forced the Rockets to settle for three Jeremiah Detmer field goals. Detmer hit a pair from 37 yards out and another from 29, closing his season by making 17 straight. Toledo's only touchdown came when Bernard Reedy returned a fourth-quarter kickoff 87 yards for a touchdown. Reedy was the only big producer on a Toledo offense held to 315 total yards. Reedy had 51 yards rushing and caught six passes for 62 yards. Toledo Quarterback Austin Dantin, who started in place of the injured Terrance Owens, was 12 of 21 passing for 132 yards. Dantin threw an interception in the third quarter to end a promising scoring drive and was replaced by Owens in the fourth quarter. Owens moved the Rockets on his first possession, but another red-zone opportunity was squelched when the Aggies snuffed Owens for no gain on a fourth-and-1 play from the 9. Toledo also was forced to adjust early without two of its best players. Linebacker Dan Molls, the nation's leading tackler, had a concussion on the opening kickoff and didn't return. Minutes later, running back David Fluellen, the nation's eighth-leading rusher, went down with an ankle injury. He finished with 38 yards on seven carries. Campbell refused to use the injuries to Moll and Fluellen as an excuse and pointed out the game was close until the final 7½ minutes.

2012 Poinsettia Bowl

The 2012 San Diego County Credit Union Poinsettia Bowl was held on December 20, 2012 at Qualcomm Stadium in San Diego, California. The eighth edition of the Poinsettia Bowl was televised on ESPN. It featured the Mountain West Conference co-champion San Diego State Aztecs (whose regular home stadium is Qualcomm) against the BYU Cougars (which had been in the MW until 2011 before playing as an FBS independent.

2012 Poinsettia Bowl	Line	1	-	2	-	3	-	4	-	Final
BYU	(-3.0)	0	-	3	-	0	-	20	-	23
San Diego State	(46.0)	3	-	3	-	0	-	0	-	6

Scoring Summary
San Diego State - Marden 27 yard Field goal
San Diego State - Marden 23 yard Field goal
BYU - Sorensen 23 yard Field goal
BYU - Van Noy fumble recovery in end zone (Sorensen kick)
BYU - Williams 14 yard run (Kick failed)
BYU - Van Noy 17 yard interception return (Sorensen kick)

Associated Press Poinsettia Bowl Game Summary - For the longest time, it seemed as if the San Diego County Credit Union Poinsettia Bowl would be touchdown-free. A ponderous field position struggle resulted in only three field goals entering the fourth quarter. Then linebacker Kyle Van Noy stepped up and scored two touchdowns on turnovers, leading Brigham Young to a 23-6 victory over San Diego State on Thursday night. With San Diego State pinned on its 3-yard line thanks to terrific punt coverage by BYU, Adam Dingwell dropped back to pass in the end zone. Van Noy broke free from the outside and knocked the ball out of Dingwell's hand and jumped on it for the game's first TD. The play was upheld after video review. Dingwell fumbled the snap on SDSU's next play from scrimmage and it was recovered by Jordan Johnson at the 14. Jamaal Williams scored on a run up the middle on the next play, BYU's second TD in 17 seconds. With 6:09 left, Van Noy intercepted Dingwell's pass and weaved 17 yards through traffic and into the end zone. Van Noy was selected the game's defensive MVP. The Cougars (8-5) won for the sixth straight time against SDSU, a former rival from the Western Athletic and Mountain West conferences. BYU went independent after the 2010 season, when it beat SDSU thanks to a controversial fumble. BYU was making its 12th bowl appearance in San Diego. The first 11 were in the Holiday Bowl, big brother to the Poinsettia Bowl. San Diego State (9-4), playing in the hometown bowl for the second time in three years, missed the chance for its first 10-win season since 1977 and had its seven-game winning streak snapped. Dingwell finished with five turnovers, including three interceptions. Four of his turnovers were in the fourth quarter. As big as the defensive plays were for the Cougars, their punt unit came up huge in pinning down the Aztecs four times in the second half. They downed two punts by senior Riley Stephenson at the 1, one at the 2 and another at the 3. They were among the six punts inside the 20. Stephenson "changed the game," Mendenhall said. Until Van Noy and Williams scored, the game was a field position struggle. San Diego State led 6-3 at halftime thanks to Chance Marden's field goals of 27 and 23 yards. Justin Sorensen kicked a 23-yarder for BYU. San Diego State's Eric Pinkins intercepted Riley Nelson's pass and returned it 39 yards for a touchdown in the second quarter but the score was negated by a penalty for blocking below the waist. SDSU ended up punting from the BYU 36. James Lark, who started at Quarterback for BYU, completed 23-of-42 passes for 244 yards and was intercepted twice. BYU's Cody Hoffman caught 10 passes for 114 yards and was named offensive MVP. Dingwell completed 12 of 29 for 144 yards. Adam Muema ran 26 times for 103 yards.

2012 Beef 'O' Brady's Bowl

The 2012 Beef 'O' Brady's Bowl, the fifth edition of the game, was held on December 21, 2012 at Tropicana Field in St. Petersburg, Florida. The game was televised on ESPN, featured the UCF Knights from Conference USA and Ball State Cardinals from the Mid-American Conference. It was the final game of the 2012 NCAA Division I FBS football season for both teams. The Knights advanced to the game after losing to the Tulsa Golden Hurricane in the Conference USA Championship Game.

2012 Beef 'O' Brady's Bowl	Line	1	-	2	-	3	-	4	-	Final
Ball State	(60.0)	0	-	7	-	3	-	7	-	17
Central Florida	(-7.0)	13	-	15	-	3	-	7	-	38

Scoring Summary
Central Florida - Murray 7 yard pass from Bortles (Moffitt kick)
Central Florida - Murray 2 yard run (Kick blocked)
Ball State - Snead 7 yard pass from Wenning (Schott kick)
Central Florida - Bortles 6 yard run (Moffitt kick)
Central Florida - Murray 5 yard pass from Bortles (Moffitt kick)
Ball State - Schott 45 yard Field goal
Central Florida - Worton 7 yard pass from Bortles (Moffitt kick)
Central Florida - Moffitt 25 yard Field goal
Ball State - Snead 16 yard pass from Wenning (Schott kick)

Associated Press Beef 'O' Brady's Bowl Game Summary - Central Florida will head into the new look Big East off an impressive showing in the Beef 'O' Brady's Bowl. The Knights dominated Ball State 38-17 on Friday night in their final game as a member of Conference USA, amassing 494 yards total offense while holding the high-scoring Cardinals to their lowest point total of the season. Bortles threw for 271 yards and three touchdowns. The red-shirt sophomore also rushed for a career-high 80 yards and scored on a 6-yard run that helped UCF (10-4) build a 21-point halftime lead. Bortles tossed first-half TD passes 7 and 5 yards to Latavius Murray, who also scored on a 2-yard run. J.J. Worton's 7-yard scoring reception made 35-10 late in the third quarter. Ball State (9-4) was hoping to finish with at least 10 wins for the third time in school history, however its high-powered offense sputtered while being held 18 points below its season average. Keith Wenning threw a 7-yard TD pass to Willie Snead early in the second quarter, but the Cardinals didn't get into end zone again until Snead scored on a 16-yard reception with 5 minutes remaining. Bortles completed 22 of 33 passes without an interception to become UCF's first 3,000-yard passer since 2002. His three TD passes were a career-best and tied the Beef 'O' Brady's Bowl record. Wenning, meanwhile, was 22 of 34 for 217 yards and two TDs for Ball State, which had a six-game winning streak snapped before an announced crowd of 21,759. UCF, one of several schools joining the Big East next season, rebounded from an overtime loss in the Conference USA title game to finish with double-digit victories for the third time since stepping up to the Football Bowl Subdivision. The Knights also won 10 in 2007 and 2010, when they were Conference USA champions. The Knights' loss to Tulsa in the Conference USA title game kept them close to home for the postseason. Instead of heading to the Liberty Bowl for the second time in three years, Coach George O'Leary and his players settled for a 100-mile trek west from Orlando to Tropicana Field, the home of major league baseball's Tampa Bay Rays. O'Leary also brought his team to St. Petersburg in 2009, losing to Rutgers by three touchdowns. Friday night's victory improved the 66-year-old coach's record to 4-5 in bowl games, including a 2-3 mark with UCF. Ball State's first bowl appearance since 2008 is the latest step in an impressive turnaround under Lembo, whose team suffered early losses to Clemson, Kent State and Northern Illinois before winning six straight down the stretch to put themselves into a position to fill the Big East's slot in the Beef 'O' Brady's game because the league didn't have enough bowl-eligible teams to meet its commitment. The Cardinals beat two teams from BCS conferences in the same season for the first time, defeating Indiana and South Florida in consecutive weeks. They had the MAC's second-most productive offense at 471.3 yards and 35 points per game and won four times by scoring the winning points in the final 2 minutes or overtime. But with UCF dominating time of possession, Ball State never really had an opportunity to get its high-octane show going. The Knights held the ball for nearly 13 minutes of the opening quarter, compiling a 159-15 advantage in total yardage. By halftime UCF had run 42 plays and gained 299 yards to build its lead to 28-7. Jahwan Edwards rushed for 89 yards on 14 carries for Ball State, which fell to 0-7-1 in eight bowl appearances. Snead had seven receptions for 78 yards.

2012 Maaco Bowl

The 2012 Maaco Bowl Las Vegas was held on December 22, 2012 at Sam Boyd Stadium in Whitney, Nevada in the Las Vegas Valley. The 21st edition of the Maaco Bowl Las Vegas was televised on ESPN. It featured the Mountain West Conference co-champion Boise State Broncos against the Washington Huskies from the Pac-12 Conference (Pac-12.

2012 Maaco Bowl	Line	1	-	2	-	3	-	4	-	Final
Washington	(44.0)	3	-	14	-	6	-	3	-	26
#20 Boise State	(-4.0)	9	-	9	-	7	-	3	-	28

Scoring Summary
Boise State – Frisina 34 yard Field goal
Washington – Coons 26 yard Field goal
Boise State – Boldewijin 17 yard pass from Southwick (Kick blocked)
Boise State – Frisina 30 yard Field goal
Boise State – Huff 34 yard pass from Potter (Pass failed)
Washington – Sankey 26 yard run (Coons kick)
Washington – Price 7 yard run (Coons kick)
Boise State – Huff 1 yard pass from Southwick (Frisina kick)
Washington – Sefarian-Jenkins 6 yard pass from Price ((Pass failed)
Washington – Coons 38 yard Field goal
Boise State – Frisina 27 yard Field goal

Associated Press Maaco Bowl Game Summary - The last two times Boise State played in the MAACO Bowl Las Vegas, there were other places the Broncos wanted to be. Not so on Saturday, when the smallest player on the team came up big in a 28-26 victory over Washington. After two straight blowouts in the Las Vegas Bowl, the Broncos had to work hard for a win sealed by a 27-yard field goal by 5-foot-5 Michael Frisina with 1:16 left. It left them feeling good about a game and a season when, unlike the last two years, there was hardly any talk about Boise State being in a BCS game. The win capped another strong year for the No. 20 Broncos (11-2), who had to overcome a 205-yard rushing game by Bishop Sankey against their normally stingy defense. Sankey also had 74 yards receiving, giving him 279 of Washington's 447 yards from scrimmage. But it was Frisina who came up with the biggest game of his career in his final game. He kicked three field goals, including the first game winner he could ever recall booting. Washington (7-6) had taken the lead for the first time on a 38-yard field goal by Travis Coons with 4:09 left when Boise State (No. 19 BCS, No. 20 AP) got a big kickoff return by freshman Shane Williams-Rhodes to the Washington 42. Joe Southwick guided the team to the 12 before Frisina hit the winning kick. Boise State sealed the win when Jeremy Ioane intercepted Keith Price's pass as the Huskies neared midfield. Sankey, who was third on the depth list when fall practice began, rushed 30 times and caught six passes in the biggest game of his career. He scored one touchdown and was the MVP of the game, despite being on the losing side. Frisina was only 12 for 17 on field goals coming into the game, but kicked three of them, including a 34-yarder to open the scoring that was his first field goal over 30 yards for the year. Southwick, meanwhile, had another efficient game, completing 26 of 38 passes for 264 yards and two touchdowns for a Boise State team that struggled offensively through much of the season before improving over its last three games. Southwick, a junior who took over from the departing Kellen Moore, also ran for 39 yards and had a punt that pinned Washington by its goal line in the fourth quarter. Boise State, which outscored Utah and Arizona State 82-24 in its two previous Las Vegas Bowl wins, looked headed for a third straight blowout when Holden Huff scored on a 34-yard pass with 5:25 left in the second quarter for an 18-3 lead. But Sankey scored on a 26-yard run on Washington's next possession, and Price scrambled for another score with 3 seconds left to make it 18-17 at halftime. The teams traded long drives in the third quarter, with Boise going 74 yards in 15 plays to open the second half, and Washington responding with a 75 yard, 12 play drive. The Huskies went for a 2-point conversion that would have tied it, but the pass was incomplete. Sankey kept Washington in the game almost by himself in the first half, scoring the first touchdown for the Huskies and gaining huge chunks of yardage against the normally stingy Bronco defense. Of the 238 yards Washington gained in the half, Sankey had 178 of them. He ran 16 times for 130 yards and stretched out two short passes for another 48 yards. Boise State was playing without starting defensive end Demarcus Lawrence, the team's sack leader. Lawrence was sent home Thursday for violating unspecified team rules, his second suspension of the season.

2012 New Orleans Bowl

The 2012 R+L Carriers New Orleans Bowl was held on December 22, 2012 at the Mercedes-Benz Superdome in New Orleans, Louisiana. The 12th edition of the New Orleans Bowl was televised on ESPN. It featured the East Carolina Pirates from Conference USA against the Louisiana–Lafayette Ragin' Cajuns from the Sun Belt Conference. The Ragin' Cajuns accepted their invitation after earning an 8-4 record in the regular season, while the Pirates advanced to the game through the C-USA's contingency plan after earning an 8-4 record. The 77 combined points scored by both teams set a New Orleans Bowl record.

2012 New Orleans Bowl	Line	1	-	2	-	3	-	4	-	Final
East Carolina	(70.0)	0	-	21	-	10	-	3	-	34
Louisiana-Lafayette	(-6.5)	7	-	24	-	6	-	6	-	43

Scoring Summary
Louisiana-Lafayette - Broadway 12 yard run (Baer kick)
Louisiana-Lafayette - Peoples 10 yard run (Baer kick)
East Carolina - Bullock 5 yard run (Harvey kick)
Louisiana-Lafayette - Harris 6 yard run (Baer kick)
Louisiana-Lafayette - Harris 68 yard run (Baer kick)
East Carolina - Hardy 19 yard pass from Carden (Harvey kick)
East Carolina - Webster 16 yard pass from Carden (Harvey kick)
Louisiana-Lafayette - Baer 50 yard Field goal
East Carolina - Harvey 45 yard Field goal
East Carolina - Bullock 13 yard run (Harvey kick)
Louisiana-Lafayette - Lawson 14 yard pass from Broadway (kick blocked)
East Carolina - Harvey 26 yard Field goal
Louisiana-Lafayette - Baer 25 yard Field goal
Louisiana-Lafayette - Baer 40 yard Field goal

Associated Press New Orleans Bowl Game Summary - Terrance Broadway wasn't projected as Louisiana-Lafayette's starting Quarterback heading into this season. Now he's a bowl game MVP. Broadway passed for 316 yards and ran for 108, helping Louisiana-Lafayette repeat as winners of the New Orleans Bowl with a 43-34 victory against East Carolina on Saturday. Alonzo Harris rushed for 120 yards and two touchdowns for the Ragin' Cajuns (9-4), who briefly squandered a three-touchdown lead before moving back in front for good on Broadway's 14-yard scoring pass to Javone Lawson late in the third quarter. Brett Baer added his second and third field goals in the fourth quarter to seal the win. Broadway, who took over as starter after senior Blaine Gautier's injury in late September, also ran for a 12-yard score. Shane Carden passed for 278 yards and two touchdowns for East Carolina (8-5) but was intercepted in Cajuns territory by Jemarlous Moten in the fourth quarter as ECU drove for a potential tying or go-ahead score. The Pirates' Reggie Bullock rushed for 104 yards and two touchdowns. Carden's touchdowns went to Justin Hardy for 19 yards and Danny Webster for 16 yards. Hardy finished with five catches for 59 yards. East Carolina's Andrew Bodenheimer had five catches for a team-high 65 yards but could not secure a crucial fourth-down pass in the final minutes as defensive back T.J. Worthy ripped the ball away in ECU territory. That allowed the Cajuns to run the clock down to 15 seconds before setting up Baer's final field goal from 40-yards out. Jamal Robinson had six catches for 116 yards for ULL, while Lawson finished with four catches for 71 yards. The Cajuns carried a 37-31 lead into the fourth quarter after Lawson for a 14-yard score in which the receiver juggled but secured the ball for a sprawling, rolling catch. The point-after kick failed, however, and East Carolina pulled to 37-34 on Warren Harvey's 26-yard field goal. Broadway's lone interception on a tipped pass then gave East Carolina the ball on the Cajuns 39, but Moten was able to step in front of Carden's long pass over the middle to help preserve the slim lead. With Lafayette a drive of about two hours west of New Orleans, red-clad Cajuns fans came in droves and made up the bulk of a record New Orleans Bowl crowd of 48,828, and they were celebrating early. Broadway's scoring run, his ninth rushing TD of the season, gave ULL a 7-0 lead on the Cajuns' first series of the game and Harry Peoples' 10-yard scoring run pushed the lead to 14-0. ECU didn't get a first down until early in the second quarter, when Carden converted on third-and-long with a pass to left sideline, which Jabril Solomon turned into a 45-yard gain. That set up Bullock's first touchdown from 5 yards out to make it 14-7. Harris' two scores had the Cajuns seemingly in command at 28-7, but ECU responded with two touchdowns in a span of 13 seconds off the clock to make it a one-score game again. First came Hardy's leaping, outstretched grab in the back of the end zone to cap a 10-play, 80-yard drive. Then Darryl Surgent fumbled a kickoff return, giving ECU the ball on the Cajuns 16. Carden found Webster over the middle for a score on the next play to make it 28-21. Louisiana-Lafayette was able to regain some momentum in the final 37 seconds of the first half, driving 47 yards on five plays to set up Baer's 50-yard field goal, which was the same distance and direction as his game-winner at the end of last year's New Orleans Bowl. The Pirates tied it in the third quarter on Harvey's 45-yard field goal and Bullock's 13-yard scoring run, capping a drive that included a converted fourth-and-3.

2012 Hawai'i Bowl

The 2012 Sheraton Hawaii Bowl was held on December 24, 2012 at Aloha Stadium in Honolulu, Hawaii in the United States. The eleventh edition of the Hawaii Bowl was televised on ESPN. It featured the SMU Mustangs from Conference USA against the Mountain West Conference co-champion Fresno State Bulldogs. The Mustangs accepted their invitation after earning a 6-6 record in the regular season, while the Bulldogs accepted their invitation after a 9-3 regular season record.

2012 Hawaii Bowl	Line	1	-	2	-	3	-	4	-	Final
Fresno State	(-13.0)	0	-	0	-	7	-	3	-	10
SMU	(62.5)	0	-	22	-	7	-	14	-	43

Scoring Summary
SMU – Gilbert 17 yard run (Hover kick)
SMU – Hover 30 yard Field goal
SMU – Safety
SMU – Line 8 yard run (Hover kick)
SMU – Hover 48 yard Field goal
Fresno State – Adams 6 yard pass from Carr (Breshears kick)
SMU – Johnson 21 yard pass from Gilbert (Hover kick)
Fresno State – Breshears 32 yard Field goal
SMU – Reed 69 yard interception return (Hover kick)
SMU – Greenbauer 83 yard interception return (Hover kick)

USA Today Hawaii Bowl Game Summary - Margus Hunt knew he had eight hours to fill on the flight over the Pacific Ocean, so he asked the SMU staff to put together film of Fresno State for him to study. He hit the Bulldogs like a tidal wave Monday night in the Hawaii Bowl. The 6-foot-8 defensive end raced around right tackle to blindside Derek Carr and force a fumble. Hunt smashed into running back Robbie Rouse on a delayed handoff and forced another fumble. On a three-man rush, he sacked Carr in the end zone for a safety. It was an inspiring performance by the senior from Estonia, and it set the tone for the Mustangs' 43-10 win. The Mustangs (7-6) also returned two interceptions for touchdowns, giving them eight for the season to tie the NCAA record set last year by Southern Miss. Hayden Greenbauer picked off Carr and returned it 83 yards with 1:14 left, the final blow to a miserable night for the Bulldogs (9-4). SMU had seven sacks, more than double the most Fresno State had given up in a game all year. Garrett Gilbert was effective with his arm and his legs, running for a 17-yard touchdown for the first score of the game and throwing a perfect strike to Darius Johnson for a 21-yard score to answer the Bulldogs' only touchdown. He rushed for 98 yards on 18 carries and threw for 212 yards. But this game was decided by the Mustangs' defense, with Hunt leading the way. He was voted the game's MVP. SMU coach June Jones has a knack for taking a chance on athletes from other sports, and he liked what he saw, from the 82-inch wingspan to the 4.7 speed in the 40. The Bulldogs turned in a dud. Fresno State, which had averaged just over 47 points in its last five games, was shut out in the first half for the first time in two years. Carr was too busy running for his life to get the Bulldogs into any kind of offensive rhythm. And when the Bulldogs finally scored with 10:21 left in the third quarter, Gilbert led the Mustangs on a 75-yard drive that he finished with a pinpoint pass to Johnson in the corner for a touchdown. It allowed Jones to walk out of Aloha Stadium with yet another win. He was the coach at Hawaii for eight years, leaving after its unbeaten regular season in 2007. Jones now has won 10 straight games in Aloha Stadium, dating to a December 2006 loss to Oregon State. Without hardly breaking a sweat. The 10 points matched the fewest Fresno State has scored this year, dating to its 20-10 loss to Boise State. Carr was 33-of-54 passing for 362 yards, but most of that came late in the game when the Bulldogs were trying to catch up. He was overwhelmed by the Mustangs' defensive front, particularly Hunt, who had two sacks, two forced fumbles and three tackles behind the line of scrimmage. After a dull, scoreless opening quarter, Gilbert shook off one tackle and scored on a 17-yard run. The defense took over from there. Hunt blew past right tackle Alex Fifita and blindsided Carr, dropping him flat as the ball came loose and was scooped up by Aaron Davis, who returned it 23 yards to the Fresno State 16 until he fumbled it out of bounds. SMU had to settle for a field goal. On the next series, Carr scrambled backward and couldn't escape an 18-yard sack to the 6, and then Hunt sacked him in the end zone for a safety. Hunt wasn't finished. On second-and-7 from the 33, Carr gave it to Robbie Rouse on a delayed handoff, right about the time Hunt showed up to disrupt the play and cause another fumble that Taylor Reed recovered. That drive went backward, and Chase Hover connected from 48 yards.

2012 Little Caesars Pizza Bowl

The 2012 Little Caesars Pizza Bowl, the 16th edition of the game, was held on December 26, 2012 at Ford Field in Detroit, Michigan. The game was televised on ESPN. Under normal circumstances, the Little Caesars Pizza Bowl would feature the eighth bowl-eligible team from the Big Ten Conference against the Mid-American Conference champions. However, with the Big Ten only fielding seven bowl-eligible teams and the MAC champion Northern Illinois Huskies playing in the 2013 Orange Bowl, the spots were open this year. This was the first meeting between these two teams.

2012 Little Caesars Pizza Bowl	Line	1	-	2	-	3	-	4	-	Final
Western Kentucky	(-6.0)	7	-	7	-	7	-	0	-	21
Central Michigan	(55.5)	14	-	3	-	0	-	7	-	24

Scoring Summary
Central Michigan - Flory 69 yard pass from Radcliffe (Harman kick)
Western Kentucky - Jakes 6 yard run (Schwettman kick)
Central Michigan - Flory 29 yard pass from Radcliffe (Harman kick)
Central Michigan - Harman 50 yard Field goal
Western Kentucky - Doyle 6 yard pass from Jakes (Schwettman kick)
Western Kentucky - Jones 1 yard run (Schwettman kick)
Central Michigan - Wilson 11 yard pass from Radcliffe (Harman kick)

Little Caesar's Pizza Bowl Game Summary - On this night, Dan Enos was fine with letting the other coach make the game's most important decision. Enos and his Central Michigan Chippewas held on for a 24-21 victory over Western Kentucky on Wednesday night in the Little Caesars Pizza Bowl, stopping the Hilltoppers on fourth-and-2 in the final minute when a field goal could have sent the game to overtime. Lance Guidry, coaching Western Kentucky on an interim basis with Bobby Petrino set to take over, went for the victory after his players made their feelings known on the matter. It didn't work out. On fourth down from the 19-yard line with 51 seconds left, Kawaun Jakes threw incomplete. Ryan Radcliff had thrown an 11-yard touchdown pass to Cody Wilson with 5:11 remaining to give Central Michigan the lead. Wilson, a senior had 10 catches for 101 yards on the night. Western Kentucky (7-6) fell just short in its first bowl since joining college football's top tier in 2009. Radcliff went 19 of 29 for 253 yards and three touchdowns, but Central Michigan (7-6) needed to rally late. Down 21-17, Zurlon Tipton appeared to have put the Chippewas ahead in the fourth quarter, but his fourth-down run was ruled short of the goal line after a review. Central Michigan forced the Hilltoppers to punt from their own end zone, and Avery Cunningham blocked it. Although the ball bounced around for a bit, the Chippewas finally secured it and took over with great field position inside the 30. Radcliff found Wilson in the back left corner of the end zone for a 24-21 lead. Western Kentucky's final drive ended when Jakes' pass intended for Jack Doyle fell incomplete. Petrino, the Hilltoppers' coach-in-waiting, was expected to be at Ford Field watching his new team, but a snowstorm forced him to scrap those plans. Western Kentucky started aggressively. Down 7-0, the Hilltoppers ran a flea-flicker on their first play from scrimmage, with Antonio Andrews running to his right, then tossing the ball back to Jakes, who found Rico Brown for a 70-yard gain. Two plays later, Jakes scored on a 6-yard run to tie it. Central Michigan answered with a 73-yard drive that ended with Andrew Flory's 29-yard touchdown reception, his second of the quarter. The offenses settled down a bit for the rest of the quarter. Both teams were backed up by a pair of terrific punts. Hendrix Brakefield's 74-yarder pinned

Central Michigan at its own 5, but Richie Hogan flipped the field position with a punt that sailed past Andrews and bounced back to the Western Kentucky 12. The 82-yard effort was returned only 4 yards. David Harman's 50-yard field goal put the Chippewas up 17-7, but Jakes threw a 6-yard touchdown pass to Doyle, with the tight end making a one-handed catch to pull Western Kentucky within three. The TD pass was the 51st for Jakes, breaking a tie with Justin Haddix atop the school's career list. Harman had a field goal blocked later in the half, and although the Chippewas were in range for another attempt in the final minute, Radcliff was sacked and fumbled. He was able to recover, but the last few seconds of the half ticked off. Western Kentucky took a 21-17 lead in the third on a 1-yard scoring run by Kadeem Jones, which capped an 80-yard drive that used 9:23. Andrews rushed for 119 yards, but he fell short of the 274 all-purpose yards he needed to break the single-season record of 3,250 set by Oklahoma State's Barry Sanders in 1988. Andrews, a junior, had 184 all-purpose yards to finish the season at 3,161. Central Michigan took a 7-0 lead on a 69-yard touchdown pass from Radcliff to Flory. Western Kentucky safety Jonathan Dowling whiffed on a tackle near midfield, and Flory was gone. Dowling had a chance to make up for that mistake early in the third quarter, but with his team down 17-14, he dropped an interception near midfield that he could have easily returned for a touchdown.

2012 Military Bowl

The 2012 Military Bowl presented by Northrop Grumman was held on December 27, 2012, at Robert F. Kennedy Memorial Stadium in Washington, D.C. The fifth edition of the Military Bowl was shown on ESPN. This was the first Military Bowl appearance as well as the first meeting between these two teams. It was played at RFK Stadium. On May 20, 2013, the bowl announced that future editions would be held at Navy–Marine Corps Memorial Stadium in Annapolis, Maryland.

2012 Military Bowl	Line	1	-	2	-	3	-	4	-	Final
San Jose State	(-7.0)	7	-	3	-	9	-	10	-	29
Bowling Green	(46.0)	3	-	3	-	7	-	7	-	20

Scoring Summary
San Jose State - Kyle 33 yard pass from Fales (Lopez kick)
Bowling Green - Tate 28 yard Field goal
Bowling Green - Tate 33 yard Field goal
San Jose State - Lopez 36 yard Field goal
Bowling Green - Samuel 8 yard run (Stein kick)
San Jose State - Team safety
San Jose State - Jones 18 yard pass from Fales (Lopez kick)
Bowling Green - Pettigrew 1 yard run (Stein kick)
San Jose State - Lopez 27 yard Field goal
San Jose State - Eskridge 1 yard run (Lopez kick)

San Jose Mercury News Military Bowl Game Summary - The best season in the major college football history of San Jose State concluded with a game that showcased how this team reached levels not before seen. Quarterback David Fales broke records, defensive end Travis Johnson delivered a key sack and Bené Benwikere made a game-changing play. Those were staples throughout the year, and they helped produce the No. 24 Spartans' 29-20 victory over Bowling Green in the Military Bowl on Thursday before 17,835 at RFK Stadium. San Jose State's 11 victories are its most since 1940, and the total is unmatched in the school's 63 years of playing at college football's highest level. It comes just two years removed from a 1-12 campaign. With interim coach Kent Baer leading the charge after Mike MacIntyre departed for Colorado, the Spartans (11-2) refused to miss a beat. They focused on an opportunity to make history and did so as MacIntyre watched with pride at home on television. Fales was the MVP after throwing for a Military Bowl-record 395 yards. He completed 33 of 43 passes to complete a season in which he set every major single-season school passing record. The Spartans have often talked about the resiliency that allowed them to rise from the bottom of the college football world. It also was a factor in overcoming obstacles against Bowling Green (8-5). Harrison Waid, the only player on the roster who had attempted a collegiate punt entering this game, left with complications from pneumonia after punting on San Jose State's opening possession. Freshman place-kicker Austin Lopez filled in, and his first punt was blocked to set up a Falcons field goal. After that, Lopez was solid. He also kicked two field goals, including a go-ahead 27-yarder to make it 22-20 with 4:43 to play. The momentum turned toward the Spartans earlier when Benwikere delivered the type of play that's become commonplace for him. San Jose State was trailing 13-10 in the third quarter and looking sluggish. Bowling Green had scored off a Spartans turnover, and SJSU went three-and-out on consecutive drives. With the Falcons punting, Benwikere rushed and found a clear path toward Falcons punter Brian Schmiedebusch. Benwikere blocked the kick, and it went out of the end zone for a safety. The offense seemed invigorated and went on a six-play scoring drive. Fales capped it with an 18-yard touchdown to Chandler Jones, who caught the ball in the flat and completely juked a defender on the sideline to reach the end zone. The Falcons regained the lead at 20-19, but Fales drove the Spartans again. SJSU reached the 10-yard line to set up Lopez's field goal that made him 17 for 17 this season. The defense secured the win when Johnson, the school's career leader in sacks, delivered the final big moment of his career. He sacked Bowling Green's Matt Schilz and forced a fumble that Keith Smith recovered with 4:22 to play. San Jose State secured the knockout blow when De'Leon Eskridge scored on a 1-yard run with 2:34 left to put an end to the drama. The only debate remaining is how do these Spartans compare with the 1937-40 teams that all won 11 or more games?

2012 Belk Bowl

The 2012 Belk Bowl was held on December 27, 2012 at Bank of America Stadium in Charlotte, North Carolina in the United States. The eleventh edition of the Belk Bowl was televised on ESPN. It featured the Duke Blue Devils from the Atlantic Coast Conference (ACC) against the Big East Conference co-champion Cincinnati Bearcats. The Bearcats accepted their invitation after achieving a 9–3 record in the regular season, while the Blue Devils accepted theirs after achieving a 6–6 record. This was the first Belk Bowl for both teams.

2012 Belk Bowl	Line	1	-	2	-	3	-	4	-	Final
Cincinnati	(-9.0)	3	-	14	-	10	-	21	-	48
Duke	(62.0)	16	-	0	-	8	-	10	-	34

Scoring Summary
Duke - Connette 5 yard run (Kick blocked)
Duke - Martin 33 yard Field goal
Duke - Foster recovered fumble in end zone (Martin kick)
Cincinnati - Miliano 45 yard Field goal
Cincinnati - McClung 25 yard pass from Kay (Miliano kick)
Cincinnati - Abernathy 41 yard pass from Kay (Miliano kick)
Cincinnati - Miliano 27 yard Field goal
Cincinnati - Winn 46 yard run (Miliano kick)
Duke - Vernon 10 yard pass from Renfree (Blakeney pass from Renfree)
Duke - Reeves 2 yard pass from Connette (Martin kick)
Cincinnati - Moore 25 yard pass from Kay (Miliano kick)
Duke - Martin 52 yard Field goal
Cincinnati - Kelce 83 yard pass from Kay (Miliano kick)
Cincinnati - Temple 55 yard interception return (Miliano kick)

Associated Press Belk Bowl Game Summary - The last month was pure chaos for Quarterback Brendon Kay and the Cincinnati Bearcats. That made Thursday night's Belk Bowl victory more rewarding. Duke running back Josh Snead fumbled at the Cincinnati 5 with 1:20 left and Kay threw an 83-yard touchdown pass to tight end Travis Kelce with 44 seconds to go, lifting the Bearcats to an improbable 48-34 win over the Blue Devils. The Bearcats won without former head coach Butch Jones and both coordinators who helped guided them to the postseason. Kay, who set a Belk Bowl record with four touchdown passes and was named the game's MVP, called it a "huge win." Almost as chaotic as their latest win. With the score tied at 34 and Duke driving for a go-ahead score, Snead fumbled, and Kay capitalized with his go-ahead scoring pass to Kelce. Nick Temple capped the wild finish with a 55-yard interception return with 14 seconds left. Kay quickly took advantage of the change in momentum after the Snead fumble, finding Kelce down the middle on a seam route. Kelce got behind the Duke defense and caught the ball in stride, racing the final 60 yards to the end zone as Blue Devils fans looked on in stunned silence. It was a play called Left Texas 60, Y Go Burst, with three receivers running seam routes. Kay also threw a 41-yard touchdown pass to Ralph David Abernathy, and 25-yard scoring strikes to Anthony McClung and Chris Moore. George Winn also ran for a 46-yard touchdown for Cincinnati. Cincinnati (10-3) finished with its fifth 10-win season in six years. Duke Quarterback Sean Renfree threw for 358 yards -- another Belk Bowl record -- for the Blue Devils (6-7), who were seeking their first bowl win since 1961. Conner Vernon, the ACC's all-time leader in receptions and receiving yards, had 190 catches for 119 yards and a touchdown in his final game for the Blue Devils. But the big play for Duke was Snead's fumble. Duke Coach David Cutcliffe said the loss was tough to swallow. Duke, which came in having allowed 51 points and an average of 294.5 yards rushing over its previous four games, struggled to stop Cincinnati after the first quarter. The Bearcats piled up 554 total yards of offense, including 130 yards on the ground by Winn. Duke wasn't too shabby on offense, either, combining with the Bearcats for a Belk Bowl-record 1,114 yards. Cincinnati trailed 16-0 before rattling off 27 straight points to seemingly take control, and the big turning point came courtesy of linebacker Greg Blair. With Duke leading 16-3 and looking for more, Renfree fired a pass over the middle for running back Jela Duncan, who lunged for the goal line but was hit by Blair and fumbled.

Blair recovered and suddenly the Bearcats had a shot. A short time later, Kay connected with McClung to cut the Duke lead to 16-10. Kay's second scoring pass to Abernathy capped a 98-yard drive in the final two minutes of the first half and gave the Bearcats their first lead. NOTES: Duke Punter Will Monday set a Belk Bowl record with a 79-yard punt. ... The two teams set a combined record for most first downs in the Belk Bowl.

2012 Holiday Bowl

The 2012 Bridgepoint Education Holiday Bowl, the 35th edition of the game, was between the Baylor Bears from the Big 12 Conference and the UCLA Bruins from the Pac-12 Conference (Pac-12), played on December 27, 2012 at Qualcomm Stadium in San Diego, California. The game was broadcast on both ESPN TV and ESPN Radio. This is the first Holiday Bowl appearance for both Baylor and UCLA, as well as the first-ever meeting between the two teams. It also marks the first time one of the Pac-12's Southern California teams has played in the Holiday Bowl.

2012 Holiday Bowl	Line	1	-	2	-	3	-	4	-	Final
Baylor	(82.0)	14	-	21	-	7	-	7	-	49
#17 UCLA	(-3.0)	0	-	10	-	3	-	13	-	26

Scoring Summary
Baylor—Martin 4 yard run (Jones kick)
Baylor—Goodley 8 yard pass from Florence (Jones kick)
Baylor—Reese 55 yard pass from Florence (Jones kick)
UCLA—Fauria 22 yard pass from Hundley (Fairbairn kick)
Baylor—Martin 26 yard run (Jones kick)
Baylor—Seastrunk 43 yard run (Jones kick)
UCLA—Fairbairn 30 yard field goal
UCLA—Fairbairn 40 yard field goal
Baylor—Martin 1 yard run (Jones kick)
Baylor—Martin 26 yard run (Jones kick)
UCLA—Evans 24 yard pass from Hundley (Pass failed)
Baylor— Florence 1 yard run (Jones kick)
UCLA—Sweet 34 yard pass from Hundley (Fairbairn kick)

UCLA Media Guide Holiday Bowl Game Summary - UCLA dropped a 49-26 decision to Baylor in the Bridgepoint Holiday Bowl played in San Diego. Redshirt freshman Quarterback Brett Hundley established a new school single-season mark for passing yardage during the contest as he threw for 329 yards and three scores. The Bruins finished the season with a 9-5 record, after playing in its first Holiday Bowl game. Baylor, the nation's leader in total offense entering the contest, improved to 8-5. After BU extended its lead to 21-0 early in the second, the Bruin defense forced a fumble and two plays later Hundley found Joseph Fauria for a 22-yard score with 6:21 to play. However, Baylor came right back to reassert its control of the game with a seven-play, 75-yard touchdown drive. The Bears scored on the next possession as well before UCLA closed the half with a 30-yard field goal by Ka'imi Fairbairn. The Bruins used another field goal by Fairbairn, this one from 40-yards out, to make the score 35-13 early in the third quarter. The Bruin defense held on BU's next possession and, after Shaq Evans' 43-yard punt return, had the ball at the Baylor 41-yard line. However, four straight incomplete passes turned the ball over and BU drove down for a touchdown to carry a 42-13 advantage into the final quarter of play. Hundley connected on a 24-yard scoring pass to Evans following another Baylor fumble, but the two-point pass failed to click. The Bruins ended the game with a 34-yard touchdown pass from Hundley to Logan Sweet. Hundley (3,740 passing yards) moved past Cade McNown's 1998 single season passing yardage mark of 3,470 on the scoring pass to Fauria. It was Fauria's 12th scoring reception of the season, a total which ranks second on the school single-season list behind J.J. Stokes' total of 17 set in the 1993 season, and his 20th career scoring catch which tied him for third on that school list. Evans caught seven passes for 82 yards, including a 24-yard scoring grab. He finished the season with 60 catches, a total which ranks eighth on the all-time school single-season list. Evans also added a season-long 43-yard punt return and finished with 132 all-purpose yards in the contest. Kendricks finished the season with a total of 150 tackles, good for third on the all-time school single-season list and the most by a Bruin player since Jerry Robinson registered 161 in 1978. The Bruins set a new school record for points scored in a season (482) on Hundley's 34-yard scoring pass to Sweet. The old mark was 477 points scored in the 1997 season.

Game notes - The Bruins' final touchdown was not reviewed during the game, but replays appeared to show that Logan Sweet was down at the 1-yard line on what was ruled a 34-yard touchdown catch. While the score of the game is officially 49–26, Baylor Head Coach Art Briles had the score changed to 49-19 on the championship rings presented to Baylor players commemorating the victory. CBSSports.com called the changing of the score "an arrogant move."

2012 Russell Athletic Bowl

The 2012 Russell Athletic Bowl was held on December 28, 2012 at the Citrus Bowl in Orlando, Florida in the United States. The 23rd edition of the Russell Athletic Bowl aired on ESPN. It featured the Virginia Tech Hokies from the Atlantic Coast Conference (ACC) against the Big East Conference co-champion Rutgers Scarlet Knights. The Scarlet Knights accepted their invitation after achieving a 9-3 record in the regular season, while the Hokies accepted theirs after achieving a 6-6 record.

2012 Russell Athletic Bowl	Line	1	-	2	-	3	-	4	-	OT	-	Final
Rutgers	(42.0)	10	-	0	-	0	-	0	-	0	-	10
Virginia Tech	(-1.0)	0	-	0	-	0	-	10	-	3	-	13

Scoring Summary
Rutgers – Greene recovered fumble in end zone (Borgese kick)
Rutgers – Borgese 36 yard Field goal
Virginia Tech – Journell 25 yard Field goal
Virginia Tech – Fuller 21 yard pass from Thomas (Journell kick)
Virginia Tech – Journell 22 yard Field goal

Notes and records - A 2012 Russell Athletic Bowl featured a record 20 combined punts and a record low 23 combined points. The bowl victory for the Hokies also marked Virginia Tech's 12th consecutive victory over Rutgers and gave the Hokies' its 21st consecutive winning season.

Associated Press Russell Athletic Bowl Game Summary - After one of its most unfulfilling seasons in recent memory, Virginia Tech desperately wanted to avoid its first losing season since 1992. Mission accomplished. Cody Journell kicked a 22-yard field goal on the first possession of overtime to help the Hokies beat Rutgers 13-10 in the Russell Athletic Bowl on Friday night. Virginia Tech won its final three games to finish 7-6. Rutgers (9-4) had a chance to tie it in overtime, but Nick Borgese missed a 42-yard field goal attempt to the right. The loss ended a run of five straight bowl victories for the Scarlet Knights and kept them from recording their first double-digit win season since 2006. The win also was the Hokies' 12th straight victory against their former Big East Conference rival. Virginia Tech trailed 10-0 at the half, then rallied in the final 30 minutes thanks to some timely turnovers and offense. Quarterback Logan Thomas struggled in the first half and finished with a pair of interceptions, but also had 192 yards passing and the game's only passing touchdown. Taylor finished the night with a team-high 11 tackles to lead a defense that held Rutgers to 67 yards in the second half. Virginia Tech cornerback Antone Exum, selected the most valuable player of the game, picked off Gary Nova's pass early in the fourth quarter to set up the tying score. He said even though the offense took its lumps early, he was never down on its effort. Rutgers seemed to be in command until the opening minutes of the fourth quarter, when turnovers and a sudden surge from the Hokies' offense quickly turned the momentum. Down 10-0, Virginia Tech took over after Rutgers missed a field goal and moved into Scarlet Knights' territory for the first time in the game on a 32-yard pass from Thomas to Dyrell Roberts. Thomas then found Corey Fuller for a 25-yard strike on the next play before the drive stalled on the 8. It forced the Hokies to settle for Journell's 25-yard field goal. Exum intercepted Nova's pass on the ensuing drive, giving the Hokies a first down on the Rutgers 21. The Hokies found the end zone three plays later on a 21-yard touchdown pass from Thomas to Fuller with 10:56 left as steady rain began to fall. Virginia Tech defensive end Tyrel Wilson then came up with the defense's second turnover of the night, recovering a fumble inside the Scarlet Knights 40 after Nova dropped a snap while lined up in the shotgun. An intentional grounding penalty on Thomas forced a punt, though, with less than 7 minutes to play. They got another chance a few series later, only to see Journell's 51-yard field goal come up short with 2:20 showing on the clock. Rutgers punted but got it back just a play later when Thomas' pass was intercepted by Brandon Jones. Hokies players honored the shooting victims of Virginia Tech and Newtown, Conn., with a decal on their helmets, then went out and stunned Rutgers with a second-half rally. Douglas Jones/USA TODAY Sports. It was defense on both sides that controlled the action in the first half as Rutgers took a 10-0 halftime lead. The Scarlet Knights were the most effective offensively, managing a modest seven first downs and a field goal. But the Scarlet Knights came up empty on their best drive of the half, failing to convert on a fourth-down pass play inside the Hokies 35. Virginia Tech struggled throughout, though, tallying only 73 yards total in the first two quarters. Thomas was also sacked twice and intercepted late in the half, which severely hampered an offense that never made it into Rutgers' territory. Penalties also bent in Rutgers' favor. Virginia Tech was penalized eight times for 60 yards. The Scarlet Knights weren't whistled for any penalties in the half. A miscue by Virginia Tech on the opening drive of the game produced the game's first score. Hokies center Caleb Farris sent his second snap of the night sailing past Thomas and into the end zone. Thomas scrambled back to pick it up, and tried to run it out, but he was instantly swarmed and lost the ball as he was tackled. It was eventually recovered by Rutgers linebacker Khaseem Greene for the touchdown. Beamer said the challenge was not to let any shortcomings from this season cloud the offseason. **Game notes:** The game was the lowest scoring the bowl's history. It surpassed Stanford's 24-3 win over Penn State in 1993. ...The game also set a bowl record with 20 punts, passing the previous record of 19 in the 1991 matchup between Alabama and Colorado.

2012 Independence Bowl

The 2012 AdvoCare V100 Independence Bowl was held on December 28, 2012 at Independence Stadium in Shreveport, Louisiana in the United States. The 37th edition of the Independence Bowl was televised on ESPN. It featured the Ohio Bobcats from the Mid-American Conference against the Louisiana–Monroe Warhawks from the Sun Belt Conference. Both the Bobcats and the Warhawks accepted their invitation after finishing at 8–4 during the regular season.

2012 Independence Bowl	Line	1	-	2	-	3	-	4	-	Final
Ohio	(59.0)	14	-	10	-	14	-	7	-	45
Louisiana-Monroe	(-6.5)	0	-	7	-	7	-	0	-	14

Scoring Summary
OHIO—Foster 3 yard pass from Tettleton (Weller kick)
OHIO—Cochran 68 yard pass from Tettleton (Weller kick)
Louisiana-Monroe—Maye 14 yard pass from Browning (Manton kick)
OHIO—Weller 38 yard field goal
OHIO—Blankenship 2 yard run (Weller kick)
OHIO—Blankenship 2 yard run (Weller kick)
OHIO—Blankenship 1 yard run (Matt Weller kick)
Louisiana-Monroe - Steed 1 yard pass from Browning (Manton kick)
OHIO—Blankenship 2 yard run (Weller kick)

Ohio University Media Guide Independence Bowl Game Summary - Ohio Football picked up its second straight bowl win on Friday afternoon, earning a dominating 45-14 victory over the University of Louisiana-Monroe in the 2012 AdvoCare V100 Independence Bowl. The Bobcat offense exploded in the win, amassing a bowl-record 556 total yards and setting multiple additional Independence Bowl records in the process. Beau Blankenship led the way on the ground for Ohio (9-4), carrying the ball 19 times for a total of 105 yards and a bowl-record four touchdowns. Friday's game marked the ninth time during the 2012 season he surpassed 100 yards on the ground, an Ohio record. Quarterback Tyler Tettleton had a very strong game for the Green and White as well, completing 14 of his 22 pass attempts for 331 yards and two touchdowns. Chase Cochran was Ohio's leading receiver, catching three passes for 162 yards and one touchdown.

2012 Meineke Car Care Bowl of Texas

The 2012 Meineke Car Care Bowl of Texas, the seventh edition of the game, was held on December 28, 2012 at Reliant Stadium in Houston, Texas. The game was broadcast on ESPN. This was not the first time the Golden Gophers and Red Raiders met in a bowl game; the two teams had previously met in the 2006 Insight Bowl, with the Red Raiders winning 44–41 in overtime.

2012 Meineke Car Care Bowl	Line	1	-	2	-	3	-	4	-	Final
Minnesota	(55.0)	10	-	7	-	7	-	7	-	31
Texas Tech	(-13.0)	14	-	10	-	0	-	10	-	34

Scoring Summary
Minnesota - Wettstein 41 yard Field goal
Texas Tech - Grant 99 yard kickoff return (Bustin kick)
Minnesota - Williams 2 yard run (Wettstein kick)
Texas Tech - Edwards 13 yard pass from Brewer (Bustin kick)
Minnesota - Kirkwood 3 yard run (Wettstein kick)
Texas Tech - Bustin 28 yard Field goal
Texas Tech - Doege 4 yard run (Bustin kick)
Minnesota - Crawford-Tufts 17 yard pass from Nelson (Wettstein kick)
Minnesota - Goodger 1 yard pass from Nelson (Wettstein kick)
Texas Tech - Ward 35 yard pass from Doege (Bustin kick)
Texas Tech - Bustin 28 yard Field goal

Associated Press Meineke Car Care Bowl Game Summary - Seth Doege and D.J. Johnson both made mistakes that cost Texas Tech on Friday night. But with the game on the line in the fourth quarter, the two seniors stepped up to save the game. Johnson, who got beat on a long play in the third quarter, returned an interception 39 yards and Ryan Bustin made a 28-yard field goal as time expired to give Texas Tech a 34-31 comeback victory over Minnesota in the Meineke Car Care Bowl. Doege found Eric Ward on a short pass, and he outran a defender for a 35-yard scoring play to pull the Red Raiders even at 31 with just more than a minute remaining. Michael Carter intercepted two of Doege's passes in the fourth quarter before the tying score, but Minnesota couldn't convert either of the turnovers into points. The Red Raiders (8-5) got their third straight bowl win to wrap up a month that began with coach Tommy Tuberville's abrupt departure for the job at Cincinnati. Texas Tech has hired Kliff Kingsbury to replace him, but interim coach Chris Thomsen led the team against Minnesota (6-7). Kingsbury was at the game, watching from a suite. Doege threw for 271 yards and a touchdown and ran for another score in front of a crowd that included 1977 Heisman Trophy winner Earl Campbell and former Texas Tech coach Spike Dykes. Freshman Philip Nelson threw for 138 yards and two scores for the Gophers, who were in a bowl game for the first time since 2009. The Red Raiders returned to a bowl after having their 18-season bowl streak snapped last year. A 1-yard touchdown pass from Nelson to Drew Goodger gave Minnesota a 31-24 lead early in the fourth quarter. Texas Tech led 24-17 at halftime but couldn't do anything offensively in the second half until the last couple of minutes. It was an ugly game for the Red Raiders, who had 13 penalties for 135 yards and lost tight end Jace Amaro when he was ejected for throwing a punch. Jakeem Grant ran for what was initially ruled a Tech touchdown late in the third quarter. Amaro threw a punch at Derrick Wells in the end zone on the play and was ejected. After the penalty, the play was reviewed and overturned. Doege threw an incomplete pass before Tech made a 32-yard field goal. But the Red Raiders had a false start penalty on the play and had to kick again and this time the Gophers blocked it. Nelson threw a 17-yard touchdown pass to Devin Crawford-Tufts, who was left uncovered in the end zone, to tie it at 24 early in the third quarter. Donnell Kirkwood scored on a 3-yard run to leave Minnesota up 17-14 early in the second. Texas Tech had a first-and-goal at the Minnesota 2 after a pass-interference call on the Gophers. But Texas Tech had to settle for a field goal after a rush for a 3-yard loss and two penalties. Minnesota's next drive started out well before turning ugly. The Gophers had made two first downs before MarQueis Gray was sacked for a loss of 7 yards. Kirkwood ran for 17 yards on the next play, but Minnesota received two 15-yard penalties on the play, one for a personal foul on lineman Zac Epping, to make it second-and-42. Epping received a second personal foul penalty on the next play to bring up third-and-49. Christian Eldred shanked the punt, giving Texas Tech the ball at the Minnesota 42. The Red Raiders capitalized on their great field position when Doege spun away from a defender in the backfield and leaped over another Gophers player near the goal line on a 4-yard touchdown run. Tech converted a fourth-and-6 play on that drive and led by seven at halftime. Minnesota's Rodrick Williams Jr. scored on a 2-yard run to give the Gophers a 10-7 lead in the first quarter. Doege lost his helmet on a 5-yard scramble on Tech's next drive and had to go out for one play. He was replaced by Michael Brewer, who found Derreck Edwards for a 13-yard touchdown pass to give the Red Raiders a 14-10 lead. Minnesota's Troy Stoudermire returned the opening kickoff 26 yards to break the NCAA record for career kickoff return yards. He finished the game with 111 to push his total to 3,615. The Gophers ended that drive with a 41-yard field goal to make it 3-0. Grant returned the ensuing kickoff 99 yards for a touchdown to put Texas Tech up 7-3.

2012 Armed Forces Bowl

The 2012 Bell Helicopter Armed Forces Bowl was held on December 29, 2012 at Amon G. Carter Stadium on the campus of Texas Christian University (TCU) in Fort Worth, Texas. The tenth edition of the Armed Forces Bowl was televised on ESPN. It featured the Rice Owls from Conference USA against the Air Force Falcons from the Mountain West Conference. The Falcons accepted their invitation after earning a 6–5 record in their first eleven games of the season, while the Owls advanced to the game per C-USA's bowl contingency plan after earning a 6-6 record. This also marked the bowl's return to Amon G. Carter Stadium after a two-year absence because of renovations to the stadium. For 2010 and 2011, the game was held at Gerald J. Ford Stadium in University Park on the campus of Southern Methodist University (SMU).

2012 Armed Forces Bowl	Line	1	-	2	-	3	-	4	-	Final
Rice	(-1.0)	7	-	0	-	7	-	19	-	33
Air Force	(60.5)	0	-	14	-	0	-	0	-	14

Scoring Summary
Rice - Taylor 16 yard pass from McHargue (Boswell kick)
Air Force - Pearson 9 yard run (Herrington kick)
Air Force - Cobb 1 yard run (Herrington kick)
Rice - Taylor 22 yard pass from Jackson (Boswell kick)
Rice - Ross 2 yard run (Boswell kick)
Rice - Boswell 24 yard Field goal
Rice - Boswell 25 yard Field goal
Rice - Taylor 34 yard pass from Jackson (Kick blocked)

Associated Press Armed Forces Bowl Game Summary - When Rice freshman Quarterback Driphus Jackson was suddenly thrust into action in the Armed Forces Bowl, he drove the Owls within 2 yards of a tying touchdown before his errant pitch. Jackson more than made up for that miscue that ended the first half. After starter Taylor McHargue was knocked out the game because of a concussion, Jackson threw for 264 yards with two second-half touchdowns to Jordan Taylor, and Rice beat Air Force 33-14 on Saturday. Rice (7-6), which had to win four in a row just to get bowl eligible, has won both of its bowl games under sixth-year coach David Bailiff. Before their 2008 Texas Bowl victory, the Owls had lost their only four bowl games since winning the 1954 Cotton Bowl. And this is a Rice team with only seven seniors, three of them tight ends. The Owls were 1-5 after a loss at Memphis on Oct. 6, and their only loss was 28-24 to Conference USA champion Tulsa. Air Force (6-7) scored on consecutive drives in the second quarter with backup Quarterback Kale Pearson in the game. But the Falcons had a season-low 214 total yards. Jackson's first series ended with a bad pitch near the goal line only 2 seconds before halftime, when the Owls trailed 14-7. It was the third lost fumble by Rice in the second quarter. Taylor, had nine catches for 153 yards and three TDs, including a 16-yarder from McHargue in the first quarter. Jackson had consecutive completions of 25 and 22 yards before a 2-yard keeper and then a 22-yard TD to Taylor on Rice's opening drive of the second half. The Owls went ahead to stay, 21-14, when Jackson hit six passes in a row to set up Charles Ross' 2-yard TD run. Jackson, who started against Houston when McHargue had a shoulder problem, completed 15 of 21 passes and rushed for 32 yards. McHargue never returned after a helmet-to-helmet collision on a 5-yard run with about 5 minutes left in the first half. He put his head down and ran into defensive back Steffon Batts and fumbled. McHargue was noticeably wobbly while being helped to the sideline. The Falcons then went 35 yards in nine plays for a 14-7 lead. Mike DeWitt converted fourth-and-1 with a 2-yard run, and Wes Cobb scored on a 1-yard run. Jackson then came in for the Owls and had keepers of 5 and 14 yards before a 23-yard pass to Taylor. After another 10-yard pass for first-and-goal from the 2 before Jackson's bad pitch. McHargue hit 6 of 8 passes for 31 yards. He stood on the sideline after halftime wearing a warmup suit and a cap. Since the Falcons' last game, senior Quarterback Connor Dietz has graduated from the academy and been commissioned as a second lieutenant in the Air Force. Dietz ran six times for 11 yards and completing only 1 of 3 passes. Pearson wasn't must better, 2-of-8 passing for 44 yards with six carries for 11 yards. But he was on the field for both of Air Force's scoring drives with a 9-yard TD run. The Falcons have made a school-record six consecutive bowl appearances under Calhoun but are 2-4 in those games (1-3 in the Armed Forces Bowl). Air Force lost four of its last five games to finish this season. Chris Boswell made field goals of 24 and 25 yards in the fourth quarter, before Jackson hit Taylor for a 34-yard TD with 1:38 left. Boswell, who made six field goals of at least 50 yards during the regular season, had apparently made a 52-yarder early in the second quarter before officials blew the whistle for an Air Force timeout. Boswell got another try but pushed it wide right with about 9 minutes left in the first half. That's when Pearson took over for Air Force, leading them 66 yards in 10 plays. He had a 15-yard pass and ended the drive with a wide sweeping run to get into the front corner of the end zone to tie the game at 7.

2012 Kraft Fight Hunger Bowl

The 2012 Kraft Fight Hunger Bowl was held on December 29, 2012 at AT&T Park in San Francisco, California. The 11th edition of the Kraft Fight Hunger Bowl was televised on ESPN2. It featured the Arizona State Sun Devils of the Pac-12 Conference (Pac-12) and the Navy Midshipmen, who were an independent. The game, won by the Sun Devils 62–28, drew 34,172 spectators. In accordance with a 2009 deal with bowl organizers, the Midshipmen accepted their invitation to play in the game on November 3 after winning six of their first nine games of the season. After the Sun Devils achieved bowl eligibility by defeating in-state rival Arizona Wildcats for a 7–5 regular-season record, the team accepted its bowl invitation on December 2. The pregame buildup focused on the contest between Navy's triple option offense and the Sun Devils' defense. After a change in Quarterbacks, the Midshipmen's rushing offense had become one of the best in the nation; however, the team's passing offense ranked near the bottom of the Football Bowl Subdivision (FBS). Arizona State's balanced offense hinged on its Quarterback efficiency, with the potential to set a number of school records for the season. Defensively the team ranked as one of the best in the nation in sacks and tackles for loss, but its rushing defense ranked 74th in yards allowed per game. Most analysts predicted a victory for the Sun Devils. Navy sold over 10,000 tickets to the game, and Arizona State sold over 5,000. The Sun Devils scored the first 21 points of the game in the first quarter, while keeping the Midshipmen scoreless. After Navy scored its first points in the second quarter, Arizona State scored two more touchdowns to bring the score to 34–7 at halftime. The Sun Devils added four more touchdowns in the third quarter, but the only additional points from the Midshipmen came from a 95-yard kickoff return for a touchdown. Navy scored the only two touchdowns of the fourth quarter, ending the game with a score of 62–28. The bowl brought both teams' won–lost records to 8–5.

2012 Kraft Fight Hunger Bowl	Line	1	-	2	-	3	-	4	-	Final
Navy	(54.5)	0	-	7	-	7	-	14	-	28
Arizona State	(-13.0)	21	-	13	-	28	-	0	-	62

Scoring Summary
Arizona State - Ross 16 yard pass from Kelly (Garoutte kick)
Arizona State - Grice 10 yard run (Garoutte kick)
Arizona State - Kelly 1 yard run (Garoutte kick)
Navy - Aiken 3 yard pass from Reynolds (Sloan kick)
Arizona State - Agwuenu 11 yard pass from Kelly (Garoutte kick)
Arizona State - Ross 52 yard pass from Kelly (Garoutte kick)
Arizona State - Ross 50 yard pass from Kelly (Garoutte kick)
Arizona State - Marshall 1 yard run (Garoutte kick)
Navy - Greene 95 yard kickoff return (Sloan kick)
Arizona State - Marshall 33 yard run (Garoutte kick)
Arizona State - Marshall 33 yard run (Garoutte kick)
Navy - Swain 46 yard run (Sloan kick)
Navy - Turner 23 yard pass from Miller (Sloan kick)

Associated Press Kraft Fight Hunger Bowl Game Summary - Taylor Kelly, Marion Grice and the rest of the Arizona State offense put an emphatic finish on coach Todd Graham's successful first season with the Sun Devils. Kelly threw four touchdown passes and ran for a fifth score to lead Arizona State to its first bowl win in seven years, a 62-28 victory over Navy in the Kraft Fight Hunger Bowl on Saturday. Offensive MVP Marion Grice ran for 159 yards and two touchdowns for the Sun Devils (8-5), who used their fast-paced spread offense to score touchdowns on their first nine possessions. The Sun Devils won their most games since 2007 and won a bowl for the first time since the 2005 Insight Bowl against Rutgers. They also capped their season by beating rival Arizona and winning a bowl, a feat they had accomplished just once in the past 33 seasons. The Midshipmen (8-5) have lost five of their last six bowl games. Among the few highlights for Navy were Keenan Reynolds' 3-yard TD pass to Matt Aiken in the first half and a 95-yard kickoff return for a score by Gee Gee Greene in the third quarter. Rashad Ross, who grew up in nearby Vallejo, started and ended the first-half outburst with touchdown receptions. His 16-yard catch from Kelly capped a 75-yard game-opening drive and he got behind the Navy defense for a 52-yard score in the final minute of the half to make it 34-7. Ross then caught a 50-yard TD pass on Arizona State's first drive of the second half to make it 41-7. Grice, playing with a heavy heart after his brother was murdered last week in Houston, scored on a 10-yard run in the first quarter and a 39-yarder in the third. He had 19 touchdowns this season, with 11 coming on the ground. "We opened our arms out for Marion," Kelly said. "We're all with him. He's in our prayers and our family. He's having a hard time in the locker room, or he'd be out here. He's all into this program. He wanted to come out and play for his brother and his family and also our brothers." Much of the talk leading up to the game was how Arizona State would handle Navy's unique triple-option offense. It turned out that the Midshipmen had much more trouble with the Sun Devils' spread, giving up 648 yards. Arizona State had seven touchdown drives of at least 60 yards in the first three quarters and had just three third-down plays in that span as Kelly easily picked apart the defense. The longest drive took just 2:43 and one of the quickest came at the end of the half when the Sun Devils went 80 yards in two plays covering 19 seconds after Nick Sloan missed a 33-yard field goal for Navy. Kelly finished 17 for 19 for 268 yards, ending the season completing a school-record 67.1 percent of his passes. He also rushed for 81 yards, scoring on a 1-yard run that made it 21-0. The Midshipmen had a few opportunities to keep the game close on offense in the first half, but Greene was unable to hold onto a pass in the end zone on fourth-and-7 from the 31 in the first quarter and Reynolds lost 3 yards on a third-and-1 keeper from the 8 before Sloan's missed field goal. Sen. John McCain, a former Navy fighter pilot who represents Arizona in Congress, handled the pregame toss. Instead of using a coin, the game sponsored by Kraft uses an Oreo, with one side being a chocolate cookie and the other vanilla. Before that, Pat Tillman Sr. presented Sun Devils defensive tackle Will Sutton the Pac-12 defensive player of the year award named after his son, the former ASU star who died as an Army ranger in Afghanistan. Sutton had 2½ sacks to win defensive player of the game as the Sun Devils kept Navy grounded until the reserves took over on defense in the fourth quarter.

2012 Pinstripe Bowl

The 2012 New Era Pinstripe Bowl was held on December 29, 2012 at Yankee Stadium in the New York City borough of The Bronx. The third edition of the Pinstripe Bowl was televised on ESPN. It featured the Big East Conference co-champion Syracuse Orange against the West Virginia Mountaineers from the Big 12 Conference. Both the Orange and the Mountaineers advanced to the game after accomplishing 7–5 records in the regular season. The Orange and the Mountaineers had a notable continuous rivalry from 1955 until

2011. This included the years in the Big East Conference, which was established in 1979. The winner of the game was awarded the Ben Schwartzwalder Trophy from its establishment in 1993. That trophy was not on the line in the Pinstripe Bowl.

2012 Pinstripe Bowl	Line	1	-	2	-	3	-	4	-	Final
West Virginia	(-4.0)	0	-	7	-	7	-	0	-	14
Syracuse	(70.0)	3	-	9	-	23	-	3	-	38

Scoring Summary
Syracuse - Krautman 25 yard Field goal
Syracuse - Safety - Lynch tackled Smith in end zone
Syracuse - Gulley 33 yard run (Krautman kick)
West Virginia - Bailey 32 yard pass from Smith (Bitancurt kick)
Syracuse - Wales 10 yard pass from Nassib (Krautman kick)
Syracuse - Gulley 67 yard run (Krautman kick)
West Virginia - Bailey 29 yard pass from Smith (Bitancurt kick)
Syracuse - Gulley 9 yard pass from Nassib (Krautman kick)
Syracuse - Safety - Smith intentional grounding in end zone
Syracuse - Krautman 36 yard Field goal

Associated Press Pinstripe Bowl Game Summary - The weather made passing at the New Era Pinstripe Bowl perilous, so Syracuse sent Prince-Tyson Gulley and Jerome Smith dashing through West Virginia and the snow. Gulley ran for a career-best 208 yards and had three touchdowns, Smith added 157 yards, and the Orange bid a blustery farewell to the Big East with a 38-14 victory over West Virginia on Saturday. Syracuse (8-5) will enter the Atlantic Coast Conference on a roll after finishing this season with six wins in its last seven games, capped by its second postseason victory at Yankee Stadium in the last three years. In a bowl game played in a baseball stadium with weather better suited for a playoff game in Green Bay, the team that plays in a dome ended up being better equipped to handle the elements. Syracuse finished with a season-high 369 yards on the ground and beat its former Big East rival from West Virginia, now playing in the Big 12, for a third straight time. Geno Smith connected with Stedman Bailey for two touchdown passes for West Virginia (7-6), but the Mountaineers' Quarterback also was sacked in the end zone in the first half and called for intentional grounding in the end zone in the third quarter to give Syracuse a second safety. Smith, who was an early Heisman Trophy front-runner as the Mountaineers got off to a 5-0 start this season, was 16 for 26 for 197 yards in the final game of his record-breaking career. The NFL awaits. Same goes for Ryan Nassib, though Syracuse didn't ask much of its talented senior Quarterback. He threw two touchdown passes and an interception. His most impressive feat on this day was surviving being driven into the cold turf by Terence Garvin on a sack in the first half. Nassib missed only one play. Snow fell just about all game, giving most of the field a white dusting. Fans were bundled and players not in the game tried to do the same. It took a while for those potent offenses -- both ranked in the top 25 nationally in yards per game -- to heat up, which seemed appropriate considering the conditions. A goal-line stand by West Virginia in the second quarter kept Syracuse out of the end zone but set up the Orange for a scoring run. Left at their own 1, the Mountaineers tried to pass out of their end zone, but Smith was smothered by blitzing linebackers Cameron Lynch and Siriki Diabate for a safety to make it 5-0 -- a baseball score, of course. The Orange followed that up with a 33-yard touchdown run by Gulley to make it 12-0 with 6:07 left in the second. The Mountaineers responded with their first sustained drive, and Bailey took a quick pass, darted and broke tackles, and scooted 32 yards to the end zone to make it 12-7. The Orange extended the lead to 12 to start the second half when they caught a break -- and a touchdown pass. Nassib's throw was tipped around the goal line but floated safely into the waiting arms of intended receiver Beckett Wales for a 10-yard score. West Virginia appeared to answer with a touchdown of its own. Andrew Buie broke free for a 28-yard TD run on fourth-and-2, but a holding call on the Mountaineers wiped out the play and sent Holgorsen on to the field screaming at the officials. It didn't help. Instead of a touchdown, a punt. Holgorsen had nothing to say about the call and was more disappointed with how his team responded. Moments later another close call, this time on a fumble by Smith that was reviewed to determine if it was an incomplete pass, went Syracuse's way, and again the Orange capitalized. On the next play, Gulley broke through the line, bounced to the outside and went 67 yards for a touchdown to make it 26-7 with 6:52 left in the third. West Virginia wouldn't let Syracuse pull away. Smith found Bailey deep down the sideline, beating one-on-one coverage for a 29-yard score 1:11 later. Right back came the Orange, nine plays, 70 yards, with Gulley taking a swing pass from Nassib 10 yards to make it 33-14. The 60th meeting between these teams, but first in a bowl, ended up being a romp in the snow for Syracuse.

Notes - Syracuse converted the first safety in Pinstripe Bowl history. Syracuse and West Virginia had previously met annually since 1955 when West Virginia was a member of the Big East. The two teams played for the Ben Schwartzwalder Trophy. The victory gave Syracuse an all-time series lead of 33-27.

2012 Buffalo Wild Wings Bowl

The 2012 Buffalo Wild Wings Bowl, the 24th edition of the game, was held on December 29, 2012 at Sun Devil Stadium in Tempe, Arizona. The game was telecast on ESPN.

2012 Buffalo Wild Wings Bowl	Line	1	-	2	-	3	-	4	-	Final
TCU	(-2.0)	7	-	6	-	0	-	3	-	16
Michigan State	(40.0)	0	-	0	-	7	-	10	-	17

Scoring Summary
TCU – Tucker 4 yard run (Oberkrom kick)
TCU – Oberkrom 47 yard Field goal
TCU – Oberkrom 31 yard Field goal
Michigan State – Burbrridge 15 yard pass from Cook (Conroy kick)
Michigan State – Bell 4 yard run (Conroy kick)
TCU – Oberkrom 53 yard Field goal
Michigan State – Conroy 47 yard Field goal

Michigan State Media Guide Game summary - Dan Conroy hit a game-winning 47-yard field goal with 1:01 remaining in the fourth quarter as Michigan State defeated TCU, 17-16, in the 2012 Buffalo Wild Wings Bowl. Le'Veon Bell led all players with 145 yards rushing on 32 carries, including a 4-yard touchdown run, and was named the Offensive Player of the Game. William Gholston earned Defensive Player of the Game honors after leading MSU with a season-high nine tackles, including a 5-yard sack. TCU jumped out to a 7-0 lead as Matthew Tucker capped a nine-play, 73-yard drive with a 4-yard TD run with 5:45 left in the first quarter. The Horned Frogs added to their lead after Jared Oberkrom connected on field goals of 47 and 31 yards in the second quarter. Michigan State got on the board with 34 seconds left in the third quarter as Connor Cook capped MSU's longest touchdown drive of the season and longest in bowl history (14 plays, 90 yards) with his first career TD pass, a 15-yard strike to Aaron Burbridge. Trailing 13-7 midway through the fourth quarter, the Spartans took advantage of a crucial TCU turnover as RJ Williamson recovered a fumbled punt return by Skye Dawson at the TCU 4-yard line. Two plays later, Bell scored on a 4-yard run, giving MSU a 14-13 lead with 7:00 remaining. TCU regained the lead, 16-14, on Oberkrom's 53-yard field goal with 2:42 left in the game, but Cook led MSU on an eight-play, 45-yard scoring drive capped by Conroy's 47-yard field goal with just over a minute remaining. On the ensuing possession, the Spartans held the Horned Frogs without a first down to seal the 17-16 win.

2012 Alamo Bowl

The 2012 Valero Alamo Bowl, the 20th edition of the game, was held on December 29, 2012 and was broadcast on ESPN. Texas was selected as a participant in the 2012 Alamo Bowl following an 8–4 regular season, during which they won their first four games before losing two games. Texas then won four straight games before losing the final two contests of the season. Facing the Longhorns were the Oregon State Beavers with a regular season record of 9–3, highlighted with wins against two top–25 teams in a six-game winning streak to start the season, including then-No. 13 Wisconsin. However, the Beavers lost three of their final six games.

2012 Alamo Bowl	Line	1	-	2	-	3	-	4	-	Final
Texas	(56.5)	3	-	7	-	7	-	14	-	31
#15 Oregon State	(-3.0)	10	-	10	-	7	-	0	-	27

Scoring Summary
Oregon State - Romaine 29 yard field goal
Texas - Jordan 40 yard field goal
Oregon State - Woods 12 yard run (Romaine kick)
Texas - Goodwin 64 yard run (Jordan kick)
Oregon State - Romaine 37 yard field goal
Oregon State - Ward 9 yard run (Romaine kick)
Texas - Ash 11 yard run (Jordan kick)
Oregon State - Woods 2 yard run (Romaine kick)
Texas - Gray 15 yard pass from Ash (Jordan kick)
Texas - Goodwin 36 yard pass from Ash (Jordan kick)

Associated Press Alamo Bowl Game Summary - David Ash threw two fourth-quarter touchdown passes, the last a 36-yard strike to Marquise Goodwin with 2:24 left, to give Texas a 31-27 comeback victory over No. 15 Oregon State in the Alamo Bowl. The Longhorns (9-4) never led before Goodwin scored his second touchdown on a deep post pattern, just a down after Texas converted a fourth-and-1 play to keep its chances alive. Storm Woods ran for 118 yards and scored two touchdowns for Oregon State (9-4). Ash was 21 of 33 for 241 yards. Ash sputtered until the fourth quarter, when he went 9 for 11 for 146 yards. Texas had no choice but to stick with the only backups two redshirt freshmen who haven't taken a snap all season. Oregon State Quarterback Cody Vaz was 15 of 28 for 194 yards. The Beavers had negative 4 yards in the fourth quarter as they were muffled by the Longhorns defense that was led by Alex Okafor, who finished with 4 1/2 sacks. The Valero Alamo Bowl marked the Beavers' 16th bowl game and OSU is 10-6 all-time in them - 5-2 under head coach Mike Riley. The dean of Pac-12 Conference coaches engineered one of the top turnarounds in the nation in 2012, with the Beavers improving to a 9-4 mark after finishing the 2011 campaign at 3-9. The six-win improvement tied Ohio State and Middle Tennessee for the best win improvements from last season. Markus Wheaton ended his Oregon State career at the Alamo Bowl, catching three passes for 37 yards - he left as the program's all-time receptions leader with 227 and is sixth with 1,244 yards. Another senior playing in his final game for the Beavers, Jordan Poyer, was tied for third on the team with five tackles, including a sack. Linebacker Michael Doctor was the team leader with 11 tackles. Oregon State found itself up 20-10 at halftime and 27-17 entering the fourth quarter but two late Texas touchdowns sealed the come-from-behind win for the Longhorns. Ash found Johnathan Gray from 15 yards out with 8:18 remaining and followed that up with a 36-yard touchdown pass to Marquise Goodwin with just 2:24 left in the game.

2012 Music City Bowl

The 2012 Franklin American Mortgage Music City Bowl was held on December 31, 2012 at LP Field in Nashville, Tennessee. The Music City Bowl was televised on ESPN. The Wolfpack accepted their invitation to the game after attaining a 7–5 regular-season record, while the hometown Commodores accepted theirs after attaining an 8–4 record.

2012 Music City Bowl	Line	1	-	2	-	3	-	4	-	Final
NC State	(52.5)	0	-	14	-	0	-	10	-	24
Vanderbilt	(-7.0)	7	-	21	-	3	-	7	-	38

Scoring Summary
Vanderbilt - Boyd 5 yard pass from Rodgers (Spear kick)
Vanderbilt - Stacy 6 yard run (Fowler kick)
NC State - Creecy 1 yard run (Sade kick)
Vanderbilt - Tate 7 yard run (Spear kick)
NC State - Palmer 94 yard kickoff return (Sade kick)
Vanderbilt - Matthews 18 yard pass from Rodgers (Fowler kick)
Vanderbilt - Spear 30 yard Field goal
NC State - Sade 24 yard Field goal
Vanderbilt - Rodgers 1 yard run (Spear kick)
NC State - Smith 19 yard pass from Glennon (Sade kick)

Associated Press Music City Bowl Game Summary - The Southeastern Conference is so strong that even Vanderbilt, yes Vandy, is winning like the Commodores haven't in nearly a century. And coach James Franklin says everyone better get used to it. Jordan Rodgers threw two touchdown passes and ran for another score as the Commodores capped their best season since 1915 by defeating North Carolina State 38-24 in the Franklin American Mortgage Music City Bowl on Monday. The Commodores finished 9-4 for their best record since going 9-1 in 1915, and it's only the third time the smallest and only private university in the SEC has won as many as nine games in a season. Vandy closed the season with seven straight wins for its longest streak since an eight-game run in 1948, and its 15 wins over the past two seasons is the program's best total since 1926 and 1927. Vanderbilt forced a season-high five turnovers, including four in the first half, and turned those into 17 points. Interim coach Dana Bible ran NC State (7-6) after Tom O'Brien was fired at the end of the regular season. It was the Wolfpack's fifth game of the season with at least four turnovers, and it helped wipe out a 424-225 advantage in total offense. Bible, who said he was head coach for another minute or two, took the blame for two of the interceptions for being aggressive. This was the 27th bowl for NC State, which had won its last two postseason games. But a team that ranked second in the Atlantic Coast Conference in turnovers couldn't overcome its own mistakes, which also included a bad shotgun snap that cost the Wolfpack 21 yards on the opening drive. Franklin got a contract extension a month ago for guiding the Dores to a second straight bowl game for the first time in school history. Franklin didn't change anything that got his Commodores here as he went for it on fourth down, used the wildcat repeatedly and even had senior running back Zac Stacy attempt a halfback pass to Rodgers. Vandy wound up running for 117 yards, with Stacy getting 107 on 25 carries, mostly in the wildcat. The Commodores took control from the opening drive, moving 65 yards for a touchdown that put them ahead to stay. Officials initially called Chris Boyd out of bounds, but the video review showed the sophomore got the toes of his right foot down for a 5-yard TD pass from Rodgers. Commodores safety Kenny Ladler picked off a Glennon pass at the North Carolina State 45 for Vanderbilt's fifth interception in three games. It was just a sign of what was to come in the first half. Johnell Thomas stripped Wolfpack freshman Shadrach Thornton late in the first quarter, and Darreon Herring stripped NC State tight end Asa Watson of the ball after a nice catch. Ladler recovered that ball. And safety Eric Samuels intercepted Glennon with 54 seconds left in the first half. Vanderbilt turned the third turnover into a touchdown, making it 14-0 in the second quarter. Stacy, the school's all-time leading rusher, scored on a 6-yard run with 10:08 left. Tony Creecy responded with a 1-yard TD run for the Wolfpack. But Vanderbilt stuck with the wildcat, and Wesley Tate scored on a 7-yard TD run for a 21-7 lead with 3:47 left in the second. Tobias Palmer, who struggled catching the ball on his first two kickoff returns, caught the next cleanly and ran untouched 94 yards for a TD that made it 21-14. Rodgers tossed his second TD pass, a screen that Matthews took 18 yards to the end zone, to restore the 14-point lead and make it 28-14 at the break. That matched the most points the Commodores had scored in any of their five previous bowl games. Rodgers ran for a 15-yard TD with 5:11 left that sealed the victory. Trey Wilson picked off a Glennon pass intended for tight end Charlie Hegedus in the end zone on the opening drive of the third quarter only to be stopped by his own teammate, tackle Jared Morse, at the NC State 35. It was the kind of mistake that cost Vandy in years past. Franklin immediately ran up to Morse yelling at the junior, making it clear that's not allowed at Vandy these days.

2012 Liberty Bowl

The 2012 AutoZone Liberty Bowl was held on December 31, 2012 at the Liberty Bowl Memorial Stadium in Memphis, Tennessee in the United States. The 54th edition of the Liberty Bowl was televised on ESPN. The Golden Hurricane advanced to the game by virtue of winning the 2012 Conference USA Football Championship Game, while the Cyclones were also eligible for the bowl game due to their 6–6 regular-season record. The two teams had previously met on September 1 at the Cyclones' home of Jack Trice Stadium in Ames, Iowa; Iowa State won that game, 38–23.

2012 Liberty Bowl	Line	1	-	2	-	3	-	4	-	Final
Iowa State	(50.5)	17	-	0	-	0	-	0	-	17
Tulsa	(-2.5)	7	-	14	-	7	-	3	-	31

Scoring Summary
Iowa State – Arceo 33 yard Field goal
Iowa State – Reeves 31 yard interception return (Arceo kick)
Tulsa – Singleton 2 yard run (Schwarz kick)
Iowa State – Brun 69 yard pass from Richardson (Arceo kick)
Tulsa – Green 8 yard run (Schwarz kick)
Tulsa – Singleton 2 yard run (Schwarz kick)
Tulsa – Singleton 1 yard run (Schwarz kick)
Tulsa – Schwarz 40 yard Field goal

Iowa State Media Guide Liberty Bowl Game Summary - Iowa State stormed out of the gates and led early but Tulsa controlled much of the rest of the game enroute to a 31-17 victory at the Liberty Bowl in front of an announced crowd of 53,687, the largest ever to witness an ISU bowl game. Jeremy Reeves returned his interception 31 yards for a touchdown to put Iowa State up 10-0 with 7:44 remaining in the first quarter. After Tulsa responded with a nine play drive that resulted in a touchdown, Sam Richardson hit Ernst Brun who scampered in for the 69-yard score to make it 17-7 at the end of the opening stanza. That would be all the scoring for the Cyclones as Tulsa responded with the final 24 points of the game. Richardson, who battled illness, finished 10- for-21 for 129 yards in the air. The redshirt freshman also had a team-high 46 yards on the ground. Brun finished with four catches for 102 yards to lead the Cyclones through the air. Senior linebacker A.J. Klein capped his career with 19 tackles and Jevohn Miller added 12 for the Cyclones.
Notes - As was forecast, there was rain throughout the game. Temperatures remained in the 40s. Ticket sales exceeded expectations, but overall attendance declined from 2011; in all, the paid attendance was 53,687.

2012 Sun Bowl

The 2012 Hyundai Sun Bowl, the 79th edition of the game, was held on December 31, 2012 at Sun Bowl Stadium in El Paso, Texas. The game, the 79th edition of the Sun Bowl, was televised in the United States on CBS. The Trojans accepted their invitation to the game after attaining a 7–5 regular-season record, while the Yellow Jackets entered the game with a 6-7 record (5-3 ACC), after losing to Florida State in the 2012 ACC Championship Game. Georgia Tech cornerback Rod Sweeting was named the game's most valuable player.

2012 Sun Bowl	Line	1	-	2	-	3	-	4	-	Final
USC	(-7.5)	0	-	7	-	0	-	0	-	7
Georgia Tech	(63.0)	0	-	7	-	7	-	7	-	21

Scoring Summary
Georgia Tech – Sims 3 yard pass from Lee (Tanner kick)
USC – Redd 9 yard pass from Wittek (Heidari kick)
Georgia Tech – Washington 1 yard run (Tanner kick)
Georgia Tech – Smith 17 yard pass from Washington (Tanner kick)

Sun Bowl Classic Game Summary - Georgia Tech needed a waiver from the NCAA to play in the postseason, and it made the most of its second consecutive trip to the Hyundai Sun Bowl. Tevin Washington threw a touchdown pass and ran for another score to help the Yellow Jackets beat Southern California 21-7 on Monday. Washington's 1-yard touchdown run in the third made it 14-7, and he found Orwin Smith for a 17-yard touchdown pass in the fourth in front of a crowd of 47,922 at Sun Bowl Stadium. The Yellow Jackets rushed for 294 yards on 63 carries while stopping a seven-bowl losing streak. They also erased some of the sting from last season's Sun Bowl, when they squandered a 24-10 fourth-quarter lead in an overtime loss to Utah. They also could have won the game on a field goal at the end of regulation but missed for the third time in the game. Georgia Tech needed a pass into the bowl season because it finished with a 6-7 record following a loss in the ACC championship game. The conference's rules prevented Georgia Tech from falling to a lesser bowl, but it looked just fine competing against the disappointing Trojans. Southern California (7-6), which was ranked No. 1 at the beginning of the season, played without injured Quarterback Matt Barkley. Max Wittek tossed a 9-yard touchdown pass to Silas Redd in the second quarter, but also threw three interceptions. USC became the first preseason No. 1 team to lose six games. It's also all but assured of becoming the school to enter the season on top of The Associated Press poll and finish unranked since Mississippi in 1964. Barkley, the first three-time captain in USC history, injured his right shoulder in a loss to UCLA and was not cleared to play his final college game. He clapped as the Trojans took the field for their first bowl game after a two-year NCAA ban. Max Wittek tossed a 9-yard touchdown pass to Silas Redd in the second quarter, but also threw three interceptions. Redd added 88 yards rushing on 17 carries. Talented receiver Robert Woods was limited to three receptions for 33 yards in what was likely his final college game. The junior said after the loss he plans to enter the NFL draft. Kiffin said he took responsibility for the lost season. Tech's David Sims had 99 yards on 17 carries, but he got plenty of help. Zach Laskey added 60 yards on six carries, Vad Lee had 52 on 10 carries and Washington had 16 attempts for 46 yards for the No. 4 rushing team in the nation. Sims also caught a 3-yard touchdown pass from Lee in the first quarter. Lee and Washington combined to go just 5-for-10 passing, but two completions went for TDs passes and two more covered 26 and 49 yards, keying two of the team's scoring drives. Tech used its two-Quarterback attack masterfully, working them in and out of the lineup and playing to their strengths. High-powered USC finished with 10 first downs and eight punts as Georgia Tech shut down the Trojans' big-play threats all afternoon. USC receiver Marqise Lee, who finished fourth in this year's Heisman voting, was held to six catches for 41 yards. Yellow Jackets cornerback Rod Sweeting had an interception and was the game's MVP. Wittek had four passes deflected at the line. His second interception came in the Tech end zone with 6:22 to go and the last came inside the Tech 10-yard line in the game's final minute. He was 14 for 37 for 107 yards. Georgia Tech cornerback Rod Sweeting was the game's C.M. Hendricks Most Valuable Player of the game. Defensive back Jamal Golden was named the John Folmer Most Valuable Special Teams player, while junior Jay Finch was selected as the Jimmy Rogers, Jr. Most Valuable Lineman.

2012 Chick-Fil-A Peach Bowl

The 2012 Chick-fil-A Bowl was held on December 31, 2012 at the Georgia Dome in Atlanta, Georgia. The 45th edition of the Chick-fil-A Bowl was televised on ESPN. Both Tigers accepted an invitation to the game after achieving a 10–2 regular season record. This was not the first time the two Tigers have met in the Chick-fil-A Bowl; the 1996 game also pitted them against each other, with LSU topping Clemson by a score of 10–7. Their first meeting was the 1958 Sugar Bowl, a national championship that LSU won in a 7-0 shutout.

2012 Chick-Fil-A Peach Bowl	Line	1	-	2	-	3	-	4	-	Final
#9 LSU	(-6.0)	7	-	7	-	10	-	0	-	24
#14 Clemson	(58.0)	7	-	6	-	0	-	12	-	25

Scoring Summary
LSU – Hill 17 yard run (Alleman kick)
Clemson – Boyd 11 yard run (Catanzaro kick)
LSU – Landry 6 yard pass from Mettenberger (Alleman kick)
Clemson – Hopkins 11 yard pass from Boyd (Catanzaro kick)
LSU – Hill 57 yard run (Alleman kick)
LSU – Alleman 24 yard Field goal
Clemson – Catanzaro 26 yard Field goal
Clemson – Hopkins 12 yard pass from Boyd (Pass failed)
Clemson – Catznzaro 37 yard Field goal

Associated Press Chick-Fil-A Peach Bowl Game Summary - Clemson got one last impressive drive from Tajh Boyd and company to record its first 11-win season since its 1981 national championship team. And Tigers coach Dabo Swinney thinks this is only the beginning. Chandler Catanzaro kicked a 37-yard field goal as time expired to give No. 14 Clemson a wild 25-24 win over No. 9 Louisiana State in the Chick-fil-A Bowl on Monday night. Trailing 24-22, Clemson (11-2) took possession on its 20 with 1:39 remaining. Boyd passed to DeAndre Hopkins for 26 yards on a fourth-and-16 play during the decisive 10-play drive. Catanzaro's kick set off a wild celebration on the field and in the stands. Some players collapsed on the field in apparent disbelief while most of Clemson's orange jerseys met in a midfield circle. Clemson reached 11 wins for only the fourth time in school history and the first time since the 12-0 1981 team. Catanzaro had an extra point blocked in the second quarter, but he said that didn't cause him to doubt his chances to make the last-second field goal. Catanzaro, a former walk-on from Greenville, S.C., made 16 of 17 field goals in the regular season. Boyd completed 36 of 50 passes for 346 yards with two touchdowns and no interceptions. He set career highs for attempts and completions while winning the game MVP award. Hopkins, who had 13 catches for 191 yards and two touchdowns, also had receptions for 7 and 13 yards in the final drive. LSU safety Greg Reid was flagged for pass interference while defending Hopkins. Jeremy Hill ran for 124 yards and two touchdowns for LSU (10-3), which carried a 24-13 lead into the final quarter. After Hopkins' second TD catch, LSU got the ball with 2:43 remaining and threw three straight passes. Only one was complete in the three-and-out series that took only about 1 minute off the clock, leaving Clemson with enough time for its winning drive against LSU's exhausted defense. Hill did not have a carry in the fourth quarter. LSU's three passes allowed Swinney to save his timeouts. Boyd said having 1:39 to stage the final drive "is like having 10, 15 minutes for us." LSU Quarterback Zach Mettenberger was sacked six times and completed 14 of 23 passes for 120 yards. He also threw for a touchdown and an interception. LSU scored 10 points off Clemson's two lost fumbles, including one by Sammy Watkins on the second play of the game that set up Hill's first touchdown. Hopkins scored on an 11-yard reception in the second quarter and a 12-yard grab in the fourth. LSU's Bennie Logan blocked Catanzaro's extra point attempt following Hopkins' first touchdown. Clemson had a chance to tie it after Hopkins' second TD, but Boyd's pass for the 2-point conversion was incomplete. Michael Ford had a 43-yard kickoff return for LSU to open the second half. On first down, Hill broke through the line for a 57-yard touchdown run. His 12th rushing touchdown broke Dalton Hilliard's LSU record for a freshman set in 1982. Clemson lost Watkins to a right ankle injury on his early fumble. X-rays were negative. Clemson already was without backup receiver Martavis Bryant, who was suspended for the game for failing to meet academic requirements. Clemson's second costly fumble came midway through the third quarter. Andre Ellington ran for 8 yards but lost the ball when hit by defensive end Sam Montgomery. Reid recovered the fumble at the Clemson 29, setting up Drew Alleman's 20-yard field goal. The injury to Watkins left the spotlight on Hopkins, Clemson's leading receiver. He had catches of 17 and 12 yards as Clemson pulled even with an 11-play drive capped by Boyd's 11-yard touchdown run. After LSU regained the lead on Mettenberger's 6-yard touchdown pass to Jarvis Landry, Hopkins had a 31-yard catch to set up his 11-yard score late in the second quarter. Hopkins' sliding grab gave him TD receptions in 10 straight games to set an Atlantic Coast Conference record. Virginia's Herman Moore had touchdown catches in nine straight games in 1990.

2013 Gator Bowl

The 2013 TaxSlayer.com Gator Bowl was held on January 1, 2013 at EverBank Field in Jacksonville, Florida. The 68th edition of the Gator Bowl was televised on espn2. It featured the Mississippi State Bulldogs from the Southeastern Conference (SEC) against the Northwestern Wildcats from the Big Ten Conference.

2013 Gator Bowl	Line	1	-	2	-	3	-	4	-	Final
Mississippi State	(55.0)	0	-	10	-	3	-	7	-	20
#21 Northwestern	(-1.5)	10	-	3	-	14	-	7	-	34

Scoring Summary
Northwestern - Williams 29 yard interception return (Budzien kick)
Northwestern - Budzien 34 yard Field goal
Northwestern - Budzien 37 yard Field goal
Mississippi State - Bell 27 yard Field goal
Mississippi State - Clark 18 yard pass from Russell (Bell kick)
Mississippi State - Bell 47 yard Field goal
Northwestern - Jones 3 yard run (Budzien kick)
Northwestern - Siemian 4 yard run (Budzien kick)
Mississippi State - Johnson 14 yard pass from Russell (Bell kick)
Northwestern - Mark 3 yard run (Budzien kick)

NUSports.com Gator Bowl Game Summary - Northwestern jumped out to a fast 13-0 lead Tuesday at the 2013 TaxSlayer.com Gator Bowl and rode an NU-bowl-record four interceptions to a 34-20 victory over Mississippi State and a 10-win season. NU's 10-3 record marks the first double-digit win season since the 1995 Big Ten Championship team, of which current head coach Pat Fitzgerald was a member. The Gator Bowl win also gives Fitzgerald his 50th as NU's head coach, making him Northwestern's all-time leader in victories by himself. The game marked NU's 11th all-time bowl appearance and fifth straight. The Wildcats' four interceptions matched the program's previous bowl best set in the 1949 Rose Bowl, which Northwestern won over California. Mississippi State QB Tyler Russell, who was responsible for all four interceptions, had thrown only six picks in the Bulldogs' 12 regular season games this year. With a game-high 10 tackles and a near interception late in the game, Jared Carpenter was named the 2013 Gator Bowl MVP. Offensively, Quarterback and Florida native Trevor Siemian finished 12-of-20 passing for 120 yards -- including several clutch third-down conversions -- and one rushing touchdown. Among his most popular targets on the day was freshman super back Dan Vitale, who led the 'Cats with seven catches for 82 yards. Sophomore Christian Jones also caught five passes for 39 yards. As they have all season, the Wildcats started fast when, on the third play from scrimmage, senior DL Quentin Williams dropped into coverage and intercepted Mississippi State's Tyler Russell. Williams went untouched 24 yards on the return for his first career touchdown and a quick 7-0 Northwestern advantage. The Bulldogs regrouped on their next drive and moved inside the Wildcats red zone, but the NU defense answered the bell again when safety Ibraheim Campbell stepped in front of a Russell pass on the sideline for his fourth career interception. NU moved the ball on its first offensive drive, marching 69 yards on 15 plays before Big Ten Kicker of the year Jeff Budzien stepped on and coolly hit a 34-yard field goal to put NU in front, 10-0. Northwestern forced another three-and-out for the Bulldogs -- a series punctuated when Tyler Scott sniffed out an MSU screen pass to force a loss on third down -- to turn the ball back over to NU. The 'Cats handed the ball to Siemian, who orchestrated a return trip for NU into the red zone. The drive culminated in Budzien's second successful kick of the day, this time a 37-yarder to increase Northwestern's lead to 13-0. The frantic pace of the first half continued when the two teams traded interceptions on consecutive plays early in the second quarter. A Colter screen pass was picked and returned 42 yards to NU's 15-yard line, but on the next play, Quentin Williams got his hand on another pass to deflect it and set up a Chi Chi Ariguzo interception, NU's third of the day. It proved to be the first of two straight drives in which the Northwestern defense stopped the Bulldogs in the red zone. A 59-yard run by Josh Robinson put the Dogs on the 2-yard line, but penalties and stout tackling by the Wildcats forced a field goal that put MSU on the scoreboard. The Bulldogs pulled within three on a tremendous catch in the back of the end zone by Arceto Clark with just 1:06 left before halftime. An interception thrown by the Wildcats on the first series out of the locker room then led to a 47-yard field goal by State's Devon Brown, knotting the score at 13. Needing to respond in a big way, Northwestern received a boost from Trevor Siemian on the ensuing series. Facing third-and-10, Siemian scrambled to his left and side armed a pass to Rashad Lawrence for 12 yards to move the sticks. The next two plays were a 27-yard completion over the middle to Demetrius Fields and a 34-yarder to Dan Vitale down to the 3-yard line. Senior Tyris Jones punched the ball in on the next play to restore a seven-point Wildcats lead. Northwestern kept momentum on its side with another drive directed by both Colter and Siemian, as a 31-yard Colter run placed the ball inside the five. Siemian then ran the read-option to perfection on the next play, walking the ball into the end zone to put NU in front by two touchdowns heading to the final period. Mississippi State cut the lead to seven with a 14-yard touchdown pass early in the fourth and forced a three-and-out on NU's next possession. With momentum shifting, Nick VanHoose stepped in front of a dying quail of a pass before returning it 39 yards to set up an eventual 3-yard Venric Mark scamper that accounted for the final score. On Mississippi State's last gasp drive, both Williams and Scott recorded sacks to set up a Victory Formation that was a long time coming.

2013 Heart of Dallas Bowl

The 2013 Heart of Dallas Bowl was played on January 1, 2013 at the Cotton Bowl in Dallas, Texas. ESPNU carried the game.

2013 Heart of Dallas Bowl	Line	1	-	2	-	3	-	4	-	Final
Purdue	(68.0)	0	-	0	-	7	-	7	-	14
Oklahoma State	(-18.0)	14	-	14	-	17	-	13	-	58

Scoring Summary
Oklahoma State - Moore 4 yard pass from Chelf (Sharp kick)
Oklahoma State - Jackson 7 yard pass from Chelf (Sharp kick)
Oklahoma State - Seaton 16 yard pass from Walsh (Sharp kick)
Oklahoma State - Smith 5 yard run (Sharp kick)
Oklahoma State - Lowe 37 yard fumble return (Sharp kick)
Oklahoma State - Sharp 20 yard Field goal
Oklahoma State - Anderson 37 yard pass from Chelf (Sharp kick)
Purdue - Cottom 32 yard pass from Marve (McCartney kick)
Oklahoma State - Sharp 21 yard Field goal
Oklahoma State - Webb 37 yard pass from Walsh (Sharp kick)
Oklahoma State - Sharp 42 yard Field goal
Purdue - Thomas 16 yard pass from Marve (McCartney kick)

Associated Press Heart of Dallas Bowl Game Summary - So much for the idea that Oklahoma State didn't care about playing in the Heart of Dallas Bowl. Clint Chelf threw three of his team's five touchdown passes and the Cowboys shook off a tough Big 12 finish by rolling up 524 yards and forcing five Purdue turnovers in a dominating 58-14 victory on Tuesday. They put together the biggest bowl win for Oklahoma State since Gundy was the Quarterback in a 62-14 rout of Wyoming in the 1988 Holiday Bowl. Chelf, was 17 of 22 for 197 yards with no interceptions. With former Purdue Quarterbacks Drew Brees and Kyle Orton watching, Robert Marve didn't get to 100 yards passing until Oklahoma State led 45-0 as the Boilermakers (6-7) fell to 0-4 on New Year's Day. The Boilermakers gave the Cowboys short fields on their first two scores after a long punt return from Josh Stewart and the first of Marve's two interceptions. Various mistakes with the game still close in the first half -- a missed field goal, a drop with a receiver behind the defense, and failing to hold on to an easy interception -- ended any hope for Purdue. New coach Darrell Hazell, hired from Kent State, also attended the game. Leading 28-0 at halftime, Oklahoma State erased any lingering doubt three plays into the second half when Justin Gilbert stripped Purdue receiver O.J. Ross on a short completion. The loose ball shot straight to Daytawion Lowe, who ran 37 yards down the sideline in front of the Purdue bench for a 35-0 lead. Lowe's score was the third fumble return for a touchdown at historic Cotton Bowl Stadium dating to the namesake bowl game that started in 1937 and moved to Cowboys Stadium in 2009. Oklahoma State's 58 points were the most in a bowl game at the Fair Park stadium, topping the 55 scored by Keyshawn Johnson and Southern California against Texas Tech in 1995. The Cowboys pushed the lead to 45-0 on Chelf's third touchdown pass, a leaping 37-yard grab in the end zone by Isaiah Anderson, who had 78 yards receiving. Higgins might have unintentionally awakened the Cowboys soon after the late-morning kickoff on a cold, overcast day when he called for a fake punt from Purdue's 13 on its first possession. The Boilermakers got a first down when punter Cody Webster ran 16 yards, but he ended up punting anyway five plays later, and Josh Stewart returned it 64 yards to the Purdue 19 to set up Oklahoma State's first score on a 4-yard pass from Chelf to Charlie Moore. Marve threw his first interception on the next possession, and a 26-yard drive ended with Chelf's 7-yard pass to Blake Jackson. J.W. Walsh had two touchdown passes for Oklahoma State after replacing Chelf in the third quarter, and freshman Wes Lunt, who won the Quarterback job in summer workouts before getting hurt during the season, played the last half of the fourth. Purdue finally scored late in the third quarter when Marve found a wide open Brandon Cottom for a 32-yard touchdown. Marve finished 21 of 34 for 212 yards and two touchdowns and two interceptions but was just 11 of 20 for 80 yards before the first scoring drive. Down 14-0, the Boilermakers had their best chance to score in the first quarter when Akeem Shavers, who had 93 yards rushing, ran 24 yards to the Oklahoma State 23. Shamiel Gary, who earlier intercepted Marve on a tipped pass, made a strong tackle in the open field on third down, and Sam McCartney missed a 34-yard field goal. The Cowboys then went 80 yards the other way, sparked by a 26-yard completion to Jackson. Oklahoma State scored on fourth-and-1 when Walsh, the short-yardage specialist, replaced Chelf and threw a 16-yard scoring pass to Jeremy Seaton.

2013 Outback Bowl

The 2013 Outback Bowl, the 27th edition of the game, held on January 1, 2013, at the Raymond James Stadium in Tampa, Florida. The game, which was telecast on ESPN.

2013 Outback Bowl	Line	1	-	2	-	3	-	4	-	Final
#11 South Carolina	(-5.5)	14	-	7	-	0	-	12	-	33
#19 Michigan	(47.5)	3	-	10	-	9	-	6	-	28

Scoring Summary
South Carolina – Byrd 56 yard pass from Shaw (Yates kick)
Michigan – Gibbons 39 yard Field goal
South Carolina – Sanders 63 yard punt return (Yates kick)
Michigan – Dileo 5 yard pass from Gardner (Gibbons kick)
South Carolina – Sanders 4 yard pass from Thompson (Yates kick)
Michigan – Gibbons 40 yard Field goal
Michigan – Wile 52 yard Field goal
Michigan – Gallon 10 yard pass from Gardner (Pass failed)
South Carolina – Sanders 31 yard pass from Shaw (Pass failed)
Michigan – Gallon 17 yard pass from Gardner (Run failed)
South Carolina – Ellington 32 yard pass from Thompson (Pass failed)

Associated Press Outback Bowl Game Summary - Steve Spurrier's plan to use two Quarterbacks in the Outback Bowl worked so well that Dylan Thompson and Connor Shaw both earned game balls. That's a first for the Head Ball Coach, who has a well-known penchant for benching struggling QBs. Except in this case, the Gamecocks' winningest coach used his talented pair of passers by design. Shaw began Tuesday's 33-28 victory over Michigan with a 56-yard touchdown pass to Damiere Byrd. Thompson closed it out by throwing a 32-yard TD strike to Bruce Ellington in the final minute to help South Carolina match the school record for victories in a season. Thompson replaced Shaw during the winning drive, covering the final 43 yards after Shaw began the march from his own 30 and kept it alive with a 6-yard completion to Ace Sanders on a fourth-and-3 play. Devin Gardner's third TD pass of the game had given Michigan a 28-27 lead. Shaw threw for 227 yards and two touchdowns after missing the Gamecocks' regular-season finale with a left foot sprain. Thompson led the Gamecocks (11-2) to a victory at archrival Clemson and threw for 117 yards and two TDs in the bowl. Gardner threw for 214 yards in his fifth start for Michigan (8-5) since Denard Robinson injured his right elbow late in the season. Robinson took some snaps at Quarterback and even attempted his first passes in a game since Oct. 27 but lined up mostly at running back and rushed for 100 yards on 23 carries. Sanders caught TD passes of 4 yards from Thompson and 31 yards from Shaw, who completed 18 of 26 passes before aggravating his foot injury and limping off during the final drive. The speedy receiver had nine catches for 92 yards and scored on a 63-yard punt return — one of four plays over 50 yards yielded by Michigan. Gardner was 18 of 36, including TD passes of 5 yards to Drew Dileo and 10 and 17 yards to Jeremy Gallon, who gave Michigan its late lead and finished with career bests of nine receptions and 145 yards. Robinson set the NCAA record for career yards rushing by a Quarterback, hiking his four-year total to 4,495 — 15 more than West Virginia's Pat White ran for from 2005-08. Robinson attempted two passes in the third quarter, both incompletions, and also ran twice on plays in which he took the snap as the Quarterback — a role he's embraced since being injured during a loss to Nebraska. South Carolina defensive end Jadeveon Clowney was quiet for much of the day but shifted momentum in the fourth quarter with a big hit on Vincent Smith that sent the running back's helmet rolling several yards backward and caused a fumble that the SEC defensive player of the year recovered to set up Shaw's TD pass to Sanders for a 27-22 lead. The TD capped a three-play sequence that began with Michigan running its second fake punt of the game, gaining 4 yards to the Wolverines 41 for what was ruled a first down, despite not appearing be one when the officials called for a measurement. South Carolina challenged the spot, but the ruling on the field was upheld. Clowney then slammed into Smith just as the Michigan runner was taking the handoff from Gardner, jarring the ball loose. Robinson was injured during the first half of Michigan's two-touchdown loss to Nebraska on Oct. 27. He missed the rest of that game, as well the next two against Minnesota and Northwestern before returning the final two weeks of the regular season to contribute in ways that didn't require him to throw the ball. Gardner threw 26 yards to Gallon, moving the Wolverines into position for Brendan Gibbons to kick a 39-yard field goal. Down 14-3 after Sanders' punt return, Michigan marched 75 yards in 11 plays to trim South Carolina's lead to four, with Robinson carrying four times for 20 yards along the way. Gardner finished the drive by flipping his touchdown pass to Dileo early in the second quarter. Michigan began the day ranked second in the nation in pass defense, allowing 155 yards per game. South Carolina matched that in the opening half alone, with most of the yardage coming on Shaw's long TD throw to Byrd and Thompson's 70-yard completion to Jones that led to Sanders' second TD for a 21-10 lead. The Wolverines turned South Carolina's only turnover into Gibbons' 40-yard field goal in the second quarter, and Matt Wile's Outback Bowl-record 52-yard field goal trimmed Michigan's deficit to 21-16. South Carolina ended on a five-game winning streak that followed consecutive losses to LSU and Florida. The Gamecocks also won 11 games last season.

The Hit - "The Hit" is widely considered to mark the turning point in the game for South Carolina and it earned a "Best Play" ESPY Award for South Carolina's Jadeveon Clowney. "The Hit" refers to a play by Defensive End Jadeveon Clowney which occurred midway during the fourth quarter of play. After a Wolverines fake punt, followed by a controversial call awarding Michigan a first down during a critical time consuming drive, Clowney gained instant fame for his violent tackle of Michigan running back Vincent Smith that came with 8:21 remaining in the fourth quarter. "The Hit" dislodged Smith's helmet and forced a fumble that Clowney himself recovered, "The Hit" set up a touchdown pass to wide receiver Ace Sanders on the next play. Although "The Hit" itself did not result in the game winning touchdown, it is considered by many to have motivated a previously lethargic Gamecock offense to rally and ultimately win the game.

2013 Capital One Bowl

The 2013 Capital One Bowl, the 67th edition of the game, was held on January 1, 2013 at the Citrus Bowl in Orlando, Florida. The game, which was broadcast on ABC. Entering the game both teams suffered a loss at their respective conference championship games. The Georgia Bulldogs, winners of the SEC Eastern Division, were ranked #3 in the BCS going into the game. They lost to #2 Alabama 32–28. Meanwhile, the Nebraska Cornhuskers, winners of the Big Ten Legends Division, were ranked #12 going into the game. They lost to unranked Wisconsin 70–31.

2013 Capital One Bowl	Line	1	-	2	-	3	-	4	-	Final
#6 Georgia	(-9.5)	16	-	7	-	8	-	14	-	45
#23 Nebraska	(62.0)	14	-	10	-	7	-	0	-	31

Scoring Summary
Georgia - Team safety
Georgia - Lynch 29 yard pass from Murray (M. Morgan kick)
Nebraska - Turner 14 yard pass from Martinez (Maher kick)
Nebraska - Compton 24 yard interception return (Maher kick)
Georgia - King 75 yard pass from Murray (Morgan kick)
Georgia - Gurley 24 yard run (Morgan kick)
Nebraska - Maher 39 yard field goal
Nebraska - Burkhead 16 yard pass from Martinez (Maher kick)
Nebraska - Burkhead 2 yard run (Maher kick)
Georgia - Conley 49 yard pass from Murray (McGowan pass from Murray)
Georgia - Marshall 24 yard pass from Murray (Morgan kick)
Georgia - Conley 87 yard pass from Murray (Morgan kick)

Nebraska Athletics Communications Capital One Bowl Game Summary - No. 16 Nebraska hung tough with No. 7 Georgia for three quarters, but a pair of Bulldog touchdown passes in the fourth quarter provided the margin in the Huskers' 45-31 loss in the Capital One Bowl. Nebraska ended its 2012 campaign with a 10-4 overall record that included a 7-1 Big Ten mark and a Legends Division title. Georgia, the SEC runner-up, finished with a 12-2 overall mark. Senior I-back Rex Burkhead led the Huskers with 140 yards and a touchdown on 25 carries, while adding four receptions for 39 yards and another score in his final game as a Husker. Burkhead, who produced his 14th 100-yard rushing performance, closed his career with 3,329 yards at No. 5 on Nebraska's all-time rushing list. He also became the 10th player in NU history with 30 career rushing touchdowns. Burkhead's 357 rushing yards on 76 attempts in four bowl games are both Nebraska records. Burkhead fueled a Nebraska running attack that rolled up 239 yards against Georgia's defense. Junior Quarterback Taylor Martinez added 46 yards on the ground to push his season rushing total past 1,000 yards. He finished with 1,019 rushing yards in 2012 as just the fourth Husker Quarterback to produce a 1,000-yard campaign. Martinez also completed 16-of-27 passes for 204 yards and two touchdowns, finishing his junior year with 2,871 passing yards for the third-best total in school history. His 3,890 total yards on the year set a Nebraska record. The Huskers ended the day with 443 yards of total offense against the Bulldogs, but Georgia responded with 589 yards of its own, including 427 yards and five touchdown passes from Quarterback Aaron Murray. Running back Todd Gurley added 119 yards and a score on the ground to lead a UGA attack that managed 160 rushing yards. Murray's pass on the first play of the fourth quarter went for a 24-yard touchdown to Keith Marshall to give UGA a 38-31 lead with 14:52 left, after the two teams entered the final quarter tied at 31. Georgia's defense then forced a three-and-out on the Huskers' first drive of the fourth quarter. UGA started the next drive at its own 15 and faced a 3rd-and-12 from the 13. But Murray hit Chris Conley on a short route across the middle and the speedster raced 87 yards untouched down the middle of the field for the game's final score with 11:03 left. The play was the longest from scrimmage by a Husker opponent in a bowl game, and the third-longest touchdown pass ever against Nebraska. Nebraska had two more chances to answer in the final quarter and drove into Georgia territory on both drives before being turned away. Georgia's special teams opened the scoring with a safety on a blocked punt just 3:21 into the game. The Bulldogs added a 29-yard pass from Murray to Arthur Lynch on the ensuing drive to take a 9-0 lead with 7:54 left in the first quarter. Martinez and the Huskers answered with a seven-play, 75-yard drive capped by Jamal Turner's 14-yard touchdown catch with 4:42 left. Turner finished with three receptions for 22 yards on the day. The Huskers took their first lead of the game on Georgia's next drive, as senior linebacker Will Compton made an outstanding interception on a screen pass from Murray. Compton raced 24 yards to the end zone with his first career interception to put the Huskers up 14-9 with 4:15 left in the opening quarter. Compton added a team-high nine tackles for the Blackshirts on the day. Georgia struck quickly to regain the lead on its next drive, as Murray heaved a 75-yard touchdown pass to Tavarres King on the first play of the ensuing drive. Husker defensive back Andrew Green was in perfect position to bat the ball away but was unable to knock it down as it fell into King's hands. King closed the day with three catches for 104 yards for the Bulldogs as one of two UGA receivers to cross the century mark. Georgia took a 16-14 lead to the second quarter and pushed the lead back to nine on Gurley's 24-yard touchdown run. Bulldog defender Damian Swann set up UGA with a short field after pulling down the first of his two interceptions of Martinez in the game. The Huskers responded with a 39-yard field goal from Brett Maher to cut the Georgia lead to 23-17 with 8:48 left in the half. The field goal also gave Maher NU's single season scoring record by a kicker. He added two more extra points in the game to finish his senior year with 119, eclipsing Kris Brown's previous school mark of 116 points in 1997. The Blackshirts stopped the Bulldogs on the ensuing drive and Burkhead took over. After Burkhead carried three straight times for a total of 13 yards to open the drive, Martinez found Kenny Bell for a 35-yard completion down the middle of the field. After a one-yard dive by Ameer Abdullah and a tack-on 11-yard facemask penalty by the Bulldogs, Martinez found Burkhead wide open down the middle for the go-ahead touchdown. Maher's extra point sent the Huskers to halftime with a 24-23 lead. Nebraska started the second half with the ball and immediately mounted the game's most sustained drive. Burkhead carried six times for 18 yards on the march, including a two-yard plunge for pay dirt to give NU a 31-23 edge with 9:36 left in the third quarter. Martinez also carried three times for 16 yards on the drive, while completing two passes for 17 yards to Bell, who finished with four catches for 60 yards on the day. Abdullah added the biggest play of the drive with his nifty 26-yard burst from the middle to the left side. The I-back finished the game with seven carries for 48 yards and closed the season with 1,137 rushing yards - the sixth-most by a sophomore in Husker history. But Nebraska's lead was short-lived, as Georgia answered with a five-play, 79-yard drive capped by Murray's 49-yard scoring strike to Conley. Conley finished with a game-high 136 receiving yards and two touchdowns on his two catches. Murray's two-point conversion pass to Rhett McGowan tied the game at 31 with 7:20 left in the quarter. The two defenses took control for the remainder of the third quarter, before Georgia produced the game's two decisive touchdown passes in the final 15 minutes.

2013 Rose Bowl

The 2013 Rose Bowl, the 99th edition of the annual game, was played on Tuesday, January 1, 2013 at the Rose Bowl Stadium in Pasadena, California. The Pasadena Tournament of Roses Association is the organizer of the game. The game matched Big Ten Conference Champions Wisconsin Badgers against the Pac-12 Conference Champions Stanford Cardinal, a rematch of the same two teams in the 2000 Rose Bowl.

2013 Rose Bowl	Line	1	-	2	-	3	-	4	-	Final
Wisconsin	(47.0)	0	-	14	-	0	-	0	-	14
#8 Stanford	(-4.0)	14	-	3	-	0	-	3	-	20

Scoring Summary
Stanford – Young 16 yard run (Williamson kick)
Stanford – Taylor 3 yard run (Williamson kick)
Wisconsin – Ball 11 yard run (Russell kick)
Stanford – Williamson 47 yard field goal
Wisconsin – Fredrick 4 yard pass from Phillips (Russell kick)
Stanford – Williamson 22-yard field goal

Milwaukee Journal-Sentinel Rose Bowl Game Recap - Barry Alvarez and the Wisconsin players no doubt earned respect with their gritty performance in the 99th Rose Bowl against favored Stanford. Yet as they had too many times during the 2012 season, the Badgers failed to make the plays they needed in the closing minutes and failed to steal a victory that was within reach. This loss, a 20-14 decision to the No. 8 Cardinal on Tuesday, came in front of a crowd of 93,359 and will burn more than any of the other near-misses the Badgers suffered during a tumultuous season that saw head coach Bret Bielema leave for

Arkansas three days after the Big Ten title game. Stanford (12-2) jumped out to a 14-0 first-quarter lead by out-scheming and out-executing UW's defense on touchdown drives of 80 and 79 yards; added two critical field goals from Jordan Williamson from 47 and 22 yards; and shut down UW's offense in the final two quarters after the Badgers had pulled to within 17-14 by halftime. As a result, Stanford won its first Rose Bowl title since the 1972 game. UW (8-6), which finished 2-5 during the regular season in games decided by seven points or fewer, lost in the Rose Bowl for the third consecutive season. As a result, Alvarez saw his Rose Bowl record fall to 3-1. UW's final chance ended with Quarterback Curt Phillips, who had made big plays with his arm and his feet, turning the ball over with 2 minutes 3 seconds left and UW trailing by six points. After Williamson's 22-yard field goal gave the Cardinal a 20-14 lead with 4:23 left, UW moved from its 25 to the Stanford 49. Facing second and 5, Phillips tried to hit tight end Jacob Pedersen over the middle. The ball was tipped at the line of scrimmage by defensive lineman Josh Mauro, however, and nickel back Usua Amanam made a diving interception at the Cardinal 42 with 2:03 left. Tailback Stepfan Taylor, who carried 20 times for 88 yards and one touchdown and was named offensive player of the game, carried three times for 14 yards after the turnover to help the Cardinal run out the clock. Quarterback Kevin Hogan hurt UW with his arm (12 of 19 for 123 yards) and his feet (seven carries, 54 yards). Stanford's defense did the most damage, however. The Cardinal limited tailback Montee Ball to 13 yards on seven carries in the second half and to 100 yards and a touchdown on 24 carries. Ball needed 150 yards to surpass former UW tailback Ron Dayne as the all-time leading rusher in the Rose Bowl. Phillips, who had a 38-yard run to set up UW's second touchdown, completed 10 of 16 passes for 83 yards and a touchdown. That was a 4-yard strike to Jordan Fredrick to help UW pull within 17-14 at halftime. Stanford limited UW to 82 yards on 25 plays in the second half after surrendering 219 yards on 37 plays in the first half. Phillips completed 7 of 8 passes for 68 yards and a touchdown in the first half. After halftime, he completed 3 of 8 attempts for 15 yards. Stanford's defense made big plays throughout. Tailback James White was stuffed for no gain on fourth and goal from the 1 in the first half, and Ball was stuffed for no gain on third and 1 from the UW 23 with 11:20 left in the game. The Badgers overcame the first stop by forcing Stanford to punt and then driving 49 yards for their first touchdown, an 11-yard run by Ball. They couldn't overcome the second stop, which occurred when nose tackle David Parry blew past center Travis Frederick to hit Ball. Stanford took advantage of a 15-yard penalty on Shelton Johnson for fair-catch interference to start from its 44. The Cardinal drove to the UW 5 before the drive stalled and Williamson kicked his second field goal of the game for a 20-14 lead. That set the stage for UW's final possession. UW had the chance to drive for a game-winning touchdown to make one last statement that it was better than its record entering the day. Stanford, 7-2 in games decided by seven points or fewer before Tuesday, instead made the victory-clinching play.
Game notes - Wisconsin Running back Montee Ball became the first player in Rose Bowl Game history to score a touchdown in three straight years. No touchdown scored in the second half for the first time since 1958, when Ohio State defeated Oregon, 10–7. (The last first half without a TD was in 2007, when USC and Michigan were tied, 3–3.) Stanford Head Coach David Shaw became the first African American head coach to win a Rose Bowl, as well as a BCS game.

2013 Orange Bowl

The 2013 Discover Orange Bowl was played on Tuesday, January 1, 2013, at Sun Life Stadium in Miami Gardens, Florida. The Orange Bowl featured ACC champions Florida State versus at-large selection and MAC champions Northern Illinois. The Florida State Seminoles clinched a berth in the 2013 Orange Bowl by winning the 2012 ACC Championship. The Northern Illinois Huskies became the first MAC team to earn a BCS berth by being the 15th ranked team in the nation. The Huskies, winners of the 2012 MAC Championship Game, became the first team from the MAC to make a BCS bowl.

2013 Orange Bowl	Line	1	-	2	-	3	-	4	-	Final
#16 Northern Illinois	(59.0)	3	-	0	-	7	-	0	-	10
#13 Florida State	(-14.0)	7	-	7	-	3	-	14	-	31

Scoring Summary
Florida State – Pryor 60 yard run (Hopkins kick)
Northern Illinois – Sims 25 yard Field goal
Florida State – Greene 6 yard pass from Manuel (Hopkins kick)
Florida State – Hopkins 25 yard Field goal
Northern Illinois – Moore 11 yard pass from Lynch (Sims kick)
Florida State – Manuel 9 yard run (Hopkins kick)
Florida State – Pryor 37 yard run (Hopkins kick)

Chicago Tribune Orange Bowl Recap - It wasn't a lost cause, but a loss on the field for Northern Illinois, which crashed the Orange Bowl party as unwanted guests from the Mid-American Conference and fell Tuesday night to favored Florida State 31-10. Jordan Lynch, the proclaimed "tough kid from the South

Side of Chicago," hoped to will himself and his NIU teammates to an upset victory before the crowd of 72,073 at Sun Life Stadium. But Lynch struggled to get anything going consistently and wound up completing just 15 of 41 passes for 176 yards and one touchdown. He was intercepted once. He also carried the ball for an Orange Bowl Quarterback-record 23 times but gained just 44 yards. Rod Carey was notably upset after the loss as his first game as head coach snapped NIU's 12-game winning streak. Florida State fullback Lonnie Pryor was named Orange Bowl MVP after rushing for 134 yards on five carries. He scored touchdowns on runs of 60 and 37 yards. Florida State led 14-3 at the half, but NIU pulled to within 17-10 going into the fourth quarter. After recovering an onside kick, NIU had the ball driving into Florida State territory in the third quarter when Terrence Brooks intercepted a Lynch pass and returned it 20 yards. The scoring began after Lynch punted 52 yards on fourth down from a shotgun formation to the Florida State 5-yard line. One play later, James Wilder Jr. ran the ball to the 20 and then Quarterback EJ Manuel hit Greg Dent for a 20-yard completion. Pryor took the next handoff and darted 60 yards for a touchdown with 5 minutes, 28 seconds remaining in the first quarter to give the Seminoles a 7-0 lead. The Florida State fullback never had had a run longer than 49 yards entering the Orange Bowl. Mathew Sims booted a 25-yard field goal to pull NIU within 7-3 late in the first quarter. The score was set up by a fake punt on fourth down when a short snap from center went to freshman Desroy Maxwell, who ran 35 yards to the Seminoles' 33. Florida State scored again with 11 seconds left in the half on a 6-yard Manuel strike to Rashad Greene that capped a 10-play, 82-yard drive to take a 14-3 lead. The Seminoles took the second-half kickoff and drove 68 yards on nine plays before Dustin Hopkins added a 25-yard field goal to extend the lead to 17-3. NIU pulled to within 17-10 on an 11-yard touchdown pass from Lynch to Martel Moore in the third quarter that culminated a six-play, 87-yard drive. The big plays were a 55-yard pass from Lynch to Akeem Daniels and a 22-yard Lynch run. The Huskies' Paris Logan then recovered Tyler Wedel's onside kick, but Lynch turned the ball over on an interception in Florida State territory. Florida State all but put the game away with an eight-play, 61-yard drive that ended when Manuel rushed for a touchdown four seconds into the final quarter for a 24-10 lead. Northern Illinois coughed it up on the next possession. Two plays later, Pryor scored from 37 yards out to make it 31-10.

2013 Sugar Bowl

The 2013 Allstate Sugar Bowl was played on Wednesday, January 2, 2013, at the Mercedes-Benz Superdome in New Orleans, Louisiana. Louisville was selected to their first Sugar Bowl after a 10-2 regular season that culminated in a share of the Big East title. Florida was picked as the other half of the matchup following an 11–1 campaign. As two touchdown underdogs, the Louisville Cardinals beat the Gators 33-23. In recognition of his performance during the game, Louisville Quarterback Teddy Bridgewater was named the game's most valuable player.

2013 Sugar Bowl	Line	1	-	2	-	3	-	4	-	Final
#22 Louisville	(47.0)	14	-	10	-	6	-	3	-	33
#4 Florida	(-14.0)	0	-	10	-	0	-	13	-	23

Scoring Summary
Louisville – Floyd 32 yard interception return (Wallace kick)
Louisville - Wright 1 yard run (Wallace kick)
Florida –Sturgis 33 yard field goal
Louisville – Wallace 27 yard field goal
Louisville - Parker 15 yard pass from Bridgewater (Wallace kick)
Florida - Jones 1 yard run (Sturgis kick)
Louisville - Copeland 19 yard pass from Bridgewater (Kick blocked)
Louisville – Wallace 30 yard field goal
Florida – DeBose 100 yard Kickoff return (Sturgis kick)
Florida - Taylor 5 yard pass from Driskel (Pass failed)

Sugar Bowl Recap by Sugar Bowl historian Marty Mulé

It was no fluke. This Sugar Bowl belonged to Louisville from start to finish. Terrell Floyd's 38-yard interception return on the game's first play set the tone; and the Gators never fully recovered. It was 14-0 after Louisville's first offensive possession, when star Quarterback Teddy Bridgewater, who constantly bought time with nimble foot work throughout the night, and completed 10 of his first 11 passes, drove his team 83 yards to the Florida 1, where Jeremy Wright scored on the ground. From then on, the Gators could get no closer than the 10-point margin in which the 79th Sugar Bowl ended. The Cardinals soared to a 24-10 halftime lead, and so flummoxed were the Gators that they started the second half with an on-sides kick - unsuccessful and made worse with two personal fouls on Florida. Bridgewater connected with Damon Copeland in the end zone and Louisville had a 30-10 lead 12 seconds into the second half. Florida would miss a pair of field goals, making its task harder, but after John Wallace kicked a 30-yard field goal for the

Cardinals in the fourth quarter, Gator speedster Andre Debose returned the kickoff 100 yards to keep Florida within range of a football miracle. With time starting to run out, Florida Quarterback Jeff Driskel - recruited over Bridgewater two years before - guided his team 97 yards. With 2:13 remaining Driskel hit Kent Taylor with a two-yard touchdown pass. The Gators had scored 13 fourth-quarter points and now had an outside chance to make up a 10-point deficit and stave off an embarrassing defeat. Improbably, they would need a two-point conversion at this point, then a successful on-sides kick, another touchdown and another two-point conversion to send the game into overtime - and avoid the stigma of becoming the biggest favorite ever to lose, not only in the Sugar but in any of the major postseason pairings in the 15-year BCS era. Driskel took the snap and rolled out to look for another open receiver. But defensive back Marcus Smith shot in untouched and sacked Driskel - effectively ending the game, securing the 22nd-ranked Cardinals' greatest victory and dooming No. 3 Florida to a humiliating setback. In the end, Louisville outhit, outsmarted, and outexecuted its more heralded opponents for the entire night. After the 24-10 halftime lead, the Cardinals never allowed the Gators to muster one of their patented second-half surges. The discombobulated Gators turned the ball over three times, and committed nine penalties for 98 yards, including one on their bench for unsportsmanlike conduct. On this night Bridgewater thoroughly outplayed the Quarterback the Gators signed instead of him (Driskel was 16-of-29 for 179 yards with a pair of costly interceptions). Bridgewater was 20-of-32 for 206 yards and two touchdowns. Louisville cornerback Andrew Johnson, who had one of two interceptions of Driskel. The game opened with a memorable coin toss as Florida was represented by the NFL's all-time leading rusher, Emmitt Smith, and 1997 Heisman Trophy winner Danny Wuerffel, while Louisville was represented by former football great Tom Jackson, as well as the man known as "The Greatest of All-Time," Louisville native Muhammad Ali.

2013 Fiesta Bowl

The 2013 Tostitos Fiesta Bowl was played on Thursday, January 3, 2013, at University of Phoenix Stadium in Glendale, Arizona. This was the only bowl game of the season to feature two top-10 ranked teams, other than the 2013 BCS National Championship Game. The game was televised on ESPN.

Conversion safety scored - An extremely rare type of football scoring occurred during the third quarter on an attempted Oregon extra point, a one-point conversion safety. The one point safety was awarded to Oregon after Kansas State ended the play while in possession of the ball in the end zone after blocking Oregon's extra point attempt. This was only the second one-point safety scored in the history of NCAA FBS competition; the other was converted by Texas A&M against Texas on November 26, 2004. Coincidentally, ESPN's Brad Nessler served as the play-by-play commentator for both games.

2013 Fiesta Bowl	Line	1	-	2	-	3	-	4	-	Final
#5 Oregon	(-8.0)	15	-	7	-	10	-	3	-	35
#7 Kansas State	(74.0)	0	-	10	-	0	-	7	-	17

Scoring Summary
Oregon – Thomas 94 yard kickoff return (Jordan run)
Oregon – Thomas 23 yard pass from Mariota (Maldonado kick)
Kansas State – Klein 6 yard run (Cantele kick)
Kansas State – Cantele 25 yard Field goal
Oregon – Barner 25 yard pass from Mariota (Maldonado kick)
Oregon – Maldonado 32 yard Field goal
Oregon – Mariota 2 yard run (Kick blocked)
Oregon – Blocked PAT recovered by defense outside end zone and tackled in end zone for one-point conversion safety
Kansas State – Hubert 10 yard pass from Klein (Cantele kick)
Oregon – Maldonado 24 yard Field goal

Associated Press Fiesta Bowl Game Summary - De'Anthony Thomas caught the opening kickoff, raced past Oregon's sideline and leaned his head into the end zone like a sprinter crossing the finish line. The track meet had started, and the fifth-ranked Ducks barely looked back after that. Triggered by Thomas' 94-yard return, Oregon bolted by No. 7 Kansas State 35-17 Thursday night at the Fiesta Bowl in what may have been coach Chip Kelly's final game with the Ducks. Teams that had that national title aspirations end on the same day, Oregon and Kansas State ended up in the desert for a marquee matchup billed as a battle of styles: The fast-flying Ducks vs. the execution-is-everything Wildcats. With Kelly reportedly talking to several NFL teams, Oregon (12-1) was too much for Kansas State and its Heisman Trophy finalist, Collin Klein, turning the game into a try-to-keep up race from the start. Thomas followed his before-everyone-sat-down kickoff return with a 23-yard touchdown catch, finishing with 195 total yards. Kenjon Barner ran for 143 yards on 31 carries and scored on a 24-yard touchdown pass from Marcus Mariota in the second quarter. Mariota later scored on a 2-yard run in the third quarter, capped by an obscure 1-point safety that went in the Ducks' favor. Even Oregon's defense got into the act, intercepting Klein twice and holding him to 30 yards on 13 carries. Whether Kelly leaves Eugene or not, he had a good run, leading the Ducks to four straight trips to BCS bowls, the last two wins. Ducks fans sure let him know how they felt, chanting "We want Chip!" just before he was handed the massive Fiesta Bowl trophy. Last year's Fiesta Bowl was an offensive fiesta, with Oklahoma State outlasting Stanford 41-38 in overtime. The 2013 version was an upgrade: Nos. 4 and 5 in the BCS, two of the nation's best offenses, dynamic players and superbly successful coaches on both sides. Oregon has become the standard for go-go-go football under Kelly, its fleet of Ducks making those shiny helmets -- green like Christmas tree bulbs for the Fiesta Bowl -- and flashy uniforms blur across the grassy landscape. Their backfield of Thomas, Barner and Mariota made up a three-headed monster of momentum, each one capable of turning a single play into a scoring drive of 60 seconds or less. Mariota has been the show-running leader, a question mark before the season who ably ran Oregon's high-octane offense as the first freshman Quarterback to start for the Ducks since Danny O'Neil in 1991. Oregon won the Rose Bowl for the first time in 95 years last season and was in position for a spot in the BCS title game this year before losing a heartbreaker to Stanford on Nov. 17. Thomas offered the first flash of speed, picking up a couple of blocks and racing toward a not-so-photo finish at the line. The Ducks, are they are apt to do, went for 2 on the point-after and converted on a trick play to go up 8-0 in the game's first 12 seconds. It was the second straight day a BCS bowl began with a quick strike; Louisville returned an interception for a touchdown against Florida on the first play of the Sugar Bowl Wednesday night. Thomas hit the Wildcats (11-2) again late in the first quarter, breaking a couple of tackles and dragging three defenders into the end zone for a catch-and-run TD that put the Ducks up 15-0. It's nothing new for Oregon's sophomore sensation: He had 314 total yards, and two long touchdown runs in the 2012 Rose Bowl. The Ducks are used to it, too, after averaging more than 50 points per game. And they kept flying. Oregon followed a missed 40-yard field goal by Kansas State's Anthony Canteleby unleashing one of its blink-and-you'll-miss-it scoring drives late in the second quarter. Moving 77 yards in 46 seconds, the Ducks went up 22-10 at halftime after Mariota hit Barner on 24-yard TD pass. Alejandro Maldonado hit a 33-yard field goal on Oregon's opening drive of the third quarter and Mariota capped a long drive with an easy 2-yard TD run to the left. Kansas State's Javonta Boyd blocked the point-after attempt, but even that went wrong for the Wildcats: Chris Harper was tackled in the end zone for a bizarre 1-point safety that put Oregon up 32-10. It was the first 1-point safety in major college football since 2004 when Texas did it against Texas A&M, STATS said. Kansas State had gone through its second revival under Snyder, the studious coach who never lost touch with the game or players young enough to be his grandchildren during a three-year retirement. The 73-year-old followed up the Manhattan Miracle by returning to lead the Wildcats back to national prominence with his attention-to-detail ways. Klein has led K-State's meticulous march this season, a fifth-year senior who plays in the mold of the college version of Tim Tebow: Gritty, humble, finds a way to win, whatever it takes. Like the Ducks, the Wildcats had their national title hopes stamped out on Nov. 17, blown out by Baylor with a rare letdown on both sides of the ball. Kansas State needed a little time to get its wheels spinning on offense, laboring early before Klein scored on a 6-yard run early in the second quarter. Klein kept the Wildcats moving in the quarter, though not toward touchdowns: Cantele hit a 25-yard field goal and missed from 40 after a false-start penalty. Klein hit John Hubert on a 10-yard touchdown pass early in the fourth quarter, but all that did was cut Oregon's lead down to 32-17. He threw for 151 yards on 17 of 32 passing.

2013 Cotton Bowl Classic

The 2013 AT&T Cotton Bowl Classic was held on January 4, 2013 at Cowboys Stadium in Arlington, Texas. The 77th edition of the Cotton Bowl Classic was televised on FOX. Both the Aggies and the Sooners accepted their invitations after finishing the regular season 10–2. The pre-game buildup was primarily focused on the two high-powered offenses, both of whom were led by strong passing attacks led by Quarterbacks Johnny Manziel and Landry Jones respectively. Both teams also had several quality wide receivers, but both were average to below average defensively. Experts were split in their prognostications, but most predicted a high-scoring game. Texas A&M defeated Oklahoma 41–13 to win the Cotton Bowl Classic and to finish the season with an 11–2 record. Manziel rushed for 229 yards during the game, a bowl record, rushing for two touchdowns and throwing for two more. Though the halftime score was 14–13 Texas A&M, the Aggies went on to score 27 unanswered second half points to win the game.

2013 Cotton Bowl Classic	Line	1	-	2	-	3	-	4	-	Final
#10 Texas A&M	(-3.0)	7	-	7	-	20	-	7	-	41
#12 Oklahoma	(72.0)	3	-	10	-	0	-	0	-	13

Scoring Summary
Texas A&M – Manziel 23 yard run (Bertolet kick)
Oklahoma – Hunnicutt 23 yard Field goal
Oklahoma – Hunnicutt 24 yard Field goal
Texas A&M – Manziel 5 yard run (Bertolet kick)
Oklahoma – Brown 6 yard pass from Jones (Hunnicutt kick)
Texas A&M – Malena 7 yard run (Bertolet kick)
Texas A&M – Williams 30 yard run (Kick failed)
Texas A&M – Swope 33 yard pass from Manziel (Hunnicutt kick)
Texas A&M – Nwachukwa 34 yard pass from Manziel (Hunnicutt kick)

Cotton Bowl Classic Game Summary - Another chapter can be added to the legend of Johnny Football after the talented freshman Quarterback dazzled over 87,000 fans at Cowboys Stadium and helped guide Texas A&M to a dominating 41-13 win over Oklahoma in the 77th AT&T Cotton Bowl Classic. On the game's opening drive, Texas A&M fans let out a thunderous roar when Manziel avoided numerous Oklahoma defenders and set the tempo with an explosive 24-yard run. Just two plays later, Manziel called his own number again and scampered for 23 more yards, but this time, he tiptoed down the sideline and leaped into the end zone to give the Aggies an early 7-0 lead. It was a played that can be described as simply amazing - something Manziel has been all season. Manziel accounted for four total touchdowns and finished the game with 229 yards on the ground and 287 yards passing enroute to being named Offensive MVP. His 516 yards of total offense broke former Texas Tech Quarterback Graham Harrell's Cotton Bowl record. The 2012 Heisman Trophy winner continued to rewrite the record book as he also set the all-time FBS bowl mark for most rushing yards by a Quarterback. But it was freshman running back Trey Williams who broke the game open with 6:30 remaining in the third quarter. The true freshman, who just a year ago helped Spring Dekaney win the 5A Division II state title at Cowboys Stadium, found a hole and dashed 30 yards to give the Aggies a commanding 27-13 lead. On the ensuing Texas A&M possession, Manziel continued to work his magic and found Ryan Swope for a 33-yard touchdown on a key fourth down. Swope led Texas A&M with eight receptions for 104 yards and became the school's all-time leading receiver in terms of yards. Midway through the fourth quarter, Manziel hammered the final nail in the coffin and put the Aggies up 41-13 with his second touchdown pass of the night, a 34-yard strike to Uzoma Nwachukwu. Oklahoma Quarterback Landry Jones set his own Cotton Bowl record with 23 completions in the first half. His biggest completion of the night came just before halftime when he cut the Texas A&M lead to one on a 6-yard touchdown pass to Justin Brown. But Jones and the entire Oklahoma offense struggled to get anything going in the second half, failing to pick up a first down on their first three possessions in the third quarter. The Sooners showed signs of life early in the game when Harris picked off a Manziel pass in the end zone. But Jones followed that up with a costly interception and gave the ball right back to the Aggies. Manziel avenged his only mistake of the game with a 5-yard touchdown run on a three-play drive off the interception. Before the season began many experts projected Texas A&M to struggle in its first year in the SEC. But the Aggies proved their doubters wrong and finished with 11 wins for the first time since 1998 including a signature victory over Alabama, which is competing for the BCS national championship. Texas A&M set an SEC record with more than 7,000 yards of total offense including 663 on Friday night. With the win over its former Big 12 foe, Texas A&M moved past Arkansas for most Cotton Bowl Classic victories by an SEC team with five.

2013 BBVA Compass Bowl

The 2013 BBVA Compass Bowl, the seventh edition of the game, was held on January 5, 2013 at Legion Field in Birmingham, Alabama. The game was telecast on ESPN. This was Pittsburgh's third consecutive appearance in the game, as well as its final game as a member of the Big East before they join the Atlantic Coast Conference in 2013. The announced attendance for the game was a BBVA Compass Bowl record 59,135, eclipsing the previous attendance record of 42,610 in the 2010 edition. The University of Mississippi defeated the University of Pittsburgh 38–17.

2013 BBVA Compass Bowl	Line	1	2	3	4	Final
Pittsburgh	(54.0)	0	10	0	7	17
Mississippi	(-4.5)	14	10	7	7	38

Scoring Summary
Mississippi - Logan 14 yard pass from Wallace (Rose kick)
Mississippi - Mackey 27 yard pass from Wallace (Rose kick)
Pittsburgh - Street 10 yard pass from Sunseri (Harper kick)
Mississippi - Sanders 18 yard pass from Wallace (Rose kick)
Pittsburgh - Harper 47 yard Field goal
Mississippi - Rose 31 yard Field goal
Mississippi - Brunetti 1 yard run (Rose kick)
Mississippi - Mathers 62 yard run (Rose kick)
Pittsburgh - Shanahan 16 yard pass from Sunseri (Harper kick)

Associated Press BBVA Compass Bowl Game Summary - Hugh Freeze needed only one year to make a winner out of a Mississippi team that was woeful in 2011. The coach noted with satisfaction that most experts didn't predict such dramatic improvement in his first season. Bo Wallace threw three touchdown passes and Ole Miss beat Pittsburgh 38-17 in the BBVA Compass Bowl on Saturday to complete an impressive turnaround. Ole Miss (7-6) took a five-win improvement over its 2-10 finish in 2011. Freeze's no-huddle, up-tempo offense produced 38 first downs and 387 yards. Pitt was held to 266 yards, its second-lowest total of the season. Wallace, chosen the game's MVP, completed 22-of-32 passes for 151 yards with three touchdowns and two interceptions. He judged his performance as only average. Pitt (6-7) struggled on offense as leading rusher Ray Graham was held out with a hamstring injury, he suffered in bowl practice. The Panthers fell behind in the opening minutes after Quarterback Tino Sunseri threw his first interception since Sept. 15 and trailed the remainder of the game. Wallace's 13-yard touchdown pass to Ja-Mes Logan gave the Rebels the 7-0 lead. Wallace added first-half touchdown passes to Randall Mackey, for 27 yards, and Vince Sanders, for 18 yards. Pitt was making its third straight appearance in the bowl. The Panthers lost to SMU in last year's game. The Panthers played their last game as a Big East team. They are moving to the Atlantic Coast Conference next season. Ole Miss backup Quarterback Barry Brunetti had a 1-yard touchdown run in the third quarter and freshman running back I'Tavius Mathers added a 62-yard scoring run midway through the fourth quarter. Pitt stayed close early with Devin Street's 10-yard pass from Sunseri in the second quarter. That was Pitt's only touchdown until Sunseri's scoring pass to Shanahan with only 2:23 remaining. Sunseri completed 16-of-32 passes for 185 yards with two touchdowns and one interception. Ole Miss had four sacks. Pitt had only one turnover in its last seven games of the regular season. It shared the nation's lead with only eight turnovers for the season. Sunseri's streak of 271 passes without an interception, the nation's longest, ended on his second throw of the Panthers' opening drive. Senquez Golson's interception, returned 17 yards to the Pitt 23, set up Wallace's touchdown pass to Logan. It was only Sunseri's third interception of the season and his first since the team's third game against Virginia Tech. Sunseri lost a fumble early in the second quarter for the Panthers' second turnover. Wallace completed his first eight passes, including two for touchdowns but his hot streak ended with two second-quarter interceptions. Kevin Harper kicked a 47-yard field goal, his longest of the season, for Pitt in the second quarter. Bryson Rose kicked a 31-yard field goal for Ole Miss and missed from 44 and 48 yards. Pitt said Graham, the team leader with 1,042 yards rushing, suffered the hamstring injury in bowl practice. Rushel Shell and freshman Malcolm Crockett, who had only 32 yards rushing in the regular season, shared the carries. Shell led the Panthers with 25 carries for 79 yards. Crockett added five carries for 18 yards. Freeze said a hamstring injury in the game limited Ole Miss started running back Jeff Scott to five carries for 16 yards. Mathers led the Rebels with 96 yards rushing on only six carries. Jaylen Walton had 10 carries for 56 yards. A strong turnout by Ole Miss Fans within driving range of Birmingham pushed attendance to 59,135, easily a bowl record. The previous high was 42,610 for the 2010 game between South Carolina and Connecticut.

2013 GoDaddy.com Bowl

The 2013 GoDaddy.com Bowl was held on January 6, 2013, at Ladd Peebles Stadium in Mobile, Alabama. The 14th edition of the bowl was televised on ESPN. The Kent State Golden Flashes of the Mid-American Conference competed against the Sun Belt Conference champion Arkansas State Red Wolves.

2013 GoDaddy.com Bowl	Line	1	-	2	-	3	-	4	-	Final
Kent State	(64.0)	0	-	10	-	3	-	0	-	13
Arkansas State	(-3.0)	0	-	14	-	3	-	0	-	17

Scoring Summary
Kent State - Archer 16 yard run (Cortez kick)
Arkansas State - Oku 10 yard run (Davis run)
Arkansas State - McKissic 31 yard pass from Aplin (Davis kick)
Kent State - Cortez 42 yard Field goal
Arkansas State - Davis 25 yard Field goal
Kent State - Cortez 26 yard Field goal

Associated Press GoDaddy.com Bowl Game Summary - Arkansas State's offense was held in check Sunday night after piling up big numbers this season. It was the defense that led the Red Wolves to a breakthrough victory. Ryan Aplin threw for 213 yards and a touchdown, J.D. McKissic caught 11 passes for 113 yards and Arkansas State edged No. 25 Kent State 17-13 to win the GoDaddy.com Bowl. Arkansas State's usually prolific offense struggled against Kent State, but the consistent Aplin-to-McKissic connection and a stingy defense was enough to help the Red Wolves (10-3) to their first bowl win since joining the Football Bowl Subdivision in 1992. Kent State (11-3) was driving late in the game when Quarterback Spencer Keith tried to scramble on fourth down and was stopped a few yards short of the marker with 52 seconds left. Linebacker Qushaun Lee made the shoestring tackle for the Red Wolves and finished with a team-leading 13 stops. Darrell Hazell roamed the Kent State sideline one more time in the Golden Flashes' first bowl game since 1972. He is leaving the program to take over at Purdue. Thompson, a veteran defensive coordinator, coached the Red Wolves after Gus Malzahn left to take the Auburn job last month. It was the second straight season Arkansas State had to play its bowl game without the coach that led it to a Sun Belt championship -- Hugh Freeze left for Mississippi in 2011 before last year's GoDaddy.com Bowl, which the Red Wolves lost 38-20 to Northern Illinois. The results were much better this time -- and the defensive-minded Thompson was especially pleased with that side of the ball. Arkansas State's offense was dominant during the last half of the regular season, averaging more than 41 points during a seven-game winning streak. But the Red Wolves had to rely on their defense in this one while the offense slowly warmed up. Kent State took a 7-0 lead on Dri Archer's 16-yard touchdown run and the margin could have been worse, but Arkansas State linebacker Nathan Herrold picked off a tipped pass in the end zone to end a promising drive for the Golden Flashes. David Oku rushed for a tying 10-yard touchdown with 5:40 remaining in the second quarter, and then Aplin hit McKissic for a 31-yard touchdown minutes later to make it 14-7. Kent State responded with a 42-yard field goal by Freddy Cortez just before halftime. The teams traded field goals in the third quarter, but neither team could score in the fourth. The Golden Flashes put together one last drive in the final minutes, with Keith completing a clutch 15-yard pass over the middle on fourth down with less than two minutes remaining. He was headed for another fourth-down conversion just four plays later but was tripped up on a scramble deep in Arkansas State territory. The Red Wolves then began to celebrate on their sideline. It was a disappointing end to an otherwise breakthrough season for Kent State, which set a school record with 11 victories, including a 10-game winning streak that lasted nearly three months. But they dropped their last two games, including a 44-37 double-overtime loss to Northern Illinois on Nov. 30 in the Mid-American Conference championship. One reason Kent State was able to win 11 games was a dynamic rushing attack that averaged more than 250 yards per game. But the duo of Archer and Trayion Durham didn't have a particularly good game against the Red Wolves. Archer, who missed much of the second half with an apparent injury, led the Golden Flashes with 77 yards rushing while Durham added 68. Aplin completed 21 of 30 passes in his final college game. The 6-foot-1, 200-pound senior owns nearly every school passing record and is the Sun Belt two-time player of the year. This wasn't one of his most spectacular games, but he was consistent, made very few mistakes and had no turnovers. That was no small feat against Kent State, which led the nation with 38 takeaways coming into the game. The Golden Flashes couldn't get one against the Red Wolves.

2013 BCS Championship Game

The 2013 Discover BCS National Championship Game took place on Monday, January 7, 2013, at Sun Life Stadium in Miami Gardens, Florida. It featured the No. 1 ranked Notre Dame Fighting Irish and No. 2 Alabama Crimson Tide. Alabama was the defending champion and represented the Southeastern Conference, which had participated in and emerged victorious from every standalone BCS Championship Game (since the format was introduced in the 2006–2007 season). Notre Dame did not belong to a conference and was the first independent team to play in the National Championship game since the start of the BCS. The National Championship game between Alabama and Notre Dame was anticipated as an historical matchup with a rich tradition in college football. Going into the holiday season after Alabama was assured a spot in the National Championship after beating Georgia in the SEC Championship, sportscasters from both sides weighed in on who was most likely to win. Despite the historical record of, at the time, 5-1 in favor of Notre Dame many sports betting centers had Alabama as a heavy favorite with point spreads favoring Alabama as high as ten points over Notre Dame. Many prominent sports writers predicted Notre Dame to win based on several factors including strong overall defense, an inconsistent Alabama team (often cited as being "exposed" against LSU and Texas A&M), and various intangibles such a destiny and generalized fatigue from the dominant performances of the Southeastern Conference. With the win, Alabama won their second straight BCS championship, their third championship in four years, and their ninth AP championship overall.

Teams - It was the seventh meeting between Alabama and Notre Dame, but the teams' first since 1987. Heading into the game, Notre Dame led the series 5-1-0, which included two bowl victories. The two teams first met in the 1973 Sugar Bowl, with the Irish defeating the Crimson Tide, 24-23. Following the game, Notre Dame was voted national champions by the Associated Press while Alabama had been declared the champion by UPI in a poll taken prior to this Sugar Bowl contest, the last time the final U.P.I./Coaches poll was announced before the bowl games.

2013 BCS Championship	Line	1	-	2	-	3	-	4	-	Final
#2 Alabama	(-10.0)	14	-	14	-	7	-	7	-	42
#1 Notre Dame	(39.5)	0	-	0	-	7	-	7	-	14

Scoring Summary
Alabama – Lacy 20 yard run (Shelley kick)
Alabama – Williams 3 yard pass from McCarron (Shelley kick)
Alabama – Yeldon 1 yard run (Shelley kick)
Alabama – Lacy 11 yard pass from McCarron (Shelley kick)
Alabama – Cooper 34 yard pass from McCarron (Shelley kick)
Notre Dame – Golson 2 yard run (Brindza kick)
Alabama – Cooper 19 yard pass from McCarron (Shelley kick)
Notre Dame – Riddick 6 yard pass from Golson (Brindza kick)

Alabama Media Guide BCS Championship Game Summary - The Alabama Crimson Tide established its dominance early on the way to a dominant performance as the Tide earned the programs 15th national championship in football with a 42-14 victory over Notre Dame in the 2013 Discover BCS National Championship Game. Playing before a Sun Life Stadium record crowd of 80,120 the Tide raced to touchdowns on their first three offensive possessions and built a lead that eventually reached 35-0 in the third quarter. The title, Alabama's third in the past four seasons, concluded a 13-1 season for the Tide while Notre Dame fell to 12-1 with the loss. Tide Quarterback AJ McCarron passed for four touchdowns and 264 yards while completing 20 of 28 at- tempts without throwing an interception. Running back Eddie Lacy rushed for 140 yards and a touchdown while averaging seven yards per carry, wide receiver Amari Cooper caught six passes for 105 yards and two scores and running back T.J. Yeldon rushed for 108 yards and a touchdown as the Tide offense flourished behind an outstanding performance by its offensive line. Alabama gained 529 total yards while exhibiting incredible balance, rushing for 265 yards and passing for 264. The Crimson Tide romped to its second consecutive BCS championship, cruising to the second-most lopsided BCS championship game victory to date. Alabama (13-1) became the third team to win three national titles in four seasons since polls started being used to crown champions in 1936, and the first since Nebraska from 1994-97. The Fighting Irish (12-1) didn't score until they were down 35-0 late in the third quarter. In a matchup of tradition-rich programs tied for the most AP national championships with eight, Notre Dame was looking for its first national championship in 24 years. The Crimson Tide got its ninth. The Crimson Tide marched with ease on the opening drive, going 82 yards on five plays to take a 7-0 lead on Lacy's 20-yard touchdown run up the middle with 12:03 left in the first quarter. Notre Dame (12-0) had allowed only two rushing touchdowns in its surprising run to the championship game. On the next Alabama possession, Lacy and the Crimson Tide went right back to work, hammering away at Notre Dame's vaunted defense. Lacy set up Alabama's second touchdown with another 20-yard run, this time to the Irish 2. Instead of running into a Notre Dame goal-line defense that has become known for goal-line stands, McCarron faked a handoff and found tight end Michael Williams all alone for the score and a 14-0 lead. Alabama made it 3 for 3 on the next drive when Yeldon scored from a yard out on the first play of the second quarter. Lacy landed one more blow with 31 seconds left in the half. McCarron dumped off to Lacy, who spun off two tacklers, and went 11 yards to make it 28-0. The Fighting Irish started the third quarter with a promising drive that ended with another Alabama highlight. HaHa Clinton-Dix made a sensational diving interception, grabbing a tipped pass and tapping his toe inches from the sideline. Alabama turned the game's first turnover into another long scoring drive. McCarron capped this one with a 34-yard touchdown pass to freshman Amari Cooper, the longest scoring pass the Irish had given up in 2012. With the score 35-0, Notre Dame finally got on the board with 4:08 left in the third. Everett Golson took an option keeper 2 yards for a touchdown to break a streak of 108 minutes, 7 seconds in which Alabama had not allowed a point in a BCS championship game, dating to the last 6 minutes of the fourth quarter of the 2009 title game against Texas at the Rose Bowl. Alabama had scored 69 straight points in that span. Alabama had 529 yards. The Irish defense came in allowing 286 per game. McCarron earned Offensive Most Valuable Player honors while linebacker C.J. Mosley earned Defensive MVP honors by virtue of his team-best 8 tackles.

2013 New Orleans Bowl

The 2013 New Orleans Bowl was held on December 21, 2013 at the Mercedes-Benz Superdome in New Orleans, Louisiana. The thirteenth edition of the New Orleans Bowl was televised on ESPN. It was Sponsored by freight shipping company R+L Carriers, the game was officially known as the R+L Carriers New Orleans Bowl.

2013 New Orleans Bowl	Line	1	-	2	-	3	-	4	-	Final
Tulane	(-1.0)	0	-	14	-	7	-	0	-	21
Louisiana-Lafayette	(49.0)	14	-	7	-	0	-	3	-	24

Scoring Summary
Louisiana-Lafayette - McGuire 27 yard run (Stover kick)
Louisiana-Lafayette - Harris 15 yard run (Brauchle kick)
Louisiana-Lafayette - Trim 82 yard interception return (Stover kick)
Tulane - Darkwa 1 yard run (Santos kick)
Tulane - Darkwa 7 yard run (Santos kick)
Tulane - Darkwa 2 yard run (Santos kick)
Louisiana-Lafayette - Stover 27 yard Field goal

Associated Press New Orleans Bowl Game Summary - With Terrance Broadway toughing out the New Orleans Bowl with a cast on his broken right forearm, Louisiana-Lafayette figured its fortunes might hinge on whether its defense could make a few big plays. Ragin' Cajun defensive backs Corey Trim and Sean Thomas answered that call. Trim returned an interception 82 yards for a touchdown, Thomas' second interception set up Hunter Stover's go-ahead field goal in the fourth quarter, and Louisiana-Lafayette held off Tulane 24-21 Saturday night for its third straight R+L Carriers New Orleans Bowl victory. Tulane set up for a 48-yard field goal try in the final seconds, but Cairo Santos, the 2012 Lou Groza award winner as the nation's best kicker, missed just left. Elijah McGuire and Alonzo Harris each had touchdowns runs for the Ragin' Cajuns (9-4), who led 21-0 on Trim's interception -- the longest in the bowl game's history -- against Nick Montana. But Tulane rallied to tie it at 21 on three TD runs by Orleans Darkwa. Curtis Johnson, who coached the Green Wave to its first bowl in 11 years, said his team appeared too emotional to function well early on. Broadway passed for 143 yards and ran for 33 but was intercepted twice and took a lot of hits in the second half before being replaced by Jalen Nixon in the fourth quarter. Broadway said he was out of shape because of his injury and cramping up. Devin Powell replaced Montana in the first half and passed for 223 yards for Tulane (7-6), but his underthrown pass that Thomas picked off was costly. Tulane's Ryan Grant had seven catches for 113 yards. It wasn't clear until kickoff who was going to play Quarterback for either team. ULL coach Mark Hudspeth had all but ruled out Broadway, who broke his throwing arm Nov. 30. Johnson said he was unsure if he could start Montana, who'd struggled much of the season with injuries, including to his throwing shoulder. Both Quarterbacks ended up starting, but only Broadway took most of the his team's snaps. Nixon's play was crucial on ULL's final offensive series, in which the Cajuns drove from their own 9 to midfield, eating up 5:45 before Tulane got the ball back on its own 5 with 1:35 left. "We milked most of the clock," Hudspeth said. "That was the drive of the game." Powell completed passes of 34 yards to Justin Shackleford and 27 yards to Grant to move the Green Wave into tying field goal range, but Santos uncharacteristically didn't come through. The Ragin' Cajuns needed six plays to produce the game's opening score. Broadway completed his first two passes for first downs, and McGuire capped the drive with a 27-yard run in which he reached for the pylon as he was knocked out of bounds. Tulane's first turnover came on a trick play in which Grant took a reverse handoff and threw deep. Thomas intercepted it and returned it to the ULL 27, setting up a six-play, 73-yard scoring drive that ended with Harris' 15-yard scoring run. The Wave was in position to halve its deficit when Montana drove Tulane inside the ULL 20. Then came Trim's interception. After that, Tulane was desperate for points, and converted on fourth-and-3 from its own 47 on Powell's 42-yard completion to Devon Breaux, setting up Darkwa's first TD. Jordan Sullen's interception at the Tulane 35 set up the Green Wave's second scoring drive, which began with Powell's 49-yard pass to Grant. That led to Darwka's second score on a 7-yard run up the middle shortly before halftime. Darkwa's tying touchdown came on a 22-yard run shortly after Derrick Strozier intercepted Broadway's attempted throw-away along the sideline, returning it 20 yards to the 17. Sullen was later knocked out by a knee to the head and carted off the field, but Johnson said he was expected to be fine.

2013 Famous Idaho Potato Bowl

The 2013 Famous Idaho Potato Bowl was played on December 21, 2013 at Bronco Stadium on the campus of Boise State University in Boise, Idaho. The seventeenth annual Famous Idaho Potato Bowl was televised on ESPN.

2013 Famous Idaho Potato Bowl	Line	1	-	2	-	3	-	4	-	Final
Buffalo	(-1.0)	0	-	10	-	0	-	14	-	24
San Diego State	(50.0)	7	-	21	-	14	-	7	-	49

Scoring Summary
San Diego State - Kaehler 29 yard run (Feer kick)
San Diego State - Muema 3 yard run (Feer kick)
Buffalo - Oliver 10 yard pass from Licata (Clarke kick)
Buffalo - Clarke 38 yard Field goal
San Diego State - Muema 8 yard run (Feer kick)
San Diego State - Denso 25 yard pass from Kaehler (Feer kick)

San Diego State - Roberts 11 yard pass from Kaehler (Feer kick)
San Diego State - Young 1 yard run (Feer kick)
Buffalo - Neutz 23 yard pass from Licata (Clarke kick)
San Diego State - Muema 30 yard run (Feer kick)
Buffalo - Lee 10 yard pass from Licata (Clarke kick)

Associated Press Famous Idaho Potato Bowl Game Summary - San Diego State had its best performance in its season finale. For coach Rocky Long, it's the kind of game he has been waiting for his team to put together all season, a win where all three phases worked together, avoided costly mistakes and took full advantage of the miscues of others. Adam Muema scored three touchdowns and rushed for 230 yards, his fourth career game with more than 200 yards on the ground. Quinn Kaehler threw for two more scores and ran for another in leading an offense that generated 460 total yards. Kaehler, who made his first start in the third game, was 15 of 28 for 211 yards, and his two TD passes helped the Aztecs (8-5, 6-2 Mountain West) pull away early. Taking advantage of a pair of costly Buffalo turnovers, the Aztecs put up 21 straight points during a 5-minute span in the second and third quarters. With less than a minute left in the first half, Aztec safety Marcus Andrews intercepted Joe Licata's pass near midfield and returned it to the 25 to set up Kaehler's first TD pass, a 25-yarder to Dylan Denso that put San Diego State up 28-10 heading into halftime. Buffalo coughed up the ball on the opening kick in the third quarter, setting up the Aztecs at the Bulls 26. Five plays later, Kaehler fired an 11-yard pass to tight end Adam Roberts at the back of the end zone to stretch the lead to 35-10. The Aztecs won eight of their last 10 games. The bowl victory is the first in the postseason since 2010 when they beat Navy in the Poinsettia Bowl and the first postseason victory outside San Diego city limits since 1969. For Buffalo coach Jeff Quinn, the turnovers were too much to overcome. Buffalo (8-5, 6-2 Mid-American Conference), playing in its second bowl game in the team's 100-year history, also was hobbled by an offense that took too long to get rolling and a defense that failed to create its own turnovers. The Bulls didn't get their first down until the 10:42 mark in the second quarter. They pulled to 14-10 late in the second quarter when Patrick Clarke kicked a 38-yard field goal. But the defense, led by MAC Defensive Player of the Year Kahlil Mack, didn't have an answer for Muema and the Aztecs on the following possession. San Diego State marched 67 yards in five plays and scored when Muema sped around left end from 8 yards out. Moments later, Licata threw his only interception. Licata was 13 of 30 for 196 yards and was sacked four times. Bull's running back Branden Oliver had for 114 yards on 28 carries, but the rest of the offense only managed 309 total yards. Mack, who was the focus of San Diego State's game plan, had just six tackles, as the Aztecs ran the other way or double-teamed him throughout. The Bulls came into the game with a plus-1.3 turnover margin, among the best in the nation. Mack recovered a fumble near midfield in the first quarter, but the offense couldn't capitalize against a defense that pressured Licata and bottled up Oliver early.

2013 New Mexico Bowl

The 2013 New Mexico Bowl was played on Saturday, December 21, 2013 at University Stadium on the campus of the University of New Mexico in Albuquerque, New Mexico. The eighth annual New Mexico Bowl was televised on ESPN. The Rams won by a score of 48–45 after they were down 15 points in the final minutes of the game; they scored a touchdown, Washington State lost two fumbles, after both of which, Colorado State scored, and after the latter of which, as time expired, they kicked a field goal to win the game.

2013 New Mexico Bowl	Line	1	-	2	-	3	-	4	-	Final
Washington State	(-4.0)	21	-	14	-	3	-	7	-	45
Colorado State	(65.0)	10	-	13	-	7	-	18	-	48

Scoring Summary
Washington State - Cracraft 25 yard pass from Halliday (Furney kick)
Washington State - Marks 1 yard pass from Halliday (Furney kick)
Colorado State - Lovett 63 yard pass from Grayson (Roberts kick)
Washington State - West 28 yard pass from Halliday (Furney kick)
Colorado State - Roberts 25 yard Field goal
Colorado State - Roberts 19 yard Field goal
Washington State - Mayle 28 yard pass from Halliday (Furney kick)
Washington State - Galvin 3 yard pass from Halliday (Furney kick)
Colorado State - Bibbs 1 yard run (Roberts kick)
Colorado State - Roberts 30 yard Field goal
Washington State - Furney 33 yard Field goal
Colorado State - Bibbs 75 yard run (Roberts kick)
Washington State - Myers 22 yard pass from Halliday (Furney kick)
Colorado State - Vaden 12 yard pass from Grayson (Roberts kick)
Colorado State - Bibbs 1 yard run (Run good)
Colorado State - Roberts 41 yard Field goal

Associated Press New Mexico Bowl Game Summary - With less than 2 minutes to play and Colorado State down by eight points, Shaquil Barrett knew the Rams needed the ball back quickly to finish an improbable comeback against Washington State. Once down by 22 points in the Gildan New Mexico Bowl, the Rams got their chance when Cougars running back Jeremiah Laufasa came barreling toward Barrett. That fumble, at the Cougars 33, set up Kapri Bibbs' 1-yard run score and Donnell Alexander's two-point conversion run that tied it at 45 with 33 seconds left. Then, Washington State's Teondray Caldwell fumbled a kickoff return at the 24, setting up Jared Roberts' 41-yard field goal as time expired gave Colorado State a 48-45 victory Saturday in the bowl season's opening game. It was a Quarterback shootout that saw close to 800 passing yards combined and a game largely dominated by Washington State until the last 2 minutes. And Colorado State did not have a led the entire game until that winning field goal. Garrett Grayson threw for 369 yards and Bibbs ran for 169 yards and three touchdowns for Colorado State (8-6). The Rams overcame three early turnovers. Meanwhile, Washington State's Connor Halliday threw touchdown passes to six receivers and finished with 410 yards for Washington State (6-7). Those six touchdown passes tied West Virginia's Geno Smith and Iowa's Chuck Long for an NCAA bowl record. After the first touchdown pass, Halliday got into a shouting match with a Colorado State coach when Halliday ran into the Rams' sideline. That exchange created a social media buzz and McElwain vowed look into it. Washington State scored 35 points in the first half but had only 10 in the second. With the game winding down, a lack of a running game forced the Cougars to stay with their spread offense and prevented them for running down the clock when ahead by 15 points in the fourth quarter. Washington State rushed for minus-10 yards total. The match-up brought together two second-year coaches working to turn around their teams' fortunes with high-octane offenses. Colorado State had not played in a postseason game since 2008. Washington State had not been in a bowl game since 2003. McElwain predicted the bowl victory would help the Rams with recruiting and said it was evidence how far the program had come.

2013 Las Vegas Bowl

The 2013 Las Vegas Bowl was played on December 21, 2013 at Sam Boyd Stadium in Whitney, Nevada in the Las Vegas Valley. The 22nd annual Las Vegas Bowl was televised on ABC and Sports USA Radio. Sponsored by motor oil manufacturer Royal Purple, the game was officially known as the Royal Purple Las Vegas Bowl.

2013 Las Vegas Bowl	Line	1	-	2	-	3	-	4	-	Final
#21 Fresno State	(66.0)	6	-	0	-	7	-	7	-	20
USC	(-5.5)	14	-	21	-	3	-	7	-	45

Scoring Summary
USC – Lee 10 yard pass from Kessler (Heidari kick)
Fresno State – Burse 8 yard pass from Carr (Kick blocked)
USC – Agholor 40 yard pass from Kessler (Heidari kick)
USC – Agholor 17 yard pass from Kessler (Heidari kick)
USC – Allen 24 yard run (Heidari kick)
USC – Lee 40 yard pass from Kessler (Heidari kick)
Fresno State – Adams 23 yard pass from Carr (Mcguire kick)
USC – Heidari 39 yard Field goal
Fresno State – Smith 41 yard interception return (McGuire kick)
USC – Allen 1 yard run (Heidari kick)

USC Media Guide Las Vegas Bowl Game Summary - QB Cody Kessler threw a Las Vegas Bowl-record and career-high 4 touchdown passes, including a pair each to WRs Marqise Lee and Nelson Agholor, and TB Javorius Allen ran for 2 more scores, while USC's defense throttled No. 21 Fresno State's potent aerial attack as the Trojans posted a convincing 45-20 victory in the 22nd Royal Purple Las Vegas Bowl in front of a sold out crowd of 42,178 fans (the second most in Sam Boyd Stadium and game history) and a national ABC-TV audience. USC, which recorded its 25th 10-win season despite a season of adversity that included 4 head coaches, was led in Las Vegas by interim head coach Clay Helton, who took over the reins after former interim head coach Ed Orgeron resigned after the regular season (incoming head coach Steve Sarkisian watched the game from the press box). It was Troy's first 14-game season in history. Fresno State, which entered the game with a school-record 11 wins (and just one loss) after capturing the inaugural Mountain West Conference championship game, will meet the Trojans again to open the 2014 season in the Coliseum. USC limited a Bulldog offense, which led the nation in passing (409.8) and was third in total offense (45.3) and fifth in scoring offense (45.3), to just 216 passing yards and 253 total yards. FSU QB Derek Carr came in leading the nation in passing (305.5) but was held to 216 yards on 29-of-54 passing (just 53.7%, well shy of his 70.1% prior to the game) with an interception. Bulldog WR Davante Adams entered the game leading the nation in receptions (10.2) and was second in receiving yards (137.1) but had just 73 yards on 9 catches. Fresno State held the ball just 18:33 and had only 61 plays (it ran the ball just 6 times for 37 yards, the fewest opponent rushes ever against USC) while converting only 2-of-14 third downs and 1-of-3 fourth downs. The Bulldogs went 3-and-out on 6 of their 14 possessions. All of FSU's scores came following USC miscues in Trojan territory, including twice on drives of less than 40 yards. The Bulldogs' 55 pass attempts were the most against USC since Oregon State's 60 in 2003. USC had 499 yards of total offense on 76 plays with 24 first downs. Its 41:27 possession time was its most since getting 41:57 against Stanford in 1989. Game MVP Kessler outplayed Carr, his longtime friend from his Bakersfield hometown, as he hit 73.3% of his passes (22-of-30) for a career-best 345 yards. He was sacked just once by the nation's leading sack team. Lee had 7 receptions for 118 yards and Agholor added 5 grabs for 94 yards, while Allen ran for 86 yards on 27 carries and caught 4 passes for another 33 yards. CB Kevon Seymour, who led USC with 7 tackles, was named the Defensive Outperformer of the Game, while sixth-year senior walk-on C Abe Markowitz, making his first start of the season, and was the Offensive Outperformer of the Game. USC opened a 35-6 lead at halftime, including scoring the final 28 points of the half. USC drove 65 yards on the game's opening series, capped by a 10-yard Kessler TD pass from Lee. After USC's ensuing onside kick recovery was negated by a penalty, the Bulldogs took only 3 plays to get in the end zone on an 8-yard Carr pass to WR Isaiah Burse. Troy came right back on its next possession, as Kessler hit Agholor with a 40-yard TD pass. The Trojans scored on their first 3 series of the second quarter, first on a 17-yard Kessler-to-Agholor pass (after FSU didn't convert a fourth down run), then on a 24-yard Allen run (following a failed FSU fake punt deep in its territory) and finally on Kessler's 40-yard throw to Lee. At halftime, USC had rolled up 326 total yards and 15 first downs to FSU's 138 total yards with 8 first downs (and just 1-of-8 on third downs), and Kessler was 14-of-18 for 244 yards passing. The Bulldogs scored early in the third quarter after recovering a USC fumbled punt, with Carr hitting Allen for a 23-yard TD. But USC responded on the next series as PK Andre Heidari nailed a 39-yard field goal. FSU S Derron Smith returned an interception 41 yards for a score at the top of the fourth quarter, but the Bulldogs went 3-and-out on their final 2 possessions. Allen's 1- yard scoring run late in the game finished the scoring.

2013 Beef 'O' Brady's Bowl

The 2013 Beef 'O' Brady's Bowl was played on December 23, 2013 at Tropicana Field in St. Petersburg, Florida. The sixth edition of Beef 'O' Brady's Bowl was televised on ESPN. Sponsored by the Beef 'O' Brady's restaurant franchise, it was officially known as the Beef 'O' Brady's Bowl St. Petersburg.

2013 Beef 'O' Brady's Bowl	Line	1	-	2	-	3	-	4	-	Final
Ohio	(63.0)	0	-	14	-	3	-	3	-	20
East Carolina	(-14.0)	14	-	3	-	0	-	20	-	37

Scoring Summary
East Carolina - Worthy 5 yard pass from Carden (Harvey kick)
East Carolina - Allen 2 yard run (Harvey kick)
Ohio - Patterson 17 yard pass from Tettleton (Yazdani kick)
Ohio - Foster 80 yard pass from Vick (Yazdani kick)
East Carolina - Harvey 41 yard Field goal
Ohio - Yazdani 29 yard Field goal
Ohio - Yazdani 28 yard Field goal
East Carolina - Cooper 31 yard run (Harvey kick)
East Carolina - Carden 14 yard pass from Worthy (Harvey)
East Carolina - Cooper 22 yard run (Kick blocked)

Associated Press Beef 'O' Brady's Bowl Game Summary - Vintavious Cooper took over the Beef 'O' Brady's Bowl in the fourth quarter in a performance reminiscent of a former East Carolina running back. Just don't bring up that comparison to Cooper. The senior rushed for a career-best 198 yards and scored two touchdowns, leading the Pirates to a 37-20 victory over Ohio on Monday. Cooper broke the Beef 'O' Brady's Bowl record for yards rushing while becoming the first East Carolina player to win a MVP award in a bowl game since Tennessee Titans star Chris Johnson ran for 223 yards against Boise State in the 2007 Hawaii Bowl. The Pirates (10-3) grabbed the lead for good on the first of Cooper's two touchdowns runs in the fourth quarter, a 31-yard burst with just under 10 minutes remaining. East Carolina's Shane Carden threw for 273 yards and one TD and scored on a pass reception. Cam Worthy caught an early 5-yard scoring pass from Carden, and then took a lateral and threw 14 yards back to Carden for a fourth-quarter TD that made it 31-20. Cooper put it well out of reach, finding an opening off left tackle and racing 22 yards for his second TD. Tyler Tettleton and Derrius Vick threw scoring passes for Ohio (7-6), which overcame an early two-touchdown deficit to lead 20-17 before Cooper put East Carolina back in front before an announced crowd of 20,053 at Tropicana Field. Breon Allen also scored on a 2-yard run for East Carolina, which won six of its final seven games to finish with the second-most victories in school history. Carden set the school record for single-season yards passing with a 13-yard throw to Isaiah Jones on the drive ended with Allen's TD, making it 14-0. He completed 29 of 45 passes while boosting his season total to 4,139 yards, breaking Dominique Davis' record total for the Pirates. Cooper ran for 90 yards in the opening quarter alone, becoming the third running back in East Carolina history to rush for 1,000 in consecutive seasons. Justin Hardy, meanwhile, had eight receptions for 59 yards, setting a school record for yards receiving in a season. He finished with nine catches, giving him 114 receptions for 1,284 yards. Ohio battled back after a slow start. Tettleton and Vick each threw a touchdown pass in a five-minute span to make it 14-all early in the second quarter. Tettleton got the Bobcats going with a 26-yard completion to Daz' Patterson on a flea flicker, and then found Patterson for a 17-yard TD on the following play. Vick and Donte Foster combined for an 80-yard score on Ohio's next offensive play for the longest scoring pass in Beef 'O' Brady's Bowl history. Foster finished with six catches for 160 yards, earning most valuable player honors for Ohio. Tettleton was 21 of 40 for 228 yards, one touchdown and three interceptions. East Carolina rebounded from a triple-overtime loss to Tulane in October to win five of its final six regular-season games. Ohio stumbled in November losses to Buffalo, Bowling Green and Kent State before finishing with a 51-23 rout of Massachusetts that helped the Bobcats secure the trip to St. Petersburg. Ohio accepted the bid to the Beef 'O' Brady's bowl after the American Athletic Conference was unable to fulfill its bowl commitments. Ball State lost to Central Florida in last year's game, making the trip when the Big East was unable to supply a team. In denying Ohio a third straight bowl victory under Solich, East Carolina stopped a four-game losing streak in bowl games, a skid that began after Johnson led the Pirates to the win in the Hawaii Bowl.

2013 Hawai'i Bowl

The 2013 Hawaii Bowl was played on December 24, 2013 at Aloha Stadium in Honolulu, Hawaii. The twelfth edition of the Hawaii Bowl, it featured the Boise State Broncos from the Mountain West Conference against the Oregon State Beavers from the Pac-12 Conference.

2013 Hawaii Bowl	Line	1	2	3	4	Final
Boise State	(65.0)	3	3	7	10	23
Oregon State	(-3.5)	17	14	7	0	38

Scoring Summary
Oregon State - Romaine 27 yard field goal
Boise State - Goodale 24 yard field goal
Oregon State - Cooks 2 yard pass from Mannion (Romaine kick)
Oregon State - Reynolds 3 yard fumble recovery (Romaine kick)
Boise State - Goodale 42 yard field goal
Oregon State - Reynolds 70 yard fumble recovery (Romaine kick)
Oregon State - Ward 9 yard run (Romaine kick)
Oregon State - Woods 5 yard run (Romaine kick)
Boise State - Ajayi 1 yard run (Goodale kick)
Boise State - Miller 85 yard pass from Hedrick (Goodale kick)
Boise State - Goodale 33 yard field goal

Oregon State Media Guide Hawaii Bowl Game Summary - Rashaad Reynolds returned two fumbles for touchdowns and the Oregon State offense racked up 454 yards to pace the Beavers to a 38-23 win over Boise State at the 2013 Sheraton Hawai'i Bowl. The Beavers took the early lead taking a 31-6 advantage into halftime. That was due in large part to the Beavers' defense, which forced two fumbles. Both were returned by Reynolds, who, in his last collegiate game, collected 10 tackles amongst the two fumble returns. The first fumble return came with OSU up 10-3 in the first quarter after a touchdown reception by Brandin Cooks and field goal by Trevor Romaine. Scott Crichton sacked Boise State Quarterback Grant Hedrick, forcing a fumble, which enabled Reynolds to pick the ball up at the Broncos' 3-yard line and make it to the end zone with ease, upping the Beavers' lead to 17-3. Reynolds scored the game's next touchdown, and in grand fashion, returning the Boise State fumble 70 yards. With the Broncos driving, cornerback Larry Scott forced a fumble from Troy Ware after a short pass. Reynolds picked it up and had a clear path to the end zone. That momentum carried over to the Oregon State offense, which scored its next two – and final – touchdowns on the ground. The first came on a 9-yard carry from Terron Ward. It came with 2:46 left in the first half and sent OSU to the 25-point lead at the break. A little more than seven minutes into the second half, the OSU offense picked up where it left off as Storm Woods carried the ball into the end zone from 5 yards out. Woods stood out offensively for the Beavers, collecting 107 yards on the ground via 16 carries. He paced the Beavers' ground game, which totaled 195 yards overall. Sean Mannion passed for 259 yards, with 60 going to Cooks, who reached that figure by way of eight catches. He finished the season with a Pac-12 Conference record 128 receptions as well as 1,730 yards, surpassing USC's Marqise Lee in both categories. Mannion's 259 passing yards gave him 4,662 for the season, surpassing Washington's Cody Pickett for the most in a single-year by a Pac-12 Quarterback. He also tossed 37 touchdowns in 2013, tied for the third-most with Andrew Luck.

2013 Little Caesars Pizza Bowl

The 2013 Little Caesars Pizza Bowl was played on December 26, 2013 at Ford Field in Detroit, Michigan. The 17th edition of Little Caesars Pizza Bowl featured the Pittsburgh Panthers from the Atlantic Coast Conference against the Bowling Green Falcons from the Mid-American Conference. Pittsburgh running back James Conner, who rushed for 229 yards, was named the game's most valuable player. The game was the final edition of the Little Caesars Pizza Bowl; it was displaced by the Quick Lane Bowl, organized by the Detroit Lions, beginning in 2014.

2013 Little Caesars Pizza Bowl	Line	1	-	2	-	3	-	4	-	Final
Pittsburgh	(50.0)	7	-	10	-	3	-	10	-	30
Bowling Green	(-5.0)	3	-	7	-	10	-	7	-	27

Scoring Summary
Bowling Green - Tate 28 yard field goal
Pittsburgh - Conner 15 yard run (Blewitt kick)
Pittsburgh - Blewitt 25 yard field goal
Pittsburgh - Boyd 54 yard punt return (Blewitt kick)
Bowling Green - Bayer 29 yard pass from Johnson (Tate kick)
Bowling Green - Gates 94 yard kickoff return (Tate kick)
Bowling Green - Tate 46 yard field goal
Pittsburgh - Blewitt 28 yard field goal
Pittsburgh - Voytik 5 yard run (Blewitt kick)
Bowling Green - Burbrink 15 yard pass from Johnson (Tate kick)
Pittsburgh - Blewitt 39 yard field goal

Bowling Green Media Guide Little Caesar's Bowl Game Summary - Chris Blewitt's field goal with 1:17 remaining gave the University of Pittsburgh a 30-27 win over the Bowling Green State University football team Thursday night (Dec. 26), in the Little Caesars Pizza Bowl at Ford Field in Detroit, Mich. The win gives the Panthers a final record of 7-6, while the Falcons end the 2013 season with a record of 10-4. Pitt freshman James Conner ran for 229 yards and a touchdown, while the Panthers' Tyler Boyd had 173 receiving yards and returned a punt 54 yards for a score. The Panthers had 487 yards of total offense to the Falcons' 289. BGSU Quarterback Matt Johnson threw for 272 yards and a pair of scores, completing 20 of 32 passes on the night. For Pitt, Tom Savage was 8-of-13 for 124 yards before leaving the game due to injury late in the first half. Chad Voytik was 5-of-9 for 108 yards in relief. Pitt had a total of seven Quarterback sacks in the game. The Pitt offense went three and out on each of the first two drives. The BGSU defense forced Pitt into three plays of negative yardage and one incomplete pass in those first two drives. On third down of each drive, Pitt picked up positive yardage, but not enough for the first down in either case. Meanwhile, the Falcons were forced to punt on their opening drive. Matt Johnson's 16-yard pass to Heath Jackson on third down was not enough to overcome a sack earlier in the possession, which ended with a 60-yard punt by Brian Schmiedebusch. But, on BG's second drive, Johnson found Shaun Joplin for gains of 18 and 17 yards, respectively, on back-to-back plays. Joplin led the BG receivers with six catches and 86 yards vs. the Panthers. The Falcons got into the red zone before the drive stalled, and Tyler Tate kicked a 28-yard field goal to give the Brown and Orange the early lead. Trailing by a touchdown at halftime, BGSU drew even at the start of the second half, as BooBoo Gates returned the opening kickoff 94 yards for a score. Tate's PAT tied the game with only 11 seconds elapsed. That Gates return tied the school record for longest kickoff return in history, matching Leon Weathersby's 94-yard return in a 1997 game at Perry Stadium. The next drive, however, saw the Panthers kick what proved to be the winning field goal. On the second play of that drive, Voytik rolled out and gained 19 yards, giving Pitt a first down at midfield. Conner gained 20 yards on the following play. Voytik handed the ball to Conner on each of the next three plays, gaining a total of nine yards. On that third down play, Conner was stopped for no gain, but on fourth down, Blewitt's 39-yard kick was good.

2013 Poinsettia Bowl

The 2013 Poinsettia Bowl was played on December 26, 2013 at Qualcomm Stadium in San Diego, California. The ninth edition of the Poinsettia Bowl was televised on ESPN. The Aggies accepted their invitation after finishing with an 8–5 record after losing in the 2013 Mountain West Championship Game to Fresno State. The Huskies, meanwhile, had their hearts set on busting the BCS once again, going undefeated in the regular season and winning the MAC West, but ultimately lost out to Bowling Green in the 2013 MAC Championship Game. This was the second meeting between these two teams. The first was in 1995, when NIU traveled to Utah State and lost 42–7.

2013 Poinsettia Bowl	Line	1	-	2	-	3	-	4	-	Final
Utah State	(-1.0)	3	-	3	-	7	-	8	-	21
#24 Northern Illinois	(58.0)	0	-	7	-	0	-	7	-	14

Scoring Summary
Utah State - Diaz 31 yard Field goal
Utah State - Diaz 39 yard Field goal
Northern Illinois - Lynch 1 yard run (Sims kick)
Utah State - Swindall 5 yard pass from Garretson (Diaz kick)
Utah State - DeMartino 1 yard run (Natson pass from Garretson)
Northern Illinois - Brescacin 15 yard pass from Lynch (Sims kick)

Associated Press Poinsettia Bowl Game Summary - Utah State allowed two 100-yard rushers all season. Jordan Lynch, the all-purpose Heisman Trophy finalist from Northern Illinois, failed to make it into that exclusive club. The Aggies' swarming defense made Lynch look average during a 21-14 victory over No. 23 Northern Illinois in the Poinsettia Bowl on Thursday night. Safety Brian Suite intercepted a pass and recovered a fumble by Lynch, who was bottled up for only 39 yards rushing. That kept him from becoming the first major college player to rush for 2,000 yards and pass for 2,000 yards in the same season. Utah State stymied a Huskies offense that had averaged nearly 42 points a game. Joey DeMartino, who went to high school and junior college in San Diego, carried 23 times for 143 yards and a touchdown for Utah State (9-5). He was the offensive MVP. Lynch was third in the Heisman Trophy voting and made The Associated Press All-America team as an all-purpose player. He extended his major college record for yards rushing for a Quarterback in a season to 1,920. He completed 20 of 35 passes for 216 yards and was sacked twice. Lynch ran for a touchdown and passed for another for NIU (12-2), which ended the season with two straight losses. The Huskies were coming off a 20-point loss to Bowling Green in the Mid-American Conference title game that cost them a BCS bid. Lynch's pass was intercepted on the first play of the third quarter by Suite, setting up a go-ahead, 5-yard touchdown pass from Darell Garretson to Brandon Swindall. The Aggies put it away when DeMartino scored on a 1-yard run with 4:14 to go for a 21-7 lead. It capped a 16-play, 80-yard drive that consumed 7:19. NIU punted four times, had two turnovers and two missed field goals, and relinquished possession on downs one time. Lynch threw a 5-yard scoring pass to Juwan Brescacin with 1:44 left to pull NIU to 21-14. NIU tried an onside kicked that USU recovered. There were four turnovers and three missed field goals. The game drew only 23,408 to 70,000-seat Qualcomm Stadium, the lowest attendance in the bowl's nine-year history. Suite also recovered Lynch's fumble in the first quarter. NIU's first five series in the second half ended with an interception, three punts and a missed field goal. The teams staggered through an unimpressive first half that included a missed field goal by each team, a shanked punt by NIU and a lost fumble by Lynch. Lynch scored on a 1-yard run with 8:17 left in the second quarter to cap a 15-play, 78-yard drive and give NIU a 7-6 lead. Lynch ended NIU's second possession by losing a fumble at midfield. Utah State responded with a 31-yard field goal by Nick Diaz. NIU's Mathew Sims was wide right on a 37-yard field goal attempt, and DeMartino had a 58-yard run to set up Diaz's 39-yard field goal.

2013 Military Bowl

The 2013 Military Bowl was played on December 27, 2013 at Navy–Marine Corps Memorial Stadium in Annapolis, Maryland. The sixth edition of the Military Bowl was televised on ESPN. The Thundering Herd finished the regular season with a 9–4 record (7–1 C-USA), champions of the Conference USA East Division. The Terrapins had a record of 7–5 (3–5 ACC). This was the first Military Bowl to be played at Navy–Marine Corps Memorial Stadium. The first five were played at RFK Stadium in Washington, D.C.

2013 Military Bowl	Line	1	-	2	-	3	-	4	-	Final
Marshall	(-2.5)	14	-	3	-	0	-	14	-	31
Maryland	(62.5)	7	-	6	-	0	-	7	-	20

Scoring Summary
Marshall - Shuler 1 yard pass from Cato (Haig kick)
Maryland - Jones 29 yard pass from Brown (Craddock kick)
Marshall - Hoskins 8 yard pass from Cato (Haig kick)
Maryland - Craddock 25 yard Field goal
Marshall - Haig 27 yard Field goal
Maryland - Craddock 33 yard Field goal
Maryland - Stinebaugh 2 yard pass from Brown (Craddock kick)
Marshall - Taliaferro 7 yard run (Haig kick)
Marshall - Hoskins 8 yard pass from Cato (Haig kick)

Associated Press Military Bowl Game Summary - Maryland had just marched 99 yards to take a fourth-quarter lead, and it was up to Marshall to either respond or succumb. With standout Quarterback

Rakeem Cato leading the way, the Thundering Herd scored two touchdowns in the final 12 minutes to pull out a 31-20 victory Friday in the Military Bowl presented by Northrop Grumman. Cato went 28 for 44 for 337 yards and three touchdowns with no interceptions. The most notable part about his performance was that he saved the best for last. Marshall (10-4) trailed 20-17 before Cato brought them back. After directing a 63-yard march to put Marshall up 24-20 with 12:05 left, Cato clinched it with an 8-yard touchdown throw to Gator Hoskins with 3:42 to play. Cato had a brilliant season before this game, throwing for 3,579 yards and 36 touchdowns. But this performance -- on a national stage against an Atlantic Coast Conference foe -- served as the perfect finish. Hoskins had six catches for 104 yards and two scores, Tommy Shuler caught nine passes for 68 yards and a touchdown, punter Tyler Williams pinned the Terrapins inside the 10 four times, and Marshall's underappreciated defense played a huge role. Maryland (7-6) scored only one touchdown after halftime, and A.J. Leggett followed Cato's final TD pass with an interception to set off a celebration among the huge gathering of Marshall Fans among the crowd of 30,163. "It's a great way to send the seniors out," Holliday said. Making its first bowl appearance under third-year coach Randy Edsall, Maryland closed out its association with the ACC by falling to the runner-up in Conference USA. The Terrapins will join the Big Ten next year. Despite the loss, Maryland had its first winning season since 2010 and finished with more victories than in Edsall's first two years combined. Brandon Ross rushed for 116 yards for Maryland, and C.J. Brown went 14 for 24 for 197 yards. Although the Terrapins amassed 391 yards, they converted only two of 14 third-down tries. After a whirlwind first half that produced 30 points and 24 first downs, the teams settled into a defensive struggle in the third quarter. Each of the first four possessions ended in punts, but on the last one Marshall pinned the Terrapins on their own 1. In the same situation earlier in the game, Maryland ran three times for 2 yards and punted. This time, the Terrapins put together a 17-play drive that included a pair of fourth down conversions and lasted for 7 minutes, 44 seconds. The 99-yard march ended with a 2-yard pass from Brown to tight end Dave Stinebaugh, giving Maryland a 20-17 lead with 14:56 left. Marshall was quick to respond. Cato completed two third-down passes, and Essray Taliaferro ran in from the 7 to make it 24-20. Brown subsequently came up short on a third-and-5 bootleg, providing Cato the opportunity to put the game away. Although the Terrapins got the stop they needed, Cato came up big during the next series. After completing a 28-yard pass to Hoskins on third-and-11, Cato connected with Hoskins again in the end zone. It was Hoskins' second touchdown of the game and 15th of the season, most in the nation for tight ends. Cato went 16 for 25 for 193 and two touchdowns in the first half to provide the Thundering Herd with a 17-13 lead. After pinning the Terrapins near their own goal line, Marshall went up 7-0 with a 37-yard drive that ended with Cato's 1-yard touchdown pass to Shuler. Maryland tied it with a 29-yard touchdown throw from Brown to Levern Jacobs, but the Thundering Herd promptly regained the lead with a lengthy march that produced an 8-yard touchdown pass from Cato to Hoskins. After Maryland kicked a field goal, Marshall got one of its own for a 17-10 lead. Near the end of the half, Maryland moved 81 yards in 10 plays to set up Brad Craddock for his second field goal. On this day, the Terrapins needed touchdowns to overcome Cato and Marshall's formidable attack.

2013 Fight Hunger Bowl

The 2013 Fight Hunger Bowl was played on December 27, 2013 at AT&T Park in San Francisco, California. It was the 12th edition of the Fight Hunger Bowl was televised on ESPN. It was the last Fight Hunger Bowl game played at AT&T Park. Washington entered the game with Quarterbacks coach Marques Tuiasosopo serving as its interim coach following the departure of Steve Sarkisian and several staff members to University of Southern California, where Sarkisian was named head coach days before the game. Though the Huskies moved quickly to hire Chris Petersen away from Boise State, Tuiasosopo coached the game. Washington featured a pair of key star players on offense, in Bishop Sankey at running back and Austin Seferian-Jenkins at tight end. Key performers on the defense included linebacker Shaq Thompson and team captain Sean Parker, a safety. BYU featured a high-powered offense that centered on dual-threat Quarterback Taysom Hill and 2014 NFL Draft prospect wide receiver Cody Hoffman. The offensive line, however, had been in shambles all season long, and was a potential area of concern. Defensively, Kyle Van Noy, an All-American who was one of the "best defenders" in program history, headlined a unit that also featured Uani 'Unga, who led the group in tackles. The game featured two female officials, which made Football Bowl Subdivision (FBS) history.

2013 Fight Hunger Bowl	Line	1	-	2	-	3	-	4	-	Final
BYU	(62.5)	0	-	16	-	0	-	0	-	16
Washington	(-4.0)	7	-	14	-	7	-	3	-	31

Scoring Summary
Washington - Bishop 11 yard run (Coons kick)
BYU - Hill 1 yard run (Sorensen kick)
Washington - Ross 100 yard kickoff return (Coons kick)
BYU - Sorensen 45 yard Field goal
BYU - Sorensen 31 yard Field goal
Washington - Bishop 11 yard run (Coons kick)
BYU - Sorensen 32 yard Field goal
Washington - Sefarian-Jenkins 16 yard pass from Price (Coons kick)
Washington - Coons 45 yard Field goal

Associated Press Kraft Fight Hunger Bowl Game Summary - A tumultuous month that started with coach Steve Sarkisian leaving for another job ended with a milestone win for Washington. Bishop Sankey ran for 95 yards and two scores to tie Washington's career touchdown record, and the Huskies went on to beat BYU 31-16 in the Fight Hunger Bowl on Friday night. Keith Price added a 16-yard TD pass to Austin Seferian-Jenkins, and John Ross returned a kick 100 yards for another score to help the Huskies (9-4) win their most games since going 11-1 and winning the Rose Bowl in 2000. The game capped a whirlwind stretch for the Huskies that began with Sarkisian leaving for Southern California. Chris Petersen was hired away from Boise State to take over at Washington, and Tuiasosopo coached the bowl game on an interim basis. The Huskies won just their second bowl game since Tuiasosopo led them to that Rose Bowl win over Purdue 13 years ago. Taysom Hill threw for 293 yards and ran for 133 yards and a score, and Justin Sorensen kicked three field goals for the Cougars (8-5), who had their four-game bowl winning streak snapped. Sorensen also missed one in the third quarter after an interception by Robertson Daniel gave BYU prime field position, and the Cougars allowed two long kickoff returns, including one for a touchdown. The defense led the way for Washington, holding the Cougars to four field goal attempts and one touchdown on five drives inside the Huskies' 30. The Huskies were much more efficient on their scoring drives, with Sankey scoring on a pair of 11-yard runs in the first half to give him 38 career touchdowns, tying the school record held by George Wilson (1923-25). Price then led a touchdown drive to open the third quarter, capping it with a well-placed throw to Seferian-Jenkins on third-and-8 to make it 28-16. Seferian-Jenkins said after the game he will leave school early to enter the NFL draft. Price went 17-for-23 for 123 yards before leaving with an apparent rib injury in the second half. Sankey also sat out the fourth quarter because of a hand injury, but it didn't matter. Backup Quarterback Cyler Miles had a 32-yard run to set up Travis Coons' 45-yard field goal that made it 31-16 midway through the fourth. A strong defensive effort led by Hau'oli Kikaha (three sacks) and John Timu (14 tackles, one sack and an interception) kept BYU off the scoreboard for the entire second half as the Huskies moved their safeties closer to the line of scrimmage to take away short passes. Tuiasosopo was aggressive in his first game as head coach, going for it twice in the first quarter on fourth-and-short. Sankey converted the first but was stopped for a 9-yard loss by Kyle Van Noy on the second try. That was one of the few times the Cougars stopped Sankey, who scored on Washington's first and last possessions of the first half to give the Huskies a 21-16 lead at the break.

2013 Texas Bowl

The 2013 Texas Bowl was played on December 27, 2013 at Reliant Stadium in Houston, Texas. It was the eighth edition of the Texas Bowl was televised on ESPN. Syracuse Quarterback Terrel Hunt, who completed 19 of his 29 passes for 188 yards and rushed for 2 touchdowns, was named the game's most valuable player. The Golden Gophers finished the regular season with a record of 8–4 (4–4 Big Ten). The Orange were 6–6 (4–4 ACC). It will be the fifth meeting between the two schools; Minnesota leads the series 3–1.

2013 Texas Bowl	Line	1	-	2	-	3	-	4	-	Final
Syracuse	(48.0)	0	-	7	-	7	-	7	-	21
Minnesota	(-4.0)	0	-	3	-	0	-	14	-	17

Scoring Summary
Syracuse - Smith 1 yard run (Norton kick)
Minnesota - Hawthorne 41 yard Field goal
Syracuse - Hunt 5 yard run (Norton kick)
Minnesota - Williams 20 yard pass from Leidner (pass failed)
Minnesota - Wolitarsky 55 yard pass from Leidner (Pass - 2 pt. conversion good)
Syracuse - Hunt 12 yard run (Norton kick)

Associated Press Texas Bowl Game Summary - Syracuse coach Scott Shafer wishes his team could have held its big lead over Minnesota and cruised to an easy win in the Texas Bowl on Friday night. But he found it fitting that the Orange had to eke out the victory, considering the number of close games they played this season. Terrel Hunt scrambled 12 yards for a touchdown with 1:14 remaining to lift Syracuse to a 21-17 victory over the Golden Gophers. Brisly Estime set up Hunt's touchdown with a 70-yard punt return. Estime would have scored if not for a tackle by punter Peter Mortell. It was the second-longest punt return in Texas Bowl history. Syracuse (7-6) led 14-3 entering the fourth quarter before Mitch Leidner threw two touchdown passes and a 2-point conversion to put the Gophers up 17-14. After the Orange regained the lead, Minnesota attempted two long passes to the end zone on the final plays. The first slipped through Drew Wolitarsky's arms, and the second, as time expired, was knocked down near the end zone. Minnesota (8-5) got a boost to start the second half when Kill returned to the sideline for the first time since Sept. 28 before Syracuse came back to send the Gophers to their sixth consecutive bowl loss and second straight in this bowl. Kill began the game in the press box, where he had observed his team since returning from a leave of absence to treat and manage his epilepsy. Kill has had five seizures on game day in two-plus seasons at Minnesota. He took the leave of absence in October and returned a couple of weeks later. Hunt finished with 188 yards passing and 74 rushing with two scores to earn MVP honors and a 10-gallon cowboy hat. Leidner finished with 205 yards passing, Maxx Williams had five receptions for 76 yards and a touchdown, and Wolitarsky had 94 yards receiving and a score. Syracuse attempted a 45-yard field goal with about 3½ minutes left, but it sailed wide right. Robert Welsh sacked Leidner on third down on the next drive to force a punt and set up the winning drive. The Gophers took their first lead when Syracuse bit on a play-action fake that left Wolitarsky wide open for a 55-yard touchdown pass that made it 15-14 early in the fourth quarter. Leidner then hit Mike Henry for the 2-point conversion to push the lead to 17-14. Players and coaches on the sideline jumped around wildly after the touchdown, while Kill smiled and stood nearly still amid the chaos. Hunt was penalized for intentional grounding on third down of the ensuing drive by Syracuse, forcing a fourth-and-25 and a punt by the Orange. Jerome Smith rushed for 74 yards and a touchdown for Syracuse, and Estime had five receptions for 47 yards. Minnesota cut it to 14-9 when Williams got in front of two defenders for a 20-yard touchdown reception from Leidner on the first play of the fourth quarter. It was the Gophers' first touchdown on offense since the second quarter of a 24-10 win over Penn State on Nov. 9. The Gophers attempted a 2-point conversion, but Leidner was sacked. The Orange used a clock-eating, 15-play drive capped by a 5-yard touchdown run by Hunt to push the lead to 14-3 with about three minutes left in the third quarter. Syracuse used run after run to pound the ball on that drive, and had an 18-yard run by Smith and a 17-yard scamper by George Morris to keep it going. Syracuse took a 7-0 lead when Smith scored on a 1-yard run early in the second quarter. That drive was helped by a nifty catch by Christopher Clark, who stretched out to grab a 19-yard reception with a defender in his face just before stepping out of bounds. Minnesota cut it to 7-3 on Chris Hawthorne's 41-yard field goal as time expired in the first half.

2013 Belk Bowl

The 2013 Belk Bowl was played on December 28, 2013 at Bank of America Stadium in Charlotte, North Carolina. It was the twelfth edition of the Belk Bowl was televised on ESPN. The game was sponsored by the Belk department store company.

2013 Belk Bowl	Line	1	-	2	-	3	-	4	-	Final
Cincinnati	(57.5)	0	-	3	-	7	-	7	-	17
North Carolina	(-2.5)	16	-	7	-	13	-	3	-	39

Scoring Summary
North Carolina - Morris 2 yard run (Moore kick)
North Carolina - Safety - Martin tackled Kay in end zone
North Carolina - Logan 78 yard kick return (Moore kick)
Cincinnati - Miliano 34 yard Field goal
North Carolina - Tabb 3 yard pass from Williams (Moore kick)
North Carolina - Switzer 86 yard punt return (Kick failed)
Cincinnati - Abernathy 15 yard run (Miliano kick)
North Carolina - Morris 1 yard run (Moore kick)
Cincinnati - Washington 10 yard run (Miliano kick)
North Carolina - Moore 40 yard Field goal

Associated Press Belk Bowl Game Summary - When North Carolina freshman Ryan Switzer reported to training camp in August he was a little miffed to learn he was third on the depth chart at punt returner. Rather than pout, the 5-foot-10, 175-pound Switzer went about working even harder to earn the starting job. The 18-year-old not only did that but capped a memorable season Saturday by returning a punt 86 yards for a touchdown to help North Carolina beat Cincinnati 39-17 for its first Belk Bowl title in four tries. It was Switzer's fifth punt return for a TD this season, tying an NCAA record. T.J. Logan returned a kickoff 78 yards for a touchdown, Marquise Williams threw for 171 yards and a score and Romar Morris had two short TD runs as the Tar Heels (7-6) won a bowl game for the first time since 2010. The victory also capped a huge turnaround for the Tar Heels, who started the season 1-5. Cincinnati (9-4) was looking to become the bowl's first back-to-back champion since Virginia did it 10 years ago, but Brendon Kay -- the MVP last year -- was limited to 181 yards passing and no touchdowns. The Tar Heels brought relentless pressure and had five sacks, including one for a safety. North Carolina came in having lost its previous three in-state Belk Bowl appearances but bolted to a 23-3 halftime lead behind a pair of long touchdown drives led by Williams and Logan's nifty kickoff return. After Morris scored on a 2-yard run to make it 7-0, Brandon Ellerbe and Kareem Martin sacked Kay in the end zone for a safety -- the first of three sacks in the opening half. On the ensuing kickoff, Logan put the Tar Heels in control by fielding the ball near the left sideline and cutting back up the middle of the field for the score. Williams made it 23-3 in the second quarter, hitting Tabb on a quick slant for a 3-yard touchdown strike. Unlike last year's Belk Bowl when Cincinnati spotted Duke 17 points and stormed back to win 48-34 behind Kay's four touchdown passes, there would be no Bearcats comeback. Switzer turned in another big special teams play in the third quarter when he fielded a punt at his own 14 exploded up the field for an 86-yard TD after several Bearcats overran the punt. The Bearcats reached the end zone on a 15-yard touchdown run by Ralph David Abernathy, but the Tar Heels answered with a methodical 13-play, 65-yard drive, with Morris scoring his second touchdown on a 1-yard plunge to make it 36-10. Fedora said he's excited about North Carolina's future as the school looks to put the memory of NCAA sanctions behind them for good. Kay said it was an emotional way to end his career at Cincinnati.

2013 Buffalo Wild Wings Bowl

The 2013 Buffalo Wild Wings Bowl was played on December 28, 2013 at Sun Devil Stadium in Tempe, Arizona. The 25th annual Buffalo Wild Wings Bowl was telecast on ESPN. The game was sponsored by the Buffalo Wild Wings restaurant franchise.

Viewing issue at Buffalo Wild Wings - Throughout Michigan, Wolverine fans decided to visit their local Buffalo Wild Wings restaurant to watch the game. However, upon arrival they learned that the restaurants were featuring UFC 168: Weidman vs. Silva 2, a mixed martial arts event held roughly that same time at the MGM Grand Garden Arena in Las Vegas, Nevada. In the state of Michigan, customers were reduced to watching the bowl game on a small number of televisions with no sound. A corporate officer of Buffalo Wild Wings welcomed viewers to the game and encouraged people to watch a bowl game at one of their restaurants and at the same time disgruntled fans at the restaurants reported via Twitter that they were in the wrong place to watch the game on big screens and with sound.

2013 Buffalo Wild Wings Bowl	Line	1	-	2	-	3	-	4	-	Final
Michigan	(55.0)	3	-	3	-	0	-	8	-	14
Kansas State	(-5.5)	14	-	7	-	0	-	10	-	31

Scoring Summary
Kansas State – Lockett 6 yard pass from Waters (Patterson kick)
Michigan – Wile 22 yard Field goal
Kansas State – Lockett 29 yard pass from Waters (Patterson kick)
Michigan – Wile 26 yard Field goal
Kansas State – Lockett 8 yard pass from Waters (Patterson kick)
Kansas State – Patterson 22 yard Field goal
Kansas State – Hubert 8 yard run (Patterson kick)
Michigan – Toussaint 3 yard run (Pass good)

Associated Press Buffalo Wild Wings Game Summary - Kansas State coach Bill Snyder saw what was coming and tried to avoid it, racing 20 yards down the sideline and out onto the field. Spry as he might be, the 74-year-old coach was no match for players young enough to be his grandchildren, turning just in time to take the full icy brunt of defensive end Ryan Mueller dumping a water bucket over his head. The architect of one of college football's biggest turnarounds during his first stint at Kansas State, Snyder and his Wildcats won their first bowl game in 11 years by rolling over Michigan 31-14 in the Buffalo Wild Wings Bowl on Saturday night. Jake Waters threw for 271 yards and connected with record-breaking receiver Tyler Lockett on three scores, helping Kansas State (8-5) end a five-game bowl losing streak. The Wildcats surged at the end of the season and were unstoppable early against Michigan (7-6), scoring on their first three possessions behind Lockett and Waters. Lockett set a school record with 10 catches for 116 yards and tied the Kansas State bowl record with his three TDs. Waters was efficient in leading Kansas State's offense, completing 21 of 27 passes and running for 42 yards. The Wildcats' defense dominated most of the night, holding Michigan to 261 total yards -- 82 of that on a final scoring drive in the fourth quarter with the game out of reach. Freshman Quarterback Shane Morris was steady in place of injured starter Devin Gardner, leading Michigan on two early scoring drives. The Wolverines settled for field goals on both and did little the rest of the way. Morris threw for 196 yards on 24-of-38 passing with an interception. Michigan's run game didn't give him much support, particularly early, and finished with 65 yards on 15 carries. Michigan's defense also had trouble stopping Kansas State most of the night, giving up 420 total yards in the Wolverines' second straight bowl loss. Kansas State finished the season strong after some early difficulties -- starting with a home loss to FCS opponent North Dakota State. The Wildcats won five of their final six games while scoring at least 31 points in each. Michigan limped to the finish after a 5-0 start, losing five of its final seven games and Gardner along the way. The redshirt junior injured his toe in the regular-season finale against Ohio State and didn't recover in time for the bowl game, leaving the Wolverines in the hands of Morris. The freshman hasn't played much over the past year, limited to four games as a high school senior due to mononucleosis and to nine pass attempts as Gardner's backup this season. Morris didn't seem to mind being thrust into the spotlight as the first Michigan Quarterback to make his first career start in a bowl game. He was helped by a conservative game plan filled with short throws early and started unleashing his big left arm by Michigan's second drive, completing 15 of 19 passes for 121 yards in the first half. The problem for the Wolverines was they couldn't finish off drives, settling for field goals of 22 and 26 yards by Matt Wile. That was good for Wile, who made one field goal all season, but not for Michigan because its defense couldn't stop the Wildcats -- particularly the Waters-to-Lockett combination. Kansas State set the tone on its opening drive, grinding out 75 yards in 15 plays and 7:51 off the clock. Lockett capped it with a 6-yard touchdown catch after the Wildcats' line gave Waters just enough time to get the throw off against Michigan's blitz. Lockett set up the next drive with a 40-yard kickoff return and capped it with a 29-yard touchdown catch, set up by Waters' pump fake that gave him separation behind Michigan's defense. Kansas State raced down the field again on its next drive, setting up Lockett's third touchdown, an 8-yarder from Waters that put the Wildcats up 21-6 at halftime. The Wildcats bogged down in the second half, but so did the Wolverines. Michigan had 23 total yards in the third quarter and failed to capitalize on the game's first turnover -- a fumble by Daniel Sams -- by going three-and-out. Kansas State's Ian Anderson hit a 22-yard field goal in the fourth quarter, John Hubert scored on a 1-yard run after Morris' interception and the Wildcats celebrated Snyder's seventh bowl victory by chasing him down the sideline for the water-bucket dump.

2013 Russell Athletic Bowl

The 2013 Russell Athletic Bowl was played on December 28, 2013 at the Florida Citrus Bowl Stadium in Orlando, Florida. The 24th edition of the Russell Athletic Bowl was televised on ESPN. The game was sponsored by the Russell Athletic uniform company. The Cardinals had a regular season record of 11–1 (7–1 American). The Hurricanes finished their season at 9–3 (5–3 ACC).

2013 Russell Athletic Bowl	Line	1	-	2	-	3	-	4	-	Final
#18 Louisville	(-4.0)	6	-	16	-	7	-	7	-	36
Miami	(58.0)	2	-	0	-	0	-	7	-	9

Scoring Summary
Miami - Safety
Louisville - Wallace 36 yard Field goal
Louisville - Wallace 43 yard Field goal
Louisville - Wallace 42 yard Field goal
Louisville - Parker 26 yard pass from Bridgewater (Wallace kick)
Louisville - Harris 12 yard pass from Bridgewater (Wallace kick)
Louisville - Perry 24 yard pass from Bridgewater (Wallace kick)
Louisville - Bridgewater 1 yard run (Wallace kick)
Miami - Edwards 2 yard run (Goudis kick)

Associated Press Russell Athletic Bowl Game Summary - Leading up to the Russell Athletic Bowl, Louisville Quarterback Teddy Bridgewater batted back questions about whether the game would be his last in college. If it was, he left plenty for the Cardinals to remember. Bridgewater threw three touchdown passes and ran for another score to help No. 18 Louisville rout Miami 36-9 on Saturday night. The Cardinals (12-1) spotted Miami (9-4) an early 2-0 lead, then dominated the rest of the way, racking up 554 total yards to the Hurricanes' 174. With Cardinals fans chanting "Teddy! Teddy!" at times throughout the game, Bridgewater, projected to be a top NFL draft pick if he comes out this summer, set a school season record with 31 touchdown passes. The Miami native also tied the school record with his 27th victory as Louisville's starter. "It meant a lot because not only because I and so many other guys going against our hometown school, but we were going against a quality opponent," he said. He was 35 for 45 for career-high 447 yards. Louisville won its second straight bowl game for its second 12-win season. On the stage during the postgame trophy presentation Bridgewater, the game's MVP, was showered again by Louisville fans who beckoned him with "One more year!" overtures. He reiterated though, that he hadn't set and decision-making timelines on deciding whether to submit his name for the NFL's early entry deadline. Louisville coach Charlie Strong said throughout the week that he was banking on his defense to help spark the Cardinals' offense. It responded with one of its best efforts of the season. Miami, playing in its first bowl game since 2010, hasn't had a bowl victory since 2006, losing four straight. The Hurricanes were returning to the postseason following a two-year, self-imposed ban during an NCAA investigation. They got on the scoreboard first with the safety. But was one of their few highlights. Hurricanes Coach Al Golden said despite the setback, they aren't going to stray too far from the foundation they've been trying to build. A big second quarter by the Cardinals, punctuated by Bridgewater's two touchdown passes helped Louisville take a 22-2 lead. The Cardinals settled for field goals early after struggling to convert on third downs inside Hurricanes' territory. That coincided with one of Bridgewater's top third-down targets -- receiver DeVante Parker -- going down on Louisville's second series of the night with an ankle injury. But those fortunes changed quickly when Parker returned in the second quarter after getting his ankle attended to by the training staff. He immediately caught three passes on a seven-play, 80-yard drive, including a capping 26-yard touchdown reception. Parker finished with nine catches for 142 yards. Miami's next possession appeared to have stalled near midfield, but an unsportsmanlike conduct penalty kept it going and eventually set up the Hurricanes with second-and-goal on the 5. Stephen Morris dropped back to pass but was grabbed and lost the ball as he was slung to the ground by Cardinals defensive end Marcus Smith. The loose ball was then recovered by Louisville's Brandon Dunn to end the threat. Louisville got it again with just under 2 minutes to play and drove 60 yards for another touchdown, scoring on Bridgewater's 12-yard pass to Michael Harris.

2013 Pinstripe Bowl

The 2013 Pinstripe Bowl was played on December 28, 2013 at Yankee Stadium in the New York City borough of The Bronx. The fourth edition of the Pinstripe Bowl was televised on ESPN. The Fighting Irish accepted their invitation after earning an 8–4 record for the season, while the Scarlet Knights accepted their invitation after earning a 6–6 record.

2013 Pinstripe Bowl	Line	1	-	2	-	3	-	4	-	Final
Rutgers	(53.0)	10	-	3	-	0	-	3	-	16
Notre Dame	(-14.5)	10	-	3	-	3	-	13	-	29

Scoring Summary
Notre Dame - Brindza 21 yard Field goal
Rutgers - Federico 36 yard Field goal
Notre Dame - Jones 8 yard run (Brindza kick)
Rutgers - Coleman 14 yard pass from Dodd (Federico kick)
Notre Dame - Brindza 38 yard Field goal
Rutgers - Federico 18 yard Field goal
Notre Dame - Brindza 26 yard Field goal
Notre Dame - Brindza 25 yard Field goal
Rutgers - Federico 47 yard Field goal
Notre Dame - Folston 3 yard run (Brindza kick)
Notre Dame - Brindza 49 yard Field goal

Associated Press Pinstripe Bowl Game Summary - This nicely sums up Tommy Rees' Notre Dame Career. The senior threw for 319 yards and no interceptions in his final college game, leading No. 25 Notre Dame to a 29-16 victory against Rutgers that was far from pretty but ultimately successful -- and an offensive lineman won the MVP award. Rees finished four years of football for the Fighting Irish packed with both memorable and forgettable moments with a solid performance, going 27 for 47. He has been "The Closer," rallying Notre Dame to victories with late drives, and "Turnover Tommy," making crushing mistakes at the most inopportune times during his time in South Bend, Ind. For his finale, against one of the worst pass defenses in the nation, Rees was mistake free and productive. He missed some throws that could have broken open the game, but, typically, he persevered. Kyle Brindza kicked five field goals for the Fighting Irish (9-4), who completed their follow-up season to last year's run to the national championship game a long way from the BCS -- facing a two-touchdown underdog that was trying to avoid a losing record. Notre Dame's play was less than inspired -- Kelly said about a dozen players were fighting a flu bug -- but the win prevented the Irish from finishing with eight victories for the third time in his four seasons. Notre Dame's TJ Jones scored on an 8-yard run in the first quarter and Rutgers star Brandon Coleman answered with a 14-yard touchdown catch soon after. Tarean Folston's 3-yard touchdown run with 3:38 in the fourth made it 26-16 and finally gave the Irish a comfortable lead. On the slick turf at Yankee Stadium, the Pinstripe Bowl turned into a field-goal kicking contest. Brindza was 5 for 6. Kyle Federico made 3 of 3 for the Scarlet Knights (6-7). The Irish dominated in yards (494-237) and time of possession (38:49) but bogged down in the red zone repeatedly. Twice Notre Dame put together double-digit play drives that ended in short field goals for Brindza. A 15-play, 90-yard march that started in the third quarter and ended in the fourth with Brindza's 25-yarder made it 19-13 Notre Dame with 12:46 left. Brindza's third field goal, a 26-yarder with 6:03 left in the third quarter, gave Notre Dame a 16-13 lead -- after the Irish caught a break. Brindza had missed from 36 yards, but Rutgers was flagged for running into the kicker to give him a second, easier, try. Senior Quarterback Chas Dodd, whose career has been like Rees' in terms of ups and downs, finished with 156 yards passing for Rutgers. Notre Dame improved to 17-6-3 at Yankee Stadium, though this ballpark in the Bronx is only a few years old and across the street from where the original House that Ruth built sat for decades. "It's great to be in New York," Kelly told what was left of bowl record crowd of 47,122 during the postgame trophy ceremony on the field after the Irish had sung the alma mater with the band in right-center field, near the Yankees bullpen. The Fighting Irish played the first football game in the new stadium back in 2010. Rees, a freshman then, helped the Irish beat Army and got to use Derek Jeter's locker. Called upon to lead the Irish this year after Everett Golson was suspended from school for academic cheating, Rees became the third Notre Dame Player to surpass 3,000 yards through the air in a season. Rees will next play in the East-West Shrine Game, trying to impress pro scouts.

2013 Armed Forces Bowl

The 2013 Armed Forces Bowl was played on December 30, 2013 at Amon G. Carter Stadium on the campus of Texas Christian University in Fort Worth, Texas. The eleventh edition of the Armed Forces Bowl (which was originally known as the Fort Worth Bowl), was televised on ESPN.

2013 Armed Forces Bowl	Line	1	-	2	-	3	-	4	-	Final
Middle Tennessee	(56.5)	3	-	3	-	0	-	0	-	6
Navy	(-6.5)	7	-	3	-	0	-	14	-	24

Scoring Summary
Navy - Reynolds 3 yard run (Sloan kick)
Middle Tennessee - Clark 43 yard Field goal
Navy - Sloan 32 yard Field goal
Middle Tennessee - Clark 24 yard Field goal
Navy - Reynolds 1 yard run (Sloan kick)
Navy - Sanders 41 yard run (Sloan kick)

Associated Press Armed Forces Bowl Game Summary - Keenan Reynolds amazes so many people with how he directs Navy's triple-option offense and keeps scoring touchdowns. As for the Quarterback, he is in awe of the company he now keeps after joining the 30-touchdown rushing club in the Midshipmen's 24-6 victory over Middle Tennessee State in the Armed Forces Bowl on Monday. Reynolds had a 3-yard score to cap the opening drive for Navy (9-4) and added a 1-yarder in the fourth quarter. Already with the NCAA record for touchdowns rushing by a Quarterback, Reynolds upped his total to 31 to match Colorado State running back Kapri Bibbs, also a sophomore, for the national lead this season. The only players with more rushing TDs in a season were Sanders (37) with Oklahoma State, and Wisconsin's Montee Ball (33). Reynolds, playing 50 years after Hall of Fame Quarterback and two-time Super Bowl champion Roger Staubach won the Heisman Trophy at Navy, still has two seasons left in college. The Midshipmen ran 10 consecutive times on the game's opening drive, with Reynolds going 3 yards to put them ahead to stay. Navy, which won for only the second time in its last seven bowl games, piled up 366 yards rushing and finished this season with five straight victories. The Blue Raiders (8-5) were held to a season low in points. They had finished the regular season with a five-game winning streak, averaging nearly 43 points a game in that stretch -- since a 34-7 loss on Oct. 12 at North Texas, about 40 miles away from the TCU campus where the bowl was played. In its previous game, just more than two weeks earlier, Navy beat Army 34-7 in the snow and freezing temperatures in Philadelphia. It was 32 degrees at kickoff on Monday, but with sunny and clear skies. Reynolds lost two fumbles, matching his total during the regular season, Middle Tennessee failed to convert into points either of the miscues. Both fumbles were recovered by linebacker T.T. Barber, the game's defensive MVP, after Navy drove inside the 20. Down 10-6 at halftime, the Blue Raiders moved to the Navy 7 on the opening drive of the second half. They went for it on fourth down instead of trying a short field goal. But fullback Corey Carmichael managed only a yard before getting taken down by Travis Bridges and George Jamison, who also had an interception. Middle Tennessee played in a bowl one year after getting snubbed with the same 8-4 record in the regular season. That was in the Sun Belt Conference before moving to Conference USA this season. Barber forced the first fumble late in the first half, jumping over the Quarterback to pounce on the ball. The other came late in the third quarter when the Midshipmen drove from their own 6 to the MTSU 14 after stopping Middle Tennessee short on a fourth-and-2. There was a scary moment in the final minute before halftime when Middle Tennessee receiver Marcus Henry and Navy cornerback Lonnie Richardson each crumpled after a hard tackle. Players from both teams quickly motioned to the sideline, and trainers sprinted to the players. Henry and Richardson were side-by-side on the ground surrounded by their teammates and medical personnel. They eventually sat up, then got up and walked gingerly off the field with help. Richardson was a second teamer pressed into extra duty after the ejection of senior safety Wave Ryder for a borderline targeting penalty midway through the second quarter. Ryder appeared to make shoulder-to-shoulder contact on the hit of receiver Tavarres Jefferson at the end of a 22-yard gain, but officials upheld Ryder's ejection after the automatic review of the play.

2013 Music City Bowl

The 2013 Music City Bowl was played on December 30, 2013 at LP Field in Nashville, Tennessee. The 16th edition of the Music City Bowl was broadcast on ESPN.

2013 Music City Bowl	Line	1	-	2	-	3	-	4	-	Final
Mississippi	(-3.0)	7	-	6	-	10	-	2	-	25
Georgia Tech	(56.5)	7	-	0	-	0	-	10	-	17

Scoring Summary
Mississippi - Wallace 17 yard run (Ritter kick)
Georgia Tech - Godhigh 8 yard run (Butker kick)
Mississippi - Moncrief 28 yard pass from Wallace (Ritter kick)
Mississippi - Wallace 10 yard run (Ritter kick)
Mississippi - Ritter 29 yard Field goal
Georgia Tech - Butker 38 yard Field goal
Georgia Tech - Waller 72 yard pass from Lee (Butker kick)
Mississippi - Safety - ball recovered in end zone

Associated Press Music City Bowl Game Summary - Bo Wallace wanted redemption for his poor play in the Egg Bowl. The Mississippi Quarterback made sure the Rebels finished the season as winners. Wallace ran for two touchdowns and threw for another score, and Ole Miss Beat Georgia Tech 25-17 Monday in the Franklin American Mortgage Music City Bowl for the Rebels' second straight bowl victory under coach Hugh Freeze. The redshirt junior Quarterback and Tennessee native made up for his three turnovers in the Egg Bowl overtime loss by throwing for 256 yards and running for 86 more, giving him the school record for total yards in a season and most completions in a season, topping Eli Manning for both. Freeze said he knew from watching Wallace prepare for this game that how the Rebels lost to rival Mississippi State last month didn't sit well with the Quarterback. Ole Miss (8-5) now has won six straight bowls and 10 of the last 11 in making up for the lone loss in that stretch in the 2000 Music City Bowl. The Rebels came in tied with Auburn and Florida State, who play Jan. 6 for the BCS national championship, for the longest bowl winning streak. Georgia Tech (7-6) has lost eight of nine bowls. The Yellow Jackets scored 10 points in the fourth quarter as they tried to rally before a safety with 4:22 left ended their last chance. Yellow Jackets lineman Adam Gotsis, who also blocked an extra point, knocked down a 32-yard field goal attempt by Andrew Ritter giving Georgia Tech the ball at their own 20 with 4:36 left trailing 23-17. But Georgia Tech lost 5 yards on the first play, then Vad Lee flipped the ball to Corey Dennis on a reverse with the receiver apparently looking to throw when he fumbled under pressure. Right tackle Ray Beno covered up the ball in the end zone for the safety. Freeze said he thought it might have been a touchdown but was glad to get some points. Johnson wishes his player had just tried to run for what he could get. Ole Miss finally punted back to Georgia Tech with 37 seconds left. Senquez Golson intercepted Lee on the next play to seal the victory for the Rebels in the bowl, sponsored by Franklin American Mortgage Company. With a month to prepare, Ole Miss shut down the nation's fourth-best rushing offense. Georgia Tech came in averaging 311.7 yards per game, and the Rebels smothered the Yellow Jackets, holding them to just 151 yards on the ground. Ole Miss held the ball for nearly 33 minutes and had a 477-298 edge in total offense. Ole Miss had a 23-7 lead when the Yellow Jackets scored 10 straight points. Harrison Butker capped a 64-yard drive with a 38-yard field goal in the opening seconds of the fourth quarter, then D.J. White intercepted a Wallace pass intended for Donte Moncrief. On the next play, Lee found Darren Waller for a 72-yard catch-and-run for a TD with 13:25 left. Wallace helped Ole Miss Lead 13-7 at halftime as he capped the opening possession for Ole Miss with a 17-yard run for a touchdown, and he connected with Moncrief on a 28-yard TD catch where the receiver went down the right sideline and then held the ball out at the pylon for the score in the second quarter. But Gotsis blocked the extra point. Ritter also missed a 29-yard field goal later in the quarter that was so low it bounced off the crossbar. Georgia Tech looked impressive with its opening 14-play, 74-yard drive, and senior Robert Godhigh scored on an 8-yard run that tied the game. The Yellow Jackets also hurt themselves with a fake punt attempt in the second when punter Sean Poole tripped short of the line of scrimmage on fourth-and-11 at midfield.

2013 Holiday Bowl

The 2013 Holiday Bowl was played on December 30, 2013 at Qualcomm Stadium in San Diego, California. The 36th edition of the Holiday Bowl was telecast on ESPN. This was only the second meeting of the teams. Although both the Red Raiders and Sun Devils were members of the Border Conference from 1932–1956, neither team faced the other until the 1999 season when both universities were members of their current athletic conferences.

2013 Holiday Bowl	Line	1	-	2	-	3	-	4	-	Final
#16 Arizona State	(-15.0)	6	-	7	-	7	-	3	-	23
Texas Tech	(72.0)	13	-	14	-	10	-	0	-	37

Scoring Summary
Texas Tech – Hall 1 yard pass from Webb (Kick failed)
Texas Tech – Grant 18 yard pass from Webb (Bustin kick)
Arizona State – Gonzales 44 yard Field goal
Arizona State – Gonzales 31 yard Field goal
Texas Tech – Marquez 23 yard pass from Webb (Bustin kick)
Texas Tech – Grant 21 yard pass from Webb (Bustin kick)
Arizona State – Foster 20 yard run (Gonzales kick)
Arizona State – Kelly 44 yard run (Gonzales kick)
Texas Tech – Davis 90 yard kickoff return (Bustin kick)
Texas Tech – Bustin 23 yard Field goal
Arizona State – Gonzales 33 yard Field goal

Associated Press Holiday Bowl Game Summary - Davis Webb helped end Texas Tech's unsightly five-game losing streak while making sure the Red Raiders' seniors had a great sendoff. The freshman threw for 403 yards and tied a Holiday Bowl record with four touchdown passes, and Texas Tech raced to a 37-23 victory over No. 14 Arizona State on Monday night. Webb tied the record set by BYU's Jim McMahon in 1980 and matched by Kansas State's Brian Kavanagh in 1995 and Texas' Major Applewhite in 2001. The Red Raiders (8-5) won for the first time since beating West Virginia on Oct. 19. Arizona State (10-4) lost its second straight. Webb completed 28 of 41 passes. He threw touchdown passes of 18 and 21 yards to Jakeem Grant, 1 yard to Rodney Hall, and 23 yards to Bradley Marquez, all in the first half. After losing their final five games by an average of 20.6 points, the Red Raiders scored on four of their first five drives to take a 27-6 lead five minutes into the second quarter. Kingsbury said the Red Raiders had seen predictions that they'd lose by 22 points. Texas Tech All-American tight end Jace Amaro had eight catches for 112 yards. He set the Football Bowl Subdivision single season record for yards receiving by a tight end with 1,352. The Sun Devils, coming off a 38-14 loss to Stanford in the Pac-12 championship game, were held to 18 points fewer than their average. They dropped to 0-4 in the Holiday Bowl dating to 1985. While Texas Tech was finding the end zone early on, Arizona State had to settle for field goals of 44 and 31 yards by Zane Gonzalez. The Sun Devils got their first touchdown when D.J. Foster scored on a 20-yard run with 7:52 left in the second quarter to close to 27-13. ASU Quarterback Taylor Kelly scored on a 44-yard run early in the third, but Reginald Davis returned the ensuing kickoff 90 yards for a touchdown to extend the Red Raiders' lead to 34-20. Kelly gained 135 yards on 25 carries but threw for only 125 yards, going 16-of-29. He was sacked three times. Foster gained 132 yards on 20 carries. Arizona State's Richard Smith couldn't hold on to a 50-yard pass from Kelly as he tripped and tumbled into the end zone with 9:50 left and the Sun Devils trailing by 14.

2013 Alamo Bowl

The 2013 Alamo Bowl was played on December 30, 2013, at the Alamodome in San Antonio, Texas. The 21st edition of the Alamo Bowl was telecast on ESPN. Texas finished the regular season with a record of 8–4 (7–2 Big 12), tied for second place in the Big 12. Oregon, ranked #10 in the BCS, finished the regular season with a record of 10-2 (7–2 Pac-12), co-champions of the Pac-12 North Division.

December 14, 2013 – Texas head coach Mack Brown announced that his resignation following the Alamo Bowl after 16 years as head coach of Longhorns, having led them to six Big 12 South Division Championships, two Big 12 Conference Championships, and the 2005 BCS National Championship with an overall record of 158–47 (.771).

2013 Alamo Bowl	Line	1	-	2	-	3	-	4	-	Final
#10 Oregon	(-14.0)	10	-	10	-	3	-	7	-	30
Texas	(67.5)	7	-	0	-	0	-	0	-	7

Scoring Summary
Oregon – Patterson 37 yard interception return (Wogan kick)
Oregon – Wogan 25 yard Field goal
Texas – McCoy 1 yard run (Fera kick)
Oregon – Wogan 32 yard Field goal
Oregon – Huff 16 yard pass from Mariota (Wogan kick)
Oregon – Wogan 39 yard Field goal
Oregon – Malone 38 yard interception return (Wogan kick)

Associated Press Alamo Bowl Game Summary - No. 10 Oregon first felt overlooked by the BCS, and then came to the Alamo Bowl overshadowed by Mack Brown's final game at Texas. But the Ducks are flying home with an attention-getting blowout. Quarterback Marcus Mariota had 386 total yards and Oregon returned two interceptions for touchdowns, spoiling Brown's emotional farewell after 16 seasons at Texas with a runaway 30-7 victory Monday night. The BCS-snubbed Ducks (11-2) dominated throughout -- even though their famously high-powered offense scored just one touchdown and repeatedly settled for field goals. Yet the rout didn't seem to completely balm the sting of not playing in a BCS bowl for the first time in five years, with Oregon players after the game still reflecting on their championship hopes derailed by November losses. Oregon coach Mark Helfrich declined to answer whether this season was a success. Brown received warm goodbyes from a sellout crowd in what was practically a home game for Texas (8-5). Even the school marching band spelled his name at halftime. But the blowout was a final reminder of why Brown is resigning after a rocky and tense season at Texas, which he led to a national championship in 2005 but couldn't reverse a sharp decline in recent years. Leaving the field for the last time with Texas, Brown flashed the "Hook 'em Horns" hand signal to the scattered remaining Longhorns fans who stuck around to the end of another humbling loss this season. His players didn't say a word while surrounding Brown and his wife, who walked side by side into the tunnel and toward the locker room. Brown said he had no regrets about making this his exit. Mariota led all rushers with 133 yards on 15 carries. He was 18 of 26 for 253 yards passing in his Heisman Trophy campaign tune up for 2014, having announced earlier this month that he was coming back for his junior season. His one touchdown pass was to Josh Huff, who turned a short pass into a spectacular 16-yard sprint to the end zone. Yet even Mariota was outscored by Oregon's defense -- and so was Texas, for that matter. Oregon's first touchdown came on the third play of the game when safety Avery Patterson intercepted an overthrown pass by Texas Quarterback Case McCoy and returned it 37 yards to the end zone. McCoy later bookended a dismal performance in his final game with another pick-six, this one returned 38 yards by linebacker Derrick Malone that sent waves of burnt orange-clad fans streaming for the exits. McCoy scored on a 1-yard rush in the first quarter for Texas' only touchdown. He finished 8 of 17 for 48 yards and was pulled at times in the second half for freshman Tyrone Swoopes. Running back Malcolm Brown was the lone offensive constant for Texas, finishing with 130 yards on 26 carries. New Texas athletic director Steve Patterson said before kickoff that he wants a successor by Jan. 15. Patterson said coaches interested in the job have come forward but wouldn't discuss potential candidates. Whoever Texas hires shouldn't expect patience from a fan base that grew accustomed to winning under Brown, and then became restless as the Longhorns slid from perennial BCS contention. Brown arrived in 1998 and went 128-27 by the end of 2009, when the Longhorns lost to Alabama in its second BCS title game in five years. He went out, however, 30-21 in his final four seasons. Texas could do a lot worse than look to Oregon for how to pull off a coaching transition. Although first-year coach Helfrich couldn't get the Ducks to a BCS bowl as Chip Kelly did in each of his four seasons, Oregon still finished with a fourth consecutive year of 11 or more victories. This was the Ducks' third consecutive bowl win. Playing before New Year's Day was a disappointing consolation for the Ducks after entering November unbeaten and ranked No. 2. Losing to Stanford dashed their national title hopes, but they'll be favorites to contend again in 2014 with Mariota back. Seldom has the Alamo Bowl hosted blowouts like this in recent years.

2013 Liberty Bowl

The 2013 Liberty Bowl was played on December 31, 2013 at Liberty Bowl Memorial Stadium in Memphis, Tennessee. The 55th edition of the Liberty Bowl was televised on ESPN.

2013 Liberty Bowl	Line	1	-	2	-	3	-	4	-	Final
Rice	(50.0)	7	-	0	-	0	-	0	-	7
Mississippi State	(-7.0)	7	-	20	-	14	-	3	-	44

Scoring Summary
Rice – Ross 1 yard run (Boswell kick)
Mississippi State – Perkins 10 yard pass from Prescott (Sobiesk kick)
Mississippi State – Shumpert 1 yard run (Sobiesk kick)
Mississippi State – Johnson 13 yard pass from Prescott (Kick blocked)
Mississippi State – Samuel 4 yard pass from Prescott (Sobiesk kick)
Mississippi State – Prescott 5 yard run (Sobiesk kick)
Mississippi State – Prescott 11 yard run (Sobiesk kick)
Mississippi State – Earhart 19 yard Field goal

Associated Press Liberty Bowl Game Summary - Dak Prescott delivered a performance that would have made his mother proud. Prescott threw three touchdown passes and ran for two more scores Tuesday as Mississippi State trounced Rice 44-7 in the most one-sided AutoZone Liberty Bowl victory in the game's 55-year history. The sophomore Quarterback delivered arguably the finest performance of his career less than two months after his mother, Peggy, died of cancer. Mississippi State (7-6) wrapped up its fourth straight winning season and prevented Rice (10-4) from winning bowl games in back-to-back years for the first time. All of Mississippi State's losses this season came against teams currently in the Top 25: No. 13 Oklahoma State, No. 2 Auburn, No. 14 LSU, No. 8 South Carolina, No. 20 Texas A&M and No. 3 Alabama. The Bulldogs became bowl eligible by closing the regular season with consecutive overtime victories over Arkansas and Ole Miss. This marks the first time since 1974 that Mississippi State has closed a season with three straight wins. Nobody faced more adversity than Prescott, who set a Liberty Bowl record by accounting for five touchdowns. Prescott was 17 of 28 for 283 yards passing and ran for 78 yards on 14 carries. Prescott's performance delighted a partisan crowd of 57,846 and capped a triumphant late-season performance amid personal tragedy for the sophomore Quarterback. Prescott came off the bench in the fourth quarter to lead Mississippi State to a 17-10 overtime victory over Ole Miss last month that earned the Bulldogs a bowl bid. Although Prescott and senior Tyler Russell had shared Quarterback duties throughout the regular season, Prescott had the job to himself in the Liberty Bowl while Russell recovered from surgery to repair a torn labrum in his throwing shoulder. Prescott responded better than anyone could have reasonably imagined. Prescott thanked his teammates, Mississippi State coach Dan Mullen, university President Mark Keenum and the entire Mississippi State community for sticking with him and helping him persevere. Prescott wasn't Mississippi State's only star on a night when the Bulldogs outgained Rice 533-145 and scored the game's final 44 points. Mississippi State's Jameon Lewis caught nine passes for 220 yards to break the Liberty Bowl receiving record held by Houston's Vincent Marshall, who had 201 yards in a 44-36 loss to South Carolina in 2006. Lewis also set the school single-game record. The Bulldogs also played dominant defense. Rice had won the Conference USA title -- its first outright league championship of any kind since 1957 -- by relying on a rushing attack that was ranked 16th among all Football Bowl Subdivision teams. Rice gained only 61 yards rushing -- 179 below its season average -- on 32 carries against Mississippi State. Charles Ross, who entered the day having rushed for 1,252 yards and 14 touchdowns this season, was held to 28 yards on 10 carries. Rice took an early lead on Ross' 1-yard touchdown run, but Mississippi State took control by reaching the end zone on six of its next seven possessions. Prescott threw first-half touchdown passes to LaDarius Perkins, Malcolm Johnson and Artimus Samuel before running for two scores in the third quarter.

2013 Independence Bowl

The 2013 AdvoCare V100 Bowl was held on December 31, 2013 at Independence Stadium in Shreveport, Louisiana. The 38th edition of the AdvoCare V100 Bowl (formerly known as the Independence Bowl was televised on ESPN.

2013 Independence Bowl	Line	1	-	2	-	3	-	4	-	Final
Arizona	(-7.5)	7	-	14	-	14	-	7	-	42
Boston College	(57.5)	3	-	3	-	0	-	13	-	19

Scoring Summary
Arizona – Carey 2 yard run (Smith kick)
Boston College – Freese 32 yard Field goal
Boston College – Freese 41 yard Field goal
Arizona – Parks 69 yard interception return (Smith kick)
Arizona – Griffey 26 yard pass from Denker (Smith kick)
Arizona – Carey 5 yard run (Smith kick)
Arizona – Denker 14 yard run (Smith kick)
Arizona – Griffey 3 yard pass from Denker (Smith kick)
Boston College – Williams 4 yard run (Run failed)
Boston College – Rouse 6 yard run (Freese kick)

Associated Press Independence Bowl Game Summary - Ka'Deem Carey took a decisive victory in a showdown between two of the nation's top running backs. Arizona's complete domination of Boston College was even more impressive. Carey rushed for 169 yards and two touchdowns, B.J. Denker threw for 275 touchdowns and two touchdowns, and the Wildcats had an easy time in a 42-19 victory over the Eagles in the AdvoCare V100 Bowl on Tuesday. It was another impressive performance for Carey in what might be his final college game. The 5-foot-10, 207-pound junior topped 100 yards rushing for a 16th straight game. Arizona coach Rich Rodriguez had plenty of praise for Carey before sneaking in a plug to campaign for a senior season. The game was billed as a matchup between two of the nation's top running backs -- Arizona's Carey and Boston College's Andre Williams. But the duel between AP All-America first team selections was one-sided. Williams, who won the Doak Walker Award over Carey, was held to 75 yards rushing and a touchdown. Boston College (7-6) didn't score a touchdown until Williams' 4-yard run early in the fourth quarter. Carey had plenty of help. Arizona (8-5) had 529 total yards and scored 35 straight points to turn a tight 7-6 game in the second quarter into a 42-6 blowout by early in the fourth. Denker completed 17 of 24 passes while Nate Phillips caught nine passes for 193 yards. Redshirt freshman Trey Griffey -- the son of former baseball star Ken Griffey Jr. -- caught two touchdown passes, including a 26-yarder just before halftime that gave the Wildcats a 21-6 lead. Arizona's six touchdowns tied an AdvoCare V100 Bowl record. Rodriguez said the offense -- and particularly Denker-- played at a high level for most of the day. Boston College's remarkable turnaround season came to a disappointing conclusion. First-year coach Steve Addazio took a team that finished with a 2-10 record in 2012 back to the postseason, but the Eagles couldn't do much of anything right Tuesday. Williams, who came into the game with 2,102 rushing yards, looked ordinary against Arizona's active defensive line. The senior never had much of a chance, usually meeting a pile of defenders right at the line of scrimmage. The Eagles' secondary struggled to contain Arizona's receivers, who repeatedly found space in the defense. Boston College's Alex Amidon caught 10 passes for 129 yards and Nate Freese made field goals from 32 and 41 yards to cap a 20-for-20 season. Both teams took to the air early. Denker completed 8 of 12 passes for 145 yards in the first half. Griffey's two touchdowns were the first of his career. Boston College looked much less comfortable throwing. Chase Rettig tossed two first-half interceptions, including one that William Parks returned 69 yards for a touchdown. Denker was selected game's Most Valuable Player on offense, and Parks took defensive honors. Carey had 116 of his 169 yards rushing in the second half. The Wildcats pushed ahead 28-6 early in the third quarter after a long drive ended with Carey's second touchdown -- a 5-yard run up the middle.

2013 Sun Bowl

The 2013 Sun Bowl was played on December 31, 2013, at Sun Bowl Stadium in El Paso, Texas. In this 80th edition of the Sun Bowl was televised on CBS and heard on the Sports USA Radio Network. UCLA finished the regular season with a record of 9–3 (6–3 Pac-12). Virginia Tech was 8–4 (5–3 ACC).

2013 Sun Bowl	Line	1	-	2	-	3	-	4	-	Final
Virginia Tech	(47.0)	7	-	0	-	3	-	2	-	12
#17 UCLA	(-7.5)	7	-	7	-	0	-	28	-	42

Scoring Summary
UCLA— Brett Hundley 7 yard run (Fairbairn kick)
Virginia Tech — Coleman 1 yard run (Branthover kick)
UCLA— Hundley 86 yard run (Fairbairn kick)
Virginia Tech — Branthover 22 yard field goal
UCLA— Perkins 5 yard run (Fairbairn kick)
UCLA— Jack 24 yard interception return (Fairbairn kick)
Virginia Tech — safety—punter stepped out of end zone
UCLA— Duarte 8 yard pass from Hundley (Fairbairn kick)
UCLA— Evans 59 yard pass from Hundley (Fairbairn kick)

Sun Bowl Classic Game Summary - The No. 17th UCLA Bruins defeated Virginia Tech, 42-12, in the 80th edition of the Hyundai Sun Bowl. The Co-C.M. Hendricks Most Valuable Player, Brett Hundley had 86- and 7-yard touchdown runs and finished with 161 yards on 10 carries. Hundley also completed 16 of 29 passes for 226 yards and two scores. Hundley and UCLA linebacker Jordan Zumwalt shared MVP honors. Zumwalt had 10 tackles and returned an interception 43 yards to set up a touchdown. The Bruins (10-3) outscored the Hokies (8-5) 28-2 in the fourth quarter. After Virginia Tech cut it to 14-10 on Michael Branthover's 22-yard field goal with 3:53 left in the third quarter, UCLA answered with a 12-play, 85-yard drive, capped by Paul Perkins's 5-yard run early in the fourth. Hokies backup Quarterback Mark Leal then threw a pass under heavy pressure that linebacker Myles Jack intercepted and returned 29 yards for a touchdown that made it 28-10. Virginia Tech, which lost starting Quarterback Logan Thomas to an injury in the second quarter, got its final points when UCLA punter Sean Covington stepped on the end line for a safety with 9:38 left. Thomas, Virginia Tech's career passing leader, left after taking a big hit along the UCLA sideline early in the second quarter. The hit resulted in a 15-yard penalty on the Bruins. UCLA pushed it to 35-12 on Hundley's 8-yard touchdown pass to Thomas Duarte with 7:31 to play. The Bruins stayed aggressive late, and Hundley fired a 59-yard scoring strike down the right sideline to Shaquelle Evans for another score with 5:49 remaining. It wasn't that easy early on, though, for UCLA, which led 14-7 at the half. Hundley had six carries for 168 yards in the half. He set the Sun Bowl record for rushing yards by a Quarterback by halftime, even though he lost 7 yards in the second to finish at 161. The Bruins rushed for 202 yards in the first half – the most rushing yards the Hokies have given up this season. UCLA finished with 250 yards. The win in the first meeting between the teams allowed UCLA to post its first 10-win season since 2005, and helped the Bruins forget last season's 49-26 loss to Baylor in the Holiday Bowl. Virginia Tech had its second-worst loss in a bowl game. Its worst was a 42-3 loss to North Carolina in the 1998 Gator Bowl. The 42 points the Hokies allowed were the second-most in a bowl game behind the 52 they gave up in a 52-49 loss to California in the 2003 Insight Bowl. While the Hokies, making their 21st consecutive bowl appearance, were able to limit UCLA's running backs to 49 yards, they had no answer for Hundley, who repeatedly gouged them for big gainers on designed Quarterback counters. Defensive Tackle Kenny Clark was named the Jimmy Rogers, Jr. Most Valuable Lineman Trophy and kicker Kaim Fairbairn was tabbed the John Folmer Most Valuable Special Teams Player.

2013 Chick-Fil-A Peach Bowl

The 2013 Chick-fil-A Bowl was played on December 31, 2013 at the Georgia Dome in Atlanta, Georgia. The 46th edition of the Chick-fil-A Bowl (formerly called the Peach Bowl), was televised on ESPN. The game was sponsored by the Chick-fil-A restaurant franchise. In a contest dominated by both teams' offensive units, Duke scored first and stayed ahead for most of the game. But with a little more than a minute left in regulation, Texas A&M returned an interception for a touchdown and ended up winning by a score of 52–48. Duke finished the regular season with a record of 10–3 (6–2 ACC) and a BCS ranking of #24. Texas A&M had a record of 8–4 (4–4 SEC) and a BCS ranking of #21. The 2013 Chick-fil-A Bowl was the first-ever meeting of the two teams.

2013 Chick-Fil-A Peach Bowl	Line	1	-	2	-	3	-	4	-	Final
#22 Duke	(75.0)	14	-	24	-	3	-	7	-	48
#20 Texas A&M	(-12.5)	3	-	14	-	14	-	21	-	52

Scoring Summary
Duke – Snead 11 yard pass from Boone (Martin kick)
Texas A&M – Lambo 45 yard Field goal
Duke – Connette 3 yard run (Martin kick)
Duke – Boone 11 yard run (Martin kick)
Texas A&M – Labhart 23 yard pass from Manziel (Lambo kick)
Duke – Crowder 59 yard pass from Boone (Martin kick)
Texas A&M – Labhart 9 yard pass from Manziel (Lambo kick)
Duke – Snead 25 yard run (Martin kick)
Duke – Martin 18 yard Field goal
Texas A&M – Labhart 19 yard pass from Manziel (Lambo kick)
Texas A&M – Carson 21 yard run (Lambo kick)
Duke – Martin 20 yard Field goal
Texas A&M – Manziel 3 yard run (Lambo kick)
Duke – Reeves 21 yard pass from Boone (Martin kick)
Texas A&M – Walker 44 yard pass from Manziel (Lambo kick)
Texas A&M – Hurd 55 yard interception return (Lambo kick)

Associated Press Chick-Fil-A Peach Bowl Game Summary - If this was Johnny Manziel's last college game he lived up to his nickname. Johnny Football led No. 20 Texas A&M to another comeback win, 52-48 over No. 22 Duke in the Chick-fil-A Bowl. The Aggies were down 38-17 at halftime but with Manziel at the helm they came back in the highest-scoring game in the bowl's history. Playing in what might be his final college game, the 2012 Heisman trophy winner threw four touchdown passes, completed 30 of 38 passes for 382 yards and ran for 73 yards and a touchdown. Toney Hurd Jr. returned an interception 55 yards that gave Texas A&M (9-4) its first lead with 3:33 remaining. It was the game's first turnover. Duke (10-4) took a 41-31 lead into the fourth quarter. The Blue Devils couldn't hold off the comeback and are still looking for their first bowl win since beating Arkansas 7-6 in the 1961 Cotton Bowl. Hurd stepped in front of receiver Johnell Barnes for the interception. Texas A&M linebacker Nate Askew ended Duke's next possession with another interception. Duke's Anthony Boone passed for 427 yards and three touchdowns but was left to regret the two interceptions, especially Hurd's. Texas A&M's defense opened the second half with its first stop of the game. The Blue Devils, successful on two fourth-down plays in the first half, were stopped on fourth down from the Texas A&M 35. Manziel then had runs of 12 and 14 yards before his highlight play of the game. On second down from the Duke 17, Manziel danced and shuffled in traffic before vaulting a defender and dumping a short pass to Travis Labhart, who scored easily for his third touchdown of the game. Josh Snead ran and caught passes for touchdowns and blocked a punt to set up a scoring run by Boone as Duke dominated the first half. Snead capped Duke's opening drive with an 11-yard touchdown catch. He had 17 carries for 104 yards and a touchdown and three catches for 21 yards and a touchdown. Juwan Thompson added 92 yards rushing for the Blue Devils and Jamison Crowder had 12 receptions for 163 yards and a touchdown. All the pregame focus on Manziel and his possible farewell game failed to address the Aggies' weakness that made the 2013 season a disappointment. Texas A&M ranked last in the Southeastern Conference and 105th in the nation in total defense and 88th in the nation in scoring defense. Duke's offense, led by Boone, ripped through the vulnerable Texas A&M defense. The Blue Devils gained 365 yards with no punts in the first half while building the three-touchdown lead.

2014 Gator Bowl

The 2014 Gator Bowl was held on January 1, 2014 at EverBank Field in Jacksonville, Florida. The 69th edition of the Gator Bowl was televised on ESPN2. The 2014 Gator Bowl marked the third time Nebraska and Georgia have played each other.

2014 Gator Bowl	Line	1	-	2	-	3	-	4	-	Final
Nebraska	(60.0)	0	-	10	-	14	-	0	-	24
#23 Georgia	(-9.0)	0	-	9	-	3	-	7	-	19

Scoring Summary
Georgia - Morgan 38 yard field goal
Nebraska - Enunwa 5 yard pass from Armstrong (Smith kick)
Georgia - Morgan 28 yard field goal
Nebraska - Smith 46 yard field goal
Georgia - Morgan 38 yard field goal
Nebraska - Abdullah 1 yard run (Smith kick)
Georgia - Morgan 30 yard field goal
Nebraska - Enunwa 99 yard pass from Armstrong (Pat Smith kick)
Georgia - Gurley 25 yard pass from Mason (Morgan kick)

Nebraska Media Guide Gator Bowl Game Summary - Heroic efforts by Blackshirt defenders and the longest play from scrimmage in Nebraska football history sent a determined bunch of Husker seniors out with a dramatic 24-19 victory over No. 22 Georgia in the TaxSlayer.com Gator Bowl at EverBank Field on New Year's Day. Nebraska, which secured its sixth consecutive nine-win season under Coach Bo Pelini, finished the 2013 campaign with a 9-4 record. Georgia closed its season at 8-5. Senior wide receiver Quincy Enunwa capped one of the top receiving careers in school history with a career-high 129 yards on four receptions to earn TaxSlayer.com Gator Bowl MVP honors. Enunwa hauled in a pair of touchdown passes on the day, including a decisive 99-yard catch from sophomore Quarterback Tommy Armstrong Jr. on 3rd-and-14 midway through the third quarter. The game-winning pass play was the longest play from scrimmage in Nebraska football and Gator Bowl history. The play was set up after Armstrong fumbled a shot-gun snap on second down and managed to recover it just inches outside the NU end zone to save the Big Red from a safety that would have trimmed the Husker lead to 17-14. Instead, Armstrong dropped eight yards deep into his own end zone on third down and unleashed a 50-yard strike to Enunwa. Nebraska's big receiver took an immediate hit from a Georgia safety but held onto the ball and bounced away from the contact, sprinting from midfield into the end zone untouched the rest of the way. The touchdown catch was Enunwa's 12th of the season, breaking a 42-year-old school record of 11 touchdown receptions previously set by Heisman Trophy winner Johnny Rodgers in 1971. The Husker lead grew to 24-12 and Georgia was jolted. The Blackshirts forced a three-and-out on UGA's next drive, and the Big Red hoped to add to the lead. But Armstrong threw behind Kenny Bell on a slant and Georgia's Shaq Wiggins intercepted it at the NU 39 on the ensuing drive. The Blackshirts kept the Bulldogs at bay for the rest of the third quarter, as Nebraska took its 12-point lead to the fourth. But Mason hit Gurley on a 25-yard touchdown pass on the first play of the fourth quarter to cut NU's margin to 24-19 with 14:49 left. While the Bulldog defense kept the Big Red offense quiet the rest of the way, the Blackshirts did the same. The young Husker defenders gave up 138 yards on the Bulldogs' final three drives, but no points to seal Nebraska's first bowl victory since winning the Gator Bowl with a 26-21 win over Clemson on Jan. 1, 2009. Nebraska produced 307 yards of total offense, including Armstrong's 163 yards on 6-of-14 passing. He threw two touchdown passes to Enunwa but did have an interception for the Huskers' only turnover of the day. Armstrong added 26 rushing yards on 10 carries. Freshman tight end Cethan Carter added one catch for 23 yards, while junior wide receiver Kenny Bell added one reception for 11 yards. Bell also returned four kicks for 72 yards, including a 31-yarder to lead the Husker return game. Junior I-back Ameer Abdullah powered the Big Red ground game on a rainy day in Jacksonville, pounding his way for 122 hard-earned yards on 27 carries with one touchdown. It was Abdullah's 11th 100-yard rushing game of the year, tying a school record for the most 100-yard games in a season held by Mike Rozier (1983), Lawrence Phillips (1994) and Ahman Green (1997). Abdullah closed the season with 1,690 yards, which ranks as the fourth-best rushing total in the storied history of Nebraska football. Abdullah added an 18-yard kickoff return to finish with 140 all-purpose yards on the day, closing the season with 1,999 all-purpose yards to rank as the third-best total in Nebraska history. The Blackshirts surrendered 416 total yards on 82 offensive plays to a Georgia offense that entered the game averaging nearly 500 yards per game. Mason completed 21-of-39 passes for 320 yards with one touchdown and one interception. He was also sacked three times by the Blackshirts, finishing with minus-18 yards rushing. Husker senior defensive end Jason Ankrah sacked Mason twice for 21 yards, while also forcing a fumble that was recovered by Mason. Sophomore end Randy Gregory notched the other sack of Mason for seven yards, while adding a tackle for three yards loss. Senior cornerback Stanley Jean-Baptiste contributed a three-yard sack of his own on Brendan Douglas to thwart a halfback pass attempt in the third quarter. Jean-Baptiste added another tackle for loss of four yards. Jean-Baptiste finished with six tackles and a breakup. Todd Gurley led the Georgia rushing attack with 21 carries for 86 yards, while hauling in a game-high seven receptions for 97 yards and UGA's only touchdown. Arthur Lynch added six catches for 69 yards but dropped the final ball of the day on 4th-and-3 from the NU 16. Safety Corey Cooper led the Blackshirts with a game-high 10 tackles - all solos, while linebacker Michael Rose added nine stops. Senior defensive tackle Thad Randle closed his career with eight tackles, including four solos. After a scoreless first quarter, Georgia took its only lead of the day on Marshall Morgan's 38-yard field goal with 10:37 left in the first half. It was the first of four field goals for Morgan on the afternoon. The Bulldog lead lasted just 1:32, before Armstrong hit Enunwa on a five-yard touchdown pass to give the Huskers a 7-3 edge with 9:05 left in the second quarter. The scoring strike came just two plays after junior cornerback Josh Mitchell recovered a fumbled punt by Georgia's Reggie Davis. The special teams miscue by UGA set the Huskers up with their best field position of the day at the Georgia 14. Morgan's second field goal of the day from 28 yards out trimmed the Husker lead to 7-6 with 6:53 left in the half, before Pat Smith answered with a season-long 46-yard field with 3:18 remaining in the second quarter. The teams went to halftime with Nebraska leading 10-9, after Morgan's third field goal of the half, again from 38 yards out, as time expired. Georgia opened the second half with the ball, but it was the Blackshirts who struck first. After the defense forced the Bulldogs into a 3rd-and-7, Mitchell came up with his second turnover of the day by intercepting a Mason pass at the UGA 42. Mitchell returned the pick four yards to the 38. Seven plays later, Abdullah plunged over the left side of the line for a one-yard touchdown to extend Nebraska's lead to 17-9 with 10:08 left in the third quarter. The short drive included an 18-yard pass from Armstrong to Enunwa, and three carries for eight yards by Abdullah. After Morgan kicked his fourth field goal of the day with 6:32 left in the quarter, this time from 30 yards, Nebraska was flagged for a block in the back on Bell's kick return. The penalty buried the Big Red at the NU 5 to start the drive. After a four-yard gain by Abdullah on first down, the fumbled snap put the Huskers in 3rd-and-14 with the back tip of the ball on the goal line. The rest is Nebraska, Gator Bowl and college football history.

2014 Heart of Dallas Bowl

The 2014 January Heart of Dallas Bowl was played on January 1, 2014 at the Cotton Bowl at Fair Park in Dallas, Texas. The fourth edition of the Heart of Dallas Bowl was televised on ESPNU. UNLV finished the regular season with a record of 7–5 (5–3 MWC), tied for third place in the Mountain West Conference West Division. North Texas had a record of 8–4 (6–2 C-USA) and were tied for second place in the Conference

USA West Division. This was the fifth all-time meeting between the two teams, and the first victory of the series for North Texas.

2014 Heart of Dallas Bowl	Line	1	-	2	-	3	-	4	-	Final
Nevada-Las Vegas	(54.5)	7	-	0	-	0	-	7	-	14
North Texas	(-6.5)	7	-	0	-	7	-	22	-	36

Scoring Summary
UNLV - Sullivan 9 yard pass from Herring (Kohorst Kick)
North Texas - Jimmerson 1 yard run (Paul kick)
North Texas - Miller 7 yard pass from Thompson (Paul kick)
North Texas - Chancellor 3 yard run (Paul kick)
North Texas - Smith 34 yard pass from Thompson (Paul kick)
UNLV - Rice 13 yard pass from Herring (Kohorst kick)
North Texas - Chancellor 15 yard run (Miller run)

Associated Press Heart of Dallas Bowl Game Summary - So much for the idea that Oklahoma State didn't care about playing in the Heart of Dallas Bowl. Clint Chelf threw three of his team's five touchdown passes and the Cowboys shook off a tough Big 12 finish by rolling up 524 yards and forcing five Purdue turnovers in a dominating 58-14 victory on Tuesday. Oklahoma State coach Mike Gundy didn't hide the disappointment of sliding down the bowl priority list with an overtime loss to Oklahoma when the rival Sooners scored in the final seconds of regulation, followed by another narrow defeat at Baylor to finish the regular season. The Cowboys (8-5), a year removed from finishing the best season in school history with a win in the Fiesta Bowl, sure didn't seem to lack motivation. They put together the biggest bowl win for Oklahoma State since Gundy was the Quarterback in a 62-14 rout of Wyoming in the 1988 Holiday Bowl. With former Purdue Quarterbacks Drew Brees and Kyle Orton watching, Robert Marve didn't get to 100 yards passing until Oklahoma State led 45-0 as the Boilermakers (6-7) fell to 0-4 on New Year's Day. The Boilermakers gave the Cowboys short fields on their first two scores after a long punt return from Josh Stewart and the first of Marve's two interceptions. Various mistakes with the game still close in the first half -- a missed field goal, a drop with a receiver behind the defense, and failing to hold on to an easy interception -- ended any hope for Purdue. Leading 28-0 at halftime, Oklahoma State erased any lingering doubt three plays into the second half when Justin Gilbert stripped Purdue receiver O.J. Ross on a short completion. The loose ball shot straight to Daytawion Lowe, who ran 37 yards down the sideline in front of the Purdue bench for a 35-0 lead. Lowe's score was the third fumble return for a touchdown at historic Cotton Bowl Stadium dating to the namesake bowl game that started in 1937 and moved to Cowboys Stadium in 2009. Oklahoma State's 58 points were the most in a bowl game at the Fair Park stadium, topping the 55 scored by Keyshawn Johnson and Southern California against Texas Tech in 1995. The Cowboys pushed the lead to 45-0 on Chelf's third touchdown pass, a leaping 37-yard grab in the end zone by Isaiah Anderson, who had 78 yards receiving. Higgins might have unintentionally awakened the Cowboys soon after the late-morning kickoff on a cold, overcast day when he called for a fake punt from Purdue's 13 on its first possession. The Boilermakers got a first down when punter Cody Webster ran 16 yards, but he ended up punting anyway five plays later, and Josh Stewart returned it 64 yards to the Purdue 19 to set up Oklahoma State's first score on a 4-yard pass from Chelf to Charlie Moore. Marve threw his first interception on the next possession, and a 26-yard drive ended with Chelf's 7-yard pass to Blake Jackson. J.W. Walsh had two touchdown passes for Oklahoma State after replacing Chelf in the third quarter, and freshman Wes Lunt, who won the Quarterback job in summer workouts before getting hurt during the season, played the last half of the fourth. Purdue finally scored late in the third quarter when Marve found a wide open Brandon Cottom for a 32-yard touchdown. Marve finished 21 of 34 for 212 yards and two touchdowns and two interceptions but was just 11 of 20 for 80 yards before the first scoring drive. Down 14-0, the Boilermakers had their best chance to score in the first quarter when Akeem Shavers, who had 93 yards rushing, ran 24 yards to the Oklahoma State 23. Shamiel Gary, who earlier intercepted Marve on a tipped pass, made a strong tackle in the open field on third down, and Sam McCartney missed a 34-yard field goal. The Cowboys then went 80 yards the other way, sparked by a 26-yard completion to Jackson. Oklahoma State scored on fourth-and-1 when Walsh, the short-yardage specialist, replaced Chelf and threw a 16-yard scoring pass to Jeremy Seaton. Trailing 21-0, the Boilermakers were in scoring range again when Marve threw high on fourth-and-2 to an open Kurt Freytag, who got a hand on the ball but couldn't make a juggling catch.

2014 Outback Bowl

The 2014 Outback Bowl was played on January 1, 2014 at Raymond James Stadium in Tampa, Florida. The 28th edition of the Outback Bowl (which was originally called the Hall of Fame Bowl) was telecast on ESPN. It was sponsored by the Outback Steakhouse restaurant franchise.

2014 Outback Bowl	Line	1	-	2	-	3	-	4	-	Final
Iowa	(49.0)	0	-	0	-	7	-	7	-	14
#14 LSU	(-7.5)	7	-	7	-	0	-	7	-	21

Scoring Summary
LSU – Jennings 2 yard run (Delahoussaye kick)
LSU – Hill 14 yard run (Delahoussaye kick)
Iowa – Weisman 2 yard run (Meyer kick)
LSU – Hill 37 yard run (Delahoussaye kick)
Iowa – Martin-Manley 4 yard pass from Beathard (Meyer kick)

Associated Press Outback Bowl Game Summary - What Anthony Jennings lacked in experience, LSU more than compensated for with a talented supporting cast in the Outback Bowl. Jennings made plenty of freshman mistakes Wednesday, however they weren't nearly as costly as they could have been for the 14th-ranked Tigers with Jeremy Hill rushing for 216 yards and two touchdowns in a 21-14 victory. The second Quarterback in school history to make his first college start in a bowl game, Jennings fretted over an interception that helped Iowa (8-5) get back in the game. But with the outcome on the line, he simply turned and handed the ball to Hill, who made sure LSU (10-3) would not lose. Craig Loston's fourth-quarter interception stopped a potential tying drive, giving Hill a chance to put the game out of reach by carrying four times for 87 yards on a six-play, 92-yard march that gave LSU (10-3) a 21-7 lead. Iowa (8-5) pulled within a touchdown for the second time in 4 minutes after Jordan Cotton returned the ensuing kickoff to the Tigers 4. Jennings ran for a first-quarter touchdown, but the true freshman struggled to hit open receivers while completing 7 of 19 passes for 82 yards. In addition to throwing an interception that Iowa's John Lowdermilk returned 71 yards, he was sacked four times while standing in for the injured Zach Mettenberger. C.J. Beathard replaced Jake Rudock at Quarterback for Iowa on the first play of the fourth quarter. His fourth-down interception stopped one promising drive, but he also tossed a 4-yard TD pass to Kevonte Martin-Manley that trimmed Iowa's deficit to 21-14 with 1:42 remaining. Lowdermilk set up Iowa's other TD -- Mark Weisman's 2-yard run in the third quarter -- with his interception return to the LSU 1. Officials initially ruled Lowdermilk, who was untouched on the return, scored. But the TD was reversed when a replay review determined the Iowa defender dropped the ball before crossing the goal line. The victory enabled LSU to finish with at least 10 wins for a school-record fourth consecutive season. The loss ended Iowa's three-game winning streak. Hill, a 235-pound sophomore who rushed with 1,401 yards and 16 TDs this season, averaged 7.7 yards per carry on 28 attempts. On the clinching drive, he delivered runs of 2, 28, 20 and, finally, 37 yards for his second touchdown. He also scored on a 14-yard run in the second quarter. Iowa was back in a bowl after staying at home with a 4-8 record in 2012. The Hawkeyes' four regular-season losses came to nationally ranked Michigan State, Ohio State, Wisconsin and Northern Illinois, teams that took a combined record of 45-6 into the Rose, Orange, Capital One and Poinsettia bowls. LSU's first trip to Tampa since 1989, when the Outback was known as the Hall of Fame Bowl, capped another successful season under Les Miles, but one that fell short of expectations for a program accustomed to contending for national titles. Besides a three-touchdown loss to Alabama, the Tigers dropped three-point decisions to SEC rivals Georgia and Mississippi, while also displaying their potential by being the only team to defeat No. 2 Auburn during the regular season. Jennings came off the bench in the closing minutes to finish a comeback victory over Arkansas in the regular-season finale, leading a 99-yard game-winning drive that he finished with a 49-yard TD pass. Miles expected Jennings to play well, citing poise as one of the 19-year-old's strongest assets. Iowa didn't have much film to study of the young Quarterback, but Hawkeyes coach Kirk Ferentz said any newcomer who entered a program such as LSU's and rose to No. 2 on the depth chart as a true freshman figured to have the makings of a star. And with a talented supporting cast around him, Jennings didn't have to carry the Tigers on his back Wednesday. Hill and receivers Odell Beckham Jr. and Jarvis Landry combined with Mettenberger this season to make LSU the first team in SEC history to feature a 3,000-yard passer, two 1,000-yard receivers and a 1,000-yard rusher in the same year. And the Tigers didn't stray from the formula that made them one of the league's top offenses. Hill broke a 42-yard run on his first carry, setting the tone against an Iowa defense that entered yielding just under 121 yards per game rushing and a little more than 303 overall, third in the Big Ten and seventh nationally. Seven plays later, Jennings finished a 77-yard drive with his 2-yard TD run.

2014 Capital One Bowl

The 2014 Capital One Bowl was played on January 1, 2014 at Florida Citrus Bowl Stadium in Orlando, Florida. The 68th edition of the Capital One Bowl (previously called the Florida Citrus Bowl) was telecast on ABC. It was sponsored by the Capital One financial services corporation.

2014 Capital One Bowl	Line	1	-	2	-	3	-	4	-	Final
#19 Wisconsin	(-1.5)	0	-	14	-	3	-	7	-	24
#8 South Carolina	(51.0)	7	-	6	-	7	-	14	-	34

Scoring Summary
South Carolina – Ellington 39 yard pass from Shaw (Fry kick)
Wisconsin – Arneson 1 yard pass from Stave (Russell kick)
South Carolina – Shaw 9 yard pass from Ellington (Kick failed)
Wisconsin – Duckworth 3 yard pass from Stave (Russell kick)
Wisconsin – Russell 35 yard Field goal
South Carolina – Ellington 22 yard pass from Shaw (Fry kick)
South Carolina – Adams 4 yard pass from Shaw (Fry kick)
Wisconsin – Doe 91 yard kickoff return (Russell kick)
South Carolina – Shaw 1 yard run (Fry kick)

South Carolina Media Guide Capital One Bowl Game Summary - Behind five touchdowns from Quarterback Connor Shaw, South Carolina (11-2) claimed a 34-24 victory over Wisconsin (9-4) in the 2014 Capital One Bowl. The Game MVP, Shaw accounted for 369 yards of offense, going 22- for-25 in the air for 312 yards and 3 TDs while also running for 48 yards on 16 carries and a score. Shaw also caught a TD pass for 9 yards. Junior Bruce Ellington caught six passes for a career-best 139 yards and two touchdowns and threw for another, while sophomore Shaq Roland pulled in six passes for 112 yards, both career bests. The Gamecocks took the lead late in the third quarter behind the senior Quarterback in his final game. Shaw found Ellington from 22 yards away to hand South Carolina a 20-17 advantage, but the duo had a much more pivotal play to keep the drive going. On 4th and 7, Ellington tipped the Shaw pass to himself before pulling it down and going out of bounds for a 22-yard gain and conversion. Shaw's arm accounted for all but three yards of the series, completing six of seven pass attempts on the drive. South Carolina's defense stepped up to start the fourth quarter to snuff out a Wisconsin drive. With 1 yard to gain, the Gamecocks twice stopped Melvin Gordon, who rushed for 143 yards in the contest, for no gain to turn the ball over on downs. The Gamecocks proceeded to drive 74 yards in six plays to take a 10-point lead. Shaw twice found Roland on the drive; the second time a 49-yard catch that saw Roland's concentration as he brought in the catch among two defenders. It was tight end Jerell Adams who scored from 3 yards out for the Gamecocks, pulling down Shaw's third TD pass. Wisconsin made it a one-score game again when Kenzel Doe found a seam and dashed 91 yards on the kickoff return, making it 27-24 in favor of the Gamecocks. On the next possession, however, Shaw drove South Carolina 88 yards for another score, wrapping the drive with Shaw's 1-yard sneak. Another big pass from Shaw to Roland, a 33-yard reception, helped keep the drive alive. The Badgers, behind backup Quarterback Curt Phillips, tried to answer on the next drive, but on 4th and 1 in the Gamecocks' territory, the pass hit Jadeveon Clowney's helmet and sophomore linebacker Kaiwan Lewis corralled it to end that drive. South Carolina gave the Badgers back the ball two plays later when Ethan Armstrong recovered the Gamecocks' fumble. After the fumble recovery, Wisconsin drove inside the 20, but Gamecock freshman linebacker Skai Moore came up with his second interception of the day in the end zone to stop the Badger threat. After the Gamecocks punted the ball back to Wisconsin, the Badgers drove again deep into South Carolina territory, but Lewis picked up the fumble on the catch-and-pitch attempt. South Carolina took the initial lead after a Wisconsin turnover toward the end of the first quarter, when Moore picked off the pass from Badger starting Quarterback Joel Stave. On the next play, Shaw hit Ellington for a 39-yard score. Wisconsin answered when Sam Arneson brought in the 1-yard pass from Stave on the tight end out, leveling the score at 7-7. The offensive duo of Shaw and Ellington handed South Carolina the lead again but in reverse from their normal. To cap the 12-play, 86-yard drive, Carolina called up a double-reverse, halfback pass, as Ellington took the second handoff before firing a strike to Shaw from 9 yards out to hand the Gamecocks a 13-7 lead. Wisconsin claimed the halftime lead when Stave found Jeff Duckworth for a 3-yard score and its PAT kick went through the uprights. The Badgers made it a 17-13 lead when Jack Russell hit a 35-yard field goal to end the Badgers' first second-half drive. Shaw finished his Gamecock career in fourth on the career passing charts with 6,074 yards, while he holds the South Carolina record with 27 wins as a starting Quarterback. The 312 passing yards ranks as the most during a single game in his senior season.

2014 Rose Bowl

The 2014 Rose Bowl was a college football bowl game that was played on January 1, 2014 at the Rose Bowl stadium in Pasadena, California. This 100th Rose Bowl Game matched Big Ten Conference Champions Michigan State Spartans against Pac-12 Conference Champions Stanford Cardinal (the defending Rose Bowl champions), a rematch of the 1996 Sun Bowl. In a game dominated by both teams' rushing offense and strong defense, Michigan State defeated Stanford by a score of 24–20. It was only the Big Ten's second

Rose Bowl victory since 2000. The contest was televised on ESPN with a radio broadcast on ESPN Radio and XM Satellite Radio. The Rose Bowl Game, themed Dreams Come True, was a contractual sell-out, with 64,500 tickets allocated to the participating teams and conferences. The remaining tickets went to the Tournament of Roses members, sponsors, City of Pasadena residents, and the general public. Tickets had a face value of $185 each, with end zone tickets selling at $150.

2014 Rose Bowl	Line	1	-	2	-	3	-	4	-	Final
#5 Stanford	(-6.5)	10	-	7	-	0	-	3	-	20
#4 Michigan State	(42.5)	0	-	14	-	3	-	7	-	24

Scoring Summary
Stanford – Gaffney 16 yard run (Williamson kick)
Stanford – Williamson 34 yard Field goal
Michigan State – Langford 2 yard run (Geiger kick)
Stanford – Anderson 40 yard interception return (Williamson kick)
Michigan State – Pendleton 2 yard pass from Cook (Geiger kick)
Michigan State – Geiger 31 yard Field goal
Michigan State – Lippett 25 yard pass from Cook (Geiger kick)
Stanford – Williamson 39 yard Field goal

Michigan State Media Guide Rose Bowl Game Summary - Fourth-ranked Michigan State won its first Rose Bowl in 26 years and fourth in program history with a 24-20 comeback victory over fifth-ranked and defending Rose Bowl Champion Stanford in the 100th Rose Bowl Game. Connor Cook, who completed 22-of-36 passes for a 332 yards to earn Offensive MVP honors, hit Tony Lippett with the game-winning, 25-yard touchdown pass with 13:22 left in the fourth quarter that put Michigan State on top, 24-17. Stanford scored on the game's opening drive as Tyler Gaffney's 16-yard touchdown run capped a seven-play, 77-yard drive for the Cardinal. Jordan Williamson's 34-yard field goal with 1:40 left in the first quarter extended Stanford's lead to 10-0. The Spartans got on the board with 10:45 on the clock in the second quarter as Jeremy Langford's 2-yard TD run cut MSU's deficit to 10-7. Stanford pushed its advantage back to 10 points at 17-7 on a Kevin Anderson 40-yard interception return for a touchdown with 2:07 remaining in the second, but the Spartans quickly responded with a seven-play, 75-yard touchdown drive that concluded with a 2-yard pass from Connor Cook to Trevon Pendleton just 28 seconds before halftime. MSU tied the score at 17 on Michael Geiger's 31-yard field goal with 12:56 left in the third quarter. A 19-yard punt return by Macgarrett Kings Jr. late in the third quarter gave Michigan State great field position on the Cardinal 27-yard line, and the Spartans took advantage as Cook found Lippett for a 25-yard TD pass on a third-and-8 play early in the fourth. Stanford trimmed the margin to 24-20 on a 39-yard field goal by Williamson with 4:15 remaining. The Cardinal got the ball one last time on its own 25-yard line with 3:06 to play, but couldn't convert a first down, as Kyler Ellsworth sealed the victory for MSU by leaping over the pile at the line of scrimmage and stopping fullback Ryan Hewitt on fourth-and-1. Ellsworth, who collected four tackles including 1.5 for losses in his first career start at linebacker, was named the Rose Bowl Game Defensive MVP.

Game notes - December 25, 2013 – Michigan State captain Max Bullough was suspended for the Rose Bowl game for violating unspecified team rules

2014 Fiesta Bowl (January)

The 2014 Fiesta Bowl was played on Wednesday, January 1, 2014, at University of Phoenix Stadium in Glendale, Arizona. In this, the 43rd annual Fiesta Bowl, the Baylor Bears, champions of the Big 12 Conference, played the UCF Knights, champions of the American Athletic Conference. The game was broadcast live on ESPN. UCF defeated Baylor by a score of 52–42, undoubtedly helped by a Fiesta Bowl Record 17 penalties for 135 yards called against Baylor, becoming the biggest underdog victors in BCS history. Baylor, who had gone into the game as a 16.5 point favorite also missed a field goal. UCF was flagged for just 4 penalties totaling 40 yards.

2014 Fiesta Bowl	Line	1	2	3	4	Final
#15 Central Florida	(71.0)	14	14	7	17	52
#5 Baylor	(-16.5)	7	13	8	14	42

Scoring Summary
Central Florida—Johnson 11 yard run (Moffitt kick)
Central Florida—Johnson 2 yard run (Moffitt kick)
Baylor—Petty 1 yard run (Jones kick)
Baylor—Norwood 30 yard pass from Petty (Kick failed)
Central Florida—Hall 50 yard pass from Bortles (Moffitt kick)
Baylor—Petty 13 yard run (Jones kick)
Central Florida—Hall 34 yard pass from Bortles (Moffitt kick)
Baylor—Petty 1 yard run (Petty run)

Central Florida—Perriman 10 yard pass from Bortles (Moffitt kick)
Central Florida—Bortles 15 yard run (Moffitt kick)
Baylor—Martin 9-yard run (Jones kick)
Central Florida—Johnson 40 yard run (Moffitt kick)
Central Florida—Moffitt 36 yard field goal
Baylor—Fuller 9 yard pass from Petty (Jones kick)

42nd Annual Fiesta Bowl Game Summary - National upstart No. 15 UCF authored one of the biggest upsets of the Bowl Championship Series (BCS) era, an offensive-flavored 52-42 victory over heavily favored No. 6 Baylor in the 43rd Tostitos Fiesta Bowl. Shattering one Tostitos Fiesta Bowl record (94 total points) and nearly breaking another (1,106 total yards, second-highest total) while running 160 offensive plays, UCF, champion of the inaugural American Athletic Conference, and Baylor, a first-time Big 12 Conference champion, both appeared in their first BCS bowl games. UCF, enroute to the biggest win in school history, never trailed and bent but didn't break in the face of Baylor's lethal offense that set the NCAA record for points in a 13-game season (681) after leading the NCAA in total offense (624.5 yards per game) and scoring (53.3 points per game) during the regular season. UCF spurted to an eye-opening 14-0 lead on 11- and two-yard rushing touchdowns by running back Storm Johnson on the Knights' first two possessions that capped marches of 76 (six plays) and 51 (five plays) yards, respectively. The Knights then survived turnovers on three consecutive second-quarter possessions — interception, interception and fumble. But the Bears only were able to turn the three takeaways into seven points, a 30-yard pass from Quarterback Bryce Petty to wide receiver Levi Norwood that pulled Baylor within 14-13 with 5:05 to play in the second quarter. UCF removed all doubt with three touchdowns and a field goal on four consecutive second-half possessions. The Knights appeared to take control with back-to-back touchdown drives to end the third quarter and begin the fourth stanza that gave the Knights a seemingly comfortable 42-28 lead with 13:37 to play. But the Bears answered with a four-play, 53-yard touchdown drive, completed by running back Glasco Martin's nine-yard six-point burst, and the UCF lead was cut to 42-35 and Baylor's offense was ready to purr. UCF calmly answered Baylor's final challenge with 10 more points on Johnson's third rushing touchdown, a 40-yard scamper, and a 36-yard Shawn Moffitt field goal. The Knight's lead had swelled to 52-35. Bortles accounted for 394 total yards (301 passing, 93 rushing) and four touchdowns (three passing, one rushing) enroute to offensive player of the game honors. His performance was closely matched by his Baylor counterpart, Petty, who was responsible for 373 total yards (356 passing, 17 rushing) and three touchdowns (two passing, three rushing). Petty's three rushing touchdowns set a Tostitos Fiesta Bowl record. Both squads boasted a 100-yard rusher; UCF's Johnson notched 124 yards on 20 carries for three touchdowns, while Baylor's Lache Seastrunk added 117 yards on 17 totes. Knight Rannell Hall led all receivers with 113 yards on four catches, good for two touchdowns. UCF linebacker Terrance Plummer, who led all tacklers with 14 stops (eight solos), was voted the game's outstanding defensive player. The Knights' 52-point output was its highest point total against a ranked team in school history. Despite allowing 42 points and 550 total yards, UCF's defense held Baylor 11.3 points and 74.5 total yards shy of its regular-season averages. Baylor also was stymied by 17 penalties for 135 yards. Both figures rank second in Tostitos Fiesta Bowl annals.

2014 Sugar Bowl

The 2014 Sugar Bowl was played on January 2, 2014, at the Mercedes-Benz Superdome in New Orleans, Louisiana. The 80th annual Sugar Bow, was broadcast live on ESPN. Oklahoma overcame the largest spread in BCS history; Alabama had been a 17½-point favorite. The previous record of 16½ points was in the 2014 Fiesta Bowl, won by the UCF Knights 52-42 over the Baylor Bears.

2014 Sugar Bowl	Line	1	-	2	-	3	-	4	-	Final
#10 Oklahoma	(51.5)	14	-	17	-	0	-	14	-	45
#3 Alabama	(-16.0)	10	-	7	-	7	-	7	-	31

Scoring Summary
Alabama – Yeldon 1 yard run (Foster kick)
Oklahoma – Bester 45 yard pass from Knight (Hunnicutt kick)
Alabama – Foster 27 yard field goal
Oklahoma – Saunders 8 yard pass from Knight (Hunnicutt kick)
Alabama – White 67 yard pass from McCarron (Foster kick)
Oklahoma – Hunnicutt 47 yard field goal
Oklahoma – Saunders 43 yard pass from Knight (Hunnicutt kick)
Oklahoma – Shepard 13 yard run (Hunnicutt kick)
Alabama – Henry 43 yard run (Foster kick)
Oklahoma – Shepard 9 yard pass from Knight (Hunnicutt kick)
Alabama – Henry 61 yard pass from McCarron (Foster kick)
Oklahoma – Grissom 8 yard fumble return (Hunnicutt kick)

Associated Press Sugar Bowl Game Summary - Hello, Trevor. Farewell, AJ. Trevor Knight's final start as a freshman sent Oklahoma's expectations soaring into 2014 while bringing a sour end to AJ McCarron's otherwise-charmed Alabama career. Knight completed a Sugar Bowl-record 32 passes for 348 yards and four touchdowns, and No. 11 Oklahoma took down the third-ranked Crimson Tide 45-31 on Thursday night. Oklahoma coach Bob Stoops had declined to announce a starting Quarterback before the Allstate Sugar Bowl, and when Knight took the field on the Sooners' first possession, Alabama's defenders couldn't have anticipated what was in store. Knight's completion percentage entering the game was 52.2. He had completed 47 passes all season before a breakout performance in which two of his TDs went for more than 40 yards. Oklahoma (11-2) needed him to play that well in the 80th Sugar Bowl, the first in which the Quarterbacks for both teams threw for more than 300 yards. The victory was a sweet one for Stoops, who last offseason called talk about the Southeastern Conference being the best league in college football "propaganda." His Big 12 team vanquished an Alabama squad that had been ranked No. 1 much of the past three seasons, winning the previous two national titles before its shot at a third straight was derailed by rival Auburn on the last play of the Iron Bowl in late November. Coach Nick Saban didn't buy the notion that his team, favored by 16 points, was too deflated from its loss to Auburn to play up to its standard. McCarron passed for 387 yards and two TDs, but his two interceptions set up Oklahoma TDs, and his fumble, returned for a score in the final minute, sealed Alabama's first two-game skid since its Sugar Bowl loss to Utah in January 2009. McCarron won 36 of his first 38 games before losing his last two. Freshman Derrick Henry's 43-yard run in the third quarter pulled Alabama to 31-24, and the Crimson Tide (11-2) forced four punts while giving up only one first down in the third quarter. But Alabama was unable to add another score before the Sooners started moving the ball again. Knight lofted a perfect pass to Lacoltan Bester for a 34-yard gain to the Alabama 9. Shortly after, Knight rolled left all the way to the sideline before rifling a touchdown strike to Sterling Shepard, making it a two-touchdown game again with 10:44 left. "The game has started to slow down for him where he's really starting to feel comfortable in what he can do," Stoops said of Knight. Henry, a 6-foot-3, 238-pound true freshman, pulled Alabama within a score once more when he turned his first career reception into a tackle-shedding, 61-yard TD with 6:22 to go. But Oklahoma was able to burn several minutes off the clock, and then the Sooners registered their seventh sack when Eric Striker stripped McCarron, and Geneo Grissom returned the ball 8 yards for a score. Both teams entered the game with defenses ranked in the top 15 nationally, but Quarterback play dominated a first half highlighted by five passing plays of 43 yards or longer, three of which went for scores. Alabama took the opening kickoff and scored in four plays. McCarron hit Amari Cooper for 15 and 53 yards, and T.J. Yeldon ran it in from the 1. Knight's first series ended when Alabama's Landon Collins made a diving interception of a tipped pass, but Oklahoma got it right back when Gabe Lynn picked off McCarron's pass on the next play. One play later, Knight found Bester down the right sideline for a 45-yard score. The Sooners took their first lead when Knight found Jalen Saunders, who reached the ball across the goal line as he was being brought down. McCarron's pinpoint pass over the middle to DeAndrew White for a 67-yard TD restored Alabama's lead early in the second quarter. The Sooners tied it at 17 on Michael Hunnicutt's 47-yard field goal, then cashed in on two more turnovers. Alabama appeared on the verge of a go-ahead score when Yeldon fumbled on the 8. The Sooners then reached midfield, where they converted a fourth-and-1. On the next play, Knight hit Saunders in stride down the right sideline for a 43-yard score. McCarron's second interception, snagged by Zack Sanchez and returned to the 13, set up Shepard's 13-yard TD around the right end.

2014 Cotton Bowl Classic

The 2014 Cotton Bowl Classic was between the #9 Missouri Tigers of the Southeastern Conference and the #13 Oklahoma State Cowboys of the Big 12 Conference. The 78th edition of the Cotton Bowl Classic took place on January 3, 2014 and was televised on FOX. AT&T Stadium, formerly known as Cowboys Stadium and located in Arlington, Texas, hosted the game for the sixth straight year. This was Missouri's third appearance in the Cotton Bowl Classic and Oklahoma State's fourth appearance. Missouri and Oklahoma State were previously conference rivals in the Big 12.

2014 Cotton Bowl Classic	Line	1	-	2	-	3	-	4	-	Final
#13 Oklahoma State	(61.5)	7	-	0	-	7	-	17	-	31
#9 Missouri	(-1.0)	7	-	10	-	0	-	24	-	41

Scoring Summary
Missouri – Josey 3 yard run (Baggett kick)
Oklahoma State – Stewart 40 yard pass from Chelf (Grogan kick)
Missouri – Lucas 40 yard pass from Mauk (Baggett kick)
Missouri – Baggett 35 yard Field goal
Oklahoma State – Seales 21 yard pass from Chelf (Grogan kick)
Oklahoma State – Grogan 25 yard Field goal
Missouri – Josey 25 yard run (Baggett kick)
Oklahoma State – Chelf 23 yard run (Grogan kick)
Missouri – Baggett 46 yard Field goal
Oklahoma State – Roland 2 yard run (Grogan kick)
Missouri – Josey 16 yard run (Baggett kick)
Missouri – Ray 73 yard fumble return (Baggett kick)

Associated Press Cotton Bowl Classic Game Summary - A slow start gave way to a bushel of points in the 2014 Cotton Bowl, with the Missouri Tigers eventually beating the Oklahoma State Cowboys, 41-31, for their 12th win of the year. Not bad a bad way to represent your conference, Gary Pinkel. Not bad at all. Neither team was able to score until Missouri cashed in on an 11-play, 50-yard touchdown drive late in the first quarter. Tiger Quarterback James Franklin -- who started the game by completing just two of his first 12 passes -- settled down enough to string a pair of completions, some solid runs by Henry Josey, and an Oklahoma State facemask penalty into seven points. Cowboy wide receiver Josh Stewart went on to tie the game just 1:16 later, scoring from 40 yards out on a ridiculous catch-and-run. Neither team scored again until Maty Mauk came in for a change of pace series -- and it was quite the change of pace. Within three plays of entering the game, the freshman Quarterback already had 69 total rushing yards. Within nine, he had the Tigers up a by seven, having thrown a 24-yard touchdown pass to Marcus Lucas. Pinkel put Franklin back in the game after that, and the senior rewarded him with a field goal drive right before the half, making it 17-7 in favor of the Tigers. The Tigers continued to lead by that score through most of the third quarter, despite Franklin's erratic play and general ineffectiveness in moving the ball -- at one point, his stat line read 10-of-30 passing for 93 yards and an interception. In fact, after going up 17-7, the Franklin-led Missouri offense stalled in place, going three and out on three consecutive third-quarter possessions. Their fourth went even worse, with Franklin fumbling a handoff that Oklahoma State recovered at the Missouri 33. Three plays later, Clint Chelf found Jhajuan Seales for a 21-yard touchdown, slicing the deficit to 17-14. They would tie it up at 17-17 thanks to a second Missouri fumble. Josey then sprinted in from 25 yards out to give the Tigers back a seven-point cushion, although that margin did not last long. Using a 23-yard touchdown run by Chelf, Oklahoma State tied the game again. They even appeared to take a 31-24 lead on a pick-six of James Franklin, but that play was called back for pass interference. Instead, the Tigers drove for a second Andrew Baggett field goal, making the score 27-24. Desmond Roland and Josey traded touchdowns after that, preserving the three-point Missouri lead. The Tigers only clinched the victory with 55 seconds to play, when Chelf was sacked and stripped from behind by Michael Sam, ending a potential game-winning drive. Shane Ray returned it 73 yards for a touchdown, and the final margin of 41-31.

2014 Orange Bowl

The 2014 Orange Bowl was played on Friday, January 3, 2014, at Sun Life Stadium in Miami Gardens, Florida. The 80th annual Orange Bowl was broadcast live on ESPN. The game was a rematch of the infamous 1978 Gator Bowl. During Ohio State's final drive, Clemson linebacker Charlie Bauman intercepted a pass thrown down the middle by OSU's Art Schlichter as time expired, giving Clemson the victory. Bauman ran towards the OSU sideline and was punched by OSU coach Woody Hayes. Clemson won 17–15, and Hayes was fired the next day, ending a long coaching career spent mostly with the Buckeyes. Ironically, Clemson won the 2014 Orange Bowl in a similar fashion as the 1978 Gator Bowl: in the final play of the game Clemson linebacker Stephone Anthony intercepted a pass thrown down the middle by OSU Quarterback Braxton Miller as time expired, clinching the victory for Clemson.

2014 Orange Bowl	Line	1	-	2	-	3	-	4	-	Final
#12 Clemson	(69.5)	14	-	6	-	14	-	6	-	40
#7 Ohio State	(-2.5)	9	-	13	-	7	-	6	-	35

Scoring Summary
Clemson – Boyd 48 yard run (Catanzaro kick)
Ohio State – Miller 33 yard run (Basil kick)
Clemson – Watkins 34 yard pass from Boyd (Catanzaro kick)
Ohio State – Safety – Penalty on Quarterback in end zone
Clemson – Bryant 3 yard pass from Boyd (Catanzaro kick)
Ohio State – Heuerman 57 yard pass from Miller (Basil kick)
Ohio State – Miller 3 yard run (Basil kick)
Ohio State – Hyde 1 yard run (Basil kick)
Clemson – Watkins 30 yard pass from Boyd (Catanzaro kick)
Clemson – Bryant 3 yard pass from Boyd (Catanzaro kick)
Ohio State – Hyde 14 yard pass from Miller (Pass failed)
Clemson – Seckinger 5 yard pass from Boyd (Pass failed)

Orange Bowl Classic Game Summary - Clemson wins a high scoring, record breaking, nail-bitter - Two of the country's most potent offenses, Clemson and Ohio State, faced off in the 80th Orange Bowl. It was the first time the two teams played each other since the 1978 Gator Bowl and the star players lived up to the hype. The Clemson Tigers were able to squeak past the Ohio State Buckeyes with a late score and an interception in the final two minutes to seal the victory. Clemson wide receiver Sammy Watkins shined as he broke the Orange Bowl record in receptions (16) and receiving yards (227). Clemson Quarterback Tajh Boyd passed for a game-high 378 yards and 5 touchdowns. He was also the game's leading rusher (20 rushes for 127 and 1 touchdown) including a 48-yard touchdown run in the opening drive of the game. After trailing 20-9, OSU stormed back behind Quarterback Braxton Miller. He finished the game with a combined 271 total yards and 3 touchdowns including a 57-yard pass to Jeff Heurman and a 3-yard touchdown run with 12 seconds left in the first half to give OSU the lead at 22-20. In the third quarter running back Carlos Hyde extended OSU's lead with a 1-yard touchdown. He finished the game with 25 rushes for 113 yards. Clemson answered with a pair of touchdowns by Martavis Bryant and Sammy Watkins and Clemson regained the lead 34-29 at the end of the third quarter. Miller's 14-yard touchdown pass to Hyde early in the fourth quarter gave OSU a one point lead after a failed two point conversion. Clemson answered back again with 5-yard pass to Stanton Seckinger to take a 40-35 lead with just over 6 minutes remaining. OSU's C.J. Barnett intercepted Boyd at midfield with 1:27 left in the game. Two plays later, Clemson's Stephone Anthony picked off Miller and prevented a last minute comeback. The instant classic was the last Orange Bowl under the Bowl Championship Series (BCS) era. **Orange Bowl Game Notes** - Clemson wide receiver Sammy Watkins was named the game's most valuable player. Watkins had 16 catches for 227 yards and 2 touchdowns. Watkins also set the Orange Bowl record for yardage with his performance.

2014 BBVA Compass Bowl

The 2014 BBVA Compass Bowl was played on January 4, 2014 at Legion Field in Birmingham, Alabama. The eighth edition of the BBVA Compass Bowl (which was originally called the Birmingham Bowl was telecast on ESPN. It was sponsored by the BBVA Compass banking company. Both the Commodores and the Cougars accepted their invitations after earning 8–4 records in their respective season schedules. This was the first BBVA Compass Bowl for both Vanderbilt and Houston, as well as the first time the schools had played each other in football.

2014 BBVA Compass Bowl	Line	1	-	2	-	3	-	4	-	Final
Vanderbilt	(-2.0)	14	-	10	-	0	-	17	-	41
Houston	(53.5)	0	-	0	-	24	-	0	-	24

Scoring Summary
Vanderbilt - Matthews 50 yard pass from Robinette (Spear kick)
Vanderbilt - Robinette 8 yard run (Spear kick)
Vanderbilt - Spear 24 yard Field goal
Vanderbilt - Matthews 50 yard pass from Robinette (Spear kick)
Houston - Farrow 6 yard run (Bullard kick)
Houston - Ambles 6 yard pass from O'Korn (Bullard kick)
Houston - Bullard 30 yard Field goal
Houston - Greenberry 67 yard pass from O'Korn (Bullard kick)
Vanderbilt - Kimbrow 21 yard run (Spear kick)
Vanderbilt - Spear 35 yard Field goal
Vanderbilt - Seymour 2 yard run (Spear kick)

Associated Press BBVA Compass Bowl Game Summary - James Franklin wanted to savor Vanderbilt's bowl win. Any public comment about his interest in another job would have to wait. Patton Robinette threw two 50-yard touchdown passes to Jordan Matthews, and Vanderbilt recovered after blowing a 24-point lead to beat Houston 41-24 on Saturday in the BBVA Compass Bowl. Robinette, starting after senior Austyn Carta-Samuels had season-ending surgery to repair a torn ACL in his left knee, also had an 8-yard scoring run as Vanderbilt built a 24-0 lead in the first half. After Houston (8-4) pulled even by scoring 24 points in the third quarter, Vanderbilt reclaimed the lead on Brian Kimbrow's 21-yard touchdown run. It was the start of 17 fourth-quarter points for the Commodores. Vanderbilt (9-4) closed the season with five straight wins, adding to Franklin's status as a possible candidate for coaching vacancies, including at Penn State and with the NFL's Browns and Redskins. The Commodores played in three straight bowl games under Franklin -- a first for the program -- and completed their first back-to-back nine-win seasons. Franklin talked after the game about Vanderbilt's returning players. He left the interview room without replying when asked if he would be back. Vandy players doused Franklin with a water bucket in the final seconds. Houston gained only 22 yards and had one first down in the first half but rallied with 24 points in the third quarter to pull even. Kenneth Farrow had a 6-yard scoring run and Deontay Greenberry and John O'Korn threw scoring passes to Markeith Ambles. Franklin joked the Houston comeback was arranged to protect the TV ratings. The Commodores regrouped with two big gains on direct snaps to running backs early in the fourth quarter. Jerron Seymour ran for 38 yards to the Houston 34. Kimbrow's touchdown run gave the lead back to Vanderbilt. Jahmel McIntosh's interception less than a minute later gave the ball back to Vanderbilt, setting up Carey Spear's 35-yard field goal. Seymour added a 2-yard scoring run with less than 2 minutes remaining. Matthews, a senior who set Southeastern Conference records for career catches and yards receiving, had five catches for 143 yards and two touchdowns and was selected the game MVP. Robinette completed only one pass to another receiver -- for 11 yards to Jonathan Krause. Robinette completed 6 of 17 passes for 154 yards with two touchdowns and an interception. Seymour had 14 carries for 46 yards. O'Korn completed 16 of 31 passes for 220 yards and two touchdowns. Daniel Spencer had three carries for 69 yards for Houston and Ambles had six catches for 105 yards and a touchdown. Matthews took advantage of a lead block by Krause to make his first touchdown catch. A forced fumble by linebacker Chase Garnham set up the Commodores' second touchdown. After Houston's O'Korn threw a pass to Greg Ward Jr., a big hit by Garnham forced the fumbled recovered by Andrew Williamson at the Houston 16. Robinette, making his third career start, scored on an 8-yard keeper on fourth down. No Houston defender was near Matthews on his second 50-yard scoring catch in the second quarter. It capped a dominant first half for the Commodores. Levine said he told his players at halftime they could make up the 24-point deficit quickly. A lost fumble by Robinette set up Farrow's 6-yard touchdown run to start Houston's third-quarter comeback. Houston built on the momentum. Spencer's 62-yard run set up O'Korn's 6-yard touchdown pass to Ambles. O'Korn's 58-yard pass to Ambles set up a 30-yard field goal by Kyle Bullard. The Cougars completed their big third-quarter comeback on O'Korn's 67-yard touchdown pass to Greenberry to tie it.

2014 GoDaddy Bowl

The 2014 GoDaddy Bowl was held on January 5, 2014 at the Ladd Peebles Stadium in Mobile, Alabama. The fifteenth edition of the GoDaddy Bowl (originally known as the Mobile Alabama Bowl) was televised on ESPN. It was sponsored by web hosting service company GoDaddy. The Cardinals, who earned a 10–2 record during the season, made their second appearance in the bowl, while the Red Wolves, who earned a 7–5 record during the season, made their third consecutive appearance in the bowl. The pregame buildup focused on the teams' respective strong offenses. For Ball State, the passing game centered on Quarterback Keith Wenning connecting with wide receiver Willie Snead. In tandem with the rushing attack fueled by a strong offensive line, one writer asserted that they would enjoy "easy pickings" against a mediocre Arkansas State defense. Unlike the Ball State offense, Arkansas State's offense focused predominantly on the rushing attack, to which both dual-threat Quarterback Adam Kennedy and running back Michael Gordon contributed.

2014 GoDaddy Bowl	Line	1	-	2	-	3	-	4	-	Final
Arkansas State	(65.0)	0	-	10	-	6	-	7	-	23
Ball State	(-8.0)	7	-	3	-	0	-	10	-	20

Scoring Summary
Ball State - Snead 9 yard pass from Wenning (Secor kick)
Arkansas State - Davis 41 yard Field goal
Ball State - Secor 26 yard Field goal
Arkansas State - Thornton 1 yard run (Davis kick)
Arkansas State - Davis 18 yard Field goal
Arkansas State - Davis 29 yard Field goal
Ball State - Secor 37 yard Field goal
Ball State - Edwards 1 yard run (Secor kick)
Arkansas State - Muse 13 yard pass from Knighten (Davis kick)

Associated Press GoDaddy.com Bowl Game Summary - Arkansas State's Allen Muse sprinted to the back corner of the end zone and then turned to look for the pass. There was Fredi Knighten's throw, hanging in the air for what seemed like forever. The game-winning, 13-yard touchdown pass eventually arrived, right into Muse's hands with 32 seconds remaining to lift Arkansas State past Ball State for a 23-20 victory in the GoDaddy Bowl on Sunday night. Ball State had a chance to tie it, but Scott Secor's 38-yard field goal attempt was blocked by fifth-year senior Ryan Carrethers as time expired. Arkansas State (8-5) won the GoDaddy Bowl for a second straight season, despite losing starting Quarterback Adam Kennedy to a knee injury in the second quarter. It was the Red Wolves' third straight trip to Mobile. Knighten rescued Arkansas State's offense, finishing with 115 yards passing and 97 yards rushing. Muse, who considered quitting football following his father's suicide three years ago, wound up with the biggest catch of the night just five plays after Ball State scored what appeared to be the decisive touchdown. Ball State (10-3) went ahead 20-16 with 1:33 remaining on a 1-yard touchdown run by Jahwan Edwards but couldn't hold the lead. Edwards finished with a game-high 146 yards rushing but had to watch as Arkansas State rallied for the win. Keith Wenning capped his Ball State career with 215 yards passing, one touchdown and one interception. He's the first Ball State Quarterback to throw for 4,000 yards in a season. For a second straight season, Arkansas State shrugged off a coaching change to win the GoDaddy Bowl. Arkansas State lost Coach Bryan Harsin to Boise State in December. He's the latest in a string of three ASU coaches, including Hugh Freeze (Mississippi) and Gus Malzahn (Auburn), who have left the program for a more high-profile job. John Thompson was the team's interim coach for a second straight season, and the veteran defensive coordinator led a staff that managed to cobble together a workable offense without Kennedy. But the Red Wolves couldn't turn productive drives into touchdowns, settling for short field goals from 18 and 29 yards during the third quarter to push ahead 16-10. It nearly came back to haunt them. But Knighten's clutch throw to Muse proved to be the difference. Ball State still had a chance to tie. The Cardinals drove downfield -- and with the help of a 15-yard personal foul penalty on Arkansas State's Andrew Tryon for a late hit -- lined up for the 38-yard field goal with 2 seconds left. But it never got past the line of scrimmage, smacking off Carrethers hands and setting off an Arkansas State celebration that quickly spilled onto the field. Ball State's normally prolific passing offense struggled early in the game. Wenning missed on four of his first five pass attempts -- and took a vicious hit on a sack by Rocky Hayes. Edwards rushed for 92 yards in the first half, including 44 yards on a 14-play drive that ended with Wenning's 9-yard touchdown pass to Willie Snead. It helped Ball State push out to a 10-3 lead by late in the second quarter, but Arkansas State responded with its own long drive just before halftime, capped by Sirgregory Thornton's 1-yard touchdown run to tie the game at 10. Wenning, a 6-foot-3, 220-pound senior, holds just about every passing record in Ball State history, but struggled in his finale. He completed 23 of 44 passes. Arkansas State has hired former North Carolina offensive coordinator Blake Anderson to be the program's fifth head coach in five seasons. Anderson attended Sunday's game but didn't coach.

2014 BCS Championship Game

The 2014 Vizio BCS National Championship Game was the national championship game of the 2013 college football season, which took place on Monday, January 6, 2014. The game featured the Auburn Tigers and Florida State Seminoles. It was the 16th and last time the top two teams would automatically play for the Bowl Championship Series (BCS) title before the implementation of a four-team College Football Playoff system. The game was played at the Rose Bowl Stadium in Pasadena, California. The game was hosted by the Pasadena Tournament of Roses. The winner of the game, Florida State, was presented with the American Football Coaches Association's "The Coaches' Trophy", valued at $30,000. Face values of tickets were $385 and $325 (end zone seats) with both teams receiving a total of 40,000 tickets. Starting immediately after the 2014 Rose Bowl Game, a fresh field was placed on top of the existing field. The field was laid on Thursday, and painting of the field began Friday. The field was completed Saturday in time for it to rest on Sunday for the game on Monday.

Auburn - The Auburn Tigers staged a large turnaround in 2013, improving from a 3–9 record in 2012 to a 12-1 record in 2013. Auburn was coached by Gus Malzahn, who was in his first season at Auburn. The Tigers began the season unranked and were picked to finish fifth in the SEC West in the SEC Media Poll. The Tigers won their first three games of the season, before losing to LSU 21-35. The Tigers then won the final eight games of the regular season to move to an 11-1 record and a SEC West division title. Auburn's regular season was capped off by two improbable victories: the Prayer at Jordan–Hare and Kick Bama Kick (Chris Davis' game-winning touchdown with a 109-yard return of a missed 57-yard field goal attempt). In the 2013 SEC Championship Game, the Tigers defeated Missouri 59-42. It was with the improbable finishes and the single-season turnaround that the Auburn Tigers were dubbed "a team of destiny."

Florida State - Florida State entered the 2013 season ranked #11 in the AP Poll. Despite losing 11 starters to the 2013 NFL Draft, the Seminoles were dominant during the 2013 season, winning by an average of 42.3 points enroute to a 13–0 record. FSU's closest game was a 48-34 victory over Boston College. The team was coached by Jimbo Fisher, who was in his fourth season at Florida State.

Game summary - The 2014 BCS National Championship Game was televised by ESPN, with Brent Musburger and Kirk Herbstreit as commentators. Other ESPN networks (including ESPN2, ESPNEWS, ESPN Classic, ESPNU, and ESPN3) provided supplemental coverage with analysis and additional perspectives of the game, which the network branded as the BCS Megacast. An estimated 26,061,000 people watched the game on ESPN, ESPN2 and ESPNEWS, for a combined Nielsen rating of 14.8.

2014 BCS Championship	Line	1	-	2	-	3	-	4	-	Final
#1 Florida State	(-9.0)	3	-	7	-	3	-	21	-	34
#2 Auburn	(67.5)	7	-	14	-	0	-	10	-	31

Scoring Summary
Florida State—Aguayo 35 yard field goal
Auburn - Mason 12 yard pass from Marshall (Parkey kick)
Auburn - Ray 50 yard pass from Marshall (Parkey kick)
Auburn - Marshall 4 yard run (Parkey kick)
Florida State - Freeman 3 yard run (Aguayo kick)
Florida State - Aguayo 41 yard field goal
Florida State - Abram 11 yard pass from Winston (Aguayo kick)
Auburn - Parkey 22 yard field goal
Florida State - Whitfield 100 yard kickoff return (Aguayo kick)
Auburn - Mason 37 yard run (Parkey kick)
Florida State - Benjamin 2 yard pass from Winston (Aguayo kick)

Game notes - Florida State's deficit of 18-points was the largest ever overcome to win the BCS championship. FSU's win also ended the Southeastern Conference's seven-year winning streak in the national championship game. Texas was the last non-SEC school to win a National Championship (2006). Quarterback Jameis Winston was named the game's offensive MVP. Winston completed 20 of his 35 passes for 2 touchdowns and 237 yards.

Aftermath - Florida State's victory earned it the 2014 BCS national championship and brought the Seminoles' season to an end with an undefeated 14–0 record. This was FSU's third national title in school history. With the loss, Auburn ended its season with a 12-2 record and a #2 ranking in the AP and Coaches polls.

Auburn Media Guide BCS Championship Game Summary - Auburn came with a blink of an eye of winning its second national championship in the last four years. FSU stole a page out of Auburn's playbook for the dramatic finish when Kermit Whitfield returned a kickoff 100 yards with 4:31 for a brief lead, and then Jameis Winston threw a 2-yard touchdown pass to Kelvin Benjamin with 13 seconds remaining to send Florida State to a 34-31 victory in the BCS Championship Game on Monday night in the Rose Bowl. It prevented the biggest comeback story in college football history, though Auburn still finished with a remarkable season and a 12-2 record. The Tigers came within seconds of winning their second national title in the last four seasons. Oh, Auburn tried to win with its usual heroics. Tre Mason broke Bo Jackson's single-season rushing record when he scored on a 37-yard run with 1:19 remaining to give Auburn a 31-27 lead. But Winston, the Heisman Trophy winner, drove the Seminoles in for the game-winner. Auburn had beaten Georgia, Alabama, and Missouri to get this far, and won four games in the final minute, or second. But not this night. Florida State was the one with the heroics. Auburn led 21-3, then found itself up 21-20 with 10:55 left in the game. Florida State took the lead in the fourth quarter, but Mason's TD run gave the Tigers a late lead. Auburn found new pages in its playbook in the first half, throwing touchdown passes to Tre Mason and Melvin Ray for the first time in their careers as Marshall outplayed the Heisman winner Winston in the first half. Marshall completed passes to seven different receivers in the first half. But even with the passing, Auburn stuck with its familiar successful formula of letting Mason run. The tailback who went for 304 yards on 46 carries hit halftime Monday night with 96 yards on 18 carries. Marshall hit the break having hit 7-of- 13 passes for 113 yards and those two touchdown. Winston was only 6-of-15 passing for 62 yards and no touch- downs, though he did set up FSU's only first-half touchdown with a nice scramble to the Auburn 3. Auburn got two early sacks against him, then forced him to fumble to set up the Tigers' third touchdown. Credit punter Steven Clark for setting up Auburn's first touchdown when he flipped the field when he kicked the ball dead at the Florida State 2. The Seminoles couldn't move it, and, after a Chris Davis punt return, the Tigers found themselves in great field position at the FSU 25. Six plays later, Marshall threw a 12-yard touchdown pass to Mason to make it 7-3 Auburn with 3:07 left in the first quarter. Auburn scored on its next possession in a most surprising way when Marshall found Ray running alone down the middle of the field for a 50-yard touchdown pass and a 14-3 lead with 13:48 left in the second quarter. Auburn kept hammering away at Winston, and, after a short run, recovered his fumble at the FSU 27. Marshall made it 21-3 when he ran around end on a 4-yard run with 5:01 left in the second quarter. Florida State got that touchdown back after successfully faking a punt, watching Winston run for 21 to the Auburn 3 and scoring on the next play on a Devonta Freeman run. That made the halftime score 21-10.

2014 New Orleans Bowl

The 2014 New Orleans Bowl was held on December 20, 2014 at the Mercedes-Benz Superdome in New Orleans, Louisiana. The fourteenth annual New Orleans Bowl was televised on ESPN.

2014 New Orleans Bowl	Line	1	-	2	-	3	-	4	-	Final
Nevada	(-1.0)	0	-	3	-	0	-	0	-	3
Louisiana-Lafayette	(62.0)	10	-	0	-	0	-	6	-	16

Scoring Summary
Louisiana-Lafayette - Bates 17 yard pass from Broadway (Stover kick)
Louisiana-Lafayette - Stover 46 yard Field goal
Nevada - Zuzo 21 yard Field goal
Louisiana-Lafayette - Stover 30 yard Field goal
Louisiana-Lafayette - Stover 35 yard Field goal

Associated Press New Orleans Bowl Game Summary - Terrance Broadway set an NCAA Division I bowl game record by completing his first 14 passes, finishing with 227 yards and a touchdown to lead Louisiana-Lafayette past Nevada 16-3 on Saturday. Hunter Stover made a career-long 46-yard field goal in the first half and added kicks of 35 and 30 yards for the Ragin' Cajuns (9-4), who completed their fourth consecutive nine-victory season with their fourth straight New Orleans Bowl win. Cody Fajardo passed for 124 yards and rushed for 49 more for Nevada (7-6), marking the second time he'd passed for more than 2,000 yards and rushed for more than 1,000 in a season. But the Wolf Pack, who had 200 or more yards rushing in each of their previous five games, gained only 89 yards on the ground against ULL and failed to score a touchdown for the first time since being shut out at Notre Dame in 2009. Still, Nevada had chances to make the game tighter. Early in the second quarter, receiver Wyatt Demps fumbled on a hit by Sean Thomas moments after a completion just inside the ULL 10, and the ball was recovered by Cajuns linebacker Dominique Tovell at the 11. Later in the quarter, Nevada had a first-and-goal at the 1, only to move back 5 yards with a false start. The Cajuns then stuffed a running play and forced two incompletions before Nevada settled for a field goal. Broadway's fast start helped keep Fajardo on the sideline but didn't amount to many points. The Cajuns scored their only touchdown on their opening possession, capped by Broadway's 17-yard pass over the middle to C.J. Bates. Stover's first field goal was the only other ULL score in the opening half. Broadway's first incompletion didn't come until 44 seconds remained in the first half, when the Cajuns were threatening again. But Brock Hekking's sack of Broadway took ULL out of field goal range. Fajardo completed 14 of 29 passes, and his incompletions included a pair of key fourth-down passes in the fourth quarter. Both Quarterbacks were sacked four times. Louisiana-Lafayette running back Elijah McGuire rushed for 99 yards and caught five passes for 54 yards, and ULL outgained Nevada 411-213. Louisiana-Lafayette possessed the ball for 36:54. Broadway finished 26 of 31 with no interceptions. He had one turnover when he fumbled on a sack.

2014 New Mexico Bowl

The 2014 New Mexico Bowl was played on December 20, 2014 at University Stadium in Albuquerque, New Mexico. The ninth annual New Mexico Bowl was televised on ESPN.

2014 New Mexico Bowl	Line	1	-	2	-	3	-	4	-	Final
Utah State	(-10.0)	7	-	0	-	7	-	7	-	21
Texas-El Paso	(45.0)	3	-	0	-	0	-	3	-	6

Scoring Summary
Texas-El Paso - Mattox 32 yard Field goal
Utah State - Myers 48 yard run (Diaz kick)
Utah State - Vigil 3 yard run (Diaz kick)
Texas-El Paso - Mattox 34 yard Field goal
Utah State - Hill 11 yard run (Diaz kick)

Associated Press New Mexico Bowl Game Summary - After yet another injury, Utah State wound up needing its fifth-string Quarterback. Fortunately for the Aggies, they had the Vigil brothers the whole way. Nick Vigil ran for a touchdown and combined with his brother to make 16 tackles as Utah State shut down UTEP 21-6 Saturday in the Gildan New Mexico Bowl. The Aggies have one of the top-ranked defenses in the nation. The Vigils, a pair of linebackers who had combined for 551 career tackles to rank first at the FBS level among active brothers, helped hold UTEP to 149 rushing yards and no touchdowns. Utah State (10-4) won a bowl game for the third straight year. UTEP (7-6) is 0-6 in postseason play since winning the 1967 Sun Bowl. Sophomore Nick Vigil scored on a 3-yard run for a 14-3 lead early in the third quarter. Kent Myers threw for 68 yards and rushed for 70, including a 48-yard touchdown run for Utah State. The freshman was the fourth Quarterback used this season by the resilient Aggies, who had been hampered by injuries. When Myers went down at the end of the first half, Wells called in Ronald Butler, a receiver and fifth-string Quarterback, to close out the half. Butler then rushed for 69 yards in two carries. Wells credited Zach Vigil and the team's seniors for helping the others throughout the game. UTEP's Aaron Jones ran for 88 yards but was held to only 3.5 yards per carry because of the strong Aggies line. He came into the game ranked 23rd nationally, rushing for an average of 112 yards. The Miners stayed close with a stingy defense, making an interception and forcing two fumbles. Yet, UTEP committed eight penalties for 75 yards. Neither team threw for a touchdown and combined for only 194 yards passing. Jameill Showers passed for 126 yards for UTEP but often found himself under pressure and couldn't create a passing game to open Jones for deeper runs. Utah State is now 4-5 in bowl games. UTEP, coming off its first winning season since 2005, is 5-9 in bowl play.

2014 Famous Idaho Potato Bowl

The 2014 Famous Idaho Potato Bowl was played on December 20, 2014 at Albertsons Stadium on the campus of Boise State University in Boise, Idaho. The eighteenth annual Famous Idaho Potato Bowl was televised on ESPN. The game was sponsored by the Idaho Potato Commission.

2014 Famous Idaho Potato Bowl	Line	1	-	2	-	3	-	4	-	Final
Western Michigan	(-1.5)	3	-	7	-	0	-	14	-	24
Air Force	(59.0)	6	-	14	-	3	-	15	-	38

Scoring Summary
Western Michigan - Haldeman 25 yard Field goal
Air Force - Davern 1 yard run (Kick failed)
Western Michigan - Davis 47 yard pass from Terrell (Haldeman kick)
Air Force - Davern 55 yard run (Conant kick)
Air Force - Rushing 1 yard run (Conant kick)
Air Force - Conant 31 yard Field goal
Western Michigan - Davis 35 yard pass from Terrell (Haldeman kick)
Air Force - Walker 60 yard fumble return (2-pt Pass good)
Air Force - Johnson 9 yard run (Conant kick)
Western Michigan - Davis 51 yard pass from Terrell (Halderman kick)

Bleacher Report Famous Idaho Potato Bowl Game Summary - The Air Force Falcons ran their way to a convincing 38-24 win Saturday at the Famous Idaho Potato Bowl over Western Michigan in rain-drenched Boise, Idaho. From start to finish, the Broncos had no answer for Air Force's vaunted triple option attack. The Falcons racked up 290 yards of offense on the ground alone, with four rushing touchdowns. Western Michigan had its chances, cutting the deficit to six points early in the fourth quarter and even taking the lead on a punt return for a touchdown before it was called back for an illegal block. A few plays later, Broncos Quarterback Zach Terrell fumbled, and it was returned for a touchdown by Air Force—a gaffe Western couldn't recover from. Terrell threw three touchdowns, all to Corey Davis and all for 35 yards or more. But far more common than the long passing plays were receiver drops, and Air Force dominated the line of scrimmage defensively all game. Air Force's stout defense was the biggest key to its win, holding outstanding freshman running back Jarvion Franklin—who averaged 120 yards per game this season—to just 26 yards on 12 carries. In the end, Western Michigan falls to 0-6 all-time in bowl games and will have to wait another year to try and get the programs first-ever bowl victory. As for Air Force, getting to 10 wins marks the school's best season in well over a decade.

2014 Las Vegas Bowl

The 2014 Las Vegas Bowl was played on December 20, 2014 at Sam Boyd Stadium in Whitney, Nevada in the Las Vegas Valley. The 23rd annual Las Vegas Bowl, it featured the Colorado State Rams of the Mountain West Conference against the Utah Utes from the Pac-12 Conference.

Teams - This was the 80th overall meeting between these two teams, with Utah leading the series 55-22-2. The last time these two teams met was in 2010.

2014 Las Vegas Bowl	Line	1	-	2	-	3	-	4	-	Final
#23 Utah	(-3.0)	21	-	3	-	7	-	14	-	45
Colorado State	(57.5)	10	-	0	-	0	-	0	-	10

Scoring Summary
Utah – Wilson 8 yard run (Phillips kick)
Utah – McClellon 16 yard pass from Wilson (Phillips kick)
Colorado State – Grayson 39 yard pass from Lovett (Roberts kick)
Utah – Booker 60 yard run (Phillips kick)
Colorado State – Roberts 41 yard Field goal
Utah – Phillips 38 yard Field goal
Utah – Wilson 15 yard run (Phillips kick)
Utah – Wilson 12 yard run (Phillips kick)
Utah – Poole 10 yard run (Phillips kick)

Associated Press Las Vegas Bowl Game Summary - Right from the start, Quarterback Travis Wilson and No. 22 Utah had Colorado State on the run in the Royal Purple Las Vegas Bowl. Wilson rushed for a season-best 91 yards, scored three touchdowns and passed for another in a 45-10 rout Saturday. The Utes, who have won 11 of their last 12 bowl games. Utah (9-4) scored on its first three possessions and used big plays that measured 36, 49 and 60 yards. They also employed what Whittingham called some "trickeration." On their first offensive snap, the Utes confused Colorado State when Wilson flipped the ball to running back Devontae Booker, who threw it back to Wilson, who then heaved it down field to Kaelin Clay for 36 yards to the Colorado State 17. Two plays later, Wilson scored from 8 yards out. Wilson rushed for a season-high 91 yards on 11 carries and completed 17 of 26 passes for 158 yards. Utah finished with 548 total yards, including 359 on the ground. Booker ran for 162 yards and a TD and Troy McCormick ran for 86. Colorado State (10-3) played a ranked team for the first time this season -- it has lost its last 16 games against teams in the Top 25. Baldwin, who started the season as the offensive coordinator, ran the team after coach Jim McElwain was hired by Florida. Garrett Grayson completed 21 of 35 passes for 242 yards, but he was unable to avoid Utah's rush in the second half when the Rams were forced to throw the ball. Utah, which led the nation with 52 sacks, dropped Grayson twice in the game, one each by Jason Fanaika and Nate Orchard. Grayson threw an interception and lost a fumble in the fourth quarter, and Utah turned both into touchdowns. Wilson ran for a 12-yard touchdown and backup running back Bubba Poole scored on a 10-yard run. Baldwin hoped to confuse Utah's defense by using multiple formations, but it didn't work. The Rams ran the ball early with little success and later couldn't mount a passing attack. Colorado State ran 19 times for a total of 12 yards. Without a running game, Grayson's job was made even more difficult. "It allows their defensive line to pin their ears back, and it's obviously something you don't want to do," Grayson said. Rams wide receiver Rashard Higgins caught seven passes for 109 yards. Utah didn't do much wrong in the opening half, taking a 24-10 lead, rolling up 327 yards and scoring on its first three possessions. The only time the Utes stumbled came on the final play of the second quarter, when a 38-yard field goal attempt by Andy Phillips hit the post. But by then, the Utes were in high gear. They combined with Colorado State to score 31 points in the first period, a Las Vegas Bowl record, and used big plays to set up each of their touchdowns. A 36-yard pass from Wilson to wide receiver Clay Kaelin on their initial drive put the Utes in position for a touchdown. Two plays later, Wilson scored on an 8-yard run. On the next possession, McCormick broke two tackles for a 49-yard sideline run to set up a second Utah score, a 16-yard TD pass from Wilson to Delshawn McClellon. Booker later ran off-tackle for a 60-yard score and a 21-7 lead late in the first quarter. Colorado State used a trick play to get its only first-half touchdown, a pitch from Grayson to wide receiver Charles Lovett, who threw back downfield to Grayson for 39 yards.

2014 Camellia Bowl

The 2014 Camellia Bowl was played on December 20, 2014 at Cramton Bowl in Montgomery, Alabama. The first edition of the Camellia Bowl, it featured the Bowling Green Falcons of the Mid-American Conference against the South Alabama Jaguars of the Sun Belt Conference. The game was played on ESPN.

2014 Camellia Bowl	Line	1	-	2	-	3	-	4	-	Final
South Alabama	(-2.5)	7	-	0	-	7	-	14	-	28
Bowling Green	(54.0)	14	-	6	-	7	-	6	-	33

Scoring Summary
Bowling Green - Lewis 44 yard pass from Knapke (Tate kick)
Bowling Green - Greene 1 yard run (Tate kick)
South Alabama - Houston 44 yard run (Sunanon kick)
Bowling Green - Tate 39 yard Field goal
Bowling Green - Tate 22 yard Field goal
South Alabama - Bridge 15 yard run (Sunanon kick)
Bowling Green - Greene 17 yard run (Tate kick)
South Alabama - Buford-Hughes 18 yard pass from Bridge (Sunanon kick)
South Alabama - Timmons 3 yard run (Sunanon kick)
Bowling Green - Lewis 78 yard pass from Knapke (Tate kick)

Associated Press Camelia Bowl Game Summary - James Knapke and Roger Lewis kicked Bowling Green's quick-strike offense up to its highest gear at just the right time. Lewis caught a 78-yard touchdown pass from Knapke with 1:04 remaining to lift Bowling Green to a 33-28 victory over South Alabama on Saturday night in the inaugural Raycom Media Camellia Bowl. The Falcons (8-6) responded one play after the Jaguars (6-7) took their first lead. Lewis, Bowling Green's freshman star, got well behind safety Roman Buchanan downfield, and Buchanan came up clutching his right hamstring. The Jaguars, playing in their first bowl game after starting the program in 2009, moved 73 yards in just under 3 minutes to momentarily move ahead. Brandon Bridge hit Danny Woodson Jr. for a 44-yard strike. Terrance Timmons had a 3-yard touchdown run after converting two third-down plays with runs. Bowling Green couldn't convert the 2-point try but Jude Adjei-Barimah picked off Bridge's pass on South Alabama's next play. The Jaguars forced a punt with 31 seconds left but were called for roughing the kicker to allow Bowling Green to run out the clock. Knapke, who earned the game's MVP honors, was 25-for-39 passing for 368 yards and two long touchdowns to Lewis, who capped the first drive with a 44-yard touchdown on a fourth-and-2 play. He became the first Bowling Green freshman to reach 1,000 yards receiving and finished with four catches for 137 yards. Gehrig Dieter had 108 yards on seven catches. Travis Greene gained only 41 yards on 20 carries but also ran for two touchdowns. Knapke took over the starting job when Matt Johnson broke his hip in the opener and led the Falcons to their first bowl win since 2004. They came in on a three-game losing streak and Knapke left with an MVP award named after Bart Starr. The Falcons' fast-paced offense had scored nine touchdowns on drives of a minute or less, so the end-of-game situation wasn't much of an "OMG" moment. Bridge rallied from a slow start to pass for 279 yards and a touchdown but was intercepted twice. Woodson gained 122 yards on six catches. South Alabama had twice closed within six points in the second half, only to watch Bowling Green return a short kickoff to near midfield. The first time produced one of many quick-strike touchdown drives for Bowling Green. On the second, the Falcons' Tyler Tate pushed an 18-yard field goal wide left with 8:25 remaining. Tate had set Bowling Green's record for field goals in a season and career. It gave the Jaguars new life but they couldn't score until two drives later. The game saw both an official and South Alabama's Jones get banged up. Jaguar's tight end Ryan Onkka caught a ball on the sideline and his feet came up and smacked Jones in the face, giving him a bloody nose. In the third quarter, side judge Craig Falkner was hurt when he apparently was struck in the right leg by an object heaved from the stands. The game itself was hard-hitting, too. Bowling Green receiver Ronnie Moore was ejected for targeting and penalized for kick return interference in the third quarter after hitting return man Jereme Jones high on a punt before Jones fielded the ball. South Alabama linebacker Maleki Harris set a school record with 18 tackles, including three for a loss. Bryan Thomas had two sacks for Bowling Green.

2014 Miami Beach Bowl

The 2014 Miami Beach Bowl was played on December 22, 2014 at Marlins Park in Miami, Florida. The first edition of the Miami Beach Bowl, it featured the American Athletic Conference co-champion Memphis Tigers against the BYU Cougars. It was televised on ESPN. Afterwards, the two teams engaged in a bench-clearing brawl. During the post-game celebration Memphis players ran towards the BYU sideline to celebrate with their fans sitting behind the BYU bench (due to the bizarre baseball stadium field layout, most of the people in attendance could only sit on the BYU side of the field). Some bumping and shoving occurred, and one Memphis player was pushed in the back by a BYU player that was allegedly also being pushed from behind. The Memphis player he pushed then turned around and (using both hands) punched/shoved the BYU player in the back of the head. As the BYU player turned his attention back to the attacker in an apparent attempt to retaliate, he threw a punch and he was attacked by 3-4 Memphis players and an all-out, bench-clearing brawl ensued. Punches and kicks were thrown by many players on both sides, one Memphis player even used a helmet as a weapon, and when it was over, numerous players walked off the field bloody and bruised. As the brawl was dying down a BYU player (Kai Nacua) can be seen coming into view and sucker punching a Memphis player (Alan Cross), who was not wearing a helmet, from behind. As the BYU player turned toward the camera's view, a bloodied bruise could be clearly seen from a punch he received while attempting to defend himself from another Memphis player earlier in the brawl.

2014 Miami Beach Bowl	Line	1	2	3	4	OT	2OT	Final
BYU	(56.0)	14	14	0	17	3	0	48
Memphis	(-1.5)	17	7	14	7	3	7	55

Scoring Summary
Memphis - Malone 33 yard pass from Lynch (Elliott kick)
BYU - Jurgens 47 yard pass from Stewart (Samson kick)
Memphis - Lynch 1 yard run (Elliott kick)
BYU - Matthews 25 yard pass from Stewart (Samson kick)
Memphis - Elliott 39 yard Field goal
Memphis - Lynch 3 yard run (Elliott kick)
BYU - Leslie 23 yard pass from Stewart (Samson kick)
BYU - Lasike 3 yard run (Samson kick)
Memphis - Lynch 1 yard run (Elliott kick)
Memphis - Cross 17 yard pass from Lynch (Elliott kick)
BYU - Samson 23 yard Field goal
BYU - Lasike 7 yard run (Samson kick)
BYU - Trout 18 yard interception return (Samson kick)
Memphis - Malone 5 yard pass from Lynch (Elliott kick)
BYU - Samson 45 yard Field goal
Memphis - Elliott 55 yard Field goal
Memphis - Proctor 11 yard pass from Lynch (Elliott kick)

Associated Press Miami Beach Bowl Game Summary - They battled for 60 minutes, then again for two overtimes and literally fought after the final play. And for Memphis, the result was a win 76 years in the making. Paxton Lynch threw four touchdown passes and rushed for three more scores, Jake Elliott kicked a 54-yard field goal to end the first extra session and Memphis wasted a pair of double-digit leads before rallying to beat BYU 55-48 in the inaugural Miami Beach Bowl on Monday. No, but it was memorable -- largely for the right reasons, though also for a scene that got out of hand at the end. Roderick Proctor caught an 11-yard pass from Lynch to put Memphis up in the second overtime, and from there things just got worse for BYU. After DaShaughn Terry sealed the win by picking off BYU Quarterback Christian Stewart in the second OT, tensions and emotions took over. Dozens of people from both sidelines spilled toward the middle of the field, many punching and grabbing. Cameras caught BYU defensive back Kai Nacua -- who had blood streaming from his face -- coming from behind to punch in the head Memphis tight end Alan Cross, who was being restrained by someone from the Tigers' staff. BYU athletic director Tom Holmoe apologized to fans via Twitter. Lynch threw for 306 yards and the four touchdowns, including a 5-yarder to Keiwone Malone with 45 seconds left in regulation -- on fourth-and-4, his second fourth-down conversion on the Tigers' final drive of regulation. And Lynch said afterward that Malone wasn't even the intended receiver. Lynch, the first player at the FBS level with at least four TD throws and three TD runs in a game since Clemson's Tajh Boyd in 2012. Malone caught two TD passes for the Tigers (10-3), who won their first bowl game since 2005 and reached double-digits in wins for the first time since 1938. The 10 wins this season match Memphis' total from the previous four seasons combined. Stewart passed for 348 yards and three touchdowns for BYU (8-5), which finished with the same record for the third straight season and fell to 0-7 all-time in the state of Florida. The Cougars rallied from 10-point deficits twice to take the lead but couldn't hold either. BYU has now lost 12 straight games in which it trailed at some point by double figures. The teams combined for four touchdowns in the first 8 minutes and Memphis led 24-14 early in the second quarter, before BYU rallied with two scores in the final 4:55 to take a 28-24 lead at intermission. Memphis opened the second half with a 13-play, 71-yard march capped by Lynch's third rushing score of the day to reclaim the lead, and the Tigers extended the edge to 38-28 after Cross caught a 17-yard pass from Lynch with 3:45 left in the third. But back came BYU again, with a field goal from Trevor Samson and -- after the Cougars stripped the ensuing return away from Memphis' Joe Craig for a fumble -- Paul Lasike's second touchdown tied it at 38-all with 10:52 left. Zac Stout's interception return for a score that put BYU on top came 3 minutes later. The Tigers, though, had the final answer.

2014 Boca Raton Bowl

The 2014 Boca Raton Bowl was played on December 23, 2014 at FAU Stadium on the campus of Florida Atlantic University in Boca Raton, Florida. The first edition of the Boca Raton Bowl, it featured the Conference USA champion Marshall Thundering Herd against the Mid-American Conference champion Northern Illinois Huskies. The game was televised on ESPN.

2014 Boca Raton Bowl	Line	1	-	2	-	3	-	4	-	Final
Marshall	(-9.5)	14	-	10	-	14	-	14	-	52
Northern Illinois	(67.5)	7	-	6	-	7	-	3	-	23

Scoring Summary
Northern Illinois - Brescacin 19 yard pass from Hare (Hagan kick)
Marshall - Reaves 93 yard kickoff return (Haig kick)
Marshall - Cato 5 yard run (Haig kick)
Marshall - Haig 28 yard Field goal
Northern Illinois - Hagan 19 yard Field goal
Marshall - Johnson 2 yard run (Haig kick)
Northern Illinois - Hagan 30 yard Field goal
Marshall - Shuler 6 yard pass from Cato (Haig kick)
Northern Illinois - Stingily 24 yard run (Hagan kick)
Marshall - Jean-Louis 11 yard pass from Cato (Haig kick)
Marshall - McManus 27 yard pass from Cato (Haig kick)
Northern Illinois - Hagan 31 yard Field goal
Marshall - Cato 4 yard run (Haig kick)

Associated Press Boca Raton Bowl Game Summary - Quarterback Rakeem Cato and receiver Tommy Shuler have played together since high school, so they were able to communicate without a lot of conversation Tuesday in their final game for Marshall. He was time and time again. Shuler and Cato capped their careers with record-setting performances in the inaugural Boca Raton Bowl to help Marshall beat Northern Illinois 52-23. Cato tied an NCAA mark for touchdown passes, threw for three scores and was voted the most valuable player. Shuler had 18 receptions for 185 yards and broke the Conference USA record for career catches with 322. Cato and Shuler were high school teammates in nearby Miami, and they gave a large throng of family and friends plenty to cheer about. Marshall finished 13-1, with its lone loss to Western Kentucky, 67-66 in overtime. Northern Illinois finished 11-3. Cato extended his streak of throwing at least one touchdown pass to 46 consecutive games. That tied the NCAA all-division record set by Central Washington's Mike Reilly. As usual, Cato's favorite target was Shuler. Cato finished the season with a school-record 40 touchdown passes. He threw for scores of 6 yards to Shuler, 11 yards to Angelo Jean-Louis and 27 yards to Deon-Tay McManus. All those touchdowns came in the second half. Cato completed 25 of 37 passes for 281 yards and ran 5 yards for a score. The game drew a crowd of less than 15,000 in Florida Atlantic's 30,000-seat stadium, but both coaches praised the inaugural event. Marshall tried a bit of trickery early in the game, when Shuler took the ball and lobbed it into the end zone to Cato for an 11-yard touchdown. But the play was negated by a penalty. The tandem did better with Cato throwing. All seven of his completions in the first half went to Shuler. Cato wore No. 31 instead of his familiar No. 12 to honor teammate Evan McKelvey, who sustained a season-ending knee injury in October. Deandre Reaves scored Marshall's first touchdown on a 93-yard kickoff return. Devon Johnson ran for 131 yards and a score for the Thundering Herd, who totaled 505 yards. The Huskies' Drew Hare threw for 225 yards and a score, and they added 200 on the ground. They outgained Marshall in the first half but trailed 24-13 because they settled for field goal tries three times and missed one. Northern Illinois pulled off a successful onside kick to start the second half but lost the ball four plays later when Arnold Blackmon stopped Cameron Stingily for no gain on fourth and 1 at midfield. The Thundering Herd mounted touchdown drives of 56, 68 and 70 yards on consecutive possessions in the second half to lead 38-20. The win gave the Thundering Herd bowl victories in consecutive seasons for the first time since 2001-02.

2014 Poinsettia Bowl

The 2014 Poinsettia Bowl was held on December 23, 2014 at Qualcomm Stadium in San Diego, California. The tenth edition of the Poinsettia Bowl was televised on ESPN. The Midshipmen accepted their invitation after earning a 7–5 record in their first 12 games of the season. The Aztecs had a record of 7–5. Navy won the game by a score of 17–16.

2014 Poinsettia Bowl	Line	1	-	2	-	3	-	4	-	Final
Navy	(53.0)	7	-	0	-	7	-	3	-	17
San Diego State	(-3.0)	10	-	3	-	3	-	0	-	16

Scoring Summary
Navy - Reynolds 1 yard run (Grebe kick)
San Diego State - Pumphrey 5 yard run (Hageman kick)
San Diego State - Hageman 43 yard Field goal
San Diego State - Hageman 37 yard Field goal
Navy - Reynolds 6 yard run (Grebe kick)
San Diego State - Hageman 30 yard Field goal
Navy - Grebe 24 yard Field goal

Associated Press Poinsettia Bowl Game Summary - Pardon coach Ken Niumatalolo for being perhaps a bit befuddled amid the euphoria of Navy's 17-16 S.D. County Credit Union Poinsettia Bowl victory against San Diego State on Tuesday night. The Midshipmen won it by not being the last team to make a critical mistake in a game full of them. Navy's Austin Grebe kicked a go-ahead, 24-yard field goal with 1 minute, 27 seconds left. The Midshipmen won it after Donny Hageman was wide right on a 34-yard field goal attempt with 20 seconds left. Hageman had made his first three field goal attempts for the Aztecs. The winning drive was set up when Navy's Chris Johnson forced and recovered a fumble by Donnel Pumphrey, who earlier set San Diego State's single season rushing record. Fullback Chris Swain converted on a fourth-and-1 and Ryan Williams-Jenkins took a pitch and ran 28 yards to help set up the game-winner by Grebe. San Diego State then got to the Navy 17 before Hageman missed. Hageman earlier made field goals of 43, 37 and 30 yards. His third field goal gave SDSU a 16-14 lead late in the third quarter. Pumphrey gained 112 yards on 21 carries to set SDSU's single season rushing record with 1,867 yards. The old record was 1,842 yards by George Jones in 1995. Navy (8-5) lost four fumbles. SDSU (7-6) had three turnovers. Reynolds ran for two touchdowns, extending his own NCAA record for scores by a Quarterback to 64. He scored on a 1-yard keeper for the game's first score and then somersaulted into the end zone at the end of a 6-yard run to give Navy a 14-13 lead midway through the third quarter. The Midshipmen won their fourth straight and for the sixth time in seven games. They've won consecutive bowl games for the second time in history. They were playing just 10 days after beating Army for the 13th straight time. Leading 16-14, SDSU went for it on fourth-and-5 from the Navy 12, but Quinn Kaehler's pass to Mikah Holder was incomplete. Navy punted on its next possession but got the ball back after Pumphrey fumbled. The Midshipmen rushed for 254 yards, led by Swain with 72 yards on eight carries. Navy improved to 2-2 in the Poinsettia Bowl. It avenged a 35-14 loss to SDSU here in 2010.

2014 Bahamas Bowl

The 2014 Bahamas Bowl was played December 24, 2014 at Thomas Robinson Stadium in Nassau in the Bahamas. The first edition of the Bahamas Bowl featured the Central Michigan Chippewas of the Mid-American Conference against the WKU Hilltoppers of Conference USA. It was televised on ESPN. By the middle of the third quarter, the Chippewas had fallen behind the Hilltoppers by a score of 49–14, but they scored four unanswered touchdowns and so near the end of the fourth quarter were down by only seven points. With one second remaining on the clock, they had the ball on their own 25 yard line. They then scored a touchdown on a play that started with a Hail Mary pass and included three lateral passes. By kicking the extra point, they could have tied the game and gone into overtime, but instead they attempted a two-point conversion for the win; however, the pass was blocked. Chippewas Quarterback Cooper Rush threw seven touchdown passes, setting a new NCAA bowl game record.

2014 Bahamas Bowl	Line	1	-	2	-	3	-	4	-	Final
Central Michigan	(67.5)	7	-	7	-	0	-	34	-	48
Western Kentucky	(-3.5)	21	-	21	-	7	-	0	-	49

Scoring Summary
Western Kentucky - Dangerfield 14 yard pass from Doughty (Schwettman kick)
Central Michigan - Davis 21 yard pass from Rush (Eavey kick)
Western Kentucky - German 12 yard pass from Doughty (Schwettman kick)
Western Kentucky - Grant 19 yard pass from Doughty (Schwettman kick)
Western Kentucky - Henry 16 yard pass from Doughty (Schwettman kick)
Central Michigan - Williams 30 yard pass from Rush (Eavey kick)
Western Kentucky - McNeal 55 yard pass from Doughty (Schwettman kick)
Western Kentucky - Allen 1 yard run (Schwettman kick)
Western Kentucky - Wales 21 yard run (Schwettman kick)
Central Michigan - Davis 12 yard pass from Rush (Eavey kick)
Central Michigan - Davis 23 yard pass from Rush (Eavey kick)
Central Michigan - Williams 10 yard pass from Rush (Eavey kick)
Central Michigan - Garland 7 yard pass from Rush (Eavey kick)
Central Michigan - Rush pass complete to Jesse Kroll for 48 yards, lateral to Deon Butler for 2 yards, lateral to Courtney Williams for 8 yards, lateral to Titus Davis for 17 yards for a touchdown (Pass failed)

Associated Press Bahamas Bowl Game Summary - Western Kentucky knows its defensive blunders on what became the final touchdown of the Bahamas Bowl will stay on highlight reels for a long, long time. That's fine with the Hilltoppers -- because they found a way to hang on for an unforgettable win. Wasting nearly every bit of a 35-point lead and giving up the most improbable of touchdowns on the final play from scrimmage, Western Kentucky overcame a record-setting seven touchdown passes from Cooper Rush and beat Central Michigan 49-48 on Wednesday in the first bowl game played outside the U.S. or Canada since 1937. Central Michigan (7-6) scored the final five touchdowns of the game, including a three-lateral, 75-yard dazzler on the final play where six Chippewas -- one center, one Quarterback and four receivers -- touched the ball. Officially, it went down as a touchdown pass to Titus Davis by Rush, his seventh scoring toss of the day, one more than anyone had ever thrown in any bowl game. Central

Michigan went for a 2-point conversion and the win, only to have it broken up by Western Kentucky's Wonderful Terry. A wonderful finish, indeed. Here's how the miracle happened: The Chippewas got the ball on their own 25 with a second remaining after a punt, trailing 49-42. Rush threw deep to Jesse Kroll, who caught the ball between three defenders at the 29. Kroll advanced the ball slightly before lateraling to Deon Butler, who got the ball to Courtney Williams just before getting tackled. Williams then tossed the ball to Davis, who caught it at the 15 and outran three Western Kentucky players to the end zone, reaching to knock over the pylon as he fell out of bounds to complete the bizarre play. Central Michigan coach Dan Enos said he originally planned to kick the extra point. He then changed his mind, a decision that's surely going to be debated. When the conversion pass hit the ground, only then could the Hilltoppers exhale. Western Kentucky Quarterback Brandon Doughty, who threw five touchdowns pass to increase his nation-leading total to 49 on the season. The ending largely overshadowed a huge day by Doughty, who threw for 486 yards. Doughty completed 31 of 42 passes for the Hilltoppers (8-5) and capped the sixth-highest single-season touchdown total in major college football history. Anthony Wales and Leon Allen added touchdown runs for the Hilltoppers. Rush threw for 485 yards. He never had more than three touchdowns in a college game and wound up being credited with five in the final 12 minutes for the Chippewas. The teams finished with 1,254 yards of offense, 647 by Western Kentucky. McNeal caught five passes for 155 yards for the Hilltoppers, who got 95 yards rushing from Wales. Davis had 147 receiving yards and four touchdown grabs, including the one on the final play, for Central Michigan. The finish was one that Brohm understandably likened to the infamous Stanford-Cal, multi-lateral finish with the Cardinal band already on the field -- known simply as "The Play" that gave the Golden Bears a 25-20 win in 1982.

2014 Hawai'i Bowl

The 2014 Hawaii Bowl was played on December 24, 2014 at Aloha Stadium in Honolulu, Hawaii. The thirteenth annual Hawaii Bowl was televised on ESPN.

2014 Hawaii Bowl	Line	1	-	2	-	3	-	4	-	Final
Fresno State	(59.5)	3	-	3	-	0	-	0	-	6
Rice	(-2.0)	16	-	0	-	7	-	7	-	30

Scoring Summary
Rice – Hairston 21 yard Field goal
Fresno State – Kroening 44 yard Field goal
Rice – Taylor 14 yard pass from Jackson (Kick failed)
Rice – Hull 69 yard pass from Jackson (Hairston kick)
Fresno State – Kroening 40 yard Field goal
Rice – Parks 40 yard pass from Jackson (Hairston kick)
Rice – Dillard 1 yard run (Hairston kick)

Associated Press Hawaii Bowl Game Summary - Two touchdown passes in a span of 19 seconds were all Driphus Jackson needed to give Rice the spark it needed in the Hawaii Bowl. The defense took it from there. Jackson had his best game of the year by passing for 318 yards and three touchdowns, and Rice set a Hawaii Bowl record by holding Fresno State without a touchdown Wednesday night in a 30-6 victory that completed a remarkable turnaround for the Owls. Rice (8-5) started the season at 0-3 and ended it with its second bowl victory in the last three years. Rice senior running back Jayson Carter -- all 4 feet, 9 inches of him -- had his second career carry for 2 yards. The walk on, who has a genetic disorder that hinders his growth, had worked with the scout team for three years before making his college debut with a 1-run gain in a win against Utah in October 2013. The Houston school with a reputation as the "Harvard of the Southwest" still won't be mistaken for a football juggernaut. But the Owls are 25-15 over the last three seasons and set a school record with their third straight trip to a bowl. Better yet, they're winning them. This one wasn't close. Even though Rice dominated early, it was tied at 3 early in the first quarter when Jackson was perfect on a fly route to Dennis Parks down the left sideline for a 53-yard gain that led to his 14-yard touchdown pass to Jordan Taylor. Brian Burrell's deep throw was intercepted on Fresno State's next play from scrimmage, and Jackson then slightly underthrew a deep ball to Mario Hull, who came back for the catch and eluded two defenders to complete a 69-yard touchdown. Fresno State (6-8), the only team with a losing record to play a bowl game this year, broke its Hawaii Bowl record for fewest points. Fresno State scored 10 points two years ago in a lopsided loss to SMU. It was the fewest points Fresno State scored all season. The Bulldogs lost to Rice for the first time -- they had a 6-0 edge from their old WAC days -- and dropped their sixth consecutive bowl game. Rice piled up 463 yards and held Fresno State to 93 yards passing, well below the Bulldogs' season average of 238 yards. Brian Burrell was 10 of 20 for 44 yards and didn't complete a pass longer than 8 yards. The Owls were coming off a 76-31 loss to Louisiana Tech in which they gave up 677 yards in a game that decided the West division of Conference USA. They redeemed themselves against the Bulldogs. The Bulldogs made enough defensive adjustments to hold Rice to one first down and 4 yards in the second quarter to at least stay in range. Their offense, however, offered little in return. Fresno State was helped by a defensive holding call on fourth-and-7 to reach the 26, but it could only manage another field goal by Koedy Kroenig from 40 yards. Late in the first half and trailing 16-6, Fresno State again went for it on fourth-and-1 from the 18. Burrell threw a quick sideline pass to Greg Watson, only for Bryce Callahan to break through a block and drop him for a 3-yard loss that kept Rice up by 10 at intermission. Callahan later picked off Burrell's deep throw, and that was the end of Burrell's night. He was replaced by Zack Greenlee, who was equally ineffective. One drive effectively sealed the game for the Owls. Jackson worked the sidelines beautifully to complete four straight passes and move Rice down the field on its second drive of the third quarter. On third-and-2, he found Parks down the sideline. Parks stiff-armed linebacker Donavon Lewis and raced into the end zone for a 40-yard touchdown and a 23-6 lead. It was Parks' first touchdown reception of the year, and he went over 100 yards receiving for the first time this season.

2014 Heart of Dallas Bowl

The 2014 Heart of Dallas Bowl was played on December 26, 2014 at the Cotton Bowl at Fair Park in Dallas, Texas. The fifth edition of the Heart of Dallas Bowl was televised on ESPN. This was the second overall meeting between these two teams, with the Bulldogs winning the first matchup in 2012.

2014 Heart of Dallas Bowl	Line	1	-	2	-	3	-	4	-	Final
Illinois	(56.5)	3	-	6	-	6	-	3	-	18
Louisiana Tech	(-6.5)	14	-	7	-	0	-	14	-	35

Scoring Summary
Louisiana Tech - Craft 16 yard run (Barnes kick)
Illinois - Zalewski 27 yard Field goal
Louisiana Tech - Dixon 80 yard pass from Sokol (Barnes kick)
Illinois - Davis 25 yard pass from O'Toole (Kick failed)
Louisiana Tech - Woods 69 yard interception return (Barnes kick)
Illinois - Young 3 yard run (Pass failed)
Illinois - Reisner 43 yard Field goal
Louisiana Tech - Dixon 1 yard run (Barnes kick)
Louisiana Tech - Martin 28 yard run (Barnes kick)

Associated Press Heart of Dallas Bowl Game Summary - Louisiana Tech's Houston Bates had a career day against his former team -- his 4 1/2 sacks in the Heart of Dallas Bowl matched the number he had in three seasons at Illinois. Bates, who graduated and transferred to finish his eligibility closer to home, was chosen MVP of the game after the Bulldogs beat the Illini 35-18 on Friday. Kenneth Dixon scored one of his two touchdowns on an 80-yard reception and Xavier Woods scored on a 69-yard interception. The Bulldogs (9-5) also got touchdown runs of 16 yards from Jarred Craft and 28 yards from Blake Martin on a dark, overcast day at the Cotton Bowl stadium. Illinois (6-7) struggled early with penalties and missed field goals but got within three points on David Reisner's 43-yard field goal early in the fourth quarters. But Dixon scored his second TD from one yard out with six minutes left to make it 28-18 and the Illini couldn't answer. Illinois appeared to have gotten a break when LaKeith Walls sacked Cody Sokol, causing him to fumble. Jihad Ward returned it 19 yards before Dixon forced a fumble and Sokol recovered. That drive was capped by Dixon's TD. Tech coach Skip Holtz then asked Bates to skip the humble answer and say what it really meant to him to win. "Unbelievable," Bates added with a huge smile. Bates had an additional sack in the closing minutes negated when a teammate couldn't get off the field in time and the Bulldogs were penalized for having 12 players on the field. Dixon became Louisiana Tech's career leader in yards rushing, finishing with 63 for a total of 3,410 in three seasons. He is also the only FBS player with both a run and a reception of at least 80 yards this season. Louisiana Tech went into the game tied for first place among FBS schools with 25 interceptions and first with 40 total turnovers forced. With Monday's two Illini turnovers, Tech converted turnovers into 198 points this season. Tech led 21-9 lead at halftime after Reilly O'Toole's pass was returned for a touchdown by Woods midway through the second, but Illinois responded with a 3-yard scoring run by Donovonn Young. The 2-point conversion failed, though, but Reisner banked in a field goal to cut the Bulldogs' lead to 3. O'Toole threw a 25-yard touchdown pass to Jon Davis early in the second quarter. He was 24 of 39 for a season-high 295 yards with one touchdown and one interception. Taylor Zalewski kicked a 27-yard FG in the first quarter for Illinois, which committed eight first-half penalties for 53 yards and missed two field goals attempts and an extra point. Sokol, who began his collegiate career in the Big Ten at Iowa, completed 14 of 28 passes for 247 yards and one touchdown. On Woods' interception, the pass was thrown ahead of Dudek, whose uniform appeared to be held by Tech's Bryson Abraham just before Woods made the grab.

2014 Quick Lane Bowl

The 2014 Quick Lane Bowl was between the Rutgers Scarlet Knights and the North Carolina Tar Heels played on December 26, 2014, at Ford Field in Detroit, Michigan. It was the first edition of the Quick Lane Bowl, replacing the Little Caesars Pizza Bowl. For 2014 bowl season the Quick Lane Bowl had contractual tie-ins with the Big Ten Conference and the Atlantic Coast Conference. The game was sponsored by Ford Motor Company through its service-center brand Quick Lane.

2014 Quick Lane Bowl	Line	1	-	2	-	3	-	4	-	Final
Rutgers	(69.0)	7	-	16	-	7	-	10	-	40
North Carolina	(-3.5)	0	-	0	-	7	-	14	-	21

Scoring Summary
Rutgers - Patton 34 yard pass from Nova (Federico kick)
Rutgers - Hicks 21 yard run (Federico kick)
Rutgers - Martin 8 yard run (Kick failed)
Rutgers - Federico 19 yard Field goal
North Carolina - Williams 1 yard run (Moore kick)
Rutgers - Turzilli 34 yard pass from Nova (Federico kick)
Rutgers - Martin 28 yard run (Federico kick)
Rutgers - Federico 31 yard Field goal
North Carolina - Tabb 7 yard pass from Williams (Moore kick)
North Carolina - Singleton 1 yard pass from Trubisky (Moore kick)

ESPN Quick Lane Bowl Game Summary - Josh Hicks and the Rutgers Scarlet Knights capped their first season in the Big Ten with a dominating effort in the inaugural Quick Lane Bowl. The freshman running back rushed for 202 yards and a touchdown and Rutgers beat North Carolina 40-21 on Friday night at Ford Field. Senior Gary Nova threw for 184 yards and two touchdowns, and freshman Robert Martin ran for 100 yards and two scores for the Scarlet Knights (8-5). Flood, the brother of a New York Police Department officer, wore an "NYPD" cap during the game, as did many of his assistant coaches and support personnel. Some Rutgers fans also wore them. Owned and operated by the NFL's Detroit Lions, the bowl replaced the Little Caesar's Pizza Bowl, which had been played in Detroit under various names since 1997. The new bowl was hoped to make a bigger impact with a Big Ten vs. ACC matchup but drew a disappointing crowd. The announced attendance was 23,876 -- smaller than all but one Pizza Bowl -- and the actual crowd appeared to be less than half of that. Rutgers led 40-7 before the Tar Heels (6-7) scored twice in the final 7 minutes. North Carolina also had two second-half touchdown passes taken away because of interference penalties. North Carolina Quarterback Marquise Williams was never able to get going, although he did throw for one score and run for another. The Scarlet Knights lost the coin toss, but got the ball when North Carolina deferred. They only needed 2:17 to take the lead, with Nova hitting a wide-open Andre Patton for a 34-yard touchdown strike. North Carolina got into Rutgers' territory its first two drives but turned the ball over on the first and punted on the second. The Tar Heels blocking a punt to take over at the 30, but the drive stalled at the 5 and a fake field goal was buried for a 4-yard loss. The Scarlet Knights answered with a 91-yard drive that ended with Hicks' 21-yard run that made it 14-0 early in the second. Rutgers then turned another Tar Heels fumble into a quick touchdown -- Martin's 8-yard run -- but missed the extra point, leaving it 20-0. The Tar Heels missed a field goal, then shanked a punt 20 yards, allowing Rutgers to kick a 19-yard field goal that made it 23-0 at halftime. Williams got North Carolina on the board with a 1-yard run, but the Scarlet Knights came back with a 34-yard pass from Nova to Andrew Turzilli to make it 30-7. Martin's second touchdown run -- this one from 28 yards -- gave Rutgers a 30-point advantage early in the fourth.

2014 St. Petersburg Bowl

The 2014 St. Petersburg Bowl, the seventh edition of the annual game, was played on December 26, 2014 at Tropicana Field in St. Petersburg, Florida. The game matched the NC State Wolfpack of the Atlantic Coast Conference against the American Athletic Conference co-champion UCF Knights.

2014 St. Petersburg Bowl	Line	1	-	2	-	3	-	4	-	Final
NC State	(49.0)	7	-	10	-	14	-	3	-	34
Central Florida	(-2.0)	3	-	7	-	3	-	14	-	27

Scoring Summary
Central Florida - Moffitt 40 yard Field goal
NC State - Samuels 18 yard pass from Thornton (Sade kick)
Central Florida - Reese 6 yard pass from Holman (Moffitt kick)
NC State - Alston 37 yard pass from Brissett (Sade kick)
NC State - Sade 19 yard Field goal
NC State - Dayes 24 yard run (Sade kick)
Central Florida - Moffitt 36 yard Field goal
NC State - Dayes 15 yard run (Sade kick)
NC State - Sade 45 yard Field goal
Central Florida - Reese 14 yard pass from Holman (Moffitt kick)
Central Florida - Reese 2 yard pass from Holman (Moffitt kick)

Associated Press St. Petersburg Bowl Game Summary - A turnaround season got a little sweeter for North Carolina State in the Bitcoin St. Petersburg Bowl. The Wolfpack took another step forward under second-year coach Dave Doeren on Friday night with a 34-27 victory over Central Florida that wasn't as close as the final score. NC State (8-5) dominated for three quarters before Justin Holman threw a pair of fourth-quarter touchdown passes to help UCF pull within seven. Jacoby Brissett threw for 262 yards and one touchdown and Matt Dayes scored on runs of 24 and 15 yards for NC State, which won just three games in its first season under Doeren. Brissett tossed a 37-yard TD pass to Johnathan Alston to put the Wolfpack ahead for good in the second quarter. Running back Shadrach Thornton got NC State going early with an 18-yard scoring pass to Jaylen Samuels. UCF (9-4) began the night ranked in the top 10 in fewest yards allowed per game, as well as pass efficiency, rushing and scoring defense. But American Athletic Conference co-champions had no answers for Brissett and a supporting cast that amassed 488 yards of total offense -- over 200 more than opponents averaged against the Knights during the regular season. Brissett was 15 of 26 with no interceptions, completing passes to eight receivers. Thornton rushed for 96 yards on 17 carries and Dayes finished with 78 yards on 13 attempts to key a ground attack that produced 188 yards. Doeren thanked his players and coaching staff and talked about Brissett's growth in his first season at NC State after transferring from Florida. Holman completed 23 of 53 passes for 291 yards for UCF, including TD passes of 6, 14 and 2 yards to Josh Reese, who had six receptions for 75 yards. Reese's second touchdown cut it to 34-20 with 11 minutes remaining. The Knights got the ball back three more times but couldn't get any closer until Holman threw his 2-yarder to Reese with 1:44 left. NC State's Tyler Purvis recovered the ensuing onside kick, and the Wolfpack ran out the clock. UCF is a year removed from arguably the biggest victory in school history, an upset of Baylor in the Fiesta Bowl that capped the Knights' first 12-win season. Going from appearing in a BCS game for the first time to ending the year in St. Petersburg for the second time in three seasons might have been perceived as a letdown except the Knights have continued to prosper after losing star Quarterback Blake Bortles to the NFL draft, where he was the third overall selection by the Jacksonville Jaguars. Holman's Hail Mary pass to Breshad Perriman as time expired gave UCF a 32-30 victory over East Carolina and a share of its second straight AAC championship. NC State is in its second season of rebuilding under Doeren, who took over after a highly successful stint at Northern Illinois. The Wolfpack went 0-8 in the ACC and 3-9 overall in 2013, and the four-game improvement in their regular-season record this year matched Mississippi State for the second biggest in the five power conferences. Brissett, who is from West Palm Beach and transferred to NC State from Florida. The 6-foot-4, 231-pound redshirt junior completed 10 of his first 12 passes for 197 yards, including his TD pass to Alston that put the Wolfpack up 14-10 early in the second quarter. NC State won a postseason game for the first time since winning the Belk Bowl in 2011, ending UCF's three-game winning streak in bowl appearances.

2014 Military Bowl

The 2014 Military Bowl was played on December 27, 2014 at Navy–Marine Corps Memorial Stadium on the campus of the United States Naval Academy in Annapolis, Maryland in the United States. The seventh annual Military Bowl, it pitted the Virginia Tech Hokies of the Atlantic Coast Conference against the American Athletic Conference co-champion Cincinnati Bearcats. The game started was televised on ESPN. It was sponsored by aerospace and defense technology company Northrop Grumman.

2014 Military Bowl	Line	1	-	2	-	3	-	4	-	Final
Virginia Tech	(51.0)	7	-	6	-	14	-	6	-	33
Cincinnati	(-2.5)	7	-	3	-	0	-	7	-	17

Scoring Summary
Cincinnati - Moore 31 yard pass from Kiel (Gantz kick)
Virginia Tech - Coleman 1 yard run (Slye kick)
Virginia Tech - Slye 45 yard Field goal
Cincinnati - Gantz 25 yard Field goal
Virginia Tech - Slye 49 yard Field goal
Virginia Tech - Malleck 1 yard pass from Brewer (Slye kick)
Virginia Tech - Stroman 12 yard fumble return (Slye kick)
Virginia Tech - Slye 38 yard Field goal
Cincinnati - Moore 43 yard pass from Colosimo (Gantz kick)
Virginia Tech - Slye 33 yard Field goal

CollegeFootballPoll.com Military Bowl Game Summary - The game took place at Navy-Marine Corps Memorial Stadium near the campus of the U.S. Naval Academy in Annapolis, Maryland. Virginia Tech was outgained but won the turnover battle as Frank Beamer oversaw operations from the coaches' booth in the press box while son, Shane, led the troops on the ground. Shane had led the team through pre-game preparations following his father's throat surgery for what was only revealed as a mild but necessary procedure. The victory clinched Virginia Tech's 22nd consecutive winning season (7-6) in its 22nd straight year with a bowl appearance. Cincinnati slipped to 9-4 for the year though the team outgained the Hokies 489-334. Two interceptions and a fumble were a large part of the downfall for the Bearcats. Cincinnati fell behind 27-10 in the 3rd quarter when Deon Clark sacked QB Greg Kiel to knock him out of the game and caused a fumble that was returned by Nigel Williams. Williams rumbled toward the goal line but was stripped of the ball, so teammate Greg Stroman recovered the loose pigskin and fought his way 12 yards to the pylon. RB J.C. Coleman ran for 157 yards and a touchdown on 25 carries to pace the Virginia Tech offense. The Bearcats entered the contest on a 7-game winning streak. Virginia Tech improved its bowl record to 11-17 while Cincinnati fell to 7-8.

2014 Sun Bowl

The 2014 Sun Bowl was played on December 27, 2014, at Sun Bowl Stadium in El Paso, Texas. In this 81st edition of the Sun Bowl, Arizona State from the Pac-12 Conference met Duke from the Atlantic Coast Conference. The game was televised on CBS and heard on the Sports USA Radio Network.

2014 Sun Bowl	Line	1	-	2	-	3	-	4	-	Final
Duke	(65.0)	3	-	14	-	0	-	14	-	31
#15 Arizona State	(-7.5)	10	-	10	-	10	-	6	-	36

Scoring Summary
Arizona State – Richard 9 yard run (Gonzales kick)
Arizona State – Gonzales 28 yard Field goal
Duke – Martin 40 yard Field goal
Arizona State – Gonzales 38 yard Field goal
Arizona State – Richard 1 yard run (Gonzales kick)
Duke – Powell 14 yard pass from Boone (Martin kick)
Duke – Crowder 68 yard punt return (Martin kick)
Arizona State – Richard 11 yard pass from Kelly (Gonzales kick)
Arizona State – Gonzales 47 yard Field goal
Duke – Barnes 14 yard pass from Boone (Martin kick)
Duke – Blakeney 12 yard pass from Crowder (Martin kick)
Arizona State – Richard 4 yard pass from Kelly (Run failed)

Sun Bowl Classic Game Summary - In a game with 792 yards of combined offense, it was an interception by Arizona State's (10-3) defensive back Kweishi Brown that sealed a 36-31 victory for the Sun Devils over Duke (9-4) in the 81st Hyundai Sun Bowl on Saturday, Dec. 27 in El Paso, Texas. Duke had the ball with under a minute remaining at the ASU 14-yard line and threw the ball to the corner of the end zone, but the pass was intercepted by Brown. The Sun Devils picked up their 10th win of the year in front of 47,809 for their second-straight Sun Bowl appearance, defeating Purdue, 27-23, in 2004. Senior Quarterback Taylor Kelly highlighted the ASU offense with 240 yards passing and 24 yards rushing for 264 of total offense. After the 81st Hyundai Sun Bowl, Kelly becomes the third player in ASU program history to tally 10,000 yards of total offense with 10,223 yards. Duke trailed 30-17 heading into the fourth quarter but battled back scoring 14-points in the fourth to take their first lead of the game with 5:03 remaining in the game. The Blue Devils took possession on an ASU turnover but turned it over on downs with 9:22 left in the fourth after the Sun Devils attempted to gain a first down on 4th-and-1. The Blue Devil offense was forced to punt at the 50-yard line but pulled off a fake punt using a 30-yard pass from punter Will Monday to wide receiver Johnell Barnes moving the ball down to the 20-yardline to keep the drive alive. That play led to a 12-yard touchdown pass from wide receiver Jamison Crowder to wide receiver Issac Blakeney. Crowder received a toss from Quarterback Anthony Boone before passing the ball to Blakeney giving Duke its first lead of the game at 31-30 after the PAT. The Sun Devils immediately responded with a 96-yard kickoff return by true freshman Kalen Ballage, who ended the game as the John Folmer Most Valuable Special Teams Player. ASU running back freshman Demario Richards, who was named the C.M. Hendricks MVP, scored on the very next play, catching a pass from Kelly. The two-point conversion was unsuccessful making it a 36-31 game with 4:45 remaining on the clock. ASU's Richards posted 41 yards on seven carries, with two touchdowns and added 22 yards on five receptions and two receiving touchdowns. Duke's Shaquille Powell had a productive day with 117 yards rushing on 29 attempts, while adding 52 yards on three receptions with one touchdown. It was his first career 100-yard game and tallied a career-best 169 total yards in the game. ASU came out on fire, scoring on its first drive of the game after getting the ball on the Duke 49-yardline. The Sun Devils used just five plays in a minute and 33 seconds as Richard followed the right guard into the end zone from nine yards out. After the Blue Devils went three-and-out on their second drive of the game, ASU put up another three points on a 28-yard field goal by Zane Gonzalez to take a 10-0 lead with 10:50 left in the first quarter. The Blue Devils would get on the board in the first quarter as placekicker Ross Martin hitting a 40-yard field goal with 2:59 left. Duke started the drive at its own 35 heading down to the ASU 22-yardline, while eating up four minutes and 33 seconds off the clock.

ASU extended its lead by 10 with 12:55 on the clock in the second quarter as Gonzalez hit a 38-yard field goal. The Sun Devils had momentum but a sack by Duke on 3-and-4 for a 12-yard loss forced the field goal attempt. Gonzalez finished the game with 12 total points off three field goals and three PATs, tying No. 4 for all-time scoring for a kicker in Hyundai Sun Bowl history. The Sun Devils decided to go for it on 4th-and-1 at the Duke 12-yard line and Kelly ran the ball up the middle for an 11-yard gain before Richard ran the ball in from 1-yard line. The point after gave ASU a 20-3 lead. Duke responded using an 8-play, 78-yard drive to pull back to within 10. The Blue Devils scored on a 14-yard pass from Anthony Boone to Powell. With 2:06 on the clock, Powell had already posted a career-high 96 total offensive yards. ASU was held to its first 3-and-out of the game and punted the ball 43-yards down to the Duke 32-yardline. Blue Devil punt returner Crowder returned the ball 68 yards for a touchdown to make it a 20-17 ballgame. The 68-yard punt return was the longest punt return since North Carolina's Marcus Wall returned a punt for 82 yards against Texas during the 1994 Sun Bowl. The Sun Devils opened the second half scoring on an eight-play, 75-yard scoring drive that was capped off by an 11-yard TD pass from Kelly to Richard. It was Richard's third score of the game, giving ASU a 27-17 lead with 11:08 remaining. Duke was driving down the field and completed a pass to Blakeney on 3rd-and-14 but the ball was stripped by ASU defensive back Kweishi Brown with the fumble recovered by Jordan Simone at the 7-yardline. The ball was returned to the ASU 36-yardline, and the Sun Devils eventually scored on a 47-yard field goal by Gonzalez to make it 30-17 game. The Blue Devils pulled to within six points at 30-24, when Boone threw a 14-yard touchdown pass to Barnes with the PAT made by Martin. It was Barnes' first career-touchdown. Arizona State freshman Marcus Hardison was named the Jimmy Rogers, Jr. Most Valuable Lineman.

2014 Independence Bowl

The 2014 Independence Bowl was played on December 27, 2014 at Independence Stadium in Shreveport, Louisiana. The 39th annual Independence Bowl, it pitted the Miami Hurricanes of the Atlantic Coast Conference against the South Carolina Gamecocks of the Southeastern Conference. The game was televised on ABC.

2014 Independence Bowl	Line	1	-	2	-	3	-	4	-	Final
Miami	(-3.5)	3	-	3	-	8	-	7	-	21
South Carolina	(62.0)	0	-	17	-	0	-	7	-	24

Scoring Summary
Miami - Badgley 27 yard field goal
Miami—Badgley 26 yard field goal
South Carolina - Cooper 78 yard pass from Thompson (Fry kick)
South Carolina - Davis 15 yard pass from Thompson (Fry kick)
South Carolina - Fry 32 yard field goal
Miami - Edwards 3 yard run (Lewis pass from Kaaya)
South Carolina - Thompson 2 yard run (Fry kick)
Miami - Dorsett 11 yard pass from Kaaya (Badgley kick)

South Carolina Media Guide Independence Bowl Game Summary - It would come down to the very last minute of the game, but the South Carolina Gamecocks (7-6) secured their 11th-straight season with a record of .500 or better thanks to a 24-21 win over Miami (6-7) in the Duck Commander Independence Bowl. A bend-but-don't-break defense helped carry the Gamecocks through the early portion of the game while the offense was still finding its footing. Despite a pair of Miami drives that went deep into Carolina territory, the Hurricanes could only muster a pair of field goals after being stopped inside the ten yard line both times. It took a big play halfway through the second quarter to shake the offense from its slow start. On second down at its own 22, Dylan Thompson hit a wide-open Pharoh Cooper on a post route down the middle for the 78-yard touchdown to move the Gamecocks ahead 7-6 with just under eight minutes to play in the first half. The yardage in just that one play matched the offense's total gains for the entire game up until that point and tied for the longest pass play in the bowl's history. The score broke the seal on the offense, which scored on the very next drive after the defense forced a three-and-out from Miami. Starting near midfield, Thompson spearheaded the scoring drive with a trio of difficult throws. After hooking up with Cooper for a 13-yard first down, he followed it up with a 35-yard strike to Damiere Byrd to get to the Hurricane five-yard line. A penalty pushed the Gamecocks back to the 15-yard line before Thompson rolled to his left and threw across his body to Mike Davis in the back of the end zone for a 14-6 lead. On the very next drive, a pass from Miami's Brad Kaaya was tipped up in the air and intercepted by Jonathan Walton. The turnover would set up a 32-yard field goal from Elliott Fry and cap the team's scoring for the half, a 17-6 lead. After struggling to stop Miami's nationally renowned rushing offense in the first quarter, the Gamecocks defense learned quickly and held the opposition to just 44 yards in the second quarter after allowing 160 in just the first two drives of the game. The third quarter was largely controlled by Miami, who drew within a field goal of tying the game after an 11-play, 93-yard drive for a touchdown and a two-point conversion. The offensive momentum for Carolina would not carry over the break, as its first four drives of the second half would go for just 71 yards on 25 plays. The Gamecocks continued to be stymied offensively early in the fourth quarter, before another game-changing moment would provide the difference. Carolina would punt the ball with seven minutes left in the game, still ahead 17- 14. On the drive's second play, Miami's Duke Johnson rushed to the right and was swarmed immediately. Gerald Dixon would emerge from the pile with the ball, but the game officials ruled that he was already down before the ball came out. After it was reviewed, however, it was decided that it was a fumble. On the ensuing possession, Thompson and Cooper would combine yet again for a big play, as the sophomore wide receiver went over the back of his defender on the under-thrown ball and hauled in the 25-yard strike to set up first-and-goal at the two yard line. On the very next play, Thompson would sell the read option fake and keep it for the touchdown, strikingly similar to his game-winner against Florida. Miami drove 72 yards in under two minutes for a touchdown to make it 24-21. With 2:16 still to play and needing to run out the clock, the Gamecocks turned to Davis to seal the win. He converted a third-and-one that would be the clincher, as it forced the Hurricanes to use their final two timeouts. In his final game in the Garnet and Black, Thompson would finish with 284 yards through the air and a pair of touchdowns to go with his rushing score. Cooper would bring in nine catches for 170 yards and earned offensive MVP honors for his efforts. Skai Moore earned defensive MVP honors.

2014 Pinstripe Bowl

The 2014 Pinstripe Bowl was played on December 27, 2014 at Yankee Stadium in the New York City borough of the Bronx. It was the fifth annual Pinstripe Bowl. Pre-game buildup focused on the teams' respective exceptional defenses, especially the matchup between Boston College's ostensibly strong rushing attack and Penn State's top-ranked rushing defense; the game was expected to be won "in the trenches". Penn State's "anemic" offense sought to finally reach its potential with a strong performance from sophomore Quarterback Christian Hackenberg.

2014 Pinstripe Bowl	Line	1	-	2	-	3	-	4	-	OT	-	Final
Boston College	(-2.5)	7	-	0	-	14	-	3	-	6	-	30
Penn State	(40.5)	7	-	0	-	7	-	10	-	7	-	31

Scoring Summary
Penn State - Godwin 72 yard pass from Hackenberg (Ficken kick)
Boston College - Hillman 49 yard run (Knoll kick)
Boston College - Phillips 19 yard pass from Murphy (Knoll kick)
Boston College - Murphy 40 yard run (Knoll kick)
Penn State - Lewis 7 yard pass from Hackenberg (Ficken kick)
Penn State - Hamilton 16 yard pass from Hackenberg (Ficken kick)
Boston College - Knoll 20 yard Field goal
Penn State - Ficken 45 yard Field goal
Boston College - Dudeck 21 yard pass from Murphy (Kick failed)
Penn State - Kyle 10 yard pass from Hackenberg (Ficken kick)

Associated Press Pinstripe Bowl Game Summary - At Yankee Stadium, Sam Ficken was Penn State's captain in the clutch. He booted a walk-off winner deep into Monument Park, kicking the extra point that Boston College could not to give the Nittany Lions a 31-30 overtime win in the New Era Pinstripe Bowl. Christian Hackenberg hit Kyle Carter for a 10-yard touchdown pass that set up Ficken's automatic kick that sent the Nittany Lions dancing on top of the Yankees' dugout. The Nittany Lions (7-6) played in a bowl game for the first time since January 2012 after the NCAA lifted the most severe sanctions levied against the program in the wake of the Jerry Sandusky child sex abuse scandal. Captain to captain, Ficken had the honor of using the retired Jeter's locker and some of the five-time World Series champion shortstop's clutch postseason play appeared to rub off. Ficken sent the game into OT with a 45-yard field goal with 20 seconds left in regulation and won it with his extra point. Tyler Murphy hit David Dudeck for a 21-yard touchdown pass on Boston College's drive. Mike Knoll shanked the extra point for the Eagles (7-6) and that was the opening Penn State needed to complete its comeback from a 21-7 deficit late in the third quarter. Penn State has played under the cloud of scandal and sanctions for most of the past four years, tearing at the fabric of the community known as Happy Valley and tarnishing the legacy of Joe Paterno. Moments after Penn State hoisted the bowl trophy on the field, Franklin took the microphone and thanked the seniors "who stayed with this program when we needed them most." The Eagles left stunned after blowing the lead and missing their eighth extra point of the season. Knoll put the Eagles ahead 24-21 on a 20-yarder with 2:10 left in the fourth. Ficken, who won the opener in Dublin with a 36-yard field goal as time expired, bookended the season with his biggest kick yet. Hackenberg threw four touchdowns and played more as he did his freshman year, when he had NFL scouts raving about first-round potential rather than this season's erratic sophomore effort. He set Penn State records for completions and yards passing (34 of 50, 371 yards) and earned MVP honors. He went over the middle and hit DaeSean Hamilton to make it 21-all with 6:48 left in the fourth. Hackenberg should have been eligible for a potential bowl game his senior season. But when the bowl ban was lifted this season, the Nittany Lions earned the chance to play in front of 49,012 fans at Yankee Stadium. Murphy threw for two touchdowns and ran for 105 yards and Jon Hilliman had 148 yards rushing and a score that helped the Eagles build a lead. Murphy found Shakim Phillips in the corner end zone for a 19-yard touchdown and a 14-7 lead early in the third. He then showed how he set the ACC's single-season record for rushing yards by a Quarterback with 1,079 yards in 2014 with a 40-yard dash that put the Eagles ahead 21-7. Hilliman, who led the team with 12 rushing TDs, broke through early with a 44-yard run that gave him more yards on one carry than three teams had in a game this season against Penn State: Central Florida (24), Massachusetts (3) and Maryland (25). He averaged a whopping 19.2 yards-per-carry on just five attempts for 101 yards in the first half. He found a huge opening late in the first quarter for a 49-yard touchdown run that tied the game at 7. The Nittany Lions scored first on Hackenberg's 72-yard TD pass to Chris Godwin down the right sideline with 5:22 left in the first. The score earned a booming "We are! Penn State!" chant from the Penn State fans.

2014 Holiday Bowl

The 2014 Holiday Bowl was played on December 27, 2014 at Qualcomm Stadium in San Diego, California. The 37th edition of the Holiday Bowl was telecast on ESPN (also on ESPN Radio).

2014 Holiday Bowl	Line	1	-	2	-	3	-	4	-	Final
#25 Nebraska	(62.5)	17	-	0	-	17	-	8	-	42
#24 USC	(-7.0)	10	-	14	-	21	-	0	-	45

Scoring Summary
Nebraska – Brown 34 Field goal
USC – Jackson 98 yard kickoff return (Heidari kick)
Nebraska – Bell 18 yard pass from Armstrong (Brown kick)
USC - Heidari 42 Field goal
Nebraska - Pierson-El 9 yard pass from Armstrong (Brown kick)
USC - Agholor 17 yard pass from (Heidari kick)
USC - Allen 2 yard run (Heidari kick)
USC – Jackson 71 yard pass from Kessler (Heidari kick)
Nebraska - Abdullah 20 yard run (Brown kick)
USC - Allen 44 yard run (Heidari kick)
Nebraska - Brown 24 Field goal
USC - Dixon 20 yard pass from Kessler (Heidari kick)
Nebraska - Westerkamp 65 yard pass from Armstrong (Brown kick)
Nebraska - Armstrong 15 yard run (Bell pass from Armstrong)

Nebraska Media Guide Holiday Bowl Game Summary - In a high-scoring shootout between two of college football's most storied programs, Tommy Armstrong Jr. racked up 422 yards of total offense, but Nebraska came up short on its final two drives of the fourth quarter in a 45-42 loss to No. 24 USC in the National University Holiday Bowl on Saturday night at Qualcomm Stadium. Both teams finished their seasons with 9-4 records, while teaming up for 1,040 yards of total offense in the game. Nebraska finished with 525 total yards, including 379 passing and 146 rushing, while the Trojans managed 515 yards, including 321 through the air and 194 on the ground. Armstrong, Nebraska's sophomore Quarterback completed a career-high 32-of-51 passes for a career-best 381 yards and three touchdowns setting NU bowl records for yardage, completions and attempts, but his Hail Mary attempt on the game's final play was batted to the ground to seal the USC victory. Armstrong added 41 rushing yards on 12 carries, including a 15-yard touchdown run on fourth down midway through the fourth quarter. He followed up his scoring run with a two-point conversion pass to Kenny Bell to cut the USC lead to 45-42 after the Huskers trailed 45-27 late in the third quarter. Armstrong and Bell also connected on Nebraska's first touchdown of the night, an 18-yard connection to give the Huskers a 10-7 lead with 8:23 left in the first quarter. Bell finished his Nebraska career with seven catches for 71 yards to push his school-record totals to 181 receptions for 2,689 yards in his four-year career. NU had opened the scoring with a Drew Brown 34-yard field goal, before USC's Adoree' Jackson uncorked a 98-yard kickoff return for a touchdown. After USC tied the game at 10 on 42-yard Andre Heidari field goal, Armstrong sent the Big Red to the second quarter with a 17-10 lead after a nine-yard touchdown pass to De'Mornay Pierson-El. Pierson-El finished the night with his first career 100-yard receiving game, hauling in eight passes for 102 yards. Although Nebraska led at the end of the first quarter, the second quarter belonged to the Trojans, who put together a pair of long touchdown drives to take a 24-17 lead to the locker room at halftime. USC pushed its lead to two scores for the first time early in the third quarter when the Trojans' Cody Kessler hit Jackson on a 71-yard touchdown strike to put USC up 31-17 with 12:01 left in the quarter. But Nebraska showed its fight, answering with a touchdown drive of its own capped by a 20-yard run from senior I-back Ameer Abdullah to make it 31-24 with 9:41 left in the third quarter. Abdullah finished his career as Nebraska's all-time all-purpose yardage leader, rushing 27 times for 88 yards and a score. He added six catches for 61 yards and three kickoff returns for 120 yards including a 49-yarder to finish with 269 all-purpose yards in the game. Abdullah finished his career No. 11 on the NCAA all-purpose yardage list with 7,168, while closing his illustrious career at No. 2 on the Nebraska rushing list with 4,588 yards. USC then answered the Javorius Allen's second touchdown run of the game, as he sprinted 44 yards to pay dirt to put the Trojans up 38-24 with 8:06 left in the third. Allen finished the game with 152 rushing yards on 26 carries. The Big Red pulled within 38-27 on Brown's 44-yard field with 2:28 left in the quarter, before the Trojans took their biggest lead of the night just 25 seconds later when Kessler connected with Bryce Dixon on a 20-yard touchdown pass to make it 45-27 with 2:03 remaining in the third. Kessler finished 23-of-39 for 321 yards with three touchdowns and one Josh Mitchell interception. Dixon finished with four catches for 44 yards, while Nelson Agholor led USC with seven receptions for 90 yards and a score. Armstrong struck again before the end of the quarter, finding Jordan Westerkamp on a 65-yard touchdown pass to make it 45-34 with 24 seconds left in the quarter. Westerkamp finished the night with three catches for 81 yards. While Armstrong's run was the only score of the fourth quarter, the Huskers drove near the USC 30 with three minutes left and faced 3rd-and-3. After a timeout, Armstrong's short pass across the middle to Pierson-El was batted down by a USC defender to set up a fourth down. On fourth down, Pierson-El came up short on a solid defensive play by the Trojans.

2014 Liberty Bowl

The 2014 Liberty Bowl was held on December 29, 2014 at Liberty Bowl Memorial Stadium in Memphis, Tennessee. The 56th edition of the Liberty Bowl was televised on ESPN.

2014 Liberty Bowl	Line	1	-	2	-	3	-	4	-	Final
Texas A&M	(67.0)	14	-	14	-	17	-	0	-	45
West Virginia	(-3.5)	20	-	7	-	3	-	7	-	37

Scoring Summary
Texas A&M - Reynolds 44 yard pass from Allen (Lambo kick)
West Virginia - Lambert 32 yard Field goal
West Virginia - Alford 45 yard pass from Howard (Lambert kick)
West Virginia - Dillon 35 yard interception return (Lambert kick)
Texas A&M - Williams 40 yard pass from Allen (Lambo kick)
West Virginia - Lambert 40 yard Field goal
Texas A&M - Kennedy 11 yard pass from Allen (Lambo kick)
West Virginia - White 49 yard pass from Howard (Lambert kick)
Texas A&M - Allen 14 yard run (Lambo kick)
Texas A&M - Lambo 26 yard Field goal
Texas A&M - Williams 18 yard run (Lambo kick)
West Virginia - Lambert 31 yard Field goal
Texas A&M - Kennedy 9 yard pass from Allen (Lambo kick)
West Virginia - Wellman 4 yard pass from Howard (Lambert kick)

Associated Press Liberty Bowl Game Summary - Texas A&M relied on big performances from freshmen all season, and the Aggies' bowl game was no different. Kyle Allen threw for four touchdowns and ran for a fifth Monday, and Texas A&M erased an early 10-point deficit to defeat West Virginia 45-37 in the Liberty Bowl. Allen, a true freshman making his fifth career start, went 22 of 35 for 294 yards to make up for an early interception that KJ Dillon returned for a touchdown. The Aggies' season leaders in sacks (Myles Garrett), all-purpose yards (Speedy Noil) and interceptions (Armani Watts) also were true freshmen. Malcome Kennedy caught two of Allen's touchdown passes, and Tra Carson rushed for a career-high 133 yards on 25 carries. Allen's 14-yard rushing touchdown in the final minute of the first half put the Aggies (8-5) ahead for good. Texas A&M has won bowl games in four straight seasons for the first time in school history. The Aggies won the Chick-fil-A Bowl last year, the Cotton Bowl two seasons ago and the Texas Bowl in 2011. West Virginia's Skyler Howard went 20 of 45 for 346 yards and three touchdowns while making his second career start in place of Clint Trickett, who announced Friday he was giving up football because of multiple concussions. Kevin White had seven catches for 129 yards and a touchdown for West Virginia (7-6). Josh Lambert made all three of his field-goal attempts. The game lived up to its billing as a shootout between two fast-paced offenses that had scored over 30 points per game while allowing more than 25 this season. This wound up as the second-highest scoring day in the Liberty Bowl's 56-game history, trailing only Louisville's 44-40 victory over Boise State in 2004. The first quarter alone featured 34 combined points, with West Virginia leading 20-14. The most notable hits of the first half came out of bounds: Sumlin ordered Michael Richardson off the sideline for the second half after videos showed the student assistant striking West Virginia players in two separate incidents. Texas A&M outlasted West Virginia by outrushing the Mountaineers 235-126 and holding West Virginia below 4 yards per carry. The Aggies had allowed 5.1 yards per rush this season. Perhaps the biggest play of the game came in the first quarter. Texas A&M trailed 17-7 when it went for it on fourth-and-5 from the West Virginia 40. The move paid off when Allen found running back Trey Williams for a touchdown. Texas A&M pulled ahead 21-20 early in the second quarter on Allen's 11-yard touchdown pass to Kennedy. Just 39 seconds later, West Virginia went back in front 27-21 on Howard's 49-yard TD throw to White. Texas A&M took over from there. The Aggies got a 28-27 lead with 53 seconds left in the half as Allen went to his right and saw a defender converging, then headed to his left and ran down the sideline for a touchdown. Texas A&M scored 17 points on its first three series of the third quarter to pad its advantage to 45-30. West Virginia cut the deficit to 45-37 on Howard's 4-yard touchdown pass to Elijah Wellman with 2:32 remaining, but the Mountaineers' offense wouldn't touch the ball again.

2014 Russell Athletic Bowl

The 2014 Russell Athletic Bowl was played on December 29, 2014 at Orlando Citrus Bowl Stadium in Orlando, Florida. This was the 25th Russell Athletic Bowl. This was the fourth overall meeting between these two teams, with Oklahoma leading the series 2–1 going into the game. The previous time these two teams met was in the 1989 Citrus Bowl, when Clemson won 13–6.

2014 Russell Athletic Bowl	Line	1	-	2	-	3	-	4	-	Final
Oklahoma	(-6.5)	0	-	0	-	0	-	6	-	6
#18 Clemson	(49.5)	17	-	10	-	13	-	0	-	40

Scoring Summary
Clemson – Scott 65 yard pass from Stoudt (Lakip kick)
Clemson – Lakip 34 yard Field goal
Clemson – Boulware 47 yard interception return (Lakip kick)
Clemson – Lakip 49 yard Field goal
Clemson – Williams 26 yard pass from Stoudt (Lakip kick)
Clemson – Stoudt 2 yard run (Lakip kick)
Clemson – Hopper 24 yard pass from Stoudt (Kick failed)
Oklahoma – Ross 11 yard run (Kick blocked)

Associated Press Russell Athletic Bowl Game Summary - Clemson Quarterback Cole Stoudt has had several moments during the 2014 season he tried hard to forget. The senior ended his career with a performance worth savoring. Stoudt threw for three touchdowns and ran for another, and 17th-ranked Clemson routed Oklahoma 40-6 in the Russell Athletic Bowl on Monday. The Tigers (10-3) reached double-digit victories for the fourth consecutive season. Clemson was 10-4 in 2011, 11-2 in 2012 and 11-2 in 2013. Oklahoma (8-5) had five turnovers, including three interceptions by sophomore Quarterback Trevor Knight. Stoudt began the season as the Tigers' starting Quarterback, before struggles cost him the job to freshman standout Deshaun Watson. Injuries to Watson gave Stoudt several opportunities to regain the spot, but he never was able to put together the kind of outing that gave the coaching staff lasting confidence. The ultimate low point came in November when Watson was lost to a knee injury in the first quarter of the Tigers' matchup at Georgia Tech. Stoudt came in to replace him but threw three interceptions in a 28-6 loss that ended Clemson's six-game win streak. Stoudt was a different presence against the Sooners on Monday, completing 26 of 36 attempts for a season-high 319 yards. He was sacked four times, but Clemson never turned the ball over. As good as Stoudt was, the Tigers' defense was equally impressive. The Tigers, which came in ranked No. 1 in the nation in total defense, held the Sooners' offense to just 275 yards. With most of the Oklahoma section of the announced crowd of 40,071 already gone from Citrus Bowl Stadium, Swinney pulled the senior starters from his defense early in the fourth quarter. It wasn't until then that the Sooners finally were able to score their first touchdown with just less than seven minutes to play. Sooners coach Bob Stoops shied away from assigning blame but acknowledged Oklahoma's lofty yearly standards aren't being met. After the loss, Sooners All-Big 12 linebacker Eric Striker said he would return for his senior season. Clemson was efficient in all phases but also was the beneficiary of three early Sooners turnovers in building a 27-0 halftime lead. A 47-yard interception return for a touchdown by Ben Boulware was part of a 17-point first quarter. Stoudt completed his first six passes and finished the half with a pair of touchdown throws -- a 65-yarder to Artavis Scott and a 26-yarder to Mike Williams. Tigers' kicker Ammon Lakip also did his part to deepen the hole for Oklahoma, connecting on a pair of field goals, including a career-long kick from 49 yards in the second quarter. The Sooners were out of sync on both sides of the ball during the opening 30 minutes. Knight was just 5-for-14, with a pair of interceptions. Samaje Perine rushed for 62 yards but also had a fumble inside the Tigers' 25 that ended the Sooners' best drive late in the second quarter. Stoops said changes were possible at Quarterback and elsewhere. Trailing 20-0, Oklahoma's defense nearly grabbed a bit of momentum when defensive end Charles Tapper appeared to tip, intercept and return Stoudt's pass for a touchdown. But the play was called back for offside. Stoudt then promptly hooked up with Williams for the Tigers' final scoring play of the half.

2014 Texas Bowl

The 2014 Texas Bowl was played on December 29, 2014 at NRG Stadium in Houston, Texas. The ninth edition of the Texas Bowl was televised on ESPN. The game was the 78th meeting of the Arkansas–Texas football rivalry, which has been played only occasionally since the Razorbacks left the Southwest Conference for the SEC in 1992.

2014 Texas Bowl	Line	1	-	2	-	3	-	4	-	Final
Arkansas	(-7.0)	3	-	21	-	0	-	7	-	31
Texas	(44.5)	0	-	7	-	0	-	0	-	7

Scoring Summary
Arkansas - McFain 32 yard Field goal
Arkansas - Wilson 36 yard pass from Allen (McFain kick)
Arkansas - Johnson fumble recovered in end zone (McFain kick)
Texas - Swoopes 9 yard run (Rose kick)
Arkansas - Hatcher 5 yard pass from Allen (McFain kick)
Arkansas - Williams 1 yard run (McFain kick)

Texas Bowl Game Summary - The 2014 Texas Bowl was dominated by Arkansas from beginning to end. The Razorbacks opened the scoring with an Adam McFain field goal in the first quarter, to give Arkansas a 3-0 lead. The second quarter proved to be very productive for the Razorback offense, as Quarterback Brandon Allen threw touchdowns passes to Demetrius Wilson and Keon Hatcher. The Arkansas defense got in on the second quarter scoring as well, as defensive lineman Taiwan Johnson recovered a Longhorn fumble in the end zone for a Razorback touchdown. Texas put together their only scoring drive in the second period, when Longhorn Quarterback Tyrone Swoopes scored on a nine yard run around the left end. The Hogs lead 24-7 at the half. Scoring was limited in the second half, as neither team put up any points in the third quarter. Arkansas running back Jonathan Williams tacked on a fourth quarter rushing touchdown, pushing the Hogs lead to 31-7. Texas would attempt a late game comeback, but Arkansas cornerback Henre' Tolliver intercepted Swoopes' final pass attempt, ending all hope for the Longhorns. That allowed the Hogs to run out the game clock and secure the 31-7 victory. Arkansas Quarterback Brandon Allen was named the Texas Bowl MVP, after passing for 160 yards and two touchdowns with no interceptions and guiding the Hog offense to 353 yards of total offense. The Razorback defense was overpowering all night against the Longhorn offense, holding Texas to only 2 yards rushing, 59 yards of total offense, forcing two turnovers, and sacking Swoopes three times. Arkansas improved to finish the season 7-6, while Texas fell to 6-7.

2014 Music City Bowl

The 2014 Music City Bowl was played on December 30, 2014 at LP Field in Nashville, Tennessee. The 17th edition of the Music City Bowl was broadcast nationally by ESPN. It featured the Notre Dame Fighting Irish, and the LSU Tigers from the SEC.

2014 Music City Bowl	Line	1	-	2	-	3	-	4	-	Final
Notre Dame	(52.5)	7	-	14	-	7	-	3	-	31
#22 LSU	(-7.5)	7	-	7	-	14	-	0	-	28

Scoring Summary
Notre Dame - Fuller 12 yard pass from Zaire (Brindza kick)
LSU - Fournette 8 yard run (Domingue kick)
Notre Dame - Zaire 7 yard run (Brindza kick)
LSU - Fournette 100 yard kickoff return (Domingue kick)
Notre Dame - Folston 6 yard run (Brindza kick)
LSU - Diarse 75 yard pass from Jennings (Domingue kick)
LSU - Fournette 89 yard run (Domingue kick)
Notre Dame - Prosise 50 yard run (Brindza kick)
Notre Dame - Brindza 32 yard Field goal

Associated Press Music City Bowl Game Summary - Notre Dame and senior kicker Kyle Brindza got the finish they had missed too often the last half of the season. Beating a Southeastern Conference team in southern territory only made it that much sweeter. Brindza hit a 32-yard field goal as time expired, and Notre Dame upset LSU 31-28 in a Franklin American Mortgage Music City Bowl shootout Tuesday. The Tigers (No. 22 CFP, No. 23 AP) were unsuccessful on a fake field goal at the end of the first half, a call that stood on review even though replays appeared to show the ball crossing the goal line. The Fighting Irish (8-5) also blocked a 40-yard field goal attempt by Trent Domingue early in the fourth quarter. Kelly watched the fake field goal on the video board and thought the Irish stopped holder Brad Kragthorpe short. LSU coach Les Miles thought Kragthorpe scored and wasn't happy the play wasn't overturned for a touchdown. Miles also wasn't pleased at the lack of better replays that might have shown Kragthorpe got the ball over the line before his knee went down. Notre Dame got the ball with 5:41 left and never gave it back, driving 71 yards in 14 plays before Brindza finished off the win. Kelly went with sophomore Malik Zaire for his first career start, but he also played senior Everett Golson, using both Quarterbacks on the winning drive. Notre Dame held the ball for 37 minutes but finished with a 449-436 edge in total offense against the SEC's toughest defense thanks only to that final drive. Golson was 4 of 5 for 50 yards passing on it, including a 12-yard completion to Ben Koyack on third-and-10. Zaire finished off the drive with a couple of rushes to set up Brindza. Brindza had missed 6 of 9 field goals in the last five games of the regular season, including a 32-yarder late in a loss to Louisville. The Fighting Irish were ranked as high as fifth before dropping four straight and five of their final six, struggling in the fourth quarter against Florida State, Northwestern, Arizona State and Louisville. Kelly set a target of controlling the ball for 9 minutes each quarter, and they beat that by a minute for the game. Zaire rushed 22 times for 96 yards and was 12 of 15 for 96 yards passing. He threw for a TD and ran for another. Golson was 6 of 11 for 90 yards passing, and Kelly said the senior needed a painkilling shot after taking a hit to his ribs earlier in the game. Fournette ran for 143 yards and two touchdowns, and the freshman also returned a kickoff 100 yards for a score. Miles said after the game he heard media reports that defensive coordinator John Chavis is leaving for Texas A&M but planned to make another pitch to keep the coach nicknamed Chief. The Tigers' final three touchdowns took all of 38 seconds. Fournette had his kick return, and his 89-yard TD run later gave the Tigers their first lead of the game at 28-21 with 6:14 left in the third quarter. In between, Anthony Jennings connected with John Diarse on a 75-yard catch-and-run touchdown. But LSU didn't score again after Fournette's TD run, the longest play from scrimmage in this bowl's history. Isaac Rochell blocked Domingue's field goal attempt with 11:56 left. Late in the first half, Notre Dame stopped LSU at the Irish 1 on a third-down pass, so the Tigers lined up for a field goal attempt. But Kragthorpe took off on a fake, bumping into teammate Terrence McGee on his way to the end zone. Officials ruled Kragthorpe short, and the call wasn't reversed.

2014 Belk Bowl

The 2014 Belk Bowl was played on December 30, 2014 at Bank of America Stadium in Charlotte, North Carolina in the United States. The thirteenth annual Belk Bowl was televised on ESPN. The game was sponsored by Charlotte-based department store chain Belk. The Bulldogs won the matchup by a final score of 37–14.

2014 Belk Bowl	Line	1	-	2	-	3	-	4	-	Final
#13 Georgia	(-7.0)	7	-	13	-	7	-	10	-	37
#20 Louisville	(56.5)	7	-	0	-	7	-	0	-	14

Scoring Summary
Georgia - Conley 44 yard pass from Mason (Morgan kick)
Louisville - Christian 11 yard pass from Bolin (Wallace kick)
Georgia - Morgan 41 yard Field goal
Georgia - Chubb 31 yard run (Morgan kick)
Georgia - Morgan 22 yard Field goal
Georgia - Michel 2 yard run (Morgan kick)
Louisville - Radcliff 6 yard run (Wallace kick)
Georgia - Morgan 37 yard Field goal
Georgia - Chubb 8 yard run (Morgan kick)

Associated Press Belk Bowl Game Summary - When Quarterback Hutson Mason went down with an injury in the second quarter, Georgia coach Mark Richt said the Bulldogs turned to plan B. "Just give it to Nick," Richt said with a wide smile. Freshman Nick Chubb took over from there, running for a career-high 266 yards and two touchdowns as No. 13 Georgia defeated 21st-ranked Louisville 37-14 in the Belk Bowl on Tuesday night. Chubb's rushing total was second highest in school history, behind only Herschel Walker's 283 yards rushing against Vanderbilt in 1980. With Chubb and four starting offensive linemen returning next season, the Georgia running game appears to be in good hands -- even with Todd Gurley headed to the NFL. Chubb finished his first season at Georgia by running for 1,323 yards and 12 touchdowns in last eight games after taking over as the primary ball carrier after the NCAA suspended Gurley for four games for taking $3,000 for autographed memorabilia and other items over two years. Gurley later sustained a season-ending knee injury in his first game back from the suspension. Chubb averaged 8 yards per carry against Louisville (No. 20 AP) and the Bulldogs (10-3) piled up 301 yards rushing against the nation's second-best run defense. Mason threw for 149 yards and a touchdown before leaving with blurred vision in the second quarter with the Bulldogs ahead 20-7. He was replaced by Brice Ramsey, whose primary duty was to hand the ball off to Chubb and watch him run. Mason said after the game he didn't have a concussion but couldn't see straight. Georgia's defense certainly contributed to the win. They came up with three interceptions, two of those by Dominick Sanders. Redshirt freshman Quarterback Kyle Bolin made his first career start for Louisville (9-4) and finished 20 of 40 for 300 yards with two interceptions and one touchdown. Backup Reggie Bonnafon threw one interception in limited playing time. Brandon Radcliff ran for 91 yards and a touchdown. The Bulldogs leaned heavily on the 5-foot-10, 228-pound Chubb after Mason left the game and Ramsey was intercepted on his first play from scrimmage. Louisville's defense came into the game allowing just 93.7 yards per game on the ground. Chubb nearly had that in the first half, rushing for 78 yards on 12 carries and a touchdown. He added an 82-yard run in the second half that led to another Georgia score. The Bulldogs roared to a 20-7 lead in the first half as Mason found wide open flanker Chris Conley down the middle of the field for a 44-yard touchdown strike for a 7-0 lead. Chubb added a 31-yard scoring run. The Bulldogs (10-3) made it a three-possession game late in the third quarter when Chubb broke free from his own 3 and raced 82 yards, setting up a 2-yard touchdown run by Sony Michel. Chubb later sealed the win with an 8-yard touchdown run. Louisville's only scores came on an 11-yard scoring strike from Bolin to Gerald Christian and a 6-yard run by Radcliff. Game notes - Chubb set a new Belk Bowl rushing record, eclipsing the 174-yard effort set by Boston College's Andrew Callender in 2004. ... DeVante Parker lived up to his billing with eight catches for 120 yards for Louisville. ... Conley led Georgia with four catches for 80 yards and the TD.

2014 Foster Farms Bowl

The 2014 Foster Farms Bowl was played on December 30, 2014 at Levi's Stadium in Santa Clara, California. The 13th edition of the Foster Farms Bowl (previously known as the Fight Hunger Bowl), featured the Stanford Cardinal from the Pac-12 Conference against the Maryland Terrapins from the Big Ten Conference. The game was televised on ESPN/ESPN Radio.

2014 Foster Farms Bowl	Line	1	2	3	4	Final
Maryland	(47.0)	0	7	0	14	21
Stanford	(-14.0)	7	21	7	10	45

Scoring Summary
Stanford - Wright 1 yard run (Williamson kick)
Maryland - Brown 1 yard run (Craddock kick)
Stanford - Wright 3 yard run (Williamson kick)
Stanford - Wright 1 yard run (Williamson kick)
Stanford - Cajuste 8 yard pass from Hogan (Williamson kick)
Stanford - Cajuste 9 yard pass from Hogan (Williamson kick)
Stanford - Seale 1 yard run (Williamson kick)
Maryland - Likely 100 yard kickoff return (Craddock kick)
Stanford - Williamson 29 yard Field goal
Maryland - Brown 2 yard run (Craddock kick)

Associated Press Foster Farms Bowl Game Summary - Everything that Stanford was trying to do most of the season came together in the final three games, and each victory was more impressive than the prior one. Kevin Hogan threw for 189 yards and two touchdowns, Remound Wright ran for three short scores, and Stanford overwhelmed Maryland 45-21 in the Foster Farms Bowl on Tuesday night. On a chilly, windy night in Silicon Valley, Stanford (8-5) blew past the Terrapins with the kind of complete performance that had eluded the Cardinal most of the year. They outgained Maryland 414 to 222 yards and looked right at home at Levi's Stadium, about 11 miles from campus. It was the most points scored in a bowl game in Stanford history. Stanford denied Maryland its first postseason win since 2010, when it beat East Carolina in the Military Bowl. The Terrapins (7-6) lost three of their last four games in their first year in the Big Ten, which included victories at Penn State and Michigan. But it was a forgettable finale for Coach Randy Edsall's team. The Terps traveled about 2,800 miles to play in the $1.3 billion home of the San Francisco 49ers and never really came out of their shells. Outgoing Quarterback C.J. Brown moved the offense early, although he was sacked six times and his receivers -- other than star Stefon Diggs -- often struggled to create separation against the nation's second-ranked scoring defense. Brown finished 15-for-27 passing for 205 yards and one interception and ran for a late touchdown. Diggs caught 10 passes for 138 yards, Wes Brown ran for a short TD early in the second quarter and William Likely returned a kickoff 100 yards for a score in the fourth after the game had become a rout. About the only other highlight for the Terps came in the first quarter, when Andre Monroe became Maryland's career sacks leader after bringing down Hogan. It was Monroe's 25th sack, passing Mike Corvino's mark of 24 from 1979-82. While the sun had shined across the Bay Area for the past week, the temperature dipped into the 40s at kickoff with a wind chill that made it feel like it was in the 30s -- frosty weather by Northern California standards. The patchy field, where the 49ers' logos could easily be seen under the school names painted in each end zone, also made quick movements tricky at the sparsely filled stadium. The Cardinal overcame the conditions -- and the absence of top playmaker Ty Montgomery (sprained right shoulder) for the second straight game -- to end a down season on an upbeat note. Stanford had made a BCS bowl each of the previous four seasons, including back-to-back Pac-12 titles, before falling back in 2014 in large part because of its inefficient offense. Not this time. Hogan, who has yet to announce whether he'll return for his final season of eligibility, completed 14 of 20 passes. Wright tied the bowl record for touchdowns rushing, and Stanford's smothering defense did the rest. Ten receivers caught passes, with Devon Cajuste (four receptions for 47 yards and two touchdowns) and tight end Austin Hooper (five receptions for 71 yards) leading the way. Electric freshman Christian McCaffrey had 138 all-purpose yards. Even fifth-year senior Ricky Seale ran for his first career touchdown -- a 1-yard plunge that put Stanford up 42-7 early in the fourth -- for a feel-good moment to cap the Cardinal's season. The performance beat out Stanford's 40-12 victory over Virginia Tech in the 2011 Orange Bowl for the program's most points scored in a bowl game.

2014 Chick-Fil-A Peach Bowl

The 2014 Peach Bowl was played on December 31, 2014 at the Georgia Dome in Atlanta, Georgia. The 47th Peach Bowl was one of the "New Year's Six" bowl games in the College Football Playoff. The game was televised on ESPN and ESPN Deportes, and broadcast on ESPN Radio and XM Satellite Radio. The 2014 Peach Bowl featured the TCU Horned Frogs of the Big 12 Conference against the Ole Miss Rebels of the Southeastern Conference.

2014 Chick-Fil-A Peach Bowl	Line	1	-	2	-	3	-	4	-	Final
#9 Mississippi	(55.5)	0	-	0	-	0	-	3	-	3
#6 TCU	(-3.5)	14	-	14	-	14	-	0	-	42

Scoring Summary
TCU – Green 31 yard pass from Listenbee (Oberkrom kick)
TCU – Green 15 yard run (Oberkrom kick)
TCU – Doctson 12 yard pass from Boykin (Oberkrom kick)
TCU – McFarland interception return (Oberkrom kick)
TCU – Listenbee 35 yard pass from Boykin (Oberkrom kick)
TCU – Doctson 27 yard pass from Boykin (Oberkrom kick)
Mississippi – Wunderlich 27 yard Field goal

Fort Worth Star-Telegram Peach Bowl Game Summary - That had to feel good. "It's a feeling that you can't really express," defensive tackle Chucky Hunter said. The only thing to do is jump and dance — that was obvious on the TCU sideline, where every player leaped as high as he could or danced his best dance after defensive end James McFarland's second-quarter interception in the end zone for a touchdown. His catch, off a pass thrown by reeling Quarterback Bo Wallace under pressure from linebacker Marcus Mallet, prompted a frenzy of yells, chest thumps, hugs and high-fives from the Horned Frogs. With one play, in an already dominating first half, the No. 6-ranked Frogs had gone up by four touchdowns against

Ole Miss in the Chick-fil-A Peach Bowl on Wednesday at the Georgia Dome and allowed themselves to release a month of bottled-up emotion. They believed they should have been in the College Football Playoff, and they played like it in a furious 42-3 rout of the No. 9 Rebels and a top SEC defense. Quarterback Trevone Boykin threw three touchdown passes, extending his school record for a single season to 33, and Doctson, who played at Mansfield Legacy, caught two touchdown passes in setting school records for yards and touchdown catches in a season. Kolby Listenbee, from Arlington Bowie, threw a wide receiver pass for a touchdown to Aaron Green, who also ran for a touchdown, as the Horned Frogs (12-1) made good on a promise to themselves to play the best game they could. Their 39-point margin of victory was the largest in Peach Bowl history, even with a scoreless fourth quarter — only their sixth scoreless quarter of the season. Even with two turnovers, TCU simply swamped Ole Miss (9-4) for the first 30 minutes. The defense simply could not be moved out of the way, and Ole Miss had no answer to protect Wallace, who took five sacks and threw three interceptions. It was a trademark performance for the defense — the four takeaways for the game gave it 40 for the year. McFarland's interception for a touchdown was the fifth interception returned for a touchdown by the Horned Frogs this year. Chris Bradley and Hunter combined for a sack, and Tevin Lawson, Paul Dawson, Terrell Lathan and McFarland also had sacks in the first half. Wallace had only five completions, and the Rebels had only four first downs. All that happened in the first 30 minutes. The defense had Ole Miss so discombobulated that there were times Wallace simply didn't know where to go with the ball. Late in the first half, as the Rebels moved into the red zone, he never saw the shotgun snap on a fourth-down play. The start of the game was everything TCU could have asked for — maybe more. Chris Hackett intercepted a third-down pass, his team-high seventh pick for the year, to give the offense the ball at the Ole Miss 35. On second down, co-offensive coordinators Doug Meacham and Sonny Cumbie went for broke. Boykin threw a backward pass to Listenbee, a high school Quarterback, who waited for Green to streak out of the backfield and then hit him with a 31-yard pass in stride in the end zone for a 7-0 lead that lit up the purple side of the stadium. After four Rebels plays and a punt, and to show the first touchdown was not a fluke, the Frogs drove 78 yards for a 14-0 lead — their ninth in 13 games this year — on Green's wide-open 15-yard run up the middle. Doctson's 12-yard touchdown catch in the second quarter, on a perfectly executed slant, made it 21-0. And a possession later, Mallet and McFarland combined for their electrifying play in the end zone and the 28-0 lead that turned the game into a celebration. Out of halftime, TCU put up two more touchdowns quickly. Ranthony Texada's 65-yard kickoff return set up Listenbee's 35-yard touchdown catch for a 35-0 lead, and on the next possession, Doctson caught a 27-yard pass for a 42-0 lead. The Frogs had made their point.

2014 Fiesta Bowl (December)

The 2014 Fiesta Bowl was played on December 31, 2014 at University of Phoenix Stadium in Glendale, Arizona. The 44th Fiesta Bowl was one of the New Year's Bowls of the College Football Playoff. The game was televised on ESPN and ESPN Deportes, and broadcast on ESPN Radio and XM Satellite Radio.

2014 Fiesta Bowl	Line	1	-	2	-	3	-	4	-	Final
#21 Boise State	(68.0)	21	-	10	-	7	-	0	-	38
#12 Arizona	(-3.0)	7	-	10	-	10	-	3	-	30

Scoring Summary
Boise State – Ajayi 56 yard run (Goodale kick)
Boise State – Anderson 57 yard pass from Hedrick (Goodale kick)
Boise State – Ajayi 16 yard run (Goodale kick)
Arizona – Solomon 1 yard run (Skowron kick)
Boise State – Ajayi 1 yard run (Goodale kick)
Arizona – Wilson 1 yard run (Skowron kick)
Arizona – Skowron 42 yard Field goal
Boise State – Goodale 36 yard Field goal
Arizona – Skowron 24 yard Field goal
Boise State – Deayon 16 yard interception return (Goodale kick)
Arizona – Grant 51 yard pass from Solomon (Skowron kick)
Arizona – Skowron 24 yard Field goal

Associated Press Fiesta Bowl Game Summary - The Boise State Broncos are no longer just trick-play ponies. But once the tricks were used up and the offensive fireworks dulled, Boise State had to grind out this VIZIO Fiesta Bowl victory with its defense. The Fiesta Bowl has brought out the best from the Boise State Broncos over the last decade, and Wednesday's game was no different. Donte Deayon returned an interception for a touchdown in third quarter and sack specialist Kamalei Correa had his biggest takedown of the season on the game's final play, lifting No. 20 Boise State to a 38-30 victory over No. 10 Arizona in the VIZIO Fiesta Bowl on Wednesday. Boise State (12-2, No. 21 AP) lived up to its unpredictable reputation in the first quarter, pulling off the Statue of Liberty play while racing to a 21-0 lead in the opening 10 minutes. Jay Ajayi scored two of his three touchdowns in the first quarter -- one on the trick play -- and finished with 134 yards rushing. Grant Hedrick was perfect through his first 14 passes and threw for 304 yards and a touchdown. Thomas Sperbeck had 12 catches for 199 yards. The bulk of those numbers came in the first half, though. Once the second rolled around, the Broncos bogged down, allowing Arizona to cut the lead to eight in the fourth quarter. The Wildcats had a final chance, using their quick-strike offense to march down the field, but Correa sacked Anu Solomon at Boise State's 10-yard on the game's last play. The Broncos charged onto the field after Correa's sack, celebrating a successful first season under Coach Bryan Harsin with their third VIZIO Fiesta Bowl victory. Not bad for a team supposedly in transition. Arizona (10-4, No. 12 AP) was overrun by Oregon in the Pac-12 Championship and seemed to still have a hangover against the Broncos. Once the Wildcats shook out of their daze, they shut down Boise State's high-powered offense and began chipping away at the lead. The problem was that they needed to take bigger chunks. Instead of scoring touchdowns, Arizona mostly dinked its way back, settling for three field goals after driving deep into Boise State's end. Turnovers also hurt. Solomon threw for 335 yards and a touchdown but had two interceptions that led to touchdowns for Boise State, including Deayon's pick six late in the third quarter. Of all the non-playoff bowls, the Fiesta had one of the most intriguing matchups: Two prolific offenses, two programs trying to make a statement with a big-bowl win. It certainly lived up to the billing at the start. The big-play Broncos burst out of the gate with long touchdowns on their first two drives: a 56-yard touchdown run by Ajayi and a 57-yard TD hookup between Hedrick and Anderson. No VIZIO Fiesta Bowl with Boise State would be complete without a Statue of Liberty play, so the Broncos did that, too. Ajayi scored on it, taking a behind-the-back handoff from Hedrick, and then stiff-arming Arizona cornerback Cam Denson to the ground on the 16-yard run. Arizona was finally able catch its breath and marched in for a 1-yard touchdown dive by Solomon. But just when the Wildcats looked like they were back in it, Solomon threw an interception, setting up a 1-yard touchdown run by Ajayi that made it 28-7. Nick Wilson scored on a 1-yard run in the second quarter, but Boise State still led 31-17 at halftime after Hedrick completed 17 of 18 passes for 272 yards. Boise State had 2 yards on 14 plays in the third quarter but took an 18-point lead Deayon's interception return. Solomon made up for it right after that, scrambling to the right before finding Samjie Grant for a 51-yard touchdown strike that made it 38-27 heading into the fourth quarter. Arizona cut it to eight on Casey Skowron's third field goal, from 32 yards, but failed to score on its final two drives.

2014 Orange Bowl

The 2014 Orange Bowl was played on December 31, 2014 at Sun Life Stadium in Miami Gardens, Florida. The 81st Orange Bowl was televised on ESPN and ESPN Deportes, and broadcast on ESPN Radio and XM Satellite Radio. Georgia Tech Quarterback Justin Thomas, who accounted for 4 total touchdowns, was named the game's most valuable player.

2014 Orange Bowl	Line	1	-	2	-	3	-	4	-	Final
#8 Mississippi State	(-6.5)	0	-	20	-	0	-	14	-	34
#10 Georgia Tech	(61.5)	14	-	7	-	21	-	7	-	49

Scoring Summary
Georgia Tech - Days 3 yard run (Butker kick)
Georgia Tech - Waller 41 yard pass from Thomas (Butker kick)
Mississippi State - Sobiesk 32 yard field goal
Mississippi State - Prescott 5 yard run (Sobiesk kick)
Mississippi State - Sobiesk 30 yard field goal
Georgia Tech - Thomas 13 yard run (Butker kick)
Mississippi State - Ross 42 yard pass from Prescott (Sobiesk kick)
Georgia Tech - Days 69 yard run (Butker kick)
Georgia Tech - Thomas 32 yard run (Butker kick)
Georgia Tech - Thomas 15 yard run (Butker kick)
Mississippi State - Wilson 7 yard pass from Prescott (Sobiesk kick)
Georgia Tech - Days 4 yard run (Butker kick)
Mississippi State - Wilson 12 yard pass from Prescott (Sobiesk kick)

Aftermath - Georgia Tech Quarterback Justin Thomas was named the game's most valuable player. Thomas completed 7 of his 12 passes for 1 touchdown, 1 interception and 125 yards. Thomas also had 121 rushing yards for 3 touchdowns.

Orange Bowl Classic Game Summary - Georgia Tech Rushes to Victory in 81st Capital One Orange Bowl - The ringing of the cowbells from Mississippi State fans that made the trip to South Florida from "Stark Vegas" and elsewhere could be heard all night, but it was the Georgia Tech faithful who rang in the New Year with a victory in the 2014 Capital One Orange Bowl. As the clock struck midnight, ushering in the year 2015, the Yellow Jackets of Georgia Tech were on stage hoisting the Capital One Orange Bowl trophy amid a backdrop of fireworks and fanfare, minutes after concluding the 2014 season with a 49-34 win over Mississippi State. As the two teams took center stage on New Year's Eve, Georgia Tech would prove quickly that they belonged. Dak Prescott threw an interception on the first drive of the game, leading to a 3-yard Synjyn Days touchdown to put the Yellow Jackets up 7-0 early in the contest. Later in the first, it was the arm of Quarterback Justin Thomas, rather than his legs, putting Georgia Tech up 14-0 with a 41-yard touchdown pass to Darren Waller. Mississippi State was not lacking in big plays itself and kept the game close throughout. The momentum was in large part due to the miraculous 42-yard Hail Mary that Mississippi State converted to end the half. Fred Ross caught the tipped pass from Dak Prescott in the end zone to bring the score within one at halftime, 21-20. The touchdown capped off a 20-point second quarter that also featured a Dak Prescott rushing touchdown and a pair of Evan Sobiesk field goals. However, in a game of runs, Georgia Tech struck next. Days' scintillating touchdown run was the first of three straight Georgia Tech touchdowns that eventually put the Yellow Jackets up 42-20 entering the fourth quarter. Despite two more touchdown passes from Dak Prescott and a Capital One Orange Bowl record 453 passing yards, the Ramblin' Wreck offense was too much as their own record setting performance, 452 team rushing yards, carried them to the win.

2015 Outback Bowl

The 2015 Outback Bowl was played on 1 January 2015 at Raymond James Stadium in Tampa, Florida. It was the 29th edition of the Outback Bowl (previously called the Hall of Fame Bowl) and featured the #17 Wisconsin Badgers from the Big Ten and the #19 Auburn Tigers from the SEC. It was nationally televised by ESPN2. It was sponsored by the Outback Steakhouse restaurant franchise.

2015 Outback Bowl	Line	1	-	2	-	3	-	4	-	OT	-	Final
#19 Auburn	(-6.5)	7	-	7	-	3	-	14	-	0	-	31
#17 Wisconsin	(64.0)	7	-	0	-	14	-	10	-	3	-	34

Scoring Summary
Wisconsin – Clement 7 yard pass from Stave (Gaglianone kick)
Auburn – Artis-Payne 2 yard run (Carlson kick)
Auburn – Louis 66 yard pass from Marshall (Carlson kick)
Wisconsin – Gordon 25 yard run (Gaglianone kick)
Auburn – Carlson 51 yard Field goal
Wisconsin – Gordon 53 yard run (Gaglianone kick)
Auburn – Uzomah 20 yard pass from Marshall (Carlson kick)
Wisconsin – Gordon 6 yard run (Gaglianone kick)
Auburn – Artis-Payne 2 yard run (Carlson kick)
Wisconsin – Gaglianone 29 yard Field goal
Wisconsin – Gaglianone 25 yard Field goal

Auburn Media Guide Outback Bowl Game Summary - Auburn played it to the end, and then some, but it wasn't enough to beat Wisconsin and Melvin Gordon in the Outback Bowl on Thursday. The Badgers won 34-31 in overtime when they made a field goal on their first possession, and Auburn missed a 45- yard try when it got the ball. Gordon rushed for 251 yards and three touchdowns, though Auburn had the lead with eight seconds left in regulation. Wisconsin tied the game a second later on a field goal and won it in the first overtime period. The end of the game was like the rest of the game, a see-saw affair that featured big runs and good plays. Auburn Quarterback Nick Marshall picked one good play, and then another, in two drives near the end that gave the Tigers two leads. That's when Auburn found the proper balance between the run and the pass. The Tigers answered two Wisconsin leads with decisive drives. Cameron Artis-Payne scored on a 2-yard run with 2:55 remaining. Before that, the Tigers had taken the lead a drive that saw Artis-Payne rip off a 21-yard run, Corey Grant run for 21, too, and Marshall throw a 21-yard touchdown pass to C.J. Uzomah. Marshall came through after that, too. He led the Tigers to the Wisconsin 7, and, on fourth down, his pass to Sammie Coates may have been a TD had it not been for pass interference. It didn't matter. Artis-Payne scored on the next play. Auburn finished the season with an 8-5 record. Wisconsin finished at 11- 3. The Tigers led at the half, but n Gordon carried four times for 55 yards, including the final 25, on the first series of the second half to tie Auburn at 14-all. On fourth-and-1, Gordon broke loose for a 53-yard touchdown run to give Wisconsin a 21-17 lead with 20 seconds left in the third quarter. But Auburn mixed it up on the Badgers from there, with Artis-Payne ripping off a 21-yard run, with Corey Grant doing the same, and with Marshall throwing a 21-yard touchdown pass to Uzomah for a 24-21 lead with 11:21 left in the fourth quarter. Auburn regained the lead on a career-long 51-yard field goal by Daniel Carlson. Wisconsin scored on its first series on a 7-yard pass from Joel Stave to Corey Clement, but the Tigers tied the game on a 2-yard touchdown run with 2:16 left in the first quarter and went ahead on a Marshall 66-yard TD pass to Ricardo Louis. Those plays, and interceptions by Trovon Reed and Jermaine Whitehead, had Auburn ahead 14-7 at the half. The first half was more of the same for Marshall, who threw for a single-game school record of 456 yards against Alabama in the previous game, then threw for 131 more in the first half against Wisconsin. Auburn hit halftime with those 131 yards passing and 46 yards rushing.

2015 Cotton Bowl Classic (January)

The 2015 Cotton Bowl Classic was played on January 1, 2015 at AT&T Stadium in Arlington, Texas. The 79th Cotton Bowl Classic was one of the "New Year's Six" bowls of the College Football Playoff. It was broadcast on ESPN, ESPN Deportes, ESPN Radio and XM Satellite Radio. In 2014, Michigan State was runner-up in the Big Ten Conference's East Division, and Baylor was Big 12 co-champion with TCU. After falling behind by 20 points, Michigan State staged a dramatic comeback in the fourth quarter to beat Baylor by a score of 42–41. This was the highest scoring Cotton Bowl ever, and the fourth bowl game in a row for Michigan State where they won after trailing at halftime.

2015 Cotton Bowl Classic	Line	1	-	2	-	3	-	4	-	Final
#7 Michigan State	(70.0)	14	-	0	-	7	-	21	-	42
#4 Baylor	(-2.5)	14	-	10	-	17	-	0	-	41

Scoring Summary
Michigan State – Langford 2 yard run (Geiger kick)
Baylor – Cannon 49 yard pass from Petty (Callahan kick)
Michigan State – Shelton 11 yard run (Geiger kick)
Baylor – Coleman 53 yard pass from Lee (Callahan kick)
Baylor – Petty 1 yard run (Callahan kick)
Baylor – Callahan 25 yard Field goal
Baylor – Cannon 74 yard pass from Petty (Callahan kick)
Baylor – Callahan 46 yard Field goal
Michigan State – Langford 2 yard run (Geiger kick)
Baylor – McGowan 18 yard pass from Petty (Callahan kick)
Michigan State – Price 8 yard pass from Cook (Geiger kick)
Michigan State – Langford 1 yard run (Geiger kick)
Michigan State – Mumphrey 10 yard pass from Cook (Geiger kick)

Michigan State Media Guide Cotton Bowl Game Summary - Michigan State (No. 7 AP, No. 8 CFP) staged its biggest comeback in bowl history with a thrilling 42-41 victory over Baylor (No. 4 AP, No. 5 CFP) in the 2015 Cotton Bowl Classic at AT&T Stadium. The game was the highest-scoring Cotton Bowl ever. Down 20 points entering the fourth quarter, 41-21, the Spartans outscored the Bears 21-0 in the final 15 minutes, including the game-winning touchdown on a 10-yard pass from Connor Cook to Keith Mumphery with just 17 seconds remaining. MSU extended its school-record bowl winning streak to four games, which also tied a Big Ten record. Cook completed 24-of-42 throws for 314 yards, two touchdowns and two interceptions. Jeremy Langford extended his school-record streak to 10 straight 100-yard rushing games, with 27 carries for 162 yards, marking the third-highest single-game rushing total by a Spartan in a bowl game. He also tied a career high and a Spartan bowl record with three rushing TDs. Langford's career-long 65-yard run off left tackle on the third play from scrimmage set up his first rushing TD of game, a 2-yard score just 2:33 into the game. Baylor quickly responded on a 49-yard pass from Bryce Petty to KD Cannon to tie the game midway through the first. The teams traded TDs again in the first quarter as R.J. Shelton scored on an 11-yard run at the 5:06 mark and Jay Lee connected with Corey Coleman on a 53-yard scoring strike at the 2:32 mark. The Bears took a 24-14 lead into halftime after Petty rushed for a 1-yard TD and Chris Callahan made a 25-yard field goal in the second quarter. Baylor pushed its lead to 34-14 early in the third as Petty again found Cannon on a deep scoring pass, this time for 74 yards, just 28 seconds into the second half, and Callahan kicked a 46-yard field goal with 11:23 remaining. The Spartans got back on the board as Langford scored his second rushing TD of the game (2 yards) at the 6:50 mark, but the Bears went back up by 20 on Petty's 18-yard TD pass to offensive lineman LaQuan McGowan with 4:03 left to make it 41-21. The Spartans started their comeback in the fourth when Cook hooked up with Josiah Price for an 8-yard TD pass less than three minutes into the quarter. Langford cut the Spartan deficit to 41-35 on a 1-yard rush with 4:55 left in the game. With Baylor still leading 41-35 and just over a minute remaining, Callahan lined up for a 43-yard field goal – and essentially the win – but Marcus Rush blocked the kick, and RJ Williamson scooped up the ball and ran 36 yards down the Spartan sideline to the Baylor 45, setting up MSU's game-winning TD drive. Cook completed a key fourth-and-10 pass to Tony Lippett for 17 yards that kept the drive alive with 33 seconds left, then found Mumphery in the back of the end zone on third-and-goal with 17 seconds left to tie the game at 41. Michael Geiger followed the TD by making his sixth point-after attempt to give the Spartans a 42-41 lead. With one final chance to win the game, Baylor was sacked twice on its last drive before Riley Bullough iced the victory on a diving interception with just two seconds remaining.

Aftermath - The win resulted in Michigan State's school record fourth straight bowl win and second straight New Year's Day bowl win. Baylor's loss made it their third in the Cotton Bowl (0-3 all time). Despite losing, Baylor Quarterback Bryce Petty and linebacker Taylor Young were awarded offensive and defensive MVP respectively. Michigan State finished the season ranked #5 in both polls (tied with Florida State in the AP poll) while Baylor finished #7 in the AP and #8 in the Coaches.

2015 Buffalo Wild Wings Citrus Bowl

The 2015 Citrus Bowl was held on January 1, 2015 at the Orlando Citrus Bowl Stadium in Orlando, Florida. The 69th edition televised by ABC. It was sponsored by the Buffalo Wild Wings restaurant franchise and is officially known at the Buffalo Wild Wings Citrus Bowl.

Missouri - The 2014 Missouri Tigers football team was led by head coach Gary Pinkel, who was in his 14th year, and played its home games at Faurot Field in Columbia, Missouri. They finished the season 11–3, 7–1 in SEC play to be champions of the Eastern Division. They represented the Eastern Division in the SEC Championship Game where they lost to Western Division champions Alabama 13–42.

Minnesota - The 2014 Minnesota Golden Gophers football team represented the University of Minnesota in the 2014 NCAA Division I FBS football season. They were led by fourth-year head coach Jerry Kill and played their home games at TCF Bank Stadium. They were a member of the West Division of the Big Ten Conference. They finished the season 8–5, 5–3 in Big Ten play to finish in a tie for second place in the West Division. They were invited to the Citrus Bowl where they lost to Missouri. It was their first New Year's Day bowl game appearance in 53 years, their previous was the 1962 Rose Bowl.

2015 Buffalo Wild Wings Bowl	Line	1	-	2	-	3	-	4	-	Final
#16 Missouri	(-4.5)	0	-	10	-	9	-	14	-	33
Minnesota	(47.0)	7	-	0	-	10	-	0	-	17

Scoring Summary
Minnesota – R. Williams 20 yard run (Santoso kick)
Missouri – Baggett 21 yard Field goal
Missouri – Sasser 25 yard pass from Mauk (Baggett kick)
Missouri – Baggett 33 yard Field goal
Minnesota – M. Williams 54 yard pass from Leidner (Santoso kick)
Missouri – Mauk 18 yard run (Pass failed)
Minnesota – Santoso 38 yard Field goal
Missouri – Hansbrough 78 yard run (Baggett kick)
Missouri – Sasser 7 yard pass from Mauk (Baggett kick)

Minnesota Media Guide Citrus Bowl Game Summary - Marcus Murphy ran for 159 yards, Russell Hansbrough added 114 yards and a touchdown and No. 16 Missouri beat Minnesota 33-17 on Thursday in the Citrus Bowl. Missouri (11-3) won its third straight bowl game to reach 11 victories for the fourth time in school history. Minnesota (8-5) trailed 19-17 entering the fourth quarter, but Missouri pulled away on Hansbrough's 78-yard touchdown run and Maty Mauk's 7-yard scoring pass to Bud Sasser. Mauk settled down to throw two TD passes after interceptions on the Tigers' first two possessions. The Tigers forced three turnovers. Minnesota Quarterback Mitch Leidner was 21 of 31 for 258 yards and a touchdown. The Tigers used an onside kick to open the third quarter to stretch out their halftime lead to 13-7. The Golden Gophers responded on the ensuing series with a 54-yard touchdown pass from Leidner to tight end Maxx Williams. Williams leaped over cornerback Aarion Penton and stepped over another defender before diving into the end zone. But Missouri quickly answered, needing just three plays after a muffed Minnesota punt for Mauk to give the Tigers a 19-14 lead on an 18-yard touchdown run. It tightened to 19-17 by the start of in the fourth quarter before Hansbrough got free and rumbled for his score that put the Tigers' up by nine with 9:28 to play. Missouri survived a disastrous offensive start to lead 10-7 at halftime in a game that started with the teams combining for three turnovers in the first 4 minutes. Missouri's Mauk opened the game by being picked off by Derrick Wells on the Tigers' third play from scrimmage. Minnesota would give it right back, though, when Leidner fumbled after being sandwiched in the backfield by defensive ends Markus Golden and Shane Ray. The Tigers then went just four more plays before Mauk's pass was intercepted for the second time, this time in the end zone by Briean Boddy-Calhoun. The Gophers finally ended the drought on the ensuing series, capping an 11-play, 80-yard drive with a 20-yard touchdown run by Rodrick Williams. It was part of a bruising first quarter that saw Minnesota gain 76 yards on the ground. That was flipped in the second quarter, as the Tigers used its own rushing attack to set up the passing game. First, following a punt, they used their best starting field position of the half to get on the board with Andrew Baggett's 21-yard field goal. Mauk then made the best of Missouri's final possession of the half, finding Bud Sasser for a 25-yard touchdown strike. In all, the Tigers outgained the Gophers 156-41 in the second quarter.

2015 Rose Bowl (CFP National Semifinal)

The 2015 Rose Bowl (officially known as the College Football Playoff Semifinal at the Rose Bowl Game presented by Northwestern Mutual) was played on January 1, 2015, at the Rose Bowl stadium in Pasadena, California. This 101st Rose Bowl Game, as a semifinal for the College Football Playoff (CFP), matched the Oregon Ducks against the Florida State Seminoles as selected by the system's selection committee to compete for a spot at the National Championship game to be played on January 12, 2015 at AT&T Stadium in Arlington, Texas. It was televised on ESPN and ESPN Deportes, and broadcast on ESPN Radio and XM Satellite Radio. The Pasadena Tournament of Roses Association organized the game. The Northwestern Mutual financial services organization sponsored the game. Oregon won the game, beating Florida State, the last undefeated team of the season, and advanced to the inaugural College Football Playoff National Championship Game, assuring that no team will finish the season with a perfect record.

Florida State - The 2014 Florida State Seminoles were led by fifth year head coach Jimbo Fisher and played their home games at Bobby Bowden Field at Doak Campbell Stadium in Tallahassee, Florida. They were members of the Atlantic Coast Conference, playing in the Atlantic Division. It was the Seminoles' 23rd season as a member of the ACC and its 10th in the ACC Atlantic Division. Florida State entered the season as the defending national champion. The Seminoles ended the regular season as the only team from a power conference without a loss but finished the season with a 13–1 record. The Seminoles won the ACC Atlantic Division for the sixth time, advancing to their fifth conference championship game, where they defeated Georgia Tech to win their fifteenth conference title. Florida State was selected to play in the inaugural College Football Playoff, losing to Oregon in the semifinal at the Rose Bowl and snapping the Seminoles' 29 game win streak. Starting Quarterback and 2013 Heisman Trophy winner Jameis Winston was the first pick in the NFL Draft.

Oregon - The 2014 Oregon Ducks were led by second-year head coach Mark Helfrich and played their home games at Autzen Stadium for the 48th straight year. They were a member of the Pac-12 Conference in the North Division. The Oregon Ducks finished the season with 13–2 overall and 8–1 in Pac–12 play. The Ducks won the Pac-12 North Division for the second time since the division's creation in 2011, advancing to the Pac-12 Football Championship Game, where they defeated the Arizona Wildcats 51–13. The Ducks played in the inaugural College Football Playoff, netting a berth in the 2015 Rose Bowl semifinal game, where they defeated the Florida State Seminoles 59–20, advancing to the 2015 College Football Playoff National Championship game facing the Ohio State Buckeyes. This was Oregon's second-ever national championship game appearance (their first was the 2011 BCS National Championship Game, in which they lost to Auburn).

Records - Oregon broke the record for the most points (59) scored in a Rose Bowl, surpassing the previous record of 49 (set in 1902, then tied in 1948 and 2008). Oregon's 41 points in the second half were also the most ever scored in one half of a Rose Bowl. Oregon set the Rose Bowl record for total offensive yards (639).

Tickets cost $225 per seat, while end zone seats cost $150. The total ticket allotment for both teams is approximately 25,000. Oregon's victory ended FSU's school-record winning streak at 29 games dating back to late in the 2012 season.

2015 Rose Bowl	Line	1	-	2	-	3	-	4	-	Final
#3 Oregon	(-9.0)	8	-	10	-	27	-	14	-	59
#2 Florida State	(72.0)	3	-	10	-	7	-	0	-	20

Scoring Summary
Florida State – Aguayo 28 yard Field goal
Oregon – Freeman 1 yard run (Pass good)
Oregon – Schneider 28 yard Field goal
Florida State – Aguayo 26 yard Field goal
Oregon – Tyner 1 yard run (Schneider kick)
Florida State – Williams 10 yard run (Aguayo kick)
Oregon – Freeman 3 yard run (Schneider kick)
Florida State – Rudolph 18 yard pass from Winston (Aguayo kick)
Oregon – Carrington 56 yard pass from Mariota (Schneider kick)
Oregon – Carrington 30 yard pass from Mariota (Schneider kick)
Oregon – Washington 58 yard fumble return (Kick blocked)
Oregon – Mariota 23 yard run (Schneider kick)
Oregon – Tyner 21 yard run (Schneider kick)

New York Times Rose Bowl Game Summary - As Jameis Winston moved forward, looking for another improbable outcome, then circled counterclockwise in desperation, Florida State's comeback magic came unraveled in spectacular fashion. On a fourth-down play Thursday late in the third quarter of the

Rose Bowl, Winston, the Seminoles' hitherto-undefeated Quarterback, spun to elude Oregon defenders, only to fall clumsily backward on the grass. The ball slipped from his grasp, took a bounce and landed in the hands of Oregon linebacker Tony Washington, who ran 58 yards for a touchdown. A taut game turned into a rout, as the up-tempo, high-scoring Ducks scored the game's final 34 points and ended Florida State's 29-game winning streak with a 59-20 victory. The Rose Bowl served as a semifinal in the inaugural season of the four-team College Football Playoff. Oregon (13-1), seeded second and searching for its first national title in football, will face No. 4 Ohio State, which defeated No. 1 Alabama in the Sugar Bowl, in the title game Jan. 12 in Arlington, Tex. "We want 'Bama!" Oregon fans in the partisan crowd of 91,322 had chanted. The Rose Bowl, played on a cool, sunny afternoon, represented a highly anticipated match between high-scoring offenses led by Heisman Trophy-winning Quarterbacks. Oregon's Marcus Mariota, the 2014 winner, completed 26 of 36 passes for 338 yards and 2 touchdowns. Then, in a span of 12:54, ending with a 21-yard touchdown run by Oregon running back Thomas Tyner, the Ducks outscored Florida State, 34-0. Oregon's 59 points represent a Rose Bowl record. The Seminoles, winner of last year's national championship, had not lost a game since the 2012 regular season. Winston, a redshirt sophomore, and Mariota, a redshirt junior, are both expected to declare for the coming N.F.L. draft. Speculation persists that they could be chosen first and second overall. Before Winston's fumble, the game unfolded as expected, with Florida State trying to keep up with Oregon's fast-motion offense. Even the officials struggled to keep up with Oregon's high-speed flair. The Ducks appeared to score their first touchdown on a 1-yard run, but officials belatedly called off the play to review the previous play, in which Charles Nelson took a pitch from Mariota, was flipped by a tackler and landed just short of the goal line. Oregon scored, again, two plays later, on Freeman's 1-yard run, and then added a surprise 2-point conversion when the holder Taylor Alie threw quickly to Torrodney Prevot. Oregon had an 8-3 lead, and the full attention of everyone in attendance. The Seminoles had a season-long habit of falling behind and coming back to win, and its previous four victories came by a total of 13 points. They kept the Ducks within reach until turnovers undid the Seminoles. Both teams gained 208 yards in the third quarter, but Florida State had four turnovers, and Oregon had four touchdowns. With Oregon leading, 18-13, the Florida State freshman tailback Dalvin Cook fumbled on the first drive of the third quarter. Five plays later, the Ducks scored on Royce Freeman's 3-yard touchdown. Winston and the Seminoles responded with Rudolph's scoring catch. Soon enough, though, Oregon receiver Darren Carrington caught a short pass from Mariota, slipped past Florida State defensive back Tyler Hunter and ran for a 56-yard touchdown. The Ducks had a 32-20 lead. The Seminoles marched to respond again but Cook fumbled once more after making a third-down reception near midfield. Two plays later, Mariota lobbed a pass to Carrington, who caught it inside the 10-yard line, eluded Hunter again and fell into the end zone. Oregon had a 39-20 lead as the sun set in California and on Florida State's chances. Only Winston could lead the type of comeback required. Instead, he spun until he fumbled wildly as he fell — "That was crazy," he said — and was greeted by defeat for the first time in 27 starts. The defenses took turns through most of the first half bending easily yet breaking stubbornly, as if leery of stepping on the colorfully painted end zones. Like marching bands, the teams made a show of moving back and forth on the field but not contributing much to the scoreboard. After the Ducks stalled at Florida State's 22-yard line looking for a second touchdown in the first quarter, the Seminoles churned downfield with a battery of running plays, slowing the pace between bursts by the quick-footed Cook, who finished with 103 yards on 15 carries. But Winston's fourth-down plunge from the 1-yard line, initially ruled a touchdown, was overturned when replays showed that his knee touched the ground before the ball reached the goal line. The Ducks used 19 plays to go 88 yards the other direction but settled for a field goal and an 11-3 lead. The Seminoles went the other direction for 13 plays and settled for a field goal. After Mariota threw his third interception of the season — a hush fell over the stadium, as if fans had just seen a comet — Florida State's all-American kicker Roberto Aguayo ended the half by missing a 54-yard field-goal attempt that struck the left upright. It was just the beginning of a string of unusual plays, none more than the one in which Winston sputtered and toppled like a tired top, symbolizing the end of Florida State's streak and Oregon's ascension to the national championship game. After the game, as remaining fans in the stands sang the "Animal House" anthem "Shout," Oregon players rushed into a jubilant locker room, some with roses clenched in their teeth. Moments after, first Fisher, then Winston, drove solemnly by on a golf cart, quietly headed somewhere out of sight.

2015 Sugar Bowl (CFP National Semifinal)

The 2015 Sugar Bowl was held on January 1, 2015 at the Mercedes-Benz Superdome in New Orleans, Louisiana. It was the 81st Sugar Bowl, and a semifinal game in the College Football Playoff. Sponsored by the Allstate insurance company, the game was officially known as the College Football Playoff Semifinal at the Allstate Sugar Bowl. The contest was televised on ESPN and ESPN Deportes, with a radio broadcast on

ESPN Radio and XM Satellite Radio. Kickoff time was set for 8:30 PM, Eastern Standard Time, but was delayed until after the end of the Rose Bowl. With 28,271,000 viewers, the game was the most watched cable television program in American history at the time.

Alabama - The Alabama Crimson Tide entered the season ranked 2nd in the AP and Coaches polls behind defending National Champions Florida State. Along with Ohio State, the Crimson Tide were considered a preseason favorite for a berth in the inaugural College Football playoff. After losing offensive coordinator Doug Nussmeier to Michigan, the Crimson Tide added former Oakland Raiders, Tennessee, and USC head football coach Lane Kiffin as their offensive coordinator. Among other changes came a change at Quarterback with a controversy between Blake Sims and Florida State transfer Jacob Coker. Initially, Coker was the favorite for the starting job; however, Sims, a more mobile Quarterback, was named the starter shortly before the season began. After a routine win against Western Carolina, the Crimson Tide then looked on to the Auburn Tigers. In the previous season, the Tigers won one of the most thrilling games in the history of college football 34–28 in the Iron Bowl with a late field goal return for a touchdown (now dubbed the "Kick Six"). In this edition of the Iron Bowl, Auburn jumped on multiple interceptions by Blake Sims to stay ahead of the Crimson Tide; however, a second half turnaround by Sims saw Alabama win the highest scoring edition of the Iron Bowl, 55–44. The next week, the #1 ranked Crimson Tide routed the SEC East Division champion Missouri Tigers, 42–13, in the SEC Championship, all but securing a #1 seed in the playoff and a Sugar Bowl berth the following morning.

Ohio State - The Ohio State Buckeyes entered the 2014 season ranked number 5 in both the AP and Coaches polls. They were an early favorite, along with Alabama, to make it to inaugural College Football Playoff. Two weeks before the season started, two-time Big Ten Offensive player of the year and Heisman Trophy candidate Braxton Miller was injured in practice. It was determined that Miller had a torn labrum which required surgery, and the Buckeyes had to look to J. T. Barrett, an unproven redshirt freshman. Following close wins against the Minnesota Golden Gophers and the Indiana Hoosiers, the Buckeyes entered their rivalry game against Michigan ranked #6 and just outside a playoff spot. In the game, Ohio State struggled early before pulling away to a 42–28 victory against their rivals. The win came at a cost, however, as J. T. Barrett was injured in the fourth quarter with a broken ankle. Following Barrett's injury during the Michigan Game, Ohio State turned to their third string Quarterback, Cardale Jones, for the Big Ten Championship game against Wisconsin. Because #4 Mississippi State lost in the Egg Bowl, Ohio State moved from #6 to #5 despite the loss of Barrett. Due to the game being Jones' first collegiate start, the Buckeyes entered as a 4.5 point underdog to the West Division champion Badgers. Ohio State, however, proved the oddsmakers wrong as Jones shined in a 59–0 rout of Wisconsin to capture the program's 35th Big Ten Championship and a potential College Football Playoff berth. The next morning, it was announced that Ohio State's win had propelled them to #4 in the final College Football Playoff rankings, securing their spot in the Sugar Bowl against #1 Alabama.

2015 Sugar Bowl	Line	1	-	2	-	3	-	4	-	Final
#4 Ohio State	(58.0)	6	-	14	-	14	-	8	-	42
#1 Alabama	(-9.0)	14	-	7	-	7	-	7	-	35

Scoring Summary
Ohio State – Nuernberger 22 yard field goal
Alabama – Henry 25 yard run (Griffith kick)
Ohio State – Nuernberger 21 yard field goal
Alabama – Cooper 15 yard pass from Sims (Griffith kick)
Alabama – Yeldon 2 yard run (Griffith kick)
Ohio State – Elliott 3 yard run (Nuernberger kick)
Ohio State – Thomas 13 yard pass from Spencer (Nuernberger kick)
Ohio State – Smith 47 yard pass from Jones (Nuernberger kick)
Ohio State – Miller 41 yard Interception return (Nuernberger kick)
Alabama – Sims 5 yard run (Griffith kick)
Ohio State – Elliott 85 yard run (Pass good)
Alabama – Cooper 6 yard pass from Sims (Griffith kick)

Associated Press Sugar Bowl Game Summary - Urban Meyer had barely sat down after the Allstate Sugar Bowl when someone told him about the score from the other semifinal game. He started to bolt from his chair, feigning a sense of urgency with another game left against a team that wiped out the defending national champion. He's not intimidated in the least. Meyer knows he's got a pretty good team, too.
Cardale Jones turned in another savvy performance in his second college start and Ezekiel Elliott ran for a Sugar-Bowl record 230 yards Thursday night, leading Ohio State to a 42-35 upset of top-ranked Alabama in the second semifinal of the College Football Playoff. The No. 4 Buckeyes (13-1) kicked off at the Superdome right after No. 2 Oregon finished its 59-20 rout of reigning champ Florida State in the Rose Bowl Presented

by Northwestern Mutual. Now, it's on to the Jan. 12 College Football Playoff National Championship Presented by AT&T in Arlington, Texas. Denied a shot at his fourth national title in six years, Alabama coach Nick Saban has no doubt Ohio State can hang with the high-scoring Ducks. This is what Meyer had in mind when he took over at Ohio State in 2012, having taken a year off from coaching after leading Florida to a pair of national titles. Coming from the Southeastern Conference, Meyer knew what he had to do. Recruit more speed. Bring a more athletic style to the plodding Big Ten. Turn Columbus into the SEC North. After just three years on the job, he's one win away from a national championship. And, for the first time in nine years, the SEC won't be part of the championship game. Jones threw for 243 yards, including a 47-yard touchdown to Devin Smith that put the Buckeyes ahead for good early in the third quarter. He also ran for 43 yards and converted a crucial third-down play with a spinning, 1-yard dive and Ohio State clinging to a 34-28 lead. On the next play, Elliott took a handoff, broke one feeble attempt at a tackle and was gone for an 85-yard touchdown that essentially clinched the victory with 3:24 remaining. Ohio State snapped a 0-for-10 futility streak against the SEC in bowl games, its only victory vacated by a scandal that cost former coach Jim Tressel his job. Alabama (12-2) didn't go down quietly. Blake Sims threw a 6-yard touchdown pass to Amari Cooper with 1:59 remaining. The Buckeyes recovered the onside kick, but Alabama got it back one more time after some questionable clock management. The Tide's final shot ended when a desperation heave into the end zone was picked off by Tyvis Powell as time ran out, Sims' third interception of the game. Jones started fall practice as Ohio State's third-string Quarterback, moved up the depth chart when star Braxton Miller sustained a season-ending shoulder injury and became the starter for the Big Ten championship game after J.T. Barrett went down with an injury. A 59-0 rout of Wisconsin showed that Jones was up to the job. His performance against Alabama gives him a chance to go down as one of the greatest replacement players in college football history. Alabama hardly looked like the defensive powerhouse that Coach Nick Saban is used to sending out, giving up 537 yards to the Buckeyes. Elliott scored on a 3-yard run with 2:55 left in first half to spark the comeback, and he wound up averaging a staggering 11.5 yards on 20 carries to earn the award as the most outstanding offensive player. For the second year in a row, Alabama's season ended at the Sugar Bowl. This one was especially painful, costing the Tide a chance to advance in college football's first playoff. But he never liked the feel of the game, even after Alabama raced to its early lead, taking advantage of a pair of turnovers and coming up with a pair of red zone stops. Shaking off an interception, Jones led one of the biggest drives of the game at the end of the first half. He completed three straight passes for 37 yards, then broke off a 27-yard run up the middle when his receivers were covered. After a timeout with 19 seconds remaining, Ohio State pulled out a trick play – and Michael Thomas pulled off one of the most spectacular catches of the season. Jones handed off to receiver Jalin Marshall on an apparent end-around, Marshall flipped it to Evan Spencer coming the other way, and Spencer suddenly pulled up and threw toward Thomas. He leaped up to make a twisting catch and somehow got his left foot down just inside the line for a 13-yard score that gave the Buckeyes all the momentum going into halftime. Ohio State kept right on going, scoring two more touchdowns to complete a stunning 28-0 spurt that pushed the Buckeyes ahead 34-21.

2015 Armed Forces Bowl

The 2015 Armed Forces Bowl was played on January 2, 2015 at Amon G. Carter Stadium on the campus of Texas Christian University in Fort Worth, Texas in the United States. The twelfth annual Armed Forces Bowl was televised on ESPN. The bowl was the first to be sponsored by aerospace and defense company Lockheed Martin (which has two of its divisions headquartered in the DFW area); as such, for sponsorship purposes the game was officially known as the Lockheed Martin Armed Forces Bowl. With less than 11 minutes left on the game clock, Houston trailed Pittsburgh by 25 points, but the Cougars went on to win 35–34. It was the biggest fourth quarter comeback in bowl history.

2015 Armed Forces Bowl	Line	1	2	3	4	Final
Houston	(54.0)	0	6	0	29	35
Pittsburgh	(-4.0)	0	17	7	10	34

Scoring Summary
Pittsburgh - Conner 1 yard run (Blewitt kick)
Houston - Farrow 2 yard run (Bullard kick)
Pittsburgh - Bennett 12 yard run (Blewitt kick)
Pittsburgh - Blewitt 52 yard Field goal
Pittsburgh - Holtz 16 yard pass from Voytik (Blewitt kick)
Pittsburgh - Conner 5 yard run (Blewitt kick)
Houston - Farrow 8 yard run (Bullard kick)
Pittsburgh - Blewitt 29 yard Field goal
Houston - Greenberry 8 yard pass from Ward (Bullard kick)
Houston - Ayers 29 yard pass from Ward (Bullard kick)
Houston - Greenberry 29 yard pass from Ward (Ward pass good)

SportsDayDFW.com Armed Forces Bowl Game Summary - After a crazy comeback featuring two crazy onside kicks, Houston interim coach David Gibbs made a crazy decision. Having watched his team improbably roar back from a 25-point fourth-quarter deficit to climb within a point of Pittsburgh with 59 seconds left, Gibbs had his Cougars go for a two-point conversion and the win rather than playing it safe and going into overtime. The decision paid off when Deontay Greenberry pulled down Greg Ward Jr.'s jump-ball pass between two defenders in the back of the end zone, giving Houston a wild 35-34 win — the biggest comeback victory ever in an NCAA bowl in regulation time. But, that decision had already been made three weeks before, during the Cougars' first practice after coach Tony Levine was fired Dec. 8. The plan wasn't, however, to fall behind 31-6, which Houston did when Pitt's James Conner, the Atlantic Coast Conference Player of the Year raced into the end zone from 5 yards out with 13:58 left in the fourth quarter. At the time, Pitt was in complete control, having outgained Houston 376 yards to 194 and holding more than a 10-minute edge in time of possession. The Panthers (6-7) rolled over the Cougars' stout defense for two drives of more than 90 yards and 6 1/2 minutes. Conner's second TD of the game seemed to be nothing more than a final flourish to an easy victory. Instead, it was the beginning of the third-largest comeback in bowl history, and the largest fourth-quarter deficit ever overcome in a bowl. It began with a swift 86-yard drive capped by Kenneth Farrow's 8-yard touchdown run. After Pitt answered with a field goal, Ward pushed the Cougars 83 yards for another TD, this one an 8-yard pass to Greenberry that closed the gap to two touchdowns with 3:41 left. Then the fireworks really began. Ty Cummings rolled an onside kick that somehow slipped underneath Pitt linebacker Nicholas Grigsby and was recovered by Houston's Tyler White. Six plays later, Ward dropped a perfect pass in the hands of Demarcus Ayers for a 29-yard score with 1:58 on the clock. On the kickoff, Cummings faked an onside to the left, then faked right, then kicked it back to the left, where the ball caromed off Grigsby and into the arms of Farrow, a former Hurst L.D. Bell star. Ward made the most of the chance, hitting Greenberry for 38 yards on the first play. On third-and-16 from the Pitt 25, Markeith Ambles ran deep down the sideline, drawing safety Reggie Mitchell with him and leaving Greenberry all alone down the seam for the touchdown. On the conversion, Ward sprinted to the right and lofted one up for Greenberry. The 6-3 junior rose over Mitchell and linebacker Bam Bradley for the winning points. The result capped an incredible quarter in which Houston put up 292 yards to Pitt's 88 and scored 29 points, 22 in the final 3:41. Ward, who had 37 passing yards through three quarters, passed for 237 yards in the fourth and ran for 28 more. Greenberry, who had been shut out until the fourth, caught four passes for 85 yards and two touchdowns.

2015 Gator Bowl

The 2015 TaxSlayer Bowl was held on January 2, 2015, at EverBank Field in Jacksonville, Florida. The 70th edition of the TaxSlayer Bowl (formerly called Gator Bowl) featured the Tennessee Volunteers of the Southeastern Conference and the Iowa Hawkeyes from the Big Ten Conference. The game was nationally televised by ESPN. It was sponsored by tax preparation software company TaxSlayer.com.

2015 Gator Bowl	Line	1	-	2	-	3	-	4	-	Final
Iowa	(51.5)	0	-	7	-	0	-	21	-	28
Tennessee	(-3.5)	21	-	14	-	7	-	3	-	45

Scoring Summary
Tennessee – Hurd 3 yard run (Medley kick)
Tennessee – Hurd 29 yard run (Medley kick)
Tennessee – Wharton 49 yard pass from Lane (Medley kick)
Tennessee – Dobbs 8 yard run (Medley kick)
Iowa – Weisman 3 yard run (Koehn kick)
Tennessee – Pearson 19 yard pass from Dobbs (Medley kick)
Tennessee – Dobbs 11 yard run (Medley kick)
Iowa – Weisman 1 yard run (Koehn kick)
Tennessee – Medley 28 yard Field goal
Iowa – Hamilton 31 yard pass from Beathard (Koehn kick)
Iowa – VandeBerg 18 yard pass from Beathard (Koehn kick)

Associated Press Gator Bowl Game Summary - Tennessee coach Butch Jones was soaked from a celebratory sideline dousing. Quarterback Joshua Dobbs carried the Most Valuable Player trophy with him all around EverBank Field. Both, as well as the rest of the Volunteers, donned championship hats for the first time in years. It was tangible proof that the program is headed in the right direction. Dobbs accounted for three touchdowns, Jalen Hurd ran for two scores and Tennessee beat Iowa 45-28 on Friday in the TaxSlayer Bowl for its first postseason victory since the Phillip Fulmer era. The Volunteers (7-6) took the momentum early Friday, scoring on their first four possessions and leading 28-0 before Iowa (7-6) managed 70 yards. Hurd, Dobbs and a bit of trickery helped Tennessee build the big lead. Hurd broke tackles on nearly every run, capping Tennessee's first possession with a 3-yard score and adding a 29-yard touchdown scamper on the next drive. Tennessee made it 21-0 late in the first quarter when Dobbs threw a lateral to running back Marlin Lane in the right flat. Lane, a senior from nearby Daytona Beach, turned and hit Vic Wharton in stride down the sideline. It was a nice send-off for Lane, one of just a handful of Tennessee's seniors. But the victory, which was Tennessee's first in the postseason since beating Wisconsin in the 2008 Outback Bowl, was more about the future. The Vols won four of their last five games, showing plenty of potential for one of the youngest teams in college football. Jones also delivered the program's first winning season since 2009. And it's not out of the question for Tennessee to be a trendy pick to contend for the Southeastern Conference's Eastern Division title in 2015. Hurd and Dobbs could be integral parts. Hurd, a freshman, had his fourth 100-yard game. He finished with 122 yards -- three shy of his career high -- and totaled the most yards on the ground by a Tennessee player in a bowl game since Travis Henry ran for 180 against Kansas State in the 2001 Cotton Bowl. Dobbs, a sophomore filling in for injured Quarterback Justin Worley, completed 16 of 21 passes for 129 yards, with a touchdown and an interception. He also ran for 76 yards and two scores. His 19-yard scoring pass to Von Pearson in the closing seconds of the first half made it 35-7. It came one play after the duo hooked up for an 11-yard gain on a ball that was tipped by a defender. It was that kind of day for Iowa, which was looking for its first postseason victory since the 2010 Insight Bowl. The Hawkeyes missed tackles, made mistakes and looked like they would end up with their worst bowl loss in school history before scoring three times in the fourth quarter. The Volunteers dominated on the field -- and in the stands. Tennessee fans vastly outnumbered Iowa fans, not surprising considering they feel good about the direction of the program under Jones and hadn't been to a bowl game in several years. Players kept them entertained, scoring their first six touchdowns in less than 3 1/2 minutes.

2015 Alamo Bowl

The 2015 Alamo Bowl was played on January 2, 2015, at the Alamodome in San Antonio, Texas. The 22nd edition of the Alamo Bowl featured the Kansas State Wildcats from the Big 12 Conference and the UCLA Bruins from the Pac-12 Conference. It was televised on ESPN and heard on the ESPN Radio. The game was sponsored by the Valero Energy Corporation and was officially known as the Valero Alamo Bowl.

2015 Alamo Bowl	Line	1	-	2	-	3	-	4	-	Final
#11 Kansas State	(-1.0)	0	-	6	-	15	-	14	-	35
#14 UCLA	(60.0)	17	-	14	-	3	-	6	-	40

Scoring Summary
UCLA – Hundley 10 yard run (Fairbairn kick)
UCLA – Fairbairn 27 yard Field goal
UCLA – Hundley 28 yard run (Fairbairn kick)
Kansas State – McCrane 47 yard Field goal
Kansas State – McCrane 29 yard Field goal
UCLA – Perkins 32 yard run (Fairbairn kick)
UCLA – Lucien 7 yard pass from Hundley (Fairbairn kick)
Kansas State – Lockett 3 yard pass from Waters (Lockett pass from Waters)
Kansas State – Robinson 2 yard run (McCrane kick)
UCLA – Fairbairn 44 yard Field goal
Kansas State – Waters 1 yard run (McCrane kick)
UCLA – Perkins 67 yard run (Fairbairn kick)
Kansas State – Lockett 29 yard pass from Waters (McCrane kick)

Associated Press Alamo Bowl Game Summary - Even with a 31-6 halftime lead, UCLA coach Jim Mora knew the Bruins had a lot of work to do to finish off Kansas State in the Valero Alamo Bowl. The No. 14 Bruins held on, beating the Wildcats 40-35 on Friday night. Kansas State coach Bill Snyder bristled at the thought that TV broadcasters might say the same thing about his Wildcats that they did about Florida State in the Rose Bowl Game presented by Northwestern Mutual. Kansas State (9-4) scored 22 of the first 25 points in the second half, cutting it to 34-28 on Quarterback Jake Waters' 1-yard run with 4:54 left. Paul Perkins countered for UCLA (10-3) with a 67-yard run with 2:20 to go. The Wildcats weren't finished. Waters threw a 29-yard touchdown pass to Tyler Lockett with 1:21 left, but Perkins recovered the onside kick for UCLA and the Bruins ran out the clock. Mora and Snyder had an awkward exchange on the field after the game. Apparently upset that Kansas State took a timeout and hit Bruins Quarterback Brett Hundley as he kneeled to down the ball on the final play, Mora quickly turned away from Snyder after barely shaking hands, then went back and got into an animated chat. It has been a week of big comebacks at bowl games. Michigan State trailed Baylor by 20 in the fourth quarter at the Goodyear Cotton Bowl Classic and won 42-41. Earlier Friday, Houston scored 29 points in the fourth quarter to beat Pittsburgh 35-34 in the Lockheed Martin Armed Forces Bowl. Waters was 31-of-48 for 338 yards but was sacked seven times -- twice by Butkus Award winner Eric Kendricks -- and threw two interceptions and lost a fumble. Lockett had 13 catches for 164 yards for Kansas State. Hundley ran for 96 yards and two touchdowns on 11 carries and passed for 136 yards. Mora has said Hundley is forgoing his senior season to enter the NFL draft. UCLA raced to a 17-0 lead in the first quarter, with Hundley scoring on runs of 10 and 28 yards. The Bruins outgained Kansas State 218-4 and had a 9-1 edge in first downs in the quarter. In the second quarter, Perkins had a 32-yard touchdown run and Hundley threw a 7-yard scoring pass to Devin Lucien. The Bruins sacked Waters five times in the half.

2015 Cactus Bowl

The 2015 Cactus Bowl was played on January 2, 2015, at Sun Devil Stadium in Tempe, Arizona. The game was televised on ESPN. Sponsored by the TicketCity ticket broker company, the game was officially known as the TicketCity Cactus Bowl. The 26th edition of the Cactus Bowl featured the Oklahoma State Cowboys from the Big 12 Conference and the Washington Huskies from the Pac-12 Conference.

2015 Cactus Bowl	Line	1	-	2	-	3	-	4	-	Final
Washington	(-6.5)	0	-	0	-	14	-	8	-	22
Oklahoma State	(56.5)	14	-	10	-	3	-	3	-	30

Scoring Summary
Oklahoma State – Castleman 1 yard run (Grogan kick)
Oklahoma State – Washington 28 yard pass from Rudolph (Grogan kick)
Oklahoma State – Grogan 40 yard Field goal
Oklahoma State – Shephard 47 yard pass from Rudolph (Grogan kick)
Washington – Mickens 31 yard run (Van Winkle kick)
Oklahoma State – Grogan 27 yard Field goal
Washington – Ross 96 yard kickoff return (Van Winkle kick)
Oklahoma State – Grogan 34 yard Field goal
Washington – Mickens 16 yard pass from Miles (Pass good)

Associated Press Cactus Bowl Game Summary - Oklahoma State went through its most difficult season under coach Mike Gundy, losing five straight games before squeaking into a bowl game. Once the Cowboys got to the Cactus Bowl, they rode a freshman Quarterback and an offensively gifted defensive tackle to a spirit-lifting victory. Mason Rudolph threw for 299 yards and two touchdowns, and 300-pound tackle James Castleman showed off his versatility with two big offensive plays lead Oklahoma State to a 30-22 victory over Washington in the TicketCity Cactus Bowl Friday night. Oklahoma State (7-6) needed a late rally over rival Oklahoma in the season finale to become bowl eligible and played the TicketCity Cactus Bowl without its most dynamic offensive player. The Cowboys closed out the season with a flourish behind Rudolph, with some help from Castleman. A freshman making his third start, Rudolph kept his composure against Washington's vaunted front seven, overcoming three turnovers to hit 17 of 26 passes. Desmond Roland kept the Huskies off-balance by tearing off big runs up the middle, finishing with 123 yards on 32 carries. Then there was Castleman. Though he had never played offense before, the beefy defensive tackle lined up in the shotgun to score on a 1-yard run in the first half, helping Oklahoma State build a 17-point halftime lead. Washington rallied to within a touchdown in the second half, but Castleman wreaked havoc again, catching a pass out of the backfield and rumbling down the sideline for a 48-yard catch that all but killed the Huskies' hopes. Washington (8-6) stumbled out of the gate on both sides of the ball in the first half in the first half before finding a rhythm on offense in the second. The hole proved to be too deep, ending coach Chris Petersen's first season with a loss. John Ross scored on a 96-yard kickoff return and Cyler Miles threw for 268 yards and a touchdown but had an interception on Washington's last-ditch drive. The Cowboys pulled off a last-minute comeback to earn a spot in the Cactus Bowl, scoring two touchdowns in the final 8 minutes to knock off Oklahoma in overtime. Tyreek Hill had the big play in that game, scoring on a 92-yard punt return with 45 seconds left, but he was dismissed from the team last month after being arrested on charges of choking and punching his pregnant girlfriend. That left Oklahoma State without its most dangerous threat against a Washington defense that has three first-team All-Americans. The Cowboys didn't seem to mind. They had no trouble against Washington's ferocious front seven on their opening drive, confidently converting a midfield fourth-and-1 to set up Castleman's 1-yard dive off left tackle. Rudolph turned it over on the next two drives, losing a fumble when he was sacked, then on a one-handed interception by Budda Baker. The freshman kept his poise, though. He caught a pass from receiver Brandon Sheperd on a trick play to set up a 28-yard touchdown pass to James Washington, who one-upped Baker with a one-handed catch in the end zone. The Sheperd-Rudolph connection worked again just before the half, this time in reverse: Rudolph on the throw, Sheperd on the catch for a 47-yard touchdown that put the Cowboys up 24-0. Washington had just as much trouble on offense, finishing with 113 total yards in the half. The Huskies finally showed signs of life on their opening drive of the third quarter, cutting into Oklahoma State's lead on Mickens' 31-yard reverse. Washington got a bad break when a punt hit one of its players and Oklahoma State recovered but held the Cowboys to Ben Grogan's 27-yard field goal. Ross took the ensuing kickoff up the middle, made a couple of jukes and raced off to a 96-yard touchdown that cut the Cowboys' lead to 27-14. Miles followed with a 16-yard touchdown pass to Mickens, trimming the lead to 30-2 with 3 1-2 minutes left. The Cowboys then turned to Castleman again and he played the receiver role well, killing off precious seconds that helped the Cowboys finish a difficult season on a positive note.

2015 Birmingham Bowl

The 2015 Birmingham Bowl was played on January 3, 2015 at Legion Field in Birmingham, Alabama. The ninth annual Birmingham Bowl saw the Florida Gators of the Southeastern Conference defeat the East Carolina Pirates of the American Athletic Conference by a score of 28–20. The game was televised on ESPN.

2015 Birmingham Bowl	Line	1	-	2	-	3	-	4	-	Final
East Carolina	(56.5)	7	-	0	-	10	-	3	-	20
Florida	(-7.0)	7	-	14	-	7	-	0	-	28

Scoring Summary
East Carolina - Hardy 3 yard pass from Carden (Harvey kick)
Florida - Poole 29 yard interception return (Hardin kick)
Florida - Lane 2 yard run (Hardin kick)
Florida - Powell 13 yard pass from Harris (Hardin kick)
East Carolina - Worthy 4 yard pass from Carden (Harvey kick)
Florida - Fulwood 86 yard pass from Harris (Hardin kick)
East Carolina - Harvey 24 yard Field goal
East Carolina - Harvey 24 yard Field goal

Associated Press Birmingham Bowl Game Summary - The Florida Gators got big plays from star cornerback Vernon Hargreaves III, Quarterback Treon Harris and two of their lesser known teammates. Harris threw an 86-yard scoring pass to mostly unheralded receiver Ahmad Fulwood, and Hargreaves intercepted a pass in the end zone late to preserve Florida's 28-20 victory over East Carolina on Saturday in the Birmingham Bowl. The big plays helped the Gators (7-5) finish a disappointing season with a winning record while new coach Jim McElwain was among the spectators. Brian Poole also scored on a 29-yard interception return and Florida's defense repeatedly turned East Carolina's high-powered offense away from the end zone. Redshirt freshman running back Adam Lane was chosen the game's MVP after rushing 16 times for 109 yards and a touchdown with Matt Jones sidelined with a shoulder injury. He had only eight carries coming into the game, all in two lopsided wins. Shane Carden was 34 of 66 for 427 yards for the Pirates (8-5), but Hargreaves' pick with 1:20 left ended his day. It was a school record for passing attempts and the most thrown against Florida. Harris left late in the third quarter with what Durkin described as an elbow injury and was replaced by former starter Jeff Driskel. Driskel ran for a first down on a third-down play on the final drive to allow Florida to run out the clock. Durkin took over for the bowl game after Will Muschamp's firing. East Carolina came in averaging 37.2 points a game but managed only a field goal in the fourth quarter and couldn't cash in on a number of flirtations with the end zone. Justin Hardy finished with 11 catches for 160 yards and Cam Worthy gained 130 yards on eight catches. Carden's take on the offense: Florida's Harris was 5 of 11 for 123 yards and two touchdowns, including the play to Fulwood on a screen pass early in the third quarter. It was the Gators' longest play from scrimmage this season. The game gave young players like Lane and Fulwood hope for more playing time under the new regime. Fulwood had just 113 yards receiving in the regular season. Driskel had 48 passing yards in what could be his final Florida game. McElwain said before the game Driskel had asked for a release from his scholarship. Florida's offense mostly sputtered without Harris, but the defense delivered. Trying to expand the lead, Driskel led the Gators into East Carolina territory before Josh Hawkins forced a fumble by receiver Chris Thompson. East Carolina drove to Florida's 27 before getting forced back by a penalty and Dante Fowler Jr.'s third sack of the game in his Gators finale. Fowler has already said he's skipping his senior season to turn pro. The Gators took over with 4:21 left and went three and out. With two incompletions, Florida burned only 44 seconds off the clock before giving it back to Carden and the Pirates' high-powered offense at their 42. Carden completed three straight passes, including a nifty catch and run by Hardy for 24 yards. Then East Carolina caught a momentary reprieve. Isaiah Jones fumbled at the end of a catch, the ball squirted away from a Florida player and Jimmy Williams dove on it at Florida's 5. Hargreaves, the Gators' All-Southeastern Conference cornerback, picked off Carden's pass two plays later.

2015 GoDaddy Bowl

The 2015 GoDaddy Bowl was held on January 4, 2015 at Ladd Peebles Stadium in Mobile, Alabama in the United States. The sixteenth edition of the GoDaddy Bowl, which featured the Toledo Rockets of the Mid-American Conference against the Arkansas State Red Wolves of the Sun Belt Conference, was televised on ESPN. The game was sponsored by web hosting service company GoDaddy.

2015 GoDaddy Bowl	Line	1	-	2	-	3	-	4	-	Final
Toledo	(-3.5)	21	-	14	-	7	-	21	-	63
Arkansas State	(68.5)	14	-	3	-	14	-	13	-	44

Scoring Summary
Toledo - Voss fumble recovery in end zone (Detmer kick)
Arkansas State - Mays 44 yard pass from Knighten (Spry kick)
Toledo - Hunt 4 yard run (Detmer kick)
Toledo - Hunt 44 yard run (Detmer kick)
Arkansas State - Houston 66 yard pass from Knighten (Spry kick)
Arkansas State - Spry 31 yard Field goal
Toledo - Hunt 29 yard run (Detmer kick)
Toledo - Covington 67 yard fumble return (Detmer kick)
Toledo - Hunt 6 yard run (Detmer kick)
Arkansas State - Mays 55 yard pass from Knighten (Spry kick)
Arkansas State - Hunter 94 yard interception return (Spry kick)
Toledo - Hunt 1 yard run (Detmer kick)
Arkansas State - Mays 27 yard pass from Knighten (Spry kick)
Toledo - Jones-Moore 10 yard run (Detmer kick)
Arkansas State - Griswold 3 yard pass from Knighten (Pass failed)
Toledo - Jones-Moore 29 yard run (Detmer kick)

Associated Press GoDaddy Bowl Game Summary - Sophomore Kareem Hunt is already one of the most accomplished running backs in Toledo history. The five seniors blocking for him were intent on ending their college careers with a victory. Combine the two and the Rockets were a running juggernaut that Arkansas State simply couldn't stop. Hunt ran for a bowl-record 271 yards and five touchdowns to lead Toledo over Arkansas State 63-44 on Sunday night. He averaged 8.5 yards per carry and scored three touchdowns in the first half as the Rockets took a 35-17 lead by halftime. The 5-foot-11, 200-pound Hunt capped a phenomenal season by slicing through Arkansas State's defense early and often. The performance easily set a GoDaddy Bowl record, topping the previous mark of 207 set by Tulsa's Tarrion Adams in 2009. Hunt, who was the game's offensive MVP, said he wished he could give the trophy to the offensive line. Toledo (9-4) ended the season on a three-game winning streak. Arkansas State (7-6) pulled within 49-38 in the fourth quarter but could get no closer. The Red Wolves were playing in their fourth straight GoDaddy Bowl and fell to 2-2 over that span. Arkansas State's Fredi Knighten threw for 403 yards and five touchdowns. It was an entertaining game that featured three defensive touchdowns, six touchdowns of at least 40 yards and Arkansas State linebacker Xavier Woodson getting kicked out of the game for "threatening an official." Big numbers were the norm, even outside of Hunt's record-setting performance. Knighten's day was tempered by two costly fumbles that were both returned for touchdowns. Arkansas State's Booker Mays caught five passes for 138 yards and three touchdowns. The two teams combined for 1,009 total yards. Toledo finished with 365 yards rushing, including 103 yards and two touchdowns by Damion Jones-Moore. Logan Woodside completed 21 of 27 passes for 176 yards. It was a frantic start to the game with two touchdowns scored in the first 90 seconds. Knighten fumbled on Arkansas State's first play and Toledo's Trent Voss recovered in the end zone to give the Rockets a 7-0 lead. The Red Wolves bounced back quickly, though, needing just five plays to tie the game on Knighten's 43-yard touchdown pass to Mays. Toledo scored two more touchdowns by the end of the first quarter -- both on runs by Hunt -- to take a 21-14 advantage. The 35 combined points in one quarter tied a GoDaddy Bowl record. Arkansas State pulled within 21-17 by midway through the second quarter, but the Red Wolves had no answer for Hunt and couldn't overcome some costly turnovers. Toledo added two more touchdowns in the waning minutes of the first half: Hunt ran for a 29-yard touchdown on a 4th-and-2 play and then 6-foot-2, 275-pound defensive Allen Covington recovered a fumble by Knighten and rumbled 67 yards for the touchdowns. It gave the Rockets a 35-17 halftime lead despite Arkansas State's 250-237 advantage in total yards. Arkansas State didn't go away until late in the fourth quarter. The Red Wolves fell behind 42-17 midway through the third quarter, but responded with two quick touchdowns, including a 94-yard interception return by Money Hunter, who is the son of Major League outfielder Torii Hunter.

2015 CFP Championship Game

The 2015 College Football Playoff National Championship (known as the 2015 College Football Playoff National Championship presented by AT&T for sponsorship reasons) took place at AT&T Stadium in Arlington, Texas on January 12, 2015. It was the inaugural College Football Playoff National Championship, replacing the BCS National Championship Game. The national title was contested through a four-team bracket system, the College Football Playoff, which replaced the previous Bowl Championship Series. This was the first championship game since 2006 that did not feature at least one SEC team, and the teams' first meeting since the 2010 Rose Bowl, which the Buckeyes won 26–17.

Before the game - AT&T Stadium (capacity 80,000) was announced as the host site in April 2013. Arlington and Tampa (Raymond James Stadium) were the only cities to submit hosting bids for the inaugural title game. Each team received 20,000 tickets. Premium seat packages for the event cost $1,899 to $3,899 apiece. The packages can include hotel accommodations, game tickets, parking access, pregame hospitality, and an on-field postgame experience. College Football Playoff announced that 1,000 tickets will be made available for purchase to fans who have signed up for a random drawing by May 1, 2014. On March 25, 2014, Dr. Pepper was announced as the official championship partner and presenting sponsor of the new College Football Playoff National Championship Trophy. The cost of a thirty-second commercial during the game broadcast reached upwards of $1 million.

Broadcasting - The game was televised by ESPN with Chris Fowler and Kirk Herbstreit as commentators, and Heather Cox and Tom Rinaldi as sideline reporters and on ESPN Deportes with Eduardo Varela and Pablo Viruega as Spanish commentators. ESPN revived the Megacast coverage it had employed during the 2014 BCS National Championship Game: other ESPN networks (including ESPN2, ESPNEWS, ESPN Classic, ESPNU, and ESPN3) supplemented coverage with analysis and additional perspectives of the game. Approximately 33.4 million watched the game. The game set a cable television record for ratings, receiving an 18.5 Nielsen rating. The game was broadcast on nationwide radio by ESPN Radio with Mike Tirico and Todd Blackledge on the call, with Holly Rowe and Joe Schad on the sidelines.

2015 CFP Championship Game	Line	1	-	2	-	3	-	4	-	Final
#3 Oregon	(-6.5)	7	-	3	-	10	-	0	-	20
#4 Ohio State	(74.5)	14	-	7	-	7	-	14	-	42

Scoring Summary
Oregon – Lowe 7 yard pass from Mariota (Schneider kick)
Ohio State – Elliott 33 yard run (Nuernberger kick)
Ohio State – Vannett 1 yard pass from Jones (Nuernberger kick)
Ohio State – Jones 1 yard run (Nuernberger kick)
Oregon – Schneider 26 yard Field goal
Oregon – Marshall 70 yard pass from Mariota (Schneider kick)
Oregon – Schneider 23 yard Field goal
Ohio State – Elliott 9 yard run (Nuernberger kick)
Ohio State – Elliott 2 yard run (Nuernberger kick)
Ohio State – Elliott 1 yard run (Nuernberger kick)

Associated Press National Championship Game Summary - Ohio State was done when Braxton Miller got hurt in August. Ohio State was done when it lost at home to Virginia Tech in September. Ohio State was done when J.T. Barrett got hurt in November. A funny thing happened: Every time the Buckeyes looked done; they kept getting better. And in the new era of college football, that was enough to earn a chance to win a championship. They took advantage of an opportunity they never would have had in the BCS, shrugging off questions about whether they belonged among college football's final four. Cardale Jones, Ezekiel Elliott and the Buckeyes won the first College Football Playoff National Championship Presented by AT&T, upsetting Marcus Mariota and Oregon 42-20 on Monday night. Behind their bullish backup Quarterback Jones and the relentless running of Elliott, the Buckeyes (14-1) completed a remarkable in-season turnaround with a dominating performance against the Ducks (13-2). Ohio State began the first major college football playoff as the fourth and final seed and was an underdog against both top-seeded Alabama and second-seeded Oregon. Plenty of people thought TCU or Baylor should have had the Buckeyes' spot. No question about it now: Ohio State is the truest champion big-time football has ever crowned, showered by golden confetti as its band played the school's unofficial anthem, "Hang on Sloopy," after the clock hit 0:00. The Buckeyes overcame two injured Heisman contenders and one awful 35-21 loss to Virginia Tech to win their first national title since the 2002 BCS championship. In the BCS, the early slip to the Hokies could have pretty much eliminated the Buckeyes from the championship race. Before the BCS's 16-year stint, it was up to The Associated Press and coaches' polls to sort out which team was best, with a little help from the bowls. The Buckeyes have three of those championships, too. Now they can add college football's newest championship trophy to the display cases at Woody Hayes Athletic Center back in Columbus. Meyer now has three titles, adding this one for his home state team to the two he won for Florida. He matches Alabama's Nick Saban as the only coaches to win a national championship at two schools. It has taken just three seasons for Meyer to put the Buckeyes -- and the Big Ten -- back on top, with a team that looks built to last. Elliott, a sophomore, was the offensive MVP and ran for 246 yards and four touchdowns on a career-high 36 carries. In the past three games -- the Big Ten championship against Wisconsin, the Allstate Sugar Bowl semifinal against Alabama and the final against Oregon -- Elliott had 696 yards rushing. Jones, who took over in the Michigan game for the injured Barrett (who had taken over at the start of the season for the injured Miller), passed for 242 yards and a touchdown and ran for score in his third career start. The 250-pound third-year sophomore proved he could keep up with Mariota -- at least on this night. Mariota passed for 333 yards and two touchdowns, but the Ducks' warp-speed spread offense missed too many red zone opportunities and couldn't unleash its running game against linebacker Darron Lee and an Ohio State front seven stacked with future NFL draft picks. Even with the benefit of four Ohio State turnovers, the Ducks were held to their lowest point total of the season, four touchdowns fewer than their average coming in. They went 2-for-12 on third downs, with two dropped passes in the first half. Oregon has done just about everything as it has blossomed into a national power over the past two decades, but it might have to continue the search for its first national championship without Mariota. Barring a major surprise, the junior is likely to turn pro -- although he said after the game that he hadn't yet decided. Elliott scored the game's last three touchdowns, finishing it off with a 1-yarder with 28 seconds left. While Elliott slipped and darted through the Ducks, Jones pushed them around and shook them off. When Jones surged and spun his way into the end zone with 4:49 left in the second quarter, it was 21-7 Ohio State, and the "O! H! I! O!" chant made the dome in North Texas sound like the horseshoe in Columbus. The Ducks were facing their largest deficit of the season. If there was any concern that fans wouldn't travel to the championship game in the new postseason system, the packed house at the home of the Dallas Cowboys, awash in Buckeyes scarlet and Ducks yellow, put that to rest. The crowd of 85,689 was as charged as that at any BCS national championship game. But by the time Elliott went in from 2 yards out with 9:44 left in the fourth to make it 35-20, it was clear this night had turned into a Buckeyes bash.

2015 Air Force Reserve Celebration Bowl

The **2015 Celebration Bowl** (officially known as the **2015 Air Force Reserve Celebration Bowl**) was played on December 19, 2015 at the Georgia Dome in Atlanta, Georgia. The inaugural Celebration Bowl game pitted the North Carolina A&T Aggies, co-champion of the Mid-Eastern Athletic Conference, versus the Alcorn State Braves, champion of the Southwestern Athletic Conference. The game kicked off at 12:00 PM (EST) and was televised live on ABC. 22nd ranked North Carolina A&T won the game, beating Alcorn State by the score of 41–34, claiming the 2015 Black college football national championship before an announced crowd of 35,528. The participants for the Celebration Bowl game are based upon the final regular season standings which determine the MEAC football champion and the SWAC football championship Game determining the SWAC representative. The MEAC representative was announced on November 22, 2015, after the release of the final Sagrin ratings. As part of the MEAC tiebreaker, the ratings determined which of the 3 Co-Champions would represent the conference in the bowl game. The SWAC representative was announced at the conclusion of the SWAC Football Championship Game which matched the top teams from the conferences' eastern and western division.

2015 Celebration Bowl	Line	1	-	2	-	3	-	4	-	Final
Alcorn State		6	-	7	-	7	-	14	-	34
North Carolina A&T		21	-	3	-	3	-	14	-	41

Scoring Summary
North Carolina A&T – Gardin 74 yard punt return (Jones Kick)
Alcorn State – Williams 84 yard punt return (2 pt conversion no good)
North Carolina A&T – Cohen 74 yard run (Jones Kick)
North Carolina A&T – Cohen 83 yard run (Kick Good)
North Carolina A&T – Jones 45 yard Field goal
Alcorn State – Baker 10 yard pass from Footman (McRaney Kick)
North Carolina A&T – Jones 43 yard Field Goal
Alcorn State – Footman 9 yard pass from George (McRaney Kick)
Alcorn State – George 11 yard pass from Footman (McRaney Kick)
North Carolina A&T – Quick 1 yard run (Jones Kick)
Alcorn State – Campbell 3 yard pass from Vessell (McRaney Kick)
North Carolina A&T – Cohen 73 yard run (Jones Kick)

NCATAggies.com Celebration Bowl Summary – There is a saying that permeates inside the Bryan Fitness and Wellness Center and Aggie Stadium on the campus of North Carolina A&T State University: If something good happens, keep playing. If something bad happens, keep playing. There was plenty of good and bad that happened to N.C. A&T during the inaugural Air Force Reserve Celebration Bowl Saturday afternoon. The Aggies withstood it all in front of a national television audience on ABC to win the school's third HBCU National Football Championship with a 41-34 victory over SWAC champion Alcorn State at the Georgia Dome. The Aggies are now 4-4 in bowl games all-time and will forever hold the distinction of being the first-ever Celebration Bowl Champion. For N.C. A&T head coach Rod Broadway, it was his first career postseason win. Some may say junior Tarik Cohen was introduced to the nation over the summer thanks to the fact his videos of doing backflips while catching one, sometimes two footballs went viral and earned him live appearances on ESPN SportsCenter. But if some around the country thought his talents only consisted of backflips, then they saw a whole new side of him on Saturday. Cohen rushed for 295 yards and three touchdowns and had some amazing runs that had Twitter nation buzzing. In fact, the Celebration Bowl was ESPN's second-highest trending event on Twitter. Cohen played a big role in that. But Cohen wanted to talk about the guys who weren't being discussed on social media. It has been a season of good and bad that would perhaps derail most teams without the Aggies motto. Not only had the play of the offensive line been brought into question, but the offense. Late in the season the Aggies struggled offensively in a 9-6 win at S.C. State. The following week the offense didn't blowout the Delaware State Hornets the way many thought they would. Then came the loss to N.C. Central where the Aggies scored 16 points, seven of them on a kickoff return. It led prognosticators to believe the combinations of the offensive struggles late in the season, Alcorn's powerful running game and the disappointment of losing to their archrival, N.C. Central two years in a row, would be too much for the Aggies to overcome. Too bad they didn't know the motto. The Aggies compiled a season-high 543 yards of offense. Senior quarterback Kwashaun Quick threw for 149 yards on 11-for-16 passing with no interceptions. Meanwhile, the Braves were held to a season low 260 yards of offense. The Aggies finished the season 10-2 overall. It is their first 10-win season in 12 years. It marks the third time in school history the Aggies have recorded double-digit wins in a season (1999, 2003, 2105). Tarik Cohen had already scored on runs of 74 and 83 and sophomore punt returner Khris Gardin had a 74-yard punt return as the Aggies led 24-6 midway through the second quarter. But an interception by freshman quarterback Kylil Carter gave the Braves the ball on the N.C. A&T 10-yard line. Lenorris Footman then completed a 10-yard pass to Aaron Baker to help the Braves halt the Aggies momentum and gain a little of their own. In fact, the Braves kept getting the breaks in their rally against A&T. A 47-yard kickoff return set the Braves up at the Aggies 49 which led to a score. With the Aggies leading 27-20 in the third quarter, the Braves also blocked a Cody Jones field goal, which led to the game-tying score at 27. The Aggies regained the lead on a 1-yard Quick touchdown, but an unsportsmanlike penalty on the ensuing kickoff gave the Braves the ball at their 48, leading to another game-tying score. The one mistake that didn't harm the Aggies eventually became the games finally turning point. Leading 41-34, Aggies punter Steven Sawicki shanked a 6-yard punt giving the Braves the ball at the 50. On 4th-and-9 from the Aggies 9, Footman's pass dropped incomplete in the final seconds to give the Aggies the win.

2015 New Mexico Bowl

The 2015 New Mexico Bowl was played on December 19, 2015 at University Stadium in Albuquerque, New Mexico. The tenth annual New Mexico Bowl was televised on ESPN.

Arizona–New Mexico football rivalry - Kit Carson Rifle - From 1938 to 1990, the winner of the rivalry took ownership of the Kit Carson Rifle. The gun is a Springfield Model 1866 rifle that is rumored to have once belonged to the famous frontier scout, Kit Carson. Game scores from each game are carved into the stock of the rifle. Prior to the 1997 Insight.com Bowl, the two schools announced that they would retire the rifle due to concerns of its history of violence against Native Americans, and it has not been used during any subsequent games between the two schools.

2015 New Mexico Bowl	Line	1	-	2	-	3	-	4	-	Final
Arizona	(-9.0)	7	-	21	-	14	-	3	-	45
New Mexico	(64.0)	3	-	14	-	14	-	6	-	37

Scoring Summary
New Mexico - Rogers 37 yard Field goal
Arizona - Jones 78 yard pass from Solomon (Skowron kick)
Arizona - Baker 27 yard run (Skowron kick)
New Mexico - Jordan 31 yard run (Rogers kick)
Arizona - Solomon 14 yard run (Skowron kick)
New Mexico - Hart-Johnson 92 yard pass from Jordan (Rogers kick)
Arizona - Richards 1 yard pass from Solomon (Skowron kick)
Arizona - Baker 32 yard run (Skowron kick)
New Mexico - Jordan 11 yard run (Rogers kick)
Arizona - Baker 4 yard run (Skowron kick)
New Mexico - Jordan 3 yard run (Rogers kick)
New Mexico - Apodaca 4 yard run (Run failed)
Arizona - Skowron 37 yard Field goal

Associated Press New Mexico Bowl Game Summary - At the beginning of the season, Arizona began with much promise after a previous Pac-12 championship appearance and a 3-0 start. The Wildcats were hit with injuries to Quarterback Anu Solomon and All-America linebacker Scooby Wright III. On Saturday, both came back to help Arizona (7-6) hold off pesky New Mexico 45-37 in a wild New Mexico Bowl. Solomon threw for two touchdowns and rushed for another score against New Mexico (7-6) in a game that saw New Mexico surge late after being down as many of 18 points. Wright had two sacks and 11 solo tackles. After the game, Wright announced he would enter the NFL draft. Arizona's high-tempo offense needed only 19:08 minutes of possession time to overwhelm New Mexico in the Lobos' first bowl appearance since 2007. Jared Baker ran for 107 yards and three touchdowns, and Cayleb Jones had 182 yards receiving and a touchdown. For Arizona, the New Mexico Bowl win comes just a year after Arizona eyed a playoff spot. Rodriguez said a bowl appearance and a victory was just fine for the team. Meanwhile, New Mexico Quarterback Lamar Jordan rushed for three touchdowns and threw a 92-yard touchdown pass to Delane Hart-Johnson before leaving in the third quarter with a knee injury. However, Jordan tossed two key interceptions -- one in Arizona's end zone and another deep in New Mexico territory. After Jordan's departure, the Lobos then turned to a committee of running backs to get New Mexico back in the game. Still, Arizona was able to hold star running back Jhurell Pressley to 75 rushing yards and no touchdowns. It was New Mexico's first bowl game appearance under Davie, a former Notre Dame Head coach who took over the program in 2012. The game at its home-field New Mexico Bowl had excited the city of Albuquerque following the long bowl drought. Arizona is 9-10-1 in bowl games. New Mexico fell to 3-8-1 in the postseason.

2015 Las Vegas Bowl

The 2015 Las Vegas Bowl was played on December 19, 2015 at Sam Boyd Stadium in the Las Vegas suburb of Whitney, Nevada. The 24th edition of the Las Vegas Bowl featured the BYU Cougars against the Utah Utes, earning the game the moniker the Holy War in Sin City (named for the "Holy War" rivalry game and the "Sin City" nickname for Las Vegas). The game sold out 24 hours after the matchup was announced. It was televised on ABC.

2015 Las Vegas Bowl	Line	1	-	2	-	3	-	4	-	Final
BYU	(49.5)	0	-	7	-	7	-	14	-	28
#20 Utah	(-2.5)	35	-	0	-	0	-	0	-	35

Scoring Summary
Utah - Williams 1 yard run (Phillips kick)
Utah - Carter 28 yard interception return (Phillips kick)
Utah - Williams 1 yard run (Phillips kick)
Utah - Hatfield 28 yard interception return (Phillips kick)
Utah - Wilson 20 yard run (Phillips kick)
BYU - Peck 3 yard pass from Mangum (Samson kick)
BYU - Benard 10 yard run (Samson kick)
BYU - Kurtz 5 yard pass from Mangum (Samson kick)
BYU - Mangum 4 yard run (Samson kick)

Associated Press Las Vegas Bowl Game Summary - BYU kept turning the ball over, and Utah kept scoring. About the only question left after five first-quarter touchdowns by the Utes was how big their Royal Purple Las Vegas Bowl rout would be. Until BYU regained its composure, that is, and made it a game for both teams to remember. Utah took advantage of a disastrous start by BYU, scoring five first-quarter touchdowns on turnovers -- including two interceptions by Tevin Carter -- before holding on Saturday to beat the Cougars 35-28. Utah used its string of first-quarter turnovers to build a 35-0 lead, then managed to hold on as BYU mounted a comeback that brought the Cougars to within one score with 3:23 left in the game. BYU couldn't get the ball back, though, losing in Bronco Mendenhall's last game after 11 years as head coach. After the game, BYU said it hired former Cougars running back Kalani Sitake as head coach. Sitake was Oregon State's assistant head coach and defensive coordinator. Carter returned one of his picks for a touchdown and another to the 1 as Utah (No. 22 CFP, No. 2 AP) romped to a 35-0 first- quarter lead in the first meeting of the two heated rivals outside of the state of Utah. BYU turned the ball over the first five times it had the ball, with freshman Quarterback Tanner Mangum throwing three interceptions and fumbling once. That was all the scoring Utah did, and it nearly cost the Utes the game. Mangum would bring BYU back, throwing two touchdown passes and rushing for another to get the Cougars close. Mendenhall's last game as BYU coach was almost over even before some of the fans settled into their seats, thanks to an opportunistic Utah defense that forced Mangum to fumble on the third play of the game. Midway through the first quarter, the Utes were already up 28-0. In a statistical quirk, BYU outgained Utah offensively (89-69) in the first quarter. But Carter and Dominique Hatfield both scored on interceptions, Joe Williams had two 1-yard touchdown runs, and Quarterback Travis Wilson added another TD on a 20-yard run. Mangum's shaky start didn't stop him from throwing for 315 yards in rallying his team. BYU dominated much of the game but couldn't quite dig itself out of the big hole. Utah (10-3) came in as a 2-point favorite in the first meeting since 2013 of schools that have campuses just 46 miles from each other. But the quick succession of turnovers -- Utah scored its first four touchdowns in a span of 3:30 -- threatened to turn the game into a rout before BYU settled down. BYU ended up with 386 yards to 197 for Utah, but the five early turnovers were the key in a game where the Utes didn't turn the ball over at all. Mendenhall, who is leaving BYU (9-4) after 11 seasons to coach at Virginia, failed in his try at win No. 100 at the school. Mendenhall, who wanted to coach the bowl game before leaving, finished his BYU career with a 99-43 record. Mangum, who earlier this season led the Cougars to last-minute comebacks against Nebraska and Boise State, never had a chance to do the same against the Utes. After bringing them within a touchdown with 3:23 left, he could only watch on the sideline as the Utes picked up two first downs and ran out the clock. BYU was down largely because of the early mistakes by the freshman, who lost a ball while scrambling on the third play of the game, then threw interceptions on the next three drives. Coming into the game, Mangum had thrown just seven picks all year. Mangum ended up completing 25 of 56 passes for 315 yards. Wilson was 9 for 16 for 71 yards. Utah, which at one point in the season was 6-0 and ranked No. 3, had 19 interceptions in the regular season, seventh best in the country. The Utes wasted no time adding to that number with two picks on tipped passes by Carter followed by a 46-yard interception return by Hatfield for a touchdown. The win before a sellout crowd of 42,213 was the ninth in 10 bowl games for Whittingham as head coach of Utah. The Utes have won 12 of their last 13 bowl games.

2015 Camellia Bowl

The 2015 Camellia Bowl was played on December 19, 2015 at Cramton Bowl in Montgomery, Alabama. The second edition of the Camellia Bowl featured the Ohio Bobcats from the Mid-American Conference against the Appalachian State Mountaineers of the Sun Belt Conference. This was the first ever meeting between the two teams. It was televised on ESPN.

2015 Camellia Bowl	Line	1	-	2	-	3	-	4	-	Final
Ohio	(55.0)	0	-	17	-	7	-	5	-	29
Appalachian State	(-7.0)	7	-	0	-	0	-	24	-	31

Scoring Summary
Appalachian State - Lamb 21 yard run (Matics kick)
Ohio - Yazdani 36 yard Field goal
Ohio - Poling 20 yard interception return (Yazdani kick)
Ohio - Ouellette 7 yard run (Yazdani kick)
Ohio - Johnson 45 yard fumble return (Yazdani kick)
Appalachian State - Burns 17 yard pass from Lamb (Matics kick)
Appalachian State - Cox 26 yard run (Matics kick)
Appalachian State - Burns 8 yard pass from Lamb (Matics game)
Ohio - Safety - Johnson tackled Cox in end zone
Ohio - Yazdani 21 yard Field goal
Appalachian State - Matics 23 yard Field goal

Associated Press Camellia Bowl Game Summary - Appalachian State and Ohio swapped huge defensive plays, gigantic momentum swings and even clutch kicks. The Mountaineers simply struck last. Zach Matics capped a wild Raycom Media Camellia Bowl with a 23-yard field goal on the final play to lift Appalachian State to a 31-29 victory over Ohio on Saturday night, capping a 17-point, fourth-quarter comeback. The Mountaineers (11-2) moved from their own 21 in the final 1:42 after rallying from a 24-7 deficit in the fourth quarter only to lose the lead again. It was their first bowl game since moving up to FBS. Quarterback Taylor Lamb had a 32-yard scramble then handed off to backup tailback Jalin Moore several times. Moore had a tackle-breaking 15-yarder and a 6-yarder to set up the kick by Matics, who missed two earlier attempts. Matics came in having made 13 of 14, missing only a 52-yarder. He was benched last season after going 1 of 5 but wiped away the earlier misses in this one. A safety and Josiah Yazdani's 21-yard field goal had restored the lead to Ohio (8-5) in a game where the Bobcats scored two defensive touchdowns after a sluggish start. MVP Marcus Cox gained 162 yards on 24 carries for Appalachian State, which set a Sun Belt Conference record for wins in just its second season in FBS. The Bobcats' final drive was finished by third-team Quarterback Greg Windham after an injury to J.D. Sprague, who had taken over for an injured Derrius Vick late in the season. Solich said Vick was only about "85 percent" healthy. Windham came in on a third down and was spun to the ground short on a run. On fourth and 1, he dropped the ball and scooped it up before hitting Kawmae Sawyer, who scampered down the right sideline for a 33-yard gain before getting knocked out of bounds to set up the go-ahead field goal. The celebration was short-lived. Appalachian State had started its own fourth-quarter comeback with a 97-yard drive and two touchdowns in a 42-second span before taking the lead. Lamb hit tight end Barrett Burns for a 17-yard touchdown pass, and they hooked up on an 8-yarder a couple of minutes later for a 28-24 lead with 11:56 left. That gave Lamb a school single season record of 31 touchdown passes. In between, Cox scampered 26 yards down the left sideline one play after Latrell Gibbs' interception. Mondo Williams then made a diving interception of another Sprague pass and Cox streaked through the middle for a 35-yard gain to set up Burns' second score. Dominated most of the first half, Ohio scored 17 points over the final 1:31. Linebacker Quentin Poling returned an interception 20 yards for a touchdown 8 seconds after a 36-yard field goal by Yazdani. Three plays later, Tony Porter recovered a botched snap to set up A.J. Ouellette's 7-yard touchdown run for a 17-7 lead. The Mountaineers had raced to a huge edge on the stat sheet, but not the scoreboard. They outgained Ohio 188-33 deep into the second quarter but led just 7-0 thanks to those two missed field goals and a failed fourth-down attempt. Appalachian State players jogged to the locker room while several of the Bobcats danced and pumped their fists. The roles were reversed by the end.

2015 AutoNation Cure Bowl

The 2015 Cure Bowl was played on December 19, 2015 at Orlando Citrus Bowl in Orlando, Florida. The first edition of the Cure Bowl featured the San Jose State Spartans of the Mountain West Conference against the Georgia State Panthers of the Sun Belt Conference. It was televised on CBS Sports Network.

2015 AutoNation Cure Bowl	Line	1	-	2	-	3	-	4	-	Final
San Jose State	(-1.0)	0	-	10	-	3	-	14	-	27
Georgia State	(55.5)	0	-	7	-	0	-	9	-	16

Scoring Summary
San Jose State - Lopez 19 yard Field goal
San Jose State - Ervin 85 yard punt return (Lopez kick)
Georgia State - Harden 38 yard pass from Arbuckle (Lutz kick)
San Jose State - Lopez 19 yard Field goal
Georgia State - Team safety
Georgia State - Boyd 19 yard pass from Arbuckle (Lutz kick)
San Jose State - Potter 42 yard run (Lopez kick)
San Jose State - Oliver 1 yard pass from Potter (Lopez kick)

Associated Press AutoNation Cure Bowl Game Summary - Kenny Potter scored on a 42-yard run and threw a 1-yard touchdown pass to Josh Oliver in San Jose State's 27-16 comeback victory over Georgia State on Saturday night in the inaugural Cure Bowl. Austin Lopez kicked a pair of 19-yard field goals, and Tyler Ervin returned a punt 85 yards for a touchdown for the Spartans (6-7). Ervin had 30 carries for 132 yards to become San Jose State's single season rushing leader with 1,601. He also set the mark for most all-purpose yards in a season with 2,637. San Jose State was one of three teams given bowl berths despite losing records. The Spartans were awarded their postseason spot based on their Academic Progress Rate of 975. Coach Ron Caragher's players came into the game determined to show they belonged in a bowl. It was the fourth consecutive bowl win for the Spartans, who also claimed victories in 1990, 2006 and 2012. Georgia State's Nick Arbuckle threw for 208 yards and two touchdowns, including a 19-yard scoring pass to Todd Boyd that gave the Panthers (6-7) a 16-13 lead early in the fourth quarter. Arbuckle also threw a 38-yard touchdown pass to Donovan Harden and set a Sun Belt Conference record for single-season passing yards with 4,368. However, the Panthers were held to 231 yards of offense — just 23 yards rushing — by a San Jose State defense that sacked Arbuckle four times and used a three-man front and different coverages that Arbuckle said he had not seen the Spartans use all year on film. With San Jose State leading 13-7, Spartans punter Michael Carrizosa set up to punt in his own end zone. The snap was high and Carrizosa could not bring it down, leading to a safety. Georgia State's Donovan Harden then returned the ensuing kick 24 yards to the San Jose State 36. Arbuckle converted the great field position, hitting Boyd with a 19-yard touchdown to put the Panthers up 16-13 with 10:46 remaining. Potter then broke loose for a 42-yard touchdown run to put San Jose State back on top 20-16. It was Potter's seventh rushing touchdown of the season, tying the school's single-season record. It also was his sixth run of more than 30 yards. Potter's 1-yard touchdown pass to Oliver was the tight end's fourth reception of the year and his first touchdown catch. Game sponsor AutoNation presented a $1 million check to the Breast Cancer Research Foundation following the end of the first quarter. At halftime, the Orlando Sports Foundation presented the BCRF with a check for $150,000. It is the largest donation ever made by a bowl game to a charitable cause. With players and coaches on both teams having been affected by cancer — San Jose State safety Simon Connette lost his mother to the disease last spring and Carrizosa's mother is fighting it — the game took on a special meaning.

2015 New Orleans Bowl

The 2015 New Orleans Bowl was played on December 19, 2015 at the Mercedes-Benz Superdome in New Orleans, Louisiana. The 15th edition of the New Orleans Bowl featured the Louisiana Tech Bulldogs from Conference USA against the Arkansas State Red Wolves of the Sun Belt Conference. It was televised on ESPN.

Teams - The game featured the Louisiana Tech Bulldogs against the Arkansas State Red Wolves. It was the 38th overall meeting between the schools, with Louisiana Tech leading the series 25–12 before this game (both had previously been in-conference foes in the Southland Conference and Big West Conference before Louisiana Tech joined the Western Athletic Conference and later Conference USA and Arkansas State joined the Sun Belt). The last meeting between these two teams was in 1998, when the Bulldogs beat the Indians 69–21 in Jonesboro.

2015 New Orleans Bowl	Line	1	-	2	-	3	-	4	-	Final
Arkansas State	(-1.0)	3	-	14	-	3	-	8	-	28
Louisiana Tech	(65.0)	10	-	7	-	17	-	13	-	47

Scoring Summary
Louisiana Tech - Dixon 9 yard pass from Driskel (Barnes kick)
Arkansas State - Houston 35 yard Field goal
Louisiana Tech - Barnes 50 yard Field goal
Louisiana Tech - Taylor 13 yard pass from Driskel (Barnes kick)
Arkansas State - Wand 1 yard run (Houston kick)
Arkansas State - Knighten 1 yard run (Houston kick)
Louisiana Tech - Barnes 20 yard Field goal
Arkansas State - Houston 37 yard Field goal
Louisiana Tech - Dixon 59 yard pass from Driskel (Barnes kick)
Louisiana Tech - Dixon 8 yard run (Barnes kick)
Louisiana Tech - Barnes 28 yard Field goal
Louisiana Football - Dixon 4 yard run (Barnes kick)
Arkansas State - Taylor 98 yard kickoff return (Pass good)
Louisiana Tech - Barnes 22 yard Field goal

Associated Press New Orleans Bowl Game Summary - Kenneth Dixon capped an extraordinary career at Louisiana Tech by setting NCAA touchdown and scoring records, all while leading the Bulldogs to a bowl victory. Dixon had 215 yards from scrimmage and scored four times to become the NCAA's career leader with 87 touchdowns and 522 points, and Louisiana Tech snapped Arkansas State's eight-game winning streak with a 47-28 triumph in the New Orleans Bowl on Saturday night. Dixon's records could fall in a few days; Navy Quarterback Keenan Reynolds takes his 85 career TDs and 512 points into the Military Bowl against Pittsburgh on Monday. If that happens, Dixon said he'd be happy for Reynolds. Driskel, a transfer from Florida, closed out his college career by passing for 458 yards and three touchdowns for Louisiana Tech (9-4), which had 687 total yards in finishing a second straight season with a bowl victory. The performance gave Driskel 4,023 yards and 27 touchdown passes for the season. Receiver Trent Taylor said the Bulldogs could not have been more pleased to see their QB close out his career with such a flourish after bouts with injuries and inconsistency at Florida. Dixon caught six passes for 113 yards and touchdowns of 9 and 59 yards. He carried 21 times for 102 yards, including scoring runs of 8 and 4 yards. He entered the game as the nation's active leader in yards rushing and finished his career with 4,480 yards on the ground. Dixon's No. 28 jersey was ripped on his first TD run. He was allowed to replace it, symbolically, with a No. 1 jersey for the remainder of the game. Quarterback Fredi Knighten accounted for 179 yards from scrimmage and scored one TD rushing for the Red Wolves (9-4), who won the Sun Belt Conference. Blaise Taylor had a 98-yard kickoff return TD for Arkansas State in the fourth quarter, but by then it was too late to mount a comeback. Arkansas State's success this season stemmed from turnovers. The Red Wolves entered the game with 26 interceptions, most in the nation. But Tech did not turn the ball over, while Arkansas State turned it over three times on two interceptions and a fumble. Arkansas State came in averaging 41 points per game but did not manage an offensive touchdown after halftime. Driskel got the Bulldogs off to a fast start, completing 10 of his first 12 passes for 170 yards and two touchdowns. He lofted long, accurate passes to set up each of the first two TDs -- a 53-yard connection with Carlos Henderson set up the first and a 45-yarder to Trent Taylor led to the second, which put Tech up 17-3. Arkansas State rallied to tie the score by halftime. Warren Wand's 1-yard score capped a 14-play, 91-yard drive that cut it to 17-10. Late in the second quarter, Blaise Taylor's 41-yard punt return gave the Red Wolves the ball on the Tech 25. Four plays later, Knighten ran it in from the 1. Tech took the lead for good on Dixon's second TD reception.

Game notes - The teams combined for 24 penalties for 263 yards, making it the most-penalized game in New Orleans Bowl history and the fifth-highest combined penalty yardage total in NCAA bowl history. "I think the officials got paid by yards tonight," Holtz said.

2015 Miami Beach Bowl

The 2015 Miami Beach Bowl was held on December 21, 2015 at Marlins Park in Miami, Florida. The second edition of the Miami Beach Bowl featured the champions from Conference USA, the Western Kentucky Hilltoppers against the South Florida Bulls of the American Athletic Conference. It was televised on ESPN.

2015 Miami Beach Bowl	Line	1	-	2	-	3	-	4	-	Final
Western Kentucky	(-3.0)	0	-	10	-	28	-	7	-	45
South Florida	(68.5)	7	-	7	-	7	-	14	-	35

Scoring Summary
South Florida - Flowers 12 yard run (Nadelman kick)
South Florida - Adams 34 yard run (Nadelman kick)
Western Kentucky - Wales 13 yard run (Schwettman kick)
Western Kentucky - Schwettman 39 yard Field goal
Western Kentucky - Norris 69 yard pass from Doughty (Schwettman kick)
Western Kentucky - Norris 55 yard pass from Doughty (Schwettman kick)
South Florida - McCants 34 yard pass from Johnson (Nadelman kick)
Western Kentucky - Fant 9 yard run (Schwettman kick)
Western Kentucky - Dangerfield 26 yard pass from Doughty (Schwettman kick)
South Florida - Adams 53 yard pass from Flowers (Nadelman kick)
South Florida - Flowers 8 yard run (Nadelman kick)
Western Kentucky - Wales 42 yard run (Schwettman kick)

Associated Press Miami Beach Bowl Game Summary - Brandon Doughty's final game at Western Kentucky perfectly epitomized his career with the Hilltoppers, with a slow start followed by a record-setting finish. Doughty threw for 461 yards and three touchdowns, and Western Kentucky overcame an early 14-point deficit to beat South Florida 45-35 in the Miami Beach Bowl on Monday. Doughty finished the season with 5,055 yards for the Hilltoppers (12-2), the 14th time in FBS history that a Quarterback has reached the 5,000 mark. His six-year career at the school -- it took him three to become the starter -- ended with these numbers: 1,023 completions, 12,855 yards and 111 touchdowns. He was probably even better than Willie Taggart thought he would be when he signed him in 2010. Taggart was Doughty's coach for his first game and the opposing coach for his last, and his Bulls (8-5) nearly stole the show from Doughty with a pair of fourth-quarter touchdowns that got them to 38-35. But Anthony Wales' second touchdown of the day, a 42-yard scamper with 5:05 left, helped seal it for the Hilltoppers. Nicholas Norris hauled in touchdown passes of 69 and 55 yards in the third quarter for Western Kentucky, and Jared Dangerfield made a highlight-caliber 26-yard TD catch over three defenders to cap a 28-point third quarter for the Hilltoppers. Quinton Flowers rushed for two touchdowns and threw for another for USF (8-5), finishing with 273 yards passing and 108 more on the ground. Marlon Mack rushed for another 108 for the Bulls, who were in a bowl for the first time since 2010 and rewarded Taggart with a three-year extension through 2020 earlier in the day. USF lost for just the second time in its last nine games. The Bulls' 597 yards of offense was the programs most ever against an FBS opponent, topped only by 745 against Florida A&M in 2011. Down 14-0 before finally getting on the scoreboard on Wales' touchdown run, the Hilltoppers -- who put up 612 yards in a game that featured 1,209 yards of offense -- seemed poised to tie the game in the second quarter after driving to the South Florida 6. And then they punted. That's right, they punted, after having first-and-goal. Another year, another oddity in a bowl game for Western Kentucky. Last year the Hilltoppers won the Bahamas Bowl despite giving up five straight touchdowns to Central Michigan -- including a three-lateral, 75-yarder as time expired, escaping with a 49-48 win only after the Chippewas' 2-point conversion try failed. This year's `what-was-that?' moment for the Hilltoppers was having a 4th-and-goal from the 38. Doughty completed five consecutive passes for 69 yards on the drive, getting his team to the USF 6. A first-and-goal rush for no gain was followed by an unsportsmanlike conduct penalty, and then sacks of 7 and 10 yards on second and third down, and that led to the punt. WKU got a field goal as the half expired to pull to 14-10, and then Doughty found Norris for the first of their two long third-quarter touchdown connections to put the Hilltoppers on top for good. And after D'Ernest Johnson connected with Tyre McCants to get the Bulls within 24-21, Doughty helped WKU answer with a score -- throwing a key block on Nacarius Fant's 9-yard double-reverse scoring run late in the third. With USF still down 10 with 3 minutes left, Flowers overthrew A.J. Legree on fourth down from the Hilltoppers 39 and Western Kentucky could finally exhale.

2015 Famous Idaho Potato Bowl

The 2015 Famous Idaho Potato Bowl was played on December 22, 2015 at Albertsons Stadium on the campus of Boise State University in Boise, Idaho. The nineteenth annual Famous Idaho Potato Bowl pitted the Akron Zips of the Mid-American Conference against the Utah State Aggies of the Mountain West Conference. The game was televised on ESPN. It is most notable for being the first bowl game victory in school history for Akron.

2015 Famous Idaho Potato Bowl	Line	1	-	2	-	3	-	4	-	Final
Akron	(46.5)	7	-	6	-	7	-	3	-	23
Utah State	(-7.5)	0	-	7	-	7	-	7	-	21

Scoring Summary
Akron - Woodson 14 yard pass from Goodman (Stein kick)
Akron - Stein 33 yard Field goal
Utah State - Swindall 9 yard pass from Myers (Warren kick)
Akron - Stein 29 yard Field goal
Utah State - Sharp 19 yard pass from Myers (Warren kick)
Akron - Alexander 2 yard run (Stein kick)
Akron - Stein 46 yard Field goal
Utah State -Swindall 2 yard pass from Keeton (Warren kick)

Associated Press Famous Idaho Potato Bowl Game Summary - When Akron placekicker Robert Stein lost his scholarship after his freshman year, he didn't quit. Instead, he fought his way back to the top of the depth chart without the free ride. And after Stein made three field goals and earned MVP honors in leading Akron to a 23-21 victory over Utah State in the Famous Idaho Potato Bowl on Tuesday, Coach Terry Bowden was delighted Stein stuck it out. Stein endeared himself to Bowden for his sacrifice -- he also became the school's all-time scoring leader with a 46-yard field goal with 8:15 remaining in the fourth quarter that proved to be the difference. He finished his career with 268 points. Akron (8-5) finished with eight wins for the first time since moving up to FBS in 1987. The record came four years to the day after the school hired Coach Terry Bowden. While Stein provided the difference in scoring, it was Akron's defense that made the lead stick. Brown, the MAC defensive player of the year, had eight tackles along with 1 1/2 sacks, 2 1/2 tackles for loss, and a critical forced fumble. Utah State (6-7) mounted a comeback behind senior Quarterback Chuckie Keeton, who threw a 2-yard touchdown pass to Hunter Sharp with 1:12 remaining to pull to 23-21. But Akron recovered the onside kick and then stopped one final flea flicker play by Utah State as time expired. While Akron averaged less than 200 yards passing per game this season, the Zips turned to the air to score the game's first points. After an incompletion, Zips Quarterback Thomas Woodson hit A.J. Coney on a 42-yard pass play. On the next play, Akron dug into its bag of tricks, scoring when receiver Tyrell Goodman hit Woodson with a 14-yard pass for the 7-0 lead. Utah State struggled to generate any offense early as the Aggies, going through three-and-out for minus-5 yards on their first four possessions. The Aggies, however, got a spark after a long punt return by Sharp set up Utah State at the Akron 31. But on third-and-8 from the Zips 18, Akron cornerback Kris Givens ripped an apparent touchdown catch out of Brandon Swindall's arms. Utah State elected to go for a first down instead of kicking a field goal, but the Akron defense held. The Zips responded with a 12-play, 59-yard drive that ended in a 33-yard field goal by Stein, pushing their lead to 10-0. Utah State wasted little time in answering. Devante Mays broke off a career-long 61-yard run before Jatavis Brown caught him at the Akron 10. Two plays later, Kent Myers hit Swindall on a 9-yard pass play. Brock Warren's extra point cut the deficit to 10-7 with 1:21 left in the half. On Akron's next possession, Utah State's defense stiffened and forced a punt with 1:00 left in the half, using two time outs to preserve time on the clock. However, it was a plan that backfired. With Utah State on the Akron 28, Brown stripped the ball loose from Myers, and Akron defensive tackle Rodney Coe scooped up the ball and rambled 56 yards to the Aggies 12 with 4 seconds left in the half. Stein booted a 29-yard field goal as time expired to give the Zips a 13-7 lead. In the second half, Utah State took its first possession 64 yards in seven plays, scoring on a 19-yard pass play from Meyers to Sharp. Warren's extra point gave the Aggies their first lead of the game at 14-13. Akron's offense could muster only two yards on its next possession but found new life after the Zips' defense recovered a fumble at the Utah State 40. Eight plays later, Donnell Alexander sprinted into the end zone from 2 yards out to help the Zips regain the lead at 20-14 with 5:43 left in the third quarter. Keeton and Myers combined for 28-of-45 passing for 232 yards and three touchdowns, while Woodson was 14 of 29 for 168 yards. Andrew Pratt set a career high with nine receptions for 94 yards to lead the Zips. Hunter Sharp had 11 catches for 93 yards. Mays led Utah State on the ground with 124 yards on 12 carries, while Woodson rushed for 47 yards to lead Akron.

2015 Boca Raton Bowl

The 2015 Boca Raton Bowl was held on December 22, 2015 at FAU Stadium on the campus of Florida Atlantic University in Boca Raton, Florida. The second edition of the Boca Raton Bowl featured the Mid-American Conference West Division co–champion Toledo Rockets against the American Athletic Conference East Division champion Temple Owls. The game was televised on ESPN.

2015 Boca Raton Bowl	Line	1	-	2	-	3	-	4	-	Final
#24 Temple	(-2.0)	3	-	0	-	6	-	8	-	17
Toledo	(49.5)	0	-	12	-	0	-	20	-	32

Scoring Summary
Temple - Jones 29 yard Field goal
Toledo - Safety - Temple fumbled ball out of end zone
Toledo - Jones 26 yard pass from Ely (Vest kick)
Toledo - Vest 38 yard Field goal
Temple - Jones 25 yard Field goal
Temple - Jones 35 yard Field goal
Toledo - Thompson 80 yard pass from Ely (Vest kick)
Toledo - Hunt 1 yard run (Kick blocked)
Temple - Patton 2 yard run (Anderson pass from Ely)
Toledo - Hunt 41 yard run (Vest kick)

Associated Press Boca Raton Bowl Game Summary - The Boca Raton Bowl trophy ceremony ended in heavy rain, and Toledo coach Jason Candle walked off the field soaking wet, declining the offer of a towel with a grin. Soggy weather couldn't dampen the celebratory mood for the Rockets, who won Candle's first game as head coach Tuesday night, beating No. 24 Temple 32-17. Phillip Ely threw for 285 yards and two touchdowns, including an 80-yarder to Cody Thompson. Candle called plays from the press box, as he has done all season. He was promoted from offensive coordinator three weeks ago when Matt Campbell took over at Iowa State. The Rockets (10-2) positioned themselves to crack the final Top 25 for the first time since 2001, the last season they won 10 games. Temple (10-4) lost for the fourth time in seven games after starting 7-0. Frequent driving rain hampered both offenses, but Ely went 20 for 28 with no turnovers. Linebacker Ja'Wuan Woodley's jarring tackle sent the ball squirting backward 15 yards through the end zone for an early safety, and the hits kept coming from the Rockets, who blitzed on virtually every play. Temple came into the game averaging 31 points but didn't reach the end zone until less than three minutes remained. Jahad Thomas, who came into the game with 1,257 yards rushing for Temple, hurt his knee late in the first half and didn't return. Thomas was held to 5 yards on eight carries, and his fumble led to the safety. Toledo entered the game ranked third in the nation in red zone defense, and three times the Rockets held Temple to short field goals. Ely and Woodley were chosen the game's most valuable players. The Rockets were nursing a 12-9 lead in the final period when they started at their 20 following a 71-yard punt. Thompson slipped behind the secondary, caught Ely's pass in stride at his 40 and veered untouched to the end zone. The play was a run-pass option. The Rockets' Thompson recovered an onside kick following Temple's touchdown, a ruling the Owls disputed. Following the recovery, Kareem Hunt scored on a 41-yard run to seal the victory. Toledo's Corey Jones broke five tackles to turn a short reception into a 26-yard score in the first half. The Rockets totaled 435 yards. They moved 36 yards in the final 1:10 of the first half and kicked a 38-yard field goal on the last play for a 12-3 lead.

2015 Poinsettia Bowl

The 2015 Poinsettia Bowl was played on December 23, 2015 at Qualcomm Stadium in San Diego, California. Boise State Broncos from the Mountain West Conference defeated the Northern Illinois Huskies from the Mid-American Conference. The game was televised on ESPN.

2015 Poinsettia Bowl	Line	1	-	2	-	3	-	4	-	Final
Boise State	(-7.0)	21	-	10	-	10	-	14	-	55
Northern Illinois	(57.0)	0	-	7	-	0	-	0	-	7

Scoring Summary
Boise State - McNichols 41 yard run (Rausa kick)
Boise State - McNichols 4 yard pass from Rypien (Rausa kick)
Boise State - McNichols 1 yard run (Rausa kick)
Boise State - Rausa 20 yard Field goal
Northern Illinois - Turner 96 yard kickoff return (Hagan kick)
Boise State - Anderson 16 yard pass from Rypien (Rausa kick)
Boise State - Rausa 27 yard Field goal
Boise State - Dhaenens 18 yard pass from Rypien (Rausa kick)
Boise State - Young 24 yard run (Rausa kick)
Boise State - Stuart 1 yard run (Rausa kick)

Associated Press Poinsettia Bowl Game Summary - Northern Illinois won the coin toss and deferred, giving Boise State the ball first. The Poinsettia Bowl was just beginning, yet it was essentially over. Jeremy McNichols scored three touchdowns, the first one 58 seconds into the game, and finished with 189 total yards as Boise State embarrassed Northern Illinois 55-7 Wednesday. The Broncos (9-4) took the opening kickoff and moved 75 yards in three plays for the fastest TD in the school's bowl history. After completions of 7 and 39 yards by Brett Rypien, McNichols ran 29 yards for a touchdown just 58 seconds in. McNichols and the Broncos kept piling on as the running back from Long Beach scored on each of the next two possessions, on a 4-yard pass from Brett Rypien and on a 1-yard run. McNichols ran 19 times for 93 yards and caught five passes for 96 yards. The sophomore came in tied with Heisman Trophy winner Derrick Henry of Alabama for the national lead with 23 TDs. Rypien, a freshman, was 29 of 40 for 377 yards and three touchdowns, with one interception. The Broncos outgained the Huskies (8-6) 654 yards to 33. The Huskies added to their misery by losing three fumbles in the first half. Tyler Gray recovered two of them. The Huskies were left disappointed in falling to 0-3 in the Poinsettia Bowl. The Huskies avoided a shutout when Aregeros Turner returned a kickoff 96 yards for a touchdown to make it 24-7 midway through the second quarter. The announced crowd of 21,501 was swallowed up by 70,000-seat Qualcomm Stadium. The Broncos led 31-7 at halftime after Tyler Rausa's 20-yard field goal and Rypien's 16-yard touchdown pass to Chaz Anderson. Rypien added an 18-yard scoring pass to Alec Dhaenens in the third quarter. The reserves took over in the fourth quarter. Backup running back Kelsey Young scored on a 24-yard run and backup Quarterback Thomas Stuart scored on a 1-yard keeper. Boise State improved to 1-1 in the Poinsettia Bowl.

2015 GoDaddy Bowl

The 2015 GoDaddy Bowl was played on December 23, 2015 at Ladd–Peebles Stadium in Mobile, Alabama. The 17th edition of the GoDaddy Bowl featured the Bowling Green Falcons of the Mid-American Conference against the Georgia Southern Eagles of the Sun Belt Conference. The game was televised on ESPN.

2015 GoDaddy Bowl	Line	1	-	2	-	3	-	4	-	Final
Georgia Southern	(62.5)	9	-	14	-	21	-	14	-	58
Bowling Green	(-5.5)	13	-	14	-	0	-	0	-	27

Scoring Summary
Georgia Southern - Ramsby 1 yard run (Koo kick)
Bowling Green - Lewis 45 yard pass from Johnson (Kick blocked)
Georgia Southern - Dobson 98 yard return of blocked P.A.T.
Bowling Green - Moore 15 yard pass from Johnson (Tate kick)
Bowling Green - Dieter 51 yard pass from Johnson (Tate kick)
Georgia Southern - Fields 26 yard run (Koo kick)
Georgia Southern - Crockett 31 yard run (Koo kick)
Bowling Green - Greene 5 yard run (Tate kick)
Georgia Southern - Upshaw 3 yard run (Koo kick)
Georgia Southern - Upshaw 80 yard run (Koo kick)
Georgia Southern - Breida 1 yard run (Koo kick)
Georgia Southern - Upshaw 8 yard run (Koo kick)
Georgia Southern - Upshaw 42 yard run (Koo kick)

Associated Press GoDaddy Bowl Game Summary - Georgia Southern Quarterback Favian Upshaw blew past Bowling Green's defensive line and linebackers and split two safeties, showing off impressive speed on his way to the end zone. But as his 80-yard touchdown run neared completion he slowed down a little and was nearly caught. Usually, the backup Quarterback with a limited role, Upshaw ran for 199 yards and four touchdowns to lead Georgia Southern over Bowling Green 58-27 in the GoDaddy Bowl on Wednesday night. Georgia Southern (9-4) won the first bowl game in school history in the first year it was eligible to go to the postseason. The program transitioned to the Football Bowl Subdivision in 2014. The Eagles prevailed thanks to their trademark running game. They had 452 yards rushing to top their nation-best season average of 355.6 yards. The 6-foot-1, 170-pound Upshaw, who was named the game's Most

Valuable Player, usually splits time with starter Kevin Ellison. But he had a much bigger role against Bowling Green -- especially in the second half. In the team's previous 12 games Upshaw had run for a total of 384 yards and two touchdowns. Bowling Green (10-4) led 27-23 at halftime, but Georgia Southern scored the final 35 points. Bowling Green was undone by a brutal stretch in the third quarter that included two fumbles by Quarterback Matt Johnson deep in the Falcons' own territory. It helped Georgia Southern score three touchdowns -- including two by Upshaw -- in three minutes and turned a 30-27 game into a blowout. The game was tight for much of the evening, but Georgia Southern started to pull away late in the third quarter when Upshaw's 80-yard touchdown run gave the Eagles a 37-27 lead. Then Bowling Green -- specifically Johnson -- fumbled away any chance at a comeback on a rain-soaked evening at Ladd-Peebles Stadium. Johnson fumbled on Bowling Green's 14 when he lost the ball as he is winding up to make a pass. Georgia Southern scored two plays later when Matt Breida ran for a 1-yard touchdown to push the advantage to 44-27. On the ensuing drive, Johnson fumbled again when trying to make a handoff at the Bowling Green 10. Two players later, Upshaw ran for the 8-yard touchdown and the rout was essentially complete. It was a surprising turn of events considering the first two quarters were full of interesting and sometimes off-the-wall, back-and-forth football. The Falcons' first touchdown came on a botched play when a bad snap forced Johnson to abandon a planned running play. He regrouped and scrambled to his right before throwing to Roger Lewis for the easy 45-yard touchdown. Georgia Southern had its share of interesting moments, too. The Eagles blocked a Bowling Green extra point and Matt Dobson returned it 98 yards for the rare two-point score. The Eagles briefly took a 23-20 lead late in the second quarter when they scored on a 31-yard pass from Ellison to Montay Crockett, which was only the team's fourth passing touchdown this season. Bowling Green responded with a quick touchdown drive -- capped by Travis Greene's 5-yard run -- to take a 27-23 lead into halftime. But the rain became more consistent after the break and Georgia Southern took advantage, capitalizing on Johnson's fumbles and slowly grinding away for their first bowl victory. Georgia Southern was an FCS-level powerhouse before jumping up to the FBS in 2014. The transition has been impressive -- the Eagles have an 18-7 record over the past two seasons. Bowling Green, which won the Mid-American Conference championship, was outgained 534 yards to 362. Johnson was 15 of 34 passing for 246 yards and three touchdowns. He finished the season with 4,946 yards passing, falling just short of becoming the 15th Quarterback at the FBS level to throw for 5,000 yards in a season.

2015 Bahamas Bowl

The 2015 Bahamas Bowl was played on December 24, 2015 at Thomas Robinson Stadium in Nassau in the Bahamas. The second edition of the Bahamas Bowl featured the Middle Tennessee Blue Raiders of Conference USA against the Western Michigan Broncos of the Mid-American Conference. It was televised on ESPN. The game is best remembered as the Broncos' first bowl victory in school history.

2015 Bahamas Bowl	Line	1	-	2	-	3	-	4	-	Final
Middle Tennessee	(65.0)	17	-	0	-	7	-	7	-	31
Western Michigan	(-3.0)	17	-	0	-	7	-	21	-	45

Scoring Summary
Middle Tennessee - James 46 yard run (Clark kick)
Western Michigan - Bogan 62 yard run (Haldeman kick)
Middle Tennessee - James 44 yard pass from Stockstill (Clark kick)
Western Michigan - Haldeman 47 yard Field goal
Middle Tennessee - Clark 12 yard Field goal
Western Michigan - Davis 80 yard pass from Terrell (Haldeman kick)
Western Michigan - Bogan 46 yard run (Haldeman kick)
Middle Tennessee - Collins 17 yard pass from Stockstill (Clark kick)
Western Michigan - Braverman 68 yard pass from Terrell (Haldeman kick)
Middle Tennessee - James 29 yard pass from Stockstill (Clark kick)
Western Michigan - Bogan 1 yard run (Haldeman kick)
Western Michigan - Bogan 1 yard run (Haldeman kick)

Associated Press Bahamas Bowl Game Summary - Considering that Western Michigan coach P.J. Fleck has made "Row the Boat" a team motto, it's only fitting the Broncos had to reach the Bahamas to finally win a bowl game. Jamauri Bogan ran for 215 yards and four touchdowns, powering Western Michigan past Middle Tennessee 45-31 on Thursday in the Bahamas Bowl for its first bowl victory. The Broncos had lost their previous six bowl games. This latest achievement comes after Western Michigan closed the regular season by beating a Toledo team that was ranked 24th at the time for the Broncos' first win over a Top 25 team. Western Michigan (8-5) also has consecutive eight-win seasons for the first time in school history after going 1-11 in 2013 during Fleck's first year. The Broncos accomplished that while facing a schedule that included Michigan State and Ohio State. Bogan broke a tie with a 1-yard touchdown run with 6:12 left, setting up the score with a 61-yard burst. He had another 1-yard scoring run with 5 minutes remaining after Rontavious Atkins' 29-yard interception return to the 4. Bogan also had 62- and 46-yard touchdown runs. He averaged 11.3 yards per carry. Zach Terrell was 18 of 26 for 297 yards and two touchdowns. Corey Davis had eight catches for 183 yards and a touchdown, and Daniel Braverman added five receptions for 101 yards and a score. Richie James had eight catches for 126 yards and two touchdowns and added a scoring run for Middle Tennessee (7-6). Brent Stockstill threw for 327 yards and three touchdowns. Stockstill was 26 of 39 and finished the season with 327 completions to break the NCAA freshman record of 321 set by Jared Lorenzen for Kentucky in 200. One year after Western Kentucky and Central Michigan combined for 12 touchdown passes in the inaugural Bahamas Bowl -- a 49-48 Western Kentucky victory -- Western Michigan and Middle Tennessee produced a similar shootout featuring six touchdowns of 40-plus yards. The game already was tied 17-all by the end of the first quarter. After a scoreless second period, the big plays resumed. Bogan gave Western Michigan its first lead with the 46-yard run on the opening drive of the second half. Middle Tennessee tied it when Christian Collins turned a short completion into a 17-yard touchdown play with 18 seconds left in the third period. Western Michigan went back in front when Braverman caught a pass about 15 yards downfield and raced along the right sideline for a 68-yard scoring strike with 12:47 left. Middle Tennessee tied it again with 9:41 left on Stockstill's 29-yard pass to James. But when Bogan scored twice more in the fourth quarter, Middle Tennessee couldn't respond. Middle Tennessee also failed to capitalize on a couple of early opportunities. With the score 17-17 in the second quarter, Middle Tennessee's Shane Tucker was stuffed by Grant DePalma and Austin Lewis on fourth-and-goal from the 1. On Middle Tennessee's next series, a holding penalty nullified an 85-yard touchdown completion from Stockstill to Collins.

2015 Hawai'i Bowl

The 2015 Hawaii Bowl was played on December 24, 2015 at Aloha Stadium in Honolulu, Hawaii. The fourteenth edition of the Hawaii Bowl featured the Cincinnati Bearcats of the American Athletic Conference against the San Diego State Aztecs from the Mountain West Conference. It was televised on ESPN.

2015 Hawaii Bowl	Line	1	-	2	-	3	-	4	-	Final
San Diego State	(-2.5)	14	-	7	-	7	-	14	-	42
Cincinnati	(56.5)	0	-	0	-	0	-	7	-	7

Scoring Summary
San Diego State - Penny 100 yard kickoff return (Hageman kick)
San Diego State - Holder 14 yard pass from Chapman (Hageman kick)
San Diego State - Gordon 16 yard pass from Pumphrey (Hageman kick)
San Diego State - Gordon 1 yard run (Hageman kick)
San Diego State - Pumphrey 2 yard run (Hageman kick)
San Diego State - Barrett 43 yard interception return (Hageman kick)
Cincinnati - Boone 1 yard run (Gantz kick)

Associated Press Hawaii Bowl Game Summary - San Diego State fullback Dakota Gordon does a lot more than just block for the Aztecs. He showed it in the Hawaii Bowl and ended up with the most valuable player award. Gordon caught a touchdown pass and ran for another score to help San Diego State rout Cincinnati 42-7 on Thursday before a sparse crowd of 14,537 at Aloha Stadium. The Aztecs (11-3) won their final 10 games to match the longest winning streak in school history. San Diego State rushed for 207 yards, topping the 200-yard mark for the 10th consecutive game, and finished with 336 yards of total offense. Donnell Pumphrey, the Mountain West offensive player of the year, had 99 yards on 25 carries. He threw a 16-yard touchdown pass to Gordon and had a 1-yard scoring run early in the fourth quarter. Gordon also had a 1-yard run and finished with four catches for 58 yards. Pumphrey finished the season with 1,653 rushing yards and Chase Price had 1,008 to become the first Aztecs teammates to run for more than 1,000 yards in a season. San Diego State coach Rocky Long said Gordon played a key role in their success. Rashaad Penny, the Mountain West special teams player of the year, returned the opening kickoff 100 yards for a touchdown Penny had his third kickoff return for a score this season — and second 100-yarder — and broke the Hawaii bowl record for the longest return. Cincinnati finished 7-5. Redshirt freshman Christian Chapman made his second straight start with starter Maxwell Smith out with a knee injury. Chapman threw a 14-yard touchdown pass to Mikah Holder to cap an 85-yard, nine-play drive on San Diego State's first offensive possession. Chapman was 8 of 11 for 113 yards and did not have an interception. The Aztecs led 14-0 after the first quarter, the ninth time this season they held an opponent scoreless in the opening quarter.

2015 St. Petersburg Bowl

The 2015 St. Petersburg Bowl was played between the Connecticut Huskies of the American Athletic Conference and the Marshall Thundering Herd of Conference USA, played on December 26, 2015 at Tropicana Field in St. Petersburg, Florida. Connecticut was selected to play in the 2015 St. Petersburg Bowl following a 6–6 regular season highlighted by a win over the otherwise-undefeated Houston Cougars to achieve bowl eligibility. The Huskies faced Marshall, who finished their regular season with a 9–3 record and for the first time since 2012 did not qualify for the Conference USA championship game.

2015 St. Petersburg Bowl	Line	1	-	2	-	3	-	4	-	Final
Connecticut	(44.5)	7	-	0	-	3	-	0	-	10
Marshall	(-3.0)	7	-	6	-	0	-	3	-	16

Scoring Summary
Marshall - Yurachek 16 yard pass from Litton (Smith kick)
Connecticut - Johnson 8 yard run (Puyol kick)
Marshall - Smith 21 yard Field goal
Marshall - Smith 29 yard Field goal
Connecticut - Puyol 52 yard Field goal
Marshall - Smith 32 yard Field goal

Associated Press St. Petersburg Bowl Game Summary - Chase Litton went 23 for 34 for 218 yards and one touchdown as Marshall won its 10th game this season by beating Connecticut 16-10 in the St. Petersburg Bowl on Saturday. Nick Smith had three field goals for Marshall (10-3), including a 32-yarder with 1:44 to play that was part of a 13-play, 80-yard march that lasted 6:35. The Thundering Herd went 13-1 a year ago and 10-4 in 2013. Bryant Shirreffs completed 10 of 17 passes for 86 yards and gained 75 yards on 19 carries for UConn (6-7), which came up short in a bid to have a winning record for the first time since 2010. UConn stopped Marshall on fourth-and-2 at the 17 on the initial drive of the second half after the Thundering Herd opted to skip a field goal try that could have made it 16-7. The Thundering Herd also failed to increase a 13-7 lead on their next possession when Smith missed a 43-yard field goal attempt with less than 3 minutes left in the third. The Huskies got within 13-10 on Bobby Puyol's 52-yard field goal with 2 seconds left in the third. Marshall took a 7-0 lead 7 minutes into the game when Litton, who played in high school in Tampa, threw a 16-yard TD pass to Ryan Yurachek. Deandre Reaves' 26-yard punt return set up Marshall at the UConn 20. Reaves also had nine receptions for 88 yards. Connecticut tied it at 7 late in the first on an 8-yard run by Ron Johnson that completed a 13-play, 75-yard drive. Marshall responded with a 13-play, 65-yard drive that concluded with Smith's 21-yard field goal that gave the Thundering Herd a 10-7 advantage 8 minutes before halftime. Smith made it 13-7 with a 29-yard field goal on the final play of the first half that finished off a 15-play, 85-yard drive. Connecticut sophomore cornerback Jamar Summers got his eighth interception of the season, including six in the last five games, early in the fourth.

2015 Sun Bowl

The 2015 Sun Bowl was played on December 26, 2015 at Sun Bowl Stadium in El Paso, Texas. The last time it snowed at the Sun Bowl was the 1987 New Year's game with West Virginia and Oklahoma State. The 82nd edition of the Sun Bowl featured the Miami Hurricanes of the Atlantic Coast Conference against the Washington State Cougars of the Pac-12 Conference. It televised on CBS.

2015 Sun Bowl	Line	1	-	2	-	3	-	4	-	Final
Miami	(62.5)	7	-	0	-	0	-	7	-	14
Washington State	(-1.5)	7	-	13	-	0	-	0	-	20

Scoring Summary
Washington State - Morrow 31 yard pass from Falk (Powell kick)
Miami - Coley 4 yard pass from Kaaya (Badgley kick)
Washington State - Powell 30 yard Field goal
Washington State - Marks 25 yard pass from Falk (Powell kick)
Washington State - Powell 25 yard Field goal
Miami - Walton 5 yard run (Badgley kick)

SBNation.com Sun Bowl Game Summary - Washington State beat Miami, 20-14, in the Sun Bowl to get its first bowl win since the 2003 Holiday Bowl, but this Sun Bowl defied its name and then some. It wasn't sunny at all. It was snowy as can be in El Paso, Texas, and that made for a lot of fun, sloppy football. This game was, predictably, a mess. Washington State games are always wild, back-and-forth affairs, while Miami isn't used to playing in the snow. This isn't what you sign up for when you accept a bid to the Sun Bowl. The first half mostly had flurries, but in the second half, the snow picked up to the point that the camera man even lost the ball at times. Essentially, the game became a big, messy snowball fight. The first half started with a bang, but it didn't quite last like some thought it would. Both teams started the game with touchdowns on their opening drives, but the points didn't keep flowing after that. Both teams turned it over once in the first half, and neither team was especially efficient converting third downs. The Cougs started to pick it up late in the second quarter, though, racking up 13 points in the final six and a half minutes to roll into halftime with a 20-7 lead as the snow flew in El Paso. The second half was more of a tug of war as the snow came down harder. It felt like Washington State was one score away from really putting the game away but repeated unsuccessful fourth down attempts kept Miami in the game. Wazzu moved the ball a bit more, but its end results were no better than Miami's. Then came the fourth quarter, which started with a 60-yard run from Miami to bring the Hurricanes within six points. Then, with the chance to take the lead late in the game, the snow struck again, as Miami fumbled at Washington State's five-yard line. But wait! Life! After forcing a punt from the Washington State end zone, the Hurricanes got the ball back on the Cougars' 28-yard line and called a halfback pass into a dang snowstorm. It did not work, and the ensuing interception essentially sealed the game for Wazzu, as players gave Mike Leach a double Gatorade bath.

2015 Heart of Dallas Bowl

The 2015 Heart of Dallas Bowl was played on December 26, 2015 at the Cotton Bowl at Fair Park in Dallas, Texas. The sixth edition of the Heart of Dallas Bowl featured the Washington Huskies of the Pac-12 Conference against the Southern Miss Golden Eagles of Conference USA. It was televised on ESPN.

2015 Heart of Dallas bowl	Line	1	-	2	-	3	-	4	-	Final
Washington	(-7.5)	14	-	7	-	10	-	13	-	44
Southern Miss	(52.0)	7	-	10	-	7	-	7	-	31

Scoring Summary
Washington - Gaskin 2 yard run (Van Winkle kick)
Southern Miss - Thomas 56 yard pass from Mullens (Brauchle kick)
Washington - Gaskin 1 yard run (Van Winkle kick)
Southern Miss - Brauchle 22 yard Field goal
Washington - Mickens 29 yard run (Van Winkle kick)
Southern Miss - Smith 1 yard run (Brauchle kick)
Washington - Van Winkle 24 yard Field goal
Southern Miss - Smith 2 yard run (Brauchle kick)
Washington - Gaskin 86 yard run (Van Winkle kick)
Washington - Van Winkle 21 yard Field goal
Washington - Gaskin 13 yard run (Van Winkle kick)
Southern Miss - Thomas 27 yard pass from Mullens (Brauchle kick)
Washington - Van Winkle 23 yard Field goal

Associated Press Heart of Dallas Bowl Game Summary - Chris Petersen's young Washington team grew up late this season, closing with a victory Saturday in the Heart of Dallas Bowl for a winning record. Myles Gaskin broke a third-quarter tie with an 86-yard run and finished with a season-high 181 yards and four touchdowns to help Washington beat Southern Mississippi 44-31 at the Cotton Bowl. The Huskies (7-6) won their last two regular-season games by a combined 97-17 over Oregon State and Washington State to become bowl eligible and then delivered Petersen's first postseason victory in his two seasons at Washington. The Huskies started 12 freshmen and sophomores with 25 of them on their two-deep depth chart. The game was played in overcast conditions with a 20-mph wind. It rained during parts of the second half as the Dallas area was placed under a tornado watch that became a tornado warning as the teams were boarding their buses to leave the stadium. Gaskin's other scores came on 2- and 1-yard runs in the first quarter and a 13-yarder in the fourth. On the 86-yarder, the freshman took a handoff inside, broke to the left sideline and shook off one final defender at the Southern Miss 35. Gaskin, the game's most valuable player, gained 170 yards in the second half on 17 carries after being held to 11 yards on nine rushes in the first half. His previous high was 155 yards against Oregon. The Golden Eagles (9-5) were seeking their first win over a Power 5 conference team since 2011. Even with the loss, they tied Washington State for the greatest improvement this season. Each went from three wins to nine. Southern Miss played without rushing leader Jalen Richard. A Southern Miss official said Richard, one of two Golden Eagles with 1,000 yards rushing this season, was held out because of an unspecified injury. Nick Mullens threw touchdowns passes of 56 and 27 yards by Michael Thomas for the Eagles, and Ito Smith added 1- and 2-yard scoring runs. Thomas had 9 catches for 190 yards. The Golden Eagles averaged 519.8 yards during the regular season, including their 45-28 loss to Western Kentucky in the Conference USA championship game. On Saturday, they gained 375. They were held to 22 net rushing yards with Smith, who gained 1,088 during the season, leading the way with 40. Gaskin's 86-yard run was the sixth-longest in school history. It came on Washington's first play from scrimmage after Southern Miss recovered a fumble near midfield to set up Smith's second touchdown run that tied it at 24. Receiver Jaydon Mickens scored Washington's other touchdown on a 29-yard run in the second quarter. Mickens took a handoff on what appeared to be an end around following a fake inside, then cut inside and was virtually untouched. The five-play, 65-yard drive included a 20-yard pass to Mickens that was upheld after a challenge from Southern Miss. Smith's 1-yard touchdown plunge through the middle followed a 36-yard catch by Thomas along the left sideline just short of the pylon. That 80-yard drive was kept alive by punter Tyler Sarrazin's 22-yard pass to Curtis Mikell on fourth-and-5 at the Golden Eagles 25. In Southern Miss' win at Rice in mid-November, Sarrazin threw for a touchdown off a fake field-goal attempt.

2015 Pinstripe Bowl

The 2015 Pinstripe Bowl was played on December 26, 2015 at Yankee Stadium in the New York City borough of the Bronx. The sixth edition of the Pinstripe Bowl was televised on ABC. This bowl marks Duke's first bowl victory in 54 years. Although Duke had a streak of 4 in bowl games, they had never won a bowl game until this one.

2015 Pinstripe Bowl	Line	1	-	2	-	3	-	4	-	OT	-	Final
Indiana	(-3.0)	0	-	17	-	14	-	10	-	0	-	41
Duke	(72.5)	10	-	7	-	10	-	14	-	3	-	44

Scoring Summary
Duke - Martin 52 yard Field goal
Duke - Wilson 85 yard run (Martin kick)
Indiana - Timian 27 yard pass from Sudfield (Oakes kick)
Indiana - Redding 17 yard run (Oakes kick)
Duke - Sirk 73 yard run (Martin kick)
Indiana - Oakes 45 yard Field goal
Duke - Martin 34 yard Field goal
Indiana - Westbrook 3 yard pass from Sudfield (Oakes kick)
Duke - Deaver 10 yard pass from Sirk (Martin kick)
Indiana - Rodriguez 10 yard run (Oakes kick)
Indiana - Oakes 27 yard Field goal
Duke - Wilson 98 kickoff return (Martin kick)
Indiana - Paige 25 yard pass from Sudfield (Oakes kick)
Duke - Sirk 5 yard run (Martin kick)
Duke - Martin 36 yard field goal

Associated Press Pinstripe Bowl Game Summary - Duke survived a wild finish at Yankee Stadium for its first bowl victory in 54 years. Ross Martin kicked a 36-yard field in overtime, and Duke held off Indiana 44-41 on Saturday night in the Pinstripe Bowl. After Martin made his kick on the first possession of the extra period, the Hoosiers' Griffin Oakes missed a 38-yard attempt to hand the Blue Devils (8-5) their first bowl victory since the 1961 Cotton Bowl. Oakes' try sailed above the right upright and was ruled wide. Oakes protested that it was good, but the kick could not be reviewed, and Duke's players poured onto the field to celebrate. Indiana coach Kevin Wilson said the potential game-tying field goal wasn't good, despite his kicker's protestations. Indiana finished the season 6-7. Duke appeared in its fourth straight bowl game, losing the previous three seasons to Cincinnati, Texas A&M and Arizona State. The dramatic finish capped a game that featured 1,203 combined yards and 56 first downs. The teams combined to establish nine offensive records in the six-year history of the game. Shaun Wilson had 282 all-purpose yards and two touchdowns for the Blue Devils, including a 98-yard kickoff return in the fourth quarter. Before getting hurt in overtime, Quarterback Thomas Sirk accounted for 318 yards and three touchdowns. Cutcliffe said he would have not been able to continue if Indiana tied it. Sirk had a 73-yard touchdown run in the first half and his 5-yard scoring run tied it with 41 seconds left. After Sirk's second TD, Oakes missed a 55-yard attempt at the end of regulation. Sirk was 17 of 37 for 163 yards and a touchdown. He also had 155 yards on the ground. Indiana's Nate Sudfeld was 28 for 51 for 389 yards and three touchdowns. Devine Redding filled in for the injured Jordan Howard (knee) and rushed for 227 yards, but it was not enough for the Hoosiers, who have not won a bowl since the 1991 Copper Bowl. Duke led 10-0 in the first quarter of what quickly became a back-and-forth game. Indiana took a 24-20 lead midway through the third when Nick Westbrook caught a 3-yard touchdown pass. But three plays after the Hoosiers' Mitchell Paige fumbled at his 19 on a punt return, Sirk connected with Braxton Deaver for a 10-yard touchdown, giving the Blue Devils a 27-24 lead. Just over 4 minutes later, Alex Rodriguez -- the Indiana running back, not the Yankees slugger -- put the Hoosiers up 31-27 with a 10-yard touchdown run. The lead grew to 34-27 when Oakes kicked a 27-yard field goal with 11:12 left, but Wilson returned the ensuing kickoff to tie it. Indiana took a 41-34 lead with 4:03 remaining when Sudfeld found Paige wide open in the back of the end zone on second-and-15 for a 25-yard scoring play.

2015 Independence Bowl

The 2015 Independence Bowl was played on Saturday, December 26, 2015 at Independence Stadium in Shreveport, Louisiana in the United States. The 40th annual Independence Bowl featured the Virginia Tech Hokies of the Atlantic Coast Conference against the Tulsa Golden Hurricane of the American Athletic Conference.

2015 Independence Bowl	Line	1	-	2	-	3	-	4	-	Final
Tulsa	(62.5)	21	-	10	-	6	-	15	-	52
Virginia Tech	(-13.5)	24	-	21	-	7	-	3	-	55

Scoring Summary
Tulsa - Brewer 48 yard run (Jones kick)
Virginia Tech - McMillian 51 yard run (Slye kick)
Tulsa - Langer 2 yard run (Jones kick)
Virginia Tech - Ford 75 yard pass from Brewer (Slye kick)
Virginia Tech - Slye 27 yard Field goal
Virginia Tech - Rogers 14 yard run (Slye kick)
Tulsa - Louie 9 yard pass from Evans (Jones kick)
Virginia Tech - Hodges 16 yard run (Slye kick)
Virginia Tech - McMillian 1 yard run (Slye kick)
Virginia Tech - Stroman 67 yard punt return (Slye kick)
Tulsa - Jones 29 yard Field goal
Tulsa - Brewer 10 yard run (Jones kick)
Virginia Tech - Edmunds 1 yard run (Slye kick)
Tulsa - Evans 9 yard run (Kick failed)
Virginia Tech - Slye 41 yard Field goal
Tulsa - Atkinson 21 yard pass from Evans (Garrett pass from Evans)
Tulsa - Garrett 36 yard pass from Evans (Jones kick)

Associated Press Independence Bowl Game Summary - Frank Beamer built a powerhouse at Virginia Tech over nearly three decades thanks to a ferocious defense and terrific special teams. In an unexpected twist, his final game with the Hokies was all about offense. But the 69-year-old coach wasn't complaining, only laughing and smiling in the aftermath of Virginia Tech's 55-52 victory over Tulsa in the Camping World Independence Bowl on Saturday night. Michael Brewer threw for 344 yards, Isaiah Ford had 227 yards receiving and Virginia Tech held off a Tulsa rally in the final minutes to send Beamer out a winner. The coach announced in November he would retire following the season and the team won three of its last four regular season games to become bowl eligible. He finished with a 238-121-2 record at Virginia Tech over 29 seasons. Virginia Tech (7-6) was playing in a bowl for the 23rd straight season. The first game of that streak also was in the Independence Bowl in 1993, when the Hokies beat Indiana 45-20. This trip was filled with plenty of offense just like in 1993 but had much more drama. Tulsa (6-7) rallied from a three-touchdown deficit in the second half to pull to 55-52 with 3:47 left. Virginia Tech's Dadi L'homme Nicolas ended Tulsa's final drive with a sack of Dane Evans on fourth down. The 107 points were the most in Independence Bowl history. Ford's 227 yards receiving on 12 catches set an Independence Bowl record. Tulsa's Evans completed 27 of 44 passes for 374 yards and three touchdowns. D'Angelo Brewer ran for 105 yards and two touchdowns. A relaxed Beamer strolled onto the field about an hour before the game, smiling and waving to fans as the Hokies went through warmups. Tulsa jumped out to a 14-7 lead, but Virginia Tech responded with 38 points over the next 19 minutes for the 45-21 advantage. The Hokies' final touchdown during that stunning run came on a 67-yard punt return by Greg Stroman -- which was fitting considering the phrase "Beamer Ball" became common during the coach's long tenure because of Virginia Tech's reputation for game-changing special teams plays. Tulsa has had a tough time on defense all season, giving up 38.6 points per game, including 66 in a loss to Memphis on Oct. 23. But the brutal performance in the first half was bad even by the Golden Hurricane's standards. Virginia Tech controlled the line of scrimmage -- gaining 370 total yards in the first two quarters -- by capitalizing on Tulsa's missed tackles, blown assignments and shoddy special teams play. Tulsa scored the final 10 points of the second quarter to pull to 45-31. The 76 combined points easily set the Independence Bowl first-half record. The Hokies controlled most of the second half, but the Golden Hurricane scored on a 21-yard touchdown from Evans to Josh Atkinson and made the 2-point conversion to pull within 55-45 with 7:35 remaining. A 36-yard touchdown from Evans to Keyarris Garrett with 3:47 left made it 55-52. But Tulsa's last gasp drive ended on Nicolas' sack. The 223-pound defensive end broke through the line and enveloped Evans before slamming him to the turf.

2015 Foster Farms Bowl

The 2015 Foster Farms Bowl was played on December 26, 2015 at Levi's Stadium in Santa Clara, California. The 14th edition of the Foster Farms Bowl (previously known as the Fight Hunger Bowl) featured the UCLA Bruins from the Pac-12 Conference against the Nebraska Cornhuskers from the Big Ten Conference. Since there were not enough bowl-eligible teams at the end of the regular season, 5–7 Nebraska was given a spot in this bowl because of its high Academic Progress Rate. Underdog Nebraska was victorious.

2015 Foster Farms Bowl	Line	1	-	2	-	3	-	4	-	Final
UCLA	(-4.5)	7	-	14	-	0	-	8	-	29
Nebraska	(61.5)	7	-	14	-	9	-	7	-	37

Scoring Summary
UCLA - Perkins 1 yard run (Fairbairn kick)
Nebraska - Cross 1 yard run (Brown kick)
UCLA - Walker 60 yard pass from Rosen (Fairbairn kick)
UCLA - Starks 26 yard pass from Rosen (Fairbairn kick)
Nebraska - Newby 3 yard run (Brown kick)
Nebraska - Janovich 1 yard run (Brown kick)
Nebraska - Morgan 22 yard pass from Armstrong (Kick failed)
Nebraska - Brown 20 yard Field goal
Nebraska - Armstrong 3 yard run (Brown kick)
UCLA - Payton 9 yard pass from Rosen (Duarte pass from Rosen)

Associated Press Foster Farms Bowl Game Summary - After a year marred by a string of close losses, Nebraska found a way to put a happy capper on a losing season. Tommy Armstrong Jr. Threw a touchdown pass and ran for another score to help Nebraska close a disappointing year by beating UCLA 37-29 in the Foster Farms Bowl on Saturday night. The Cornhuskers (6-7) scored 30 straight points after falling behind 21-7 early to overpower the Bruins (8-5) and give Nebraska something to build on heading into Coach Mike Riley's second season. Stanley Morgan Jr. gave Nebraska the lead for good with a one-handed, 22-yard catch in the third quarter and Imani Cross, Terrell Newby and Andy Janovich all ran for scores for the Cornhuskers. Armstrong completed 12 of 19 passes for 174 yards and ran for 76 more to lead the way for Nebraska, which had a season high with 326 yards rushing. Josh Rosen threw for 319 yards and three touchdowns for the Bruins. They ended what had once been a promising season with losses to Southern California and in the bowl game. Nebraska only got the chance to play in a bowl because there were not enough six-win teams to fill all 80 slots and the Cornhuskers made the most of the opportunity by taking the game over in the third quarter. After tying the game with two late touchdowns in the second quarter, Nebraska outgained UCLA 196 to 1 in the third quarter behind a dominant running game. The Cornhuskers gained 151 yards on the ground alone in the third quarter with the run game setting up Morgan's touchdown catch that made it 27-21 and then leading the way on two more scoring drives that ended in a Drew Brown's field goal and Armstrong's 3-yard run in the opening minute of the fourth to make it 37-21. UCLA responded with a 9-yard TD pass from Rosen to Jordan Payton and a 2-point conversion to get within eight. Ka'imi Fairbairn missed a 46-yard field goal after a botched shotgun snap by the Bruins and Rosen threw an interception in the end zone on fourth down from the 32 with 2:54 to play to end UCLA's chances at a comeback. After losing four games this season in the final 10 seconds of regulation or overtime, the Huskers were happy to be able to get that late stop to seal a victory. The Bruins broke out to a 21-7 lead when Rosen threw a 60-yard touchdown to Kenneth Walker III and a 26-yarder to Nate Starks. The other UCLA touchdown came when Paul Perkins ran it in from the 1 a play after Rosen completed a 22-yard pass to Thomas Duarte on fourth-and-1. Nebraska got back-to-back TD drives to tie it 21 at the half. Cornhusker's safety Nate Gerry was ejected late in the second quarter for targeting on a swing pass to Perkins. It was the second straight game that Gerry was ejected for targeting. After the game, Nebraska defensive tackle Maliek Collins announced he will skip his senior season to enter the NFL draft.

2015 Military Bowl

The 2015 Military Bowl was played on December 28, 2015 at Navy–Marine Corps Memorial Stadium in Annapolis, Maryland. The eighth edition of the Military Bowl featured the Pittsburgh Panthers of the Atlantic Coast Conference against the hometown Navy Midshipmen of the American Athletic Conference. It was televised on ESPN.

2015 Military Bowl	Line	1	-	2	-	3	-	4	-	Final
Pittsburgh	(52.5)	7	-	0	-	14	-	7	-	28
Navy	(-3.0)	14	-	7	-	10	-	13	-	44

Scoring Summary
Pittsburgh - Henderson 100 yard kickoff return (Blewitt kick)
Navy - Reynolds 1 yard run (Grebe kick)
Navy - Reynolds 5 yard run (Grebe kick)
Navy - Carmona 11 yard pass from Reynolds (Grebe kick)
Navy - Brown 26 yard run (Grebe kick)
Navy - Grebe 35 yard Field goal
Pittsburgh - Ollison 4 yard pass from Peterman (Blewitt kick)
Pittsburgh - Whitehead 22 yard fumble return (Blewitt kick)
Navy - Gulley 15 yard run (Grebe kick)
Pittsburgh - Ollison 45 yard run (Blewitt kick)
Navy - Reynolds 9 yard run (Kick blocked)

Associated Press Military Bowl Game Summary - It was appropriate that Keenan Reynolds' final touchdown at Navy thrust him into the NCAA record book and secured a milestone victory for the Midshipmen. Reynolds wrapped up his record-setting college career in spectacular fashion: by running for three scores and throwing for another to lead Navy past Pittsburgh 44-28 on Monday in the Military Bowl presented by Northrop Grumman. After the Midshipmen let a 24-point cushion dwindle to 38-28, Reynolds capped a nine-play drive with a 9-yard touchdown run with 4:19 remaining. It was his 88th career touchdown, which broke a tie with Kenneth Dixon of Louisiana Tech for most in FBS history. It was classic Reynolds, given that he broke a slew of records and won a whole lot of games during his four-year run at the Naval Academy. Reynolds ran for 144 yards on 24 carries, completed nine of 17 passes for 126 yards and had a reception for 47 yards on a trick play. He leaves Navy (11-2) as the FBS career leader in touchdowns and points (530). His 4,559 yards rushing are the most by a Quarterback in FBS history, as he passed Pat White and Denard Robinson with Monday's game. With Reynolds leading the way, the Midshipmen completed their first 11-win season in 135 years of football. That, more than all his personal accomplishments, is what Reynolds will remember. The bowl win was the first game for the Midshipmen since they beat Army and Coach Ken Niumatalolo decided to stay at Navy instead of taking the head-coaching job at BYU. Niumatalolo was glad he stuck around for Reynolds' finale. Qadree Ollison rushed for 73 yards and scored two touchdowns for Pitt. Nate Peterman threw a touchdown pass but was intercepted three times. That added up to a disappointing ending for the Panthers (8-5) in their first season under Coach Pat Narduzzi. In the end, though, they couldn't cope with Reynolds. After Quadree Henderson returned the opening kickoff 100 yards for Pitt, Navy went up 21-7 at halftime and built a 31-7 lead midway through the third quarter. Pittsburgh scored two touchdowns in 17 seconds to close to 31-21 but could not complete the comeback. The victory marked the first time Navy has won three straight bowl games. Playing before a sellout crowd of 36,352 in its home stadium, Navy used its triple-option attack to overwhelm a team that went 6-2 in the ACC and ranked 20th in the nation against the run. The Midshipmen finished with 590 yards of offense, including 417 on the ground and 114 by fullback Chris Swain. After Henderson weaved from end zone to end zone for the game-opening score, Reynolds directed a 75-yard drive that ended with his 1-yard touchdown run. Later in the first quarter, Reynolds capped a 14-play march with a 5-yard touchdown. Navy's next touchdown came on an 11-yard pass from Reynolds to Tyler Carmona. Niumatalolo momentarily abandoned the triple option in the third quarter in favor of a bit of trickery. Reynolds pitched the ball to fullback Shawn White, then went around the right side of the line for a catch-and-run that set up a 26-yard touchdown jaunt by Demond Brown. It was 31-7 before Peterman threw a 4-yard touchdown pass to Ollison, and a 22-yard fumble return by Jordan Whitehead got Pitt within 10 points. After Navy scored another touchdown, Ollison ran for a 45-yard score to make it 38-28. But this was to be Reynolds' day. In his final significant drive with the Midshipmen, he converted three third downs and drew the Panthers offside on a fourth-and-3. Soon after that, he walked off the field for the final time.

2015 Quick Lane Bowl

The 2015 Quick Lane Bowl was played between the Central Michigan Chippewas of the Mid-American Conference and the Minnesota Golden Gophers of the Big Ten Conference played on December 28, 2015, at Ford Field in Detroit, Michigan. It was the second edition of the Quick Lane Bowl. The game was televised on ESPN2. Although Minnesota finished with a below .500 record, they were allowed to participate in a bowl game after only 77 teams qualified for 80 available bowl spots. Minnesota was selected as one of three 5-7 teams to fill the final bowl spots due to their APR scores.

Central Michigan Chippewas - The 2015 Central Michigan Chippewas football team were led by first-year head coach John Bonamego and played their home games at Kelly/Shorts Stadium. They were members of the West Division of the Mid-American Conference.

Minnesota Golden Gophers - The 2015 Minnesota Golden Gophers football team were led by fifth-year head coach Jerry Kill, who retired October 28, 2015 due to health reasons. Tracy Claeys replaced Kill on an interim basis and was named head coach two weeks later. The Gophers play their home games at TCF Bank Stadium. They are a member of the West Division of the Big Ten Conference. Minnesota finished the regular season with a record of 5-7. Despite finishing below .500, the Gophers were invited to the Quick Lane Bowl versus Central Michigan due to there not being enough bowl eligible teams and Minnesota's high Academic Performance Rating.

2015 Quick Lane Bowl	Line	1	-	2	-	3	-	4	-	Final
Central Michigan	(49.5)	0	-	7	-	0	-	7	-	14
Minnesota	(-6.0)	3	-	7	-	3	-	8	-	21

Scoring Summary
Minnesota - Santoso 22 yard Field goal
Central Michigan - Rush 1 yard run (Eavey kick)
Minnesota - Maye 11 yard pass from Leidner (Santoso kick)
Minnesota - Santoso 42 yard Field goal
Central Michigan - Ross 13 yard run (Eavey kick)
Minnesota - Leidner 13 yard run (Maye pass from Leidner)

Associated Press Quick Lane Bowl Game Summary - Minnesota coach Tracy Claeys made no apologies for taking his team to a bowl with a losing record. The Golden Gophers made the most of their opportunity. Quarterback Mitch Leidner ran 13 yards for a touchdown with 4:26 remaining, and the Golden Gophers held on for a 21-14 win over Central Michigan in the Quick Lane Bowl on Monday night. Minnesota ended a trying season on a positive note. Coach Jerry Kill retired in late October because of continued difficulty managing his epilepsy and his job, and Claeys took over. The Gophers were 5-7 after the regular season but were able to play on because not enough teams reached six wins to fill all the bowls. All three teams that went to bowls at 5-7 -- Minnesota, Nebraska and San Jose State -- ended up winning. Central Michigan (7-6) took a 14-13 lead with 11:08 remaining on a 13-yard touchdown run by Romello Ross. Minnesota responded by driving 74 yards in 13 plays. Leidner ran for the go-ahead touchdown, then threw to KJ Maye for a 2-point conversion. CMU drove back into Minnesota territory, but Cooper Rush threw an ill-advised pass while being pulled down from behind, and his attempt to avoid a sack backfired when Briean Boddy-Calhoun intercepted the ball with 2:10 to play. Both teams had to overcome plenty of adversity this season. Minnesota had to play on after Kill's retirement. He was an honorary captain for the Gophers at the pregame coin toss Monday. CMU coach John Bonamego was diagnosed with cancer in his left tonsil and underwent treatment before the season. That was a tough way for him to begin his first season at the helm at CMU. Rush ran for the game's first touchdown Monday, scoring from 1 yard out to give CMU a 7-3 lead early in the second quarter. The Gophers took a 10-7 lead into halftime thanks to an 11-yard touchdown pass from Leidner to Maye. It was 13-7 in the third when an onside kick by Minnesota was unsuccessful, giving the Chippewas the ball at midfield. CMU wasn't able to do anything with that field position, but after a failed fourth down by Minnesota early in the fourth, the Chippewas went 56 yards in four plays. CMU took the lead on the run by Ross. Minnesota appeared to have him stopped at about the 3-yard line, but the Chippewas were able to push the pile into the end zone. Ross ran for 100 yards on 19 carries, but Rush was pretty well contained. CMU's single season record holder for yards passing, Rush went only 15 of 29 for 145 yards with an interception. Leidner was 24 of 30 for 223 yards with a touchdown and an interception. Last season, CMU scored on a lateral-filled play as time expired in the Bahamas Bowl, although the Chippewas lost to Western Kentucky when they went for 2 and didn't convert. This year, Central Michigan had the ball at its own 30 with 4 seconds to play, but the game ended when Rush was sacked by De'Vondre Campbell. The announced attendance was 34,217 despite a winter storm that was passing through Michigan. Having a local team surely helped boost the number of fans. Last year's game between North Carolina and Rutgers drew 23,876.

2015 Armed Forces Bowl

The 2015 Armed Forces Bowl was played on December 29, 2015 at Amon G. Carter Stadium on the campus of Texas Christian University in Fort Worth, Texas. The 13th edition of the Armed Forces Bowl featured the California Golden Bears of the Pac-12 Conference against the Air Force Falcons of the Mountain West Conference. It was televised on ESPN.

2015 Armed Forces Bowl	Line	1	-	2	-	3	-	4	-	Final
California	(-5.5)	14	-	21	-	17	-	3	-	55
Air Force	(70.0)	7	-	14	-	8	-	7	-	36

Scoring Summary
Air Force - Owens 1 yard run (Strebel kick)
California - Enwere 1 yard run (Anderson kick)
California - Treggs 30 yard pass from Goff (Anderson kick)
Air Force - Williams 16 yard run (Strebel kick)
California - Powe 5 yard pass from Goff (Anderson kick)
California - Lawler 24 yard pass from Goff (Anderson kick)
Air Force - Roberts 1 yard run (Strebel kick)
California - Lawler 14 yard run (Anderson kick)
California - Powe 12 yard run (Anderson kick)
California - Anderson 29 yard Field goal
Air Force - McVey 57 yard pass from Roberts (Owens pass from Roberts)
California - Lawler 25 yard pass from Goff (Anderson kick)
Air Force - Robinette 15 yard pass from Roberts (Strebel kick)
California - Anderson 30 yard Field goal

Associated Press Armed Forces Bowl Game Summary - If Jared Goff is headed to the NFL early, California's junior Quarterback replaced a couple of pretty big names in the record books in his final college game. How about Aaron Rodgers and Marcus Mariota. Goff threw for 467 yards and six touchdowns, and the Bears won in the postseason for the first time in seven years, beating Air Force 55-36 in the Armed Forces Bowl on Tuesday. The 6-foot-4 Goff was already the season leader two times over in passing yards and touchdowns at Rodgers' alma mater. Now he has Mariota's Pac-12 record for touchdowns with 43 a year after the former Oregon star threw 42 in leading the Ducks to the national championship game before going No. 2 overall in the NFL draft to Tennessee. Not enough? OK, how about breaking Rodgers' Cal record for passing yards in a bowl game -- 394 yards in a 52-49 win over Virginia Tech in the 2003 Insight Bowl. That was a full season before Green Bay drafted Brett Favre's eventual replacement in the first round. Cal fans were chanting "One more year!" while celebrating the victory. Goff had three of his scoring tosses in a span of five plays in the second quarter as the Bears (8-5) broke a 14-14 tie and cruised while setting a school postseason scoring record in a rematch of the 2007 Armed Forces Bowl, also won by Cal (42-36). Receiver Kenny Lawler had three touchdowns for Cal, which last made the postseason in a 21-10 loss to Texas in the Holiday Bowl in 2011. The Bears' last bowl win was 24-17 over Miami in the 2008 Emerald Bowl near their Bay Area campus. Weakened by the targeting ejection of secondary anchor Weston Steelhammer on Air Force's third defensive play, the Falcons (8-6) lost for the fourth time in five Armed Forces appearances since 2007. Goff, who was Cal's first freshman starting Quarterback in 2013, has started all 37 games as the Bears bounced back from 1-11 his first year to 5-7 last year. He was 25 of 37 with no interceptions while breaking Armed Forces records for passing yards and touchdowns. While Goff fell short of his career record of seven touchdown passes in a game from a 59-56 double-overtime win against Colorado last season, he added another Pac-12 mark with 4,719 yards. It was another successful Texas homecoming for Dykes, the son of former Texas Tech coach Spike Dykes. The Bears won for the second time this season in the Lone Star State after beating Texas 45-44 in September. Steelhammer, Air Force's leader in tackles and interceptions at safety, was ejected after hitting Bryce Treggs moments after a pass had gone by the Cal receiver. The junior dropped his head as the announcement was made, and coach Troy Calhoun angrily waved his arms at officials. Karson Roberts threw for two touchdowns and had 69 yards rushing and another score for Air Force. Jacobi Owens, the leader of one of the nation's best rushing attacks, had 83 yards and a touchdown. The Falcons lost their last three games, including the Mountain West Conference championship to San Diego State, and dropped to 1-9 at TCU's Amon G. Carter Stadium. Cal took control on a sequence that started with Goff's perfect deep throw to Maurice Harris, who reached out with his left hand to redirect the ball to his body and cradled it on his way out of bounds for a 40-yard gain to the Air Force 5. Goff found Darius Powe on the next play for one of Powe's two scores and a 21-14 lead. The Bears got the ball back immediately on a fumble when Roberts lost control trying to run the option, and Goff hit Lawler in stride in the end zone for a 24-yard score. Lawler had five catches for 75 yards. After an Air Force punt, Goff moved the Bears 78 yards on three completions, with a 55-yarder to Treggs setting up a 14-yard score to Lawler. Treggs had 143 yards and a touchdown.

2015 Russell Athletic Bowl

The 2015 Russell Athletic Bowl was played on December 29, 2015 at the Orlando Citrus Bowl in Orlando, Florida. The 26th edition of the Russell Athletic Bowl featured the North Carolina Tar Heels of the Atlantic Coast Conference against the Baylor Bears of the Big 12 Conference. It was televised on ESPN.

2015 Russell Athletic Bowl	Line	1	-	2	-	3	-	4	-	Final
#10 North Carolina	(-2.5)	7	-	10	-	14	-	7	-	38
#18 Baylor	(74.0)	14	-	14	-	14	-	7	-	49

Scoring Summary
North Carolina - Fritts 9 yard pass from Williams (Weiler kick)
Baylor - Hawthorne 6 yard run (Callahan kick)
Baylor - Hawthorne 6-yard run (Callahan kick)
North Carolina - Weiler 32 yard Field goal
Baylor - Jefferson 11 yard run (Callahan kick)
Baylor - Jefferson 27 yard run (Callahan kick)
North Carolina - M. Williams 4 yard run (Weiler kick)
North Carolina - M. Williams 1 yard run (Weiler kick)
Baylor - T. Williams 3 yard run (Callahan kick)
Baylor - Jefferson 80-yard run (Callahan kick)
North Carolina - Howard 27 yard pass from M. Williams (Weiler kick)
Baylor - T. Williams 1 yard run (Callahan kick)
North Carolina - Singleton 7 yard pass from M. Williams (Weiler kick)

Associated Press Russell Athletic Bowl Game Summary - When it was at full strength this season, Baylor had the most productive offense in college football. Even without several of their key pieces, the Bears proved they could be just as impressive. Johnny Jefferson rushed for three touchdowns and a record 299 yards, and No. 18 Baylor ran past No. 10 North Carolina 49-38 in the Russell Athletic Bowl on Tuesday night. Despite missing two Quarterbacks, an award-winning receiver, and a 1,000-yard running back, the Bears' No. 1-ranked scoring offense stayed creative, pounding out 645 yards rushing and 756 total yards -- both records for this bowl. Devin Chafin added 161 yards and a touchdown, and Terence Williams rushed for 97 yards and two touchdowns for the Bears (10-3). North Carolina (11-3) tried to match Baylor's scoring output but had a key fumble in the third quarter that stifled its comeback efforts. Tar Heels Quarterback Marquise Williams passed for 243 yards and three scores and rushed for two more. Elijah Hood added 118 yards rushing. The win was Baylor's first bowl victory since 2012, snapping a string of two consecutive bowl losses. The biggest question leading up to Tuesday's matchup was how Baylor's offense would adapt with Quarterbacks Seth Russell (neck injury) and Jarrett Stidham (broken ankle), Biletnikoff Award winner Corey Coleman (hernia surgery), and running back Shock Linwood (broken foot) all sidelined. The answer became apparent early on. Though sophomore Chris Johnson started the day at Quarterback, five different players -- Johnson, his backup Lynx Hawthorne, and running backs Jefferson, Chafin, and Terence Williams -- all took snaps from center for the Bears within the first two series. They continued to use the quintet in multiple Wildcat formations throughout the game. Coach Art Briles did not address the media after the game, but his son and offensive coordinator Kendal Briles said using the Wildcat sets were always part of the game plan. North Carolina kept pace as best it could and scored on its opening possession of the second half to cut what had been an 18-point first-half deficit to 28-24. Baylor needed just eight plays to go up 35-24 following 3-yard touchdown run by Williams. The Tar Heels started their next drive with a 67-yard run by Hood to get back into the red zone. But two plays later T.J. Logan fumbled at the goal line after being hit by Aiavion Edwards and it was scooped up by Baylor's Orion Stewart for a touchback. The Bears took advantage, and on their first play after the changeover scored on an 80-yard scamper by Jefferson that put them in front 42-24. Fedora said he thought the Bears would throw the ball more with Johnson at Quarterback or would have the level of success they did rushing the ball. Baylor turned it over on downs on the opening possession of the game but scored on each of its next four drives of the first half to take 28-10 lead. The Bears' play calling was varied and creative throughout, using a deluge of direct-snaps, jet sweeps and an occasional pass to keep the Tar Heels' secondary honest. The result was a rash of chunk plays, including 10 Bears running plays of more than 10 yards in the first half alone. For the half, Baylor finished with 358 rushing yards, breaking the previous record of 325 rushing yards set by Illinois against Virginia in 1999. Jefferson was the most active, rushing for 173 yards and a pair of touchdowns. Linebacker Edwards said getting to 10 wins after closing the regular season with two tough losses is a positive sign for the Bears.

2015 Arizona Bowl

The 2015 Arizona Bowl was between the Nevada Wolf Pack and the Colorado State Rams played on December 29, 2015, at Arizona Stadium in Tucson, Arizona. It was the inaugural edition of the Arizona Bowl. In an unusual circumstance for a postseason bowl game, both teams were from the Mountain West Conference. The previous non–championship bowl to feature two teams from the same conference was the 1979 Orange Bowl.

2015 Arizona Bowl	Line	1	-	2	-	3	-	4	-	Final
Nevada	(-4.5)	3	-	16	-	3	-	6	-	28
Colorado State	(55.5)	0	-	13	-	7	-	3	-	23

Scoring Summary
Nevada - Zuro 19 yard Field goal
Nevada - Zuro 37 yard Field goal
Colorado State - Stevens 1 yard run (Bryan kick)
Nevada - Butler 77 yard run (Zuro kick)
Colorado State - Bryan 20 yard Field goal
Nevada - Mitchell 96 yard kickoff return (Kick failed)
Colorado State - Bryan 29 yard Field goal
Nevada - Zuro 40 yard Field goal
Colorado State - Odon 9 yard run (Bryan kick)
Colorado State - Bryan 38 yard Field goal
Nevada - Butler 4 yard run (Run failed)

Associated Press Arizona Bowl Game Summary - The inaugural Arizona Bowl was ridiculed for having two teams from the same conference, both with mediocre records. The stands had vast empty spaces. Many TV viewers were unsure where to find the game. It ended up being quite a show, particularly the closing flourish. James Butler scored on a 4-yard run with 1:06 left and Nevada benefited from a late gaffe by Colorado State's Jordon Vaden to beat the Rams 28-23 in the Arizona Bowl Tuesday night. Colorado State (7-6) trailed most of the game before taking the lead on Wyatt Bryan's 38-yard field goal with just under 4 minutes left. The Wolf Pack (7-6) responded quickly, marching 72 yards in eight plays to set up Butler's tackle-breaking touchdown run. Nick Stevens orchestrated a quick-hitting drive in the final minute with no timeouts, but Vaden was unable to get out of bounds at Nevada's 12-yard line and time ran out on the Rams. Butler ran for 189 yards and Elijah Mitchell scored on a 96-yard kickoff return in the bowl battle between Mountain West Conference teams. Stevens threw for 310 yards and a touchdown for the Rams. Colorado State earned a trip to a bowl game in its first season under coach Bobo, overcoming a 2-4 start by winning its final four games. Nevada clinched its bowl berth with a win over San Jose State on Nov. 14 but closed the season with consecutive losses. The reward for both teams was what amounted to an extra conference game in the first non-playoff bowl game between teams from the same conference since the 1979 Orange Bowl. Mountain West officials pleaded with anyone they could to prevent an all-MWC bowl game and Commissioner Craig Thompson issued a lengthy statement once the bowl slots were announced. The Rams and Wolf Pack didn't really care who they faced. This was a bowl game, a chance to end the season with a win. The Rams got it off to a rough start, losing the ball on their opening drive when Stevens was hit as he was about to throw and fumbled. Colorado State later reached Nevada's 4-yard line but turned the ball over on downs when Izzy Matthews was stopped on fourth-and-inches. The Rams finally got going on their next drive, reaching the 1-yard line after Rashard Higgins turned a slant into a 38-yard reception with a string of broken tackles. Colorado State punched it in this time, with Steven scoring on a 1-yard sneak the next play. The Rams kept racking up yards, though had to settle for two field goals by Bryan, including a 29 yarder just before halftime. Colorado State had a 302-169 advantage in total yards, yet trailed 19-13 at halftime thanks to missed opportunities, including a dropped TD pass by Higgins. Nevada had to settle for a pair of field goals early before its explosive running game finally showed up in the second quarter, when Butler burst up the middle for a 77-yard touchdown. The next big play came on special teams: Mitchell took a kickoff up the middle, made a juke and was gone for a 96-yard touchdown, Nevada's first kickoff return for a score since 1998. The Rams kept rolling to open the second half, setting up Jasen Oden for a 9-yard touchdown run through a mammoth hole on the right side. Both teams struggled offensively the rest of the half until the late fireworks in what was supposed to be a dud of a bowl.

2015 Texas Bowl

The 2015 Texas Bowl was played on December 29, 2015 at NRG Stadium in Houston, Texas. The tenth edition of the Texas Bowl was televised on ESPN.

2015 Texas Bowl	Line	1	-	2	-	3	-	4	-	Final
#20 LSU	(-7.0)	14	-	7	-	21	-	14	-	56
Texas Tech	(74.0)	6	-	7	-	7	-	7	-	27

Scoring Summary
LSU - Fournette 2 yard run (Domingue kick)
Texas Tech - Grant 46 yard pass from Mahomes (Pass failed)
LSU - Chark 79 yard run (Domingue kick)
LSU - Fournette 44 yard pass from Harris (Domingue kick)
Texas Tech - Grant 3 yard pass from Mahomes (Hatfield kick)
Texas Tech - Davis 31 yard pass from Mahomes (Hatfield kick)
LSU - Fournette 43 yard run (Domingue kick)
LSU - Fournette 4 yard run (Domingue kick)

LSU - Harris 26 yard run (Domingue kick)
Texas Tech - Grant 4 yard pass from Mahomes (Hatfield kick)
LSU - Fournette 2 yard run (Domingue kick)
LSU - Williams 2 yard run (Domingue kick)

Associated Press Texas Bowl Game Summary - LSU coach Les Miles wasn't at all surprised by Leonard Fournette's performance in the AdvoCare V100 Texas Bowl. At this point, Miles is used to seeing his All-America running back take over games. Fournette scored five touchdowns and ran for 212 yards as the Tigers (No. 20 CFP, No. 22 AP) used a big third quarter to pull away for a 56-27 win over Texas Tech on Tuesday night. Fournette's five touchdowns (four rushing, one receiving) tied the record for most total touchdowns in a bowl game, matching seven previous performances. LSU's 56 points set the school record for scoring in a bowl game. Texas Tech (7-6) cut the lead to one early in the third quarter before the Tigers (9-3) scored 21 straight points, with two touchdowns by Fournette, to make it 42-20 entering the fourth. Fournette had two rushing touchdowns of 2 yards, ran for TDs of 43 and 4 yards, and took a screen pass 44 yards for another score. The Texas Bowl MVP described his performance succinctly. Patrick Mahomes threw for 370 yards and four touchdowns for Texas Tech but was under heavy pressure all night. He was sacked six times and scrambled away from probably 10 more. Miles thought his defense set a tone for the game by limiting Tech to minus-5 yards on the first drive. Jakeem Grant set a Texas Tech bowl record with three touchdown receptions. The Tigers believe their offense was helped by having coordinator Cam Cameron on the sideline instead of up in the booth, where he had been all season. It was the 10th 100-yard rushing game and fourth 200-yarder this season for Fournette, who extended his LSU single-season rushing record to 1,953 yards. LSU outrushed Texas Tech 384-29 as the Tigers took advantage of a run defense that was one of the worst in the nation. Fournette joined Alabama's Derrick Henry as the only running backs in Southeastern Conference history to rush for more than 1,900 yards in a season. Fournette's 162.8 yards per game lead the nation. Brandon Harris threw for 254 yards with a touchdown and an interception and ran for another score for LSU. Dakota Allen intercepted a pass by Harris early in the third quarter, and Texas Tech made it 21-20 on a 31-yard touchdown reception by Reginald Davis three plays later. Fournette was stopped for no gain on one carry on LSU's next drive and managed just 2 yards on the next one. But Texas Tech couldn't corral him on his next run, and he broke free for 43 yards to give him the LSU record for rushing touchdowns in a season with 20 and push the lead to 28-20. The Red Raiders were driving on their next possession when Rickey Jefferson intercepted a pass that was deflected on the LSU 1-yard line. Fournette pushed LSU's lead to 35-20 on a 4-yard touchdown run after the interception. Trey Quinn had a 46-yard reception to set up that score. Harris made it 42-20 when he ran 26 yards for a touchdown with 9 seconds left in the third quarter. Grant had a 4-yard reception for Texas Tech that made it 42-27 early in the fourth. Fournette sailed into the end zone Superman style on a 2-yard run with about 8 minutes left. He got going early when he shed one defender and hurdled another on a 35-yard run on his second carry. He finished that drive with a 2-yard touchdown run to give LSU a 7-0 lead. Texas Tech closed the gap when Grant grabbed a 46-yard touchdown pass, but the 2-point conversion failed, and the score was 7-6. D.J. Chark ran 79 yards for a touchdown on LSU's next play to make it 14-6. One Texas Tech defender caught up to him at about the 10-yard line, but Chark simply dragged him into the end zone for the longest run in Texas Bowl history. Fournette pushed LSU's lead to 21-6 when he took a screen pass 44 yards for his first career touchdown catch with about 6 1/2 minutes left in the second quarter. He wasn't that excited about the reception.

2015 Birmingham Bowl

The 2015 Birmingham Bowl was played on December 30, 2015 at Legion Field in Birmingham, Alabama in the United States. The tenth annual Birmingham Bowl was televised on ESPN.

2015 Birmingham Bowl	Line	1	-	2	-	3	-	4	-	Final
Auburn	(-3.0)	10	-	0	-	7	-	14	-	31
Memphis	(64.0)	0	-	10	-	0	-	0	-	10

Scoring Summary
Auburn - Carlson 20 yard Field goal
Auburn - Johnson 8 yard run (Carlson kick)
Memphis - Elliot 53 yard Field goal
Memphis - Ball 56 yard interception return (Elliot kick)
Auburn - Smith 11 yard pass from Johnson (Carlson kick)
Auburn - Johnson 5 yard run (Carlson kick)
Auburn - Robinson 4 yard run (Carlson kick)

Associated Press Birmingham Bowl Game Summary - Jeremy Johnson and Auburn found a measure of redemption and, finally, something to celebrate in their season finale. The Tigers' former starting Quarterback came off the bench to run and pass for touchdowns and the similarly maligned defense contained Memphis Quarterback Paxton Lynch throughout in Auburn's 31-10 victory Wednesday in the Birmingham Bowl. Johnson capped a disappointing season by sparking a sputtering offense that scored three touchdowns in a five-minute span starting late in the third quarter. Auburn (7-6) avoided the first losing season of Gus Malzahn's 11-year college coaching career. An Auburn defense without a coordinator didn't allow an offensive touchdown for Memphis (9-4) and its star Quarterback. Malzahn announced the hiring of LSU defensive coordinator Kevin Steele after the game. Johnson gave Auburn a 17-10 lead with an 11-yard touchdown pass to Jason Smith. He ran 17 yards on his second play from scrimmage and opened the fourth quarter with a 5-yard touchdown run on his third. Marcus Davis set up two of the touchdowns with punt returns of 28 and 56 yards. Game MVP Jovon Robinson, who is from Memphis, effectively put the game away with a 4-yard touchdown set up by Davis' 56-yard return down to the 6 early in the fourth. He finished with 126 yards on 27 carries and smashed his way to a fourth-down conversion to set up Johnson's touchdown pass. Lynch never got going and Memphis was running the ball down three touchdowns in the fourth quarter. He finished 16-of-37 passing for 108 yards -- his lowest total since the opener against Missouri State -- with an interception in the end zone off a deflected pass. Memphis had been gunning for a program first: back-to-back 10-win seasons. The only Memphis points in this one came on Reggis Ball's interception return and Jake Elliott's 53-yard field goal. Auburn outgained Memphis 402-205 in total yards in the first game since defensive coordinator Will Muschamp left to become South Carolina's head coach. A defense that struggled much of the season played perhaps its best game. Malzahn announced before the game that Sean White, not Johnson, would start the game. White threw two interceptions, and Ball returned the second 53 yards for touchdown to tie it at 10 late in the first half. Johnson made his snaps count, including a handoff for Robinson's fourth-quarter touchdown. He opened the season as a potential Heisman Trophy contender, was benched and reclaimed the job when White sustained a knee injury. He ran for 26 yards on three carries but only attempted one pass. White was 8 of 13 for 103 yards. Memphis had three interceptions in the first half to wipe out a 10-0 deficit and forge a halftime tie. Elliott's field goal came after Smith was picked off on a trick play. Then Ball swiped White's fourth-down pass in the backfield with nothing but green in front of him.

2015 Belk Bowl

The 2015 Belk Bowl was played on December 30, 2015 at Bank of America Stadium in Charlotte, North Carolina. The fourteenth annual Belk Bowl was nationally televised by ESPN.

2015 Belk Bowl	Line	1	-	2	-	3	-	4	-	Final
NC State	(61.5)	0	-	14	-	7	-	7	-	28
Mississippi State	(-6.0)	14	-	17	-	6	-	14	-	51

Scoring Summary
Mississippi State - Ross 14 yard pass from Prescott (Graves kick)
Mississippi State - Wilson 28 yard run (Graves kick)
Mississippi State - Ross 33 yard run (Graves kick)
NC State - McKever 82 yard pass from Brissett (Bambard kick)
NC State - Samuels 48 yard run (Bambard kick)
Mississippi State - Malone fumble recovery in end zone (Graves kick)
Mississippi State - Graves 39 yard Field goal
NC State - Brissett 3 yard run (Bambard kick)
Mississippi State - Holloway 10 yard pass from Prescott Kick failed)
Mississippi State - Holloway 55 yard pass from Prescott (Graves kick)
Mississippi State - Williams 33 yard run (Graves kick)
NC State - Samuels 1 yard run (Bambard kick)

Associated Press Belk Bowl Game Summary - Dak Prescott was determined to put an exclamation point on his impressive career at Mississippi State. He did just that Wednesday. Prescott threw for a Belk Bowl-record 380 yards and four touchdowns on a rain-soaked field in Mississippi State's 51-28 victory over North Carolina State. Selected the game MVP, Prescott completed 25 of 42 passes and ran for 47 yards joining Colin Kaepernick, Tim Tebow, Dan LeFevour as the only players in FBS history to throw for 9,000 yards and run for 2,500 yards in their career. That's some high praise from Mullen, who was Tebow's offensive coordinator at Florida. Prescott threw two touchdown passes to Brandon Holloway in the second half to break it open for the Bulldogs, who finished the season 9-4 after being picked to finish last in the SEC West in the preseason poll. Wide receiver Fred Ross had seven catches for 74 yards and a touchdown and scored on a 33-yard reverse. De'Runnya Wilson added five catches for 96 yards and a touchdown to help the Bulldogs break the Belk Bowl scoring record. North Carolina State's Jacoby Brissett threw for one score and ran for another but had two early interceptions that led to Mississippi State's first 14 points. Brissett had only thrown four interceptions all season coming into the game. The Bulldogs led 31-

14 at the half before Prescott put the game away. He lobbed his third TD pass of the game to Holloway over a blitzing defense to put the Bulldogs up 37-21 late in the third quarter. The senior Quarterback hit Holloway in stride on a go route along the right sideline for a 55-yard touchdown in the fourth quarter. Holloway finished with 78 yards on four catches. Mississippi State's defense set the tone early. On the first play from scrimmage, defensive end Jonathan Calvin hit Brissett as he released the ball and linebacker Gerri Green came up with the diving interception on the slick field at the Wolfpack 26. Five plays later, Ross hauled in a pass from Prescott in the left flat, turned up the left sideline and raced 14 yards for a score. Brissett had another pass picked off later in the first quarter and Prescott capitalized by finding Wilson for a 28-yard scoring strike. Mississippi State made it 21-0 when Ross scored on a 33-yard reverse. Brissett did battle back. He hooked up with former defensive end Pharoah McKever on an 82-yard scoring strike on a blown coverage to get NC State on the board, and Jaylen Samuels raced 46 yards for a touchdown to trim the lead to seven. But that was as close as the Wolfpack would get. The Bulldogs made it a two-possession game when left guard Justin Malone bent over to pick up a loose ball in the end zone after Prescott fumbled on a Quarterback draw. Doeren believes a young Wolfpack (7-6) team has a bright future.

2015 Music City Bowl

The 2015 Music City Bowl was played on December 30, 2015 at Nissan Stadium in Nashville, Tennessee. The 18th edition of the Music City Bowl was broadcast nationally by ESPN. It featured the Louisville Cardinals from the ACC, and the Texas A&M Aggies from the SEC.

2015 Music City Bowl	Line	1	-	2	-	3	-	4	-	Final
Texas A&M	(51.0)	7	-	7	-	0	-	7	-	21
Louisville	(-3.0)	20	-	0	-	7	-	0	-	27

Scoring Summary
Louisville - Jackson 6 yard run (Wallace kick)
Louisville - Crum 2 yard pass from Jackson (Kick failed)
Texas A&M - Carson 9 yard run (Bertolet kick)
Louisville - Jackson 61 yard run (Wallace kick)
Texas A&M - Seals-Jones 4 yard pass from Hubenak (Bertolet kick)
Louisville - Towbridge 17 yard pass from Jackson (Wallace kick)
Texas A&M - Kirk 29 yard pass from Hubenak (Bertolet kick)

Associated Press Music City Bowl Game Summary - Lamar Jackson put on quite a show for most of the Music City Bowl. Then he had to stand around and watch the Louisville defense polish off his record-setting night. Jackson ran for a career-high and Music City Bowl-record 226 yards and two touchdowns and threw for two more scores to help Louisville beat Texas A&M 27-21 on Wednesday night. After Louisville went three-and-out late, the Cardinals' defense sealed the victory by forcing the Aggies to turn it over on downs with 1:39 remaining. The freshman, making his first start since Oct. 30, finished with a bowl-record 453 total yards, and set the Louisville career rushing mark before the end of the first quarter in giving the Cardinals a 20-7 lead they never lost. Jackson ran for 126 yards in the first 15 minutes, including a 61-yard scoring run. Louisville (8-5) won its third bowl in their past four trips and first since 2013. The Cardinals also won for the eighth time in 10 games after starting the season 0-3. Texas A&M (8-5) became the first Southeastern Conference team to lose this bowl season. The Aggies made it interesting in the final minutes with their third-string Quarterback making his first career start. Josh Hubenak started after both Kyle Allen and Kyler Murray transferred this month. Hubenak shook off five sacks and two turnovers to throw for 307 yards, including a 29-yard touchdown pass to Christian Kirk with 4:54 left that pulled the Aggies to 27-21. Texas A&M nearly had first-and-goal at the Cardinals 6, but a review showed Kirk did not maintain possession of the ball on his catch. That left Hubenak two more chances inside the final 2 minutes. The Cardinals batted down a pass, then Hubenak was incomplete throwing into the end zone. The Aggies lost their second straight overall and snapped a four-game bowl winning streak. Aggies wide receiver Josh Reynolds set Music City Bowl records with 11 catches for 177 yards. Louisville linebacker Devonte Fields had three sacks, and Louisville safety Josh Harvey-Clemons stripped Hubenak of the ball and intercepted a pass -- both in the third quarter. Jackson had no such issues as he passed Stefan LeFors' previous career rushing mark of 756 yards between 2002 and 2004. He showed off the speed that Petrino wants to bring to the Atlantic Coast Conference, running through, around and over the Aggies. The Louisville Quarterback set a bowl rushing record, topping the 187 yards Marion Barber had for Minnesota had in 2004. He also set the total offense mark, topping the 424 set by Mike Glennon of North Carolina State in 2012. Jackson also became the third Quarterback to run and throw for at least 200 yards in a bowl game, joining Vince Young in 2006 and Johnny Manziel in 2012. Louisville senior linebacker James Burgess' career ended on the Cardinals' first defensive play of the game. He was flagged, then ejected for targeting Texas A&M wide receiver Damion Ratley on a hit that left both the receiver and Cardinals cornerback Shaq Wiggins on the ground for a few minutes. He didn't return until late in the first quarter with a strained lower back. Aggies defensive end Myles Garrett, who came in leading the SEC in sacks, had a quiet night aside from one sack, giving him a career-high 12 1/2 for the season.

2015 Holiday Bowl

The 2015 Holiday Bowl was played on December 30, 2015 at Qualcomm Stadium in San Diego, California. The 38th edition of the Holiday Bowl was telecast on ESPN (also on ESPN Radio).

Teams - This was the seventh overall meeting between these two teams, with USC leading the series 6–0 before this game. The last time these two teams met was in 1966 when #5 USC defeated the unranked Badgers 38-3 in a regular season non-conference game.

2015 Holiday Bowl	Line	1	-	2	-	3	-	4	-	Final
USC	(-3.5)	0	-	7	-	7	-	7	-	21
#23 Wisconsin	(50.0)	0	-	13	-	7	-	3	-	23

Scoring Summary
Wisconsin - Gaglianone 38 yard Field goal
Wisconsin - Clement 6 yard run (Gaglianone kick)
USC - Davis 1 yard run (Wood kick)
Wisconsin - Gaglianone 33 yard Field goal
Wisconsin - Traylor 4 yard pass from Stave (Gaglianone kick)
USC - Davis 1 yard run (Wood kick)
USC - Rogers 7 yard pass from Kessler (Wood kick)
Wisconsin - Gaglianone 29 yard Field goal

Associated Press Holiday Bowl Game Summary - After more than six decades, the Wisconsin Badgers have finally beaten the Southern California Trojans. Rafael Gaglianone kicked a 29-yard field goal with 2:27 left to lift No. 23 Wisconsin to a 23-21 victory against Southern California in the Holiday Bowl on Wednesday night. Gaglianone's third field goal gave Wisconsin (10-3) its first win in seven tries against USC (8-6). The teams hadn't met since 1966, and two of USC's wins in the series were in the Rose Bowl, in 1953 and 1963. Wisconsin's Sojourn Shelton intercepted Cody Kessler with 1:44 left. Kessler was hit from behind by Cichy. In the third quarter, Cichy sacked Kessler on three straight plays. The Trojans got to the 50 in the final seconds before Kessler threw four straight incompletions. USC, which beat Nebraska in last year's Holiday Bowl, had taken a 21-20 lead on Kessler's 7-yard touchdown pass to Darreus Rogers with 10:19 left. Kessler was flushed from the pocket but scrambled around. Rogers got open and made a leaping catch. Gaglianone also had field goals of 28 and 33 yards. Wisconsin was in control for much of the game. Corey Clement scored on a 6-yard run midway through the second quarter for a 10-0 lead. Joel Stave threw a 4-yard scoring pass to tight end Austin Traylor for a 20-7 lead midway through the third quarter. The Trojans gained some momentum with Justin Davis' second TD run of the game, with 5:34 left in the third quarter. On USC's next possession, Cichy broke through to sack Kessler three straight times, for a total loss of 24 yards. Davis' first TD was a 1-yard dive over the top on fourth down in the second quarter. That drive was kept alive on a 34-yard pass from Cody Kessler to Adoree' Jackson on fourth-and-4 from the 36. Kessler was 18 of 32 for 221 yards. Stave was 18 of 27 for 217 yards.

2015 Chick-Fil-A Peach Bowl

The 2015 Peach Bowl was played on December 31, 2015 at the Georgia Dome in Atlanta, Georgia. The 48th Peach Bowl is one of the New Year's Eve bowl games. The game was televised on ESPN and ESPN Deportes, and broadcast on ESPN Radio and XM Satellite Radio.

Background - Florida State had started the season 6–0 before a loss to Georgia Tech on the final play of the game dropped them from #9 to #17 ranked. A loss to then ranked #3 ranked Clemson curtailed hopes for Atlantic Division title hopes in the Atlantic Coast Conference. This was the Seminoles' first Peach Bowl since 2010. Houston, in their first year under newly hired Tom Herman, raced off to a 10–0 start and a #13 ranking, but a loss to Connecticut opened a chance for Navy to swoop in and win the division title. However, the Cougars beat the Midshipmen handily to win the West Division and qualify for the first-ever American Athletic Conference championship game. Their victory over Temple the following week gave Houston their first conference title since 2006. Since the Cougars were the highest ranked "Group of Five" ranked team, they were selected to play in the Peach Bowl. This was their first major bowl appearance since the 1985 Cotton Bowl Classic.

2015 Chick-Fil-A Peach Bowl	Line	1	-	2	-	3	-	4	-	Final
#14 Houston	(56.5)	7	-	14	-	0	-	17	-	38
#9 Florida State	(-7.5)	3	-	0	-	7	-	14	-	24

Scoring Summary
Houston - Ward 7 yard run (Cummings kick)
Florida State - Aguayo 20 yard Field goal
Houston - Allen 20 yard pass from Ayers (Cummings kick)
Houston - Ward 6 yard run (Cummings kick)
Florida State - Cook 1 yard run (Aguayo kick)
Houston - Cummings 39 yard Field goal
Florida State - Rudolph 65 yard pass from Maguire (Aguayo kick)
Houston - Allen 17 yard pass from Ward (Cummings kick)
Florida State - Wilson 14 yard pass from Maguire (Aguayo kick)
Houston - Jackson 2 yard run (Cummings kick)

Game notes - Houston's 13th win of the season was also Houston's 13th win all time against Florida State. Houston is 13-2-2 all-time against Florida State

Associated Press Peach Bowl Game Summary - Greg Ward Jr. and the Houston Cougars showed they could thrive in a big-game atmosphere against a big-name opponent. Ward ran for two touchdowns and threw for another, leading Houston past turnover-plagued Florida State 38-24 in the Peach Bowl on Thursday. Florida State, which won the national championship two years ago, was favored by seven points. Florida State's Sean Maguire, who was carted off the field with a sprained left ankle late in the first quarter, returned but threw four interceptions. Dalvin Cook was held to 33 yards rushing with a touchdown and a lost fumble. That left the Seminoles with five turnovers -- half their total of 10 in 12 regular-season games. Houston scored the most points allowed by Florida State this season. The No. 9 Seminoles (10-3), who trailed 21-3 at halftime, tried to rally with two fourth-quarter touchdown passes by Maguire. Fisher said X-rays showed no structural damage to Maguire's ankle. Maguire said the injury "limited some stuff, but it was fine." Ward threw for 238 yards and ran for 67 yards for No. 14 Houston (13-1). Houston safety Trevon Stewart and cornerback William Jackson III each had two interceptions. Stewart recovered a fumble. Ward, the junior who started at wide receiver early last season before becoming a full-time Quarterback, had touchdown runs of 7 and 6 yards. He left the game briefly after taking a hit in the third quarter and was shaken up again with about 4 minutes remaining. Ward returned to take the final snaps of the game, raising his arm in celebration before laying on his back, wallowing in the confetti which fell from the Georgia Dome roof. He was named offensive MVP of the game. Houston backup Quarterback Kyle Postma's 29-yard run set up Ryan Jackson's game-clinching 2-yard touchdown run with about 2 minutes left. Ward completed 25 of 41 passes with one touchdown and one interception. Houston's only loss this season, to Connecticut, came when Ward was out with an injury. He kept the Florida State defense off-balance by leading the Cougars' fast-tempo, no-huddle attack. Maguire's 65-yard scoring pass to Travis Rudolph cut Houston's lead to 24-17 early in the fourth quarter. Ward answered with a 17-yard touchdown pass to Chance Allen, who was left uncovered as Florida State sent a defensive back on a blitz. Maguire added a scoring pass to Jesus Wilson later in the final quarter. Maguire was hurt in the first quarter when hit by Adams. Maguire couldn't put pressure on his left leg as he was supported by trainers before leaving the field on a cart. When Maguire was out, backup J.J. Cosentino completed only 1 of 4 passes for 5 yards. Maguire returned midway through the second quarter with the ankle wrapped. The Seminoles were without Quarterback Everett Golson, the Notre Dame transfer who began the season as the starter but was away from the team for the bowl game for personal reasons. Maguire's last interception came with 25 seconds remaining. He completed 22 of 44 passes for 392 yards with two touchdowns and four interceptions. The Cougars won 13 games for the second time in school history, following the 2011 season.

2015 Orange Bowl (CFP National Semifinal)

The 2015 Capital One Orange Bowl was played on December 31, 2015 at Sun Life Stadium in Miami Gardens, Florida. The 82nd Orange Bowl was a College Football Playoff semifinal with the winner of the game competing against the winner of the 2015 Cotton Bowl: Alabama Crimson Tide football in the 2016 College Football Playoff National Championship, which will take place at University of Phoenix Stadium in Glendale, Arizona. This was the fifth overall meeting between these two teams, with the series tied 2–2. The game was a rematch of the previous year's Russell Athletic Bowl, which Clemson won 40–6. The game was televised on ESPN and ESPN Deportes, and broadcast on ESPN Radio and XM Satellite Radio.

Clemson - Clemson began the season ranked number 12, and to kick off the season, won their first 3 games. In their 4th game, they faced the undefeated and 6th ranked Notre Dame Fighting Irish, with both teams having playoff aspirations. Despite leading for most of the game, the game came down to a key 2 point conversion stop by Clemson, essentially sealing the game for the Tigers. The Tigers then won 4 more games to finally reach the number 1 ranking in all the polls, just in time for a huge matchup with the defending ACC Champions, the Florida State Seminoles. Despite losing for most of the first half, Clemson came back in the 2nd half to win the game, 23-13. The Tigers then won the rest of their games, including a matchup with North Carolina in the ACC Championship game. Clemson won the game 45-37, to give Clemson their first ACC Championship since 2011.

Oklahoma - Oklahoma began their season ranked number 19 in the preseason poll, but they won their first 4 games to rise to number 10 in the polls. In their 5th game, they were matched against Texas, a team that was currently 1-4 and unranked. Oklahoma, despite being huge favorites, were stunned by the Longhorns 24-17, which dropped them to 4-1 and lowered their ranking to 19. Oklahoma responded strong to the loss, churning out 4 straight wins before looking at an extremely tough 3 game stretch which included the undefeated Baylor Bears, the 1 loss TCU Horned Frogs, and the undefeated Oklahoma State Cowboys. First off, they had to go up against the number 4 ranked Baylor Bears. They beat them, 44-34, and rose to the number 7 spot in the polls. Then they had to play the number 11 ranked TCU Horned Frogs. Oklahoma dominated for most of the game, and even led 30-13 in the 4th Quarter. However, TCU mounted a furious comeback and had nearly tied the game up at 30, down 1, when TCU coach Gary Patterson decided to go for 2 at the end of the game. TCU was unable to convert the 2 point conversion, and Oklahoma survived. Then they had to play the undefeated Oklahoma State Cowboys, who had serious championship aspirations. However, Oklahoma destroyed their in-state rivals 58-23, and clinched the Big 12 Title.

2015 Orange Bowl	Line	1	-	2	-	3	-	4	-	Final
#4 Oklahoma	(-3.5)	7	-	10	-	0	-	0	-	17
#1 Clemson	(62.5)	3	-	13	-	14	-	7	-	37

Scoring Summary
Oklahoma - Perine 1 yard run (Seibert kick)
Clemson - Huegel 26 yard Field goal
Clemson - Watson 5 yard run (Huegel kick)
Clemson - Huegel 36 yard Field goal
Oklahoma - Seibert 22 yard Field goal
Clemson - Huegel 43 yard Field goal
Oklahoma - Andrews 11 yard pass from Mayfield (Seibert kick)
Clemson - Gallman 1 yard run (Huegel kick)
Clemson - Renfrow 35 yard pass from Watson (Huegel kick)
Clemson - Gallman 4 yard run (Huegel kick)

Capital One Orange Bowl Game Summary - After giving away momentum and trailing 17-16 at halftime, No. 1 Clemson roared back in the second half, shutting out No. 4 Oklahoma, and beating the Sooners 37-17 in the Capital One Orange Bowl and advancing to the national championship game. The Tigers (14-0) will be playing for their first national championship since they won it in 1981 with 22-15 victory over Nebraska in the 1982 Orange Bowl. Oklahoma, who had a seven-game winning streak snapped, finished 12-2 before a crowd of 67,615 at Sun Life Stadium. Clemson, who beat Oklahoma 40-6 in the 2014 Russell Athletic Bowl, will play Alabama, a 38-0 winner over Michigan State, in Glendale, Ariz. on Jan. 11. The Tigers become the eighth team to enter the national championship game with 14 wins. Five of those teams have won the title, but none of them have finished with 15 wins. Clemson's offense led by Quarterback Deshaun Watson and running back Wayne Gallman rolled by 533 yards on Oklahoma's defense. Watson, the game's Most Outstanding Player, had 145 yards in 24 carries rushing with a 5-yard touchdown and completed 16 of 30 passes for 187 yards with a 35-yard touchdown pass to Hunter Renfrow. Watson's rushing yards and attempts were Orange Bowl records for a Quarterback. Gallman rushed for 150 yards in 26 carries with touchdowns of 1 and 4 yards. He had 111 yards on 19 carries in the second half. The Tigers finished 530 yards on offense and outgained the Sooners 225 to 121 yards in the second half. Greg Huegel kicked field goal of 26, 36 and 43 yards to complete Clemson's scoring and set a school record for field goal in a season at 25. Oklahoma Quarterback Baker Mayfield completed 26 of 41 for 311 yards with and 11-yard pass to Mark Andrews, but he also had two interceptions. Samaje Perine led the OU rushers with 58 yards on 11 carries and 1-yard touchdown. Trailing 17-16 with 1:29 left in the half, Clemson didn't back down. The Tigers drove to the Sooners' 15. On third down, Watson tried to hit tight end Jordan Leggett in the back of the end zone. Oklahoma's Zack Sanchez outfought the taller Leggett and intercepted the pass leaving the Sooners with the halftime lead. Clemson took the second half kickoff, much like Oklahoma did to start the game, and drove 75 yards in 12 plays with Gallman running 1 yard for a 23-17 lead after only 4:09 had elapsed. Oklahoma drove to the Clemson 30 one possession later where it faced a fourth down. There, Coach Bob Stoops gambled and gave the ball to Perine, and he was stopped by Kendall Joseph. From there, it was downhill for the Sooners. Clemson scored two more times as Watson threw 35 yards to Renfrow who beat Steven Parker, and Gallman ran 4 yards for the final score. Based on the game's opening possession, it looked as if Oklahoma might have a big offensive day. The Sooners took the kickoff and went 75 yards in 10 plays with Perine gaining 33 yards in 5 carries including the final 1-yard touchdown run. Following a 24-yard punt by Oklahoma's Austin Seibert, Clemson went 19 yards in 9 plays but settled for a 26-yard Huegel field goal, cutting the deficit to 7-3. Oklahoma's next three possessions were halted by a 14-yard sack of Mayfield by Shaq Lawson, a 15-yard unsportsmanlike conduct penalty on Dimitri Flowers, and a 7-yard sack of Mayfield by Ben Boulware and Richard Yeargin. Clemson rewarded its defense by scoring on three straight possessions. The momentum turned on a fourth and 4 play from the OU 44 when punter Andy Teasdall completed a 31-yard pass to defensive tackle Christian Wilkins. Two plays later, Watson scored on a 5-yard run and 10-7 lead. The last time Teasdall tried a fake punt was against North Carolina in the ACC Championship game, but it was not called then. Swinney left Teasdall on the bench at halftime to consider his decision, but he obviously did not lose confidence in his punter's throwing ability. Huegel added field goals of 36 and 43 yards for a 16-10 lead with 2:17 left before halftime. This time, Oklahoma answered by going 67 yards in 10 plays for a 22-yard Seibert field goal pulling to within 16-10. Mayfield's 19-yard pass to Sterling Shepard on third and 4 from the Clemson 23 was the big play. On its next possession, the Sooners retook the lead on Mayfield's 11-yard pass to Andrews completing a 4 play, 76-yard drive. The big play was a 42-yard pass from Mayfield to Westbrook who beat Cordrea Tankersley. Clemson drove to the Oklahoma 15, but Watson's interception prevented the Tigers from taking the lead. It was one of several times when the offense didn't get touchdowns in the red zone, only this time it was a turnover, not a field goal that ended their hopes. Still, it set up what was coming in the second half.

2015 Cotton Bowl Classic (December) (CFP National Semifinal)

The 2015 Cotton Bowl Classic was played on December 31, 2015 at AT&T Stadium in Arlington, Texas. The 80th Cotton Bowl Classic was a College Football Playoff semifinal with the winner of this game competing against Clemson, the winner of the 2015 Orange Bowl in the 2016 College Football Playoff National Championship, which will take place at University of Phoenix Stadium in Glendale, Arizona. The game was broadcast on ESPN, ESPN Deportes, ESPN Radio and XM Satellite Radio.

2015 Cotton Bowl Classic	Line	1	-	2	-	3	-	4	-	Final
#3 Michigan State	(45.5)	0	-	0	-	0	-	0	-	0
#2 Alabama	(-10.0)	0	-	10	-	21	-	7	-	38

Scoring Summary
Alabama - Henry 1 yard run (Griffith kick)
Alabama - Griffith 47 yard Field goal
Alabama - Ridley 6 yard pass from Coker (Griffith kick)
Alabama - Jones 57 yard punt return (Griffith kick)
Alabama - Ridley 50 yard pass from Coker (Griffith kick)
Alabama - Henry 11 yard run (Griffith kick)

Associated Press Cotton Bowl Game Summary - The loss still stung. It burned Alabama so badly to be beaten in the College Football Playoff semifinals last season that the Crimson Tide were determined to handle business differently this time around. The players said they were more focused and promised to be more prepared, more precise in their execution and more relentless in their effort. Nick Saban said he saw something in his team going into the College Football Playoff semifinal at the Goodyear Cotton Bowl Classic that he had never seen before. Michigan State claimed it was ready for a 15-round brawl, but the Tide knocked out the Spartans early on Thursday night like a nonconference cupcake. No. 2 Alabama 38, No. 3 Michigan State 0. It was the largest shutout in Cotton Bowl history. Alabama (13-1) will face No. 1 Clemson (14-0) on Jan. 11 in Arizona looking for its fourth national title in nine seasons under Saban, who improved to 9-0 against his former assistants, with all nine wins coming by double digits. The Tide took it but not the way they had done for so much of this season -- at least offensively. Instead of pounding away at a Michigan State defense that was stacked to stop Heisman Trophy winner Derrick Henry from running wild, Alabama aired it out. Jake Coker played the game of his career, including connecting with Calvin Ridley for two touchdowns and going 25-for-30 for a career-best 286 yards. Conventional wisdom on beating Alabama was to take away the run and make Coker, the promising Florida State transfer who sat on the bench most of last season, win the game. Clemson might have to come up with a new plan. The Tide looked like a team with no weaknesses against overmatched Michigan State (12-2). The freshman Ridley was brilliant, streaking by defenders on deep throws and outfighting them on jump balls. He caught eight passes for 138 yards. Jonathan Allen and the ferocious Tide defensive front sacked Connor Cook four times and allowed the Spartans only one trip into the red zone -- which ended with Cyrus Jones intercepting a pass at the goal line. Jones added a high-stepping 57-yard punt return touchdown for the Tide, who hardly even had to use the 242-pound Henry. He ran 20 times for 75 yards and scored two touchdowns. The last made it 38-0 halfway through the fourth quarter. The celebration at that point was pretty tame on the Alabama sideline.

The Bama fans were having fun, though. They broke out the "S-E-C!" chant and sang along to "Sweet Home Alabama" with that familiar "Roll, Tide, Roll!" AT&T Stadium in North Texas had turned into Tuscaloosa West. Alabama won twice this season on the Dallas Cowboys' home field, with the first win coming in a season-opening 35-17 victory over Wisconsin. The Cowboys are currently 1-6 at home. The Tide are the only team to be playing in the College Football Playoff each of its first two seasons. Last season, the Crimson Tide couldn't get past the semifinals, upset by Ohio State in the Allstate Sugar Bowl. Heading into another game as big favorites against the Big Ten champions, the Tide players said all week that their focus was better and their attitude more serious. The Tide players talked about how some players were too concerned about where they would be drafted or partying on Bourbon Street last season. In chilly Dallas, there was nothing to do but practice, and that was fine by them. The players set the curfews this week. In by midnight the first two days in town and by 11 p.m. the last two. Michigan State embraced its role as the underdog and came in expecting to slug it out with the Tide. The Spartans' offensive line watched video of the 1971 Ali-Frazier fight to prepare. Alabama broke through in the second quarter by going deep to Ridley for 50 yards to the 1. Running behind the blocks of defensive linemen A'Shawn Robinson and Jarran Reed, Henry punched it in for his SEC-record breaking 24th touchdown, and with 5:36 left in the first half, it was 7-0 Tide. It felt like more. It would only get worse. It was Alabama at its best, and it looked downright terrifying to be on the other end.

Chapter 2 – 2016-2020
2016 Outback Bowl

The 2016 Outback Bowl was played on January 1, 2016, at Raymond James Stadium in Tampa, Florida. It was the 30th edition of the Outback Bowl (previously called the Hall of Fame Bowl), featuring the #13 Northwestern Wildcats from the Big Ten and the #23 Tennessee Volunteers from the SEC. It was televised on ESPN2. It was sponsored by the Outback Steakhouse restaurant franchise.

Series history - In their only series game, the 1997 Florida Citrus Bowl, Tennessee won 48–28.

2016 Outback Bowl	Line	1	-	2	-	3	-	4	-	Final
#12 Northwestern	(48.5)	0	-	6	-	0	-	0	-	6
Tennessee	(-9.5)	7	-	10	-	7	-	21	-	45

Scoring Summary
Tennessee - Dobbs 14 yard run (Medley kick)
Tennessee - Medley 35 yard Field goal
Northwestern - Jackson 5 yard run (Kick failed)
Tennessee - Kamara 11 yard run (Medley kick)
Tennessee - Hurd 3 yard run (Medley kick)
Tennessee - Dobbs 18 yard run (Medley kick)
Tennessee - Kelly 1 yard run (Medley kick)
Tennessee - Berry 100 yard interception return (Medley kick)

Associated Press Outback Bowl Game Summary - The architect of Tennessee's resurgence won't be happy until the Volunteers are perennial championship contenders again. Butch Jones, nevertheless, is proud of the progress the Vols have made in his three seasons as coach and confident the program is on solid footing as it moves into 2016. Friday's 45-6 victory over No. 12 Northwestern in the Outback Bowl not only capped Tennessee's best season in eight years but showcased some of the young talent that gives the Vols a chance to keep climbing. Joshua Dobbs threw for 166 yards and ran for two touchdowns, while Outback MVP Jalen Hurd rushed for 130 yards and one TD for the Vols (9-4), who finished with at least nine wins for the first time since 2007. Evan Berry put a punctuation mark on the team's sixth consecutive win by returning one of Tennessee's four interceptions 100 yards for a TD in the closing seconds. Northwestern (10-3) sputtered offensively and was unable to keep up the stronger, faster Vols defensively in falling short on a bid to finish with a school-record 11 victories. Dobbs completed 14 of 25 passes. The dual-threat Quarterback ran 12 times for 48 yards, including a highlight-reel burst around right end in which he dove for his second TD after picking up a bobbled snap and tight-roping his way up the sideline to make it 31-6 early in the fourth quarter. Hurd scored on 3-yard run in the third quarter and, despite playing with a sore hamstring, became the first Tennessee player to top 100 yards rushing in two bowl games. The 6-foot-4, 240-pound sophomore ran for 122 yards in the Vols' victory over Iowa in last year's Taxslayer Bowl. The 100-yard performance was the ninth of Hurd's career, sixth this season. Both teams ended the regular season on five-game winning streaks, Tennessee finishing strong after a 3-4 start that included losses to Alabama, Oklahoma, Florida and Arkansas by a combined 17 points and Northwestern rebounding from lopsided Big Ten losses to Michigan and Iowa in consecutive weeks in October. The Vols won the only previous meeting between the schools, 48-28 in the 1997 Florida Citrus Bowl. They improved to 3-1 in the Outback, where Tennessee beat Boston College on Jan. 1. 1993 and Wisconsin to finish with a 10-4 record eight years ago -- the last time the Vols appeared in the SEC championship game and won at least nine games. Northwestern's Clayton Thorson, one of just eight freshmen in the Football Bowl Subdivision since 2008 to lead his team to 10 wins, was 8 of 20 passing for 57 yards and two interceptions. The Wildcats, whose three losses came by a combined score of 123-16, were outgained 420 yards to 261. Justin Jackson averaged over 5 yards per carry in rushing for 74 yards and one TD, a 5-yard run that finished a 12-play, 75-yard drive in the second quarter to trim Tennessee's lead to 10-6. The Wildcats missed the extra point, and it was pretty much downhill from there.

2016 Buffalo Wild Wings Citrus Bowl

The 2016 Citrus Bowl was held on January 1, 2016 at the Orlando Citrus Bowl in Orlando, Florida. The 70th edition was televised by ABC. It was sponsored by the Buffalo Wild Wings restaurant franchise and is officially known as the Buffalo Wild Wings Citrus Bowl.

Teams - The game featured the Michigan Wolverines of the Big Ten Conference, and the Florida Gators of the Southeastern Conference in their third meeting against each other, with all three matchups coming in January bowl games in Florida.

2016 Buffalo Wild Wings Citrus Bowl	Line	1	-	2	-	3	-	4	-	Final
#18 Michigan	(-3.5)	7	-	10	-	14	-	10	-	41
#17 Florida	(40.0)	7	-	0	-	0	-	0	-	7

Scoring Summary
Michigan - Johnson 4 yard run (Allen kick)
Florida - Harris 2 yard pass from Callaway (MacInnes kick)
Michigan - Chesson 31 yard pass from Rudock (Allen kick)
Michigan - Allen 21 yard Field goal
Michigan - Perry 3 yard pass from Rudock (Allen kick)
Michigan - Houma 2 yard run (Allen kick)
Michigan - Johnson 8 yard pass from Rudock (Allen kick)
Michigan - Allen 25 yard Field goal

Associated Press Citrus Bowl Game Summary - Michigan and Florida's Buffalo Wild Wings Citrus Bowl matchup was supposed to play out as an evenly matched struggle between two of the top defenses from the Big Ten and Southeastern Conference. Someone forgot to tell the Wolverines. Jake Rudock threw for 278 yards and three touchdowns and Michigan's defense dominated throughout in the No. 14 Wolverines' 41-7 victory over No. 19 Florida on Friday in the Citrus Bowl. There were some questions surrounding how effective Rudock would be after being knocked out of Michigan's regular-season finale against Ohio State with a left shoulder injury. He dismissed any notions about his health almost immediately in the Wolverines' first bowl victory since 2012. Michigan (10-3) had three touchdown drives of at least 70 yards and finished with 503 yards of offense against a Florida defense that entered the game ranked sixth nationally. Rudock credited the coaching staff's game plan and scouting efforts with putting him and his teammates in optimum situations. He also had lots of support on the ground from tailback De'Veon Smith, who finished with 109 yards rushing and two scores. Leading by 10 at the half, Michigan scored on each of its first two possessions in the third quarter to take a 31-7 lead. Michigan's defense played without safety Jabrill Peppers, who sat out with an undisclosed injury. But the Wolverines didn't miss him, holding the Gators (10-4) to 28 total yards in the second half. Florida Quarterback Treon Harris had his moments early. But he also had a costly interception in the end zone late in the first half that stifled the Gators' attempt to stay in the game. Michigan took a 17-7 lead into halftime thanks largely to the efficiency of the Wolverines passing attack. Michigan's receivers did a great job creating lanes for Rudock to throw to and ran crisp routes to open up deep-play opportunities. The best example was on Rudock's 31-yard touchdown pass to Jehu Chesson early in the second quarter that put Michigan up 14-7. Chesson used a double move, initially faking an inside slant, to strand and separate from cornerback Vernon Hargreaves III. Despite some unsteady outings to end the regular season, Harris managed the Gators' offense well for most of the first half. Florida seemed poised to keep pace early on, tying the game at 7 in the first quarter with an efficient eight-play, 75-yard drive. The series was capped with a fake reverse pass from receiver Antonio Callaway to Harris. But on the series following Chesson's touchdown, Harris made a poor decision while getting chased toward the sideline, tossing a third-down pass from just outside the red zone into a crowded end zone. The pass was intercepted by Jarrod Wilson. The Wolverines drove down on the next series and added a field goal to extend their lead to 10.

2016 Fiesta Bowl

The 2016 Fiesta Bowl was played on January 1, 2016 at University of Phoenix Stadium in Glendale, Arizona. The 44th Fiesta Bowl was one of the New Year's Bowls of the College Football Playoff. The game was televised on ESPN and ESPN Deportes, and broadcast on ESPN Radio and XM Satellite Radio. Coincidentally, it took place 10 years after the 2006 Fiesta Bowl, which was also played by Ohio State and Notre Dame. That was also the last time Notre Dame participated in the Fiesta Bowl.

2016 Fiesta Bowl	Line	1	-	2	-	3	-	4	-	Final
#8 Notre Dame	(57.0)	0	-	14	-	7	-	7	-	28
#7 Ohio State	(-4.5)	14	-	14	-	7	-	9	-	44

Scoring Summary
Ohio State – Elliot 2 yard run (Nuernberger kick)
Ohio State – Thomas 15 yard pass from Barrett (Nuernberger kick)
Notre Dame – Adams 3 yard run (Yoon kick)
Ohio State – Elliot 1 yard run (Nuernberger kick)
Ohio State – Elliot 1 yard run (Nuernberger kick)
Notre Dame – Kizer 1 yard run (Yoon kick)
Notre Dame – Brown 4 yard pass from Kizer (Yoon kick)
Ohio State – Elliot 47 yard run (Nuernberger kick)
Ohio State – Nuernberger 37 yard Field goal

Notre Dame – Fuller 81 yard pass from Kizer (Yoon kick)
Ohio State – Nuernberger 38 yard Field goal
Ohio State – Nuernberger 35 yard Field goal

Associated Press Fiesta Bowl Game Summary - Ezekiel Elliott bulldozed his way into the end zone in the first half, showing off his strength as Ohio State's drive capper. He flashed his speed in the second, becoming the showstopper as he raced up the middle for a long run. Those skills should translate well in the NFL. They certainly worked out for the Buckeyes over the past three seasons. Notre Dame overcame injuries all season to reach the Fiesta Bowl. But against an elite Ohio State team, the bad luck finally caught up to the Irish. Elliott ran for 149 yards and matched a Fiesta Bowl record with four touchdowns to close the curtain on his college career, sparking No. 7 Ohio State's prolific offense in a 44-28 win over No. 8 Notre Dame on Friday. The Buckeyes (12-1) were left out of the College Football Playoff thanks to an inopportune loss. They might leave the desert wondering what could have been after blowing past another late-season playoff contender. Ohio State rolled past the Fighting Irish (10-3) in the BattleFrog Fiesta Bowl, quick hitting its way to one scoring drive after another and 496 total yards. Elliott, who's leaving school early for the NFL, scored on three short runs in the first half and left Notre Dame defenders flailing as he raced past them for a 47-yard score to open the second. J.T. Barrett gave the Buckeyes some balance, throwing for 211 yards and a score with 96 yards rushing in the highest-scoring game against Notre Dame's defense this season. Ohio State's seniors finished 50-4, tying the Football Bowl Subdivision record set by Boise State's 2011 class for most wins in a four-year span. The Fighting Irish had some good offensive moments behind DeShone Kizer after Buckeyes star defensive end Joey Bosa was ejected for targeting in the first quarter. They just couldn't keep up with the blistering Buckeyes after a string of injuries, including losing do-everything linebacker Jaylon Smith to a knee injury in the first quarter. Notre Dame missed its CFP chance by four points -- two-point losses to Clemson and Stanford. Ohio State lost to Michigan State in its penultimate game and had to watch the Spartans join fellow one-loss teams Alabama and Oklahoma in the playoff. Those just-misses turned the Fiesta Bowl into a talent show, with NFL-caliber players dotting rosters from both teams. Two of the best players were gone before the first quarter ended. Smith, the Butkus Award winner as the nation's best linebacker, had to be helped off four minutes in after suffering what Kelly said was a significant leg injury. Bosa, projected as a top-10 NFL draft pick, was gone a few minutes later after driving the top of his helmet into the chest of Kizer, long after the Notre Dame Quarterback had released the ball. Ohio State had its way with Notre Dame's defense without Smith in the lineup, racing down the field for scores like a seven-on-seven drill. Elliott, another potential first-round pick, was the Buckeyes' punctuation mark, scoring on a pair of 1-yard runs and another from 2 yards. Barrett accounted for the other score, finding Michael Thomas on a 15-yard TD to put Ohio State up 28-14 at halftime. Elliott showed off his speed to open the second half, blurring through a hole for his 47-yard touchdown to match the Fiesta Bowl record set by Arizona State's Woody Green against Missouri in 1972. Notre Dame took advantage of Ohio State's Bosa-less defense a few times, although not enough to keep pace with the Buckeyes. Kizer was the key, moving the Irish down the field to set up a 3-yard touchdown run by Josh Adams and on another drive that he capped himself with a 1-yard score. It was his 10th rushing TD, most by a Notre Dame Quarterback in one season. Kizer connected with Chris Brown on a 4-yard touchdown pass to open the second half, pulling the Irish within a touchdown. After a quiet first three quarters, Will Fuller finally got a chance to show off his speed, using a quick move to create space before racing off on an 81-yard touchdown. The second-longest TD reception in Fiesta Bowl history pulled the Fighting Irish within 38-28, but they got no closer. Kizer threw for 284 yards and two touchdowns on 22-of-37 passing but had an interception and lost a fumble.

2016 Rose Bowl

The 2016 Rose Bowl was played on January 1, 2016 at the Rose Bowl stadium in Pasadena, California. This 102nd Rose Bowl Game matched the Big Ten Conference West Division champion Iowa Hawkeyes against the Pac-12 Conference champion Stanford Cardinal. Stanford defeated Iowa 45–16 to win the Lathrop K. Leishman trophy. The contest was televised on ESPN with a radio broadcast on ESPN Radio and XM Satellite Radio. The Pasadena Tournament of Roses Association was the organizer of the game. The Rose Bowl Game was a contractual sell-out, with 64,500 tickets allocated to the participating teams and conferences. The remaining tickets are distributed to the Tournament of Roses members, sponsors, City of Pasadena residents, and the general public. Ticket prices were $150 and $185.

Iowa - The Iowa Hawkeyes, as the Big Ten West Division Champions, were back in the Rose Bowl after 25 years, last appearing in the 1991 Rose Bowl. Their last win in Pasadena was against the California Bears, 38–12 in the 1959 Rose Bowl. Prior to the 2016 Rose Bowl, they were 2–3 in Rose Bowl games. In the 2015 season, the team was nearly undefeated before the Rose Bowl, losing only the Big Ten Championship Game to Michigan State 16–13. Iowa wore its black jerseys.

Stanford - The Stanford Cardinal, 11-2 (8-1 in conference), were playing their fifteenth Rose Bowl game (and their third Rose Bowl Game in four years) by winning the Pac-12 Championship Game over USC 41–22. Prior to the 2016 Rose Bowl, they were 6–7–1 in Rose Bowl games, last winning over Wisconsin 20–14 in 2013. They lost the 2014 Rose Bowl to Michigan State 20–24. Stanford wore its white jerseys.

2016 Rose Bowl	Line	1	-	2	-	3	-	4	-	Final
#5 Stanford	(-6.0)	21	-	14	-	3	-	7	-	45
#6 Iowa	(51.5)	0	-	0	-	3	-	13	-	16

Scoring Summary
Stanford – McCaffrey 75 yard pass from Hogan (Ukropina kick)
Stanford – Hogan 8 yard run (Ukropina kick)
Stanford – Meeks 66 yard interception return (Ukropina kick)
Stanford – McCaffrey 63 yard punt return (Ukropina kick)
Stanford – Rector 31 yard pass from Hogan (Ukropina kick)
Stanford – Ukropina 31 yard Field goal
Iowa – Koehn 39 yard Field goal
Iowa – VandeBerg 31 yard pass from Beathard (Koehn kick)
Iowa – Wadley 31 yard pass from Beathard (Koehn kick)
Stanford – Rector 42 yard pass from Hogan (Ukropina kick)

New records - 368 was the most all-purpose yards per game set by Christian McCaffrey of Stanford. Thirty five was the most points scored in the first half by Stanford in a Rose Bowl game.

Associated Press Rose Bowl Game Summary - Stanford barely missed out on the College Football Playoff, and Christian McCaffrey almost won the Heisman Trophy. McCaffrey and the mighty Cardinal didn't miss a thing in their Rose Bowl romp over Iowa. McCaffrey caught a 75-yard touchdown pass on the opening snap and returned a punt 66 yards for another score while setting the Rose Bowl record with 368 all-purpose yards, propelling No. 6 Stanford to a 45-16 victory against the No. 7 Hawkeyes on Friday. Kevin Hogan passed for 223 yards and three TDs in his final game for the Cardinal (12-2), who won the Rose Bowl for the second time in three trips over the past four years for this unlikely football powerhouse. McCaffrey was sublime in his debut at the Granddaddy of Them All, breaking the all-purpose yards record set by Wisconsin's Jared Abbrederis in 2012. McCaffrey finished second behind Alabama's Derrick Henry in the Heisman voting, but the speedy sophomore left no doubt about his brilliance with one of the most dynamic performances in the 102-game history of the Rose Bowl. He had 172 yards rushing, 105 yards receiving and 91 on kick returns, putting an appropriate cap on the season in which he set the NCAA record for all-purpose yards. McCaffrey also became the first player ever to rack up more than 100 yards rushing and 100 yards receiving in a Rose Bowl. Stanford and Iowa finished in the final two spots outside the College Football Playoff field, but the Cardinal showed they belong among the best with their 12th win in their final 13 games. With a powerful offensive line and a sturdy defense, they also ruined the first trip to Pasadena in 25 years for the Hawkeyes (12-2), who followed up their remarkable 12-0 regular season with two postseason losses. C.J. Beathard passed for 239 yards and two fourth-quarter touchdowns for the Hawkeyes, whose thousands of fans proudly filling the venerable stadium with old gold and black. The faithful had painfully little to cheer after Iowa fell behind in the opening seconds, putting a daylong damper on Kirk Ferentz's first Rose Bowl after 17 years as a head coach. Just 11 seconds in, Hogan hit McCaffrey with a TD pass down the middle. After Hogan rushed for an 8-yard score and Quenton Meeks returned an interception 66 yards for another TD, the Cardinal had the highest-scoring first quarter in the Rose Bowl's lengthy history. The rout was really on after McCaffrey's 63-yard TD return in the opening minute of the second, and Stanford comfortably sat on its 35-point halftime lead while improving to 7-7-1 in the Rose Bowl in school history. Michael Rector caught two touchdown passes for Stanford, which reigned atop the Pac-12 and conquered the Rose Bowl again with Coach David Shaw's brand of simple, powerful football. That style has led to a renaissance for Stanford, which beat Wisconsin in the 2013 Rose Bowl and lost to Michigan State two years ago in the 100th edition. Hogan became the third Quarterback to start three Rose Bowls, but he hadn't thrown a TD pass in the game until he hit McCaffrey over the middle on the opening snap. It was the second-longest TD pass in Rose Bowl history and the longest play given up all season by the stingy Iowa defense. Hogan then showed off his elusiveness on a TD run to cap a 74-yard drive, and Meeks erased Iowa's first solid drive with a TD interception return down the Stanford sideline. Iowa had never trailed by more than seven points at any point in its magical season, which included the first 12-0 start in school history before a narrow loss to Michigan State in the Big Ten title game. McCaffrey then took a return through the heart of Iowa's coverage unit, juking Iowa linebacker Josey Jewell on the way to his first TD on a punt return this season. Stanford even got creative — or cruel, depending on your perspective. Hogan appeared to fake a fumble in the second quarter before popping up and throwing to an untouched

Rector for a 31-yard score making it 35-0 at halftime. Iowa avoided a shutout on Marshall Koehn's 39-yard field goal late in the third quarter, prompting huge cheers and a confetti shower from the Hawkeyes' band. Matt VandeBerg and Akrum Wadley caught Beathard's late scoring passes.

2016 Sugar Bowl

The 2016 Sugar Bowl was held on January 1, 2016 at the Mercedes-Benz Superdome in New Orleans, Louisiana. This 81st Sugar Bowl was televised on ESPN and ESPN Deportes, with a radio broadcast on ESPN Radio and XM Satellite Radio.

2016 Sugar Bowl	Line	1	-	2	-	3	-	4	-	Final
#16 Oklahoma State	(70.5)	3	-	3	-	7	-	7	-	20
#12 Mississippi	(-7.5)	10	-	24	-	7	-	7	-	48

Scoring Summary
Oklahoma State – Grogan 26 yard Field goal
Mississippi – Wunderlich 34 yard Field goal
Mississippi – Core 31 yard pass from Kelly (Wunderlich kick)
Mississippi – Treadwell 34 yard pass from Kelly (Wunderlich kick)
Mississippi – Treadwell 10 yard pass from Kelly (Wunderlich kick)
Mississippi – Wunderlich 38 yard Field goal
Oklahoma State – Grogan 31 yard Field goal
Mississippi – Tunsil 2 yard run (Wunderlich kick)
Mississippi – Wilkins 36 yard run (Wunderlich kick)
Oklahoma State – Walsh 2 yard run (Grogan kick)
Mississippi – Treadwell 14 yard pass from Kelly (Wunderlich kick)
Oklahoma State – Walsh 8 yard run (Grogan kick)

Associated Press Sugar Bowl Game Summary - Mississippi's Chad Kelly was throwing touchdown passes and Laquon Treadwell was catching them in the Allstate Sugar Bowl on Friday night. No surprise there. But that touchdown run by 305-pound left tackle Laremy Tunsil, who nimbly grabbed a lateral and jogged untouched into the end zone? That caught a few people off guard -- including an overwhelmed Oklahoma State defense that had no answer for the Rebels. Behind 375 total yards from Quarterback Chad Kelly, Ole Miss raced to a 48-20 win over Oklahoma State in the Allstate Sugar Bowl on Friday night. No. 12 Ole Miss cruised to a 48-20 victory over No. 16 Oklahoma State to help the Southeastern Conference improve to 6-2 in bowl games this season with three teams still playing. The Rebels (10-3, No. 16 AP) showed plenty of playbook moxie during the win, jumping out to a 34-6 lead at halftime by mixing their standard offense with a few trick plays that kept the Cowboys reeling all night. Kelly, who was selected the game's most valuable player, threw for 302 yards and four touchdowns, including three to Treadwell. Kelly's four touchdown passes, and Treadwell's three touchdown catches tied Sugar Bowl records. Kelly completed 21 of 33 passes and ran for 73 yards on 10 carries. Oklahoma State (10-3, No. 13 AP) lost its final three games after 10 straight wins. The Cowboys fell into a 41-6 hole midway through the third quarter and never mounted a legitimate challenge. Mason Rudolph was 18-of-31 for 179 yards for Oklahoma State. Ole Miss outgained Oklahoma State 554-366 in total yards. Gundy said Rudolph wasn't the same Quarterback in the Sugar Bowl after battling a foot injury in November. Ole Miss was embarrassed a year ago in a 42-3 loss to TCU in the Peach Bowl, and players vowed throughout the past month that the outcome would be much different. They were right. Ole Miss started off a little shaky after a couple of early penalties helped Oklahoma State advance down the field. The Cowboys eventually kicked a short field goal for a 3-0 lead. That was the end of the good news for the Cowboys, who were playing in the Sugar Bowl for the first time since 1946. The Rebels' offense got on track later in the first quarter when Kelly hit a wide-open Cody Core for a 31-yard touchdown that made it 10-3 and started the onslaught. Treadwell added two touchdown catches in the first half and completed a 45-yard pass after a lateral on a trick play. His second touchdown catch gave Ole Miss a 24-3 lead. The Ole Miss fans -- who were cheering for the Rebels at the Sugar Bowl for the first time since 1970 -- were already in a frenzy when one more trick play by Freeze brought down the house. Even Archie Manning, the Rebels' Quarterback in 1970, was impressed. With 5 seconds remaining in the second quarter, Kelly ran right and then fired back across his body to Tunsil, who caught the lateral and jogged into the end zone for a 2-yard rushing touchdown. Ole Miss Fans roared, and the "S-E-C! S-E-C!" chant started in the Superdome: The Rebels had scored on their final six possessions of the first half, and this one was essentially over. For Oklahoma State, it was a rough ending to what started as a promising season. The Cowboys were in the middle of the playoff conversation in November after 10 straight wins, but losses to Baylor, Oklahoma and then Ole Miss exposed their defense. They gave up a combined 151 points in those three losses.

2016 Gator Bowl

The 2016 TaxSlayer Bowl was held on January 2, 2016 at EverBank Field in Jacksonville, Florida. The 71st edition of the TaxSlayer Bowl (formerly called Gator Bowl) featured the Penn State Nittany Lions of the Big Ten Conference against the Georgia Bulldogs of the Southeastern Conference. It was televised on ESPN. The game's naming rights sponsor was tax preparation software company TaxSlayer.com.

2016 Gator Bowl	Line	1	-	2	-	3	-	4	-	Final
Penn State	(44.5)	0	-	3	-	0	-	14	-	17
Georgia	(-6.5)	3	-	14	-	7	-	0	-	24

Scoring Summary
Georgia – Morgan 44 yard Field goal
Penn State – Davis 34 yard Field goal
Georgia – Mitchell 44 yard pass from Godwin (Morgan kick)
Georgia – Godwin 17 yard pass from Lambert (Beless kick)
Georgia – Michel 21 yard run (Beless kick)
Penn State – Lewis 17 yard pass from McSorley (Davis kick)
Penn State – Hamilton 20 yard pass from McSorley (Davis kick)

Post-game effect - In the immediate aftermath of the game, Penn State Quarterback Christian Hackenberg thanked his teammates, offensive coordinators, and former head coach Bill O'Brien before announcing he would forgo his final year of NCAA eligibility and enter the NFL Draft, and in doing so, he ended his three-year tenure with the Nittany Lions during which, in the words of LNP sports columnist Mike Gross, "he did everything he could" to help a program in transition.

Associated Press Gator Bowl Game Summary - After watching Terry Godwin execute the trick play in practice, Georgia interim coach Bryan McClendon was having second thoughts about calling it in the bowl game. His players and coaches convinced him otherwise. It may have been the best decision of McClendon's short-lived coaching career. Godwin threw a 44-yard touchdown pass that got the Bulldogs going and caught a 17-yarder later, doing a little bit of everything in Georgia's 24-17 win over Penn State in the TaxSlayer Bowl on Saturday. And it helped the Bulldogs (10-3) win their fifth consecutive game to close the season, send McClendon out a winner in his head-coaching debut and give the senior class its 40th career victory. Incoming coach Kirby Smart was in attendance for part of the game and had to like what he saw. Despite a makeshift coaching staff -- Georgia used different offensive and defensive coordinators -- the Bulldogs turned in one of their most complete performances since September. It helped that Penn State (7-6) played more than half the game without star Quarterback Christian Hackenberg. Hackenberg left in the second quarter with a right shoulder injury, hurt when linebacker Roquan Smith tackled him. Hackenberg stayed in the game and threw four more passes but grabbed his shoulder between plays. He headed to the locker room after an incompletion and returned for the second half in street clothes. He said he wanted to play, but team officials told him no. Hackenberg declared for the NFL draft after the game. A junior and the school's all-time leader in passing yards (8,457) and touchdowns (48), Hackenberg completed 8 of 14 for 139 yards against Georgia. Trace McSorley replaced Hackenberg and threw a 17-yard touchdown pass to Geno Lewis on the first play of the fourth quarter and then a 20-yard strike to DaeSean Hamilton with 6:14 to play. Hamilton's leaping grab between two defenders made it close, a welcome change given many of the games on New Year's Eve and New Year's Day. The Bulldogs responded with a 50-yard drive that could have sealed the victory, but they failed to convert a fourth-and-2 play at the 23. McClendon decided to go for it because kicker Marshall Morgan injured an ankle on a kickoff and backup Collin Barber missed a 48-yarder in the third quarter. Penn State took over with 1:52 remaining and no timeouts. McSorley converted two fourth-down plays, but eventually ran out time. His final pass, a Hail Mary to the end zone, was batted down as time expired. The Nittany Lions lost their fourth in a row to end Coach James Franklin's second season. Georgia led 24-3 late in the third after Sony Michel carried 260-pound defensive end Garrett Sickels into the end zone. Michel started right, made a cut and then gave Sickels a 7-yard ride before stretching across the goal line. Had it not been for Godwin that might have been Georgia's top highlight. Godwin accounted for two scores in the second quarter. He lined up in the wildcat, took the snap and then launched a high, deep pass to Malcolm Mitchell. Godwin was on the receiving end of a touchdown just before halftime.

2016 Liberty Bowl (January)

The 2016 Liberty Bowl was held on January 2, 2016 at Liberty Bowl Memorial Stadium in Memphis, Tennessee. The 57th edition of the Liberty Bowl will feature the Kansas State Wildcats of the Big 12 Conference against the Arkansas Razorbacks of the Southeastern Conference. It was televised on ESPN.

2016 Liberty Bowl	Line	1	-	2	-	3	-	4	-	Final
Kansas State	(56.0)	10	-	3	-	10	-	0	-	23
Arkansas	(-13.5)	14	-	10	-	7	-	14	-	45

Scoring Summary
Kansas State – Dimel 10 yard run (McCrane kick)
Arkansas – Collins 22 yard run (Hedlund kick)
Kansas State – McCrane 36 yard Field goal
Arkansas – Cornelius 13 yard run (Hedlund kick)
Arkansas – Collins 13 yard run (Hedlund kick)
Arkansas – Hedlund 26 yard Field goal
Kansas State – McCrane 21 yard Field goal
Kansas State – Dimel 48 yard pass from Cook (McCrane kick)
Arkansas – Sprinkel 6 yard pass from Allen (Hedlund kick)
Kansas State – McCrane 32 yard Field goal
Arkansas – Collins 14 yard run (Hedlund kick)
Arkansas – Walker 10 yard run (Hedlund kick)

Associated Press Liberty Bowl Game Summary - Just in case this ends up being his last college game, Arkansas' Alex Collins made it one to remember. Collins ran for 185 yards and three touchdowns and Arkansas capped its late-season surge with a 45-23 victory over Kansas State on Saturday in the AutoZone Liberty Bowl. Collins, who has rushed for over 1,000 yards each of the last three seasons, indicated after the game he hadn't decided whether to return for his senior year or enter the NFL draft. Ranked 18th to open the season, Arkansas stumbled through a 1/3 start that knocked the Razorbacks out of the Top 25. The Razorbacks (8-5) turned things around won six of their last seven games. Arkansas snapped Kansas State's three-game winning streak in front of a sellout crowd of 61,136, the fourth-largest crowd in the game's 57-year history. Kansas State (6-7) finished a season below .500 for the first time since Bill Snyder began his second stint as coach in 2009. Arkansas' Brandon Allen was 20 of 26 for 315 yards with one touchdown and one interception. Kansas State's Kody Cook, starting at Quarterback for the first time, went 12 of 24 for 163 yards with a touchdown. The game pitted two friends and former colleagues against each other. Arkansas coach Bret Bielema worked as an assistant coach on Snyder's Kansas State staff from 2002-03. When Arkansas was struggling early this season, Bielema even sought Snyder for advice. Snyder added some intrigue to this game by making a Quarterback switch. Cook had been Kansas State's second-leading receiver during the regular season while also backing up Quarterback Joe Hubener. Cook took the first snaps for Kansas State on Saturday and remained the Quarterback until the game was out of reach. Snyder said Cook had earned the starting assignment with his practice performance. Although Cook played well enough to keep Kansas State relatively close, he couldn't do anything about his defense's inability to slow down Collins, who was largely responsible for helping Arkansas reach the end zone on three straight first-half drives. Collins had touchdown runs of 22 yards and 13 yards in the first 17 minutes. His total of three touchdown runs tied a Liberty Bowl record. He also had a 68-yard kickoff return that set up Jared Cornelius' 13-yard touchdown on an end around. Kansas State trailed 31-23 late in the third quarter and appeared ready to make a stop when Arkansas knocked out the Wildcats with a one-two punch. Facing third-and-13, Allen found All-America tight end Hunter Henry down the left sideline for a 43-yard completion. On the next play, Collins spun away from a couple of defenders, eluded the grasp of a third and dragged a couple more into the end zone for a 14-yard touchdown with 12:04 remaining. Kansas State wouldn't threaten again. The game had a scary moment late in the second quarter when Arkansas' Dominique Reed was carted off the field on a stretcher. Reed lay on the ground for several minutes after making a 15-yard reception. Replays appeared to show him taking a blow to the side of the head at the end of the play. Reed was taken to the hospital for precautionary reasons, but Bielema said the junior receiver was in the locker room after the game.

2016 Alamo Bowl

The 2016 Alamo Bowl was played on January 2, 2016, at the Alamodome in San Antonio, Texas. The 23rd edition of the Alamo Bowl featured the TCU Horned Frogs from the Big 12 Conference and the Oregon Ducks from the Pac-12 Conference. It was televised on ESPN and heard on ESPN Radio. The game was officially known as the Valero Alamo Bowl. The Horned Frogs trailed 31-0 at halftime, but an injury to Oregon Quarterback Vernon Adams Jr. just before the halftime break would result in a scoreless second half for the Ducks. TCU scored on all 9 possessions after halftime, completing the comeback in the second half with a late field goal. The two teams traded touchdowns in the first overtime and field goals in the second. The Horned Frogs scored in the third extra period, failed their 2 point conversion, but held the Ducks out of the end zone. The 31-point comeback tied the largest comeback in NCAA college football bowl game history with the 2006 Insight Bowl.

2016 Alamo Bowl	Line	1	2	3	4	OT	2OT	3OT	Final
#11 TCU	(73.5)	0	0	17	14	7	3	6	47
#15 Oregon	(-7.5)	21	10	0	0	7	3	0	41

Scoring Summary
Oregon – Carrington 37 yard pass from Adams (Schneider kick)
Oregon – Freeman 4 yard run (Schneider kick)
Oregon – Freeman 5 yard run (Schneider kick)
Oregon – Brooks-James 5 yard run (Schneider kick)
Oregon – Schneider 47 yard Field goal
TCU – Oberkrom 24 yard Field goal
TCU – Austin 26 yard pass from Kohlhausen (Oberkrom kick)
TCU – Kohlhausen 2 yard run (Oberkrom kick)
TCU – Oberkrom 34 yard Field goal
TCU – Green 2 yard run (Jones pass from Kohlhausen)
TCU – Oberkrom 22 yard Field goal
TCU – Porter 7 yard pass from Kohlhausen (Oberkrom kick)
Oregon – Freeman 1 yard run (Schneider kick)
Oregon – Schneider 44 yard Field goal
TCU – Oberkrom 46 yard Field goal
TCU – Kohlhausen 8 yard run (Pass failed)

Associated Press Alamo Game Summary - Thrust into the starting role in place of the suspended star Quarterback, TCU's Bram Kohlhausen made the absolute most of his final chance with the Horned Frogs -- in historic fashion. Not just for his team, but for the family that could join him at the Valero Alamo Bowl and those who couldn't. Starting in place of Trevone Boykin, who was suspended after a bar fight two days earlier, Kohlhausen led the No. 11 Horned Frogs back from 31 points down for a 47-41, triple-overtime victory over No. 15 Oregon on Saturday night in the Alamo Bowl. Kohlhausen passed for 351 yards and accounted for four touchdowns, running in for the winner in the third overtime. The comeback tied the record for the largest deficit overtime to win a bowl game, matching Texas Tech's win over Minnesota in the 2006 Insight Bowl. Down 31-0 at halftime, TCU coach Gary Patterson changed shirts and his team changed gears, racing for 31 second-half points before winning in 3 OTs. After it was over, Kohlhausen talked stadium security into letting his mother join the celebration on the field. The person not there was his father, Bill, who died Nov. 7 of cancer. Kohlhausen, who had played spot duty this season, was thrust into the spotlight on Thursday when Boykin was arrested and suspended after a bar fight in San Antonio's famed River Walk district. Kohlhausen started his career at Houston, left for junior college and walked on at TCU (11-2). He had never started a major college game until his final one and did his best to mimic Boykin, especially in the second half with tough runs and pinpoint passing as TCU stormed back. He twice came back from hard hits that forced him out of the game. TCU coach Gary Patterson said. It didn't look possible when Oregon (9-4) was rolling to a 28-0 lead behind standout senior Quarterback Vernon Adams Jr., and led 31-0 at halftime. Adams passed for 197 yards and a touchdown and led the Ducks on four consecutive touchdown drives, eluding sacks and throwing downfield as Oregon rolled early. But Oregon stopped in its tracks when Adams was hurt on a rare called run for him. Adams knocked heads with TCU linebacker Derrick Kindred, left the game and never returned. Jeff Lockie drove Oregon to a field goal that made it 31-0 at halftime, but the Ducks stalled there. TCU scored on all of its possessions in the second half and overtime… The Horned Frogs started their march back with 17 points in the third quarter, twice scoring touchdowns on fourth down. Kohlhausen threw a touchdown pass to Jaelen Austin, then ran 2 yards for his first score. TCU was gaining confidence with each play while Oregon seemed stuck in neutral. Lockie, who had played in relief of Adams when he was injured earlier this season, couldn't move the offense as the TCU-dominated crowd of nearly 65,000 revved up. Jaden Oberkrom's 22-yard field goal with 19 seconds left tied it, and TCU scored first in the first overtime when Kohlhausen hit Emanauel Porter for a 7-yard touchdown. Oregon answered with Royce Freeman's third touchdown run. After the teams exchanged field goals in the second overtime, Kohlhausen sneaked around the right end on an option, and seemingly disappeared behind his blockers until he was in the end zone. TCU's 2-point conversion pass attempt failed, but Oregon's final chance to tie and keep the game going ended with an incomplete pass on fourth down near the goal line. TCU players stormed the field when the game was over.

Aftermath - Two days after the game, Oregon coach Mark Helfrich demoted defensive coordinator Don Pellum to linebackers coach. Pellum, a former Ducks linebacker who had been involved with the program for more than 30 years as a player, administrator, and coach, had been criticized for the shortcomings of Oregon's defense in 2015. Shortly after Kohlhausen was named offensive MVP for the game, Quarterback of the All-Bowl team, and he found out that TCU had begun the process of placing him on scholarship for his final semester in spring 2016.

2016 Cactus Bowl

The 2016 Cactus Bowl was played on January 2, 2016 at Chase Field in Phoenix, Arizona. This was the twenty-seventh edition of the Cactus Bowl, which was originally known as the Copper Bowl and then as the Buffalo Wild Wings Bowl. It was televised on ESPN. The 2016 Cactus Bowl marked the game's return to Chase Field, its home from 2000 until 2005, after a ten-year absence during which the game was played at Sun Devil Stadium in Tempe, Arizona. The move was made due to a reconstruction project at Sun Devil Stadium that rendered the facility unusable during the college football offseason and would see Chase Field host the Cactus Bowl through 2019.

2016 Cactus Bowl	Line	1	-	2	-	3	-	4	-	Final
West Virginia	(-3.0)	9	-	13	-	14	-	7	-	43
Ariozna State	(62.5)	3	-	15	-	14	-	10	-	42

Scoring Summary
West Virginia – Lambert 21 yard Field goal
West Virginia – Lambert 31 yard Field goal
Arizona State – Gonzales 37 yard Field goal
West Virginia – Lambert 27 yard Field goal
Arizona State – Lucien 19 yard pass from Bercovici (Gonzales kick)
West Virginia – Gibson 59 yard pass from Howard (Lambert kick)
Arizona State – Gonzales 19 yard Field goal
West Virginia – Shorts 10 yard pass from Howard (Kick blocked)
Arizona State – White 2 point conversion return
Arizona State – Gonzales 35 yard Field goal
Arizona State – White 2 yard pass from Bercovici (Gonzales kick)
West Virginia – Jennings 64 yard pass from Howard (Lambert kick)
Arizona State – White 33 yard pass from Bercovici (Gonzales kick)
West Virginia – Shorts 17 yard pass from Howard (Lambert kick)
Arizona State – Gonzales 48 yard Field goal
Arizona State – Chambers 58 yard pass from Bercovici (Gonzales kick)
West Virginia – Sills 15 yard pass from Howard (Lambert kick)

WVUIllustrated Cactus Bowl Game Summary - Arizona St. (6-7) only had to travel 11 miles from its home Sun Devil Stadium to Chase Field. Meanwhile, it was a 2,080-mile trek from Milan Puskar Stadium to Chase Field for West Virginia (8-5). Head coach Dana Holgorsen, Quarterback Skyler Howard, and the rest of the Mountaineer offense, must've taken notes about flying during the plane ride, as WVU employed the air-raid offense, picking up a large majority of its yardage through the air. Howard set the WVU record for most passing yards in a bowl game and broke the Cactus Bowl record for the same stat in the Mountaineers 43-42 win to end the season on a high note. West Virginia made trips inside the red zone in three of its first four drives of the game but could only come away with nine points as Josh Lambert kicked three field goals. Arizona St. had offensive struggles early on, as well, gaining just 42 yards in the opening quarter, compared to the Mountaineers who gained 236 yards. Despite WVU heavily outgaining ASU for much of the first half, the Mountaineers couldn't gain the necessary yardage on third down, unable to convert on each of their first seven third-down attempts. The Sun Devils, though, were the first team to find the end zone, as Devin Lucien caught a pass along the left sideline, and reached the football over the goal line on an impressive second effort. Arizona State's touchdown drive was aided by a 16-yard punt return by Tim White that put ASU across midfield. The Sun Devils led 10-9 with 10 minutes remaining in the second quarter. Two possessions later, WVU regained the lead with two big pass plays. Howard completed a 21-yard pass over the middle of the field to Ka'Raun White. He then lofted a pass down the near sideline to Shelton Gibson, who slowed down just enough to catch the ball, and then turned on the afterburners to outrun two Sun Devil defenders. Both catches gave both WVU wide outs 100 yards receiving for the game. White finished with four catches and 116 yards, while Gibson ended the game with four receptions for 143 yards and a score. Lambert's PAT gave West Virginia a six-point lead. Arizona St. pieced together a lengthy drive and threatened to once again get in the end zone. The WVU defense had other plans, though, stopping consecutive ASU runs from the one-yard line, and forcing the Sun Devils to kick a field goal with 2:53 remaining in the opening half. Howard once again marched the offense down field, taking eight plays to travel 75 yards. He completed a 16-yard pass to White, a 22-yard strike to a wide-open Daikiel Shorts, and a 17-yard pitch and catch to Jordan Thompson put WVU inside the red zone at the five-yard line. Smallwood lost five yards on first down, but on second down Howard tossed a 10-yard pass to the back, right corner of the end zone that fell right into the hands of a diving Shorts for a touchdown. ASU scored five points in the final 33 second of the half, blocking the PAT and returning it for a safety, and then turning good field position into a field goal. WVU lead by just four points, 22-18, at halftime despite gaining 139 more yards on offense. Howard threw for 334 of his total 532 yards in the first half. The ASU offense continued to put points on the board coming out of the break, quickly going 66 yards to score a touchdown and take a three-point lead. The air-raid attack continued for WVU on its next drive as Howard connected with Gary Jennings for a 64-yard scoring play to re-gain the lead, 29-25. ASU and WVU traded touchdowns once again, the Sun Devils scoring as result of multiple broken tackles from WVU defenders, and the Mountaineers finding the end zone with the second Howard-to-Shorts-touchdown combination of the game. WVU led 36-32 at the end of the third quarter. Arizona State's Zane Gonzalez converted on a 48-yard field goal early in the fourth to pull the Devils within one point. The Sun Devil's took the lead with just under five minutes remaining with the help of questionable officiating, and a lack of WVU tackling. Linebacker Jared Barber was called for a personal foul for hitting Quarterback Manny Wilkins, who kept running after it appeared he had been tackled. Three plays later, Mike Bercovici completed a pass to Gary Chambers, who eluded multiple Mountaineer defenders enroute to pay dirt on a 58-yard scoring play that gave ASU a 42-36 lead with 4:56 remaining. Howard and company weren't done, as the offense put together a 10-play drive that required two third-down conversions, including a 24-yard rush by Wendell Smallwood on 3rd and 22. Two passes later, Howard set the Cactus Bowl record with his fifth touchdown pass, completing this one to David Sills. 43-42 Mountaineers. Arizona State had one last chance after a dropped pass on third down set up the Sun Devils with 4th and 10 at midfield. Bercovici's pass fell incomplete, tipped by Barber over the middle of the field. With the win, West Virginia wins its first bowl game since the 2011 Orange Bowl. It also marks the best finish WVU has had since joining the Big 12 Conference.

2016 CFP Championship Game

The 2016 College Football Playoff National Championship was played at University of Phoenix Stadium in Glendale, Arizona on January 11, 2016. The game was played between the winners of two pre-designated semifinal bowls played on December 31, 2015: the No. 1 Clemson Tigers, who beat the No. 4 Oklahoma Sooners 37-17 at the Orange Bowl, coached by Dabo Swinney in his 8th season with Clemson, and the No. 2 Alabama Crimson Tide, who beat No. 3 Michigan State Spartans 38-0 at the Cotton Bowl Classic, coached by Nick Saban.

Broadcasting - The game was broadcast in the United States by ESPN, ESPN Deportes, and ESPN Radio, with Chris Fowler and Kirk Herbstreit as commentators on TV, and Eduardo Varela and Pablo Viruega as Spanish commentators. As in 2015, ESPN provided Megacast coverage of the game, with enhanced feeds and perspectives on various ESPN television channels and WatchESPN.

2016 CFP Championship Game	Line	1	-	2	-	3	-	4	-	Final
#2 Alabama	(-6.5)	7	-	7	-	7	-	24	-	45
#1 Clemson	(50.5)	14	-	0	-	10	-	16	-	40

Scoring Summary
Alabama – Henry 50 yard run (Griffith kick)
Clemson – Renfrow 31 yard pass from Watson (Huegel kick)
Clemson – Renfrow 11 yard pass from Watson (Huegel kick)
Alabama – Henry 1 yard run (Griffith kick)
Alabama – Howard 53 yard pass from Coker (Griffith kick)
Clemson – Huegel 37 yard Field goal
Clemson – Gallman 1 yard run (Huegel kick)
Alabama – Griffith 33 yard Field goal
Alabama – Howard 51 yard pass from Coker (Griffith kick)
Clemson – Huegel 31 yard Field goal
Alabama – Drake 95 yard kickoff return (Griffith kick)
Clemson – Scott 15 yard pass from Watson (Pass failed)
Alabama – Henry 1 yard run (Griffith kick)
Clemson – Leggett 24 yard pass from Watson (Huegel kick)

Associated Press National Championship Game Summary - The last step toward making Alabama's run of championships under Nick Saban the greatest in college football history was the toughest. The Crimson Tide needed all their power and speed. They needed all their talent and steely resolve. When that alone couldn't do it, it was up to one gutsy trick to help win the fourth national title of the Saban dynasty. Derrick Henry, O.J. Howard and Kenyan Drake hit No. 1 Clemson with long touchdowns, and No. 2 Alabama outlasted the dynamic play Deshaun Watson to win the College Football Playoff championship 45-40 on Monday night. The Crimson Tide (14-1) won their three previous championship game appearances in runaway fashion. This game was an instant classic -- a relief for fans who had sat through the blowouts that turned the New Year's Six lineup into a dud. Alabama has just won the national title, but we're already looking to next year. A College Football Playoff with Art Briles and Jim Harbaugh? We're in. The Pac-12 shut out again? Oh boy. With 10:34 left in the fourth quarter and Alabama having just tied the game at 24-24, Saban took a gamble to try to keep the ball away from Watson. He called for an onside kick called "pop kick" from Adam Griffith, and Alabama defensive back Marlon Humphrey caught it over the shoulder at midfield. Tide turned. "It was tough. It really was," said Saban, who now has more national titles than every other coach but Bear Bryant, the man who first made Alabama synonymous with college football greatness. Moments later, Alabama took back the lead for good. For the second time, Clemson (14-1) lost track of the tight end Howard in coverage, and Jake Coker hit him in stride deep for a 51-yard touchdown to make it 31-24 with 9:45 left. Clemson and Watson proved to be every bit Alabama's equal. The Tigers just kept coming. Watson led Clemson to a field goal to make it 31-27, and boom! Another Alabama big play. Drake broke free and streaked down the sideline for a 95-yard kickoff-return touchdown, diving the last 5 yards to the pylon. Watson threw his third touchdown pass to make it 38-33 with 4:40 left, and then Alabama went back to its workhorse Heisman Trophy winner. Henry plunged into the end zone for his third touchdown of the game to make it 45-33 with 1:07 left. Watson threw another touchdown pass to cap a wild 40-point fourth quarter but would not get another chance. Clemson's onside kick went out of bounds. Coker took a knee, and after a two-year drought that felt like eternity in Tuscaloosa, Alabama was back on top. After a loss to Ole Miss in mid-September, there were doubters. Saban used them to fuel his team. "There weren't many people earlier in the year who thought they could do it," he said. The Crimson Tide became the second team in college football's poll era, dating back to 1936, to win four titles in seven seasons. Alabama joins Notre Dame, which won four titles from 1943-49, but those Fighting Irish never even played in bowl games, nevertheless two playoff games. For Saban, it is his fifth national championship -- four in his nine seasons at Alabama -- leaving him only one short of Bryant for the most titles in history. Watson gave the Tide all they could handle, throwing for 405 yards and four touchdowns, and conjured up memories of Vince Young's miraculous performance for Texas in the 2006 Rose Bowl that derailed Southern California's dynasty. The sophomore, who finished third in the Heisman Trophy voting, had 478 total yards against a loaded Tide defense and bested Young's 467 yards against the Trojans. But Watson couldn't finish the job the way Young did in Pasadena, California, and win the national title. Instead, Saban and the Tide raised another trophy, their first in this new playoff system, and got another confetti shower. It is the Tide's 11th national title in the poll era -- 10 AP and one coaches' poll -- and more than any other school. Alabama was a unanimous No. 1 in the final AP poll and Clemson finished No. 2. The Tide hit Clemson early with Henry, who scored the game's first touchdown on a 50-yard burst through the middle. He finished with 158 yards on 36 carries. Howard was the offensive player of the game with five catches for 208 yards, including a 63-yarder that set up Alabama's final score. After Watson and walk-on Hunter Renfrow hooked up for two touchdowns to give Clemson a 14-7 lead at the end of the first quarter, Henry tied it up with a 1-yard plunge. Back and forth it went. Alabama had never been challenged like this in a championship game under Saban. Alabama pulled away from Texas for Saban's first Tide title to end the 2009 season. Alabama blanked LSU for the next in 2011 and crushed Notre Dame to repeat in 2012. Trying to become the first FBS team to go 15-0, Clemson did not crumble under the force of Alabama's might. But all those five-star recruits and future NFL players who dot the Alabama roster showed they also have plenty of resiliency and toughness. And Saban, the quintessential CEO Coach, showed he had a little riverboat gambler in him. That onside kick stunned the stadium and Clemson and brought a big grin to the face of the country's most serious coach. The Tide will send another batch of players to the NFL this year, as Saban always does. There is another wave ready to roll.

2016 Air Force Reserve Celebration Bowl

The **2016 Air Force Reserve Celebration Bowl was** played on December 17, 2016, at the Georgia Dome in Atlanta, Georgia. The second Celebration Bowl game matched the champion of the Mid-Eastern Athletic Conference, against the champion of the Southwestern Athletic Conference, the two historically black division I conferences.

2016 Celebration Bowl	Line	1	-	2	-	3	-	4	-	Final
North Carolina Central		3	-	0	-	0	-	6	-	9
Grambling State		0	-	0	-	10	-	0	-	10

Scoring Summary
North Carolina Central – McClaren 23 yard Field Goal
Grambling – Carter 32 yard run (Wallace Kick)
Grambling – Wallace 26 yard Field Goal
North Carolina Central – Atkinson 39 yard pass from Bell (Kick Blocked)

GSUtigers.com Celebration Bowl Game Summary - The Grambling State University Tiger football (11-1) team capped off an amazing season with a Historically Black College and University National Championship on Saturday afternoon in the Air Force Reserve Celebration Bowl. The Tigers took the

Georgia Dome by storm and bested the North Carolina Central University Eagles, 10-9. The victory was hard fought as, for the second time this season; the G-Men were held scoreless in the first half. NCCU (9-3) seemed to have Grambling's number when it came to the offensive side of the ball in the first two quarters of play. The Tigers offense was held to 17 plays for 73 yards. DeVante Kincade finished the first half going 9-of-21 with one interception for 111 yards and was sacked three times. Grambling's receivers combined for seven catches for 98 yards in the first half. NCCU's Brandon McLaren scored the only points of the first half as he drilled a 23 yard field goal with 6:05 left in the first quarter. In the second half of play, the Tigers came out with a renewed spirit and began to put together a drive. Grambling's "Golden Curtain" defense halted the Eagles to bring up a quick four downs and give the offense a crack at the end zone. The G-Men began to utilize the running game to pound the ball into the heart of North Carolina Central's defense. Eventually, the hard work began to pay off with yardage and a touchdown. *Martez Carter* found the end zone for Grambling's first touchdown of the game with a 32 yard run and *Jonathan Wallace* tacked on the point after with 9:14 left in the third quarter, 7-3. The Tigers earned a few more points as Wallace hung a field goal on board after GSU's drive stalled with 2:50 left in the third quarter, 10-3. In the last quarter of the game, each team tried to impose their will on the other. Grambling was able to hold the Eagles to just one first down and seven rushes for four yards. The fourth quarter was also one of momentum swinging plays. The first swing happened when *Jameel Jackson* intercepted Malcolm Bell's pass at the Grambling 33 yard line with 5:41 left in the game to give the momentum back to the G-Men. The drive stalled and the Tigers were forced to punt with 4:03 left in the game. The second swing came when Bell connected with Quentin Atkinson for a 39 yard touchdown with 2:14 left, 10-9. The third moment happened when *Joseph McWilliams* blocked the Eagles extra point, and the ball was scooped up by *De'Arius Christmas* to prevent the game from being tied. When North Carolina Central regained possession, the team attempted an onside kick that was almost successful but was called back because of two penalties. On the replay of the kickoff, NCCU couldn't capture lightening twice as Grambling's *Chad Williams* came up with the ball on the Eagles 42 yard line with 2:12 left. As time wound down, it would be *Verlan Hunter* who put the nail in the coffin as he made a 12 yard catch from Kincade to pick up the first down with 1:00 left. The Tigers last plays of the season were the victory formation for two straight plays. Kincade finished the day going 15-of-31 with one interception, 149 yard, and was sacked three times. Hunter was the leading receiver for Grambling with four catches for 35 yards, the longest being 18 yards. Carter led the running back corps for GSU with 12 carries for 109 yards, one touchdown, and averaging 9.1 yards per carry. The G-Man defense was anchored by Jackson with five solo tackles and one interception. Carter was named Air Force Celebration Bowl Offensive Most Valuable Player while Jackson claimed the Defensive MVP honor. Grambling also set a Celebration Bowl record with 20 first downs. Bell went 18-of-32 for two interceptions, 240 yards, one touchdown and was sacked twice. He also led in rushing for NCCU with 13 carries for 31 yards. The Eagles defensive leader was Reggie Hunter as he racked up 8.5 total tackles and one tackle for a loss of one yard.

2016 New Mexico Bowl

The 2016 New Mexico Bowl was played on December 17, 2016 at University Stadium in Albuquerque, New Mexico. The eleventh annual New Mexico Bowl was aired on ESPN.

2016 New Mexico Bowl	Line	1	-	2	-	3	-	4	-	Final
Texas-San Antonio	(54.0)	3	-	3	-	0	-	14	-	20
New Mexico	(-9.0)	7	-	3	-	6	-	7	-	23

Scoring Summary
Texas-San Antonio - Falcon 23 yard Field goal
New Mexico - McQuarley 1 yard run (Sanders kick)
Texas-San Antonio - Falcon 28 yard Field goal
New Mexico - Sanders 52 yard Field goal
New Mexico - Gipson 10 yard run (Kick failed)
Texas-San Antonio - Stevens 16 yard pass from Sturm (Falcon kick)
New Mexico - McQuarley 1 yard run (Sanders kick)
Texas-San Antonio - Taylor 6 yard pass from Sturm (Falcon kick)

Associated Press New Mexico Bowl Game Summary - Coach Bob Davie waited a long time for this moment. It had been quite a while for his New Mexico Lobos, too. Davie earned his first career bowl victory when the Lobos, boosted by a pair of short touchdown runs from Richard McQuarley, beat Texas-San Antonio 23-20 Saturday in the New Mexico Bowl. Davie had been 0-4 in bowls -- three when he coached at Notre Dame, then last year with the Lobos in this event. The Lobos (9-4) posted just their second bowl victory in a half-century. The Lobos' previous postseason win came in the 2007 New Mexico Bowl over Nevada. Before that, it was a victory in the 1961 Aviation Bowl. In his fifth season at New Mexico, Davie completed the turnaround of a program that won three total games in the three seasons before his arrival.

The Lobos lost last year's New Mexico Bowl to Arizona. Jarveon Williams ran for 125 yards for the Roadrunners (6-7), who lost in their first bowl appearance in the program's six-year history. Despite the hype around New Mexico's triple-option threat and the Lobos leading the nation in rushing, the Roadrunners ran for more yards than the Lobos. New Mexico Quarterback Lamar Jordan rushed for 81 yards and threw a 34-yard pass to Dameon Gamblin that set up McQuarley's 1-yard burst for a 23-13 lead with 2:22 left. Dalton Sturm threw two TD passes for Texas-San Antonio, including a 4-yard toss to JaBryce Taylor with 25 seconds remaining. The Roadrunners failed to recover an onside kick. Six Lobos combined for 219 yards rushing. New Mexico was able to keep UTSA's big-play receivers mostly in check amid windy conditions.

2016 LAS VEGAS BOWL

The 2016 Las Vegas Bowl was played on December 17, 2016, at Sam Boyd Stadium in Las Vegas, Nevada. The twenty-fifth annual Las Vegas Bowl aired on ABC. Houston entered the game with a 9-3 record (AAC) and was coached by Major Applewhite (Interim) after Tom Herman left to take the Texas head coaching job. San Diego State, coached by Rocky Long, entered the game 10-3 and were Mountain West Champions.

2016 Las Vegas Bowl	Line	1	-	2	-	3	-	4	-	Final
Houston	(-4.5)	10	-	0	-	0	-	0	-	10
San Diego State	(50.5)	0	-	6	-	14	-	14	-	34

Scoring Summary
Houston - Cummings 31 yard Field goal
Houston - Ward 2 yard run (Cummings kick)
San Diego State - Baron 23 yard Field goal
San Diego State - Baron 28 yard Field goal
San Diego State - Pumphrey 32 yard run (Baron kick)
San Diego State - Smith 54 yard interception return (Baron kick)
San Diego State - Anderson 28 yard pass from Chapman (Baron kick)
San Diego State - Washington 7 yard run (Baron kick)

San Diego State media guide Las Vegas Bowl Game Summary - Donnel Pumphrey broke the NCAA career rushing record Saturday in his college finale, running for 115 yards and a touchdown in San Diego State's 34-10 victory over Houston in the Las Vegas Bowl. Pumphrey passed former Wisconsin star Ron Dayne's mark of 6,397 yards on a 15-yard run early in the fourth quarter, with teammates swarming him on the sideline, and wrapping up his sensational career in his Nevada hometown with 6,405 yards. Pumphrey's senior total of 2,133 yards rushing ranks in the top 10 for an FBS player. Ron Smith returned an interception 54 yards for a touchdown, Curtis Anderson caught a 28-yard touchdown pass from Christian Chapman, Juwan Washington ran for a touchdown, and John Baron kicked two field goals for the Aztecs (11-3). They overcame a 10-0 first-quarter deficit against the Cougars (9-4) for their second consecutive bowl win. Neither the victory nor Pumphrey's record-setting performance seemed likely after Houston's defense absolutely smothered the Aztecs in the first quarter. Led by freshman Ed Oliver, Houston had seven tackles for loss on San Diego State's first 16 plays. Pumphrey had minus-1 yard rushing on seven carries in the first quarter and the Aztecs didn't have a first down until the first play of the second quarter - on a penalty for running into the kicker. "The first quarter, they came out with more intensity than we did, at least their defensive side of the ball," Pumphrey said. But Pumphrey started to gash Houston on the perimeter, giving San Diego State the lead for good on a 32-yard touchdown run late in the third quarter, and the defense intercepted four of Houston Quarterback Greg Ward Jr.'s passes in the second half. Ward threw for 229 yards and had a 2-yard touchdown run, tying Bryce Beall's school record of 39 rushing touchdowns. Houston finished with 254 yards of total offense and just 25 yards rushing.

2016 CAMELLIA BOWL

The 2016 Camellia Bowl was held on December 17, 2016 at Cramton Bowl in Montgomery, Alabama. The third annual edition of the Camellia Bowl, Sponsored by television broadcasting company Raycom Media, it is officially known as the Raycom Media Camellia Bowl.

2016 Camellia Bowl	Line	1	-	2	-	3	-	4	-	Final
Appalachian State	(-1.5)	7	-	7	-	14	-	3	-	31
Toledo	(59.5)	7	-	7	-	14	-	0	-	28

Scoring Summary
Appalachian State - Hopkins 16 yard pass from Lamb (Rubino kick)
Toledo - Roberts 15 yard pass from Woodside (Vest kick)
Appalachian State - Cox 13 yard run (Rubino kick)
Toledo - Hunt 26 yard run (Vest kick)
Appalachian State - Lamb 13 yard run (Rubino kick)
Toledo - Thompson 4 yard pass from Woodside (Vest kick)
Appalachian State - Evans 94 yard kickoff return (Rubino kick)
Toledo - Hunt 1 yard run (Vest kick)
Appalachian State - Rubino 39 yard Field goal

Raycom Media Camellia Bowl Game Summary - Each year, the Raycom Media Camellia Bowl must live up to the hype of its predecessor. The inaugural game was decided in the final 64 seconds. The second game was won by a field goal as time expired. There were no last-minute heroics in the 2016 game, just an exciting game that featured a back-and-forth scoring battle that wasn't decided until a final field goal attempt sailed wide right with 1:48 remaining that allowed Appalachian State to pull out a 31-28 win in front of an estimated crowd of 20,300 at Cramton Bowl on Saturday night. Appalachian State finished 10-3, winning 21 games and a pair of Camellia Bowls in their first two years of FBS bowl eligibility. Toledo finished 9-4, losing the Mid-American West title to Western Michigan 55-35, then to the Mountaineers to put a damper on the 2016 season. First two games featured comebacks by one of the participants but that wasn't the case on Saturday as the score was tied at the end of each of the first three quarters. Much of the pre-game focus was on the matchup between Appalachian State's vaunted defense and Toledo Quarterback Logan Woodside, who leads the NCAA with 45 passing touchdowns this season. Woodside lived up to the billing, setting a bowl record by completing 69.2 percent of his passes, going 18 of 26 for 247 yards and two touchdowns. If Appalachian State was going to win with its offense, most analysts would have concluded, it would have been behind the tailback tandem of Marcus Cox and Jalin Moore. And while Cox did finish with 143 yards and a touchdown on 22 carries to become the only Mountaineer to ever gain 1,000 yards in four consecutive seasons and the 22nd player to reach the 5,000-yard career plateau, he was overshadowed by the feet of his Quarterback. Lamb rushed for a career-high 126 yards and a touchdown on just nine carries, repeatedly turning third-and-long plays into crucial first downs. The Mountaineers' first scoring drive featured two third-and-long conversions with Lamb's arm, another touchdown came on Lamb's 13-yard run at left end and a third came on Darrynton Evans' 94-yard kickoff return. Each time, the Rockets answered, never taking the lead but tying the game after every Appalachian State touchdown. Finally, a Mountaineer drive stalled, and freshman Michael Rubino kicked a 39-yard field goal with 5:14 remaining. When the Rockets faced the same situation minutes later, Candle took a delay penalty to set up a 30-yard attempt by Jameson Vest, but the sophomore pushed the kick wide right. Satterfield, who defeated Ohio on a last-second field goal last year, figured he still had some Camellia Bowl magic left. As it turned out, he was able to simply run out the clock.

2016 AutoNation CURE BOWL

The 2016 Cure Bowl was played on December 17, 2016 at Camping World Stadium in Orlando, Florida. The second annual edition of the Cure Bowl is sponsored by automotive retailer AutoNation, the game is officially known as the AutoNation Cure Bowl. Arkansas State (8-4) of the Sun Belt Conference played Central Florida (6-6) of the American Athletic Conference. The game was televised by CBS Sports Network.

2016 AutoNation Cure Bowl	Line	1	-	2	-	3	-	4	-	Final
Arkansas State	(51.0)	17	-	0	-	7	-	7	-	31
Central Florida	(-4.0)	0	-	10	-	3	-	0	-	13

Scoring Summary
Arkansas State - Edmonds recovered blocked punt in end zone (Williams kick)
Arkansas State - Williams 22 yard Field goal
Arkansas State - Sanders 28 yard pass from Hansen (Williams kick)
Central Florida - Oldham 11 yard pass from Milton (Wright kick)
Central Florida - Wright 45 yard Field goal
Arkansas State - Sanders 75 yard pass from Hansen (Williams kick)
Central Florida - Wright 34 yard Field goal
Arkansas State - Sanders 17 yard pass from Hansen (Williams kick)

Associated Press AutoNation Cure Bowl game summary - Arkansas State senior wide receiver Kendall Sanders admits that he was pushed by his coaches and even teammates when he didn't want to be at times this season. The Texas transfer came around as the Red Wolves' season progressed in his lone year with the program. Sanders finally put it all together in his final appearance Saturday night, catching five passes for 127 yards and three touchdowns in a 31-13 rout of UCF in the AutoNation Cure Bowl. It was almost like vindication for Sanders who missed two years of football after leaving the Longhorns under the controversy of a sexual assault case in which he was acquitted last year. Sanders speed opened up opportunities for big plays all night with Quarterback Justice Hansen connecting with Sanders on touchdown passing plays of 12, 75 and 17 yards for a career night. His 75-yard touchdown reception on the third play of the second half set the tone for remainder of the game as the Red Wolves (8-5) went up by a commanding 24-10 just 51 seconds into the third quarter. Sanders got by the safety, broke a tackle and outran the secondary to the end zone. It was a fitting ending to college career that was about perseverance. The Red Wolves also received major contributions from their defense and special teams. Arkansas State's defensive front, led by defensive end Ja'Von Rolland-Jones, swarmed UCF Quarterback McKenzie Milton all night, giving him little time to find open receivers. But the special teams unit also came through big, contributing two turnovers that led to touchdowns and also blocking a punt for a touchdown. For first-year UCF coach Scott Frost the biggest takeaway was learning how much more his team must grow to take the next step.

2016 NEW ORLEANS BOWL

The 2016 New Orleans Bowl was held on December 17, 2016 at Mercedes-Benz Superdome in New Orleans, Louisiana. The 16th annual edition of the New Orleans Bowl was sponsored by freight shipping company R+L Carriers, the game was officially known as the R+L Carriers New Orleans Bowl. Southern Miss won the game by a score of 28–21.

2016 New Orleans Bowl	Line	1	-	2	-	3	-	4	-	Final
Southern Mississippi	(-5.5)	14	-	0	-	7	-	7	-	28
Louisiana-Lafayette	(56.5)	7	-	7	-	0	-	7	-	21

Scoring Summary
Southern Miss - Smith 11 yard run (Shaunfield kick)
Southern Miss - Smith 6 yard pass from Mullens (Shaunfield kick)
Louisiana-Lafayette - Jennings 4 yard run (Artigue kick)
Louisiana-Lafayette - Ray 12 yard run (Artigue kick)
Southern Miss - Staggers 5 yard pass from Mullens (Shaunfield kick)
Southern Miss - Smith 1 yard pass from Mullens (Shaunfield kick)
Louisiana-Lafayette - Jennings 3 yard run (Artigue kick)

Game Summary (by Hattiesburg American) - Southern Miss sent its seniors out victorious. Nick Mullens led the way, throwing for 346 yards in his final game as a Golden Eagle. Junior Allenzae Staggers was on the receiving end of most of Mullens' handiwork. He broke New Orleans Bowl records with 11 catches for 230 yards enroute to a 28-21 victory over Louisiana-Lafayette at the Mercedes-Benz Superdome on Saturday. The victory is Southern Miss' fourth in five trips to the New Orleans Bowl. The Golden Eagles have scored at least 28 points in all five New Orleans Bowl contests. Jay Hopson's squad finished 7-6 in his first season as coach. The Ragin' Cajuns finished 6-7. While Mullens and Staggers accumulated the eye-popping statistics, junior running back Ito Smith put points on the board. Smith scored a pair of rushing touchdowns and collected one receiving score. Southern Miss jumped out to a 14-0 lead in the first quarter. Smith's 11-yard scoring gallop with 9:39 left in the first put the Golden Eagles up 7-0, and he followed that up with a 6-yard touchdown catch just more than 2 minutes later. But the Ragin' Cajuns battled back to tie the game in the second quarter. The Sun Belt Conference member scored on a 4-yard run by Quarterback Anthony Jennings to narrow the gap to 14-7 with 3:15 left in the first quarter. With 7:28 left in the first half, Dion Ray found the end zone to knot things up. That's where it stood at halftime. The Golden Eagles took the lead for good with 10:42 to play in the third quarter when Mullens hooked up with Staggers on a 5-yard scoring toss. Smith tacked on his third touchdown early in the fourth quarter to put Southern Miss up by two scores. ULL capitalized on Mullens' only interception of the game when Jennings scored on a 3-yard run with 5:10 remaining to cut into the Golden Eagles' deficit again to 28-21. The Ragin' Cajuns had a shot to tie the game inside the final minute of play, but the Golden Eagle defense held them off the scoreboard. Smith finished the game with 138 yards rushing. Mullens' 346 passing yards broke a Southern Miss bowl record.

2016 MIAMI BEACH BOWL

The 2016 Miami Beach Bowl was held on December 19, 2016 at Marlins Park in Miami, Florida. The third annual edition of the Miami Beach Bowl featured the Central Michigan Chippewas against the Tulsa Golden Hurricane. This was the third meeting between the schools, with the all-time series tied 1–1. The most recent meeting was on October 17, 1987, where the Chippewas defeated the Golden Hurricane by a score of 51–21.

2016 Miami Beach Bowl	Line	1	-	2	-	3	-	4	-	Final
Central Michigan	(66.0)	3	-	0	-	0	-	7	-	10
Tulsa	(-13.0)	10	-	17	-	21	-	7	-	55

Scoring Summary
Tulsa - Atkinson 5 yard pass from Evans (Jones kick)
Tulsa - Jones 46 yard Field goal
Central Michigan - Eavey 26 yard Field goal
Tulsa - Jones 44 yard Field goal
Tulsa - Lucas 13 yard pass from Evans (Jones kick)
Tulsa - Minter 4 yard pass from Evans (Jones kick)
Tulsa - Flanders 17 yard run (Jones kick)
Tulsa - Lucas 28 yard pass from Evans (Jones kick)
Tulsa - Lucas 11 yard pass from Evans (Jones kick)
Tulsa - Brubaker 66 yard interception return (Jones kick)
Central Michigan - Hayes 13 yard run (Eavey kick)

Central Michigan Athletic Communications Miami Beach Bowl game summary - Central Michigan knew its Miami Beach Bowl opponent had an explosive offense. Tulsa's defense was pretty good too. The Golden Hurricane rolled up 581 total yards Monday as it routed the Chippewas, 55-10, at Marlins Park. The loss ended CMU's season at 6-7, its first sub-.500 season since 2011. Tulsa (10-3) entered the game averaging 522.8 yards per game. It built a 27-3 halftime lead, then hit the gas in the second half and scored nearly at will. Central Michigan Quarterback Cooper Rush, vying to become the all-time Mid-American Conference leader in passing yardage, finished with 241 yards. He needed to throw for 253 yards to supplant former Chippewa Dan LeFevour atop the list. Rush, a senior from Lansing, finished his four-year career as the CMU starter with 12,894 yards and 90 touchdown passes. He goes down as one of the very best to have ever played at CMU. Tulsa Quarterback Dane Evans completed 28 of 38 pass attempts for 304 yards and five touchdowns and was named the game's most valuable player. CMU simply could not match Tulsa's high-octane and quick-paced offensive attack, which produced 34 first downs. The Golden Hurricane never huddled on offense and the Chippewas never forced a punt all game long. Jahray Hayes scored CMU's lone touchdown on a 13-yard run in the fourth quarter, long after the game had been decided. Brian Eavey kicked a 26-yard field goal to account for the Chippewas' other points.

2016 BOCA RATON BOWL

The 2016 Boca Raton Bowl was played on December 20, 2016 at FAU Stadium in Boca Raton, Florida. The third annual edition of the Boca Raton Bowl participants were the University of Memphis Tigers of the AAC and the Western Kentucky Hilltoppers, who won the championship of Conference USA. This was the sixth meeting between the schools, with the all-time series tied 2–2–1.

2016 Boca Raton Bowl	Line	1	-	2	-	3	-	4	-	Final
Western Kentucky	(-7.0)	14	-	14	-	16	-	7	-	51
Memphis	(78.5)	10	-	7	-	7	-	7	-	31

Scoring Summary
Memphis - Pollard 45 yard pass from Ferguson (Elliott kick)
Western Kentucky - Donatell 4 yard pass from White (Simcox kick)
Memphis - Elliott 33 yard Field goal
Western Kentucky - Lamp 9 yard run (Simcox kick)
Western Kentucky - Norris 37 yard pass from White (Simcox kick)
Memphis - Miller 7 yard pass from Ferguson (Elliott kick)
Western Kentucky - Wales 2 yard run (Simcox kick)
Western Kentucky - Taylor 41 yard pass from White (Simcox kick)
Western Kentucky - Wales 1 yard run (Simcox kick)
Memphis - Miller 10 yard pass from Ferguson (Elliott kick)
Western Kentucky - Simcox 21 yard Field goal
Memphis - Miller 45 yard pass from Ferguson (Elliott kick)
Western Kentucky - Wales 1 yard run (Simcox kick)

Game Summary - The game started with both high-powered offenses stalling and going three-and-out. Memphis scored on their second drive, and the Hilltoppers responded with a touchdown of their own. Memphis's third drive ended with a field goal, while WKU pulled a trick play on first and goal - QB Mike White lateraled the ball to offensive lineman Forrest Lamp, who caught the ball and ran nine yards for the touchdown, giving Western Kentucky a four point lead. With 1:10 left in the first quarter, Western Kentucky defender Joel Iyiegbuniwe was ejected on a questionable targeting call when he hit Memphis's Tony Pollard with his facemask while Pollard was attempting to catch the ball. The first quarter ended 14-10, WKU. The Tigers' fourth drive ended 48 seconds into the second quarter when kicker Jake Elliott hit the left upright on a 45-yard field goal, keeping the score 14-10. The Hilltoppers extended their lead to 11 with just under twelve minutes left in the 2nd as they capped their fourth drive with a 37-yard touchdown pass. Memphis responded just two minutes later with a touchdown pass of their own, cutting the lead back down to four. WKU then marched down the field, taking just under seven minutes, and scored on a 2-yard rush to culminate a 13 play drive, and took a 28-17 lead into halftime. The Hilltoppers got the ball to start the second half and, on the fourth play of the third quarter, scored on a 41-yard touchdown pass, extending their lead to 18. Memphis turned the ball over on downs on their ensuing drive, but WKU was unable to capitalize as kicker Skyler Simcox missed a 45-yard field goal, the second missed FG of the game. Memphis then got the ball back but fumbled on the very next play to give the Hilltoppers possession on the Tigers' 21. Unlike the last, Western Kentucky capitalized on this turnover, and scored in three plays to extend their lead to 24 after the PAT was missed. With 6:18 left in the 3rd, WKU came close to losing another of their defenders (Juwan Gardner) to another targeting call, though this one was overturned. Memphis scored a touchdown on the next play, cutting the lead down to 17. Western Kentucky opened their next drive with a 38-yard pass on a flea flicker and a 32-yard rush, but then stalled on the 4-yard line and settled for a 21-yard field goal, extending the lead to 20. With 2:14 left in the 3rd, Memphis lost offensive lineman Trevon Tate after he received his second unsportsmanlike conduct penalty of the game. Clearly shaken, Tigers QB Riley Ferguson threw an interception on the next play, and WKU took over on the Memphis 30; Ferguson was injured on the play. WKU stalled on their ensuing drive, and the third quarter ended 44-24, Western Kentucky. Memphis's first drive of the fourth quarter resulted in a turnover on downs (their second of the game), and WKU took over on their own 29. Western Kentucky punted, and, on 4th & 12 of their next drive, Memphis threw a 45-yard touchdown pass to pull within 13. Western Kentucky added to their lead with just over two minutes to go in the game as Player of the Game Anthony Wales found the end zone from 1 yard out.

2016 POINSETTIA BOWL

The 2016 Poinsettia Bowl was played on December 21, 2016 at Qualcomm Stadium in San Diego, California. The 12th edition of the Poinsettia Bowl was aired on ESPN. It was sponsored by San Diego County Credit Union. This was the 78th meeting between the schools, with BYU leading the all-time series 44–30–3. From 1921 until 2010, BYU and Wyoming had been in the same conference, being together in the Rocky Mountain Athletic Conference, the Mountain States Conference, the Western Athletic Conference, and the Mountain West Conference until BYU football went independent after 2010.

2016 Poinsettia Bowl	Line	1	-	2	-	3	-	4	-	Final
BYU	(-7.0)	7	-	3	-	7	-	7	-	24
Wyoming	(56.0)	0	-	0	-	7	-	14	-	21

Scoring Summary
BYU - Mangum 3 yard run (Almond kick)
BYU - Almond 27 yard Field goal
Wyoming - Hill 4 yard run (Rothe kick)
BYU - Balderree 5 yard pass from Mangum (Almond kick)
BYU - Williams 36 yard run (Almond kick)
Wyoming - Gentry 9 yard pass from Allen (Rothe kick)
Wyoming - Gentry 23 yard pass from Allen (Rothe kick)

BYU Athletic Communications Poinsettia Bowl game summary - On a rare wet and rainy night at Qualcomm Stadium, BYU capped off its 2016 season with a wild 24-21 win over Wyoming in the 2016 San Diego County Credit Union Poinsettia Bowl on Wednesday. BYU (9-4) led 24-7 in the fourth quarter, but a furious Cowboy (8-6) comeback made it a thriller in the final minutes. Wyoming cut the advantage to 24-21 and had the ball at the Cougar 32-yard line with 1:22 to play before senior Kai Nacua picked off a pass heading near the end zone to end the final threat of a comeback. The win was BYU's first bowl win since its last trip to the Poinsettia Bowl in 2012 when the Cougars defeated San Diego State 23-6. Senior running back Jamaal Williams put on a show in his final game at BYU, running for 210 yards and one touchdown on 26 carries. He finished his career with the most rushing yards in school history with 3,901 and the most games of 100 rushing yards or more with 16. Nacua's interception was his sixth of the year and 14th of his career. Dayan Lake also had a takeaway, giving BYU 21 interceptions in 2016, tied for No. 2 nationally after the game. Harvey Langi led the team with 16 tackles, a career high, while Butch Pau'u and Fred Warner had 11 and 10 tackles, respectively. Wyoming's punter fumbled the snap near the end of the first quarter at the Cowboy 3-yard line. Quarterback Tanner Mangum scrambled and punched it in for a rushing score to put BYU up 7-0 with 38 seconds to play after a slow and soggy first quarter. Mangum threw an interception on the next Cougar possession and Wyoming ran it back to the BYU 39-yard line. The Cougar defense forced a field goal attempt, and a fake was snuffed out as Langi batted down a pass attempt. BYU took over at its own 25-yard line midway through the second frame. BYU was able to get three points on the next possession at the 3:08 mark in the second quarter with a 27-yard field goal from Rhett Almond. The Cougars took a 10-0 lead into halftime. Out of the break, Wyoming went 60 yards on its first drive, capped by a 4-yard touchdown run to cut BYU's lead to 10-7 after a drive over eight minutes long. BYU answered in its first possession of the half. Mangum completed 4 of 5 passes on the drive, capped off with a completion on a desperation throw on to the end zone that bounced off of multiple players' hands before falling into Tanner Balderree's arms for a 5-yard touchdown. Nick Kurtz had a 39-yard reception to set up the score. With 2:42 left in the third quarter, BYU had a 17-7 lead. On the first play following a targeting call that ejected defensive back Micah Hannemann near the end of the third quarter, Lake stepped in front of a pass and intercepted it for his third pick of the year, returning it 14 yards to the BYU 45-yard line. The Cougars cashed in five plays later when a Jonah Trinnaman block helped spring Williams for a 36-yard touchdown scamper to make it 24-7 less than a minute into the fourth quarter. The back and forth scoring continued when Wyoming made it 24-14 after a 9-yard touchdown pass with 7:35 left in the game. The Cowboys continued to fight with another touchdown from Wyoming wide receiver Tanner Gentry (his second of the game) with 2:11 to go to make things interesting at 24-21. BYU failed to convert on the next drive and had to punt it back to Wyoming with 1:52 remaining. The Cowboys took over at midfield. After getting to the 32-yard line, Wyoming's Quarterback tried to extend the play and threw across his body for the end zone, but Nacua jumped in front and picked it off to seal BYU's victory. BYU finishes the season 9-4 with a bowl victory in head coach Kalani Sitake's first season at the helm.

2016 FAMOUS IDAHO POTATO BOWL

The 2016 Famous Idaho Potato Bowl was played on Thursday, December 22, at Albertsons Stadium in Boise, Idaho. The twentieth annual edition of the Famous Idaho Potato Bowl was sponsored by the Idaho Potato Commission.

2016 Famous Idaho Potato Bowl	Line	1	-	2	-	3	-	4	-	Final
Idaho	(64.5)	0	-	20	-	21	-	20	-	61
Colorado State	(-16.0)	0	-	7	-	7	-	36	-	50

Scoring Summary
Colorado State - Johnson 52 yard pass from Stevens (Bryan kick)
Idaho - Saunders 2 yard run (Kick failed)
Idaho - Saunders 26 yard run (Rehkow kick)
Idaho - Sannon 6 yard pass from Linehan (Rehkow kick)
Idaho - Linehan 7 yard run (Rehkow kick)
Idaho - Watson 74 yard pass from Linehan (Rehkow kick)
Idaho - Sannon 16 yard pass from Linehan (Rehkow kick)
Colorado State - Gallup 12 yard pass from Stevens (Bryan kick)
Idaho - Duckworth 5 yard run (Rehkow kick)
Colorado State - Johnson 72 yard pass from Stevens (Bryan kick)
Idaho - Frysinger 54 yard pass from Linehan (Rehkow kick)
Colorado State - Gallup 60 yard pass from Stevens (Bryan kick)
Idaho - Saunders 12 yard run (Kick failed)
Colorado State - Gallup 3 yard pass from Stevens (Bryan kick)
Colorado State - Dawkins 22 yard run (Bryan kick)
Colorado State - Matthews 1 yard run (Johnson pass from Stevens)

Famous Idaho Potato Bowl Game Summary - The 2016 Famous Idaho Potato Bowl was broadcast by ESPN. Idaho kicked off to start the game and Rams returner Jake Schlager opened the game with a 46-yard return. After an unsportsmanlike conduct penalty, the Rams started their first drive at their own 40. They marched the ball down to the Idaho 21, where they failed to convert a 4th & 1. Idaho's first drive started at their own 21, but they stalled and went three-and-out, and CSU got the ball on their own 42. The Rams' second drive was cut short after two plays when Rams QB Nick Stevens's pass was intercepted over the middle by Jayshawn Jordan at the Idaho 41. The Vandals again went three-and-out and punted back to Colorado State, and the punt was downed at the CSU 40. CSU's third drive ended in a punt that rolled into the end zone, and the Vandals took over at their own 20. For the third time, Idaho went three-and-out, and Colorado State took the ball on their own 36 yard line. The Rams punted right back to Idaho and the Vandals took the ball on their own 25. This drive ended in a punt, and CSU took over on their own 16. The Rams took over on their own 16 and drove to their own 48, where they threw a 52-yard touchdown pass for the first points of the game. They kicked off to Idaho and the Vandals started their fifth drive on their own 35. Idaho jumpstarted their offense with their first big play of the game, a 36-yard pass down to the CSU 2; they scored on the next play to pull within one after the extra point was missed. Idaho's kickoff resulted in a touchback, and the Rams got the football on the 25. A false start and two incompletions didn't help the offense, and CSU punted it right back to Idaho, who took over at their own 38. Yet again, the Vandals made a statement with a deep pass: this time a 33-yard pass, and again they scored on the next play. They took the lead on a 26-yard scamper from RB Isaiah Saunders, his second of the game. CSU returned the kickoff to the 27. After gaining one first down, the Rams punted again, and Idaho started their seventh drive on their own 15. Idaho squibbed the kickoff and CSU started the last drive of the second half on their own 17 with 14 seconds left. They ran one play and the clock expired. Idaho received the kick to open the second half; they started their drive on the 31. Idaho's offense came out ready to play as they marched the ball down the field and capped the drive with their fourth touchdown in their last four drives. Colorado State's first drive of the third quarter included a third down conversion, yet still ended in a punt, which was downed on the 21. Idaho's next drive was capped by yet another touchdown, upping their lead to 27. The Rams started their second drive of the second half on their own 39. Two incompletions and a sack later, Colorado State punted, and Idaho took over on the 9. The Vandals would be forced to punt on this drive, but the punt was muffed, and Idaho got the ball right back on the CSU 14. It took them just three more plays to punch it in and extend their lead to 34. The Rams' next possession finally saw something productive happen on offense: back-to-back long passes going for 47 and 24 yards that took them down to the Idaho 20. An unsportsmanlike conduct penalty took the ball down to the 7, and two plays later the Rams found the end zone and snapped Idaho's streak of 41 unanswered points. Idaho's offense didn't let up, though, as they scored within two minutes of the start of the fourth quarter to extend their lead to 34. CSU responded, though, with a 72-yard touchdown pass on a blown coverage. Idaho responded with yet another long touchdown pass - this time Jordan Frysinger caught a long ball with one hand while being interfered with. Idaho went back up by 34 with 9:27 left in the game. On the first play of their next drive, the Rams found the end zone again on a long pass; a 60-yard touchdown pass made the score 55-28 with 9:06 left. Colorado State's onside kick was unsuccessful, and Idaho responded with yet another touchdown: an Isaiah Saunders 12-yard rush to make it 61-28 after the PAT was missed. Once again, Colorado State found the end zone; this time from 3 yards out on a pass play. Again, the onside kick was unsuccessful. The first drive of the fourth quarter not to result in a touchdown came with 3:12 to go when Idaho went three-and-out and was forced to punt back to CSU, who took over on their own 16. With 2:42 to play, Nick Stevens went for another long pass but was intercepted at the Idaho 20 by D.J. Hampton. Idaho went three-and-out and punted back to the Rams, who started their next drive of the game on the 43 and resulted in a 22-yard touchdown rush from CSU's Dalyn Dawkins, making the score 61-42. With just over a minute left in the game, Colorado State recovered their onside kick at the CSU 46 and gained 39 yards on the first play of that possession. The second play got them inside the five and 2 plays later they scored their fifth touchdown of the fourth quarter on a 1-yard rush by Izzy Matthews. The two-point conversion was good on a Stevens to Johnson pass, and the score was 61-50.

2016 ARMED FORCES BOWL
LOUISIANA TECH 48   NAVY 45

The 2016 Armed Forces Bowl was played on December 23, 2016 at Amon G. Carter Stadium in Fort Worth, Texas. This was the third meeting between the schools, with Navy winning both previous ones.

2016 Armed Forces Bowl	Line	1	-	2	-	3	-	4	-	Final
Louisiana Tech	(-7.5)	17	-	14	-	0	-	17	-	48
Navy	(67.5)	7	-	17	-	7	-	14	-	45

Scoring Summary
Louisiana Tech - Higgins 1 yard run (Barnes kick)
Louisiana Tech - Barnes 22 yard Field goal
NAVY - Abey 3 yard run (Moehring kick)
Louisiana Tech - Taylor 19 yard pass from Higgins (Barnes kick)
NAVY - Bonner 64 yard pass from Abey (Moehring kick)
NAVY - Abey 2 yard run (Moehring kick)
Louisiana Tech - Henderson 3 yard pass from Higgins (Barnes kick)
NAVY - Moehring 40 yard Field goal
Louisiana Tech - Taylor 51 yard pass from Higgins (Barnes kick)
NAVY - High 24 yard run (Moehring kick)
Louisiana Tech - Scott 12 yard run (Barnes kick)
NAVY - High 9 yard run (Moehring kick)
Louisiana Tech - Henderson 4 yard pass from Higgins (Barnes kick)
NAVY - Perry 30 yard run (Moehring kick)
Louisiana Tech - Barnes 32 yard Field goal

Star-Telegram Armed Forces Bowl game summary - Louisiana Tech's recipe for winning on Saturday was built by the now-calloused bare hands of Trent Taylor and Carlos Henderson in an Armed Forces Bowl game that came down to the guy wearing the cleanest jersey. Taylor, the game's MVP, had game-record totals of 12 catches for 233 yards and two touchdowns, and Henderson added 129 yards and two TDs for the Bulldogs, who defeated No. 25 Navy 48-45 on a 32-yard field goal off the foot of Jonathan Barnes in the closing seconds at TCU's Amon G. Carter Stadium. Their Quarterback Ryan Higgins passed for 409 yards and four TDs on 29-of-40 passing for the Bulldogs, who finished 2016 at 9-5 and captured their third bowl victory in consecutive years, unprecedented at Louisiana Tech. Taylor had a TD reception of 19 yards and another of 51 yards just before the half. Henderson, who had a Louisiana Tech-bowl record 215 all-purpose yards, had TD scores of 3 and 4 yards. The Bulldogs started their decisive campaign at their own 15 with 3:40 left in the game and drove the ball to Navy's 15 in nine plays. The made field-goal was sweet justice for Barnes who missed two field goals, including one to start the fourth quarter in a one-point loss to Arkansas in the Bulldogs' season opener. Taylor leaves Louisiana Tech as one of the school's most prolific receivers, including becoming only the second player in school history to go over 4,000 yards receiving. Troy Edwards was the other. Over his career, Taylor has 20 games of 100 or more yards. In addition to the Bulldogs snapping a two-game skid, the triumph was also a feather in the cap for Conference USA, which is now 4-1 in the post-season. If fans came to watch a defensive struggle, they came to the wrong game, which turned out to be the highest-scoring Armed Forces Bowl, surpassing last year's 55-36 Cal win over Air Force. The teams combined for 956 total yards, and each did it their way. Of Louisiana Tech's 497 total, 409 yards were generated through the pass. Out of its triple-option offense, Navy (9-5) racked up 459 total yards, including 300 rushing. After throwing two interceptions in his first career start, against Army on Dec. 10, Navy Quarterback Zach Abey more resembled a seasoned starter on Saturday. Abey had 273 total yards and accounted for three touchdowns, two on short runs and a 64-yard pass to Darryl Bonner. The Bulldogs put Navy in a 10-0 hole to start the game. Louisiana Tech started the game's first drive at the Navy 16 after Henderson's 82-yard return on the opening kickoff. On the fourth play of the game from the 1, Higgins snuck into the end zone to give Louisiana Tech an early touchdown lead. The Bulldogs then turned Prince Sam's fumble recovery off Navy's first possession into a Jonathan Barnes 22-yard field goal to make the score 10-0. Abey's 3-yard TD run got the Midshipmen on the board and set off a run. After misfires to open receivers over the top, Abey finally connected with Bonner, who raced down the middle of the field for the Midshipmen's second score to cap a two-play, 23-second drive. Abey's 2-yard scoring run marked the game's first lead change, putting Navy up 21-17 at the 11:17 mark of the second quarter. Tied at 24-all just before half, Louisiana Tech moved the ball to midfield, and from there Higgins dialed up his star receiver a second time, hitting Taylor for a 51-yard score to cap a six-play drive.

2016 BAHAMAS BOWL

The 2016 Bahamas Bowl was played on December 23, 2016 at Thomas Robinson Stadium in Nassau in the Bahamas. The third edition of the Bahamas Bowl featured the Eastern Michigan Eagles of the Mid-American Conference against the Old Dominion Monarchs of Conference USA.

2016 Bahamas Bowl	Line	1	-	2	-	3	-	4	-	Final
Eastern Michigan	(63.0)	0	-	0	-	17	-	3	-	20
Old Dominion	(-5.0)	3	-	7	-	7	-	7	-	24

Scoring Summary
Old Dominion - Davis 34 yard Field goal
Old Dominion - Pascal 47 yard pass from Washington (Davis kick)
Eastern Michigan - Bailey 5 yard pass from Roback (Fricano kick)
Old Dominion - Fulgham 31 yard pass from Washington (Davis kick)
Eastern Michigan - Niupalau 5 yard pass from Roback (Fricano kick)
Eastern Michigan - Fricano 24 yard Field goal
Old Dominion - Duhart 5 yard pass from Washington (Davis kick)
Eastern Michigan - Fricano 19 yard Field goal

Bahamas Bowl game summary - Old Dominion, making the school's first bowl appearance since the football program restarted in 2009, held off Eastern Michigan 24-20 to win the 2016 Popeye's Bahamas Bowl. Led by Offensive Player of the Game running back Ray Lawry and his 133 rushing yards, the Monarchs (10-3) left the Bahamas with a six-game win streak and their first bowl trophy. Quarterback David Washington added 188 passing yards and three touchdowns for ODU. Eastern Michigan Quarterback Brogan Roback did all he could to keep the Eagles (7-6) in the game, throwing for 300 yards and two second-half touchdowns, but it was not enough to help EMU to a title in their first bowl game in 29 years. Eastern Michigan dominated the time of possession, holding the ball 32:30 to the Monarchs' 27:30, and converted on a season-high 13 third downs, but it was the Old Dominion defense that made one final stand late in the fourth quarter. ODU senior linebacker TJ Ricks was named Defensive Player of the Game after finishing with nine tackles, including one for a loss. Through the first 30 minutes, Old Dominion was the only team able to put points on the board, holding a 10-0 lead at the half. It was the eighth time this season the Monarchs led a game at the break. ODU got on the board first when Brad Davis connected on a 34-yard field goal for a 3-0 lead with 7:43 remaining in the first quarter. The 16-play, 58-yard drive appeared to stall at midfield when the Monarchs faced a fourth-and-two situation. Wilder dialed up a fake punt, calling a direct snap to running back Jeremy Cox, who drove the ball three yards for the first down. Old Dominion extended its lead to 10-0 behind a 47-yard touchdown pass from Washington to Zach Pascal.

The six-play, 80-yard drive began with Anthony Wilson picking off Roback in the end zone for a touchback, and the drive took just 2:23. Unlike the first half, both teams' offenses came out of the locker rooms on fire. Each team found the end zone in the first five minutes of action in the third quarter. After receiving the kickoff to start the second half, Roback put the Eagles on the board, driving his team 76 yards in 2:50, capped off by a five-yard strike to wide receiver Sergio Bailey to cut the Old Dominion lead to 10-7. It didn't take long for the Monarchs to respond, as Washington found Travis Fulgham downfield for a 31-yard touchdown with no defender in sight to push the ODU lead to 17-7 with 9:50 remaining in the third quarter. Roback hit Johnnie Niupalau for a five-yard touchdown pass, capitalizing on another quick drive to pull to 17-14 with 7:25 left in the third quarter. A 24-yard field goal by Eastern Michigan's Paul Fricano with 12 seconds remaining in the third tied the game at 17-17. Opening the fourth quarter, Washington drove Old Dominion 72 yards in 2:09 to put the Monarchs back on top 24-17 after hitting Jonathan Duhart on a five-yard TD pass in the corner of the end zone – his third passing touchdown of the game. Fricano connected on a 19-yard field goal with 9:08 to play to cut the Monarchs lead to 24-20. The Eagles had a chance late, driving the ball to midfield, but couldn't keep their drive going, punting the ball back to Old Dominion. ODU ran out the final 5:21 to secure the victory.

2016 DOLLAR GENERAL BOWL

The 2016 Dollar General Bowl was played at Ladd Peebles Stadium in Mobile, Alabama on December 23, 2016. The 18th edition of the Dollar General Bowl (previously called the GoDaddy Bowl) featured the Ohio Bobcats of the Mid-American Conference versus the Troy Trojans of the Sun Belt Conference. This was the second meeting between the schools; the first meeting was in the 2010 New Orleans Bowl, where the Trojans defeated the Bobcats by a score of 48–21.

2016 Dollar General Bowl	Line	1	-	2	-	3	-	4	-	Final
Ohio	(49.5)	7	-	10	-	3	-	3	-	23
Troy	(-6.0)	14	-	7	-	7	-	0	-	28

Scoring Summary
Troy - Chunn 1 yard run (Kay kick)
Ohio - White 44 yard pass from Windham (Zervos kick)
Troy - Chunn 3 yard run (Kay kick)
Ohio - Zervos 33 yard Field goal
Troy - Thompson 11 yard pass from Silvers (Kay kick)
Ohio - Reid 5 yard pass from Windham (Zervos kick)
Troy - Chunn 4 yard run (Kay kick)
Ohio - Zervos 47 yard Field goal
Ohio - Zervos 37 yard Field goal

Associated Press Dollar General Bowl game summary - The Troy Trojans polished off their best season as an FBS program thanks largely to a defense that kept taking the ball away. Jordan Chunn had three short touchdown runs and the Trojans intercepted four passes and recovered a fumble in a 28-23 victory over Ohio in the Dollar General Bowl on Friday night. The Trojans (10-3) finished off their first 10-win season since moving up to the FBS in 2001, thanks largely to a defense that came up with three big fourth-quarter stops. The first Sun Belt Conference team to crack the Top 25, Troy forced 18 turnovers in its last five games. This time it was mainly a defense that hounded Quarterback Greg Windham into mistakes and kept delivering stops. The result was a win in the program's first bowl game since 2010. The Bobcats (8-6) settled for field goal attempts twice in the fourth quarter, making one, and got one more chance from their own 15 with 2:20 left and no timeouts. They managed one first down, but Windham couldn't throw for another one under heavy pressure. Louie Zervos had made a 37-yard field goal with 4:01 left to cut Troy's lead to 28-23. They had first down from the 12 before a personal foul penalty against lineman Jake Pruehs. Solich said he wasn't sure what happened to prompt the flag. Chunn found little room to run except near the goal line against the nation's sixth-ranked run defense. He had 56 yards on 20 carries to earn offensive MVP honors. Deondre Douglas gained 113 yards on six catches. Ohio's Jordan Reid had 12 catches for 162 yards. Troy's fourth interception came courtesy of 315-pound defensive tackle Trevon Sanders. One play later, Chunn powered in for a touchdown and a 28-17 third-quarter lead. Linebacker Justin Lucas made another big one when he was closing in on Windham when the ball came right to him to set up Troy's third touchdown. He earned game MVP honors. Rashad Dillard was credited with three pressures on Windham and was the defensive MVP.

2016 HAWAII BOWL

The 2016 Hawaii Bowl was played on December 24, 2016 at Aloha Stadium in Honolulu, Hawaii. The 15th edition of the Hawaii Bowl featured the Middle Tennessee Blue Raiders from Conference USA against the Hawaii Rainbow Warriors from the Mountain West Conference. It was aired on ESPN. This was the second time that the Hawaii Bowl featured a team with a losing record, after Fresno State in the 2014 Hawaii Bowl. This was the second meeting between the schools.

2016 Hawaii Bowl	Line	1	-	2	-	3	-	4	-	Final
Hawaii	(70.0)	14	-	21	-	10	-	7	-	52
Middle Tennessee	(-7.5)	14	-	7	-	7	-	7	-	35

Scoring Summary
Middle Tennessee - Mathers 20 yard run (Rooker kick)
Middle Tennessee - James 51 yard pass from Stockstill (Rooker kick)
Hawaii - Unga 18 yard pass from Brown (Sanchez kick)
Hawaii - Lakalaka 1 yard run (Sanchez kick)
Hawaii - Brown 2 yard run (Sanchez kick)
Hawaii - Henderson 68 yard interception return (Sanchez kick)
Middle Tennessee - Lee 3 yard pass from Stockstill (Rooker kick)
Hawaii - Kemp 39 yard pass from Brown (Sanchez kick)
Hawaii - Sanchez 23 yard Field goal
Middle Tennessee - Andrews 10 yard pass from Stockstill (Rooker kick)
Hawaii - Unga 12 yard pass from Brown (Sanchez kick)
Middle Tennessee - Lee 13 yard pass from Stockstill (Rooker kick)
Hawaii - Collie 4 yard pass from Brown (Sanchez kick)

Associated Press Hawaii Bowl game summary - Hawaii has already come quite a ways in one season under Coach Nick Rolovich, and that culminated in snapping a decade-long skid on Saturday night. Dru Brown threw for 274 yards and four touchdowns and Hawaii overcame an early deficit to beat Middle Tennessee 52-35 in the Hawaii Bowl. The Rainbow Warriors (7-7) amassed 500 yards of total offense and their highest-scoring output this season to end on a three-game winning streak. The Christmas Eve victory marks their first bowl win since 2006, an unlikely end to a season that began with losses in three of the first four games under Rolovich. Brown completed 20 of 30 passes without an interception. He had a 2-yard touchdown run and was sacked just once. Brown has nine touchdowns to zero interceptions in his last two games. Tight end Metuisela Unga caught two of Brown's scoring strikes, an 18-yarder in the first quarter for Hawaii's first score and a 12-yarder late in the third. Diocemy Saint Juste ran for 170 yards on 25 carries. Hawaii turned three Middle Tennessee turnovers into 21 points. It fell behind 14-0 just over 5 minutes into the game but scored the next 28 points and never relinquished the lead. Brent Stockstill started at Quarterback for the Blue Raiders (8-5) after missing the last three games with a broken collarbone. He finished 30 of 51 passing for 432 yards. Stockstill threw four touchdown passes -- two to Richie James -- and was intercepted twice. James caught nine passes for 175 yards. It was his 14th game of 100 or more receiving yards in his career. Middle Tennessee posted 542 yards of total offense. Hawaii took a 35-21 lead into halftime.

2016 ST. PETERSBURG BOWL

The 2016 St. Petersburg Bowl was played on December 26, 2016 at Tropicana Field in St. Petersburg, Florida. The ninth edition of the St. Petersburg Bowl featured the Miami Redhawks from the Mid-American Conference against the Mississippi State Bulldogs from the Southeastern Conference.

2016 St. Petersburg Bowl	Line	1	-	2	-	3	-	4	-	Final
Miami-Ohio	(57.5)	3	-	6	-	7	-	0	-	16
Mississippi State	(-14.5)	0	-	7	-	7	-	3	-	17

Scoring Summary
Miami-Ohio - Dowd 18 yard Field goal
Miami-Ohio - Gardner 6 yard pass from Ragland (Kick failed)
Mississippi State - Fitzgerald 2 yard run (Graves kick)
Miami-Ohio - Smith 1 yard pass from Ragland (Dowd kick)
Mississippi State - Fitzgerald 44 yard run (Graves kick)
Mississippi State - Graves 36 yard Field goal

Associated Press St. Petersburg Bowl game summary - Mississippi State's sideline erupted in celebration, relieved to escape with a victory to end a challenging season. Nick Fitzgerald rushed for 142 yards and two touchdowns in another strong performance by the dual-threat Quarterback; however, the heavily favored Bulldogs had to block a field goal in the closing seconds to hold off Miami (Ohio) 17-16 in the St. Petersburg Bowl on Monday. Instead, both the Bulldogs (6-7) and the RedHawks (6-7), who won six straight games to become bowl eligible, finished with losing marks. Fitzgerald, who led the Southeastern Conference in total offense, scored on runs of 2 and 44 yards on the way to his eighth 100-yard rushing performance of the season. The redshirt sophomore also completed 13 of 26 passes for 126 yards. Gus Ragland threw for 257 yards and two touchdowns for Miami. He also threw his first interception of the

season early in the fourth quarter, and Mississippi State turned the mistake into a 36-yard field goal that put the Bulldogs ahead with 12:03 remaining. The RedHawks drove the ball deep into Bulldogs territory on their next two possessions, turning the ball over on downs at the Mississippi State 32 midway through the fourth quarter and reaching the 17 before Dowd had his kick blocked with 5 seconds left. James Gardner and Ryan Smith caught TD passes for Miami, which also had an extra-point blocked in the opening half.
PERSEVERANCE - Miami became the first team in NCAA history to start 0-6 and finish the regular season 6-6. The senior class that entered school in 2013 had a 5-37 record before the RedHawks began their six-game winning streak in mid-October.

2016 QUICK LANE BOWL

The 2016 Quick Lane Bowl was played at Ford Field in Detroit, Michigan, on December 26, 2016. The third edition of the Quick Lane Bowl featured the Maryland Terrapins of the Big Ten Conference and the Boston College Eagles of the Atlantic Coast Conference. This was the twelfth meeting between the schools, with Boston College leading the all-time series 8–3 coming into the game. Notably, Boston College and Maryland had been together in the ACC from 2005 until 2013, after which Maryland left to join the Big Ten.

2016 Quick Lane Bowl	Line	1	-	2	-	3	-	4	-	Final
Maryland	(-1.0)	0	-	13	-	14	-	3	-	30
Boston College	(43.5)	6	-	23	-	7	-	0	-	36

Scoring Summary
Boston College - Hillman 1 yard run (Kick failed)
Boston College - Sweeney 2 yard pass from Towles (Knoll kick)
Boston College - Knoll 22 yard Field goal
Maryland - Johnson 62 yard run (Greene kick)
Boston College - Towles 20 yard pass from Smith (Knoll kick)
Maryland - Johnson 30 yard run (Pass failed)
Boston College - Walker 49 yard pass from Towles (Kick failed)
Boston College - Kavalec recovered fumble in end zone (Knoll kick)
Maryland - Morgan 63 yard pass from Hills (Greene kick)
Maryland - Jacobs 52 yard pass from Hills (Greene kick)
Maryland - Greene 23 yard Field goal

Associated Press Quick Lane Bowl game summary - Boston College feels right at home playing at Ford Field. The Eagles, who improved to 2-0 all time at the Lions' stadium, surged to a big lead over Maryland and held on for a 36-30 win at Monday's Quick Lane Bowl. Boston College (7-6), which also won over Toledo, 51-25, in the 2002 Motor City Bowl at Ford Field, finished 2016 with three straight wins. The Eagles ended the regular season with victories over Connecticut and Wake Forest to become bowl eligible. Attendance was announced at 19,117, although it appeared closer to 10,000. Monday's win snapped a five-game bowl losing streak and gave Boston College its first postseason victory since beating Michigan State, 24-21, in the 2007 Champs Sports Bowl. It was a disappointing finish for Maryland (6-7), which hoped to build momentum for next season and give first-year coach DJ Durkin, a former defensive coordinator at Michigan, positive recruiting leverage moving forward. Maryland had four turnovers, including a fumble in its own end zone that Boston College recovered for a third-quarter touchdown, and committed 11 penalties for 86 yards. Boston College, which built a 36-13 third-quarter advantage, allowed Maryland to fight back and make it interesting. The Terps scored two touchdowns, including Perry Hills' 52-yard pass to Levern Jacobs, to cut the deficit to 36-27. Maryland had a chance to get closer with 4 minutes left in the game, but Hills fumbled on Boston College's 2-yard line, and it was recovered by Eagles linebacker Matt Milano. On Boston College's ensuing possession, running back Jon Hilliman fumbled on his own 5 and Maryland's Azubuike Ukandu recovered, leading to Adam Greene's 23-yard field goal to make it 36-30 with 2:55 left. Maryland forced a Boston College punt with 1:57 remaining but was not able to score. Eagles fifth-year senior Quarterback Patrick Towles finished with 151 yards passing and two touchdowns. He also caught a 20-yard scoring pass from receiver Jeff Smith on a trick play, putting his team ahead, 23-7, in the second quarter. Boston College junior defensive end Harold Landry, an All-America second-team selection by the Associated Press, had four tackles, 1.5 sacks, an interception, two pass break-ups and a Quarterback hurry. Hills passed for 229 yards and two touchdowns, while sophomore running back Ty Johnson had 159 yards and two touchdowns, including a 62-yarder to cut Boston College's lead to 16-7. Boston College and Maryland were former rivals in the ACC before Maryland joined the Big Ten in 2014. The Eagles lead the all-time series, 9-3, and have won four consecutive games against the Terps.

2016 INDEPENDENCE BOWL

The 2016 Independence Bowl was played on December 26, 2016 at Independence Stadium in Shreveport, Louisiana. The 41st annual Independence Bowl featured the NC State Wolfpack of the ACC against the Vanderbilt Commodores of the SEC. This was the third meeting between the schools, with Vanderbilt winning the two previous ones. The most recent meeting was in the 2012 Music City Bowl, where the Commodores defeated the Wolfpack by a score of 38–24.

2016 Independence Bowl	Line	1	-	2	-	3	-	4	-	Final
NC State	(-6.5)	0	-	14	-	14	-	13	-	41
Vanderbilt	(46.5)	3	-	0	-	7	-	7	-	17

Scoring Summary
Vanderbilt - Openshaw 52 yard Field goal
NC State - Samuels 9 yard pass from Finley (Haskins kick)
NC State - Samuels 55 yard pass from Finley (Haskins kick)
NC State - Gallaspy 5 yard pass from Finley (Haskins kick)
NC State - Samuels 17 yard pass from Finley (Haskins kick)
Vanderbilt - Webb 30 yard run (Openshaw kick)
Vanderbilt - Blasingame 1 yard run (Openshaw kick)
NC State - Hines 100 yard kickoff return (Haskins kick)
NC State - Clark 30 yard interception return (No kick)

Associated Press Independence Bowl game summary - North Carolina State Quarterback Ryan Finley has a simple philosophy when it comes to getting do-everything threat Jaylen Samuels involved with the offense. The method of choice on Monday was by air, and Finley found Samuels for three touchdowns passes in North Carolina State's 41-17 win over Vanderbilt in the Independence Bowl. North Carolina State (7-6) won three of its final four games to finish with a winning record. The Wolfpack built a 28-3 lead by midway through the third quarter -- largely thanks to Samuels' touchdown catches of 9, 55 and 17 yards -- and then held off a brief Vanderbilt rally. Samuels was named the game's Most Valuable Player on offense and his three touchdown catches were an Independence Bowl record. Finley, who completed 19 of 30 passes for 235 yards, hit Samuels six times for 104 yards. North Carolina State coach Dave Doeren said Samuels' big night wasn't necessarily planned, but when Vanderbilt loaded the defense to stop the run, he was the man who was open. The 5-foot-11, 223-pound junior often has had an unorthodox role on the offense and is listed as a tight end and fullback. Vanderbilt (6-7) had a lot of momentum going into the game thanks to surprising wins over Mississippi and Tennessee to end the regular season. But the Commodores' offense -- which scored a combined 83 points against the Rebels and Volunteers -- struggled for most of the night. Vanderbilt's Kyle Shurmur completed just 19 of 46 passes for 158 yards and three interceptions. Even so, the Commodores briefly made things interesting, closing to 28-17 early in the fourth quarter. But that's when NC State's Nyheim Hines responded with a 100-yard touchdown on a kickoff return to put the game out of reach.

DEFENSIVE MVP - North Carolina State's Airius Moore was named the game's defensive MVP after leading the Wolfpack with nine tackles, including two sacks.

2016 HEART OF DALLAS BOWL

The 2016 Heart of Dallas Bowl was played at the Cotton Bowl in Dallas, Texas, on December 27, 2016. The seventh Heart of Dallas Bowl featured the Army Black Knights versus the North Texas Mean Green of Conference USA. This was the sixth meeting between the schools, with Army previously leading the all-time series 4–1. The most recent meeting was earlier in the season, on October 22, 2016, where the Mean Green defeated the Black Knights by a score of 35–18, marking the first time North Texas had ever beaten Army.

2016 Heart of Dallas Bowl	Line	1	-	2	-	3	-	4	-	OT	-	Final
Army	(-10.5)	12	-	12	-	7	-	0	-	7	-	38
North Texas	(47.0)	7	-	14	-	7	-	3	-	0	-	31

Scoring Summary
ARMY - Wolfolk 5 yard run (Kick failed)
North Texas - Wilson 22 yard run (Moore kick)
ARMY - Campbell 70 yard run (Run failed)
ARMY - Wolfolk 1 yard run (Run failed)
ARMY - Davidson 6 yard run (Pass failed)
North Texas - Wilson 22 yard pass from Morris (Moore kick)
North Texas - Bussey 27 yard pass from Morris (Moore kick)
ARMY - Bradshaw 65 yard run (Wilson kick)
North Texas - Wilson 18 yard pass from Morris (Moore kick)
North Texas - Moore 37 yard Field goal
ARMY - Asberry 3 yard run (Wilson kick)

UPI Heart of Dallas Bowl game summary - Jordan Asberry scored on a 3-yard touchdown run in overtime as Army outlasted North Texas 38-31 on Tuesday in the Zaxby's Heart of Dallas Bowl before a sun-splashed crowd of 39,177 at the venerable Cotton Bowl Stadium in Dallas. After Asberry's scoring run, the Army defense held North Texas without a first down, forcing a desperation pass from Alec Morris on fourth-and-9 that was batted away to secure the victory. Army rolled the dice in overtime, opting to go for touchdown rather than a field goal on fourth down from the North Texas 3-yard line. But the gamble worked as Asberry took an option pitch and found his way into the end zone to give the Black Knights the lead. Army (8-5) ran off nearly 10 1/2 minutes on a final fourth-quarter drive that began at its own 4-yard line and ended on a missed fourth-down conversion at the North Texas 30 with 2:18 to play. That was enough time for the Mean Green to move into field-goal range for Trevor Moore, whose 37-yard kick with 28 seconds to play in regulation tied the game at 31 and forced overtime. Quarterback Ahmad Bradshaw ran for 129 yards for Army, including a 65-yard touchdown in the third quarter. Darnell Woolfolk added 119 yards and two touchdowns for the Black Knights. The eight wins are the most for Army since the 1996 team when it was 10-2. North Texas (5-8) was led by Alec Morris's 304 yards and three touchdowns passing. The Mean Green earned a berth in the bowl game on the strength of its Academic Progress Rate when there were not enough 6-6 or better teams eligible for the postseason. Of the 128 Football Bowl Subdivision schools, North Texas ranked 10th in APR and was second among non-eligible teams. Army scored on its first four possessions, getting a pair of touchdown runs from Darnell Woolfolk from 5 and 3 yards away, respectively, a rousing 70-yard TD dash by Tyler Campbell on a picture-perfect option pitch from Bradshaw and a 6-yard run up the middle by fullback Andy Davidson. Blake Wilson's extra-point kick after the first touchdown missed wide left, and the Black Knights failed on 2-point conversion attempts following the other three TDs but still earned a 24-7 lead. North Texas responded after Woolfolk's first touchdown with a six-play, 66-yard drive that culminated in a 22-yard scoring run from Wilson, but the Mean Green were forced to punt on their next two possessions. Wilson found the end zone again with 2:26 to play in the first half on a 22-yard catch from Morris. The touchdown cut Army's advantage to 24-14 and swung momentum into North Texas' favor for the first time. North Texas moved even closer on its final possession of the first half, moving 68 yards in 1:40 to a 27-yard TD pass from Morris to Rico Bussey with 10 seconds remaining until intermission. Army outgained North Texas 332-245 in the first half, with 294 of the Black Knights' yardage coming on the ground. Bradshaw ripped off his 65-yard touchdown run on its first possession of the third quarter, pushing the Black Knights' lead to 31-21. The drive began at the Army 13-yard line after Elijah Riley's interception of Morris. Army returned the favor late in the third quarter when Malik McGue muffed a punt that was recovered by North Texas' Kenny Buyers at the Black Knights' 18-yard line. On the ensuing snap, Morris found Tyler Wilson for a touchdown that brought the Mean Green to within 31-28.

2016 MILITARY BOWL

The 2016 Military Bowl was played at Navy–Marine Corps Memorial Stadium in Annapolis, Maryland, on December 27, 2016. The ninth edition of the Military Bowl featured the American Athletic Conference champion Temple Owls versus the Wake Forest Demon Deacons of Atlantic Coast Conference. This was the second all-time meeting between the schools; the previous one was on November 1, 1930, when the Owls defeated the Demon Deacons by a score of 36–0.

2016 Military Bowl	Line	1	-	2	-	3	-	4	-	Final
#24 Temple	(-10.5)	7	-	3	-	10	-	6	-	26
Wake Forest	(41.5)	14	-	17	-	0	-	3	-	34

Scoring Summary
Temple - Jennings 48 yard pass from Walker (Boumerhi kick)
Wake Forest - Serigne 41 yard pass from Wolford (Weaver kick)
Wake Forest - Hines 20 yard pass from Wolford (Weaver kick)
Wake Forest - Carney 11 yard run (Weaver kick)
Wake Forest - Weaver 25 yard Field goal
Wake Forest - Colburn 3 yard run (Weaver kick)
Temple - Boumerhi 45 yard Field goal
Temple - Jennings 58 yard pass from Walker (Boumerhi kick)
Temple - Boumerhi 24 yard Field goal
Temple - Boumerhi 32 yard Field goal
Temple - Boumerhi 38 yard Field goal
Wake Forest - Weaver 30 yard Field goal

Associated Press Military Bowl game summary - When Wake Forest fans look back at 2016, perhaps they will remember an exciting victory in the Military Bowl as the culmination of the team's first winning season in eight years. At least, that's what Demon Deacons coach Dave Clawson would like to believe. Wake Forest attached a positive ending to a season marred by scandal, using a strong performance by Quarterback John Wolford to beat heavily favored Temple 34-26 on Tuesday in the Military Bowl. After throwing an interception on the first series of the game -- a turnover Temple used to take a 7-0 lead -- Wolford helped the Demon Deacons rattle off 31 straight points before halftime. Wolford left with a neck strain in the third quarter with the score 31-17. Wake Forest (7-6) then withstood a comeback bid by Temple (10-4) to secure its first bowl victory since 2008. That gave the Demon Deacons something to talk about this offseason beside a troubling spy story. According to a Wake Forest investigation, broadcaster Tommy Elrod leaked or attempted to leak game plan information to at least three opponents. Though Elrod has not released a public statement on the scandal, the school has since fired him. The scandal was dubbed "Wakey Leaks." Despite the distraction, the Demon Deacons snapped a three-game losing streak and won for only the second time since Oct. 8. Wolford, a junior, completed 10 of 19 passes for 183 yards and two scores. Though he wasn't there at the finish, he certainly did enough while in the game. His backup, redshirt freshman Kyle Kearns, went 4 for 10 for 60 yards and an interception. Seeking the first 11-win season in school history, Temple came in as an 11-point favorite. A 48-yard pass from Phillip Walker to Adonis Jennings on the Owls' first offensive play gave them their only lead. Down 31-7 late in the first half, Temple used a 19-point run to close to 31-26 with 3:56 left. Wake Forest then used an 80-yard kickoff return by John Armstrong and the resulting field goal to make it an eight-point game with 1:59 left. Temple came in with a seven-game winning streak after capturing the American Athletic Conference title with a 34-10 rout of Navy on this same field Dec. 3. Foley took the reins after Matt Rhule was hired by Baylor on Dec. 6. The Owls subsequently signed Florida defensive coordinator Geoff Collins as their new head coach, and he got a first-hand look at his new team on Tuesday. Walker finished his career by going 28 for 49 for 396 yards and two touchdowns, both to Jennings. He was sacked four times, including a pivotal 22-yarder on second down from the Wake Forest 6 preceding the Owls' final field goal.

2016 HOLIDAY BOWL

The 2016 Holiday Bowl was played at Qualcomm Stadium in San Diego, California, on December 27, 2016. The 39th edition of the Holiday Bowl featured the Minnesota Golden Gophers of the Big Ten Conference versus the Washington State Cougars of the Pac-12 Conference. This was Minnesota's first appearance in the Holiday Bowl. On December 15, Minnesota players threatened to boycott all football activity, including participation in the 2016 Holiday Bowl, in protest a decision to suspend ten players from the team. The suspension was made as a result of school investigation into sexual assault charges from the beginning of school year. The legal process had already run its course, with no charges filed. On December 17, the Golden Gophers ended their boycott and announced they would play. Had Minnesota continued its boycott, Northern Illinois was first in line to replace them in the Holiday Bowl.

2016 Holiday Bowl	Line	1	-	2	-	3	-	4	-	Final
Minnesota	(61.0)	0	-	3	-	7	-	7	-	17
Washington State	(-8.5)	3	-	3	-	0	-	6	-	12

Scoring Summary
Washington State - Powell 26 yard Field goal
Minnesota - Carpenter 43 yard Field goal
Washington State - Powell 41 yard Field goal
Minnesota - Brooks 13 yard pass from Leidner (Carpenter kick)
Minnesota - Smith 9 yard run (Carpenter kick)
Washington State - Sweet 8 yard pass from Falk (Pass failed)

Associated Press Holiday Bowl game summary - After a few days of turmoil and perhaps more to come, the Minnesota Golden Gophers played lights-out in shutting down Luke Falk and the Washington State Cougars to win the Holiday Bowl. Shannon Brooks caught a tipped pass from Mitch Leidner for a 13-yard, go-ahead touchdown in the third quarter and Minnesota, mired in controversy, won 17-12 on Tuesday night. The Golden Gophers (9-4) were looking to regroup after backing down from a threat to skip this game if their teammates suspended after the investigation weren't reinstated. The players backed down amid pressure from many who read details of the allegations. Brooks' TD catch was one of the few exciting plays in an otherwise pedestrian edition of what traditionally has been one of the country's most exciting bowl games. WSU cornerback Marcellus Pippins reached up with his right hand and deflected Leidner's pass in the end zone, but it went right to Brooks for the TD and a 10-6 lead. That capped an 84-yard, 10-play drive on Minnesota's first possession of the second half. WSU (8-5) ended on a three-game losing streak and was held to its lowest point total of the season. The Cougars had scored more than 50 points four times this season, a school record. The Golden Gophers frustrated Falk most of the game, holding him to 264 yards -- 86 below his average -- on 30-of-51 passing. Falk didn't crack 200 yards until the final minutes, when he led a drive capped by an 8-yard TD pass to Kyle Sweet. After three tries due to Minnesota penalties, the conversion attempt failed. Minnesota then recovered an onside kick. Falk came in having completed 71 percent of his passes in throwing for 4,204 yards and 37 touchdowns. The Cougars were ranked second in the nation in passing. Falk was intercepted by Adekunle Ayinde on fourth down with 3:05 left. That set up Rodney Smith's 9-yard TD run with 2:06 left for a 17-6 lead. WSU lead 6-3 after a lackluster first half that included just three field goals. The Cougars crossed the 50 just twice, getting field goals of 26 and 41 yards by Erik Powell. Powell's second field goal was set up when Nnamdi Oguayo hit Leidner and forced a fumble that Isaac Dotson recovered at the Golden Gophers' 38. Minnesota got a 43-yard field goal by Emmit Carpenter in the second quarter.

2016 CACTUS BOWL

The 2016 Cactus Bowl was held on December 27, 2016 at Chase Field in Phoenix, Arizona. This was the twenty-eighth edition of the Cactus Bowl, which was previously known as the Copper Bowl, the Insight.com Bowl, the Insight Bowl, and the Buffalo Wild Wings Bowl. The bowl featured the Baylor Bears of the Big 12 Conference against the Boise State Broncos of the Mountain West Conference. Baylor opened the year 6–0 to become bowl eligible. They raised in the polls to as high as #8 in the AP poll and a tie for #6 in the coaches poll. However, the Bears would finish the season on a six-game losing streak to finish in the season 6–6. The team had to also deal all season with the ongoing Baylor University football scandal. Boise State opened the season 7–0 and climbed to #13 in the AP and coaches poll before losing to Wyoming and dropping in the polls. The Broncos won their next three games and rose back up to #19 in the polls and were in position to be the highest ranked team from the Group of 5 until a season ending loss to Air Force which dropped them out of the polls, the Mountain West Championship Game, and contention for the Group of 5 spot in a New Year's Six.

2016 Cactus Bowl	Line	1	-	2	-	3	-	4	-	Final
Boise State	(-7.0)	0	-	6	-	0	-	6	-	12
Baylor	(70.5)	7	-	14	-	3	-	7	-	31

Scoring Summary
Baylor - Cannon 30 yard pass from Smith (Callahan kick)
Boise State - Rausa 24 yard Field goal
Baylor - Cannon 68 yard pass from Smith (Callahan kick)
Baylor - Hasty 5 yard run (Callahan kick)
Boise State - Rausa 26 yard Field goal
Baylor - Callahan 34 yard Field goal
Baylor - Zamora 14 yard pass from Smith (Callahan kick)
Boise State - Wilson 28 yard pass from Rypien (Pass failed)

Associated Press Cactus Bowl game summary - Baylor played all season under the shadow of a sexual assault scandal that cost coach Art Briles his job last May. The Bears lost their prolific Quarterback to a gruesome ankle injury and spiraled downward with a long losing streak. Winning a bowl game in a rout won't wash any of that away, but it sure was nice to end a difficult season on a positive note. KD Cannon had 14 catches for a Cactus Bowl-record 226 yards and two touchdowns, helping the Bears close out a challenging season with a 31-12 victory over Boise State on Tuesday night. Despite the lingering sexual assault scandal, Baylor (7-6) managed to play well to start the season, winning its first six games. Once the season turned, it was hard to get it back. Quarterback Seth Russell suffered a season-ending ankle injury, the scandal carried on and the losses piled up, six straight to end the regular season. The Bears went out with a win by revving up their quick-hitting offense again behind freshman Quarterback Zach Smith, who threw for 375 yards and three scores. Boise State (10-3) tried to keep up with the Bears but struggled in the red zone: two field goals, an interception in the end zone and a failed fourth down try. The result was the worst postseason loss in program history. Smith had some ups and downs in three games after Russell broke his ankle but had a month to prepare for the Cactus Bowl. The freshman from Texas was sharp with the extra work, completing 28 of 39 passes. He also threw a 14-yard touchdown pass to Ishmael Zamora in the fourth quarter to put Baylor up 31-6. Boise State's Brett Rypien moved the Broncos' offense but had his share of mistakes. He threw an interception at the Baylor 5-yard line on Boise State's second drive and had an overthrow on what would likely have been a touchdown later in the first quarter, forcing the Broncos to settle for a field goal. Rypien also threw an interception in the end zone in the second quarter. He finished with 305 yards and a touchdown on 32-of-51 passing with two interceptions and a lost fumble.

2016 PINSTRIPE BOWL

The 2016 Pinstripe Bowl was played on December 28, 2016 at Yankee Stadium in the New York City borough of the Bronx. The seventh edition of the Pinstripe Bowl featured the Pittsburgh Panthers of the Atlantic Coast Conference against the Northwestern Wildcats of the Big Ten Conference. This was the seventh meeting between the schools, with the series tied at 3–3.

2016 Pinstripe Bowl	Line	1	-	2	-	3	-	4	-	Final
Pittsburgh	(-3.5)	3	-	7	-	7	-	7	-	24
Northwestern	(63.0)	0	-	14	-	7	-	10	-	31

Scoring Summary
Pittsburgh - Blewitt 46 yard Field goal
Northwestern - Jackson 8 yard run (Mitchell kick)
Northwestern - Jackson 16 yard run (Mitchell kick)
Pittsburgh - Weah 69 yard pass from Peterman (Blewitt kick)
Pittsburgh - Peterman 5 yard run (Blewitt kick)
Northwestern - Jackson 40 yard run (Mitchell kick)
Pittsburgh - Aston 6 yard pass from DiNucci (Blewitt kick)
Northwestern - Dickerson 21 yard pass from Thorson (Mitchell kick)
Northwestern - Mitchell 37 yard Field goal

Associated Press Pinstripe Bowl game summary - Justin Jackson has the last name made for the bright lights at Yankee Stadium. He had the kind of postseason game worthy of the setting. Jackson made his case in the home of the Yankees to become Northwestern's Mr. December. Unlike Hall of Fame slugger Reggie Jackson, the Wildcats' stud running back did his damage one step at a time instead of one swing. Jackson ran for 224 yards and three touchdowns to power Northwestern to only its third bowl victory, 31-24 over No. 22 Pittsburgh in the Pinstripe Bowl on Wednesday night. Jackson was the straw that stirred Northwestern's offense in the Bronx and helped etch this performance alongside the 1948 Rose Bowl and 2012 Gator Bowl victories in the program's oft-futile history. Jackson, the game's MVP, was awed by the lights and monuments at the stadium. But it was a more discreet spot in the locker room Northwestern borrowed from the Yankees that really bowled over Jackson. Jackson had TD runs of 8 and 16 yards in the second quarter, then went deep on a 40-yard burst in the third that left one defender face down on the turf following a fantastic fake and gave the Wildcats (7-6) a 21-17 lead. Rallying without injured Quarterback Nathan Peterman and running back James Conner, Pitt yanked the lead away in the fourth on a short TD pass before it collapsed the rest of the quarter. The Wildcats turned a fourth-and-1 into a 21-yard play-action TD pass that made it 28-24 and a hit late field goal for a seven-point lead. The Panthers (8-5), who had wins over No. 2 Clemson and Big Ten champion Penn State, still had time to spoil Northwestern's upset bid with a late drive for the tying score. Scott Orndoff failed to hang on to backup Quarterback Ben DiNucci's strike in the end zone on third down. DiNucci had his fourth-down pass picked off by Jared McGee, who helped bust up the previous pass play, to clinch the win for the Wildcats. Northwestern's defense made the stops late. Jackson carried the Wildcats to a celebration on a purple-glittered baseball field. Jackson stiff-armed one defender, then bowled over a second for a 16-yard score that helped Northwestern take a 14-10 lead into halftime. After some confusion over his final rushing total, Jackson fell just shy of setting the Pinstripe Bowl mark of 227 yards by Indiana's Devine Redding. Peterman, who threw for 253 yards, gave Pitt a 17-14 lead on a 5-yard scamper in the third. Peterman's solid outing ended late in the quarter when he was sandwiched between two defenders and his head slammed the turf. DiNucci was picked on Pitt's final drive with 30 seconds left in the game and the Wildcats would get their kicks from storming the field in a frenzy. Conner, who capped a triumphant return from Hodgkin lymphoma, suffered a brutal helmet-to-helmet blow to the head late in the first half and did not return. Unlike some draft prospects, Conner played the bowl game even though he decided to skip his senior season and declare for the NFL draft. The 6-foot-2, 240-pound Conner, who had 1,060 yards rushing and 20 total touchdowns entering the game, was far from a sure-fire early NFL pick. Conner was stuffed when he tried to go over the top on a failed fourth-down try in the first quarter.

2016 RUSSELL ATHLETIC BOWL

The 2016 Russell Athletic Bowl was played on December 28, 2016 at the Camping World Stadium in Orlando, Florida. The 27th edition of the Russell Athletic Bowl featured the Miami Hurricanes of the Atlantic Coast Conference against the West Virginia Mountaineers of the Big 12 Conference.

2016 Russell Athletic Bowl	Line	1	-	2	-	3	-	4	-	Final
#14 West Virginia	(58.0)	7	-	0	-	7	-	0	-	14
Miami	(-3.0)	0	-	21	-	10	-	0	-	31

Scoring Summary
West Virginia - McKoy 6 yard run (Molina kick)
Miami - Richards 51 yard pass from Kaaya (Badgley kick)
Miami - Lewis 3 yard pass from Kaaya (Badgley kick)
Miami - Berrios 26 yard pass from Kaaya (Badgley kick)
Miami - Njoku 23 yard pass from Kaaya (Badgley kick)
West Virginia - Howard 4 yard run (Molina kick)
Miami - Badgley 30 yard Field goal

Associated Press Russell Athletic Bowl game summary - Miami fans asked Brad Kaaya to end the school's 10-year bowl-victory drought, and he delivered. Now they have another request. "One more year! One more year!" they chanted at Kaaya on Wednesday night, after he threw four touchdown passes to help Miami top No. 14 West Virginia 31-14 in the Russell Athletic Bowl. And it's easy to see why they're clamoring for the school's most prolific Quarterback to return. Kaaya completed 24 of 34 passes for 282 yards for Miami (9-4) - and went 18 for 19 in one dazzling stretch, the lone incompletion in that span being a drop. The four TDs tied both a Miami bowl record and Kaaya's collegiate best. Skyler Howard passed for 134 yards and ran for a touchdown for West Virginia (10-3), which fell to 3-17 against Miami. Kennedy McKoy also had a touchdown run for the Mountaineers, who committed 11 penalties and allowed four sacks. West Virginia came in averaging more than 500 yards per game. Miami held the Mountaineers to 229. The Hurricanes had lost six straight bowl games and punted on their first six possessions Wednesday. But Kaaya finally got rolling, and Miami soon had total control. Kaaya connected with Ahmmon Richards, Malcolm Lewis and Braxton Berrios for touchdowns in the final 6:30 of the first half to get Miami rolling and found David Njoku for another touchdown on the first possession of the second half.

2016 FOSTER FARMS BOWL

The 2016 Foster Farms Bowl was played on December 28, 2016 at Levi's Stadium in Santa Clara, California. It was the 15th edition of the Foster Farms Bowl; the game featured the Utah Utes from the Pac-12 Conference against the Indiana Hoosiers from the Big Ten Conference. The 2016 edition was the first under its new management, as it is now run by the San Francisco 49ers NFL team. Utah finished their regular season 8-4. This was Utah's second trip to the Foster Farms Bowl, with the previous appearance being during the 2005–06 bowl season when they won against Georgia Tech by a score of 38–10 in the 2005 Emerald Bowl. Indiana finished their season 6–6. This bowl marked the Hoosiers' eleventh bowl game (they were 3–7 in bowl games previously) and they were seeking their first bowl victory since the 1991 Copper Bowl, when they beat Baylor 24–0.

2016 Foster Farms Bowl	Line	1	-	2	-	3	-	4	-	Final
Indiana	(54.0)	7	-	10	-	0	-	7	-	24
#19 Utah	(-3.5)	10	-	7	-	6	-	3	-	26

Scoring Summary
Indiana - Paige 7 yard pass from Lagow (Oakes kick)
Utah - Phillips 30 yard Field goal
Utah - Williams 16 yard run (Phillips kick)
Utah - Huntley 1 yard run (Phillips kick)
Indiana - Oakes 24 yard Field goal
Indiana - Westbrook 36 yard pass from Diamont (Oakes kick)
Utah - Phillips 48 yard Field goal
Utah - Phillips 41 yard Field goal
Indiana - Redding 3 yard run (Oakes kick)
Utah - Phillips 27 yard Field goal

Associated Press Foster Farms Bowl game summary - Whenever it seems Joe Williams won't be available to Utah, he comes back and delivers. Williams returned from a four-week retirement early in the season to help solidify a broken-down running back position. Then in the bowl game, he overcame an illness that forced him to miss a team meeting the night before and capped his career in style. Williams ran for 222 yards and a touchdown; Andy Phillips kicked a 27-yard field goal with 1:24 to play and Utah beat Indiana 26-24 on Wednesday night in the Foster Farms Bowl for its 14th victory in its past 15 bowl games. Williams had to check out of the game several times but shook off his own costly fumble to run for 64 yards on the final drive, setting up Phillips' fourth field goal of the night. Tyler Huntley ran for another score and the Utes (9-4) forced three turnovers to spoil Tom Allen's coaching debut at Indiana and improve Whittingham's bowl record to 10-1. Allen took over the Hoosiers (6-7) after Kevin Wilson's sudden resignation this month. Allen had finished his first season at Indiana as defensive coordinator and is now tasked with rebuilding the team as he did in his one year with the defense. He appeared to be off to a good start when the Hoosiers rallied from 10 points down to take a 24-23 lead early in the fourth quarter on Devine Redding's 3-yard run following a fumble by Utah's Zach Moss. Indiana failed to capitalize on

Williams' fumble when Griffin Oakes missed a 40-yard field goal attempt with 5:34 left. That set the stage for Utah's final drive. Indiana's last-gasp chance ended when Richard Lagow was hit on a desperation heave near midfield, sending the Hoosiers to their fourth straight bowl loss since their last win in the 1991 Copper Bowl.

2016 TEXAS BOWL

The 2016 Texas Bowl was played on December 28, 2016 at NRG Stadium in Houston, Texas. Sponsored by the It was the eleventh edition of the Texas Bowl, it featured the Kansas State Wildcats of the Big 12 Conference against the Texas A&M Aggies of the Southeastern Conference. This was the first meeting between the two teams since Texas A&M left the Big 12 Conference after the 2011 season.

2016 Texas Bowl	Line	1	-	2	-	3	-	4	-	Final
Texas A&M	(-4.0)	7	-	7	-	7	-	7	-	28
Kansas State	(56.5)	7	-	16	-	3	-	7	-	33

Scoring Summary
Texas A&M - Ford 7 yard run (LaCamera kick)
Kansas State - Pringle 79 yard pass from Ertz (Patterson kick)
Kansas State - Ertz 5 yard run (Patterson kick)
Texas A&M - Seals-Jones 3 yard pass from Knight (LaCamera kick)
Kansas State - Patterson 40 yard Field goal
Kansas State - Heath 52 yard run (Patterson kick)
Texas A&M - Reynolds 4 yard pass from Knight (LaCamera kick)
Kansas State - Patterson 25 yard Field goal
Kansas State - Ertz 1 yard run (Patterson kick)
Texas A&M - Reynolds 15 yard pass from Knight (LaCamera kick)

Associated Press Texas Bowl game summary - Kansas State was unbeatable against teams from Texas in the regular season, and that didn't change on Wednesday night in the Texas Bowl. Jesse Ertz threw for 195 yards and a touchdown and ran for two more scores in Kansas State's 33-28 victory over Texas A&M. He had 67 yards rushing to give him 1,012 this season. The victory improved the Wildcats to 5-0 against teams from the Lone Star State this season after they downed Texas Tech, Texas, Baylor and TCU earlier this year. Ertz had a 79-yard touchdown pass and scoring runs of 1 and 5 yards to help give Kansas State its fourth straight win and first bowl victory since the 2013 Buffalo Wild Wings Bowl. The Wildcats (9-4) led 33-21 after Ertz bulled into the end zone on a 1-yard run with nine minutes left. Ertz set up the score with a 20-yard run two plays earlier. The Aggies (8-5) cut it to 33-28 on Josh Reynolds' 15-yard TD reception about a minute later. Texas A&M attempted to convert a fourth-and-8 with about two minutes left, but Trevor Knight's pass was short, to give Kansas State the ball back and allow the Wildcats to run out the clock. Reynolds had a Texas A&M bowl-record 12 receptions for 154 yards and two touchdowns and Knight threw for 310 yards with three touchdowns and one interception as A&M dropped its second straight bowl game. Texas A&M got to 23-21 when Reynolds made a 4-yard touchdown catch with about seven minutes left in the third quarter. A 25-yard field goal by Ian Patterson extended Kansas State's lead to 26-21 with about three minutes remaining in the quarter. A highlight of that drive came on a 36-yard run John Silmon. The Aggies took a 7-0 lead when Keith Ford scored on a 7-yard run on their first possession. Kansas State tied it when Ertz connected with Byron Pringle, and he dashed down the field for a 79-yard touchdown run later in the first quarter. The Wildcats took the lead when Ertz stiff-armed Justin Evans on a 5-yard touchdown run early in the second quarter. But Myles Garrett blocked the extra point to make it 13-7. A 3-yard reception by Ricky Seals-Jones put A&M back on top 14-13 soon after that. But Kansas State regained the lead with a 40-yard field goal before pushing the lead to 23-14 on a 52-yard run by Dominique Heath just before halftime.

2016 BIRMINGHAM BOWL

The 2016 Birmingham Bowl was played on December 29, 2016 at Legion Field in Birmingham, Alabama. The eleventh annual Birmingham Bowl featured the South Florida Bulls from the American Athletic Conference against the South Carolina Gamecocks from the Southeastern Conference.

2016 Birmingham Bowl	Line	1	-	2	-	3	-	4	-	OT	-	Final
South Florida	(-10.0)	15	-	14	-	10	-	0	-	7	-	46
South Carolina	(58.0)	0	-	14	-	10	-	15	-	0	-	39

Scoring Summary
South Florida - Flowers 4 Yard Run (Wilcox pass from Kean)
South Florida - Flowers 4 Yard Run (Behr kick)
South Carolina - Hurst 25 Yard pass from Bentley (Fry kick)
South Florida - Flowers 1 Yard Run (Behr kick)
South Carolina - Samuel 3 Yard pass from Bentley (Fry kick)
South Florida - Johnson 37 Yard pass from Flowers (Behr kick)
South Carolina - Samuel 4 Yard Run (Fry kick)
South Florida - Behr 21 Yard Field goal
South Florida - Fullwood 47 Yard Interception Return (Behr kick)
South Carolina - Fry 43 Yard Field goal
South Carolina - Edwards 9 Yard pass from Bentley (Fry kick)
South Carolina - Turner 1 Yard Run (Hurst pass from Bentley)
South Florida - Dillon 25 Yard pass from Flowers (Behr kick)

Associated Press Birmingham Bowl game summary - South Florida's Quinton Flowers says there were a lot of big-name college football programs that thought he could be a star player. As a running back. Or maybe as a safety. But Flowers knew he could be a great Quarterback. And on Thursday in the Birmingham Bowl against a team from the Southeastern Conference, he proved it once again. Flowers ran for three touchdowns and threw for two more -- including what proved to be the winner in overtime -- to help No. 25 South Florida beat South Carolina 46-39. Flowers said South Carolina coach Will Muschamp -- who was then at Florida -- was among the coaches who wanted him to switch positions. Muschamp got an up-close look at Flowers' Quarterback skills on Thursday. South Florida (11-2) squandered a 39-21 lead in the second half but recovered for its school-record 11th victory. Flowers threw a 25-yard touchdown pass on the first play of overtime, finding Elkanah Dillon in the end zone. South Carolina's overtime drive ended after Jake Bentley was sacked by Mike Love on fourth down. Bentley fumbled and Khalid McGee recovered to end the game. It was a sweet ending for a South Florida program that has had a lot of upheaval during December. Coach Willie Taggart left for Oregon after the regular season and former Texas Coach Charlie Strong was hired a few days later. But the Bulls, who played Thursday under interim coach T.J. Weist, pushed aside the distractions and finished their season with another win. Flowers, who was selected the game's Most Valuable Player, completed 23 of 32 passes for 261 yards and ran for 105 yards on 21 carries. The Bulls controlled the game for most of the afternoon, but the Gamecocks rallied to tie it at 39 with 1:11 remaining on A.J. Turner's 1-yard touchdown run and a 2-point conversion. Bentley completed 32 of 43 passes for 390 yards, three touchdowns and two interceptions. Deebo Samuel caught 14 passes for 190 yards and a touchdown. Muschamp said he was pleased with the offense. It was the defense -- specifically the lack of an effective pass rush against Flowers -- that left him frustrated. South Carolina (6-7) was hurt by five turnovers, including a pick-six thrown by Bentley that Tajee Fullwood returned 47 yards.

2016 BELK BOWL

The 2016 Belk Bowl was played on December 29, 2016. The game featured the Arkansas Razorbacks of the Southeastern Conference and the Virginia Tech Hokies of the Atlantic Coast Conference. With its 2016 Belk Bowl appearance, Virginia Tech extended its bowl streak to 24 consecutive games. The streak is the longest active bowl streak in the NCAA.

2016 Belk Bowl	Line	1	-	2	-	3	-	4	-	Final
Arkansas	(-10.0)	17	-	7	-	0	-	0	-	24
#22 Virginia Tech	(58.0)	0	-	0	-	21	-	14	-	35

Scoring Summary
Arkansas - Hedlund 38 yard Field goal
Arkansas - Allen 1 yard run (Hedlund kick)
Arkansas - O'Grady 28 yard pass from Allen (Hedlund kick)
Arkansas - Hatcher 12 yard pass from Allen (Hedlund kick)
Virginia Tech - Evans 4 yard run (Slye kick)
Virginia Tech - Rogers 3 yard pass from Evans (Slye kick)
Virginia Tech - Cunningham 5 yard pass from Evans (Slye kick)
Virginia Tech - McMillan 6 yard run (Slye kick)
Virginia Tech - Evans 1 yard run (Slye kick)

Virginia Tech Media Relations Belk Bowl game summary - Virginia Tech Quarterback Jerod Evans accounted for four second-half touchdowns and Tech's defense forced four turnovers in the second half, as the No. 22 Hokies rallied from a 24-0 halftime deficit to knock off Arkansas 35-24 in the Belk Bowl played Thursday night at Bank of America Stadium. With the win, the Hokies finished the season with a 10-4 record, recording at least 10 wins for the first time since 2011 and for the 14th time in program history. The Hokies also won their third straight bowl game for the first time in school history. The Hokies' 24-point rally was the biggest since 1987 and believed to be the biggest in school history. Tech turned the ball over twice in the first half, and the Razorbacks scored 10 points off of those – part of their 24-point barrage. But Tech's Chuck Clark arguably turned the game, forcing a fumble on Arkansas first possession of the second half. Woody Baron recovered for the Hokies, and Evans scored on a 4-yard run for Tech's first score of the game. Arkansas turned it over four times in the second half – and the Hokies scored touchdowns after every one of them. A Tremaine Edmunds interception led to a 5-yard touchdown pass from Evans to tight end Chris Cunningham with 4 minutes left in the third quarter that cut the lead to 24-21. Tech took its first lead of the game on a 6-yard touchdown run by Travon McMillian with 12:03 left in the game. The Hokies then iced it when Terrell Edmunds' interception led to a 1-yard touchdown run by Evans with 6:41 remaining that accounted for the final margin. "I think it [the turnovers] changed the game completely," said Tech's Anthony Shegog, who recorded an interception and forced a fumble in the game. Evans completed 21 of 33 for 243 yards, with two touchdowns and an interception to lead the Hokies. He also rushed for 87 yards and two scores.

2016 ALAMO BOWL

The 2016 Alamo Bowl was played on December 29, 2016 at the Alamodome in San Antonio, Texas. The game featured the Oklahoma State Cowboys, of the Big 12 Conference, and the Colorado Buffaloes, of the Pac-12 Conference. It was the two teams' first meeting since 2009 and the first since Colorado's departure from the Big 12 Conference in 2011. The game was the 24th edition of the Alamo Bowl and was sponsored by the San Antonio-based company, Valero Energy. The teams played each other annually from 1960–1997, as members of the Big Eight Conference, and twice every four years in Big 12 competition. The Buffaloes heading into this contest held a 26–19–2 record over Oklahoma State.

2016 Alamo Bowl	Line	1	-	2	-	3	-	4	-	Final
#10 Oklahoma State	(64.0)	3	-	14	-	14	-	7	-	38
#12 Colorado	(-3.0)	0	-	0	-	0	-	8	-	8

Scoring Summary
Oklahoma State - Grogan 28 yard Field goal
Oklahoma State - Carson 10 yard run (Grogan kick)
Oklahoma State - Washington 5 yard pass from Rudolph (Grogan kick)
Oklahoma State - Jarwin 6 yard pass from Rudolph (Grogan kick)
Oklahoma State - Seales 23 yard pass from Rudolph (Grogan kick)
Colorado - Liufau 6 yard run (Lindsay pass from Liufau)
Oklahoma State - Hill 37 yard run (Grogan kick)

UPI Alamo Bowl game summary - The mantra for Oklahoma State in the run-up to its game against Colorado in the Valero Alamo Bowl was to be the most physical team on the field, to exploit the Buffaloes' man-defense with deep passes and to draw on its experience in bowl games to overcome the inexperienced Pac 12-South champions. The No. 10 Cowboys checked off all those goals in spades and looked impressive doing so as they manhandled No. 12 Colorado 38-8 on Thursday before a crowd of 59,815 in the Alamodome. Mason Rudolph threw for 314 yards and touchdowns to three different receivers, but the Oklahoma State defense was just as important in this wire-to-wire win, limiting the normally potent Buffaloes' offense to 182 yards through the first three quarters. Oklahoma State ruled the trenches throughout and outhit the Buffaloes while recording three sacks and nine tackles for a loss and knocking Colorado starting Quarterback Tony Liufau out of the game for a quarter. Rudolph (22-of-32 passing) connected with James Washington on a 5-yard scoring pass at the end of the second quarter. He hit Blake Jarwin with a TD throw from 6 yards out and added a 23-yard touchdown pass to Jhajuan Seales in the third quarter to give the Cowboys (10-3) a 31-0 lead. Liufau (195 yards passing) scooted in for a 6-yard touchdown run to get the Buffaloes on the board with 5:28 to play. He then passed to Phillip Lindsay for a 2-point conversion, but it was far too late for the Buffaloes (10-4). Justice Hill roared up the middle untouched for a 37-yard TD in the waning minutes to push the score to 38-8. Hill led the Cowboys with 100 yards on 19 carries. Washington had 171 yards receiving on nine catches for Oklahoma State before leaving the game with an injured finger in the third quarter. Lindsay racked up 166 total yards (103 receiving on six catches and 63 on the ground on 14 carries) for Colorado. The Buffaloes were outscored 79-18 in their final two games. Oklahoma State owned the first 19 minutes, forging a 10-0 lead on the strength of a 28-yard field goal by Ben Grogan on the Cowboys' opening possession and a 10-yard touchdown run by Chris Carson at the 11:15 mark of the second quarter. The latter score came on the snap after a nifty throwback pass from Rudolph to Carson and back to Rudolph that gained 24 yards and allowed Oklahoma State to a short field at the Colorado 10-yard line.

In between Oklahoma State's two early scores, the Buffaloes produced one significant drive on offense, moving 65 yards in 14 plays to a missed 47-yard field goal attempt by Chris Graham. The Cowboys pushed their lead to 17-0 with seven minutes to play in the second quarter on a 5-yard touchdown pass from Rudolph to Washington. The score culminated a seven-play, 66-yard drive for Oklahoma State and put the Cowboys firmly in control. Oklahoma State enjoyed a 282-153 edge in total yards in the first half, with most of that advantage coming through the air (216-106). The Cowboys averaged 7.2 yards per play in the first half as compared with 4.9 yards per snap for Colorado. Colorado walked off the gridiron with its collective head held high after playing in a bowl for the first time since 2007.

2016 LIBERTY BOWL

The 2016 Liberty Bowl was played on December 30, 2016 at Liberty Bowl Memorial Stadium in Memphis, Tennessee. The 58th edition of the Liberty Bowl featured the Georgia Bulldogs of the Southeastern Conference against the TCU Horned Frogs of the Big 12 Conference.

2016 Liberty Bowl	Line	1	-	2	-	3	-	4	-	Final
Georgia	(48.5)	7	-	7	-	7	-	10	-	31
TCU	(-3.0)	9	-	7	-	7	-	0	-	23

Scoring Summary
Georgia - Michel 4 yard run (Blankenship kick)
TCU - Hatfield 40 yard Field goal
TCU - Hill 10 yard run (Kick failed)
TCU - Diarse 10 yard pass from Hill (Hatfield kick)
Georgia - Michel 33 yard pass from Eason (Blankenship kick)
Georgia - Wims 4 yard pass from Eason (Blankenship kick)
TCU - Diarse 9 yard pass from Hill (Hatfield kick)
Georgia - Blankenship 30 yard Field goal
Georgia - Chubb 13 yard run (Blankenship kick)

Associated Press Liberty Bowl game summary - No matter how difficult it was to find running room early on, Georgia kept trying to establish its ground attack. That approach eventually paid off. Nick Chubb and Sony Michel combined to rush for 229 yards and two touchdowns Friday as Georgia came from behind in the fourth quarter to beat TCU 31-23 in the Liberty Bowl. Chubb rushed for 142 yards and a touchdown on 17 carries, while Michel ran for 87 yards and a score on 16 attempts. Michel also had a 33-yard touchdown catch. The two juniors already have announced that they plan to return to school for their senior seasons. Held in check for much of the game, Chubb closed the third quarter with a 48-yard burst that set up Rodrigo Blankenship's field goal to put Georgia ahead 24-23 with 13:27 left. Chubb then rushed for 57 yards in the final period, including a 13-yard touchdown with 2:48 remaining. Georgia (8-5) restored some pride to the Southeastern Conference. The SEC had entered the day with a 1-4 bowl record, a major step back for a league that went 9-2 in bowl games last year to set a record for bowl victories. The Bulldogs also sent TCU (6-7) to only its third losing year in Gary Patterson's 16 full seasons as coach. Missed opportunities proved costly for the Horned Frogs, who led 16-7 in the first half and carried a 23-21 advantage into the fourth quarter. Brandon Hatfield was wide right on a 47-yard field goal attempt that would have put TCU ahead with 7:57 remaining. He earlier had missed an extra point attempt as well as a 41-yard field goal. Both of Hatfield's missed field goals came after Trenton Thompson sacked Kenny Hill in third-down situations. Thompson set a Liberty Bowl record with three sacks and was named the game's most valuable player. After Hatfield missed his 47-yarder, Georgia went on a 70-yard touchdown drive to extend its lead to 31-23. Deandre Baker clinched the victory by breaking up Hill's fourth-and-4 pass from the Georgia 44 with 1:14 remaining. Hill threw a pair of touchdown passes to John Diarse and ran for a third score, but he was sacked five times and lost a fumble. Georgia's Jacob Eason was 12 of 21 for 164 yards with two touchdown passes.

MOVING INTO SECOND - Chubb's 142-yard rushing performance increased his career total to 3,424 and made him the second-leading rusher in Georgia history. Chubb overtook Los Angeles Rams running back Todd Gurley, who rushed for 3,285 yards in his college career. The school record is held by Herschel Walker, who ran for an SEC-record 5,259 yards from 1980-82.

2016 SUN BOWL

The 2016 Sun Bowl was played on December 30, 2016 at the Sun Bowl Stadium in El Paso, Texas. It featured the Stanford Cardinal and the North Carolina Tar Heels.

2016 Sun Bowl	Line	1	-	2	-	3	-	4	-	Final
#16 Stanford	(-2.5)	7	-	6	-	3	-	9	-	25
North Carolina	(54.5)	7	-	0	-	10	-	6	-	23

Scoring Summary
North Carolina - Switzer 19 yard pass from Trubisky (Weiler kick)
Stanford - Love 49 yard pass from Chryst (Ukropina kick)
Stanford - Ukropina 44 yard Field goal
Stanford - Ukropina 33 yard Field goal
Stanford - Ukropina 43 yard Field goal
North Carolina - Weiler 37 yard Field goal
North Carolina - Brown 5 yard run (Weiler kick)
Stanford - Lloyd 19 yard interception return (Pass failed)
Stanford - Ukropina 27 yard Field goal
North Carolina - Howard 2 yard pass from Trubisky (Run failed)

Sun Bowl game summary - It took almost every second of the 60 minutes played to determine the winner of the 83rd Hyundai Sun Bowl as two storied universities, Stanford and North Carolina, fought down to the wire before the 16th-ranked Cardinal eventually prevailed 25-23 over the Tar Heels in front of 42,166 fans. UNC (8-5) trailed by eight with 1:34 left in the game and had to drive 97 yards to try and tie the game after a Stanford (10-3) punt pinned them at the 3-yard line. Tar Heel Quarterback Mitch Trubisky showed why he is considered one of the top Quarterback prospects for the NFL, bouncing back from three previous turnovers to lead UNC down the field on that final drive. Trubisky began the drive with a 13-yard completion to All-ACC first teamer Ryan Switzer. The big pass play came a few plays later after Trubisky hit his big 6-5 target Bug Howard down the sideline for a 44-yard completion that took the ball from the UNC 28-yard line to the Stanford 28-yard line. Once again it was Switzer and Howard that would wrap up the drive as a 27-yard completion to Switzer placed the ball at the 1-yard line with just over 30 seconds remaining. After a run that lost a yard and an incomplete pass, Trubisky seemed to be in trouble on third down but somehow escaped, scrambled and eventually found Howard in the end zone with 25 seconds left to get within a two-point conversion of tying the game. But the biggest name on the Cardinal defense came up big during the two-point conversion as defensive end and eventual C.M. Hendricks MVP award winner Solomon Thomas sliced through the Tar Heel offensive line and got to Trubisky before he had a chance to get a pass off. A failed onside kick would close UNC's chances and give Stanford its third Sun Bowl victory and first in 20 years. The future NFL prospect Thomas finished with seven tackles, two for losses, a sack and the biggest play of the game. He is the first defensive player to win the Sun Bowl MVP since UCLA linebacker Jordan Zumwalt was named Co-MVP in 2013 and the first defensive lineman to win the award since Oregon State's Victor Butler won the award in 2008. Trubisky finished 23-of-39 for 280 yards but had three costly turnovers including two interceptions and a fumble. On the Stanford side, senior Quarterback Ryan Burns relieved starter Keller Chryst after he got injured in the first quarter. Burns finished 6-of-12 for 86 yards. Leading the charge for the Cardinal was running back Bryce Love, who was playing in place of Stanford's All-American Christian McCaffrey. Love finished with 119 yards on the ground on 21 carries including a career-high 59-yard romp. He also caught a 49-yard touchdown pass. The Tar Heels would take an early 7-0 lead, only to see the Cardinal score 16-straight points, mainly off the leg of place kicker Conrad Ukropina who tied a Sun Bowl record with four field goals in the game enroute to being named the John Folmer Most Valuable Special Teams Player. The Tar Heels struck first to open the scoring. After holding the Cardinal to a three-and-out on their first possession, Trubisky led UNC on a 10-play, 71-yard drive that culminated with a 19-yard touchdown pass from Trubisky to Switzer. The touchdown connection was Trubisky's 29th passing touchdown of the season, a new school record. The rest of the first-half scoring, however, belonged to the team from the Pac-12 as Stanford would rally for the final 13 points of the first stanza. The Cardinal immediately evened the score following the Tar Heel touchdown drive with a quick touchdown drive of their own. The drive, which only took six plays and less than three minutes, culminated with a 49-yard touchdown pass Chryst to Love. Love's first touchdown reception of the season knotted the game at 7-7 midway through the first quarter. Stanford then had an eventful third possession that started around midfield after a UNC three-and-out. After an early personal foul flag for a late hit against the Tar Heels, the Cardinal seemed to have their second-straight touchdown after Chryst hit JJ Arcega-Whiteside in the corner of the end zone for an apparent 27-yard score. The called was looked at and after further review it was determined that the ball hit the ground before the catch, thus negating the score. On the next play from scrimmage, Chryst ran down the field on a Quarterback keeper, but did not get up after the tackle. He had to be helped off the field with an apparent knee injury and would not return to the game. Burns, who started the first seven games of the season for Stanford, would play the rest of the game. Burns gained positive yardage on his first play from scrimmage, but a delay of game penalty and a sack would stall the drive. The Cardinal would have to settle for an Ukropina 44-yard field goal a few plays into the second quarter that would give them their first lead of the game. On UNC's following possession, Trubisky would have his first turnover as Stanford's Dallas Lloyd intercepted a pass and returned it 45 yards to the Tar Heel 35-yard line. However, the Cardinal could not move the ball and came away empty after Ukropina missed on a 36-yard attempt that hit the left upright. Ukropina would redeem himself, however, after Trubisky fumbled the ball after apparently running into an official with under two minutes left in the half. Ukropina nailed a 33-yarder, his school record 20th of the season, as Stanford led 13-7 at the half. UNC kicker Nick Weiler tried to cut into the Cardinal lead during the first possession of the second half, but his 51-yard field goal attempt sailed wide left. The middle portion of the third quarter saw the teams add a field goal to their score as Ukropina hit a 43-yard field goal and Weiler redeemed himself with a 37-yarder. Down six, the Tar Heels turned to senior running back T. J. Logan to help them regain the lead. Logan's running led a 9-play, 68-yard drive that culminated in a 5-yard touchdown run by freshman Jordan Brown, his first career touchdown. UNC regained the lead 17-16 with just over two minutes left in the third. Lloyd once again came up big for Stanford a couple of plays into the fourth quarter as the senior safety once again intercepted a Trubisky pass, this time running it back 19 yards for a pick-six that once again gave the Cardinal the lead, this time at 22-17 after a failed two-point conversion attempt. Ukropina's record-tying fourth field goal with 3:23 left gave Stanford a 25-17 lead that set up the game's final dramatic moments.

2016 MUSIC CITY BOWL

The 2016 Music City Bowl was held on December 30, 2016 at Nissan Stadium in Nashville, Tennessee. It featured the Tennessee Volunteers, from the Southeastern Conference (SEC), and the Nebraska Cornhuskers, from the Big Ten Conference. The game was the third all-time meeting between these two teams, with Nebraska leading the series 2–0 going into the game.

2016 Music City Bowl	Line	1	-	2	-	3	-	4	-	Final
#24 Nebraska	(59.0)	0	-	7	-	7	-	10	-	24
#21 Tennessee	(-9.5)	0	-	21	-	3	-	14	-	38

Scoring Summary
Tennessee - Kelly 28 yard run (Medley kick)
Tennessee - Dobbs 10 yard run (Medley kick)
Nebraska - Reilly 38 yard pass from Fyfe (Brown kick)
Tennessee - Dobbs 2 yard run (Medley kick)
Tennessee - Medley 46 yard Field goal
Nebraska - Reilly 9 yard pass from Fyfe (Brown kick)
Tennessee - Dobbs 3 yard run (Medley kick)
Nebraska - Brown 45 yard Field goal
Nebraska - Fyfe 9 yard run (Brown kick)
Tennessee - Malone 59 yard pass from Dobbs (Medley kick)

Associated Press Music City Bowl game summary - Joshua Dobbs finished his Tennessee career making one final move, helping All-America defensive lineman Derek Barnett figure out how to lead the band in "Rocky Top." The duo led Tennessee in celebrating after beating No. 24 Nebraska 38-24 on Friday at the Music City Bowl. Dobbs ran for three touchdowns and 118 yards and threw for 291 yards and another score, while Barnett got the sack, he needed to break a tie with the late Reggie White for the school career record. The Volunteers (9-4) beat a Big Ten team in a bowl for a third straight year and notched their first win in three tries against the Cornhuskers. It's the first time Tennessee has won three straight bowls since 1994-1996 when Peyton Manning was Quarterback for the Vols. Tennessee took a 14-0 lead in the second quarter and outgained Nebraska 521-318 in total offense in the bowl sponsored by Franklin American Mortgage. Nebraska (9-4) ended the season with two straight losses. The Cornhuskers lost four of their final six after rising as high as No. 7 in the rankings. Ryker Fyfe, the fifth-year former walk-on started for injured Quarterback Tommy Armstrong Jr. He pulled Nebraska within a touchdown in the fourth quarter. Fyfe threw two TD passes to Brandon Reilly and ran for a 9-yard TD with 10:02 left in the fourth to pull the Cornhuskers within 31-24. Dobbs answered with a 59-yard TD pass to Josh Malone for the final margin, and Nebraska coach Mike Riley said Dobbs' athleticism was a factor.

2016 ARIZONA BOWL

The 2016 Arizona Bowl was played at Arizona Stadium in Tucson, Arizona on December 30, 2016. The second edition of the Arizona Bowl, the game featured the South Alabama Jaguars of the Sun Belt Conference versus the Air Force Falcons of the Mountain West Conference.

2016 Arizona Bowl	Line	1	-	2	-	3	-	4	-	Final
South Alabama	(54.0)	14	-	7	-	0	-	0	-	21
Air Force	(-14.5)	3	-	18	-	17	-	7	-	45

Scoring Summary
South Alabama - Magee 75 yard pass from Davis (Patterson kick)
Air Force - Strebel 25 yard Field goal
South Alabama - Ayoola 2 yard run (Patterson kick)
South Alabama - Davis 4 yard run (Patterson kick)
Air Force - Strebel 22 yard Field goal
Air Force - Cleveland 14 yard run (Strebel kick)
Air Force - Owens 1 yard run (Robinette pass from Worthman)
Air Force - Robinette 75 yard pass from Worthman (Strebel kick)
Air Force - Williams 6 yard run (Strebel kick)
Air Force - Strebel 37 yard Field goal
Air Force - Owens 22 yard run (Strebel kick)

Associated Press Arizona Bowl game summary - Air Force could not get its usually reliable triple option rolling. South Alabama's defenders clogged the inside lanes and used their speed to keep the Falcons from getting to the edge. Air Force countered by going to the air, something it rarely does. Arion Worthman threw for 207 yards to balance out Air Force's run-heavy offense, Jacobi Owens scored two touchdowns and the Falcons overcame a sluggish start to beat South Alabama 45-21 in Arizona Bowl on Friday. Worthman had 71 yards on 21 carries. Air Force (10-3) struggled to get its triple-option going, falling into an 18-point first-half hole. Once the Falcons got rolling, they couldn't be stopped, scoring 42 straight points to turn it into a rout. Worthman was the trigger, jump-starting Air Force's option while completing 7 of 10 passes, including a 75-yard touchdown to Jalen Robinette to open the second half. The surprise contribution from Worthman — he had 339 total yards entering Friday — caught the Jaguars off-guard and opened the run game a little more for the Falcons. South Alabama (6-7) appeared to be headed toward its first bowl win after jumping on the Falcons early, starting with Dallas Davis' 75-yard touchdown pass to Josh Magee on the game's first play. The Jaguars couldn't sustain their early offensive success or stop the Falcons to lose a bowl game for the second time in three seasons. Davis threw for 245 yards and a touchdown, but also had an interception and lost a fumble. Magee had five catches for 154 yards. South Alabama landed the first blows by hitting a few long passes. Davis followed his opening TD throwing by hitting Chris Lewis on a 51-yard pass to set up Dami Ayoola's 2-yard TD run. Davis next found Magee on a 37-yard pass, then scored himself on a 4-yard run that put the Jaguars up 21-3. South Alabama also seemed to have the combination for stopping Air Force's tricky triple-option, the Falcons to a pair of field goals into the second quarter. Air Force finally unlocked its option late in the half after hitting a couple of mid-range passes. Ronald Cleveland scored on 14-yard run, then Owens on a 2-yard run after Santo Coppola returned Davis' fumble to 1-yard line. Once down 21-3, Air Force found itself at halftime after converting the 2-point conversion. The Falcons took their first lead by doing exactly what South Alabama did to open the game: a 75-yard TD pass on the first play of the second half, from Worthman to Robinette. Tyler Williams later took a pitch left to the pylon for a 6-yard TD and Owens scored on a 22-yard run to put Air Force up 45-21, well on its way to ending the season with a victory.

2016 ORANGE BOWL

The 2016 Capital One Orange Bowl was played on December 30, 2016 at the Hard Rock Stadium in Miami Gardens, Florida. The game matched the Michigan Wolverines of the Big Ten Conference against the Florida State Seminoles of the Atlantic Coast Conference (ACC). Dalvin Cook, running back for the Seminoles, was named the game's MVP. The contest was televised on ESPN. After finishing their regular season with a 10–2 record, the Wolverines were selected to their third Orange Bowl appearance. This will be their 45th bowl game appearance, the 11th-highest total all-time among FBS schools. After finishing their regular season with a 9–3 record, the Seminoles were selected to their 10th Orange Bowl appearance, the third most Orange Bowl appearances by any team. This will be their 46th bowl game appearance. This was the third meeting between the two schools, with the all-time series tied at 1–1; the most recent previous meeting was in 1991, when the Seminoles defeated the Wolverines by a score of 51–31 in Ann Arbor, Michigan. The other meeting occurred in 1986 when the Wolverines defeated the Seminoles by a score of 20–18, a game also played in Ann Arbor.

2016 Orange Bowl	Line	1	-	2	-	3	-	4	-	Final
#6 Michigan	(50.5)	3	-	3	-	9	-	17	-	32
#10 Florida State	(-7.0)	17	-	3	-	0	-	13	-	33

Scoring Summary
Florida State - Cook 2 yard run (Aguayo kick)
Michigan - Allen 19 yard Field goal
Florida State - Aguayo 42 yard Field goal
Florida State - Murray 92 yard pass from Francois (Aguayo kick)
Michigan - Allen 28 yard Field goal
Florida State - Aguayo 38 yard Field goal
Michigan - Allen 37 yard Field goal
Michigan - McCray 14 yard interception return (Pass failed)
Florida State - Francois 3 yard run (Aguayo kick)
Michigan - Hill 8 yard pass from Speight (Allen kick)
Michigan - Evans 30 yard run (Darboh pass from Speight)
Florida State - Murray 12 yard pass from Francois (Kick blocked)
Michigan - Metellus returned blocked PAT for 2 points

Associated Press Orange Bowl game summary - Renegade, the horse that serves as Florida State's mascot, took an uncharacteristic tumble while prancing on the field before kickoff. The horse got up and was just fine. Hours later, Florida State collapsed -- and like Renegade, recovered with a flourish. Deondre Francois' 12-yard touchdown pass to Nyquan Murray with 36 seconds left put No. 10 Florida State ahead for good, and the Seminoles topped No. 6 Michigan 33-32 in a frantic, down-to-the-wire Orange Bowl on Friday night. It capped a simply wild final few minutes of a game that Florida State controlled most of the way before needing a rally in the final moments. Dalvin Cook rushed for 145 yards and a touchdown for Florida State (10-3), which led 17-3 and 20-6 early -- and was up by 12 midway through the fourth quarter before falling behind. Francois completed only 9 of 27 passes but made the most of them, throwing for 222 yards and connecting with Murray for two scores. Chris Evans had a 30-yard touchdown run and Khalid Hill an 8-yard scoring catch in the final minutes for Michigan (10-3), which also got a defensive conversion when Josh Metellus ran a blocked extra point back after the second Francois-Murray TD. But Michigan turned the ball over on its final possession, and the Seminoles held on to win after the teams combined for 23 points and two lead changes in the final 5:22. The Wolverines played without Heisman Trophy finalist Jabrill Peppers, their do-everything guy who couldn't go because of a bad left hamstring, and lost standout tight end Jake Butt to what was believed to be a serious knee injury in the second quarter. Wilton Speight was 21 for 38 passing for 163 yards for Michigan, which got a 14-yard interception return from Mike McCray for a touchdown. Florida State was in total control, but the game turned midway through the fourth when Trey Marshall was ejected for targeting on a punt return -- giving Michigan a short field on which to start its comeback. Marshall missed an amazing finish. Hill's scoring grab was Michigan's first offensive TD of the night, and Evans' run with 1:57 left gave the Wolverines their first lead. It lasted 81 seconds. Florida State's Keith Gavin swung momentum back to the Seminoles with a 66-yard kickoff return right up the middle -- setting up the drive where his team would take the lead for good. Francois lobbed one up perfectly for Murray, and the Seminoles escaped.

ORANGE RECORDS - Francois' scoring pass to Murray in the first quarter was the longest TD throw in Orange Bowl history, the 92-yarder topping the mark set in 1959 when Oklahoma's Brewster Hobby connected with Ross Coyle on what became a 79-yard score against Syracuse. Francois also was part of the shortest interception return for a TD in the game's history, when McCray ran his back 14 yards late in the third.

2016 BUFFALO WILD WINGS CITRUS BOWL

The 2016 Citrus Bowl (December) was played on December 31, 2016 at the Camping World Stadium in Orlando, Florida. The 71st edition of the Citrus Bowl, the game was nationally televised by ABC.

2016 Buffalo Wild Wings Citrus Bowl	Line	1	-	2	-	3	-	4	-	Final
#19 LSU	(-3.0)	0	-	16	-	10	-	3	-	29
#15 Louisville	(59.5)	3	-	3	-	0	-	3	-	9

Scoring Summary
Louisville - Creque 24 yard Field goal
LSU - Jeter 1 yard pass from Etling (Delahoussaye kick)
LSU - Guice 1 yard pass from Etling (Delahoussaye kick)
LSU - Safety (Jackson tackled in end zone)
Louisville - Creque 47 yard Field goal
LSU - Guice 70 yard run (Delahoussaye kick)
LSU - Delahoussaye 42 yard Field goal
Louisville - Creque 30 yard Field goal
LSU - Delahoussaye 25 yard Field goal

Associated Press Citrus Bowl game summary - For much of the first half Saturday, LSU sophomore running back Derrius Guice found little room to work as Louisville's defensive front filled the gaps and swarmed to the ball. But the second half of the Buffalo Wild Wings Citrus Bowl was a different story. The game slowed down and Guice took the time to let the blocks develop before hitting the holes. Finally, he popped a 12-yard run off left tackle and then the big one came the next play when he burst up the middle, broke a tackle and then was off to the races for a 70-yard touchdown early in the third quarter that all but closed the door on the 15th-ranked Cardinals and sealed the 19th-ranked Tigers 29-9 victory at Camping World Stadium. Guice, earned the Citrus Bowl MVP after finishing his day with 138 yards and a rushing touchdown while also catching a 1-yard touchdown pass. The spotlight has been on Guice since star running back Leonard Fournette announced earlier this month that he would not play in the Tigers' bowl game so that he can focus on getting his injured ankle healthy to begin his path toward an NFL career. Guice had filled in nicely for Fournette during the season and Saturday was no different as his clock-draining runs and the Tigers' (8-4) suffocating defense limited Louisville's Heisman Trophy-winning Quarterback Lamar Jackson. Guice made explosive plays running the ball and catching it, but his most memorable play may have come on special teams in the fourth quarter when he took a kickoff return 50 yards, steamrolling Cardinals kicker Blanton Creque near the sideline in the process. It was the perfect capper on a breakout season while delivering a glimpse of is in store for next season.

2016 TAXSLAYER BOWL (GATOR BOWL)

The 2016 TaxSlayer Bowl was played on December 31, 2016 at EverBank Field in Jacksonville, Florida. The 72nd edition of the TaxSlayer Bowl (formerly the Gator Bowl) featured the Georgia Tech Yellow Jackets of the Atlantic Coast Conference against the Kentucky Wildcats of the Southeastern Conference. It was aired on ESPN. This was the 20th overall meeting between the two teams, with Georgia Tech holding an 11–7–1 series lead coming into the game. The previous time the two teams met was in 1960, when both teams were members of the Southeastern Conference. Georgia Tech was led by head coach Paul Johnson. The Yellow Jackets began the season 3–0, before losing three games in a row to become 3–3 halfway through the season. Georgia Tech went 5–1 the second half of the season, ending their regular season in a 28–27 victory over their rivals Georgia. This was Georgia Tech's eighth appearance in the TaxSlayer Bowl/Gator Bowl; in their prior appearances they were 3–4. Kentucky was led by head coach Mark Stoops. The Wildcats began the season 0–2 before going 5–1 in their next 6 games. They then lost back-to-back games against Georgia and Tennessee before winning their final two games of the regular season, ending the regular season in a 41–38 victory over their rivals Louisville. This was Kentucky's first bowl game since the 2011 BBVA Compass Bowl and was their first appearance in the TaxSlayer Bowl/Gator Bowl.

2016 Taxslayer Bowl	Line	1	-	2	-	3	-	4	-	Final
Georgia Tech	(-3.0)	10	-	10	-	3	-	10	-	33
Kentucky	(61.0)	0	-	3	-	0	-	15	-	18

Scoring Summary
Georgia Tech - Davis 38 yard fumble return (Butker kick)
Georgia Tech - Butker 23 yard Field goal
Kentucky - MacGinnis 37 yard Field goal
Georgia Tech - Thomas 21 yard run (Butker kick)
Georgia Tech - Butker 52 yard Field goal
Georgia Tech - Butker 44 yard Field goal
Kentucky - Baker 20 yard pass from Johnson (MacGinnis kick)
Georgia Tech - Butker 26 yard Field goal
Kentucky - Johnson 21 yard run (Conrad from Johnson)
Georgia Tech - Mills 3 yard run (Butker kick)

Associated Press TaxSlayer (Gator) Bowl game summary - Dedrick Mills got a shoutout, some head nods and several high-fives as he walked toward the interview room at EverBank Field. And those came from opposing players. The freshman was an even bigger hit inside Georgia Tech's locker room and in the stands. Mills ran for a career-high 169 yards and a touchdown, leading the Yellow Jackets to a 33-18 victory against Kentucky in the TaxSlayer Bowl on Saturday. It was the seventh-most rushing yards in bowl history, earning Mills the Most Valuable Player trophy and making some forget about his two suspensions this season. Playing without running back Marcus Marshall, who decided to transfer after the regular-season finale, Georgia Tech (9-4) turned to Mills to handle the workload against Kentucky (7-6). The newcomer from nearby Waycross, Georgia, delivered. With dozens of friends and family members in attendance, he carried a career-high 31 times as the Yellow Jackets won back-to-back bowl games for the first time in more than a decade. He got plenty of help, too, as Tech won its fourth consecutive game. Senior P.J. Davis returned a fumble 38 yards for a touchdown. Fellow linebacker Terrell Lewis blocked a punt late in the first half that set up one of Harrison Butker's four field goals. Thomas added a 21-yard TD run in his final collegiate game.

VERBAL EXCHANGE - Stoops and Johnson exchanged words in the first quarter. Stoops initially seemed upset that two of his players were injured on consecutive plays. But Stoops said he took issue with something someone on Tech's sideline said. "I have great respect for Coach Johnson, but nobody else over there is going to say a word to me," he said.

2016 Chick-Fil-A Peach Bowl (National Semifinal)

The 2016 Peach Bowl was played on December 31, 2016 at the Georgia Dome in Atlanta, Georgia. The 49th Peach Bowl was a College Football Playoff semifinal, with the winner of this game advancing to play the winner of the 2016 Fiesta Bowl in the 2017 College Football Playoff National Championship. This was the final edition of the Peach Bowl contested in the Georgia Dome, as the stadium is scheduled to be demolished once its replacement, Mercedes-Benz Stadium, opens in 2017. The game was televised on ESPN with a radio broadcast on ESPN Radio. The winner of the game received the George P. Crumbley Trophy, named for the founder of the original Peach Bowl. This was the fifth meeting between the schools, with Alabama having won all four previous encounters.

2016 Chick-Fil-A Peach Bowl	Line	1	-	2	-	3	-	4	-	Final
#4 Washington	(50.5)	7	-	0	-	0	-	0	-	7
#1 Alabama	(-12.5)	7	-	10	-	0	-	7	-	24

Scoring Summary
Washington - Pettis 16 yard pass from Browning (Van Winkle kick)
Alabama - Scarbrough 18 yard run (Griffith kick)
Alabama - Griffith 41 yard Field goal
Alabama - Anderson 22 yard interception return (Griffith kick)
Alabama - Scarbrough 68 yard run (Griffith kick)

Associated Press Chick-fil-A Peach Bowl game summary - For Nick Saban and the Alabama Crimson Tide, it would be unimaginable to end a season any other way. Once again, they'll be playing for a national title. Going old school on playoff newcomer Washington, top-ranked Alabama relied on a stifling defense and the bruising runs of Bo Scarbrough to wear down the Huskies for a 24-7 victory Saturday in the Chick-fil-A Peach Bowl semifinal game. Saban isn't satisfied. He never is. Saban, will be seeking his fifth national title in the last eight years at Alabama, a remarkable run that has stamped him perhaps the greatest coach in college football history. The Crimson Tide (14-0) scored 10 points off turnovers, including Ryan Anderson's interception return for a touchdown late in the first half, and Scarbrough's 68-yard TD run in the fourth quarter finished off the Huskies. Scarbrough totaled 180 yards and two scores, garnering offensive MVP honors. Not bad for a backup. Seeking its second straight title, Alabama heads to Tampa, Florida, for the Jan. 9 championship game rematch against Clemson which blanked Ohio State 31-0 at the Fiesta Bowl. No. 4 Washington (12-2) reached the College Football Playoff with a remarkable turnaround season after struggling much of the last two decades -- including a 0-12 debacle in 2008. But Jake Browning and the Huskies' high-powered offense were no match for Alabama's top-ranked defense, even after an impressive drive gave them an early 7-0 edge. The Tide began to exert its dominance late in the first quarter when Anthony Averett stripped the ball away from John Ross on a screen pass. Jonathan Allen recovered, giving Alabama possession at the Washington 40 and setting up Adam Griffith's 41-yard field goal for a 10-7 lead. Anderson made an even bigger defensive play with just over a minute to go in the half. With the blitzing Foster bearing down on him, Browning desperately heaved a pass into the flats for Lavon Coleman. But Anderson peeled off to make the pick, knocked Coleman over in the process and was off to the end zone on a 26-yard return that made it 17-7 at the half. For Alabama, it was the 11th defensive touchdown of the season. Any hopes of a Washington comeback were snuffed out by Scarbrough, a starter at most schools but not for the deep, talented Tide. On a simple running play to the left, he appeared to be stopped by two players just short of the line of scrimmage. But Scarbrough somehow managed to stay on his feet and -- boom! -- he was gone. Streaking down the field in front of the Alabama bench, he avoided another defender with a subtle deke, cut back toward the middle of the field at the Washington 30 and outran everyone to the end zone. Scarbrough also scored Alabama's first touchdown with a bruising, 18-yard run.

UGLY ENDING - A scuffle broke out after Minkah Fitzpatrick's interception in the closing seconds, leading to a pair of unsportsmanlike conduct penalties against Alabama. Several Washington players were shaken up while chasing down Fitzpatrick, but they all managed to walk off the field while the officials sorted things out. Two Alabama players -- linebacker Reuben Foster and defensive back Ronnie Harrison -- headed to the locker room before the game was over. But they were sent off by their coaches, not the officials. "They were taking some cheap shots," Foster said.

2016 Fiesta Bowl (National Semifinal)

The 2016 PlayStation Fiesta Bowl (December) was played on December 31, 2016 at the University of Phoenix Stadium in Glendale, Arizona. This 46th Fiesta Bowl Game was a College Football Playoff semifinal with the winner of the game competing against the winner of the 2016 Peach Bowl in the 2017 College Football Playoff National Championship. The winning team will receive the Molina Fiesta Bowl Trophy. Clemson became just the second team in college football history to shut out Ohio State (11-2) in a bowl game, joining California in the 1921 Rose Bowl. The game also marked the first time that Buckeyes head coach Urban Meyer was shut out in his career, in about 193 games, and his second major loss to Dabo Swinney in the past four seasons. The game also marked the second consecutive advance to the CFP National Championship game by the Clemson football program. This was the third meeting between the schools, with Clemson having won both previous matchups.

2016 Fiesta Bowl	Line	1	-	2	-	3	-	4	-	Final
#3 Ohio State	(-1.0)	0	-	0	-	0	-	0	-	0
#2 Clemson	(56.5)	10	-	7	-	7	-	7	-	31

Scoring Summary
Clemson - Huegel 45 yard Field goal
Clemson - Watson 1 yard run (Huegel kick)
Clemson - Fuller 30 yard pass from Watson (Huegel kick)
Clemson - Watson 7 yard run (Huegel kick)
Clemson - Gallman 7 yard run (Huegel kick)

New York Times Fiesta Bowl game summary - Bring on 'Bama. The confetti still were falling at University of Phoenix Stadium when Clemson players and fans began calling out last year's national champion. It continued throughout the on-field celebration and in the postgame media session. The second-seeded Tigers have waited a calendar year for revenge, and now they have their shot against undefeated Alabama following their 31-0 whitewashing of No. 3 Ohio State in the Fiesta Bowl on Saturday night. A year ago, on the same field, Clemson (13-1) fell just short of its first championship since 1981, dropping a gut-wrenching 45-40 decision to the Crimson Tide. After the loss, Quarterback Deshaun Watson told reporters the Tigers would be in Tampa, Fla., a year later, and here they are, following this utter decimation of the Buckeyes. It's no surprise they will meet Alabama, the No. 1 seed who advanced with a 24-7 victory over fourth-seeded Washington in the Peach Bowl in Atlanta. Clemson, meanwhile, was impressive, making a mockery of its underdog status. A majority of the 71,279 fans in attendance wore O.S.U. scarlet red, but Watson and Co. made themselves at home, looking nothing like the inconsistent team that had several close calls against inferior opponents during the regular season. They became just the second team to shut out Ohio State (11-2) in a bowl game, joining California in the 1921 Rose Bowl, and handed the Buckeyes the worst loss of the Urban Meyer era by far. In 193 previous games, none of his teams ever had been shut out. It also was Ohio State's most lopsided loss since falling 35-3 to USC on Sept. 14, 2008. Clemson coach Dabo Swinney now has defeated Meyer in the Fiesta Bowl twice in the last four years and has Clemson (13-1) one win away from its first title since 1981. Perhaps reading Meyer's book paid off, as Swinney planned to do this week. Clemson dominated virtually every category, outgaining Ohio State (11-2) 458-208 and nearly tripling them in first downs 24-9. Ohio State's opportunistic secondary intercepted Watson twice, but the Heisman Trophy runner-up otherwise had his way with the Buckeyes' third-ranked scoring defense, producing 344 total yards and three touchdowns. As he has done all year, Watson spread the ball around — he connected with eight different receivers — and used his legs when needed. But the star of the evening was Clemson's overlooked defense. It swallowed up Meyer's high-powered offense, the big defensive front overpowering the Buckeyes' offensive line, making Ohio State one-dimensional and jumping on the short passing patterns to limit Ohio State to short gains. Clemson sacked J.T. Barrett three times and had 10 tackles behind the line of scrimmage. Lacking that big-play threat down the field, the Buckeyes were handcuffed. Clemson safety Jadar Johnson criticized Barrett's throwing ability during the week, and the Ohio State Quarterback did little to distinguish himself, held to minus-2 yards rushing and throwing two interceptions. For months, Alabama felt like the inevitable national champion. But Saturday, against arguably a better opponent, Clemson looked like a juggernaut. Despite an inconsistent regular season, the Tigers believe they can beat the Crimson Tide. Last year's narrow loss is proof they can play with Nick Saban's dynamo.

2017 OUTBACK BOWL

The 2017 Outback Bowl was played on January 2, 2017 at Raymond James Stadium in Tampa, Florida. The 31st annual Outback Bowl featured the Iowa Hawkeyes from the Big Ten Conference and the Florida Gators from the Southeastern Conference. The game was nationally televised by ABC, and its title sponsor was the

Outback Steakhouse restaurant franchise. This was the fourth overall meeting between the teams and was the third time the Gators and Hawkeyes played each other in the Outback Bowl, with each team having won one of the previous meetings. This was also the fifth time each school played in the Outback Bowl.

2017 Outback Bowl	Line	1	-	2	-	3	-	4	-	Final
#20 Florida	(-1.0)	3	-	7	-	7	-	13	-	30
#21 Iowa	(41.0)	3	-	0	-	0	-	0	-	3

Scoring Summary
Iowa - Duncan 36 yard Field goal
Florida - Pineiro 44 yard Field goal
Florida - Thompson 85 yard pass from Appleby (Pineiro kick)
Florida - Goolsby 6 yard pass from Appleby (Pineiro kick)
Florida - Gardner 50 yard interception return (Pineiro kick)
Florida - Pineiro 25 yard Field goal
Florida - Pineiro 48 yard Field goal

Associated Press Outback Bowl game summary - No. 20 Florida dominated the Outback with stingy defense and a persistent offense that did its job, too. Chauncey Gardner, Jr., returned one of his two fourth-quarter interceptions 58 yards for a touchdown, and graduate transfer Austin Appleby threw for 222 yards and two TDs to pace Monday's 30-3 rout of No. 21 Iowa. With Gardner grabbing game MVP honors, the Gators (9-4) held up their end of what many expected to be a day defense ruled, especially considering Florida entered ranked 115th in the nation in total offense -- five spots ahead of the sputtering Hawkeyes. Conversely, the teams were sixth and 24th, respectively, in total defense. Mark Thompson scored on an 85-yard pass play in the first half and Appleby, who spent the past four seasons at Purdue, tossed a 6-yard TD pass to DeAndre Goolsby to break the game open late in the third quarter. Florida (9-4) rebounded from lopsided losses to archrival Florida State and No. 1 Alabama, scoring more points on Iowa (8-5) than the Hawkeyes allowed to Michigan, Illinois and Nebraska combined while ending the regular season on a three-game winning streak. Iowa's C.J. Beathard led an early field goal drive and managed to get his team close to the end zone on two other occasions. Florida's defense stiffened both times, stopping the Hawkeyes on downs at the Gator 3 in the second quarter and forcing them to settle for a 30-yard field goal that sailed wide right midway through the third quarter. Appleby, who began his career at Purdue against Iowa, shrugged off throwing interceptions on Florida's first two drives of the day to finish 14 of 25 passing. Akrum Wadley ran for 115 yards, giving Iowa a pair of 1,000-yard rushers in the same season for the first time. The junior finished with 1,081, and LeShun Daniels wound up with 1,058 after gaining 45 Monday.

TURNING POINT - Beathard directed the best drive of the game by either team, moving Iowa from its own 36 to inside the Florida 10 with help from runs of 27 yards by Akrum Wadley and 11 yards by LeShun Daniels, plus an 18-yard pass to tight end George Kittle on third-and-14 from the Gators 28. Three plays later, Beathard dropped back to throw before scrambling for a 6-yard gain near the goal line. The Hawkeyes thought he scored, but officials ruled him down at the 1. Daniels was dropped for a 2-yard loss on fourth down.

2017 COTTON BOWL CLASSIC

The 2017 Cotton Bowl Classic was played on January 2, 2017, at AT&T Stadium in Arlington, Texas. The 81st Cotton Bowl Classic was broadcast on ESPN, ESPN Deportes, ESPN Radio and XM Satellite Radio. Western Michigan was selected as an at-large as the highest ranked College Football Playoff (CFP) Group of Five team while Wisconsin was chosen as an at-large out of the Big Ten Conference. This was the fifth meeting between the schools, with Wisconsin leading the all-time series 4–1. This was the first Cotton Bowl for both teams.

2017 Cotton Bowl Classic	Line	1	-	2	-	3	-	4	-	Final
#12 Western Michigan	(53.5)	0	-	7	-	3	-	6	-	16
#8 Wisconsin	(-9.0)	14	-	3	-	0	-	7	-	24

Scoring Summary
Wisconsin - Clement 2 yard run (Endicott kick)
Wisconsin - Ogunbowale 1 yard run (Endicott kick)
Western Michigan - Terrell 2 yard run (Hampton kick)
Wisconsin - Endicott 30 yard Field goal
Western Michigan - Hampton 27 yard Field goal
Wisconsin - Fumigalli 8 yard pass from Hornibrook (Endicott kick)
Western Michigan - Davis 11 yard pass from Terrell (Kick failed)

Associated Press Cotton Bowl game summary - Troy Fumagalli had highlight catches for Wisconsin even before the big tight end's leaping 8-yard touchdown in the fourth quarter and his 26-yard gain on third down that effectively wrapped up the Cotton Bowl victory. The game's offensive MVP also had a nifty one-handed grab on third down with his left hand -- the one missing an index finger since right after his birth -- to extend the eighth-ranked Badgers' opening touchdown drive. There was another leaping two-handed catch in the first half of a 24-16 victory Monday that denied Western Michigan a perfect season. Fumagalli had seven passes thrown his way, and the 6-foot-6 junior caught six of them. The last two clinched the third consecutive bowl victory for the Big Ten runner-up Badgers (11-3). After his TD catch between two defenders in the back of the end zone with 12:26 left made it 24-10, Western Michigan (13-1) took 9 minutes to score. Wisconsin was able to run out the clock after Fumagalli's big play on third-and-8. With their "Row the Boat" mentality inspired by Fleck, the 12th-ranked Broncos (13-1) went from one win during his first season in Kalamazoo three years ago to the last FBS team other than No. 1 Alabama this season with a chance to be undefeated. The Badgers, who finished with 11 wins for the fourth time in seven seasons, were clearly bigger and stronger -- especially up front. Their offensive line averaged about three inches and 45 pounds more than the WMU defensive front. Wisconsin set the tone early, with rushing touchdowns on its first two drives to lead 14-0 against the Group of Five team. Fumagalli's TD came three plays after a rare interception by senior Zach Terrell, who finished with 33 touchdowns and four picks -- the last by Wisconsin linebacker T.J. Edwards. Terrell combined with All-America receiver Corey Davis for 51 career touchdowns, tying the FBS record on an 11-yarder on fourth down with 3:27 left. Even with cornerback Sojourn Shelton's arms wrapped around him in the back of the end zone, Davis broke free to make the catch.

2017 ROSE BOWL

The 2017 Rose Bowl was played on January 2, 2017 at the Rose Bowl stadium in Pasadena, California. This 103rd Rose Bowl Game matched the Big Ten Conference champions Penn State Nittany Lions against the USC Trojans of the Pac-12 Conference, a rematch of the 1923 and 2009 Rose Bowls, the former the first appearance for either team in the bowl and the latter the most recent appearance for either team. USC received the Lathrop K. Leishman trophy for winning the game. The contest, played on January 2 in keeping with the game's standard practice when New Year's Day falls on a Sunday, was televised on ESPN with a radio broadcast on ESPN Radio and XM Satellite Radio. The Pasadena Tournament of Roses Association was the organizer of the game. The Rose Bowl Game was a contractual sell-out, with 64,500 tickets allocated to the participating teams and conferences. The remaining tickets were distributed to the Tournament of Roses members, sponsors, City of Pasadena residents, and the general public. Ticket prices were $150 and $210.

The Trojans started the year with a dismal 1–3 record, but after a Week 4 loss at No. 24 Utah the Trojans reeled off an eight-game winning streak, including an upset win over No. 4 Washington to break them into the Top 25 where they have remained since. USC was led by freshman Quarterback Sam Darnold, 1,000-yard rusher Ronald Jones II, receivers JuJu Smith-Schuster, Darreus Rogers and Deontay Burnett, defensive end Porter Gustin, and all-purpose player Adoree Jackson. They were coached by Clay Helton, who led them to a 9–3 season (after going 5–4 in 9 games as interim head coach last season). The team wore its white jerseys. The Nittany Lions started the season off 2–2 after losses to Pitt and No. 4 Michigan but finished the regular season on a 9–game winning streak, including a pivotal 4th-quarter comeback victory over #2 Ohio State that led to Penn State receiving a Top-25 national ranking for the first time since 2011. Penn State added a Big Ten Championship with a comeback win over #6 Wisconsin to close out the season. The Nittany Lions were led by sophomore duo Quarterback Trace McSorley and 1,000+ yard rusher Saquon Barkley and junior wide receiver Chris Godwin. They came into the game 11–2 (8–1 Big Ten), a big improvement from the last two seasons under head coach James Franklin (finished 7–6 both seasons). The team wore its dark jerseys. The Nittany Lions and Trojans had previously played nine times, with USC leading the series 5–4, and had played twice in the Rose Bowl in (1923 and 2009) with USC winning both games. The 2017 match was the highest scoring game in the bowl's history, with a total of 101 points, breaking the record set five years earlier at the 2012 Rose Bowl game.

2017 Rose Bowl	Line	1	-	2	-	3	-	4	-	Final
#9 USC	(53.5)	13	-	14	-	8	-	17	-	52
#5 Penn State	(-9.0)	0	-	21	-	28	-	0	-	49

Scoring Summary
USC - Burnett 26 yard pass from Darnold (Boermeester kick)
USC - Boermeester 22 yard Field goal
USC - Boermeester 44 yard Field goal
Penn State - Barkley 24 yard run (Davis kick)
USC - Burnett 3 yard pass from Darnold (Boermeester kick)
Penn State - Godwin 30 yard pass from McSorley (Davis kick)
USC - Rogers 3 yard pass from Darnold (Boermeester kick)
Penn State - Gesicki 11 yard pass from McSorley (Davis kick)
Penn State - Barkley 79 yard run (Davis kick)
Penn State - Godwin 72 yard pass from McSorley (Davis kick)
Penn State - McSorley 3 yard run (Davis kick)
USC - Smith-Schuster 13 yard pass from Darnold (McNamara pass from Darnold)
Penn State - Barkley 7 yard pass from McSorley (Davis kick)
USC - Jones 3 yard run ((Boermeester kick)
USC - Burnett 27 yard pass from Darnold (Boermeester kick)
USC - Boermeester 46 yard Field goal

Associated Press Rose Bowl game summary - After 98 combined points and 1,040 yards of spectacular offensive play, the highest-scoring Rose Bowl in history rested on the left foot of a Southern California kicker who had already missed two field goals. Matt Boermeester somehow blocked out the cacophonous tension in the chilly air. He focused only on securing a perfect ending to an epic evening. His technique was sound. His kick was true. And the Trojans got their storybook finish in Pasadena. Boermeester hit a 46-yard field goal as time expired, and No. 9 USC rallied from a 14-point deficit in the fourth quarter for a 52-49 victory over No. 5 Penn State on Monday night in the 103rd edition of the Granddaddy of Them All. Freshman Sam Darnold passed for 453 yards and five touchdowns while leading a stirring comeback by the Trojans (10-3), who won their ninth consecutive game and triumphed in their first Rose Bowl since 2009. USC trailed 49-35 with nine minutes to play but persevered to win one of the greatest Rose Bowls ever played. Deontay Burnett, who had three TD receptions, caught a tying 27-yard scoring pass from Darnold with 1:20 left to cap an 80-yard drive in 38 seconds with no timeouts available. Leon McQuay III then intercepted an ill-advised long pass by Trace McSorley and returned it 32 yards to the Penn State 33 with 27 seconds left. In an instant, the Trojans went from preparing for overtime to having a chance to win. The Trojans set up Boermeester, and the junior confidently drilled the Rose Bowl winner, sprinting away as it went through the south uprights and set off pandemonium on the hallowed field. McSorley passed for 254 yards and threw two of his four touchdown passes to Chris Godwin for the Nittany Lions (11-3), whose nine-game winning streak ended in heartbreaking fashion. Saquon Barkley rushed for 194 yards and two TDs as the Nittany Lions (12-2) followed up their 21-point comeback in the Big Ten title game with another ferocious rally, only to watch the Trojans rally back. With one jaw-dropping play after another from two talent-laden offenses, the teams obliterated the combined Rose Bowl scoring record in the third quarter, surpassing Oregon's 45-38 victory over Wisconsin in the 2012 game.

2017 SUGAR BOWL

The 2017 Sugar Bowl was played on January 2, 2017 at the Mercedes-Benz Superdome in New Orleans, Louisiana. This 83rd Sugar Bowl was played between the Oklahoma Sooners of the Big 12 Conference and the Auburn Tigers of the Southeastern Conference. It is sponsored by the Allstate insurance company; the game is officially known as the Allstate Sugar Bowl.

2017 Sugar Bowl	Line	1	-	2	-	3	-	4	-	Final
#17 Auburn	(66.5)	7	-	6	-	0	-	6	-	19
#7 Oklahoma	(-2.0)	0	-	14	-	14	-	7	-	35

Scoring Summary
Auburn - Cox 3 yard run (Carlson kick)
Oklahoma - Andrews 13 yard pass from Mayfield (Seibert kick)
Auburn - Carlson 49 yard Field goal
Oklahoma - Mixon 3 yard run (Seibert kick)
Auburn - Carlson 39 yard Field goal
Oklahoma - Westbrook 7 yard pass from Mayfield (Seibert kick)
Oklahoma - Mixon 4 yard run (Seibert kick)
Oklahoma - Perine 2 yard run (Seibert kick)
Auburn - Harris 1 yard pass from Johnson (No PAT attempt)

Associated Press Sugar Bowl game summary - Heisman Trophy finalists Baker Mayfield and Dede Westbrook connected one last time for a touchdown. Joe Mixon emerged from his recent controversy with big plays that had teammates lifting him off his feet in celebration. Samaje Perine put his name in Oklahoma's record books. Seventh-ranked Oklahoma had plenty to celebrate after a 35-19 triumph over

No. 17 Auburn in the Sugar Bowl on Monday night, including a 10th-straight victory. Mayfield passed for 296 yards and two touchdowns. Mixon heard boos from Auburn fans, who also shouted derisive comments regarding a recently publicized video of him punching a woman in the face in 2014. Mixon, who served a season-long suspension in 2014 and has apologized for the assault, also drew cheers from crimson-clad Oklahoma fans with his play. His two short touchdown runs were among the highlights of a performance in which he gained 180 yards from scrimmage -- 91 rushing on 19 carries and 89 receiving on five catches. Mixon didn't answer questions about the boos or the reasons for them, saying only he wanted to celebrate with his teammates. Perine rushed for 86 yards, three more than he needed to set Oklahoma's career rushing record. "Our backs pound people and it wears on people," Mayfield said. Auburn (8-5), which wound up in the Sugar Bowl despite dropping its last two Southeastern Conference games to Georgia and Alabama, entered the game hopeful that it would be buoyed by the return of Quarterback Sean White, who'd missed the Tigers' final two games with a throwing shoulder injury. White led Auburn to a touchdown on its first series -- Chandler Cox's 3-yard run on fourth down -- but the Quarterback left the game for good in the first half with a broken right forearm. John Franklin III backed up White but also hurt his throwing arm, Malzahn said, so Jeremy Johnson got into the game. The Tigers' offense was inconsistent, increasing pressure on Auburn's 20th-ranked defense to keep the Sooners' fast-paced, high-powered attack in check. Mixon broke loose for a 35-yard run in the third quarter that set up his second TD, which he scored from 4 yards out by diving for the pylon. Early in the fourth quarter, Perine took a direct snap for a 2-yard TD that made it 35-13. With the Sooners (11-2) pulling away for their second Sugar Bowl triumph in four years, Auburn fans started filing out.

2017 CFP NATIONAL CHAMPIONSHIP

The 2017 College Football Playoff National Championship was played at Raymond James Stadium in Tampa, Florida, on January 9, 2017. It was the third College Football Playoff National Championship. The national title was contested through a four-team bracket system, the College Football Playoff, which replaced the previous Bowl Championship Series National Championship Game. In the three-game playoff, the Clemson Tigers defeated the Ohio State Buckeyes in the Fiesta Bowl, and the Alabama Crimson Tide defeated the Washington Huskies in the Peach Bowl. The resulting championship game between Clemson and Alabama became a rematch of the previous year's championship game, which Alabama won, 45–40. The Tigers won the game, 35–31, after coming back from a 14–0 deficit earlier in the game. Clemson scored the game-winning touchdown with one second left in the game. Clemson's Deshaun Watson and Ben Boulware were named the Offensive and Defensive Most Valuable Players, respectively.

2017 CFP Championship Game	Line	1	-	2	-	3	-	4	-	Final
#2 Clemson	(51.0)	0	-	7	-	7	-	21	-	35
#1 Alabama	(-6.5)	7	-	7	-	10	-	7	-	31

Scoring Summary
Alabama - Scarbrough 25 yard run (Griffith kick)
Alabama - Scarbrough 37 yard run (Griffith kick)
Clemson - Watson 8 yard run (Huegel kick)
Alabama - Griffith 27 yard Field goal
Clemson - Renfrow 24 yard pass from Watson (Huegel kick)
Alabama - Howard 68 yard pass from Hurts (Griffith kick)
Clemson - Williams 4 yard pass from Watson (Huegel kick)
Clemson - Gallman 1 yard run (Huegel kick)
Alabama - Hurts 30 yard run (Griffith kick)
Clemson - Renfrow 2 yard pass from Watson (Huegel kick)

Game Summary - Alabama opened the game with a three-and-out, and Clemson failed to capitalize, turning the ball over on downs after failing to convert a 4th & 1. On Alabama's ensuing drive, Bo Scarbrough opened the game's scoring with a 25-yard rushing touchdown. The first quarter ended with Alabama leading Clemson, 7–0. Scarbrough scored again in the second quarter, on a 37-yard rush to increase Alabama's lead to 14–0. Clemson Quarterback Deshaun Watson scored the Tigers' first touchdown of the game on an eight–yard run with six minutes left in the second quarter. The game went to halftime with Alabama leading, 14–7. The Tigers turned the ball over on their first drive in the second half; their fumble was recovered by Ryan Anderson and returned to Clemson's 16 yard line – the Tide increased their lead to 10 after converting a 27-yard field goal. Clemson cut the lead to three with seven minutes left in the third quarter after Watson found Hunter Renfrow over the middle for a 24-yard touchdown pass. After an injury to Scarbrough, the Tide came out and scored on a 68-yard pass from Jalen Hurts to O. J. Howard on the next play; this put Alabama back up by ten points with 1:53 left in the third quarter, which ended with Alabama leading Clemson, 24–14. Clemson scored just three plays into the final quarter as

Watson threw a touchdown pass to Mike Williams; this cut the lead down to 24–21. With 4:38 to go in the game, Clemson took their first lead in the game after Wayne Gallman scored on a one-yard touchdown rush; Alabama got the ball back on their own 32 yard line with 4:38 remaining in the game. The drive came to a 3rd & 16, on which Jalen Hurts found Ar'Darius Stewart for a 15-yard pass to set up a 4th & 1, which the Tide converted via a Damien Harris 5-yard rush. Hurts found the end zone on a 30-yard rush just a few plays later to give Alabama the lead back, 31–28. Clemson took possession of the ball with 2:01 on the clock and the ball on their own 36 yard line. After another long catch by Mike Williams, the drive came to a 3rd & 3 on the Alabama 32 yard line, which was converted on a pass to Renfrow to the Alabama 26 yard line with 0:19 left. The next play saw Watson find Jordan Leggett on a pass down to the Tide 9 yard line with 0:14 left. Watson threw to the end zone on 1st & Goal; the pass was overthrown, and the clock stopped with 0:09. On 2nd & Goal, Watson targeted Mike Williams, who was tripped in the end zone. The resulting pass interference call gave the Tigers 1st & Goal with the ball placed on the 2-yard line with 0:06 left. On the next play, Watson threw a touchdown pass to Renfrow with 0:01 left in the game, putting Clemson back in the lead, 35–31. After Clemson recovered an onside kick attempting to run out the clock, the game ended with a kneel-down and Clemson won the National Championship Game. Watson, who went 36-for-56 (64%) on pass attempts for 420 yards with three passing touchdowns, and ran for 43 yards and one rushing touchdown, was named the game's Offensive Most Valuable Player. Ben Boulware, who recorded six tackles, including one for a loss of yards, was named the Defensive Most Valuable Player.

2017 Air Force Reserve Celebration Bowl

The **2017 Celebration Bowl** was played on December 16, 2017 at the Mercedes-Benz Stadium in Atlanta, Georgia. This third Celebration Bowl game matched the champion of the Mid-Eastern Athletic Conference, against the champion of the Southwestern Athletic Conference, the two historically black division I conferences. The game kicked off at 12:00 PM (EST) and was televised live on ABC, as the kickoff game to the 2017 Bowl season

Pre-Game Buildup – Pregame media coverage of the game focused the similarities between Grambling and North Carolina A&T, and the shared history between the two programs. Both the A&T and Grambling are previous Celebration Bowl champions and the last two HBCU national champions, with A&T winning the inaugural game in 2015 and Grambling winning in 2016.

2017 Celebration Bowl	Line	1	-	2	-	3	-	4	-	Final
Grambling State	(-5.5)	0	-	7	-	0	-	7	-	14
North Carolina A&T	(49.5)	0	-	7	-	7	-	7	-	21

Scoring Summary
North Carolina A&T – Cartwright 11 yard pass from Raynard (Ruiz Kick)
Grambling – Jones 2 yard pass from Kincaide (Orozco Kick)
North Carolina A&T – Cartwright 29 yard run (Ruiz Kick)
Grambling – Carter 29 yard pass from Kincaide (Orozco Kick)
North Carolina A&T – Raynard 1 yard run (Ruiz Kick)

NCATAggies.com Celebration Bowl Summary – In Major League Baseball, the unbreakable record appears to be Joe DiMaggio's 56-game hitting streak. In the NBA, it is perhaps Wilt Chamberlain's 100 points. On Saturday, America may have witnessed another unbreakable record happen in sports, live on ABC. In the world of black college football, where teams must play Division I-FBS programs (who are sometimes named Florida State, Clemson and Arkansas) for revenue, the seventh-ranked North Carolina A&T Aggies football team went an undefeated 12-0, won the Black College Football National Championship and improved to 2-0 in the third edition of the Celebration Bowl with a 21-14 win over No. 12 Grambling State (11-2) at Mercedes-Benz Stadium. It may be a while before an unbeaten team emerges from black college football. Yes Lawd. N.C. A&T is the first-ever Mid-Eastern Athletic Conference school to finish the entire season undefeated. They are the first Division I-AA black college football team to finish a season unbeaten and untied and they broke the school and conference record for wins with 12. What makes Saturday's outcome even more special, fun and humbling is the fact that 10 years ago today, the Aggies were coming off their second straight 0-11 season. Today, they are the kings of black college football, they're a top-10 team in the Football Championship Subdivision, and they went from winless to unbeaten. Aggie Pride! N.C. A&T won in true championship folklore. With the game tied at 14, the Aggies took over the ball at their own 44-yard line with 1:42 remaining in the game. On 2nd-and-10, one of the many crucial moments of the game occurred. N.C. A&T quarterback and MEAC Offensive Player of the Year Lamar Raynard dumped a short pass over the middle to All-MEAC first-team running back Marquell Cartwright. As Cartwright made his initial move up the field, he started to bobble the ball and it eventually hit the Mercedes-Benz turf. A GSU defender picked the ball up as if it were a fumble and returned the other way.

Before he got too far, the officials ruled the play an incomplete pass. GSU coach Broderick Fobbs wasn't so sure, so he challenged the play. The call of incomplete pass was upheld, costing the Tigers their final timeout. Raynard then proceeded to lead his team to another championship. He completed a 19-yard pass to Gardin. Raynard then tried to complete another pass to his high school teammate, Cartwright, and this time it was successful. Cartwright took the catch and run play to the GSU 18 before junior Elijah Bell made an amazing catch for a 15-yard gain to the GSU 3. He was the final catch of his 10-reception, 95-yard day. The Aggies, who were victims of a goal line stand earlier in the game, would not be denied with the game on the line. After a 2-yard Cartwright run, the Aggies hurried to the line and snuck Raynard through for a 1-yard touchdown with 38 seconds remaining. Cartwright was named the game's offensive MVP after finishing with 110 yards and a touchdown on 20 carries. His three receptions for 54 yards and a touchdown gave him 164 all-purpose yards against the Tigers. Another Aggies running back, current Chicago Bear Tarik Cohen, was the game's offensive MVP two years ago when the Aggies won the Celebration Bowl. Two dominant programs gave everyone their money's worth. The Aggies got on the board first as Cartwright caught an 11-yard pass from Raynard. GSU quarterback Devante Kincade was a problem for the Aggies all afternoon. He had 225 yards passing and two touchdowns and another 93 yards rushing on 16 carries. He led the Tigers on an 8-play, 70-yard drive to the game at 7 in the second quarter. GSU and Kincade tried to take its first lead of the game in the third quarter. On 2nd-and-goal from the 7, All-America cornerback Mac MCcain came up with his sixth interception of the season to halt the Tigers drive. N.C. A&T used the big play to drive 80 yards to take the lead on a Cartwright 29-yard TD run. GSU tied the game at 14 on a 29-yard TD pass from Kincade to Martez Carter to open the fourth quarter.

2017 NEW ORLEANS BOWL

The 2017 New Orleans Bowl was played on December 16, 2017, at the Mercedes-Benz Superdome in New Orleans, Louisiana, United States. The 17th edition of the New Orleans Bowl began at 1 P.M. EST and aired on ESPN. It was the eleventh all-time meeting between the schools; with Troy's victory, it now leads the series 9–2. The Trojans and Mean Green played together in the Sun Belt from 2004 until 2012, when North Texas joined Conference USA.

2017 New Orleans Bowl	Line	1	-	2	-	3	-	4	-	Final
Troy	(-5.0)	15	-	7	-	21	-	7	-	50
North Texas	(61.5)	7	-	13	-	3	-	7	-	30

Scoring Summary
Troy – Anderson 1 yard run (Sumpter Kick)
Troy – Anderson 2 yard run (2 pt conversion good)
North Texas – Bussey 12 yard pass from Fine (Moore Kick)
Troy – Willis 7 yard pass from Silvers (Sumpter Kick)
North Texas – McDonald 56 yard fumble recovery (2 pt conversion no good)
North Texas – Lawrence 13 yard pass from Fine (Moore Kick)
Troy – Silvers 1 yard run (Sumpter Kick)
Troy – McCormick 59 yard pass from Silvers (Sumpter Kick)
North Texas – Moore 24 yard Field Goal
Troy – Johnson 20 yard pass from Silvers (Sumpter Kick)
Troy – Willis 10 yard pass from Silvers (Sumpter Kick)
North Texas – Smiley 17 yard pass from Fine (Moore Kick)

Troytrojans.com New Orleans Bowl Game Summary – Brandon Silvers accounted for five touchdowns and Troy's defense recorded six sacks as the Trojans systematically dismantled North Texas, 50-30, Saturday at the Mercedes-Super Dome in the R&L Carriers New Orleans Bowl. Troy set the New Orleans Bowl record and the school's bowl record for points in a game against their former conference foe. The meeting was the first between the two since North Texas left the Sun Belt for Conference USA; the Trojans have now won nine of the 11 meetings between the two schools all-time. Silvers was named the New Orleans Bowl MVP after completing 24-of-31 passes for 305 yards and four touchdowns, while rushing for another score. Silvers became the school's all-time leader in career touchdowns responsible for with 87 as he passed Corey Robinson's 84. Troy (11-2) finished the season with 11 wins for just the eighth time in school history and the first at the FBS level. The Trojans have now won 22 of their last 27 games dating back to the 2015 season and are one of just 10 schools in the country with at least 21 wins over the past two seasons. The Trojans, who were playing without eight normal players on its two-deep, wasted no time showing the Mean Green (9-5), the C-USA West Division champions, what they were in for Saturday afternoon.

Silvers completed his first 10 pass attempts of the game and Josh Anderson scored twice on the ground in the game's first five minutes and 39 seconds. Anderson finished with a career-best 113 yards on 22 carries in the game. His second score followed one of three fumbles recovered by the Trojan defense. Jamal Stadom dropped Mason Fine for a loss 10 yards behind the line of scrimmage and Sam Lebbie fell on the loose ball. Troy held North Texas to -8 yards rushing in the game thanks to the six sacks and 11 tackles for loss – the Trojans finished the season with 112 tackles for loss, a new school record. It marked the eighth time this season that Troy held an opponent under 100 yards rushing, a new FBS record. North Texas scored two late touchdowns in the second quarter to turn a 15-point deficit into just a 22-20 halftime score. Following a 7-yard touchdown pass from Silvers to Damion Willis, the Mean Green returned a fumble 56-yards for a touchdown and got a late Fine touchdown pass. That was the last good thing to happen for the Mean Green as Troy came out of the break determined to show its former conference mate what they left behind when they left the league. Silvers opened the second half scoring with a 2-yard touchdown run and found Tevaris McCormick from 59-yards out – the longest pass in Troy's bowl history – just over three minutes later to give Troy a 36-20 lead. The large Troy contingent in the Superdome had more to cheer about on a 20-yard touchdown pass from Silvers to John Johnson with 2:02 to play in the quarter. Willis and Silvers connected again with just over four minutes left to seal the game for Troy. Willis set a Troy bowl record with 11 catches while his 135 receiving yards were the second most in a bowl game in school history. McCormick added five catches for 107 yards making the pair the first since 2013 to top over 100 yards receiving in the same game. Fine, the Conference USA Offensive Player of the Year, finished 30-of-54 for 303 yards with three touchdowns and two interceptions. Troy held Fine to -58 yards rushing in the game. Stadom finished with a pair of tackles for loss, while Cedarius Rookard had a game-high nine tackles and two pass break ups. Lebbie added two stops behind the line with a sack in addition to forcing a fumble.

2017 AUTO NATION CURE BOWL

The 2017 Cure Bowl was held on December 16, 2017, at Camping World Stadium in Orlando, Florida, with kickoff at 2:30 PM local time. The game was broadcast on the CBS Sports Network. The third annual edition of the Cure Bowl featured Georgia State Panthers of the Sun Belt Conference and the Western Kentucky Hilltoppers of Conference USA.

2017 Cure Bowl	Line	1	-	2	-	3	-	4	-	Final
Western Kentucky	(-5.0)	7	-	3	-	0	-	7	-	17
Georgia State	(54.5)	10	-	3	-	7	-	7	-	27

Scoring Summary
Georgia State – Wright 42 yard Field Goal
Western Kentucky – Yelder 54 yard pass from White (Nuss Kick)
Georgia State – Kirk 26 yard run (Wright Kick)
Western Kentucky – Nuss 38 yard Field Goal
Georgia State – Wright 37 yard Field Goal
Georgia State – Carter 42 yard pass from Manning (Wright Kick)
Georgia State – Neal 1 yard run (Wright Kick)
Western Kentucky – Yelder 4 yard pass from White (Nuss Kick)

Georgiastatesports.com Cure Bowl Game Summary – Led by Most Valuable Player Conner Manning and a record-setting effort by the defense, Georgia State earned the first bowl victory in school history with a 27-17 win over Western Kentucky in the AutoNation Cure Bowl at Camping World Stadium. The win also gave the Panthers (7-5, 5-3 Sun Belt) their school-record seventh victory of the season under first-year head coach Shawn Elliott and secured their first winning season as an FBS program. Manning, the senior signal-caller, completed 20 of 28 passes for 276 yards and one touchdown while directing a GSU offense that also rushed for 143 yards. Georgia State accomplished that while essentially playing without top weapon Penny Hart, who was battling an ankle injury and was limited to a handful of snaps. The Georgia State defense limited Western Kentucky's (6-7, 4-4 CUSA) high-powered offense to 349 yards. By collecting six sacks, including two by senior Mackendy Cheridor, the Panthers set a school record by holding WKU to a net of minus-two yards rushing. Leading 13-10, the Panthers used a flea flicker to take a 10-point lead in the third quarter. After two flips, Manning got the ball back and found freshman tight end Roger Carter all alone for a 42-yard touchdown and a 20-10 advantage with 5:55 left in the third quarter. The touchdown was set up by Hart's lone catch of the game, a 27-yard reception to WKU 42-yard line. In the fourth quarter, the Panthers effectively sealed the game a 16-play, 74-yard drive that ate up nine minutes on the clock. The drive started after Jerome Smith's interception, and Kyler Neal tallied the clinching score on a 1-yard run to put GSU ahead 27-10 with 5:50 left in the game. Georgia State got on the scoreboard first with Brandon Wright's 42-yard field goal on the Panthers' opening possession, giving GSU a 3-0 lead midway through the first quarter. Then the teams traded quick touchdowns on a total of just five plays. First, WKU needed just two plays to score, including White's 54-yard touchdown pass to Deon Yelder. But the Panthers' answer was almost as quick. Devin Gentry rushed for 10 yards, and then Manning found Tamir Jones down the left sideline for 49 yards to the WKU 26. On the next play, Demarcus Kirk broke through the middle of the line and rambled 26 yards for the score to regain the lead at 10-7 with 6:19 to play in the first quarter. In the second quarter, the teams exchanged field goals, with Wright's second three-pointer of the day, this one from 37 yards, giving GSU a 13-10 lead with nine minutes left in the first half. Late in the half, the Panthers had an apparent touchdown pass called back when Jonathan Ifedi's knee was ruled to have touched the ground before he took off for the end zone, so the halftime lead remained 13-10.

2017 LAS VEGAS BOWL

The 2017 Las Vegas Bowl was played on December 16, 2017, at Sam Boyd Stadium in Whitney, Nevada. The twenty-sixth annual Las Vegas Bowl was aired on ABC. This was Boise State's fourth trip to the Las Vegas Bowl, while it was Oregon's third. This was the third meeting between the schools, with Boise State having won both previous meeting. The most recent prior meeting was on September 3, 2009, when the Broncos defeated the Ducks by a score of 19–8

2017 Las Vegas Bowl	Line	1	-	2	-	3	-	4	-	Final
#25 Boise State	(62.5)	14	-	10	-	7	-	7	-	38
Oregon	(-7.0)	0	-	14	-	0	-	14	-	28

Scoring Summary
Boise State – Wolpin 1 yard run (Hoggarth Kick)
Boise State – Wilson 26 yard pass from Rypien (Hoggarth Kick)
Boise State – Hoggarth 39 yard Field Goal
Boise State – Kaniho 53 yard interception return (Hoggarth Kick)
Oregon – Dye 86 yard fumble recovery (Schneider Kick)
Oregon – Robinson 100 yard interception return (Schneider Kick)
Boise State – Dhaenens 13 yard pass from Rypien (Hoggarth Kick)
Oregon – Schooler 24 yard pass from Herbert (Schneider Kick)
Boise State – Wolpin 1 yard run (Hoggarth Kick)
Oregon – Redd 8 yard pass from Herbert (Schneider Kick)

Broncosports.com Las Vegas Bowl Game Summary – Cedrick Wilson caught 10 passes for 221 yards and a touchdown, Kekaula Kaniho returned an interception 53 yards for a score and No. 25 Boise State beat Oregon 38-28 in the Las Vegas Bowl on Saturday. Brett Rypien threw for 362 yards and two touchdown passes -- with two interceptions -- to help the Broncos (11-3) break a three-game losing streak against Power 5 opposition. Ryan Wolpin rushed for two touchdowns. Troy Dye and Tyree Robinson each scored a defensive touchdown, and Justin Herbert was 26 of 36 passing for 233 yards with two touchdowns and two interceptions for the Ducks (7-6) in new head coach Mario Cristobal's debut. Boise State forced four turnovers in the first half, taking a 14-0 lead in the first quarter on Wolpin's 1-yard touchdown run and Rypien's 26-yard scoring pass to Wilson. Haden Hoggarth added a 39-yard field goal before an off-balance Herbert heaved a pass toward the sideline that was easily picked off and run back by Kaniho, who also had a strip-sack. Oregon clawed back into it with two defensive touchdowns in the final minute of the first half. Dye recovered a fumble on a botched Statue of Liberty handoff and returned it 86 yards for a touchdown with 37 seconds remaining to get the Ducks on the scoreboard. A 65-yard reception by Wilson to set the Boise State single-season record for yards receiving got the Broncos right back in the red zone, but Robinson picked off Rypien's pass in the end zone and took it back 100 yards on the longest interception return in school history with 7 seconds remaining to make it 24-14. Boise State outgained Oregon 294-77 in the first half and reached Ducks' territory on eight of 10 possessions. After Alec Dhaenens caught a 13-yard touchdown pass from Rypien in the third quarter, the Ducks pulled back within 31-21 on a 24-yard scoring thrown from Herbert to Brendan Schooler with 10:07 remaining. Oregon had a chance to cut it to a one-possession game, but Herbert was sacked near midfield, and Boise State drove 86 yards in 11 plays capped by Wolpin's second 1-yard touchdown run.

2017 NEW MEXICO BOWL

The 2017 New Mexico Bowl was played at Dreamstyle Stadium in Albuquerque, New Mexico on December 16, 2017. The game was the 12th edition of the New Mexico Bowl and featured the Marshall Thundering Herd of Conference USA and the Colorado State Rams of the Mountain West Conference.

2017 New Mexico Bowl	Line	1	-	2	-	3	-	4	-	Final
Marshall	(58.5)	0	-	21	-	10	-	0	-	31
Colorado State	(-3.0)	0	-	14	-	0	-	14	-	28

Scoring Summary
Marshall – Brady 76-yard touchdown reception from Litton (Vedvik kick)
Colorado State – Clark 5-yard touchdown reception from Stevens (Bryan kick)
Marshall – Yurachek 15-yard touchdown reception from Litton (Vedvik kick)
Colorado State – Stevens 9-yard touchdown run, Bryan kick
Marshall – Davis 68-yard touchdown run, Vedvik kick
Marshall – King 90-yard touchdown run, Vedvik kick
Marshall – Vedvik 21 yard Field Goal
Colorado State – Clark 24-yard touchdown reception from Stevens, Bryan kick
Colorado State – Stevens 1-yard touchdown run, Bryan kick

HerdZone.com New Mexico Bowl Game Summary – Marshall rose above the elevation in Saturday's Gildan New Mexico Bowl. The program stood tall in the shadow of the Sandia Mountains, which loom large -- as high as 10,678 feet -- to the east of the host city. In the end, the Thundering Herd put together a peak performance in front of an ESPN audience, using a pair of 100-yard rushers and a 100-yard receiver to out-offense one of the nation's top offenses, Colorado State, in a 31-28 win. The victory is Marshall's sixth consecutive bowl win and 11th in 12 bowl game trips. The Herd entered the opening day of bowl season as the winningest bowl team, by percentage, among FBS teams, and undefeated in bowl games under coach Doc Holliday. Those bowl traditions were protected after the Herd survived a two-touchdown rally by the Rams in the fourth quarter. But after quarterback Chase Litton hit tight end Ryan Yurachek for an 8-yard gain on third-and-5 in the twilight of the fourth quarter, Litton and the offense went into victory formation and the postgame celebration started at midfield. Equipment staff hurriedly passed out white bowl champions hats as Holliday and Yurachek smiled and hugged for an interview on ESPN. The team huddled on stage as junior receiver Tyre Brady and sophomore defensive lineman Channing Hames were honored as the Offensive MVP and Defensive MVP, respectively. Brady caught six passes for 165 yards and one touchdown, the third-most receiving yards in New Mexico Bowl history. Hames dominated defensively, leading the team in tackles, recording 1.5 sacks, 2.5 tackles for a loss and two quarterback hurries. But while they were the MVPs, others starred on national television. Marshall junior running back Keion Davis established a new career high with 141 rushing yards on 18 carries, including a 68-yard touchdown that was the longest run of his career. Fellow running back Tyler King, a freshman, only carried six times, but covered 106 yards and scored on a 90-yard run that equaled the school record for the longest rush. Overall, the Herd outgained the nation's No. 10 offense 501-390, distributing its yardage almost equally between the passing game (262) and run game (239). Defensively, Marshall sacked the Rams five times, even though CSU entered the game having allowed only eight sacks in 12 games. Marshall and Colorado State scored on five consecutive possessions in the second quarter, and then the Herd took over in the third quarter for good. MU's defense held the potent Rams offense scoreless in the third quarter, with all three CSU drives ending in a punt (15 total plays for 40 combined yards). Meanwhile, the Herd offense stayed in rhythm from the second quarter, first receiving a record-breaking run by King, who zigged and zagged his way to a 90-yard touchdown run with 12:12 left of the third quarter. King's run put the Herd up 28-14 and set a New Mexico Bowl record by 13 yards. Colorado State entered Saturday's bowl game with the high-powered offense in FBS, but it was Marshall that struck first. Litton dropped a perfect ball into the arms of Brady, who raced down the left sideline for a 76-yard touchdown on the fourth play of the second quarter (the first play of the drive for MU). The touchdown connection is tied for the third-longest in New Mexico Bowl history and gave the Herd a 7-0 lead with 14:29 left. The pass was the longest for Litton this season, and the longest reception of Brady's career. The Rams answered on the ensuing drive, as quarterback Nick Stevens engineered a lengthy 15-play, 75-yard touchdown drive that chewed six minutes and 12 seconds off the clock. CSU tied it at 7-7 when Stevens, a senior, found Detrich Clark in the right flat for an easy 5-yard score. It did not take long for Marshall to answer. Litton found Yurachek, who earlier in the game extended his streak of consecutive games with a reception to 42 games (tying a school record), for a 15-yard touchdown with 6:07 left of the second quarter. The score gave Herd a 14-7 lead. The touchdown was set up by another long connection between Litton and Brady. Litton found the junior receiver between the hashes for a 47-yard gain to the CSU 18-yard line. Litton found Yurachek in the end zone two plays later. The scoring continued Colorado State's next drive when Stevens found the middle of the field open and comfortably ran into the end zone for a touchdown to tie the game at 14-14 with 4:41 left of the second quarter. And as was the case the entire second quarter, Marshall had an answer on offense. On the second play of the ensuing drive, Davis found running room on the right side and broke free, then shook off tackles on his way into the end zone for a 68-yard touchdown run. It was the fifth-longest rush in New Mexico Bowl history. Davis' touchdown came 45 seconds after Colorado State's score and gave the Herd a 21-14 advance it would carry into halftime. Marshall's largest lead came with 4:10 left of the third quarter when Kaare Vedvik booted a 21-yard field goal to make it 31-14. Colorado State, however, scored a pair of fourth quarter touchdowns to trim the deficit to 31-28. Stevens connected with Clark again, this time from 24 yards out, to make it 31-21 with 12:55 to go. Stevens added a touchdown in a quarterback sneak with 6:37 left to make it a 3-point game, and then the Herd defense made one last stand when the Rams had a chance to tie or take the lead to preserve the win.

2017 CAMELLIA BOWL

The 2017 Camellia Bowl was played at the **Cramton Bowl in Montgomery, Alabama**, on December 16, 2017. The game was the fourth edition of the **Camellia Bowl** and was televised on ESPN.

2017 Camellia Bowl	Line	1	-	2	-	3	-	4	-	Final
Middle Tennessee	(60.5)	7	-	14	-	7	-	7	-	35
Arkansas State	(-3.5)	3	-	7	-	7	-	13	-	30

Scoring Summary
Arkansas State – Williams 20 yard Field Goal
Middle Tennessee – West 45 yard run (Rooker Kick)
Middle Tennessee – Sanders 54 yard fumble recovery (Rooker Kick)
Arkansas State – Hansen 1 yard run (Williams Kick)
Middle Tennessee – Garnett 31 yard pass from Stockstill (Rooker Kick)
Middle Tennessee – Thomas 2 yard run (Rooker Kick)
Arkansas State – McIniss 20 yard pass from Hansen (Williams Kick)
Arkansas State – Wand 2 yard pass from Hansen (Williams Kick)
Middle Tennessee – Tucker 30 yard pass from Stockstill (Rooker Kick)
Arkansas State – Booker 41 yard pass from Hansen (Williams Kick)

Goblueraiders.com Camellia Bowl Game Summary – Just as it's done all season, Middle Tennessee showed an incredible amount of resiliency Saturday night in taking down Arkansas State for the Raycom Media Camellia Bowl championship, its first bowl victory since 2009. Despite a four-hour marathon game, a late A-State comeback, committing three turnovers, suffering a rough outing from their quarterback and injuries keeping some key guys sidelined, the Blue Raiders were undeterred in the 35-30 win. The victory snapped a four-game bowl losing streak for the Blue Raiders (7-6) and pushed their record against their old Sun Belt Conference rival Red Wolves (7-5) to 10-5. Redshirt sophomore quarterback *Brent Stockstill* had a rough outing but came up big when it mattered most. With just over 12 minutes remaining and the Blue Raiders nursing a 28-23 lead, he hit senior *Shane Tucker* over the middle for a 30-yard touchdown two plays after connecting with sophomore *CJ Windham* for 34 yards. The TD halted a 13-0 A-State run and essentially put the finishing touches on the win. Stockstill had thrown just five interceptions in six games played this season going into Saturday but had three on the night. He finished 19-of-32 for 232 yards and two TDs. His first pass of the game was off target and picked, then on the Blue Raiders' third drive a questionable call wound up being his second INT in eight pass attempts. Another pass was picked in the third quarter. Instead of dropping their heads after the turnovers, Middle Tennessee's resilient defense simply went to work against the Red Wolves' nationally 11th-ranked offense. The Blue Raider stop squad gave up just three points off the first two turnovers, allowing MT to hold a 7-3 lead after the first quarter thanks to a 45-yard rushing score from redshirt sophomore *Terelle West*. Then, they forced and recovered a red-zone fumble after Stockstill's third-quarter INT, preserving a 28-17 lead. Holding tough after the turnovers was far from the end of the story for Middle Tennessee's defense. The Blue Raider stoppers also forced plenty of takeaways, picking off A-State quarterback Justice Hansen once and coming up with two fumble recoveries. The most exciting play of the night for MT's defense came in the second quarter. After a Middle Tennessee punt, the Red Wolves took over, looking to turn around a 7-3 MT advantage. On third down in Raider territory, Hansen dropped back to pass but was immediately pressured by a blitzing *Darius Harris*. The redshirt junior linebacker came up with the sack and got a hand on the ball, forcing a fumble that was scooped up and returned by senior *D.J. Sanders* 54 yards for a touchdown. It was Sanders' fourth career defensive score to add to three pick sixes. Harris was named the game's Most Valuable Player after racking up a game-high and career-high-tying 12 tackles with the sack and forced fumble. He also had two pass breakups. Sanders finished with 10 tackles and a sack in his final collegiate game. On the offensive side, running backs West and *Tavares Thomas* were a two-headed attack. West had 65 yards and a TD on 10 carries, while Thomas finished with 49 yards and a TD on 16 attempts. Tucker led the way in the receiving department with four catches for 63 yards and a score, while Windham also had 63 yards on three receptions. Sanders and Tucker were just two of the 14 seniors who leave this year's team being bowl eligible all four years, or five for some.

2017 BOCA RATON BOWL

The 2017 Boca Raton Bowl was played on December 19, 2017, at FAU Stadium in Boca Raton, Florida. The fourth edition of the Boca Raton Bowl featured the Conference USA champion Florida Atlantic Owls against the Mid-American Conference East Division champion Akron Zips. Kickoff was scheduled for 7:00 PM EST and the game aired on ESPN. It was sponsored by the Cheribundi beverage company, the game was officially known as the Cheribundi Tart Cherry Boca Raton Bowl. Although FAU Stadium is the Owls' usual home field, the Zips served as the designated home team for the game. This was Florida Atlantic's third bowl game in school history, first since 2008, and first Boca Raton Bowl; the Owls won both of their previous bowl games (the 2007 New Orleans Bowl and the 2008 Motor City Bowl). This was Akron's third bowl game in school history, first since 2015, and first Boca Raton Bowl; the Zips previously lost one bowl game (the 2005 Motor City Bowl) and won one bowl game (the 2015 Famous Idaho Potato Bowl).

2017 Boca Raton Bowl	Line	1	-	2	-	3	-	4	-	Final
Florida Atlantic	(23.5)	7	-	14	-	15	-	14	-	50
Akron	(65.5)	0	-	3	-	0	-	0	-	3

Scoring Summary
Florida Atlantic – Wright 4 yard pass from Driskel (Joseph Kick)
Akron – Gasser 19 yard Field Goal
Florida Atlantic – Driskel 3 yard run (Joseph Kick)
Florida Atlantic – Singletary 6 yard run (Joseph Kick)
Florida Atlantic – Singletary 2 yard run (Joseph Kick)
Florida Atlantic – Wright 13 yard pass from Driskel (Joseph Kick)
Florida Atlantic – Driskel 7 yard run (Joseph Kick)
Florida Atlantic – Singletary 26 yard run (Joseph Kick)

Associated Press Boca Raton Game Summary – Lane Kiffin's first bowl game at Florida Atlantic was the perfect microcosm of his first season with the Owls. Slow start. Super finish. And the future could be even better. Devin Singletary ran for 124 yards and three touchdowns, Jason Driskel accounted for four scores and FAU rolled past Akron 50-3 in the Boca Raton Bowl on Tuesday night -- finishing the season on a 10-game winning streak, and with Kiffin having agreed to terms on an extension that, in theory, would keep him at FAU for another 10 years. That seems unlikely, of course. Then again, so did a program with nine wins in the last three years combined rolling through 2017 this way. The Owls were 1/3 in late September. They never lost again, the 10 wins coming by an average of 24.8 points and capped by a win in FAU's first bowl appearance since 2008. Singletary finished with 32 touchdowns this season for the Owls (11-3), who matched the school record for wins in a season -- set during the team's run to the Division I-AA semifinals in 2003. Driskel threw for 270 yards and two touchdowns, plus ran for two more scores for FAU. The Owls had a massive turnaround in Kiffin's first year and may have an even brighter future. Earlier Tuesday, a person with knowledge of the negotiations told The Associated Press that FAU and Kiffin have agreed to extend his contract six more years through 2027. The days of being called out with an overhead projector as he was by Al Davis in Oakland or fired on a tarmac like he was at USC, or facing weekly questions about his job security like he was at Alabama, are over. He's at FAU for as long as he wants to be. The new deal isn't signed, but the sides will get there. Kato Nelson threw for 80 yards for Akron (7-7). And Kiffin held nothing back. FAU got three touchdowns on fourth-down tries, unsuccessfully tried an onside kick in the first quarter, went for a 2-point conversion in the third quarter to make it 36-3 and even tried a halfback pass in the fourth quarter with a 47-point lead. The Owls didn't punt on their first nine possessions, getting seven touchdowns and two missed field goals out of those. Even on the last play of the game, FAU threw a pass -- a 10-yard gain, one that gave the Owls a 582-146 edge in total yards. The Owls left no doubt: Only two bowl games since 2000 had a bigger margin of victory than FAU's 47-point romp in this one.

2017 FRISCO BOWL

The 2017 Frisco Bowl was held on December 20, 2017, at Toyota Stadium in Frisco, Texas. The first annual Frisco Bowl, it featured the Louisiana Tech Bulldogs of Conference USA and the SMU Mustangs of the American Athletic Conference. It began at 7:00 PM CST and aired on ESPN.

2017 Frisco Bowl	Line	1	-	2	-	3	-	4	-	Final
Louisiana Tech	(71.0)	21	-	21	-	6	-	3	-	51
SMU	(-4.0)	3	-	7	-	0	-	0	-	10

Scoring Summary
Louisiana Tech – Smith 1 yard run (Barnes Kick)
Louisiana Tech – Robertson 45 yard interception return (Barnes Kick)
SMU – Williams 25 yard Field Goal
Louisiana Tech – Veal 6 yard pass from Smith (Barnes Kick)
Louisiana Tech – Lewis 23 yard interception return (Barnes Kick)
Louisiana Tech – Veal 27 yard pass from Smith (Barnes kick)
Louisiana Tech – McKnight 11 yard pass from Smith (Barnes Kick)
SMU – Quinn 9 yard pass from Hicks (Williams Kick)
Louisiana Tech – Barnes 28 yard Field Goal
Louisiana Tech – Barnes 43 yard Field Goal
Louisiana Tech – Barnes 41 yard Field Goal

Associated Press Frisco Bowl Game Summary - A fumble by SMU on the first snap of the game set the tone for Louisiana Tech in a 51-10 victory in the Frisco Bowl on Wednesday night. J'mar Smith threw three touchdown passes and ran for a score, Louisiana Tech's defense scored twice, and the Bulldogs ended their fourth straight season with a bowl victory. Smith completed 15 of 23 passes for 216 yards, and Teddy Veal caught four passes for 84 yards for Louisiana Tech (7-6). The Bulldogs led 42-10 at the half. SMU (7-6) fumbled on its first offensive snap and turned it over on its first three drives and six times overall. It was a disappointing debut for SMU coach Sonny Dykes against his former school. Dykes was 22-15 at Louisiana Tech from 2010 to 2012 before leaving for California in 2013. Dykes was fired by Cal a year ago and spent this season as an offensive analyst at TCU before SMU hired him to replace Chad Morris on Dec. 11. With most of the staff joining Morris at Arkansas, Dykes elected to coach the bowl game and installed graduate assistant G.J. Kinne as offensive coordinator for the bowl game. It didn't have the desired effect. Smith gave the Bulldogs a 7-0 lead on a 1-yard sneak with 7:43 remaining in the first quarter. Louisiana Tech had a short field to work with after Secdrick Cooper returned an interception 31 yards to the SMU 30. Amik Robertson returned an interception 55 yards for a touchdown less than a minute later, pushing the lead to 14-0. SMU held onto the ball on its fourth drive but couldn't reach the end zone and settled for a field goal after stalling at the 8. On the ensuing kickoff, Jaqwis Dancy had a 65-yard return, setting up a 6-yard touchdown pass from Smith to Veal for a 21-3 lead. Louisiana Tech returned another interception for a touchdown early in the second quarter. This time, Darryl Lewis had a 23-yard return down the sideline for a 28-3 lead. Smith added touchdown passes to Veal and Kam McKnight, helping Louisiana set a school record for first-half points in a bowl game. Trey Quinn scored SMU's touchdown on a 9-yard pass late in the second quarter. Hicks completed 19 of 33 passes for 127 yards.

2017 GASPARILLA BOWL

The 2017 Gasparilla Bowl was played on December 21, 2017, at Tropicana Field in St. Petersburg, Florida. The tenth annual Gasparilla Bowl began at 8:00 PM EST and aired on ESPN. This was Temple's first Gasparilla Bowl and the third consecutive (and seventh overall) bowl game for the Owls, extending the longest bowl streak in school history. This was FIU's third bowl game in school history and second Gasparilla Bowl; the Panthers had previously played in the 2011 game (when it was known as the Beef 'O' Brady's Bowl), losing to Marshall by a score of 20–10.

2017 Gasparilla Bowl	Line	1	-	2	-	3	-	4	-	Final
Temple	(-7.0)	0	-	7	-	7	-	14	-	28
Florida International	(56.5)	0	-	0	-	3	-	0	-	3

Scoring Summary
Temple – Nutile 4 yard run (Boumerhi Kick)
Florida International – Borregales 27 yard Field Goal
Temple – Hood 1 yard run (Boumerhi Kick)
Temple – Wright 45 yard pass from Nutile (Boumerhi Kick)
Temple – Armstead 5 yard run (Boumerhi Kick)

Associated Press Gasparilla Bowl Game Summary – Frank Nutile threw for 254 yards and a touchdown to lead the Owls to a 28-3 victory over Florida International in the Gasparilla Bowl on Thursday night. Nutile teamed with Isaiah Wright on 45-yard TD play in the fourth quarter and also scored on a 4-yard run to give the Owls (7-6) an early lead. He completed passes of 13 and 17 yards to escape a first-and-30 hole before throwing 39 yards to Adonis Jennings to set up another TD. The victory was the fourth in five games for Temple, which rebounded from a 3-5 start to finish with a winning record. The Owls, American Athletic Conference champions a year ago, won a bowl game for the first time since the 2011 New Mexico Bowl. FIU (8-5) matched a school record for victories in its first year under Butch Davis, the former Miami, North Carolina and Cleveland Browns coach. The Panthers played most of the night without quarterback Alex McGough, who left in the opening quarter with what Davis said was a fractured collarbone. Maurice Alexander replaced him but had limited success throwing the ball and was intercepted twice. Nutile finished 17 of 27 passing with no interceptions and was named game MVP. He threw 13 yards to Keith Kirkwood and 17 yards to Isaiah Wright on consecutive plays before Jennings' long reception moved the Owls into position to go up 14-3 on David Hood's 1-yard TD run. Wright's TD reception made it 21-3 midway through the fourth quarter. Ryquell Armstead also scored on a 5-yard run for Temple. Alexander completed 16 of 33 passes for 162 yards for FIU. The Panthers were unable to run the ball consistently to take pressure off the backup quarterback, finishing with 88 yards on the ground and avoiding a shutout with Jose Borregales' 27-yard field goal in the third quarter. Temple's defense set a Gasparilla Bowl record with seven sacks. LB William Kwenkeu led the way with two. The Owls also forced three turnovers, including a fumble that Freddie Booth-Lloyd recovered to set up Armstead's late TD.

2017 BAHAMAS BOWL

The 2017 Bahamas Bowl was played on December 22, 2017, at Thomas Robinson Stadium in Nassau in the Bahamas. The fourth annual Bahamas Bowl, It began at 12:30 PM EST and aired on ESPN. 2017 was the Blazers' first season back on the football field following a two-year hiatus (the program had originally been dropped, but massive public outcry led to its reinstatement a year later). After finishing their regular season 8–4, the Blazers accepted their invitation to the Bahamas Bowl. This was the first bowl game for UAB since the 2004 Hawaii Bowl where they lost to the Hawaii Warriors by a score of 59–40. After finishing their regular season 8–4, the Bobcats accepted their invitation to the Bahamas Bowl. This was Ohio's eighth bowl appearance in the last nine seasons, and their first appearance in the Bahamas Bowl.

2017 Bahamas Bowl	Line	1	-	2	-	3	-	4	-	Final
Alabama-Birmingham	(54.5)	0	-	3	-	3	-	0	-	6
Ohio	(-6.5)	13	-	14	-	14	-	0	-	41

Scoring Summary
Ohio – Knock 2 yard pass from Rourke (Zervos Kick)
Ohio – White 56 yard pass from Rourke (Kick no good)
Ohio – Brown 74 yard run (Zervos Kick)
UAB – Vogel 34 yard Field Goal
Ohio – Brown 9 yard run (Zervos Kick)
UAB – Vogel 25 yard Field Goal
Ohio – Brown 25 yard run (Zervos Kick)
Ohio – Brown 14 yard run (Zervos Kick)

Associated Press Bahamas Bowl Game Summary – Ohio coach Frank Solich knew his Bobcats were better than their record showed. You'll get no argument from UAB. Dorian Brown rushed for 152 yards on just 12 carries and scored four touchdowns, Nathan Rourke threw for two scores and Ohio beat UAB 41-6 in the Bahamas Bowl on Friday. It was a stirring comeback for the Bobcats, who lost their last two games of the regular season to miss a shot at the Mid-American Conference title. Ohio (9-4) averaged 38.9 points per game during the season, setting a school record with 467 points scored, and the Bobcats exhibited that prowess in the opening half of this one, using big plays to build an insurmountable 27-3 halftime lead. Brown, a redshirt senior, scored on runs of 74, 9, 25 and 14 yards, two in the second quarter and two in the third as he carried the load for injured A.J. Ouellette. Brown's heroics were too much for the Blazers, a feel-good team seeking its first bowl victory on just its second try. The loss spoiled the end of a remarkable first season back for UAB (8-5), which was predicted to struggle and didn't. UAB President Ray Watts had cut the football program in December 2014 because a university report deemed it too expensive. After public outcry, football was reinstated, but NCAA rules required the school to skip the 2016 season to help the players who stuck it out re-adjust to competing at the top level of college football. The Blazers, under Conference USA Coach of the Year Bill Clark, responded by winning a school-record eight games and finished second in the conference's West Division. They won six of their final eight games. On this day, though, they ran out of miracles. The high-scoring Bobcats have a veteran offensive line with more than 100 starts and they repeatedly took advantage of that experience. Rourke had plenty of time to throw, and when the Bobcats decided to run, holes were there. They finished with a 249-99 edge on the ground. Ohio raced to a 13-0 lead in the first quarter, pretty much sticking to the ground until the end of an 11-play drive. After the Blazers were called for two penalties in the red zone, Rourke hit DL Knock for a 19-yard touchdown midway through the period. Rourke then stunned the Blazers with a bomb. After a nifty 23-yard punt return by the elusive Papi White, Rourke took advantage of UAB's preoccupation with the run game and hit White on a play-action pass for a 56-yard touchdown and a 13-0 lead. Brown's 74-yard run early in the second boosted the lead to 20-0. When UAB finally mounted a promising drive, the Blazers had to settle for Nick Vogel's 34-yard field goal midway through the second quarter. Spencer Brown, who broke the UAB school record for freshman rushing yards with 1,329, finished with 37 yards on 13 carries.

2017 FAMOUS IDAHO POTATO BOWL

The 2017 Famous Idaho Potato Bowl was played on Friday, December 22, 2017, at Albertsons Stadium in Boise, Idaho. The 21st annual Famous Idaho Potato Bowl, was sponsored by the Idaho Potato Commission. With a temperature of 37 °F (3 °C) at kickoff, the game started at 2:05 pm MST (4:05 pm EST) and was broadcast by ESPN. Central Michigan finished their regular season with an 8–4 record overall (6–2 in conference). This was their first Famous Idaho Potato Bowl. Wyoming finished their regular season with a 7–5 record overall (5–3 in conference). This was their first Famous Idaho Potato Bowl.

2017 Famous Idaho Potato Bowl	Line	1	-	2	-	3	-	4	-	Final
Central Michigan	(47.0)	7	-	0	-	7	-	0	-	14
Wyoming	(-2.5)	21	-	6	-	3	-	7	-	37

Scoring Summary
Wyoming – Scott 23 yard pass from Allen (Rothe Kick)
Wyoming – Conway 11 yard pass from Allen (Rothe Kick)
Central Michigan – Ward 74 yard pass from Morris (Armstrong Kick)
Wyoming – Johnson 45 yard pass from Allen (Rothe Kick)
Wyoming – Rothe 27 yard Field Goal
Wyoming – Rothe 28 yard Field Goal
Wyoming – Rothe 20 yard Field Goal
Central Michigan – Ward 3 yard run (Armstrong Kick)
Wyoming – Granderson 58 yard fumble return (Rothe Kick)

Associated Press Famous Idaho Potato Bowl Game Summary – When Wyoming junior quarterback Josh Allen stepped onto the stage to accept his MVP trophy following the Cowboys' 37-14 victory over Central Michigan on Friday in the Famous Idaho Potato Bowl, it didn't take long for the chant to begin. Surrounded by teammates and a throng of Wyoming fans, Allen couldn't resist the moment and hoisted the trophy over his head before declaring his intentions to skip his senior season to enter the NFL draft. Allen missed the final two regular-season games with a sprained right shoulder, resulting in a pair of close losses. In warmups, he looked anxious to return to the field and didn't disappoint the Wyoming contingent on hand for his final collegiate game. Allen completed 11 of 19 passed for 154 yards and three touchdowns without an interception. He didn't have to do much thanks to Wyoming's suffocating defense. But when the Cowboys needed Allen, he produced. Allen's first touchdown pass to open the scoring was a 23-yard bullet to Jared Scott. But the potential top 10 draft pick showed off the arm strength and accuracy that has scouts drooling with a 45-yard strike that hit C.J. Johnson in stride in the end zone. However, Allen's performance didn't have to be all that impressive thanks to a defense that forced eight turnovers. Central Michigan (8-5) had won five straight. The eight turnovers broke the previous Famous Idaho Potato Bowl record of six. Wyoming entered the game first in the nation in turnover margin, but second in forced turnovers with 30 behind Central Michigan, which had 31. But with an 8-0 advantage, Wyoming will likely finish at the top of both rankings after the bowl season concludes. Wyoming took a 21-7 lead in the first quarter. Wyoming's offense struggled in the red zone after the first quarter, settling for three field goals in three trips. Central Michigan struggled everywhere on the field, watching promising drives end on turnovers or other drives stunted due to Wyoming's relentless pass rush. The Cowboys had a season-high five sacks. Late in the third quarter, Central Michigan found a spark and cut the deficit to 30-14. The Chippewas strung together a seven-play, 65-yard drive that ended on a 3-yard run by Jonathan Ward. But Central Michigan failed to build on that momentum, losing it all on a scoop and score. After a strip sack by Youhanna Ghaifan, Wyoming defensive end Carl Granderson took the fumble and rumbled 58 yards for the touchdowns.

2017 BIRMINGHAM BOWL

The 2017 Birmingham Bowl was held on December 23, 2017, at Legion Field in Birmingham, Alabama. The twelfth edition of the Birmingham Bowl featured the Texas Tech Red Raiders of the Big 12 Conference against the South Florida Bulls of the American Athletic Conference. It was the first ever meeting between the two schools. Kickoff was scheduled for 11:00 AM CST and the game aired on ESPN. This was the Red Raiders' first Birmingham Bowl. South Florida entered the game as the defending Birmingham Bowl champion, their 2016 team having defeated the South Carolina Gamecocks, 46–39 in overtime. This was the Bulls' third Birmingham Bowl; in addition to their 2016 victory, the 2006 Bulls defeated the East Carolina Pirates, 24–7 in the inaugural game when it was known as the PapaJohns.com Bowl.

2017 Birmingham Bowl	Line	1	-	2	-	3	-	4	-	Final
Texas Tech	(65.0)	10	-	0	-	14	-	10	-	34
#23 South Florida	(-2.0)	3	-	7	-	7	-	21	-	38

Scoring Summary
Texas Tech – Hatfield 26 yard Field Goal
South Florida – Nadelman 25 yard Field Goal
Texas Tech – Coutee 5 yard pass from Shimonek (Hatfield Kick)
South Florida – McCants 21 yard pass from Flowers (Nadelman Kick)
Texas Tech – Cantrell 3 yard pass from Shimonek (Hatfield Kick)
South Florida – Saloman 17 yard pass from Flowers (Nadelman Kick)
Texas Tech – King 4 yard run (Hatfield Kick)
South Florida – Flowers 5 yard run (Nadelman Kick)
Texas Tech – Hatfield 33 yard Field Goal
South Florida – Valdez-Scantling 64 yard pass from Flowers (Nadelman Kick)
Texas Tech – Vasher 25 yard pass from Shimonek (Hatfield Kick)
South Florida – McCants 26 yard pass from Flowers (Nadelman Kick)

Gousfbulls.com Birmingham Bowl Game Summary - Quinton Flowers cemented a stellar legacy as the program's most outstanding player as he accounted for 417 total yards and five touchdowns to lead the Bulls to a thrilling 38-34 comeback win over Big 12 foe Texas Tech in Saturday's Birmingham Bowl. The game's most valuable player for the second straight season, Flowers capped off his four-touchdown pass day with a 26-yard scoring toss to Tyre McCants that put USF ahead for the final time with 16 seconds remaining. Flowers' final throw as a Bull, and his 71st career TD toss, helped USF (10-2) repeat as Birmingham Bowl champions and post back-to-back double-digit win seasons for the first time in program history. Flowers (Miami), who entered the game with 27 school records, finished his career with The American's total offense record (11,802 yards) and became just the fourth player in FBS history to eclipse 8,000 passing yards and 3,500 rushing yards. With 106 yards on the ground Saturday, his 16th career 100-yard game, Flowers also became USF's career rushing leader with 3,672 yards in his second straight 1,000-yard rushing season. It was one of seven additional school marks he added under his name on the day to give him 34 on his career. Marquez Valdes-Scantling set a new USF season receiving record (879 yards) with three catches for 133 yards and a touchdown after putting the Bulls ahead for the first time with a 64-yard score with 4:26 remaining. McCants also helped USF produce 561 yards of offense with six catches for 88 yards and two touchdowns. Darnell Salomon completed a solid sophomore season with four receptions for 47 yards and USF's second TD catch of the day from 17 yards out. Senior defensive tackle Deadrin Senat registered a career-high three sacks while the USF defense used two interceptions to move up to a tie for the national pick lead with 20. Deemed a shootout heading into the action, the Birmingham Bowl began with both defenses keeping things close early on. Trailing 10-3, USF's defense delivered with Jaymon Thomas' first-career interception in the end zone. He returned it to the Bulls' 18 with 3:18 left in the half. Senat also stepped up with three first-half sacks, including one on fourth down deep in USF territory in the opening quarter. Senat's third sack helped set USF up for a late score that tied the game at 10-10. McCants hauled in a 21-yard touchdown catch with 51 seconds left and Devin Abraham's team-leading fifth interception of the season gave the Bulls more momentum heading into the break. No. 23/24 USF's offense continued to heat up with Flowers' 17-yard touchdown pass to Salomon that tied the score at 17-17 midway through the third quarter. After grabbing USF's career rushing lead, Flowers used his feet to get the Bulls back on even ground once again. Flowers' 41st-career rushing touchdown from 5 yards out tied the game up at 24-24 with 9:30 remaining. Texas Tech took a 27-24 lead with 5:02 left on a 33-yard Clayton Hatfield field goal. Needing a big play, Flowers found Valdes-Scantling for a 64-yard touchdown on the Bulls second play on the ensuing drive to give the Bulls their first lead of the game, 31-27, on a drive that took just 44 seconds. The Red Raiders (6-7) pulled back ahead with 1:31 remaining on 25-yard pass from Nic Shimonek to T.J. Vasher. But Flowers and the Bulls were not going to be denied from securing their fifth bowl victory in the past six trips.

2017 ARMED FORCES BOWL

The 2017 Armed Forces Bowl was played on December 23, 2017, at Amon G. Carter Stadium on the campus of Texas Christian University in Fort Worth, Texas. The fifteenth edition of the Armed Forces Bowl was scheduled for 2:30 PM CST and the game aired on ESPN. This was the third time that Army and San Diego State played each other; the Aztecs won both previous meetings. Immediately following their 31–28 overtime win over Temple to become bowl-eligible, the Black Knights officially accepted their invitation. This was the Black Knights' second Armed Forces Bowl, following their victory over the SMU Mustangs in the 2010 Armed Forces Bowl by a score of 16–14. This was the Aztecs' first Armed Forces Bowl.

2017 Armed Forces Bowl	Line	1	-	2	-	3	-	4	-	Final
San Diego State	(-6.5)	7	-	14	-	7	-	7	-	35
Army	(46.0)	7	-	14	-	0	-	21	-	42

Scoring Summary
San Diego State – Penny 81 yard run (Baron Kick)
Army – Bradshaw 19 yard run (Wilson Kick)
San Diego State – Penny 32 yard run (Baron Kick)
Army – Woolfolk 7 yard run (Wilson Kick)
Army – Davidson 4 yard run (Wilson Kick)
San Diego State – Washington 78 yard run (Baron Kick)
San Diego State – Penny 49 yard run (Baron Kick)
Army – Bradshaw 27 yard run (Wilson Kick)
San Diego State – Penny 4 yard run (Baron Kick)
Army – Woolfolk 1 yard run (2 pt conversion good)
Army – Riley 29 yard fumble return (No kick)

Goarmywestpoint.com Armed Forces Bowl Game Summary — In what has become typical Army West Point football games, the Black Knights persevered here Saturday afternoon in thrilling fashion to win the 2017 Lockheed Martin Armed Forces Bowl, 42-35, over San Diego State. In a contest that featured four tie scores and four lead changes, a gutsy two-point conversion call by Army head coach *Jeff Monken* determined the outcome. After a *Darnell Woolfolk* one-yard rush pulled Army to within 35-34 with 18 seconds left, SDSU called two timeouts which allowed the Black Knights enough time to draw up the perfect two-point attempt call. With team captain *Ahmad Bradshaw* under center, the senior stepped back and pitched it to sophomore *Kell Walker*, who dashed home for the score. Ball game. SDSU did have 12 seconds to work with, but after returning the kickoff to the 40-yard line, the Aztecs were sacked for a loss of 10 yards before also being tagged with an intentional grounded call. Senior *Alex Aukerman* was credited with his seventh sack of the season when he took down Christian Chapman. Timeout San Diego State. On the ensuing play, the designated visiting team tried some laterals before fumbling at the 29-yard line into the hands of *Elijah Riley* who dashed into the end zone. Pandemonium ensued, and the entire Black Knights team met the sophomore in the corner of the field to celebrate their second-consecutive bowl victory in as many years. Army has now won back-to-back bowls games for the first time since the 1984 and 1985 seasons (Cherry Bowl and Peach Bowl). The Black Knights matched their program record for wins with Saturday's outcome (10) and broke last season's rushing touchdown mark with 50 on the year after five in the contest. Bradshaw led the team in rushing with his 12th 100-yard rushing game after compiling 180 in the contest. He also became the all-time single-season service-academy leading rusher in the contest and wrapped up his senior season with 1,746. Woolfolk chipped in 87 yards and two touchdowns to register his sixth multi-score game of the year. *Andy Davidson* muscled key yardage all game and finished with 81 on the day. Bradshaw did complete a pass with a six-yard connection to *Camden Harrison* in the third quarter. *Jaylon McClinton* racked up a team-best six tackles. He was followed closely by *James Nachtigal* with five. To go along with his sack, Aukerman also notched his first career interception.

2017 DOLLAR GENERAL BOWL

The 2017 Dollar General Bowl was played on December 23, 2017, at Ladd–Peebles Stadium in Mobile, Alabama, United States. The 19th edition of the Dollar General Bowl was the Mountaineers' first Dollar General Bowl. This was the Rockets' third Dollar General Bowl; their record in prior games was 2–0, having previously defeated the UTEP Miners 45–13 in the 2005 game (when it was known as the GMAC Bowl) and having subsequently defeated the Arkansas State Red Wolves 63–44 in the January 2015 game (when it was known as the GoDaddy Bowl). Kickoff was scheduled for 6:00 PM CST and the game aired on ESPN.

2017 Dollar General Bowl	Line	1	-	2	-	3	-	4	-	Final
Appalachian State	(61.0)	7	-	13	-	7	-	7	-	34
Toledo	(-6.0)	0	-	0	-	0	-	0	-	0

Scoring Summary
Appalachian State – Moore 7 yard run (Staton Kick)
Appalachian State – Moore 7 yard run (Staton Kick)
Appalachian State – Staton 29 yard Field Goal
Appalachian State – Staton 23 yard Field Goal
Appalachian State – Moore 31 yard run (Staton Kick)
Appalachian State – Williams 3 yard run (Staton Kick)

Appstatesports.com Dollar General Bowl Game Summary — A record-setting quarterback, senior Taylor Lamb delivered one final handoff after his last game in an Appalachian State uniform. He gave a game ball to Scott Satterfield. In a festive locker room, App State's players responded to Lamb's heartfelt speech and touching gesture by chanting their head coach's name. There were plenty of reasons to celebrate a 34-0 shutout of high-scoring Toledo in the Dollar General Bowl at Ladd-Peebles Stadium on Saturday night. Four forced turnovers by the Mountaineers' dominant defense and a career-high three rushing touchdowns from Jalin Moore triggered a postseason victory that was, for a change, devoid of late-game drama. Winning in Alabama for the third straight December, App State stands alone as the only program to claim a bowl victory in each of its first three years after the complete transition to the FBS classification. After erasing a 24-7 deficit and prevailing 31-29 against Ohio on a last-second field goal in the 2015 Camellia Bowl, then using a tiebreaking field goal to claim a 31-28 win against Toledo last year at the same site in Montgomery, Ala., the Mountaineers (9-4) were in control from start to finish in the Mobile rematch with the Rockets (11-3). Named the Dollar General Bowl MVP after accounting for 125 of his team's 327 rushing yards, Moore opened the scoring on a 7-yard touchdown run less than 11 minutes into the game, added another 7-yard touchdown early in the second quarter and surpassed 1,000 yards for the second straight season on his 31-yard touchdown that produced a 27-0 lead midway through the third quarter. App State's defense forced senior quarterback Logan Woodside into the first three-interception game of his career while recording four sacks and limiting Toledo to 146 total yards — or 364 below its season average. The Rockets had scored in the first half of their last 45 games, and a team averaging 39.2 points was shut out for the first time since 2009. It didn't even move inside App State's 35-yard line all night. Defensive MVP Anthony Flory's 19-yard interception return set up Moore's first touchdown, Chandler Staton kicked one of his two short field goals after Austin Exford recovered a fumble forced by Kaiden Smith on a second-quarter kickoff return and Desmond Franklin's interception of a deep throw near the end zone stopped Toledo's initial attempt to rally from a 20-0 halftime deficit. Flory returned the ball from App State's 45 to the Toledo 36 on his first career interception, and Moore rolled into the end zone after consecutive runs of 15, 10 and 7 yards. Despite hurting his shoulder on his first carry Saturday, adding another injury to a long list that forced him to sit out the equivalent of three games this year, Moore managed to rush for 1,037 yards as a junior. He became the sixth App State player with back-to-back seasons of 1,000 rushing yards thanks to a late surge in which the Mountaineers — behind a restructured, improved offensive line with two standout seniors — had 1,007 yards on the ground in their final three victories. They outscored their opponents 128-24 in those games. True freshman Malik Williams capped the scoring by rushing for a 3-yard touchdown on the first play of the fourth quarter, and sophomore cornerback Clifton Duck recorded his sixth interception of the season midway through the final period, raising his total to 11 in two seasons. With the outcome decided between champions from the Sun Belt and Mid-American conferences, the only question that remained was whether the Mountaineers would keep Toledo scoreless. Its final drive began with a sack by App State senior Devan Stringer, who joined senior Caleb Fuller (1.5 sacks among his 3.0 tackles for loss), junior Okon Godwin (1.0 sack) and senior Eric Boggs (half a sack) in bringing down Woodside behind the line of scrimmage. Postseason shutouts are rare, as Clemson and Alabama (twice) are the only other FBS programs with one in a bowl game since 2010. The Mountaineers notched their second postseason shutout in the modern era, adding to a 19-0 victory against Georgia Southern in the 1987 FCS playoffs, and contributed to the first shutout in the 19-year history of the Dollar General Bowl. App State regained possession for the last time with 2:28 left, and Lamb took one more snap before exiting the field to cheers along with senior linemen Beau Nunn and Colby Gossett, the right-side tandem with a combined 87 starts in their careers. Lamb wasn't quite done, as he had one more huddle to address in a victorious locker room.

2017 HAWAII BOWL

The 2017 Hawaii Bowl was played on December 24, 2017, at Aloha Stadium in Honolulu, Hawaii. The sixteenth edition of the Hawaii Bowl featured the Houston Cougars from the American Athletic Conference against the Fresno State Bulldogs from the Mountain West Conference. Houston entered the game with an overall record of 7–4 (5–3 in conference), while Fresno State entered the game with a 9–4 overall record (7–2 in conference). This was the first meeting between the schools.

2017 Hawaii Bowl	Line	1	-	2	-	3	-	4	-	Final
Fresno State	(52.0)	0	-	13	-	7	-	13	-	33
Houston	(-2.5)	7	-	3	-	10	-	7	-	27

Scoring Summary
Houston – Oliver 1 yard run (Novikoff Kick)
Fresno State – McMaryion run (Camacho Kick)
Fresno State – Camacho 27 yard Field Goal
Houston – Novikoff 31 yard Field goal
Fresno State – Camacho 38 yard Field Goal
Houston – Novikoff 31 yard Field goal
Fresno State – McMaryion 6 yard run (Camacho Kick)
Houston – Myres 94 yard blocked field goal return (Novikoff Kick)
Fresno State – Camacho 33 yard Field Goal
Fresno State – Camacho 26 yard Field Goal
Fresno State – Bryant 44 yard interception return (Camacho Kick)
Houston – Bonner 2 yard pass from King (Novikoff Kick)

Associated Press Hawaii Bowl Game Summary – Marcus McMaryion could not have envisioned this success when he joined Fresno State four months ago. McMaryion threw for a career-best 342 yards and Jimmy Camacho made four field goals to help Fresno State beat Houston 33-27 on Sunday in the Hawaii Bowl. The Oregon State-transfer completed 33 of 48 passes to tie the Hawaii bowl record for completions set by Hawaii's Colt Brennan against Arizona State in 2006 and matched by Fresno State's Derek Carr against SMU in 2012. The Bulldogs (10-4) had their first 10-win season in five years and completed the biggest turnaround in FBS this season. They went 1-11 last year and became just the second team in FBS history to go from double-digit losses one season to double-digit wins the next. The Cougars (7-5) were seeking their fifth consecutive season of eight or more wins. Camacho was busy in his final game for Fresno State. He attempted six field goals, with makes of 27, 38, 26 and 33 yards, but missed a 56-yarder in the second quarter -- which would have been a career long -- and had a 24-yard try blocked and returned for a touchdown in the third quarter. Camacho broke the Hawaii Bowl record for field goals. Fresno State finished with 480 yards of total offense to Houston's 341. Defensive tackle Ed Oliver, the first underclassman to win the Outland Trophy, had his first career carry -- a 1-yard touchdown run -- to cap Houston's first scoring drive in the first quarter. Camacho lined up a 24-yard field goal attempt late in the third quarter, but it was blocked by Houston's Jeremy Winchester and returned 94 yards for a touchdown by Alexander Myres. The Bulldogs took the lead for good on Camacho's 26-yard field goal with 13:57 left to play and stretched the lead to 26-20 with his 33-yarder with six minutes remaining. Jaron Bryant's 44-yard interception return for a TD off a deflection with 3:49 wrapped up the win. D'Eriq King's pass was batted up in the air by defensive end Robert Stanley and fell into the hands of Bryant, who maneuvered his way along the left sideline for the score. KeeSean Johnson caught eight passes for 95 yards for Fresno State and went over the 1,000-yard mark for the season. Steven Dunbar, one of two senior receivers for the Cougars, had seven receptions for 168 yards. McMaryion and Dunbar were selected as the game's most valuable players for each team.

2017 HEART OF DALLAS BOWL

The 2017 Heart of Dallas Bowl was played on December 26, 2017, at the Cotton Bowl in Dallas, Texas. The 8th edition of the Heart of Dallas Bowl, it was sponsored by fast food chicken restaurant Zaxby's, and was officially known as the Zaxby's Heart of Dallas Bowl. The game featured the Utah Utes from the Pac-12 Conference against the West Virginia Mountaineers from the Big 12 Conference.

2017 Heart of Dallas Bowl	Line	1	-	2	-	3	-	4	-	Final
Utah	(-7.0)	7	-	10	-	0	-	13	-	30
West Virginia	(56.0)	0	-	3	-	3	-	8	-	14

Scoring Summary
Utah – Moss 58 yard run (Gay Kick)
West Virginia – Staley 28 yard Field goal
Utah – Huntley 2 yard run (Gay Kick)
Utah – Gay 29 yard Field Goal
West Virginia – Staley 26 yard Field Goal
Utah – Huntley 2 yard run (Gay Kick)
Utah – Gay 26 yard Field Goal
Utah – Gay 24 yard Field Goal
West Virginia – White 18 yard pass from Chugonov (2 pt pass good)

Utahutes.com Heart of Dallas Bowl Game Summary – The University of Utah football program posted a 30-14 win over the West Virginia Mountaineers, finishing the season 7-6 overall. The Utes held the Mountaineers to just 153 yards of total offense, including 29 yards rushing and just six first downs. Utah had a balanced game offensively with 197 rushing yards and 165 yards through the air, finishing the game with three rushing scores and three field goals. Tyler Huntley finished the game 12-for-26 (0 TD, 0 INT) for 165 passing yards, adding 57 rushing yards and two rushing scores. Zack Moss led the Utes in rushing with

150 yards for his fifth game with 100-plus yards on the ground, also scoring his 10th rushing touchdown of the season. Darren Carrington II racked up 62 yards on four receptions with Raelon Singleton adding 52 yards on two catches. Wrapping up things on special teams was Matt Gay, kicking in three field goals and scoring 12 points. Utah struck first after the Ute defense forced a three-and-out to get the ball on their own 17-yard-line. Just three plays later, Moss broke free for a career-long 58-yard rushing touchdown to put the Utes up 7-0 with 11:37 on the clock in the first quarter. Donavan Thompson and Kavika Luafatasaga led the Utes in tackles with six each with Lowell Lotulelei contributing four tackles that included 1.5 sacks and 2.5 tackles for loss. Cody Barton and Julian Blackmon were also key contributors against the Mountaineers with Barton recording two fumbles recoveries and Blackmon coming away with his fourth interception of the year. Blackmon was named the game's Most Valuable Player. The Utah defense was stingy in the first quarter, holding West Virginia to just 38 yards of total offense, including -3 rushing. The Mountaineers were only able to convert on one third down in the first quarter, punting three times. It was the Utah defense that stepped up again, holding WVU to just a field goal to start the second quarter. The Mountaineers were able to knock in a 28-yarder with 13:09 left to play, cutting the Utah lead to 7-3, ending an 11-play, 67-yard drive. Utah extended its lead with 5:46 left in the second quarter after the Ute specials teams came up big. Cody Barton came up with a fumble recovery on a WVU punt return, giving the Utes the ball back on the Mountaineer 13-yard-line. With the Utes in scoring territory, Utah got to the two-yard-line with Huntley sneaking it into the end zone for the two-yard score, putting the Utes up 14-3. It was a quick scoring drive, taking 1:19 off the clock for three plays and 13 yards. The Utes wasted no time getting another three points on the scoreboard after Matt Gay punched in a 29-yard field goal with 1:08 remaining in the second quarter. The field goal gave Utah a 17-3 advantage heading into halftime, ending a nine-play, 56-yard drive. West Virginia took advantage of a special teams play after Utah fumbled the ball on a punt to put up a field goal in the third quarter, converting a 28-yarder to make it 17-6 with 6:43 left. It would be the only points of the quarter after both teams struggled to get going offensively. Utah scored right out of the gate in the fourth quarter with Huntley finding the end zone for the second time in the game, scoring on another two-yard quarterback keeper to give Utah a 24-6 lead with 13:59 remaining in the game. It didn't take long for Utah to add to its stat line after Barton recovered his second fumble of the game to give the Utes the ball back with 13:16 on the clock. The Utes started its drive on the West Virginia 15-yard-line, eventually giving Gay the go-ahead 26-yard field goal to make it 27-6 at the 11:38 mark. The Utes made it a 24-point game with 4:15 left to play in the game when Gay sent in his third field goal of the game, recording a 24-yarder to give Utah a 30-6 lead. After a Julian Blackmon interception put the Utes on the WVU 26-yard-line, Utah was able to score on its eight-play, 20-yard drive. West Virginia scored its only touchdown of the game late, after Ka'Ruan White was found in the end zone for an 18-yard reception, making it 30-14 with 1:58 on the clock. It would be the last points of the game after Utah was able to run out the clock and claim the 30-14 victory.

2017 QUICK LANE BOWL

The **2017 Quick Lane Bowl** was played at Ford Field in Detroit, Michigan, on December 26, 2017. The game featured the Duke Blue Devils of the Atlantic Coast Conference and the Northern Illinois Huskies of the Mid-American Conference. This was the first meeting between the schools. The fourth annual Quick Lane Bowl was sponsored by Quick Lane tire and auto centers.

2017 Quick Lane Bowl	Line	1	-	2	-	3	-	4	-	Final
Duke	(-5.5)	14	-	12	-	7	-	3	-	36
Northern Illinois	(47.0)	0	-	14	-	0	-	0	-	14

Scoring Summary
Duke – Jones 1 yard run {Holmquist Kick}
Duke – Wilson 1 yard run {Holmquist Kick}
Northern Illinois – Harbison 25 yard run {Hagan Kick}
Northern Illinois – Wesley 67 yard pass from Childers {Hagan Kick}
Duke – Rahming 33 yard pass from Jones {Holmquist Kick}
Duke – Wilson 11 yard pass from Jones {2 pt. pass no good}
Duke – Brown 7 yard run {Holmquist Kick}
Duke – Holmquist 24 yard Field Goal

Detroit News Quick Lane Bowl Game Summary - Duke dominated the opening quarter of the Quick Lane Bowl, jumping out to a 14-0 lead before defeating Northern Illinois 36-14 before an announced crowd of 20,252 fans Tuesday evening. Duke scored midway through the first quarter when sophomore quarterback Daniel Jones scored on a 1-yard run on fourth down. Then, Duke (7-6) gladly accepted a belated Christmas present when Northern Illinois went for a fake punt on fourth down … and 18 … from its own end zone and the pass by punter Matt Ference fell incomplete, giving the ball to Duke at the 11 and the

Blue Devils scored three plays later on Shaun Wilson's 1-yard run to open up a 14-0 cushion. After Duke's second TD, the Blue Devils held advantages on total yards (94-0) and plays run (20-10) in addition to the lead. Jones finished 27-of-40 for 252 yards and two TDs while also rushing for 86 yards and a score. His performance brought back memories of his effort in a 41-17 rout of No. 20 Northwestern when he threw for 305 yards and two TDs and rushed for 108 yards and two scores. Northern Illinois bounced back from its slow start, showing its big-play ability with redshirt freshman quarterback Marcus Childers finding Spencer Tears for 44 yards to set up Tre Harbison's 25-yard TD run. And Northern Illinois would score less than two minutes later when Childers found Javan Wesley for a 67-yard TD pass to pull even at 14 with 12:22 left in the second quarter. Jones was at his best during the final two drives of the half, showing his ability as a dual-threat quarterback by moving the chains with both his arm and his legs. First, Jones picked up a pair of first downs on runs, then went up top to find T.J. Rahming for a 33-yard TD pass for a 20-14 lead. Then, in the final minutes Jones connected on all five of his pass attempts for 54 yards, the final one when he hit Wilson in the right flat and the Blue Devils' senior running back did the rest for an 11-yard TD, reaching the end zone after taking advantage of a big block from tackle Evan Lisle. In the first half against Northern Illinois, Jones connected on 16-of-23 for 178 yards and two TDs and ran for 28 yards and a score. Northern Illinois had a chance of cutting into the lead early in the third quarter when Childers connected with Wesley for 42 yards to the Duke 18, but Duke's defense made some big plays to force a 40-yard field goal and holder Josh Orne got up for a possible run but turned right into cornerback Mark Gilbert for a loss. Duke took advantage of the strong defensive stop by moving 67 yards on 11 plays to open up a 33-14 lead with Brittain Brown's seven-yard run. Northern Illinois — which also failed to convert on fourth and three from the Duke 41 on an option run late in the first quarter — went to 0-for-4 on fourth down when Childers misfired on fourth and three from the Duke 33 late in the third. Still, it was the fake punt that left everyone shaking their heads. It was the first bowl trips for the teams to Ford Field, but Northern Illinois had made several appearances before at Ford Field while playing in the Mid-American Conference Championship game. The outcome put the MAC at 1-4 in bowl games this season with all the setbacks being lopsided.

2017 CACTUS BOWL

The 2017 Cactus Bowl was held on December 26, 2017, at Chase Field in Phoenix, Arizona. The game was the twenty-ninth edition of the Cactus Bowl, which was originally known as the Copper Bowl, Insight Bowl and then as the Buffalo Wild Wings Bowl. The bowl featured the Kansas State Wildcats of the Big 12 Conference against the UCLA Bruins of the Pac-12 Conference. Kansas State won, 35–17. Kansas State and UCLA had met three times previously, most recently in the 2015 Alamo Bowl, with UCLA leading the series, 2–1.

2017 Cactus Bowl	Line	1	-	2	-	3	-	4	-	Final
Kansas State	(-6.0)	7	-	0	-	14	-	14	-	35
UCLA	(59.0)	3	-	14	-	0	-	0	-	17

Scoring Summary
UCLA – Molson 44 yard Field Goal
Kansas State – Delton 68 yard run (McCrane Kick)
UCLA – Lasley 52 yard pass from Modster (Molson Kick)
UCLA – Howard 70 yard pass from Modster (Molson Kick)
Kansas State – Delton 1 yard run (McCrane Kick)
Kansas State – Heath 8 yard pass from Delton (McCrane Kick)
Kansas State – Barnes 41 yard run (McCrane Kick)
Kansas State – Delton 3 yard run (McCrane Kick)

Associated Press Cactus Bowl Game Summary - Bill Snyder stood on a makeshift stage in the middle of a baseball stadium with a roof, a sparkling trophy at his side depicting a football sailing through cactus uprights. If this was the end of his storied coaching career at Kansas State, it sure was a great way to go out. Alex Delton ran for 158 yards and accounted for four touchdowns, leading the Wildcats to a 35-17 Cactus Bowl victory over UCLA on Tuesday night in what could be Snyder's final game. Delton replaced Skylar Thompson late in the first quarter and scored on runs of 68 yards, 3 yards and 1 yard. Alex Barnes added 117 yards and a touchdown for the Wildcats, who rushed for 345 yards. Kansas State (8-5) struggled in the first half against UCLA's potent offense but shut down the Bruins in the second to give Snyder his 210th - and possibly last - win with the Wildcats. UCLA (6-7) played without top NFL prospect Josh Rosen, who's recovering from a concussion, and built a 10-point halftime lead without its star quarterback. The Bruins' offensive success didn't carry over into the second half and their defense had a hard time containing Delton, saddling interim coach Jedd Fisch with a loss in his last game before Chip Kelly takes over the program. Snyder turned around one of the nation's worst programs after taking over in 1989, leading the Wildcats to eight straight bowl appearances after un-retiring in 2008. He says he has not decided whether he will return for a 27th season or retire again to spend time with his family. The 78-year-old coach made a quarterback change in the first quarter of the Cactus Bowl after Thompson threw an interception. Delton had an immediate impact, bursting up the middle for a 68-yard touchdown run. Snyder opted to go for it on fourth-and-goal from the 1 in the third quarter, and Delton came through again, bulling his way through a massive pile - with some help from his teammates. Kansas State's Denzel Goolsby recovered Bolu Olorunfunmi's fumble at the Bruins 24-yard line on the next play from scrimmage, and Delton hit Dominique Heath for an 8-yard touchdown to give the Wildcats the lead. UCLA turned it over on downs - after a successful fake punt - and Kansas State turned its fourth-down try into a touchdown, with Alex Barnes putting the Wildcats up 28-17 with a 41-yard run. Kansas State ended UCLA's comeback hopes with an eight-minute drive capped by Delton's final TD run. Rosen, expected to leave for the NFL after his junior year, was in uniform and warmed up before the game, but Devon Modster trotted out to the huddle. The Bruins still had their big-play game going even without Rosen, building a 17-7 halftime lead on two long TD passes by Modster. UCLA's offensive roll ended with halftime. The Bruins had 100 total yards and three first downs in the second half. If this was the final game of Snyder's career, the Wildcats sent him out on a high note with a dominant second-half performance.

2017 INDEPENDENCE BOWL

The 2017 Independence Bowl was played on December 27, 2017, at Independence Stadium in Shreveport, Louisiana. The 42nd annual Independence Bowl featured the Southern Miss Golden Eagles of Conference USA against the Florida State Seminoles of the Atlantic Coast Conference. This was the twenty-third meeting between the schools, with Florida State holding a 13–8–1 advantage. They had most recently played in 1996, when the Seminoles defeated the Golden Eagles by a score of 54–14. The contest was televised on ESPN, with kickoff at 1:30 PM (EST).

2017 Independence Bowl	Line	1	-	2	-	3	-	4	-	Final
Southern Miss	(48.0)	6	-	0	-	7	-	0	-	13
Florida State	(-11.5)	7	-	16	-	10	-	9	-	42

Scoring Summary
Southern Miss – Griggs 5 yard run (Kick no good)
Florida State – Tate 20 yard pass from Blackman (Aguayo Kick)
Florida State – Akers 14 yard pass from Blackman (Aguayo Kick)
Florida State – Aguayo 29 yard Field Goal
Florida State – Tate 10 yard pass from Blackman (Aguayo Kick)
Florida State – Aguayo 39 yard Field Goal
Florida State – Patrick 2 yard run (Aguayo Kick)
Southern Miss – Robinson 13 yard pass from Griggs (Shaunfield Kick)
Florida State – Tate 17 yard pass from Blackman (Aguayo Kick)
Florida State – Aguayo 39 yard Field Goal

Orlando Sentinel Independence Bowl Game Summary - Florida State quarterback James Blackman and running back Cam Akers became the first true freshman duo to start for the Seminoles at their positions in school history. They saved their best performances of their first college football season for Wednesday's season finale and will likely provide new FSU coach Willie Taggart a bright future to build on offensively after earning valuable experience this season. Akers broke FSU all-time leading rusher Dalvin Cook's school record for rushing yards by a freshman while Blackman threw four touchdowns to earn Independence Bowl offensive MVP honors following FSU's 42-13 win over Southern Miss. Akers, a former five-star standout and the highest rated recruit to ever sign with the Seminoles, finished the game with 94 yards rushing, to finish his freshman season with 1,024 yards. Cook rushed for 1,008 yards rushing as a freshman in 2014. Akers is now ahead of Cook's pace but will have plenty of work to do to reach Cook's all-time school record of 4,464 yards rushing from 2014-16. As for Blackman, he completed 18 of 26 passes for 233 yards with three of his four touchdown passes thrown in the first half. Blackman, 18, said the 12 bowl practices helped him regroup after a turnover-prone season. He finished this season completing 57.2 percent of his passes for 15 touchdowns with 11 interceptions. Junior receiver Nyqwan Murray, FSU's leading receiver entering the bowl game, did not play in the bowl game after suffering a concussion. Fifth-year senior defensive back Nate Andrews, one of the few remaining players from FSU's 2013 national championship team, earned defensive MVP honors after the game. He had six tackles and one pass deflection.

2017 PINSTRIPE BOWL

The 2017 Pinstripe Bowl was played on December 27, 2017, at Yankee Stadium in the New York City borough of the Bronx. The eighth edition of the Pinstripe Bowl featured the Boston College Eagles of the Atlantic Coast Conference against the Iowa Hawkeyes of the Big Ten Conference. It was the first meeting between the two. It was sponsored by the New Era Cap Company; the game was officially known as the New Era Pinstripe Bowl. The contest was televised on ESPN, with kickoff at 5:15 PM (EST).

2017 Pinstripe Bowl	Line	1	-	2	-	3	-	4	-	Final
Iowa	(-2.0)	3	-	7	-	7	-	10	-	27
Boston College	(46.0)	7	-	10	-	0	-	3	-	20

Scoring Summary
Iowa – Recinos 24 yard Field Goal
Boston College – Dillon 4 yard run (Lichtenberg Kick)
Iowa – Fant 8 yard pass from Stanley (Recinos Kick)
Boston College – Sweeney 39 yard pass from Wade (Lichtenberg Kick)
Boston College – Lichtenberg 30 yard Field Goal
Iowa – Wadley 5 yard run (Recinos Kick)
Iowa – Recinos 38 yard Field Goal
Boston College – Lichtenberg 24 yard Field Goal
Iowa – Kulick 1 yard run (Recinos Kick)

Reuters News Service Pinstripe Bowl Game Summary — Akrum Wadley knew he had 40 tickets to give out to family and friends to watch him serve as Iowa's top running threat. Those close to him might not have anticipated watching him dash through tacklers on special teams as well. Performing as a kick returner for the first time since the second week of the season, Wadley produced 283 all-purpose yards, helping Iowa to a 27-20 victory over Boston College on Wednesday at frigid Yankee Stadium. Wadley finished with 171 yards on five kickoff returns, including a 72-yard return that set up Iowa's first touchdown early in the second quarter. He also gained 88 yards on the ground, including a 27-yard scamper down the left sideline that set up fullback Drake Kulick's tiebreaking 1-yard plunge with 3:09 remaining in the fourth. Wadley, who is from Newark, N.J., finished his four-year career at Iowa (8-5) by stepping in for regular return man Ihmir Smith-Marsette, who was injured during a practice last week. Wadley's showing helped the Hawkeyes snap a seven-year gap between bowl wins on a night when the temperature at kickoff was 23 degrees and the wind-chill factor made it feel like 12. Iowa finished with 101 rushing yards and 317 yards on kickoff returns thanks to Wadley, who entered the game with four career kickoff returns totaling 100 yards. The ability to create favorable field position earned Wadley MVP honors. He also broke the school record for kickoff return yardage in a bowl game, surpassing the mark of 169 yards set by C.J. Jones in the 2003 Orange Bowl against USC. Wadley's performance on the ground wasn't even the best in the eighth edition of the game at the current Yankee Stadium. Boston College freshman AJ Dillon gained 157 yards on 32 attempts but only 11 in the final 15 minutes. The Eagles (7-6) committed three turnovers, leading to 10 Iowa points. Dillon (1,589 yards) finished with the third-highest single-season rushing total in school history. However, his performance was negated by an uncharacteristic showing from a team, which came in ranked 19th nationally in turnover margin and couldn't contain Wadley on special teams. Iowa's Nate Stanley completed 8 of 15 passes for 99 yards, connecting with Noah Fant on a first-half touchdown. Miguel Recinos added a pair of field goals for the Hawkeyes. Wade finished 16 of 27 for 208 yards for Boston College. Sweeney caught seven passes for 137 yards and a touchdown, and Colton Lichtenberg kicked two field goals for the Eagles. Boston College took a 7-3 lead after the opening quarter when Dillon barreled in from 4 yards out with five seconds remaining. Dillon's TD occurred five plays after the Eagles gained 12 yards on a fourth-and-8. Wadley returned the ensuing kickoff 72 yards, and the Hawkeyes took a 10-7 lead an 8-yard pass to Fant less than two minutes into the second. The Eagles regained the lead at 14-10 on a 39-yard pass to Sweeney about four minutes later and took a 17-10 lead on a 30-yard field goal by Lichtenberg with 1:29 remaining in the half. Iowa tied the game at 17 midway through the third quarter when Wadley rushed to the left side from 5 yards out. The Hawkeyes settled for a 38-yard field goal by Recinos with 11:32 left in the fourth moments after T.J. Hockenson dropped a potential TD pass, but Boston College tied at 20 nearly 3 1/2 minutes later, a 24-yard field goal by Lichtenberg. Boston College DE Harold Landry did not play due to an ankle injury. Iowa CB Josh Jackson recorded his eighth interception of the season with 1:18 remaining. He tied the school record shared by Desmond King (2015), Lou King (1981) and Nile Kinnick (1939). Boston College fell to 0-2 in the Pinstripe Bowl. The Eagles also lost 31-30 in overtime to Penn State in 2014.

2017 FOSTER FARMS BOWL

The 2017 Foster Farms Bowl was played on December 27, 2017, at Levi's Stadium in Santa Clara, California. The 16th edition of the Foster Farms Bowl, the game featured the Arizona Wildcats from the Pac-12 Conference against the Purdue Boilermakers from the Big Ten Conference. It was sponsored by the Foster Farms poultry company. This was Arizona's first trip to the Foster Farms Bowl; they entered the game with a record of 9–10–1 in prior bowl appearances. Their last bowl win was at the 2015 New Mexico Bowl, when they defeated New Mexico 45–37. This bowl marked the Boilermakers' eighteenth bowl appearance (they were 9–8 in prior bowl games) and they were seeking their first bowl victory since the 2011 Little Caesars Pizza Bowl, when they beat Western Michigan 37–32.

2017 Foster Farms Bowl	Line	1	-	2	-	3	-	4	-	Final
Arizona	(-2.5)	14	-	0	-	14	-	7	-	35
Purdue	(64.0)	14	-	17	-	0	-	7	-	38

Scoring Summary
Purdue – Mahoungou 31 yard Pass from Sindelar {Evans kick}
Arizona – Poindexter 31 yard Pass from Tate {Pollack kick}
Arizona – Ellison 29 yard Pass from Tate {Pollack kick}
Purdue – Phillips 42 yard Pass from Sindelar {Dellinger kick}
Purdue – Phillips 22 yard Pass from Sindelar {Dellinger kick}
Purdue – Knox 13 yard run {Dellinger kick}
Purdue – Evans 26 yard Field goal
Arizona – Ellison 40 yard Pass from Tate {Pollack kick}
Arizona – Johnson 40 yard Pass from Tate {Joshua Pollack}
Arizona – Brown 24 yard Pass from Tate {Pollack kick}
Purdue – Mahoungou 38 yard Pass from Sindelar {Dellinger kick}

Purduesports.com Foster Farms Bowl Game Summary - Elijah Sindelar threw a 38-yard touchdown pass to Anthony Mahoungou with 1:44 remaining and Purdue capped coach Jeff Brohm's first season in dramatic style with a 38-35 victory over Arizona in the Foster Farms Bowl on Wednesday. The Boilermakers (7-6) had squandered a 17-point halftime lead when Khalil Tate threw his fifth touchdown pass with 3:21 remaining to give the Wildcats (7-6) the lead. But Sindelar responded with a 75-yard drive that ended with the deep throw into the end zone to Mahoungou, giving the Boilermakers their first winning record since 2011 and first bowl win over a major conference team since beating Washington in the 2002 Sun Bowl. Purdue had won only nine games in the previous four seasons before Brohm arrived. Sindelar threw for 396 yards and four touchdowns, with Mahoungou (118 yards) and Gregory Phillips (149) each topping the 100-yard mark and catching two touchdown passes. Tate was just as good, showing he can win with his arm as well as he can with his legs that carried him to 1,353 yards rushing in the regular season. Tate threw for 302 yards and five touchdowns, but his late interception to Jacob Thieneman ended the comeback attempt. Brohm pulled out all the stops, going for it three times on fourth down, calling a couple of flea-flickers and using an innovative trick play to set up a field goal at the end of the first half that made it 31-14. The Boilermakers took over at their 32-yard line with 56 seconds left after Tate lost a fumble. Purdue appeared to be taking a knee on the play to run out the clock, but running back D.J. Knox was crouching hidden behind a guard. Sindelar then handed the ball to Knox, who waited an instant and then ran around left end for a 30-yard gain that helped set up the field goal.

2017 TEXAS BOWL

The 2017 Texas Bowl was played on December 27, 2017, at NRG Stadium in Houston, Texas. Sponsored by the Academy Sports + Outdoors sporting goods company, it was officially known as the Academy Sports + Outdoors Texas Bowl. The twelfth edition of the Texas Bowl, the game featured the Texas Longhorns of the Big 12 Conference against the Missouri Tigers of the Southeastern Conference. This was the teams' 24th meeting. Prior to the game, Texas led the series 17–6. This was their first match-up since Missouri left the Big 12 Conference after the 2011 season.

2017 Texas Bowl	Line	1	-	2	-	3	-	4	-	Final
Texas	(62.0)	14	-	7	-	2	-	10	-	33
Missouri	(-3.0)	0	-	7	-	9	-	0	-	16

Scoring Summary
Texas – Young 22 yard pass from Buechele (Rowland Kick)
Texas – Burt 7 yard pass from Ehlinger (Rowland Kick)
Missouri – Witter 4 yard run (McCann Kick)
Texas – Wheeler 38 yard fumble return (Rowland Kick)
Missouri – Johnson 79 yard pass from Lock (2 pt. conversion no good)
Missouri – McCann 28 yard Field Goal
Texas – Safety – tackled Missouri player in end zone
Texas – Rowland 41 yard Field goal
Texas – Foreman 18 yard run (Rowland Kick)

Bleacher Report Texas Bowl Game Summary: The Texas Longhorns defeated the Missouri Tigers 33-16 in the Texas Bowl at Houston's NRG Stadium on Wednesday night to capture their first bowl win in five years. The triumphant effort was largely without flash, but the Longhorns parlayed two Tigers turnovers into nine points through a second-quarter scoop-and-score and a third-quarter safety to take pressure off an offense that didn't produce big plays. Quarterbacks Sam Ehlinger and Shane Buechele combined to complete 17 of 29 passes for 167 yards and two touchdowns, while Longhorns rushers totaled 42 carries for 113 yards and a score. Those shortcomings meant plenty of work for punter Michael Dickson—who was named the game's MVP for his outstanding performance. The 2017 Ray Guy Award winner finished the night with 11 punts for a staggering 452 yards. Ten of those attempts landed inside the 20-yard line, including eight that settled at or inside the 10-yard line. And while Missouri outgained Texas, 390-280, a 3-of-14 third-down conversion rate meant quarterback Drew Lock and Co. were never able to establish a rhythm. Lock, who's considering leaving Missouri and declaring for the 2018 NFL draft, finished 18-of-34 for 269 yards and one touchdown, which came in the form of a 79-yard laser to Johnathon Johnson on the first play of the third quarter. However, that was as good as things would get for the Tigers. The Longhorns' safety with 1:10 remaining in the third quarter put them back up by a touchdown, and a 41-yard Joshua Rowland field goal less than three minutes into the final frame gave them all the cushion they needed.

2017 MILITARY BOWL

The 2017 Military Bowl was played at Navy–Marine Corps Memorial Stadium in Annapolis, Maryland, on December 28, 2017. The game was the 10th edition of the Military Bowl and featured the Virginia Cavaliers of the Atlantic Coast Conference and the Navy Midshipmen of the American Athletic Conference. The Virginia Cavaliers finished the regular season with a 6–6 record. This was the team's first appearance in the Military Bowl and their first bowl appearance since 2011. The Navy Midshipmen had a 6–6 record in the regular season. This was the team's third appearance in the Military Bowl; they lost in 2008 (when the game was the EagleBank Bowl) and won in 2015.

2017 Military Bowl	Line	1	-	2	-	3	-	4	-	Final
Virginia	(50.0)	7	-	0	-	0	-	0	-	7
Navy	(-2.5)	14	-	14	-	14	-	7	-	49

Scoring Summary
Virginia – Reed 98 yard run (Meija Kick)
Navy – Abey 1 yard run (Moehring Kick)
Navy – Perry 22 yard run (Moehring Kick)
Navy – Perry 19 yard run (Moehring Kick)
Navy – Abey 1 yard run (Moehring Kick)
Navy – Abey 5 yard run (Moehring Kick)
Navy – Abey 20 yard run (Moehring Kick)
Navy – Abey 1 yard run (Moehring Kick)

Associated Press Military Bowl Game Summary — Two quarterbacks put on one heck of a show for Navy in the Military Bowl. Backup Zach Abey scored five touchdowns, starter Malcolm Perry ran for 114 yards and two scores and the Midshipmen rolled to a surprisingly easy 49-7 victory over Virginia on Thursday. After Virginia's Joe Reed took the opening kickoff 98 yards for a touchdown, the Midshipmen (7-6) got two TDs apiece from Perry and Abey in taking a 28-7 halftime lead. Perry left in the third quarter with a foot injury, leaving Abey to score on runs of 5 and 20 yards to make it 42-7 in a game Navy entered as a 1 1/2-point favorite. The Midshipmen rolled up a Military Bowl-record 452 yards rushing, including 101 by Chris High and 88 by Abey, who began the season as the starter before losing the job. Going back and forth with Perry and Abey might be the way to go in 2018. After scoring on a 1-yard run with 11:11 remaining, Abey sat down after becoming the fifth player in FBS history to rush for five TDs in a bowl game. Playing in their first bowl since 2011, the Cavaliers (6-7) could not contain Navy's triple option and had no success moving the ball. Seeking its first winning season in six years, Virginia instead absorbed its sixth loss in seven games. They're currently in the second tier of the Atlantic Coast Conference, and at least on this day not nearly as good as Navy. Virginia senior Kurt Benkert came in with a school-record 3,062 yards passing this season, along with 25 touchdown passes. In this one, he went 15 for 34 for 133 yards and an interception, and the Cavaliers finished with a season-low 175 yards in offense. After Reed went the distance with the opening kickoff, Navy responded with a 69-yard drive that ended with a 1-yard run by Abey. The Midshipmen then forced a three-and-out, and Perry finished an eight-play drive with a 22-yard touchdown run for a 14-7 lead. Perry scored from 19 yards out and Abey concluded the first-half scoring with a 1-yard TD. By then, Reed's kickoff return was irrelevant.

2017 CAMPING WORLD BOWL

The 2017 Camping World Bowl was played on December 28, 2017, at the Camping World Stadium in Orlando, Florida. The 28th edition of the Camping World Bowl featured the Oklahoma State Cowboys of the Big 12 Conference against the Virginia Tech Hokies of the Atlantic Coast Conference.

2017 Camping World Bowl	Line	1	-	2	-	3	-	4	-	Final
#22 Virginia Tech	(60.5)	7	-	0	-	7	-	7	-	21
#17 Oklahoma State	(-6.5)	3	-	10	-	14	-	3	-	30

Scoring Summary
Oklahoma State – Ammendola 33 yard Field Goal
Virginia Tech – Jackson 76 yard run (Slye Kick)
Oklahoma State – Ammendola 36 yard Field Goal
Oklahoma State – Hill 1 yard run (Ammendola Kick)
Oklahoma State – Stoner 17 yard pass from Rudolph (Ammendola Kick)
Virginia Tech – Kumah 9 yard pass from Jackson (Slye Kick)
Oklahoma State – Washington 65 yard pass from Rudolph (Ammendola Kick)
Virginia Tech – Jackson 5 yard run (Slye Kick)
Oklahoma State – Ammendola 38 yard Field Goal

Associated Press Camping World Bowl Game Summary: They started playing football at Oklahoma State 116 years ago, and never in that span had there been a run of three consecutive 10-win seasons. Until now. Mason Rudolph threw for 351 yards and a pair of touchdowns on his way to winning game MVP honors, James Washington had a long touchdown grab and became Oklahoma State's career receiving yards leader, and the 17th-ranked Cowboys beat No. 22 Virginia Tech 30-21 in the Camping World Bowl on Thursday night. Washington caught five passes for 126 yards, giving him 4,472 for his career and passing Rashaun Woods for the school mark. Justice Hill ran for 120 yards and another score for the Cowboys (10-3). Josh Jackson ran for two scores and threw for another for the Hokies (9-4), including a rush that got Virginia Tech within 27-21 with 5:40 remaining. Deshawn McClease ran for 124 yards, a Virginia Tech season-best, but the Hokies were hurt by two turnovers in Oklahoma State territory. Hill came through with perhaps the play of the night. Facing a third-and-11 with 3:30 left, Hill took a handoff, went left, waited for a lane to open -- and broke loose for a 31-yard gain down to the Hokies' 18. Matt Ammendola's 38-yard field goal with 2:34 left put the Cowboys up by nine, essentially sealing the outcome. Virginia Tech outgained the high-octane Cowboys, 518 yards to 492. A pair of big missed Hokie opportunities helped Oklahoma State take a 13-7 lead at the break. An 18-play, 10-minute drive that got to the Oklahoma State 1 resulted in no points when the Hokies fumbled a snap away. And after the Cowboys took the lead late in the half, Jackson had a wide-open Henri Murphy down the middle for what would have been a 54-yard score. But the pass was overthrown, the Hokies never led again, and Rudolph and Washington got the winning ending they sought. Rudolph ended his college career with no less than 52 school records. His two touchdown throws gave him 37 on the season, tying Brandon Weeden's school mark. And he came into the game needing 175 yards to break Weeden's season passing record, eclipsing that in the third quarter.

2017 ALAMO BOWL

The 2017 Alamo Bowl was played on December 28, 2017, at the Alamodome in San Antonio, Texas. The 25th annual Alamo Bowl featured the Stanford Cardinal of the Pac-12 against the TCU Horned Frogs of the Big 12. This was the third meeting between the schools; TCU won both games to lead the series 2–0. The contest was televised on ESPN, with kickoff at 8:00 PM (CST).

2017 Alamo Bowl	Line	1	-	2	-	3	-	4	-	Final
#15 Stanford	(49.5)	14	-	7	-	10	-	6	-	37
#13 TCU	(-3.0)	3	-	7	-	13	-	16	-	39

Scoring Summary
Stanford – Love 15 yard run (Toner Kick)
TCU – Bunce 38 yard Field Goal
Stanford – Arcega-Whiteside 18 yard pass from Costello (Toner Kick)
Stanford – Arcega-Whiteside 14 yard pass from Costello (Toner Kick)
TCU – Hill 6 yard run (Bunce Kick)
TCU – Hill 27 yard pass from White (Bunce Kick)
Stanford – Love 69 yard run (Toner Kick)
TCU – White 11 yard pass from Hill (Bunce Kick)
Stanford – Toner 27 yard Field Goal
TCU – Reagor 93 yard pass from Hill (2 pt pass failed)
TCU – White 76 yard punt return (Bunce Kick)
Stanford – Arcega-Whiteside 4 yard pass from Costello (2 pt pass failed)
TCU – Bunce 33 yard Field Goal)

Associated Press Alamo Bowl Game Summary – Kenny Hill passed for two touchdowns, ran for another and even caught one as No. 13 TCU rallied from a big early deficit to beat 15th-ranked Stanford 39-37 in the Alamo Bowl on Thursday night. Cole Bunce's 33-yard field goal with just over 3 minutes to play won it for the Horned Frogs (11-3), who trailed 21-3 before storming back behind big plays from Hill and a 76-yard punt return from Desmon White. TCU rallied from 31 down in to beat Oregon in the 2015 Alamo Bowl. Stanford (9-5) running back Bryce Love, a Heisman Trophy finalist, rushed for 145 yards and had a 69-yard touchdown run in the third quarter. K.J. Costello had three touchdown passes to J.J. Arcega-Whiteside, the last one giving Stanford a 37-36 lead. Hill then drove TCU to Bunce's game winner. The Horned Frogs defense sealed it with an interception by Innis Gaines with 2:01 left. Hill finished with 314 yards passing, a team-high 60 yards rushing and caught a 27-yard TD pass from White in his final game. Love finished with the season with 2,118 yards rushing, the school's single-season record. The Horned Frogs defended Love about as well as anyone this season despite the long touchdown run. Most important, they didn't let him take over the game in the second half, which let Hill and the offense rally. When the running game wasn't working, the TCU defense could get after Costello, who struggled under pressure after his quick start. The Cardinal were doomed by the big play just when they had a chance to put the game away. After pinning TCU deep, Hill connected with Jalen Reagor on a 93-yard touchdown pass early in the fourth quarter. White, who earlier had a costly fumble, then gave TCU its first lead with his punt return touchdown.

2017 HOLIDAY BOWL

The 2017 Holiday Bowl was played at SDCCU Stadium in San Diego, California, on December 28, 2017. The 40th edition of the Holiday Bowl featured the Michigan State Spartans of the Big Ten Conference versus the Washington State Cougars of the Pac-12 Conference. This was Michigan State's first appearance in a Holiday Bowl. The Spartans finished the 2017 regular season at 9–3 and were second in the B1G East Division (7–2). The team had upset wins over then-#7 Michigan and then-#7 Penn State. Their three losses were all against teams that finished in the AP Top 20 (#14 Notre Dame, #20 Northwestern and #5 Ohio State). This was Washington State's fourth appearance in the Holiday Bowl, having lost to #14 Brigham Young in 1981, having defeated #5 Texas in 2003, and having lost to Minnesota in 2016. The Cougars finished the 2017 regular season at 9–3 and were third in the Pac-12 North Division (6–3). The season featured wins against then-#5 USC and then-#18 Stanford.

2017 Holiday Bowl	Line	1	-	2	-	3	-	4	-	Final
#21 Washington State	(47.5)	3	-	0	-	7	-	7	-	17
#19 Michigan State	(-2.5)	0	-	21	-	14	-	7	-	42

Scoring Summary
Washington State – Powell 45 yard Field Goal
Michigan State – White 15 yard pass from Lewerke (Coghlin Kick)
Michigan State – Davis 49 yard pass from Lewerke (Coghlin Kick)
Michigan State – Scott 3 yard run (Coghlin Kick)
Michigan State – White 10 yard pass from Lewerke (Coghlin Kick)
Michigan State – Terry 6 yard run (Coghlin Kick)
Washington State – Martin 14 yard pass from Hilinski (Powell Kick)
Washington State – Martin 15 yard pass from Hilinski (Powell Kick)
Michigan State – Scott 28 yard run (Coghlin Kick)

Associated Press Holiday Bowl Game Summary – Brian Lewerke threw for 213 yards and three touchdowns, and LJ Scott ran for 110 yards and two scores for No. 18 Michigan State, which took advantage of Luke Falk's absence to rout No. 21 Washington State 42-17 in the Holiday Bowl on Thursday night. Lewerke also rushed for 73 yards for Michigan State (10-3), which reached double digits in wins for the eighth time in program history. Falk, who was photographed earlier in the week with a cast on his left wrist, went through warmups but came out in street clothes at game time. He was replaced by redshirt sophomore Tyler Hilinksi, who made his first start and eighth appearance of the season. It's unclear precisely when Falk injured the wrist on his non-throwing hand, but he had issues with it throughout the season. Coach Mike Leach refused to give specifics during the week. Hilinski led WSU (9-4) to a 45-yard field goal by Erik Powell on the Cougars' second drive, but the Cougars were overpowered by the Spartans. Lewerke threw the first of two TD passes to Cody White, a 7-yarder midway through the second quarter, when he was flushed to the left but found the receiver in the back of the end zone. On MSU's next possession, Lewerke took the snap and glanced at his running back, which froze the secondary and allowed Felton Davis III to get wide open for a 49-yard scoring pass. Scott scored on a 3-yard run to give the Spartans a 21-3 halftime time. Early in the third, Lewerke rolled left and had his pass tipped, but a sliding White caught it for a 7-yard touchdown. Lewerke, who finished 13 of 21, was hit hard on a keeper in the third quarter and came out for a few plays. His backup, Damion Terry, scored on a 6-yard keeper to make it 35-3. The Cougars closed the gap when Hilinski threw a 14-yard touchdown pass to Tay Martin late in the third quarter and a 15-yarder to Tay in the fourth quarter. Scott scored on a 28-yard burst up the middle with about six minutes left to play. Hilinski was 39 of 50 for 272 yards and two touchdowns, with one interception. It was the second straight lackluster Holiday Bowl for Leach's Cougars, who lost 17-12 to Minnesota last year. Besides being without Falk, leading receiver Tavares Martin Jr. was kicked off the team after the regular season and third-leading receiver Isaiah Johnson-Mack left the squad. Michigan State's LJ Scott had his third 100-yard game of the season and ninth of his career. Felton had four catches for 118 yards.

2017 BELK BOWL

The 2017 Belk Bowl was played at Bank of America Stadium in Charlotte, North Carolina on December 29, 2017. The game was the 16th edition of the Belk Bowl. The Wake Forest Demon Deacons finished the 2017 regular season with a 7–5 record. The game was the team's second appearance in the bowl; they made their first appearance in 2007, when the game was known as the Meineke Car Care Bowl. The Texas A&M Aggies finished the 2017 regular season with a 7–5 record. The game was the team's first appearance in the bowl. The game was sponsored by department store chain Belk.

2017 Belk Bowl	Line	1	-	2	-	3	-	4	-	Final
Wake Forest	(-3.5)	17	-	21	-	3	-	14	-	55
Texas A&M	(62.0)	14	-	14	-	14	-	10	-	52

Scoring Summary
Texas A&M – Oliver blocked punt return (LaCamera Kick)
Texas A&M – Williams 2 yard run (LaCamera Kick)
Wake Forest – Washington 50 yard pass from Wolford (Weaver Kick)
Wake Forest – Hines 7 yard pass from Wolford (Weaver Kick)
Wake Forest – Weaver 28 yard Field Goal
Wake Forest – Hines 7 yard pass from Wolford (Weaver Kick)
Wake Forest – Bates 59 yard punt return (Weaver Kick)
Texas A&M – Kirk 52 yard pass from Starkel (LaCamera kick)
Wake Forest – Serigne 37 yard pass from Wolford (Weaver Kick)
Texas A&M – Kirk 10 yard pass from Starkel (LaCamera Kick)
Texas A&M – Kirk 19 yard pass from Starkel (LaCamera Kick)
Wake Forest – Weaver 27 yard Field Goal
Texas A&M – Ford 1 yard run (LaCamera Kick)
Texas A&M – LaCamera 19 yard Field Goal
Wake Forest – Carney 1 yard run (Weaver Kick)
Texas A&M – Ausbon 13 yard pass from Starkel (LaCamera Kick)
Wake Forest – Colburn 1 yard run (Weaver Kick)

Associated Press Belk Bowl Game Summary - Wake Forest coach Dave Clawson called it a fitting ending to senior quarterback John Wolford's adversity-filled career -- one where nothing seemed to come easy. The four-year starter who battled through two difficult sack-filled 3-9 seasons to begin his career, threw for 400 yards and four touchdowns to help Wake Forest beat Texas A&M 55-52 in the Belk Bowl on Friday. Clawson said Wolford, who was named the game's Most Valuable Player, deserves every accolade he receives given how he helped put the Wake Forest program back on the map with toughness and tenacity. It was Wake Forest's second straight bowl season with a bowl win and its first eight-win season since 2008. The Demon Deacons won seven games last season. For Texas A&M (7-6), the future now belongs to Jimbo Fisher, who will coach next season. Interim coach Jeff Banks coached the team Friday. The teams combined for 1,260 yards and 107 points, tied for the fourth-highest scoring game in college bowl history. The record is the 2011 GMAC Bowl where Marshall and East Carolina combined for 125 points. Running back Matt Colburn ran for 150 yards and provided the go-ahead score with 2:18 left in the game. Wake Forest's defense stopped the Aggies on downs on their final drive to seal the win, which was no easy task considering Texas A&M's potent offense. Aggies quarterback Nick Starkel threw for a Belk Bowl-record 499 yards and four touchdowns -- three of those to NFL-ready wide receiver Christian Kirk, who caught 13 passes for 189 yards. But Wolford got the win. Scotty Washington had nine catches for 138 yards and a touchdown for the Demon Deacons, while tight end Cam Serigne had nine catches for 112 yards and a score. Tabari Hines added eight receptions for 58 yards and two touchdowns. Clawson said he had a feeling it would be a shootout. Wake Forest spotted Texas A&M (7-6) a 14-point first quarter lead following a pair of special teams miscues but rattled off 31 straight points in a span of 11 minutes, 16 seconds to take a 31-14 lead in the second quarter. Texas A&M battled back to take the lead late in the third quarter behind Starkel and Kirk.

2017 SUN BOWL

The 2017 Sun Bowl was played at Sun Bowl Stadium in El Paso, Texas, on December 29, 2017. The game was the 84th Sun Bowl. The Wolfpack finished the 2017 regular season with an 8–4 record under Coach Dave Dorean; the most wins Dorean has had at his tenure at NC State to date. The game was the team's first appearance in the Sun Bowl, and their second straight bowl win. Shortly after at the NFL draft, the entire NC State defensive line was selected in the first four rounds along with their running back, Nyheim Hines. Arizona State finished the 2017 regular season with a 7–5 record. The game was the team's sixth appearance in the Sun Bowl.

2017 Sun Bowl	Line	1	-	2	-	3	-	4	-	Final
NC State	(-4.5)	7	-	21	-	3	-	21	-	52
Arizona State	(62.0)	0	-	10	-	0	-	21	-	31

Scoring Summary
NC State – Hines 5 yard run (Bambard Kick)
NC State – Hines 5 yard run (Bambard Kick)
Arizona State – Ruiz 24 yard Field Goal
NC State – Hines 5 yard run (Bambard Kick)
Arizona State – Harry 6 yard pass from Wilikins (Ruiz Kick)
NC State – Meyers 25 yard pass from Finley (Bambard Kick)
NC State – Bambard 26 yard Field Goal
NC State – Gallaspy 23 yard run (Bambard Kick)
Arizona State – Wilkins 1 yard run (Ruiz Kick)
Arizona State – Williams 19 yard pass from Wilkins (Ruiz Kick)
NC State – Samuels 2 yard run (Bambard Kick)
Arizona State – Darby 20 yard pass from Wilkins (Ruiz Kick)
NC State – Gallaspy 2 yard run (Bambard Kick)

Associated Press Sun Bowl Game Summary – North Carolina State's offense came up big in a Sun Bowl matchup that was supposed to be about defense. Nyheim Hines had three of North Carolina State's Sun Bowl-record six rushing touchdowns to help the Wolfpack beat Arizona State 52-31 on Friday. Hines' three scoring runs were all from 5 yards. Hines was named the game's MVP. He helped the team score on four of five first-half possessions to fuel the rout. Hines finished with 72 yards on 16 carries for North Carolina State (9-4). The Wolfpack played in their fourth consecutive bowl game and sixth in seven years under Coach David Doeren. Reggie Gallaspy added 79 yards and two touchdowns on 12 carries for the Wolfpack, Ryan Finley completed 24 of 29 passes for 318 yards and a score, and Stephen Louis had three catches for 115 yards. Arizona State (7-6) played its final game under fired coach Todd Graham, with former NFL coach Herm Edwards taking over the program. The Sun Devils had four turnovers. Manny Wilkins was 25 of 40 for 352 yards and three touchdowns for the Sun Devils. He also threw three interceptions. N.C. State played without defensive end Bradley Chubb. Chubb, a projected top-10 pick in the NFL draft, announced before the game that he wouldn't play. It marked the second year in a row that the biggest star at the game didn't play. Last year, Stanford running back Christian McCaffrey skipped it. The 42 points scored in the fourth quarter set a Sun Bowl record for points in a quarter. The 45 points in the second half tied a game record, and the 83 total points was the second most in game history. N.C. State is 17-13-1 in bowl games and won its first appearance in the Sun Bowl. Hines is the first Wolfpack rusher to have consecutive 1,000-yard seasons since 1977-78. Receiver Kelvin Harmon had four catches for 24 yards, pushing him over 1,000 yards for the season. All-purpose back Jaylen Samuels had seven catches for 46 yards, setting the team record for catches in a career. Arizona State is 14-15-1 in bowls and 3-2-1 in the Sun Bowl. Running back Demario Richard had 50 yards to become the first ASU runner with multiple 1,000-yard seasons since 1974-75.

2017 MUSIC CITY BOWL

The 2017 Music City Bowl was played on December 29, 2017, at Nissan Stadium in Nashville, Tennessee. The 20th annual Music City Bowl featured the Northwestern Wildcats (9–3) from the Big Ten Conference and the Kentucky Wildcats (7–5) from the Southeastern Conference (SEC). This was only the second time that Kentucky and Northwestern had played against each other. Their previous match-up was on October 20, 1928, and was won by Northwestern, 7–0.

2017 Music City Bowl	Line	1	-	2	-	3	-	4	-	Final
Kentucky	(51.5)	7	-	7	-	0	-	9	-	23
#20 Northwestern	(-8.0)	3	-	14	-	0	-	7	-	24

Scoring Summary
Kentucky – Snell 3 yard run (MacGinnis Kick)
Northwestern – Kuhbander 33 yard Field goal
Northwestern – Jackson 5 yard run (Kuhbander Kick)
Northwestern – Jackson 2 yard run (Kuhbander Kick)
Kentucky – Johnson 3 yard run (MacGinnis Kick)
Northwestern – Queiro 26 yard interception return (Kuhbander Kick)
Kentucky – MacGinnis 48 yard Field Goal
Kentucky – Johnson 9 yard run (2 pt pass failed)

Associated Press Music City Bowl Game Summary – Go ahead and question Northwestern coach Pat Fitzgerald's decisions to go for it over and over on fourth down, even late in a move that nearly cost the Wildcats dearly. His defense had their coach's back. The Wildcats broke up Kentucky's 2-point conversion, and No. 21 Northwestern held off Kentucky 24-23 on Friday in a Music City Bowl that might be remembered more for injuries, ejections and a wild finish. Justin Jackson ran for 157 yards and two touchdowns as Northwestern (10-3) finished off back-to-back bowl wins in consecutive years for the first time in program history. The Wildcats notched their second 10-win season in three years and third in six under Fitzgerald. The senior class also won its 27th game for the best stretch in more than a decade. Both starting quarterbacks left in the first half with injuries, though Kentucky's Stephen Johnson returned early in the third quarter. Kentucky lost running back Benny Snell Jr. to an ejection for contact with an official early in the second quarter, and Northwestern lost leading tackler and linebacker Paddy Fisher before halftime when he was ejected for targeting. Kentucky (7-6) still had a chance to win after Fitzgerald tried to convert his fifth fourth down of the game only to turn it over for the fourth time on downs -- this time at his own 39 with 2:31 left. Johnson ran for his second TD of the second half with 37 seconds left. Kentucky coach Mark Stoops went for the 2-point conversion rather than play for overtime. Johnson couldn't connect with Tavin Richardson on the pass. That cost Kentucky a chance at its best season since 2007 and a second straight bowl loss. With quarterback Clayton Thorson knocked out early in the second with an injured right knee, Northwestern outran Kentucky 333-65. Safety Kyle Quiero provided the winning margin taking Northwestern's second interception 26 yards for a TD with 7:49 left.

2017 ARIZONA BOWL

The 2017 Arizona Bowl was played on December 29, 2017, at Arizona Stadium in Tucson, Arizona, United States. The third edition of the Arizona Bowl featured the New Mexico State Aggies of the Sun Belt Conference against the Utah State Aggies of the Mountain West Conference. It was the 38th all-time meeting between the schools, with Utah State leading the series 30–7. From 1984 until 2000, and again from 2003 until 2012, New Mexico State and Utah State were members of the same conference, spanning the Big West, Sun Belt and WAC until Utah State joined Mountain West in 2013. This was New Mexico State's fourth bowl game in school history and their first since the 1960 Sun Bowl, which coincidentally saw them play against Utah State; New Mexico State won that game by a score of 20–13. New Mexico State's appearance in this Arizona Bowl snapped their 56-year bowl less streak, which was the longest in all of FBS. This bowl was also New Mexico State's final game as a member of the Sun Belt before going independent for 2018. This was Utah State's first Arizona Bowl. Kickoff was scheduled for 3:30 PM MST and the game aired on CBS Sports Network.

2017 Arizona Bowl	Line	1	-	2	-	3	-	4	-	OT	Final
New Mexico State	(64.0)	10	-	3	-	0	-	7	-	6	26
Utah State	(-5.5)	7	-	6	-	0	-	7	-	0	20

Scoring Summary
New Mexico State – Brown 24 yard Field goal
Utah State – Scarver 96 yard kickoff return (Eberle Kick)
New Mexico State – Huntley 100 yard kickoff return (Brown Kick)
Utah State – Eberle 24 yard Field Goal
New Mexico State – Brown 33 yard Field Goal
Utah State – Eberle 30 yard Field Goal
Utah State – Hunt 1 yard run (Eberle Kick)
New Mexico State – Scott 11 yard pass from Rogers (Brown Kick)
New Mexico State – Rose 21 yard run

Associated Press Arizona Bowl Game Summary – The Arizona Bowl is not typically the type of game where fans storm the field. Certainly not for a team that finished 7-6. But this has been a long, arduous wait for New Mexico State fans. All those losing seasons, all that disappointment, all that time between bowl games. Storm away, Aggies. You've earned it. Larry Rose III scored on a 21-yard run in overtime and New Mexico State won in its first bowl game in 57 years, beating Utah State 26-20 in the Arizona Bowl on Friday night. Utah State (6-7) had the ball first in overtime and Dominik Eberle hit the right upright on a 29-yard field goal attempt, sending a groan through the Utah State crowd. Eberle made 16 for 18 field goals during the regular season but missed three in the Arizona Bowl. New Mexico State won it when Jones burst through a hole on the left side, sending the Aggies and their fans rushing onto the Arizona Stadium field. Jones finished with 142 yards on 16 carries. The third Arizona Bowl started with some early fireworks on special teams. Utah State's Savon Scarver returned a kickoff 96 yards for a touchdown in the first quarter, then New Mexico State's Jason Huntley took the ensuing kickoff 100 yards for a score. The excitement leveled off considerably until LaJuan Hunt scored on a 1-yard run in the fourth quarter, set up by a shanked punt from New Mexico State's Payton Theisler. New Mexico State's Tyler Rogers, held in check most of the game, answered by moving the Aggies on a 69-yard scoring drive, capped by his 11-yard touchdown pass to Jaleel Scott that tied it at 20. A video review overturned the initial call that Scott was out of bounds. Rogers, who was second nationally with 347 yards passing per game during the regular season, threw for 191 yards and touchdown with two interceptions. This was a rematch 57 years in the making. New Mexico State had not been to a bowl game since the 1960 Sun Bowl. The opponent: Utah State. Utah State went to eight bowls after that, including six of the last seven. New Mexico State went into a bowl-less tailspin, finishing with a losing record 44 times since that last bowl game. It had 14 straight losing seasons, including a 0-12 mark in 2005, before winning its final two games this season to finally get back to bowling. The long-awaited rematch turned into the Special Teams Bowl in the first half. New Mexico State's Dylan Brown made two field goals, Eberle made two and missed two, and each team had a kickoff return for a touchdown. After a third quarter of defensive stops and punting, both teams found the end zone to send the game overtime -- and, later, New Mexico State's fans onto the field. Utah State racked up 441 yards of offense and kept Rogers from having a big game but had a rough night on special teams. New Mexico State made its first postseason game in nearly six decades a memorable one by rallying for a victory.

2017 COTTON BOWL

The 2017 Cotton Bowl Classic was played at 7:30 pm CST on December 29, 2017 at AT&T Stadium in Arlington, Texas. The 82nd Cotton Bowl Classic was broadcast on ESPN, ESPN Deportes, ESPN Radio and XM Satellite Radio. Prior to kickoff, the Trojans led the all-time series 13-9-1; the most recent game was on September 12, 2009, where the Trojans defeated the Buckeyes by a score of 18-15, scoring with 1:05 remaining in the game to go ahead to stay. USC had won the last 7 games in the series, with Ohio State's last win coming in the 1974 Rose Bowl. This is the eighth time that the schools met in a bowl game. The previous seven bowl meetings were all in the Rose Bowl, most recently in 1985—a game the Trojans won, 20–17. With the Ohio State victory, the all-time series between the schools now stands at 13-10-1 in favor of USC.

2017 Cotton Bowl	Line	1	-	2	-	3	-	4	-	Final
#8 USC	(65.0)	0	-	7	-	0	-	0	-	7
#5 Ohio State	(-9.5)	7	-	17	-	0	-	0	-	24

Scoring Summary
Ohio State – Barrett 1 yard run (Nuernberger Kick)
Ohio State – Nuernberger 26 yard Field Goal
Ohio State – Webb 23 yard interception return (Nuernberger Kick)
Ohio State – Barrett 28 yard run (Nuernberger Kick)
USC – Jones 1 yard run (McGrath Kick)

Cotton Bowl Classic Game Summary - Whenever conference champions tangle in postseason play it tends to grab attention. And, when the teams involved are Ohio State and USC, it makes for a matchup of mega proportions. These two college football bluebloods made the 83rd Goodyear Cotton Bowl a highly anticipated attraction. Both teams sported identical 11-2 records with lofty national rankings. The Buckeyes checked in at No. 5 in the final College Football Playoff rankings while the Trojans finished up the regular season at No. 8. For the first time, Ohio State and USC clashed in a bowl game outside of their celebrated Rose Bowl skirmishes. The Classic would be their eighth bowl matchup against one another and their 24th meeting overall with USC holding a 13- 10-1 advantage in the series. The Trojans had recorded seven consecutive victories over the Buckeyes, a streak that spanned 44 years. While the Trojans held the historical edge, Ohio State came to North Texas with something to prove. The Buckeyes had barely missed landing a berth in the national semifinals. And, it was J.T. Barrett, OSU's brilliant senior quarterback, who seized the moment offensively. Playing in his final collegiate game and just two hours away from his hometown of Wichita Falls, Barrett rushed for two touchdowns and threw for 114 yards to lead the Buckeyes to a compelling victory over USC. The Buckeye defense took control less than two minutes into the game. USC quarterback Sam Darnold had just connected with standout receiver Deontay Burnett for 16 yards and an apparent first down. That's when cornerback Kendall Sheffield unloaded on Burnett to force a fumble. Safety Damon Webb scooped up the loose football and rambled 20 yards to the USC 19. It was the first of four costly turnovers for the Trojans and the Buckeyes were quick to capitalize. A nine-yard pass to Marcus Baugh moved OSU to the USC six, and freshman running back J.K. Dobbins carried for five more yards to the one. Barrett then cashed in for the touchdown to give Ohio State an early 7-0 lead with 12:25 on the clock. Soon, the Buckeyes were on the move again. A USC punt pinned the Buckeyes on their eight-yard line. But, a key third-down pass from Barrett to receiver Austin Mack covered 33 yards and gave Ohio State room to breathe at the Buckeye 43. Barrett and Mack hooked up again two plays later for a 15-yard gain to the USC 40. The drive eventually stalled just inside the Trojan 10 as the opening period came to an end. On the first play of the second quarter, in came junior placekicker Sean Nuernberger to boot a 26-yard field goal and push the Buckeyes to a 10-0 advantage. More fireworks erupted seconds later when Webb picked off Darnold on a first down pass and sprinted 23 yards to the end zone to pad the Ohio State lead at 17-0. The Buckeyes' final score came on the heels of yet another fumble when Darnold was sacked by defensive end Tyquan Lewis after the Trojans marched 65 yards from their own 12 to the Ohio State 23. Linebacker Jerome Baker grabbed the loose ball and ran 13 yards before being hauled down at the Buckeyes' 41. Barrett passed for 16 yards to Mike Weber out of the backfield to move inside USC territory and a facemask penalty tacked 15 more yards onto the play. The Buckeyes were back in scoring position at the 28. After calling timeout with 5:36 left to play in the half, Barrett raced 28 yards for his second touchdown of the game and Ohio State was well in command, 24-0. USC finally got untracked with the recovery of a fumbled punt return at the Buckeye 15. Darnold, the first Trojan quarterback in history to pass for more than 4,000 yards in a single season, jumped on the turnover and fired a pass to tight end Daniel Imatorbhebhe at the one. Two plays later, tailback Ronald Jones scored to trim the Buckeye lead to 24-7. USC fought back and played well in the second half, but by that point the damage had been done. Ohio State's suffocating defense continued to harass Darnold. USC mounted one last drive in the game's final seven minutes only to see it stall at the Ohio State 18 with just 31 seconds to play. Three years earlier, Ohio State had defeated Oregon 42-20 at AT&T Stadium to claim the first national title of the College Football Playoff era. Now, the Buckeyes added the Field Scovell Trophy to their collection and left Arlington with a resounding 24-7 victory over a longtime rival.

2017 GATOR BOWL

The 2017 TaxSlayer Bowl was played on December 31, 2017, at EverBank Field in Jacksonville, Florida. The 73rd edition of the Gator Bowl featured the Louisville Cardinals of the Atlantic Coast Conference against the Mississippi State Bulldogs of the Southeastern Conference.

2017 Taxslayer Gator Bowl	Line	1	-	2	-	3	-	4	-	Final
Louisville	(-6.5)	7	-	14	-	3	-	3	-	27
#24 Mississippi State	(60.5)	14	-	3	-	0	-	14	-	31

Scoring Summary
Mississippi State – Williams 5 yard run (Christman Kick)
Louisville – Standberry 5 yard pass from Jackson (Creque Kick)
Mississippi State – Thompson 14 yard run (Christman Kick)
Louisville – Jackson 13 yard run (Creque Kick)
Mississippi State – Christman 23 yard Field Goal
Louisville – Smith 11 yard pass from Jackson (Creque Kick)
Louisville – Creque 23 yard Field Goal
Mississippi State – Thompson 2 yard run (Christman Kick)
Louisville – Creque 31 yard Field Goal
Mississippi State – Thompson 1 yard run (Christman Kick)

Hailstate.com Gator Bowl Game Summary: Closing out the 2017 season, Mississippi State (9-4, 4-4 SEC) defeated Louisville (8-5, 4-4 ACC) 31-27 in the TaxSlayer Bowl Saturday at EverBank Field. Coached by an interim staff led by Greg Knox, the Bulldogs put on an impressive display in all facets of the game, highlighted by big plays on each side of the ball. With the win, the Bulldogs registered their third-consecutive bowl triumph while also improving to 13-8 all-time in bowl games. The Cardinals fell to 11-11 in bowl appearances. With junior quarterback Nick Fitzgerald out with an ankle injury, true freshman Keytaon Thompson made his first-ever start at quarterback and put on a record-breaking performance in the win. Thompson finished 11-of-20 passing for 127 yards and one interception, while also rushing 27 times for 147 yards and three touchdowns. Ultimately, MSU racked up 404 yards of offense behind Thompson's leadership. Junior safety Mark McLaurin was named the TaxSlayer Bowl MVP after recording three interceptions on the day, contributing to four total picks the Bulldogs had in the game. MSU also recorded six pass break-ups and six sacks, capping a strong day by the defense. UL led 21-17 at halftime and 24-17 through three quarters, but State rallied to outscore Louisville 14-3 in the final period on the strength of two of Thompson's three rushing touchdowns as well as two of McLaurin's three interceptions.

2017 LIBERTY BOWL

The 2017 Liberty Bowl was played on December 30, 2017, at Liberty Bowl Memorial Stadium in Memphis, Tennessee. The 59th edition of the Liberty Bowl featured the Iowa State Cyclones against the Memphis Tigers. This is the third Liberty Bowl for Iowa State, having previously played in the 1972 and 2012 editions of the game.

2017 Liberty Bowl	Line	1	-	2	-	3	-	4	-	Final
Iowa State	(67.5)	7	-	7	-	7	-	0	-	21
#18 Memphis	(-3.5)	7	-	3	-	10	-	0	-	20

Scoring Summary
Iowa State – Butler 52 yard pass from Kempt (Owens Kick)
Memphis – Miller 10 yard pass from Moser (Patterson Kick)
Iowa State – Lanning 2 yard run (Owens Kick)
Memphis – Patterson 34 yard Field Goal
Memphis – Mayhue 36 yard pass from Ferguson (Patterson Kick)
Iowa State – Lazard 5 yard pass from Kempt (Owens Kick)
Memphis – Patterson 30 yard Field Goal

Associated Press Liberty Bowl Game Summary – Iowa State proved its season-long bid to raise its standards was more than just a slogan. Allen Lazard tied a Liberty Bowl record with 10 catches and put Iowa State ahead with a remarkable 5-yard touchdown reception in the third quarter Saturday, and the Cyclones beat No. 19 Memphis 21-20 on the Tigers' home field. The victory gave Iowa State (8-5) its first bowl victory since a 2009 Insight Bowl triumph and marked the Cyclones' third win over a Top 25 team this season. That's the step forward Iowa State had in mind when it made "Raise The Standard" its team motto. Iowa State's progress was evident in the way it held on to win after its only lost fumble of the season. Iowa State was attempting to become the first Football Bowl Subdivision team to go an entire season without losing a fumble. The Cyclones led 21-20 and had third-and-goal from the 1 when David Montgomery fumbled as he was crossing the goal line. As replay officials reviewed the play, Campbell told his players he hoped the call wasn't overturned because it would enable the Cyclones to show how they'd matured since a heartbreaking 20-19 loss to Kansas State in their regular-season finale. Memphis (10-3) drove to the Iowa State 40 but lost the ball when Riley Ferguson overthrew Phil Mayhue on fourth-and-10 with 1:52 remaining. Iowa State ran out the clock from there. Iowa State pulled ahead 21-17 with 4:28 left in the third quarter when Kyle Kempt's pass appeared to get deflected just before Lazard caught it in the back of the end zone. The touchdown came after a roughing-the-passer penalty on Genard Avery wiped out an interception by Memphis' Curtis Akins and gave the Cyclones first-and-goal. Lazard had 142 yards receiving in his final college game and was named the Liberty Bowl's most valuable player. The only other players to catch 10 passes in a Liberty Bowl were Louisville's Deion Branch in 2000 and Arkansas' Bobby Joe Edmonds in 1984. Memphis had the benefit of playing a bowl game on its home field -- where it hadn't lost all season -- although enough Iowa State fans traveled to the game to make the sellout crowd of 57,266 an even split. Lazard's 10th touchdown catch of the season set an Iowa State record. Memphis' Anthony Miller had four catches for 55 yards and a touchdown to end the year with 96 catches for 1,462 yards, breaking his own school single-season records in both categories.

2017 FIESTA BOWL

The 2017 Fiesta Bowl was played on December 30, 2017, at University of Phoenix Stadium in Glendale, Arizona. The 47th Fiesta Bowl was televised on ESPN and ESPN Deportes, and broadcast on ESPN Radio and XM Satellite Radio, with the kickoff set for 4:00 PM ET (2 PM MT). The Nittany Lions entered the game with a 10–2 record, with their two losses coming in conference play in consecutive weeks by a combined four points at #6 Ohio State and at #24 Michigan State. The Huskies finished the season 10–3, 7–2 in Pac-12 play to win a share of the North Division title with Stanford. Due to their head-to-head loss to Stanford, they did not represent the North Division in the Pac-12 Championship Game. This was only the third time that Penn State and Washington played each other, and the Nittany Lions had won both previous meetings. The most recent game was 34 years earlier in Honolulu at the 1983 Aloha Bowl, where Penn State defeated the Huskies13–10. The first meeting was in 1921, where Penn State defeated the Washington Sun Dodgers 21–7 on December 3 in Seattle. The Nittany Lions had appeared in six previous Fiesta Bowls: 1977, 1980, 1982, 1987, 1992, and 1997, winning all six. This was the Huskies' first Fiesta Bowl appearance.

2017 Fiesta Bowl	Line	1	-	2	-	3	-	4	-	Final
#12 Washington	(54.5)	0	-	14	-	7	-	7	-	28
#9 Penn State	(-3.0)	14	-	14	-	7	-	0	-	35

Scoring Summary
Penn State – Hamilton 48 yard pass from McSorley (Davis Kick)
Penn State – Barkley 2 yard run (Davis Kick)
Washington – Browning 1 yard run (Vizcaino Kick)
Penn State – Sanders 1 yard run (Davis Kick)
Penn State – Barkley 92 yard run (Davis Kick)
Washington – Gaskin 13 yard run (Vizcaino Kick)
Washington – Fuller 28 yard pass from Browning (Vizcaino Kick)
Penn State – Hamilton 24 yard pass from McSorley (Davis Kick)
Washington – Gaskin 69 yard run (Vizcaino Kick)

GoPSUSports.com Fiesta Bowl Game Summary - Penn State quarterback Trace McSorley eclipsed 400 yards of total offense and became the school's all-time bowl game passing leader to lead the No. 9 Nittany Lions past No. 11 Washington (10-3), 35-28, in the 2017 PlayStation Fiesta Bowl Saturday in University of Phoenix Stadium. Penn State improved to 7-0 all-time in the Fiesta Bowl to finish the 2017 season 11-2. It marks the first time since the 2008 and 2009 seasons that the Nittany Lions posted back-to-back 11-win seasons. McSorley led a Penn State offense that totaled a program bowl-record 545 yards of offense, as he completed 32-of-42 passes for 342 yards and two touchdowns, while rushing 12 times for 60 yards. McSorley was particularly strong on third downs, completing 12-of-12 passing attempts for 194 yards and two touchdowns, resulting in 11 of Penn State's 13 third down conversions - its most since 2008. McSorley completed passes to nine different receivers, with DaeSean Hamilton catching five passes for 110 yards and two touchdowns to lead the group. McSorley was named the game's offensive MVP, while safety Marcus Allen was named the defensive MVP. Allen had a team-high six solo tackles and tied for the team lead with seven total tackles. Running back Saquon Barkley also had a record-breaking performance, setting a Fiesta Bowl and Penn State bowl record with a 92-yard touchdown run, also tying Penn State's all-time longest run record. He finished with 137 yards rushing and two touchdowns, while also catching a team-high seven receptions and totaling 38 yards receiving. Penn State led the game from its opening possession until the end, with Washington getting no closer than a touchdown. The Nittany Lions' 35 points scored snapped a 26-game streak of holding opponents to less than 30 points. Washington entered the game with the leading FBS rushing defense at 92.3 yards per game and had allowed just one play of more than 40 yards this season, however Penn State rushed for 203 yards and had two plays go for more than 40 yards. The Nittany Lions possessed the ball for nearly 10-and-a-half minutes in the first quarter, as quarterback Trace McSorley went 11-for-15 passing for 121 yards and a touchdown and was also the leading rusher with 26 yards. Barkley added 23 yards on the ground with a touchdown and also caught two passes for 12 yards.
Penn State received the opening kickoff and was first on the scoreboard, as McSorley completed a 48-yard touchdown pass to DaeSean Hamilton on the opening drive. Washington was poised to force a three-and-out initially, but Barkley kept the drive alive with a 12-yard reception on third-and-10. Penn State's defense did force a three-and-out on its first action on the field to get the offense back on the field. The Nittany Lions passed midfield on a 17-yard completion to Gesicki, but McSorley was intercepted going to Gesicki on a deep pass to the back of the end zone by Byron Murphy. Penn State forced another three-and-out on defense as Tyrell Chavis sacked Browning on third-and-11, leading to an 11-play, 64-yard Penn State touchdown drive capped by a 2-yard Barkley touchdown run. The Lions faced just one third down before reaching the red zone and converted it as DaeSean Hamilton hauled in a 9-yard reception at the Washington 40-yard line. The very next play, McSorley connected with Saeed Blacknall for 20 yards to the Washington 20, and then Barkley rushed for 8 yards to the 12. On third-and-goal from the 2, Barkley punched through the left side of the line for the touchdown. Washington's first first down came on a roughing the passer penalty on its ensuing possession, and it took advantage by following with a trick play, as wide receiver Andre Baccellia tossed a 52-yard pass to Will Dissly down to the Penn State 12. On the first play of the second quarter, Jake Browning called his own number for a 1-yard touchdown sneak.
Browning's touchdown run opened the quarter and pulled Washington within a touchdown, but the Nittany Lions responded with another touchdown drive. A 26-yard completion to Gesicki moved Penn State to midfield, and an 11-yard completion to Juwan Johnson advanced the Lions to the Washington 35. After an incompletion, McSorley found DeAndre Thompkins at the 1-yard line, setting up a 1-yard touchdown run for Miles Sanders. Washington gained one first down after the kickoff, but a sack by Kevin Givens and Parker Cothren for a loss of 10 resulted in a four-play drive and punt. It then took just two plays

for Penn State to score again, as Barkley broke free for a 92-yard touchdown run, tying Penn State's longest run record and breaking both the Penn State bowl and the Fiesta Bowl records, both previously held by Chafie Fields (84 yds, 1997). Penn State forced Washington's third three-and-out and earned strong field position at its own 40 after a punt, but a fumble on a backwards pitch on the first play of the new drive was recovered by Washington's Ryan Bowman. It took the Huskies six plays to find the end zone, as Myles Gaskin found a hole for a 13-yard touchdown run. Barkley finished the half with two touchdowns and 126 yards rushing on nine carries, while McSorley completed 18-of-24 passes for 219 yards and a touchdown. Washington received the kickoff to open the second half and used tempo to rattle off 13 plays in 4 minutes, 59 seconds on an 80-yard touchdown drive. Browning threw a 28-yard touchdown pass to Aaron Fuller to pull the Huskies back within a touchdown at 28-21. Penn State answered with an eight-play, 70-yard touchdown drive that was ignited by a 24-yard McSorley run and capped with a 24-yard touchdown toss to DaeSean Hamilton with 5:59 remaining in the quarter. A Shareef Miller sack on third down forced another Washington three-and-out and put Penn State's offense back on the field to finish out the quarter. Over the end of the third quarter and start of the fourth quarter, Penn State drove 53 yards on 13 plays to the Washington 18, but a McSorley pass was deflected by Ben Burr-Kirven and intercepted by Austin Joyner at the 19. Both teams traded punts, and then Gaskin rushed 69 yards for a touchdown to bring Washington within a touchdown at 35-28 with 6:52 to go. Penn State was able to bleed the clock down to 38 seconds with 13 plays, converting three third downs before Barkley was stopped 1 yard short on third-and-2. A false start penalty then moved the Lions back to the UW 28 on fourth down, and a Tyler Davis 45-yard field goal attempt missed wide right, giving the Huskies the ball back with 34 seconds remaining. However, the Nittany Lions forced three incompletions, forcing a desperation lateral play on fourth down with just a few seconds remaining, and Brandon Smith recovered the loose ball to ice the win.

2017 ORANGE BOWL

The 2017 Orange Bowl was played on December 30, 2017 at the Hard Rock Stadium in Miami Gardens, Florida. The contest was televised on ESPN with a radio broadcast on ESPN Radio, kickoff was at 8:00 PM (EST). The 84th Orange Bowl, the game was sponsored by the Capital One financial services organization and was officially known as the Capital One Orange Bowl. Prior to kickoff, the all-time series between the two teams was tied at 2 games apiece; the most recent meeting being at the 2009 Champs Sports Bowl, where the Badgers defeated the Hurricanes by a score of 20–14.

2017 Orange Bowl	Line	1	-	2	-	3	-	4	-	Final
#6 Wisconsin	(-6.5)	3	-	21	-	3	-	7	-	34
#11 Miami	(45.5)	14	-	0	-	7	-	3	-	24

Scoring Summary
Wisconsin – Gaglianone 35 yard Field Goal
Miami – Homer 5 yard run (Badgley Kick)
Miami – Dallas 39 yard run (Badgley Kick)
Wisconsin – Davis 20 yard pass from Hornibrook (Gaglianone Kick)
Wisconsin – Taylor 16 yard pass from Hornibrook (Gaglianone Kick)
Wisconsin – Davis 5 yard pass from Hornibrook (Gaglianone Kick)
Miami – Cager 38 yard pass from Rosier (Badgley Kick)
Wisconsin – Gaglianone 47 yard Field goal
Miami – Badgley 41 yard Field goal
Wisconsin – Davis 6 yard pass from Hornibrook (Gaglianone Kick)

Associated Press Orange Bowl Game Summary – Alex Hornibrook threw four touchdown passes, three of them to Danny Davis, and No. 6 Wisconsin ended a season with the most wins in program history with a victory over No. 11 Miami, 34-24, in the Orange Bowl on Saturday night in Miami Gardens, Fla. Jonathan Taylor finished his record-setting freshman season with 130 rushing yards on 26 carries for the Badgers (13-1), who rallied from an early 14-3 deficit. Taylor finished the year with 1,977 yards, a Football Bowl Subdivision record for a freshman. A. J. Taylor also had a scoring catch for Wisconsin and mimicked ripping Miami's "Turnover Chain" off the neck of his teammate Kendric Pryor. The Badgers dominated time of possession, holding the ball for nearly 40 minutes. Hornibrook completed 23 of 34 passes for 258 yards, going 20 for 25 in the final three quarters. Travis Homer and Deejay Dallas had rushing scores for Miami, which was in the Orange Bowl for the 10th time and lost on its home field for the first time in 2017. Lawrence Cager had a touchdown catch for the Hurricanes, while quarterback Malik Rosier was 11 for 26 passing for 203 yards — with three interceptions. The Hurricanes had a chance to get within a touchdown midway through the fourth, but Michael Badgley's chip-shot field goal went off the right upright. By the time the Hurricanes got the ball back, most of their fans were gone and only 1 minute 37 seconds remained. Rosier was picked off for a third time 18 seconds later, and the Badgers ran out the clock. The Big Ten is 7-0 in bowls this season.

2018 OUTBACK BOWL

The 2018 Outback Bowl was played on January 1, 2018, at Raymond James Stadium in Tampa, Florida. The 32nd annual Outback Bowl was nationally televised on ESPN2, and its title sponsor is the Outback Steakhouse restaurant franchise. After finishing their regular season with an 8–4 record, the Wolverines were selected to their sixth Outback Bowl appearance, the most Outback Bowl appearances by any team. This was their 46th bowl game appearance, the 11th-highest total all-time among FBS schools. After finishing their regular season with an 8–4 record, the Gamecocks were selected to their fifth Outback Bowl appearance, tying them with four other teams for the second-most Outback Bowl appearances. This was their 22nd bowl game appearance. South Carolina won the previous meeting against the Michigan Wolverines in the 2013 Outback Bowl, by a score of 33–28.

2018 Outback Bowl	Line	1	-	2	-	3	-	4	-	Final
Michigan	(-9.0)	6	-	3	-	10	-	0	-	19
South Carolina	(41.5)	0	-	3	-	13	-	10	-	26

Scoring Summary
Michigan – Nordin 35 yard Field Goal
Michigan – Nordin 26 yard Field Goal
South Carolina – White 45 yard Field goal
Michigan – Nordin 45 yard Field Goal
Michigan – Mason 1 yard run (Nordin Kick)
Michigan – Nordin 48 yard Field Goal
South Carolina – Dowdle 18 yard pass from Bentley (2 pt conversion no good)
South Carolina – Edwards 21 yard pass from Bentley (White Kick)
South Carolina – Smith 53 yard pass from Bentley (White Kick)
South Carolina – White 22 yard Field Goal

Associated Press Outback Bowl Game Summary – Will Muschamp envisions championships in South Carolina's future. Lots of them. Jake Bentley threw for 239 yards and two touchdowns Monday to pace the win, which gave the Gamecocks (9-4) at least nine wins in a season for just the seventh time. Bentley shrugged off a slow start to toss scoring passes of 21 yards to Bryan Edwards and 53 yards to Shi Smith, the latter giving his team a 23-19 lead early in the fourth quarter. The sophomore said once the Gamecocks began to have some success, the offense's confidence grew. Michigan (8-5) finished with its first three-game losing streak under Coach Jim Harbaugh. The Wolverines turned the ball over five times after halftime, including an end zone interception that denied them an opportunity to regain the lead with just under eight minutes to go. The loss also cost the Big Ten a clean sweep of bowl games involving conference members. The league entered 7-0, looking to go unbeaten in postseason play for the first time since 1998 when it went 5-0. Bentley was 19 of 32 passing with one interception. Rico Dowdle, playing for first time since breaking his leg against Tennessee on Oct. 14, began South Carolina's comeback from a 19-3 deficit with a 17-yard TD run. Brandon Peters had a tough day for Michigan, completing 20 of 44 passes for 186 yards and two interceptions. His second pick, with 1:05 remaining, sealed South Carolina's second Outback Bowl victory over the Wolverines in five years. Quinn Nordin accounted for most of Michigan's scoring, kicking field goals of 35, 26, 45 and 48 yards. Fullback Ben Mason scored on a 1-yard run in helping Michigan build its 16-point lead. Peters, who returned to the lineup after missing the regular-season finale against Ohio State with a concussion, was hoping to make it more difficult for Harbaugh to replace him next season -- even if Shea Patterson is one of coach's options. Patterson plans to transfer to Michigan from Mississippi, a program hit with sanctions, and to petition the NCAA to allow him to be immediately eligible. South Carolina leads the all-time series between the team 3-1, including a 33-28 victory in the 2013 Outback Bowl. Michigan's lone win came in 1985.

2018 CHICK-FIL-A PEACH BOWL

The 2018 Peach Bowl was played on January 1, 2018, between the UCF Knights and the Auburn Tigers. It was the 50th edition of the Peach Bowl, and the first Peach Bowl to be played in Mercedes-Benz Stadium, after spending the previous 25 editions in the now demolished Georgia Dome. The game was televised on ESPN and ESPN Deportes, and broadcast on ESPN Radio and XM Satellite Radio. Entering the game, the Tigers led the all-time series with the Knights, 3–0; the most recent matchup saw the Tigers defeat the Golden Knights (as the Knights were then known as) by a score of 28–10 on November 6, 1999, in Auburn. McKenzie Milton had a breakout game for the UCF Knights with 245 passing yards throwing for two touchdowns and a rushing touchdown. Jarrett Stidham had 331 passing yards throwing for one touchdown with two interceptions. UCF had 411 total yards compared to Auburn Tigers 421 total yards. However, the Tigers had three turnovers with Knights only having one. Shaquem Griffin had 12 tackles and one and a half sacks in the win for the Knights. Griffin was later named the game's defensive MVP, with Milton the offensive MVP.

2018 Chick-Fil-A Peach Bowl	Line	1	-	2	-	3	-	4	-	Final
#10 Central Florida	(66.0)	0	-	13	-	7	-	14	-	34
#7 Auburn	(-10.5)	3	-	3	-	14	-	7	-	27

Scoring Summary
Auburn – Carlson 25 yard Field Goal
Central Florida – Wright 33 yard Field Goal
Central Florida – Milton 18 yard run (Wright Kick)
Auburn – Carlson 45 yard Field Goal
Central Florida – Wright 45 yard Field Goal
Auburn – Hastings 26 yard pass from Stidham (Carlson Kick)
Auburn – Johnson 4 yard run (Carlson Kick)
Central Florida – Anderson 12 yard pass from Milton (Wright Kick)
Central Florida – Snelson 8 yard pass from Milton (Wright Kick)
Central Florida – Burkett 75 yard interception return (Wright Kick)
Auburn – Stove 7 yard run (Carlson Kick)

Associated Press Chick-Fil-A Peach Bowl Game Summary – McKenzie Milton wanted to throw a blanket of 13 wins and no losses over the College Football Playoff. After Milton and Central Florida capped a perfect season, he suggested it was time to respect the Knights, even if they weren't invited to the playoff. Milton threw two touchdown passes and ran for 116 yards with another touchdown, leading No. 10 UCF to a 34-27 Peach Bowl win over No. 7 Auburn on Monday. UCF (13-0) led 34-20 before having to stop a late Auburn comeback. Antwan Collier's interception in the end zone with 24 seconds remaining clinched the win. The UCF players launched a joyous postgame celebration, rolling around in confetti on the field while wearing T-shirts that read 'Champions.' The Knights won in their final game with Coach Scott Frost, who stayed with the team through the bowl game after accepting an offer to become the new coach at Nebraska, his alma mater. Frost will bring most of his UCF assistants to Nebraska. The Knights thought they deserved a higher ranking after winning the American Athletic Conference and leading the nation in scoring. They made a strong statement by beating Auburn (10-4). Auburn was held to 90 yards rushing on 44 carries. More dominance: The Knights sacked Jarrett Stidham six times. Auburn had only one sack. After Auburn took a 20-13 lead in the third quarter on a 4-yard run by Kerryon Johnson, Milton threw a 12-yard touchdown pass to Otis Anderson to tie the game. Milton, under pressure, zipped an 8-yard scoring pass to Dredrick Snelson early in the fourth to give the Knights the lead. Chequan Burkett's 45-yard interception return for a touchdown pushed the lead to 14 points. Auburn suffered its second straight loss at Mercedes-Benz Stadium, where it was beaten by Georgia in the Southeastern Conference championship game one month ago. Johnson, who said he was almost fully recovered from a late-season shoulder injury, ran for 71 yards. UCF led 13-6 at halftime despite being held under 14 points at the break for the first time this season. Frost lofted the football-shaped Chick-fil-A Peach Bowl trophy before passing it on to his players. Milton was named offensive MVP. Shaquem Griffin, who had 12 tackles including 1 1/2 sacks, was defensive MVP. The Knights passed every test, including on the line of scrimmage, as they proved they could match speed and strength with the Tigers. Milton overcame a slow start after completing only 3 of 17 passes for 30 yards in the first half. He completed 16 of 35 passes for 242 yards with two touchdowns and no interceptions. The Tigers couldn't maintain momentum after opening the second half with two touchdowns for a 20-13 lead. Stidham completed 28 of 43 passes for 331 yards with one touchdown and two interceptions.

2018 CITRUS BOWL

The 2018 Citrus Bowl was played on January 1, 2018, at Camping World Stadium in Orlando, Florida. This was the 72nd edition of a game that has been played annually since 1946, under several different names. The game was nationally televised on ABC. Notre Dame, making their first appearance in the Citrus Bowl, was the designated visiting team. LSU, the designated home team, appeared in the game for the second season in a row, and fifth time overall. For the second year in a row, no Big Ten team appeared in the Citrus Bowl; since Wisconsin committed to the Orange Bowl, the Citrus Bowl was allowed to pick Notre Dame or an Atlantic Coast Conference team. This was the fourth bowl meeting between the Fighting Irish and Tigers, with LSU winning twice previously, and Notre Dame once. LSU prevailed 27–9 in the 1997 Independence Bowl, and 41–14 in the 2007 Sugar Bowl, and Notre Dame won 31–28 in the 2014 Music City Bowl. Notre Dame and LSU met eight times in the regular season between 1970 and 1998, with the Irish holding a 5–3 edge.

2018 Citrus Bowl	Line	1	-	2	-	3	-	4	-	Final
#14 Notre Dame	(53.0)	0	-	3	-	3	-	15	-	21
#17 LSU	(-2.0)	0	-	0	-	7	-	10	-	17

Scoring Summary
Notre Dame – Yoon 46 yard Field Goal
LSU – Guice 20 yard pass from Etling (Gonsoulin Kick)
Notre Dame – Yoon 49 yard Field Goal
LSU – Guice 2 yard pass from Etling (Gonsoulin Kick)
Notre Dame – Young 6 yard pass from Book (2 pt pass good)
LSU – Gonsoulin 17 yard Field Goal
Notre Dame – Boykin 55 yard pass from Book (Yoon Kick)

UND.com Citrus Bowl Game Summary — Notre Dame Football coach Brian Kelly talks all the time about playing for 60 minutes. He talks about how, in a tight game, it comes down to somebody having to make a play. So, when the Irish and LSU, two 9-3 football teams ranked three slots apart in the final College Football Playoff standings, took the field Monday afternoon at Camping World Stadium, maybe it shouldn't have come as any surprise that it came down to who made the late-game plays. Though even the most ardent Irish supporters might not have predicted that it would be reserve quarterback Ian Book and backup-turned starter receiver Miles Boykin hooking up for the game-winning Notre Dame Touchdown pass with 88 seconds to go. Kelly told Boykin a few days ago during practice that Boykin would end up being the Citrus Bowl MVP. So, play hard for 60 minutes and good things will happen? Boykin as the MVP? Turns out Kelly was right on both accounts. And on an unlikely Florida weather day that better resembled a November Saturday in South Bend, the Irish did just enough to defeat LSU 21-17. In the Notre Dame team's mental edge session just before the squad left its team hotel Monday morning, Kelly made certain his players didn't forget what they did in 2017. Kelly also pointed out Wisconsin's stick-to-it resolve in the Orange Bowl Saturday night against Miami. Then the Irish watched the high points of their regular season, all set to "Ready or Not" by the Fugees. Most of the early going proved a defensive slog. There were five combined first-period punts, and three times in a row the Irish began drives at their own 13-yard line or worse. The first 10 possessions combined produced seven punts, two missed field goals (both by LSU) and one possession that ended on downs (Notre Dame's first). Notre Dame finally broke through with a 46-yard Justin Yoon field goal with four seconds until halftime. Book was sacked three times on the drive, but he also completed three of his four passes for 33 yards and had another big third-down conversion run of 21 yards. Meanwhile the first of the two LSU missed field goals came after the Tigers had second and goal at the Irish one and twice were turned away. A steady, misty drizzle prompted two muffed attempted punt returns by LSU and another muff on a long snap on a Tiger punt. The Irish wasted a nifty three-and-out defensive effort on LSU's opening possession of the third period, only to see the Tiger punt bounce off a Notre Dame defender's leg. From there LSU drove 43 yards, the last 20 on a Danny Etling throw to Derrius Guice for the first touchdown of the day. Book threw an interception at the LSU 11, then the Irish defense responded with a third-down sack of Etling. Yoon helped by adding another field goal, this one from 49 yards, to make it 7-6 at the end of three periods. Remember those first 10 possessions that produced no points? Yoon's second field goal began a streak of five consecutive combined possessions that turned into three touchdowns and a pair of three-pointers. LSU drove 75 yards on 12 plays, with another Etling-to-Guice TD pass making it 14-6. Notre Dame came right back with its own 75-yard march (10 plays). A Dexter Williams 31-yard run kick-started the drive, Book threw to Boykin for 29 and then he finished it with a six-yard TD throw to Michael Young. The Irish went for two, with Book flipping a shovel pass to Josh Adams. The officials called it short, but review reversed the call and made it a 14-14 game with 7:49 left. LSU looked like it might have broken Notre Dame's back with a 76-yard, 12-play drive that knocked 5:46 off the clock. But the Irish defense again saved the day at the goal line, with a third-down completion from Etling to Guice coming barely short of the goal. The Tiger field goal made it a 17-14 LSU lead at 2:03. Book went to work, finding Chris Finke over the middle for 18 yards. Then came the play of the day. Book fired it deep along the LSU sideline toward Boykin in a spot where only Boykin had a chance to catch it. Boykin somehow hauled it in with one hand and maneuvered deftly past and through two LSU defenders for 55 yards to score with 1:28 remaining. Notre Dame's pass defense then came up impressively, forcing incompletions on all six of Etling's passes — with Julian Love making a pair of break-ups. The Irish survived despite running 14 fewer plays and losing the time of possession competition 37:32 to 22:28. Once Book replaced Brandon Wimbush, he connected on 14 of his 19 throws for 164 yards and the pair of TDs. He also ran it for 36 yards. Kelly pointed out Yoon (his field goals kept the Tigers from separating), linebacker Te'von Coney (he had seven solo tackles and 10 assists) and Young (the freshman had his first TD catch). And there were plenty more. If the Irish had lost the Citrus Bowl, Kelly wasn't about to let a single game eliminate all the progress and good things his players achieved in 2017. But he's been around long enough to understand how much perception counts. The Irish bounced back from two losses in their last three regular-season games to defeat a team from the vaunted Southeastern Conference and win a New Year's Day bowl game for the first time in a while. The Irish (10-3) spent the late afternoon in Orlando flipping oranges to each other as they fell out of the winning bowl trophy. That's because they are Citrus Bowl champions on a day when every one of those inches counted.

2018 ROSE BOWL (National Semifinal)

The 2018 Rose Bowl was played on January 1, 2018 at the Rose Bowl stadium in Pasadena, California. The 104th Rose Bowl Game was a semifinal for the College Football Playoff (CFP), matching two of the top four teams selected by the system's selection committee. Georgia and Oklahoma competed for a spot at the 2018 College Football Playoff National Championship game, to be played on January 8, 2018, at Mercedes-Benz Stadium in Atlanta, Georgia. The game lasted four hours and five minutes. With 26.8 million viewers on ESPN, the game ranked as the fifth most-viewed cable program of all time. The game was televised on ESPN and ESPN Deportes, and broadcast on ESPN Radio and XM Satellite Radio, with the kickoff at 5 p.m. ET (2 p.m. local time). The Pasadena Tournament of Roses Association organized the game.

In the 2018 Rose Bowl, This was the first meeting between the University of Georgia and the University of Oklahoma football teams. Traditionally, the Rose Bowl pits the winners of the Big Ten Conference and Pac-12 Conference. However, any teams may be selected every three years, when the Rose Bowl is a CFP semifinal. The Big 12 and SEC champions traditionally meet in the Sugar Bowl. The 2018 Sugar Bowl was used as the other semifinal this year, allowing any team to be selected. Georgia won their only previous Rose Bowl appearance when their 1942 team, which claims a national championship, beat the Pacific Coast Conference (predecessor to the Pac-12) champion UCLA 9–0 in 1943, a matchup which occurred prior to the Big Nine-PCC agreement. Oklahoma won their only previous Rose Bowl appearance when their 2002 team beat the then Pac-10 champion Washington State 34–14 in 2003, a matchup which occurred since Big Ten champion Ohio State was selected for the Fiesta Bowl, which was being used as that year's BCS National Championship Game, and Oklahoma was selected to replace them.

2018 Rose Bowl	Line	1	2	3	4	OT	2OT	Final
#3 Georgia	(-2.5)	7	10	14	14	3	6	54
#2 Oklahoma	(62.5)	14	17	0	14	3	0	48

Scoring Summary
Oklahoma – Brown 13 yard pass from Mayfield (Seibert Kick)
Georgia – Michel 13 yard pass from Fromm (Blankenship Kick)
Oklahoma – Anderson 9 yard run (Seibert Kick)
Oklahoma – Anderson 41 yard run (Seibert Kick)
Georgia – Michel 75 yard run (Blankenship Kick)
Oklahoma – Seibert 38 yard Field Goal
Oklahoma – Mayfield 2 yard pass from Lamb (Seibert Kick)
Georgia – Blankenship 55 yard Field Goal
Georgia – Chubb 50 yard run (Blankenship Kick)
Georgia – Michel 38 yard run (Blankenship Kick)
Georgia – Wims 4 yard pass from Fromm (Blankenship Kick)
Oklahoma – Flowers 11 yard pass from Mayfield (Seibert Kick)
Oklahoma – Parker 46 yard fumble return (Seibert Kick)
Georgia – Chubb 2 yard run (Blankenship Kick)
Georgia – Blankenship 38 yard Field Goal
Oklahoma – Seibert 33 yard Field Goal
Georgia – Michel 27 yard run

Boston Globe Rose Bowl Game Summary – Sony Michel burst through the line for a 27-yard touchdown run to give No. 3 Georgia a 54-48 victory Monday night against No. 2 Oklahoma, winning the first overtime Rose Bowl and sending the Bulldogs to the College Football Playoff championship game. Michel, who had a fumble in the fourth quarter returned for a go-ahead Oklahoma touchdown, ran for 181 yards and three scores for the Bulldogs (13-1), but none bigger than the last one in the second overtime. In the final game of his great career, Oklahoma's Baker Mayfield threw for 287 yards and two touchdowns, and caught a touchdown pass that gave the Sooners a 17-point lead with six seconds left in the first half. But the Heisman Trophy winner could not get the Sooners into the end zone in the first overtime when a touchdown would have ended the game. The first overtime Rose Bowl was also the highest scoring, surpassing last year's 52-49 USC victory against Penn State. There was a lot more on the line in this one, which will go down as one of the greatest Granddaddies of Them All. After an offside penalty on Georgia gave Oklahoma a first down on third and 5 in the second OT possession, the Sooners stalled again, and Austin Seibert came out for a 27-yard field goal. Leaping through the line, Lorenzo Carter got his outstretched hand on the kick and the ball fluttered down short of the uprights. Any score would have ended it for the Bulldogs, and on the second play Michel slipped one tackle and was home free. The Bulldogs sprinted off the sideline and toward the corner of the end zone to mob Michel. Confetti rained down. Meanwhile, Mayfield stood motionless on the sideline for several seconds, bent over with his hands on his knees and head down. Mayfield battled flu-like symptoms the week leading into the game, but he played just fine. Michel and his running mate Nick Chubb were awesome for Georgia. Chubb ran for 145 yards and two touchdowns, including a 2-yarder on a direct snap with 55 seconds left in regulation to tie it. Both teams settled for field goals in the first overtime, first Georgia's Rodrigo Blankenship from 38 to make it 48-45. Then it was Mayfield's turn. A touchdown would have sent the Sooners to Atlanta, but on a third and 2 from the 17, Georgia All-America linebacker Roquan Smith nailed Jordan Smallwood a yard short of the first down. Seibert kicked a 33-yarder and the Bulldogs and Sooners played on, but not for much longer. The first meeting between the storied programs was an instant classic. The Bulldogs came in with the sixth-best defense in the country, but Mayfield and the Sooners sliced it up in the first half, including a nifty reverse pass to the Heisman Trophy-winning quarterback that made it 31-14 with six seconds left in the second quarter. Oklahoma had 360 yards in the first half. Georgia coach Kirby Smart said the defense "stunk it up" in the first half, but there were no dramatic changes in the second. Oklahoma managed only 171 yards and one touchdown in the second half and OT. Oklahoma linebacker Caleb Kelly lowered a shoulder into Michel trying to turn the corner on a sweep and the ball popped loose. Steven Parker picked it up on the bounce, tight-roped the sideline, and raced 46 yards for a score to put the Sooners up, 45-38, with 6:52 left in the fourth. With 3:22 left in the fourth, Georgia freshman quarterback Jake Fromm led a game-tying drive, capped by Chubb's TD run.

2018 SUGAR BOWL (National Semifinal)

The 2018 Sugar Bowl was held on January 1, 2018 at the Mercedes-Benz Superdome in New Orleans. The 84th Sugar Bowl game, it matched two of the top four teams selected by the Selection Committee to compete for a spot at the 2018 College Football Playoff National Championship played on January 8, 2018, at Mercedes-Benz Stadium in Atlanta, Georgia. The contest was televised on ESPN and ESPN Deportes, with a radio broadcast on ESPN Radio and XM Satellite Radio, with kickoff at 8:00 PM CT (9:00 PM ET). This was the third consecutive year in which Clemson and Alabama met in the CFPs, though the previous two meetings were in the CFP Championship Game.

2018 Sugar Bowl	Line	1	-	2	-	3	-	4	-	Final
#4 Alabama	(-3.5)	10	-	0	-	14	-	0	-	24
#1 Clemson	(46.5)	0	-	3	-	3	-	0	-	6

Scoring Summary
Alabama – Pappanastos 24 yard Field Goal
Alabama – Ridley 12 yard pass from Hurts (Pappanastos Kick)
Clemson – Spence 44 yard Field goal
Clemson – Spence 42 yard Field Goal
Alabama – Payne 1 yard pass from Hurts (Pappanastos Kick)
Alabama – Wilson 18 yard interception return (Pappanastos Kick)

Associated Press Sugar Bowl Game Summary - Nick Saban is back in his comfort zone. Let others run up the points. He'll take a defensive slugfest every time. Especially when it gives Alabama another shot at a national title. In a game where every yard was a struggle, the Crimson Tide defenders took matters into their own hands. They accounted for a pair of touchdowns just 13 seconds apart in the third quarter to turn an offensive slog into a 24-6 rout of defending national champion Clemson in the Sugar Bowl semifinal game Monday night. Sure, it was quite a contrast to the first two meetings in the Alabama-Clemson trilogy, both high-scoring classics with the national title on the line, not to mention the Rose Bowl semifinal that preceded it. Georgia knocked off Oklahoma 54-48 in a double-overtime thriller that wasn't decided until the Alabama was on its second possession in the Big Easy. There would be no drama in the nightcap. With Deshaun Watson off to the NFL, top-ranked Clemson (12-2) simply had no answer for the Tide's latest group of defensive standouts, setting up an all-Southeastern Conference showdown for the national title -- with Saban matched against his former defensive coordinator, Georgia coach Kirby Smart. Leading only 10-6 after a turnover to start the second half handed Clemson a field goal, the fourth-ranked Tide (12-1) quickly snuffed out any thoughts of a repeat title for the Tigers. It began with 308-pound defensive tackle Da'Ron Payne picking off a wobbly pass after besieged Clemson quarterback Kelly Bryant was hit as he threw. Payne rumbled 21 yards on the return, shedding one would-be tackler with a deft open-field move and drawing a 15-yard personal foul penalty when he was finally dragged down with a horse collar tackle. After Alabama drove to a first down at the Clemson 1, Payne re-entered the game -- presumably to add another big body for blocking purposes. Instead, he slipped open near the right pylon on a play fake and hauled in a touchdown pass, even managing to get both feet down before the celebration commenced beyond the sideline. A bit shell-shocked by that turn of events, Clemson was thoroughly demoralized after its next offensive play. Bryant's pass deflected off the hands of Deon Cainand was intercepted by linebacker Mack Wilson, who returned it 18 yards for another TD. They could've called it right then. The Tide, which began the season in Atlanta beating Florida State, will return to Mercedes-Benz Stadium next Monday night to face No. 3 Georgia and give Saban a shot at his sixth title, which would match Bear Bryant. Saban has four championships in the last eight years at Alabama, along with a BCS title at LSU during the 2003 season. This is eerily reminiscent of Alabama's run to the 2011 championship, another season when the Tide didn't even win its own division or play for the SEC title. That year, Saban's team lost at home to LSU during the regular season but got a second chance against the top-ranked Tigers with the biggest prize on the line -- in the Sugar Bowl, no less. On that night in the Big Easy, Alabama defense didn't allow LSU to cross midfield until the closing minutes of a suffocating 21-0 victory. This defensive performance was nearly as impressive. Clemson was held to 188 yards -- 260 yards below its season average -- and never reached the end zone. Bryant was sacked five times and the Tigers were held to 64 yards on the ground. Alabama played it tough right to the end, denying Clemson on a fourth-down pass into the end zone with just over a minute remaining. Clearly, the Tide was still ticked off about the way last season ended, giving up a TD pass with 1 second remaining to hand Clemson the national title. Clemson receiver Hunter Renfrow was known as the Tide Killer. Not this time. After hauling in four TD passes in the last two national championship games -- including, of course, the title winner a year ago -- Renfrow was held to just 31 yards on five receptions. All his catches came in fourth quarter with Alabama comfortably ahead.

2018 CFP CHAMPIONSHIP GAME

The 2018 College Football Playoff National Championship was was played at Mercedes-Benz Stadium in Atlanta, Georgia on January 8, 2018. The Alabama Crimson Tide defeated the Georgia Bulldogs 26–23, coming back from a 13–0 deficit at halftime to secure the win in overtime. True freshman quarterback Tua Tagovailoa and defensive tackle Daron Payne were respectively named the offensive and defensive players of the game. Alabama and Georgia advanced to the national championship after winning the semifinal games hosted by the Sugar Bowl and Rose Bowl Game respectively in January 2018.

2018 CFP Championship Game	Line	1	-	2	-	3	-	4	-	OT	Final
#4 Alabama	(-3.0)	0	-	0	-	10	-	10	-	6	26
#3 Georgia	(45.0)	0	-	13	-	7	-	0	-	3	23

Scoring Summary
Georgia – Blankenship 41 yard Field Goal
Georgia – Blankenship 27 yard Field Goal
Georgia – Hardman 1 yard run (Blankenship Kick)
Alabama – Ruggs 6 yard pass from Tagovailoa (Pappanastos Kick)
Georgia – Hardman 80 yard pass from Fromm (Blankenship Kick)
Alabama – Pappanastos 43 yard Field Goal
Alabama – Pappanastos 30 yard Field Goal
Alabama – Ridley 7 yard pass from Tagovailoa (Pappanastos Kick)
Georgia – Blankenship 51 yard Field Goal
Alabama – Smith 41 yard pass from Tagovailoa

CFP Championship Game Summary – After winning the coin toss, Alabama deferred to the second half and Georgia received the ball to begin the game. After two plays, quarterback Jake Fromm attempted a pass downfield and was intercepted by Tony Brown. Alabama began their first drive of the game, and, after eleven plays, that drive ended with kicker Andy Pappanastos missing a 40-yard field goal. The teams each had three-and-outs for the game's first two punts. During Georgia's ensuing drive, the quarter ended, with no score. After a failed third down conversion, on the second play of the second quarter, Georgia kicker Rodrigo Blankenship hit a 41-yard field goal to open the scoring and put Georgia in the lead by three. Alabama's ensuing drive went nowhere, as they gained four yards on three plays and punted. Georgia took the ball and drove down the field and found themselves with a first and goal at the Alabama 10-yard-line; the Tide defense held, however, and the Bulldogs settled for a second field goal and took a 6–0 lead with just over seven and a half minutes until half. On Alabama's next drive, the Georgia defense held yet again and Alabama's JK Scott punted for the third time. Just prior to the punt, Georgia wide receiver Javon Wims was shown walking to the locker room, reportedly with a left shoulder injury. Both defenses then forced punts, and Georgia took back over with 1:19 remaining in the half on their own 31-yard-line. Nine plays later, on Alabama's 1-yard-line, Mecole Hardman took a direct snap, faked a handoff, and ran into the end zone for the game's first touchdown, putting Georgia up 13–0 going into halftime. Because they deferred the coin toss, Alabama received the ball first in the second half. They started their drive on their own 22-yard-line. Tua Tagovailoa, Alabama's backup quarterback, started the second half for the Tide; that drive quickly resulted in a three-and-out. The initial punt was blocked, but an erroneous offside call gave the Tide another chance to punt. Georgia started their drive on their own 36-yard-line but punted on 4th & 17. Alabama took over on their own 44-yard-line. The teams then traded touchdowns on consecutive drives; Alabama scored their first points of the game on a 6-yard pass from Tagovailoa to Ruggs, but Georgia immediately responded with an 80-yard touchdown connection from Fromm to Mecole Hardman, putting Georgia up 20–7. On the second play of Alabama's ensuing drive, Tagovailoa, while scrambling to the left, threw into traffic and was intercepted by Georgia's Deandre Baker. Up 13, the Bulldogs took over possession of the ball on Alabama's 39-yard-line. The Tide defense responded immediately, however, as Raekwon Davis intercepted a Jake Fromm pass on the first play of Georgia's drive, returning the pick to the UGA 40-yard-line. The Tide gained fifteen yards on six plays and kicker Andy Pappanastos avenged his earlier miss with a 43-yard field goal that put Bama within ten. The teams then traded punts. Just prior to Alabama's punt, it was announced that an Alabama defensive back, Kyriq McDonald, had collapsed on the sideline; the situation was described as a "serious medical emergency". He was loaded onto a medical stretcher awake and conscious. Georgia could not muster anything on offense that drive and punted. The fourth quarter saw Tagovailoa lead the Tide to come back and tie the game at 20 with 3:49. With three seconds remaining in the game, Andy Pappanastos missed a potential game-winning 36-yard field goal to the left, sending the game to overtime. In overtime, Georgia had an unsuccessful drive that resulted in both a three-and-out, and a 13-yard loss sack to Fromm. Georgia opted to attempt a 51-yard field goal, which they successfully made. On Alabama's first offensive play in overtime, Tagovailoa was sacked for a 16-yard loss, but immediately followed that with a game-winning 41-yard touchdown pass to DeVonta Smith, in a play that has since been called "2nd and 26" by fans. Tagovailoa was named the offensive player of the game, and Daron Payne was named the defensive player of the game.

2018 Air Force Reserve Celebration Bowl

The 2018 Air Force Reserve Celebration Bowl was played on December 15, 2018, with kickoff at 12:00 p.m. EST. It was the only bowl to feature FCS teams. It was the fourth edition of the Celebration Bowl. The Air Force Reserve resumed its role as the title sponsor after a one-year absence. The North Carolina A&T Aggies (NC A&T) were announced as the MEAC representative on November 17, following the conclusion of games involving itself and Florida A&M (FAMU), the conference front-runners. However, FAMU lost the Florida Classic to arch-rival Bethune-Cookman, 33–19, while NC A&T defeated North Carolina Central, 45–0, giving them the conference championship and Celebration Bowl bid. Alcorn State defeated Southern in the SWAC Championship Game on December 1 to secure their berth in the Celebration Bowl. The Braves enter the bowl with a 9–3 record (6–1 in conference regular season play).

2018 Celebration Bowl	Line	1	-	2	-	3	-	4	-	Final
North Carolina A&T	(-7.0)	7	-	10	-	7	-	0	-	24
Alcorn State	(46.5)	3	-	3	-	10	-	6	-	22

Scoring Summary
North Carolina A&T – Leslie 17 yard pass from Raynard (Ruiz Kick)
Alcorn State – McCullough 29 yard Field Goal
North Carolina A&T – Ruiz 36 yard Field Goal
North Carolina A&T – Bell 27 yard pass from Raynard (Ruiz Kick)
Alcorn State – McCullough 25 yard Field Goal
Alcorn State – Johnson 30 yard run (McCullough Kick)
Alcorn State – McCullough 29 yard Field Goal
North Carolina A&T – Wilson 79 yard kickoff return (Ruiz Kick)
Alcorn State – Johnson 59 yard run (2 pt conversion failed)

Associated Press Celebration Bowl Game Summary – Lamar Raynard passed for 292 yards and two touchdowns and Malik Wilson returned a kickoff for the game-sealing touchdown Saturday as North Carolina A&T held off Alcorn State to win the Celebration Bowl 24-22, and the Aggies captured their second straight HBCU national championship and third in four years. The Celebration Bowl kicks off the bowl season by matching up the champions of two historically black leagues, the Mid-Eastern Athletic Conference and the Southwestern Athletic Conference, at Mercedes-Benz Stadium. Raynard, a senior who finished his career with a 35-2 record as a starter, did most of his damage in the first half with touchdown passes of 17 yards to Zachary Leslie and 27 yards to Elijah Bell as North Carolina A&T (10-2) built a 17-3 lead in the second quarter. Alcorn State (9-4) stormed back in the third quarter. De'Shawn Waller tallied 116 of his 167 rushing yards on just four carries in the period while playing about six miles east of where he grew up. The Braves pulled within 17-16 on a 30-yard touchdown run by quarterback Noah Johnson, the

SWAC Offensive Player of the Year, and a 29-yard field goal with 51 seconds left in the quarter. Johnson rushed for 120 yards and passed for 128. Wilson countered immediately, fielding the short kickoff on the left side of the field. He took off diagonally toward the middle and then cut up the right sideline for a 79-yard score. It was the senior's school-record fourth kickoff return for a touchdown this season alongside scores of 98, 99 and 100 yards. Johnson scored on a 59-yard option keeper early in the fourth quarter to pull the Braves within 24-22. Johnson rolled out on the ensuing two-point conversion try, and his pass to a sliding Chris Harris was ruled incomplete. Alcorn State punted on its next possession with 5:55 remaining and didn't get the ball back as North Carolina A&T put together a game-ending 11-play drive. Other than the clock-eating final drive, the Aggies were stymied on offense in the second half, with Wilson's kickoff return bailing them out. The Aggies entered the game ranked No. 1 in the HBCU poll and No. 11 in FCS. The Braves bullied North Carolina A&T in the second half, with 258 of their 328 total rushing yards on 20 carries. They flipped the script from when these teams met in the first Celebration Bowl in 2015. In that one, they lost 41-34 when North Carolina A&T running back Tarik Cohen, now with the Chicago Bears, rushed for 295 yards. Alcorn State played without starting wide receiver Dayall Harris, who did not make the trip to Atlanta for disciplinary reasons. The senior was the Braves' fourth-leading receiver during the regular season with 28 catches in 11 games, with four touchdowns and a team-leading 15.8-yard average per reception.

2018 NEW MEXICO BOWL

The 2018 New Mexico Bowl was played on December 15, 2018, with kickoff scheduled for 2:00 p.m. EST (12:00 p.m. local MST). It was the 13th edition of the New Mexico Bowl. The game featured Utah State from the Mountain West Conference and North Texas from Conference USA (C-USA). This was the eighth all-time meeting against the Mean Green and the Aggies, with Utah State leading the series, 4–3; this meeting was the first in a bowl game. The Aggies entered the bowl with a 10–2 record (7–1 in conference). Due to the resignation of head coach Matt Wells, who accepted the same position with the Texas Tech Red Raiders on November 29, the Aggies were coached in the bowl game by interim head coach Frank Maile. Utah State previously appeared in the 2014 New Mexico Bowl, defeating UTEP. The Mean Green entered the bowl with a 9–3 record (5–3 in conference). This was the first appearance by North Texas in a New Mexico Bowl.

2018 New Mexico Bowl	Line	1	-	2	-	3	-	4	-	Final
Utah State	(-7.0)	14	-	24	-	7	-	7	-	52
North Texas	(67.5)	7	-	0	-	6	-	0	-	13

Scoring Summary
Utah State – Vaughns 72 yard pass from Love (Eberle Kick)
North Texas – Torrey 2 yard run (Hedlund Kick)
Utah State – Bright 26 yard run (Eberle Kick)
Utah State – Love 9 yard run (Eberle Kick)
Utah State – Vaughns 37 yard pass from Love (Eberle Kick)
Utah State – Greene 67 yard pass from Love (Eberle Kick)
Utah State – Eberle 42 yard Field Goal
North Texas – Guyton 75 yard pass from Martin (Kick blocked)
Utah State – Bright 3 yard run (Eberle Kick)
Utah State – Tarver 13 yard pass from Love (Eberle Kick)

Associated Press New Mexico Bowl Game Summary – Utah State walked into the New Mexico Bowl with one of its best records in school history but uncertainty. Its head coach, Matt Wells, left to take the Texas Tech job. Interim coach Frank Maile had to prepare the Aggies with an army of graduate assistants and an announcement a new coach was coming next month. North Texas, meanwhile, was coming into Albuquerque with experienced coach Seth Littrell and highly touted quarterback Mason Fine. The Aggies pushed those distractions aside Saturday. Jordan Love threw for 359 yards and four touchdowns and Jalen Greene had six catches for 151 yards and a score to help Utah State rout North Texas 52-13. Maile directed the Aggies (11-2) even after Utah State announced former head coach Gary Andersen would return. However, Andersen opted not to attend the bowl game and let Maile finish what he started. Love completed 21 of 43 passes with one interception. D.J. William had two interceptions, helping Utah State ground high-flying North Texas (9-4). Aaren Vaughns caught two passes for 109 yards and two scores for the Aggies, Gerold Bright ran for 103 yards and two touchdowns on 16 carries, and Darwin Thompson added 93 yards on 21 carries. Maile said he did his best to get the offense ready. The rest was up the players, he said. Love said receivers were able to get open, find space and get yards after the catch. Fine was injured in the first quarter, and the Mean Green ended up using four quarterbacks. Jalen Guyton had four catches for 103 yards a score. Littrell said Utah State was the best team the Mean Green faced all season. When Fine came up limping following a nine-yard run in the first quarter, the whole complexion of game changed. After the game, North Texas officials announced that Fine had a severe left strained hamstring. This is the second time in three years that Fine most of or all of the Mean Green's bowl game after a shoulder injury kept him out of the 2016 Heart of Dallas Bowl. Littrell said Fine left with a "pretty bad" hamstring injury but couldn't give more details.

2018 AUTO NATION CURE BOWL

The 2018 Cure Bowl was played on December 15, 2018, with kickoff scheduled for 1:30 p.m. EST. It was the fourth edition of the **Cure Bowl**, and sponsored by automotive retailer **AutoNation**, the game was officially known as the AutoNation Cure Bowl. The game was played between the **Tulane Green Wave** from the **American Athletic Conference (AAC)** and the **Louisiana Ragin' Cajuns** from the **Sun Belt Conference**. Both teams made their first appearance in a Cure Bowl. This game was the 27th all-time meeting against the Ragin' Cajuns and the Green Wave, with Tulane leading the series 22–4; this was their second meeting in a bowl. Louisiana won the Sun Belt West Division title, earning a berth in the inaugural Sun Belt Championship, where they lost to Appalachian State. The Ragin' Cajuns entered the bowl with a 7–6 record (5–3 in conference). Tulane received and accepted a bid to the Cure Bowl on December 2. The Green Wave, who were co-champions of the West Division of the AAC, entered the bowl with a 6–6 record (5–3 in conference).

2018 Auto Nation Cure Bowl	Line	1	-	2	-	3	-	4	-	Final
Tulane	(-3.0)	21	-	3	-	3	-	14	-	41
Louisiana-Lafayette	(60.5)	7	-	3	-	7	-	7	-	24

Scoring Summary
Louisiana – Calais 38 yard run (Pfau Kick)
Tulane – Bradwell 15 yard run (Glover Kick)
Tulane – Encalade 38 yard pass from McMillan (Glover Kick)
Tulane – Jones 1 yard run (Glover Kick)
Tulane – Glover 38 yard Field goal
Louisiana – Pfau 43 yard Field Goal
Louisiana – Mitchell 3 yard run (Pfau Kick)
Tulane – Glover 26 yard Field Goal
Louisiana – Jackson 13 yard pass from Nunez (Pfau Kick)
Tulane – Bradwell 4 yard run (Glover Kick)
Tulane – McMillan 16 yard run (Glover Kick)

Associated Press Auto Nation Cure Bowl Game Summary – From a 2-5 start to Cure Bowl champions. Tulane (7-6) capped a turnaround season under Coach Willie Fritz with a 41-24 victory over Louisiana-Lafayette on Saturday, the Green Wave's first postseason win in 16 years. Darius Bradwell rushed for a career-best 150 yards and two touchdowns and graduate transfer Justin McMillan improved to 5-1 as the team's starting quarterback by tossing a first-quarter TD pass to Terren Encalade and running for a late score in the 29th meeting in an intrastate rivalry that dates to 1911. Bradwell scored on runs of 15 and 4 yards while setting bowl records for rushing attempts (35) and yards for Tulane (7-6), which won a bowl game for the first time since the 2002 Hawaii Bowl. The Green Wave also got a rushing TD from Amare Jones and outgained the Ragin' Cajuns 337 yards to 84 on the ground to improve to 23-6 all-time against the Rajun' Cajuns. Lousiana-Lafayette coach Bill Napier said he didn't want the result to leave a "blackeye" on what the Sun Belt Conference runner-up accomplished in its first season under him. The Ragin' Cajuns (7-7), coming off a loss to Appalachian State in the Sun Belt championship game, rallied from a 24-7 deficit to pull within three points on Jarrod Jackson's 15-yard TD reception with just over 10 minutes remaining. McMillan put the game away, leading a 75-yard drive Bradwell finished with his second TD and later scoring himself on a 16-yard run that put Tulane up 41-24. Andre Nunez completed 8 of 17 passes for 136 yards and one TD, however Louisiana-Lafayette's productive running tandem of Trey Ragas and Elijah Mitchell were not a factor after falling behind early. Tulane won four of five down the stretch in the regular season to not only qualify for its first bowl berth in five years, but also finish with a winning record (5-3 AAC West Division) in league play for the first time since 2014. McMillan was one of the keys, providing consistent quarterback play while throwing for more than 1,100 yards and accounting for 13 touchdowns -- nine passing and four rushing. The graduate transfer from LSU, where he appeared on only two games from 2015-17, was 11 of 18 passing with one interception Saturday. He finished with 217 yards total offense -- 145 passing and 72 rushing.

2018 LAS VEGAS BOWL

The 2018 Las Vegas Bowl was played on December 15, 2018, with kickoff scheduled for 3:30 p.m. EST (12:30 p.m. local PST). It was the 27th edition of the Las Vegas Bowl, was played between Arizona State of the Pac-12 Conference and Fresno State of the Mountain West Conference. This was the fourth all-time meeting against the Sun Devils and the Bulldogs, with Arizona State leading the series, 3–0; this was their first meeting in a bowl game. The Sun Devils entered the bowl with a 7–5 record (5–4 in conference). The Sun Devils' last Las Vegas Bowl appearance came in 2011. As the Mountain West champion, they received and accepted a bid to the Las Vegas Bowl on December 2. The Bulldogs entered the bowl with an 11–2 record (7–1 in conference). The Bulldogs' last Las Vegas Bowl appearance came in 2013.

2018 Las Vegas Bowl	Line	1	-	2	-	3	-	4	-	Final
Arizona State	(53.5)	7	-	10	-	3	-	0	-	20
#19 Fresno State	(-6.0)	10	-	7	-	7	-	7	-	31

Scoring Summary
Fresno State – Fuller 39 yard Field Goal
Fresno State – Kelly 70 yard interception return (Fuller Kick)
Arizona State – Williams 3 yard pass from Wilkins (Ruiz Kick)
Arizona State – Benjamin 17 yard run (Ruiz Kick)
Fresno State – McMaryion 10 yard run (Fuller Kick)
Arizona State – Ruiz 20 yard Field goal
Arizona State – Ruiz 44 yard Field Goal
Fresno State – Rivers 68 yard run (Fuller Kick)
Fresno State – Rivers 5 yard run (Fuller Kick)

Associated Press Las Vegas Bowl Game Summary – Running back Ronnie Rivers might be the embodiment of Fresno State's turnaround. It wasn't guaranteed Rivers would be able to play this season after sustaining a foot injury in spring practice, and he was limited by a shoulder injury late in the year. But Rivers was there, leading the way as the Bulldogs completed their journey after going 1-11 two seasons ago. Rivers rushed for 212 yards and two touchdowns to help No. 19 Fresno State beat Arizona State 31-20 in the Las Vegas Bowl on Saturday. Anthoula Kelly had a 70-yard interception return for a touchdown, and Marcus McMaryion rushed for a touchdown and was 15-of-29 passing for 176 yards to help Fresno State (12-2) set a school record for wins in a season. Rivers put Fresno State back in front 24-20 with a 68-yard touchdown run up the middle in the third quarter and had a 5-yard scoring run in the fourth quarter to seal it. The Bulldogs were 2-0 against Pac-12 opponents this season, also beating UCLA 38-14 in September. Fresno State was able to overcome turnovers on three consecutive drives in the second half, including when McMaryion threw the first of two interceptions to set up Brandon Ruiz's 44-yard field goal that gave Arizona State a 20-17 lead. Dejonte O'Neal also fumbled off the pylon when reaching out to score on a throwback screen. Eno Benjamin rushed for 118 yards a one touchdown for the Sun Devils (7-6) in their third straight bowl loss. Manny Wilkins threw for 129 yards, with a 3-yard scoring pass to Kyle Williams and two interceptions. First-year coach Herm Edwards put the loss on the failure to score points off takeaways, getting three points following the three Fresno State turnovers. Arizona State had 63 yards of offense in the second half. Benjamin set the school single-season rushing record on a 13-yard run in the second quarter, finishing with 1,642 yards rushing to break Woody Green's mark of 1,565 yards in 1972. Wilkins said he did not sustain an injury despite taking a hit to the knee on the final pass of his college career, which was intercepted by Juju Hughes.

2018 CAMELLIA BOWL

The 2018 Camellia Bowl was played on December 15, 2018, with kickoff scheduled for 5:30 p.m. EST (4:30 p.m. local CST). It was the fifth edition of the Camellia Bowl. This was the first meeting between the two programs. Georgia Southern entered the bowl with a 9–3 record (6–2 in conference). The Eagles had previously played in one bowl game, winning the 2015 GoDaddy Bowl over Bowling Green: before 2014. Eastern Michigan entered the bowl with a 7–5 record (5–3 in conference). This was the Eagles' second bowl game in the last three years, having also played in the 2016 Bahamas Bowl where they were defeated by Old Dominion, 24–20.

2018 Camellia Bowl	Line	1	-	2	-	3	-	4	-	Final
Georgia Southern	(-3.0)	7	-	10	-	0	-	6	-	23
Eastern Michigan	(45.5)	0	-	7	-	7	-	7	-	21

Scoring Summary
Georgia Southern – Werts 26 yard run (Bass Kick)
Eastern Michigan – Lyle 1 yard pass from Glass (Ryland Kick)
Georgia Southern – Werts 5 yard run (Bass Kick)
Georgia Southern – Bass 50 yard Field Goal
Eastern Michigan – Jackson 75 yard pass from Glass (Ryland Kick)
Georgia Southern – Bass 35 yard Field Goal
Eastern Michigan – Jackson 5 yard pass from
Georgia Southern – Bass 40 yard Field Goal

Associated Press Camellia Bowl Game Summary – Tyler Bass found a way to top his last-play 50-yard field goal to end the first half. Bass kicked a 40-yarder as time expired to give Georgia Southern a 23-21 victory over Eastern Michigan in the Camellia Bowl on Saturday night. Shai Werts kept the winning drive alive with a 29-yard scramble on fourth-and-10. Bass came on for his third field goal after Wesley Fields' two runs pushed Georgia Southern (10-3) 7 yards closer. Georgia Southern completed the biggest turnaround in the Football Bowl Subdivision this season, going from 10 losses to 10 wins. Eastern Michigan (7-6) had delivered its own big fourth-down play to take the lead for the first time. Mike Glass threw a 5-yard touchdown pass to Arthur Jackson with 3:33 left on fourth-and-4, followed by Chad Ryland's extra point. Georgia Southern took over at its own 25 with a triple-option offense that attempted fewer passes than every FBS team but Army. Werts completed a 15-yard pass to tight end Ellis Richardson, but Georgia Southern fittingly covered most of the 52 yards with runs. Werts ran for 79 yards and two first-half touchdowns while completing 4 of 7 passes for 33 yards to receive Most Valuable Player honors. His biggest play came on the fourth-and-10. Wesley Kennedy III gained 107 yards on nine carries. Eastern Michigan's Glass completed 17 of 25 passes for 204 yards and three touchdowns, including a 75-yarder to Jackson on the opening play of the second half. He had missed the final two games of the regular season with a right leg injury and had only two previous starts. Glass found Jackson in the back of the end zone to cap a 16-play, 75-yard drive that consumed more than six minutes.as it turns out, it left too much time on the clock.

2018 NEW ORLEANS BOWL

The 2018 New Orleans Bowl was on December 15, 2018, with kickoff scheduled for 9:00 p.m. EST (8:00 p.m. local CST). The teams previously met three times (1974, 1989, and 1992) with Middle Tennessee holding a 2–1 edge in the series. Blue Raider quarterback Brent Stockstill is the son of head coach Rick Stockstill. Due to the resignation of head coach Scott Satterfield, who took the same position with the Louisville Cardinals on December 4, the Mountaineers were coached in the bowl game by interim head coach Mark Ivey.

2018 New Orleans Bowl	Line	1	-	2	-	3	-	4	-	Final
Middle Tennessee	(49.0)	3	-	3	-	7	-	0	-	13
Appalachian State	(-6.5)	0	-	24	-	14	-	7	-	45

Scoring Summary
Middle Tennessee – Holt 24 yard Field Goal
Appalachian State – Staton 22 yard Field Goal
Appalachian State – Hennigan 30 yard pass from Williams (Staton Kick)
Appalachian State – Thomas 8 yard pass from Williams (Staton Kick)
Appalachian State – Pearson 1 yard pass from Thomas (Staton Kick)
Middle Tennessee – Holt 33 yard Field Goal
Appalachian State – Sutton 17 yard pass from Thomas (Staton Kick)
Appalachian State – Peoples 63 yard run (Staton Kick)
Middle Tennessee – Upton 43 yard pass from Stockstill (Holt Kick)
Appalachian State – Sutton 11 yard pass from Thomas (Staton Kick)

Associated Press New Orleans Bowl Game Summary – While the future of Appalachian State interim coach Mark Ivey is unknown, Mountaineers players left no doubt about how much they appreciated the way he handled his lone game in charge, carrying him off the field in triumph. Appalachian State receiver Malik Williams passed for two touchdowns on trick plays, quarterback Zac Thomas caught a scoring pass and threw for three more, and the Mountaineers routed Middle Tennessee 45-13 in the New Orleans Bowl on Saturday night. Camerun Peoples had a 63-yard touchdown run for the Mountaineers (11-2), who gave Ivey, a former Appalachian State player, a victory in what might have been his only chance to coach his alma mater. Ivey -- who'll soon be replaced by North Carolina State offensive coordinator Eli Drinkwitz -- looked determined to make his lone game as interim coach a memorable one. Appalachian State even tried a surprise onside kick in the first half -- and it might have worked if Clifton Duck had not snatched the high-bounding ball just before it had covered the mandatory 10 yards for a legal touch by the kicking team. That was one of few things that didn't go right for the Mountaineers, but Middle Tennessee

(8-6) could not take advantage of it. Three plays later, Tae Hayes' interception and 27-yard return set up Appalachian State on the Blue Raiders 41. Soon after, Williams connected on his second TD pass, which the former high school QB threw to Thomas after taking a pitch from running back Darrynton Evans on a reverse. Middle Tennessee's Brent Stockstill was 25-of-37 passing for 330 yards, one touchdown and two interceptions. Williams' first TD passing came after he caught a backward pass from Thomas near the right edge of the field and launched a 30-yard strike down the sidelined to Thomas Hennigan. Thomas threw his first touchdown pass in the final minute of the first half, when he found Henry Pearson from a yard out. In the second half, he hit Corey Sutton for TDs of 17 and 11 yards. He finished 15 of 24 for 177 yards, but also was intercepted twice by safety Reed Blankenship.

2018 BOCA RATON BOWL

The 2018 Boca Raton Bowl was held on December 18, 2018, with kickoff scheduled for 7:00 p.m. EST. It was the fifth edition of the Boca Raton Bowl. The Boca Raton Bowl was the first of three 2018–19 bowl games featuring two conference champions, along with the Orange Bowl and Rose Bowl. In just the second season since restarting its football program, the UAB Blazers defeated the Northern Illinois Huskies, 37–13, earning UAB their first-ever bowl victory.

2018 Boca Raton Bowl	Line	1	-	2	-	3	-	4	-	Final
Alabama-Birmingham	(-1.0)	10	-	17	-	10	-	0	-	37
Northern Illinois	(41.0)	7	-	3	-	3	-	0	-	13

Scoring Summary
Alabama-Birmingham – Ubosi 70 yard pass from Johnston (Vogel Kick)
Alabama-Birmingham – Vogel 25 yard Field Goal
Northern Illinois – Harbison 1 yard run (Gantz Kick)
Alabama-Birmingham – Brown 3 yard pass from Johnston (Vogel Kick)
Northern Illinois – Gantz 27 yard Field Goal
Alabama-Birmingham – Ubosi 46 yard pass from Johnston (Vogel Kick)
Alabama-Birmingham – Vogel 35 yard Field Goal
Northern Illinois – Gantz 21 yard Field Goal
Alabama-Birmingham – Ubosi 66 yard pass from Johnston (Vogel Kick)
Alabama-Birmingham – Vogel 42 yard Field Goal

Associated Press Boca Raton Bowl Game Summary – Two seasons after shutting down its football program, UAB closed out the year on an electrifying note. Tyler Johnston III threw for 373 yards and four touchdowns, three of them to Xavier Ubosi, and UAB beat Northern Illinois 37-13 in the Boca Raton Bowl on Tuesday night. Ubosi had seven catches for 227 yards for the Conference USA champion Blazers (11-3), who got their first-ever bowl victory in three appearances. UAB played in its second consecutive bowl since the program was reinstated after the self-imposed hiatus. Northern Illinois (8-6), the Mid-American Conference champion, has lost six consecutive bowl games since beating Arkansas in the 2012 GoDaddy.com Bowl. Johnston, who took over the starting job for the injured A.J. Erdely at midseason, set career highs in passing yards and touchdown passes, and Ubosi's 227 yards were the third-most receiving in a game in school history. Ubosi came into the game ranked second in the country at 21.8 yards per catch, and his TD receptions covered 70, 46 and 66 yards. All-American Spencer Brown, who entered with 1,167 rushing yards and a school-record 16 touchdowns, caught a 3-yard shovel pass for a score and had 78 yards on the ground. UAB's 10th-ranked defense harassed Huskes quarterback Marcus Childers, sacking him five times and forcing two fumbles (one lost). He finished 22 of 29 for 179 yards and had 35 yards rushing on 18 carries. NIU led the nation with 50 sacks, but never got to Johnston. Johnston hit Ubosi in stride for a 70-yard TD just 18 seconds after the opening kickoff. After a penalty on a punt gave the Blazers a fourth-and-1 opportunity that they converted, the duo connected again with 5:11 remaining in the first half for a 24-10 lead. The Huskies cut it to 27-13 early in the third, but a little over two minutes later, Johnston found Ubosi down the sideline for his third score. Nick Vogel kicked three field goals for UAB.

2018 FRISCO BOWL

The 2018 Frisco Bowl was played on December 19, 2018, with kickoff scheduled for 8:00 p.m. EST (7:00 p.m. local CST). It was the second edition of the Frisco Bowl. In the game, the Ohio Bobcats shut out the San Diego State Aztecs, 27–0. This was the first meeting between the two programs. The Bobcats entered the bowl with an 8–4 record (6–2 in conference), having won 5-of-6 to close their regular season. The Aztecs entered the bowl with a 7–5 record (4–4 in conference), having lost 4-of-5 to close their regular season.

2018 Frisco Bowl	Line	1	-	2	-	3	-	4	-	Final
San Diego State	(47.5)	0	-	0	-	0	-	0	-	0
Ohio	(-2.0)	3	-	14	-	3	-	7	-	27

Scoring Summary
Ohio – Zervos 30 yard Field Goal
Ohio – Rourke 9 yard run (Zervos Kick)
Ohio – Rourke 1 yard run (Zervos Kick)
Ohio – Zervos 26 yard Field Goal
Ohio – Meyer 35 yard pass from Rourke (Zervos Kick)

Associated Press Frisco Bowl Game Summary – Ohio running back A.J. Ouellette doesn't think of Frank Solich as the oldest head coach in FBS. He sees him as the guy who stuck around a smaller program long enough to run it for going on 15 years. Ouellette gave Solich and the Bobcats a little something to build on in his final game. The senior had his fourth straight 100-yard game with 164 yards rushing, quarterback Nathan Rourke accounted for all three touchdowns and Ohio rolled to a 27-0 victory over San Diego State in the drizzly Frisco Bowl on Wednesday night. Ohio (9-4) finished with six wins in seven games and won a second straight bowl game under Solich, who became the oldest head coach in FBS at 74 before bowl season when 79-year-old Bill Snyder retired at Kansas State. Solich spent 19 years on Tom Osborne's staff at Nebraska before replacing the coach at his alma mater in 1998. After six years in charge of the Cornhuskers, Solich was forced out following a 9-3 season, a year after a 7-7 record that ended a streak of 40 straight winning seasons. A year later, he took the Ohio job and has taken the Bobcats to 10 bowls in 14 seasons. San Diego State was shut out in a bowl for the first time since its first postseason appearance -- a 53-0 loss to Hardin-Simmons in the 1948 Harbor Bowl at long-since-demolished Balboa Stadium in San Diego. The Aztecs had 44 of their 287 yards on one run by Juwan Washington while losing a fourth straight game in a season for the first time in eight years under coach Rocky Long. The fourth-best run defense in FBS gave up a season-high 215 yards rushing to Ohio. San Diego State's first meeting with Ohio was its first loss in 15 games against Mid-American Conference teams. The 27-point margin ended a streak of 10 straight games decided by single digits for the Aztecs, which the school said was the longest such streak since at least 1980.

2018 GASPARILLA BOWL

The 2018 Gasparilla Bowl was played on December 20, 2018, with kickoff scheduled for 8:00 p.m. EST. It was the 11th edition of the game originally known as the St. Petersburg Bowl and renamed before its 2017 playing as the Gasparilla Bowl. This was the first time for the bowl to be played at Raymond James Stadium in Tampa, as the prior 10 editions of the bowl were held at Tropicana Field in nearby St. Petersburg. The Thundering Herd entered the bowl with an 8–4 record (6–2 C-USA). The game was the team's 15th overall bowl appearance and third appearance in the Gasparilla Bowl. The Herd previously played in the 2011 edition and 2015 edition, winning against FIU and Connecticut, respectively. The Bulls entered the bowl with a 7–5 record (3–5 AAC), having lost their final five regular season games. The game was the team's 10th overall bowl appearance and second appearance in the Gasparilla Bowl. The Bulls previously played in the 2008 edition, winning against Memphis.

2018 Gasparilla Bowl	Line	1	-	2	-	3	-	4	-	Final
Marshall	(-3.0)	21	-	7	-	3	-	7	-	38
South Florida	(50.0)	7	-	3	-	10	-	0	-	20

Scoring Summary
Marshall – Green 10 yard run (Rohrwasser Kick)
Marshall – Johnson 1 yard run (Rohrwasser Kick)
South Florida – St. Felix 38 yard pass from McCants (Weiss Kick)
Marshall – Knox 8 yard run (Rohrwasser Kick)
Marshall – Davis 5 yard run (Rohrwasser Kick)
South Florida – Weiss 22 yard Field Goal
South Florida – Weiss 31 yard Field Goal
Marshall – Rohrwasser 28 yard Field Goal
South Florida – St. Felix 33 yard pass from Barnett (Weiss Kick)
Marshall – Davis 16 yard run (Rohrwasser Kick)

Associated Press Gasparilla Bowl Game Summary —Isaiah Green completed 17 of 25 passes for 221 yards, Cousin Keion Davis ran for two touchdowns and Marshall beat South Florida 38-20 in the Gasparilla Bowl on Thursday night. Marshall, 6-0 in bowl games under head coach Doc Holliday, gained 503 years. The Thundering Herd (9-4) had 282 rushing yards and 221 through the air. Green also had a touchdown run in the first quarter, while Davis' second TD -- from 16 yards out -- put the Thundering Herd ahead 38-

20 with 6 1/2 minutes to play. Davis had 94 yards on 14 carries, while Brenden Knox gained 93 yards on 12 rushes -- all during the first half. Knox left with a broken hand, giving Davis extended playing time. Davis entered with 308 rushing yards and one TD in eight games. Blake Barnett, slowed by shoulder and ankle injuries, replaced Chris Oladokun for South Florida 10 minutes into the game and completed 11 of 23 passes for 212 yards. Barnett, a transfer from Arizona State who also started one game for Alabama in 2016, sat out two of the Bulls' previous three games. Green scored on a 10-yard dash and Anthony Anderson had an one-yard TD run over a 37-second span as Marshall took a 14-0 lead with 4:43 left in the first. The second score was set up by Darius Hodge's fumble recovery and 29-yard return after Barnett couldn't handle a high snap. After USF wide receiver Tyre McCants took a direct snap and threw a 38-yard touchdown pass to Randall St. Felix, the Thundering Herd went up 21-7 during the final minute of the first on Knox's eight-yard TD run. St. Felix had six receptions for a school-bowl record 165 yards. Marshall has outscored its opponent 101-39 in the first quarter this season. Davis' 5-yard run made it 28-7 with 90 seconds left in the second. USF got to 28-10 on Coby Weiss' 22-yard field goal four seconds before halftime. South Florida settled for a 31-yard field goal by Weiss on a second half opening 14-play drive. Marshall countered with Justin Rohrwasser's 28-yard field before Barnett connected on a 33-yard scoring pass with St. Felix that cut the Bulls deficit to 31-20 late in the third.

2018 BAHAMAS BOWL

The 2018 Bahamas Bowl was played on December 21, 2018. It was the fifth edition of the Bahamas Bowl. The Panthers entered the bowl with an 8–4 record (6–2 in conference). FIU's usual starting quarterback, James Morgan, was unavailable for the game due to a sore shoulder, resulting in backup Christian Alexander getting the start. The Rockets entered the bowl with a 7–5 record (5–3 in conference). This was the fourth matchup between these two teams, with FIU holding a 2–1 lead in the series. They met in the 2010 Little Caesars Pizza Bowl, which FIU won, 34–32.

2018 Bahamas Bowl	Line	1	-	2	-	3	-	4	-	Final
Florida International	(57.5)	0	-	14	-	7	-	14	-	35
Toledo	(-7.0)	10	-	0	-	7	-	15	-	32

Scoring Summary
Toledo – Koback 3 yard run {Vest Kick}
Toledo – Vest 28 yard Field Goal
Florida International – Jones 6 yard run {Borregales Kick}
Florida International – Palmer 36 yard pass from Alexander {Borregales Kick}
Toledo – Johnson 7 yard pass from Peters {Vest Kick}
Florida International – Jones 30 yard run {Borregales Kick}
Florida International – Alexander 16 yard run {Borregales Kick}
Toledo – Johnson 2 yard pass from Peters {Thompson pass from Peters}
Florida International – Jones 18 yard run {Borregales Kick}
Toledo – Johnson 43 yard pass from Peters {Vest Kick}

Associated Press Bahamas Bowl Game Summary - FIU fumbled away the opening kickoff, gave up a touchdown 23 seconds into the game and found itself trailing by double digits by the end of the first quarter. They needed a comeback. And Anthony Jones might know more about comebacks than anyone on the FIU roster. Jones -- one of two FIU players who were victims of a drive-by shooting in September -- rushed for three touchdowns, including the clincher with 41 seconds remaining as the Panthers topped Toledo 35-32 on Friday in the Bahamas Bowl. Jones tied a school record with the three scores, and FIU (9-4) set a school record with its ninth win of the season. Jones and offensive lineman Mershawn Miller were shot in the city of Opalocka, Florida -- just north of downtown Miami -- on the afternoon of Sept. 6. Miller was hit in the arm; Jones was shot in the back and the bullet exited just under his eye. He lost about 20 pounds in the days afterward, during which he was fed by tube. Eli Peters had three touchdown passes and threw for 264 yards for Toledo (7-6), which fell in a bowl game for the third consecutive year. Jon'Vea Johnson had two of those TD grabs, and Diontae Johnson had six catches for 98 yards and a score for the Rockets. It was FIU's second bowl victory. The other came in 2010 -- also against Toledo. Jones scored on runs of 6, 30 and 18 yards for the Panthers. Sterling Palmer caught a touchdown pass and Maurice Alexander rushed for another score for FIU. Christian Alexander completed 17 of 26 passes for 209 yards and a touchdown for FIU. The Panthers got a huge fourth-down conversion on a pass hauled in by Tony Gaiter IV with 2:40 remaining, the biggest play in a drive where Jones capped the win with his final TD run -- the 18-yarder that sealed the win. FIU played without starting quarterback James Morgan, who has an arm injury. Morgan completed 65 percent of his passes for 2,727 yards and 26 touchdowns in the regular season. FIU also didn't have running back Shawndarrius Phillips, who was left home after a domestic battery charge stemming from a June case became known this month. And yet, the Panthers had more than enough. They got on the board when Jones got his first rushing score of the day early in the second quarter, took a 14-10 lead into the half and grabbed the lead for good on Jones' 30-yard run with 3:47 left in the third quarter. The Rockets scored with two seconds remaining in the game on a 43-yard touchdown pass from Peters to Jon'Vea Johnson, a play where the clock originally ran down to zero before some time was added. The Rockets then tried an onside kick, which FIU linebacker Sage Lewis recovered. Jones became the sixth player to rush for three touchdowns in a game for FIU, and the first since Kedrick Rhodes did it in a loss to Louisiana in 2011. Toledo finished the year with 525 points, the second most in school history. The Rockets scored 549 points in 2011, and this season's total was 16 better than the 509 they posted last season.

2018 FAMOUS IDAHO POTATO BOWL

The 2018 Famous Idaho Potato Bowl was held on December 21, 2018. The programs previously had met five times, most recently in 1970, with BYU holding a 3–2 edge. This was Western Michigan's second appearance in the Famous Idaho Potato Bowl, having lost to Air Force in the 2014 edition. BYU became the first independent team to play in the Famous Idaho Potato Bowl.

2018 Famous Idaho Potato Bowl	Line	1	-	2	-	3	-	4	-	Final
Western Michigan	(52.0)	0	-	10	-	0	-	8	-	18
BYU	(-10.0)	7	-	0	-	28	-	14	-	49

Scoring Summary
BYU – Collie 26 yard pass from Wilson (Southam Kick)
Western Michigan – Bogan 33 yard run (Peddie Kick)
Western Michigan – Peddie 37 yard Field Goal
BYU – Collie 8 yard pass from Wilson (Southam Kick)
BYU – Burt 37 yard run (Southam Kick)
BYU – Hifo 70 yard pass from Wilson (Southam Kick)
BYU – Ghanwoluko 1 yard run (Southam Kick)
BYU – Milne 5 yard pass from Wilson (Southam Kick)
Western Michigan – Eleby 1 yard run (Reed pass from Eleby)
BYU – El-Bakri 1 yard run (Southam Kick)

Associated Press Famous Idaho Potato Bowl Game Summary – At the Famous Idaho Potato Bowl pregame news conference Thursday, BYU coach Kalani Sitake set high expectations when asked about how he thought quarterback Zach Wilson would play. Sitake didn't get it from everyone, but he did from Wilson. The BYU freshman was 18-of-18 passing for 317 yards and four touchdowns, and the Cougars beat Western Michigan 49-18 on Friday. Selected the game MVP, Wilson tied the NCAA bowl record for completion percentage set by Riley Skinner at 11-for-11 for Wake Forest in the 2008 EagleBank Bowl. Wilson and Skinner are the only players in FBS history to post a 100 percent completion percentage in a bowl game (minimum 10 pass attempts). Wilson's 18 straight completions are second-most in an NCAA bowl game behind Georgia's Mike Bobo, who had 19 straight against Wisconsin in the 1998 Outback Bowl. His four passing touchdowns also tied a BYU bowl game record. In the first half, BYU (7-6) struggled to sustain momentum offensively and had just 115 yards, despite Wilson completing all eight of his attempts, mostly on short routes. The ground game had a total of 20 yards on 17 carries. But with BYU down 10-7 at halftime, Sitake unleashed Wilson in the second half. The Cougars' 28-point third quarter started with an 8-yard pass from Wilson to Dylan Collie. Then, after a 37-yard TD run by Riley Burt, Wilson hit Aleva Hifo on a 70-yard scoring strike. Despite the record-setting performance, Wilson admitted afterward that he had no idea his day was going so well statistically. Western Michigan (7-6), which was without starting quarterback Jon Wassink due to a foot injury, rolled up 192 yards of offense in the first half with freshman Kaleb Eleby.

2018 BIRMINGHAM BOWL

The 2018 Birmingham Bowl was played on December 22, 2018. It was the 13th edition of the Birmingham Bowl. The Birmingham Bowl matchup announced on December 2 featured Wake Forest from the Atlantic Coast Conference (ACC), rather than an SEC team, to face Memphis from The American. The two programs previously met four times, each team winning twice, between 1964 and 1967. The Demon Deacons entered the bowl with a 6–6 record (3–5 in conference). The Tigers entered the bowl with an 8–5 record (5–3 in conference).

2018 Birmingham Bowl	Line	1	-	2	-	3	-	4	-	Final
Memphis	(-2.0)	14	-	14	-	0	-	6	-	34
Wake Forest	(71.5)	7	-	17	-	6	-	7	-	37

Scoring Summary
Wake Forest – Surratt 9 yard pass from Newman (Sciba Kick)
Memphis – Pollard 41 yard run (Patterson Kick)
Memphis – Taylor 1 yard pass from White (Patterson Kick)
Memphis – Claybrooks 37 yard interception return (Patterson Kick)
Wake Forest – Sciba 36 yard Field Goal
Memphis – Pollard 97 yard kickoff return (Patterson Kick)
Wake Forest – Newman 1 yard run (Sciba Kick)
Wake Forest – Newman 17 yard run (Sciba Kick)
Wake Forest – Sciba 49 yard Field goal
Wake Forest – Sciba 39 yard Field Goal
Memphis – Taylor 9 yard run (2 point pass failed)
Wake Forest – Newman 1 yard run (Sciba Kick)

Associated Press Birmingham Bowl Game Summary – Jamie Newman's season started on a sour note and finished on a sweet one. Newman ran for a 1-yard touchdown with 34 seconds left to cap a big performance and Wake Forest's comeback in a 37-34 victory over Memphis in the Birmingham Bowl on Saturday. The quarterback who lost the competition for the starting job in fall camp, then replaced an injured Sam Hartman, delivered big play after big play in a storybook ending to the season. Even after that go-ahead score, the Demon Deacons (7-6) had to wait to celebrate until Riley Patterson's 43-yard field goal attempt went wide right as time expired. Both teams scored touchdowns over the final 1:15. Memphis (8-6) lost a big lead for the second straight game after jumping ahead by 18 points in the first half. Voted the game MVP, Newman ran for three touchdowns and passed for a fourth to lead Wake Forest, throwing for 328 yards and rushing 23 times for 91 more. He led the Demon Deacons on a 75-yard drive starting at the 1:15 mark, covering most of it with completions of 49 and 20 yards to Alex Bachman. He rebounded from an early sack on that last scoring drive, and from a pick-six in the first half, too. Bachman's second catch was reviewed, and the spot was upheld at the 1-yard line after his right arm hit the pylon. Newman kept the ball for the go-ahead score. Bachman finished with seven catches for 171 yards. Memphis swiftly moved into position to at least tie the game. Brady White found an open Joey Magnifico on the right sideline for a 44-yard gain, with the tight end battling for extra yards down to the 17. The Tigers went backward after that, though, including a false start penalty after Patterson lined up to attempt a game-tying kick. In the Tigers' last outing, they had led by 17 points against No. 7 UCF in the American Athletic Conference championship game, only to lose 58-41. Subbing for All-America running back Darrell Henderson, Patrick Taylor Jr. had given Memphis the lead with a 9-yard touchdown to cap a 14-play, 88-yard drive. Before that, the Tigers had come up empty on nine consecutive drives. Tony Pollard scored on a 97-yard kickoff return to tie the NCAA career mark with seven. Memphis also scored on a 37-yard interception return by Chris Claybrooks. Memphis lost its fourth straight bowl game and second straight big lead. Ran for 207 yards without Henderson, who skipped the game to prepare for the NFL draft. Wake Forest outgained Memphis 529-378 in total yards. Last five bowl wins have all come after early deficits, including four double-digit holes.

2018 ARMED FORCES BOWL

The 2018 Armed Forces Bowl was played on December 22, 2018. It was the 16th edition of the Armed Forces Bowl. On December 18, it was announced that the game had officially sold out of tickets, the first such sellout in the Armed Forces Bowl's 16-year history. The bowl originally planned to invite teams from the Big 12 Conference and the American Athletic Conference (The American). When fourth-ranked Oklahoma was selected for the College Football Playoff, a Big 12 bowl tie-in was left open. Army, an FBS Independent, was selected to fill this opening, facing off with The American member Houston. The Black Knights subsequently won the Army–Navy Game on December 8 and entered the bowl with a 10–2 record. The Cougars entered the bowl with an 8–4 record (5–3 in conference).

2018 Armed Forces Bowl	Line	1	-	2	-	3	-	4	-	Final
Houston	(56.0)	0	-	7	-	0	-	7	-	14
#22 Army	(-6.5)	14	-	28	-	14	-	14	-	70

Scoring Summary
Army – Hopkins 1 yard run (Abercrombie Kick)
Army – Hopkins 77 yard run (Abercrombie Kick)
Army – Jones 23 yard fumble return (Abercrombie Kick)
Houston – Booker 3 yard pass from Tune (Witherspoon Kick)
Army – Hopkins 1 yard run (Abercrombie Kick)
Army – Hopkins 2 yard run (Abercrombie Kick)
Army – Hobbs 11 yard run (Abercrombie Kick)
Army – Hopkins 1 yard run (Abercrombie Kick)
Army – Slomka 3 yard run (Abercrombie Kick)
Army – Asberry 15 yard pass from Thomas (Abercrombie Kick)
Houston – Tune yard run (Witherspoon Kick)
Army – Thomas 20 yard run (Abercrombie Kick)

Associated Press Armed Forces Bowl Game Summary - Army quarterback Kelvin Hopkins Jr initially ran right before cutting back the other way and eluding a tackler. He sent two other defenders sliding to the ground when he switched directions again and took off toward the end zone. That nifty 77-yard run was one of his Armed Forces Bowl-record five rushing touchdowns as the No. 22 Black Knights overwhelmed Houston 70-14 on Saturday to reach 11 wins for the first time in program history. The Black Knights' (11-2) 56-point win tied the FBS record for largest margin of victory in a bowl game, set by Tulsa in its 63-7 win over Bowling Green in the 2008 GMAC Bowl. Army scored 70 points in a game for the first time since 1955, when it scored 81 against Furman, according to ESPN Stats & Information. The win was its ninth straight since an overtime loss at playoff team Oklahoma exactly three months earlier. Houston (8-5) lost for the fourth time in five games since starting 7-1 and getting into the AP Top 25 poll for one week in late October. The injury-plagued Cougars suffered their most-lopsided loss in their 27 bowl games, and their biggest loss overall since a 66-10 loss at UCLA during the 1997 regular season. Hopkins ran 11 times for 170 yards before coming out of the game midway through the third quarter when it was 49-7. He also completed the first 1,000-yard passing season for Army since 2007. He was 3-of-3 passing for 70 yards, including a 54-yarder that set up one of his three 1-yard TD plunges. He also had a 2-yard TD run. Army got 507 of its 592 total yards on the ground in its highest-scoring game this season -- and the most points in the program's nine bowl appearances. The Black Knights won a bowl for the third consecutive year, including last year's Armed Force Bowl over San Diego State. On the first play of the second quarter, on Houston's first snap after Hopkins' long TD run, Cameron Jones had a 23-yard fumble return for a score after James Nachtigal forced the turnover when he sacked Clayton Tune. While Hopkins had his left arm in a sling after the game, he said he was "a little banged up" and that it was just a precaution. The junior quarterback's 77-yarder on the last play of the first quarter made it 14-0. Tune, the true freshman filling in for injured playmaker D'Eriq King, was 21-of-32 passing for 230 yards and was sacked 10 times. He was responsible for both Houston TDs, a 3-yard pass to Romello Brooker in the second quarter and a 6-yard run with 6 1/2 minutes left. The Cougars didn't have King or NFL-bound defensive tackle Ed Oliver. King, who will be back next season, was responsible for 50 touchdowns in 11 games before knee surgery. Oliver missed four games because of a bruised right knee, then skipped the bowl game to focus on preparing for the NFL draft. After a 10-loss season as freshmen, the Black Knights senior class won 29 games the past three seasons. They finished with back-to-back seasons of at least 10 wins. Army is an AP Top 25 team for the first time since 1996, the Academy's only other 10-win season.

2018 DOLLAR GENERAL BOWL

The 2018 Dollar General Bowl was played on December 22, 2018. It was the 20th edition and sponsored by the Dollar General Chain of variety stores. The Trojans entered the bowl with a 10–3 record (7–1 in conference). The Bulls had a 10–3 record on the year (7–1 in conference), losing to Northern Illinois in the MAC Championship Game.

2018 Dollar General Bowl	Line	1	-	2	-	3	-	4	-	Final
Buffalo	(-2.5)	7	-	10	-	7	-	8	-	32
Troy	(51.5)	7	-	7	-	7	-	21	-	42

Scoring Summary
Buffalo – Patterson 11 yard run (Mitcheson Kick)
Troy – Eafford 60 yard pass from Smith (Sumpter Kick)
Buffalo – Marks 1 yard run (Mitcheson Kick)
Troy – Willis 7 yard pass from Smith (Sumpter Kick)
Buffalo – Mitcheson 41 yard Field Goal
Troy – Smith 2 yard run (Sumpter Kick)
Buffalo – Hill 93 yard fumble return (Mitcheson Kick)
Troy – Willis 2 yard pass from Smith (Sumpter Kick)
Troy – Davis 45 yard pass from Smith (Sumpter Kick)
Buffalo – Osborn 3 yard pass from Jackson (2 point conversion good)
Troy – Davis 20 yard run (Sumpter Kick)

Associated Press Dollar General Bowl Game Summary – Troy's offense limped through November with a handful of injuries, and a subpar game against Appalachian State in the regular-season finale cost the Trojans a shot at winning the Sun Belt Conference title. After a few weeks of rest, the Trojans were healthy for the Dollar General Bowl. It made all the difference. Sawyer Smith threw for 320 yards and four touchdowns, B.J. Smith and Sidney Davis ran for touchdowns and Troy beat Buffalo 42-32 on Saturday night. Troy coach Neal Brown said the victory was gratifying, even if the win was slightly bittersweet. Troy (10-3) secured the hard-fought win on Davis' 20-yard touchdown run with 3:09 remaining, a play after Buffalo's Tyree Jackson fumbled to give the Trojans possession. It was the Bulls' third lost fumble. The entertaining game had several big swings in momentum, especially during a strange third quarter that featured Buffalo scoring seven points despite not running an offensive play. Troy took a 21-17 lead on Smith's 2-yard touchdown run with 9:47 left in the third and then immediately recovered an onside kick. The Trojans were driving for another score before a B.J. Smith fumble bounced into the hands of Buffalo's Tyrone Hill, who ran 93 yards for a touchdown to give the Bulls a 24-21 lead. Troy jumped ahead 35-24 after two quick touchdowns in the fourth quarter and held off Buffalo's final rally. Sawyer Smith's favorite target was Damion Willis, who caught 13 passes for 101 yards and two touchdowns. The quarterback said even though the Trojans made a few mistakes in the second half, he could feel momentum building. Buffalo's Jackson threw for 274 yards with a touchdown and an interception. The quarterback said the Bulls made some uncharacteristic mistakes that caused a sour end to the season. Buffalo (10-4) took the early 7-0 lead on Jaret Patterson's 11-yard touchdown run less than two minutes into the game. The drive was helped by a spectacular 51-yard pass completion that bounced off K.J. Osborn's hands and pinballed between a few defenders before being caught by Antonio Nunn. Troy bounced back quickly with its own huge gain through the air -- a 60-yard touchdown from Sawyer Smith to Tray Eafford. The game stayed tight throughout the first half and Buffalo took a 17-14 lead late in the second quarter on Adam Mitcheson's 41-yard field goal. The Bulls had the halftime lead despite three turnovers, including two fumbles. It's a disappointing loss for the Bulls, who are still looking for their first bowl win in program history. Buffalo dominated at times, but the four turnovers proved to be tough to overcome. The Trojans secured their third straight 10-win season, which is the longest such streak in program history. Sawyer Smith was excellent, and Troy finally got its run game going in the second half. The Trojans were also able to capitalize on Buffalo's turnovers.

2018 HAWAII BOWL

The 2018 Hawaii Bowl was played on December 22, 2018, in Honolulu, Hawaii. It was the 17th edition of the Hawaii Bowl. This was the first time since 2007 that the bowl was not played on Christmas Eve. Sponsored by the SoFi personal finance company, the game was officially called the SoFi Hawaii Bowl. The game was played between the Hawaii Rainbow Warriors of the Mountain West Conference and the Louisiana Tech Bulldogs of Conference USA (C–USA). The teams had faced each other 10 times, with Hawaii holding an 8–2 lead in the series; both teams previously were members of the Western Athletic Conference. This was Louisiana Tech's first trip to the Hawaii Bowl; it was Hawaii's eighth time in this bowl. The Rainbow Warriors ended the regular season with an 8–5 overall record, 5–3 in conference. The Bulldogs compiled a 7–5 regular season record, 5–3 in conference.

2018 Hawaii Bowl	Line	1	-	2	-	3	-	4	-	Final
Hawaii	(-1.0)	0	-	7	-	0	-	7	-	14
Louisiana Tech	(61.5)	3	-	0	-	21	-	7	-	31

Scoring Summary
Louisiana Tech – Hale 24 yard Field Goal
Hawaii – Sharsh 24 yard pass from Cordeiro (Meskell Kick)
Louisiana Tech – Tucker 5 yard run (Hale Kick)
Louisiana Tech – Dancy 58 yard pass from Smith (Hale Kick)
Louisiana Tech – Smith 4 yard run (Hale Kick)
Hawaii – Brown 7 yard pass from McDonald (Meskell Kick)
Louisiana Tech – McKnight 39 yard run (Hale Kick)

Associated Press Hawaii Bowl Game Summary – Skip Holtz felt the need to refocus his players after they spent the better part of a week in paradise. The sixth-year Louisiana Tech coach dressed down his team one night before the bowl game and it certainly appeared to pay off. J'Mar Smith threw a touchdown pass and ran for another score in a big third quarter to lead Louisiana Tech to a 31-14 win over Hawai'i in the SoFi Hawai'i Bowl on Saturday night. The Bulldogs (8-5) rallied from a 7-3 halftime deficit to secure their fifth bowl victory in as many seasons, a program first. Defensive end Jaylon Ferguson, who had 2 1/2 sacks to become the NCAA's career leader, said Holtz's fiery talk ignited the Bulldogs. Smith threw for 285 yards on 19-of-31 passing with an interception. He tossed a 58-yard touchdown to Jaqwis Dancy and scored on a 4-yard run that was part of a 21-point third quarter. Louisiana Tech took the lead for good on Israel Tucker's 5-yard TD run with 10:27 left in the third. Ferguson set the sacks record when he dropped Hawai'i quarterback Chevan Cordeiro for a 2-yard loss late in the third quarter. "The play that it happened on wasn't by me, but created by the effort on the back end," said Ferguson, who finished the season with 17 1/2 sacks. His 45 career sacks broke the previous mark set by Arizona State's Terrell Suggs. "Coming into the game, that wasn't my goal. The goal was to win the game in Hawaii. I could have had zero sacks tonight if we won the game," said Ferguson, selected MVP of the game along with Hawaii defensive end Kendall Hune. Hawai'i played without wide receiver John Ursua, who leads the nation with 16 touchdown catches. Ursua, sidelined with an undisclosed injury, was ruled out just minutes before the start of the game. The Bulldogs had a Hawai'i Bowl-record nine sacks, four by Willie Baker. Amik Robertson had two of their three interceptions. It was the most sacks allowed in a game by Hawai'i. The Rainbow Warriors (8-6) were just 2 of 14 on third down and got penalized 12 times for 140 yards. Hawai'i is 6-6 in bowl games and 4-4 in the Hawai'i Bowl. The Rainbow Warriors lead the series against Louisiana Tech 8-3. The Bulldogs entered with the 28th-best pass defense in the country, allowing just 193.6 yards per game. They held Hawai'i's ninth-ranked passing offense to 168 yards, well below its average of 321.2 yards. Three of four starters in the secondary will be back for Louisiana Tech next season. While it was the Bulldogs' first appearance in the Hawai'i Bowl, it was Holtz's second win in two trips to the postseason game. He previously coached East Carolina to a 41-38 victory over Boise State in the 2007 Hawai'i Bowl. While the Rainbow Warriors were denied their second Hawai'i Bowl victory in three seasons, they still improved by five wins from last year's 3-9 record and finished with the program's first winning season since 2010. All but three of 22 starters are expected to return next year.

2018 FIRST RESPONDERS BOWL

The 2018 First Responder Bowl was scheduled for December 26, 2018, at the Cotton Bowl Stadium in Dallas. The ninth overall staging of the bowl, this was the first edition since being rebranded; its prior six editions were the Heart of Dallas Bowl, preceded by the TicketCity Bowl in its first two stagings. The game was delayed in the first quarter, after Boston College took a 7–0 lead, and went into a weather delay due to lightning. Repeated lightning strikes near the stadium forced further delays; under NCAA rules, any lightning within eight miles of a stadium triggers a mandatory 30-minute delay, and the delay is extended with additional strikes. The game was cancelled about two hours later amid forecasts that the severe weather would continue throughout the day and night. The game is considered a no-contest for the teams involved. This is believed to be the first postseason game at the FBS-level (or its predecessors) that was cancelled due to weather. NCAA records reflect only two prior postseason cancellations—a 1941 charity game between San Jose State and Hawaii that was cancelled following the attack on Pearl Harbor; and a 2013 Division II game, the C.H.A.M.P.S. Heart of Texas Bowl, between Ouachita Baptist and Tarleton State that was cancelled due to severe weather.

2018 QUICK LANE BOWL

The 2018 Quick Lane Bowl was held on December 26, 2018, at Ford Field in Detroit. It was the fifth edition of the Quick Lane Bowl and sponsored by Quick Lane tire and auto centers. The game was contested between Minnesota from the Big Ten Conference and Georgia Tech from the Atlantic Coast Conference (ACC). This was the first meeting between these teams. The Golden Gophers entered the bowl with a 6–6 record (3–6 in conference). The Yellow Jackets entered the bowl with a 7–5 record (5–3 in conference). In the weeks prior to the game, head coach Paul Johnson announced that this would be his last game coaching.

2018 Quick Lane Bowl	Line	1	-	2	-	3	-	4	-	Final
Minnesota	(57.0)	10	-	3	-	7	-	14	-	34
Georgia Tech	(-5.0)	0	-	3	-	7	-	0	-	10

Scoring Summary
Minnesota – Carpenter 31 yard Field goal
Minnesota – Johnson 18 yard pass from Morgan (Carpenter Kick)
Minnesota – Carpenter 27 yard Field Goal
Georgia Tech – Wells 44 yard Field Goal
Minnesota – Ibrahim 3 yard run (Carpenter Kick)
Georgia Tech – Cottrell 20 yard run (Wells Kick)
Minnesota – Ibrahim 1 yard run (Carpenter Kick)
Minnesota – Johnson 30 yard pass from Morgan (Carpenter Kick

Associated Press Quick Lane Bowl Game Summary – Mohamed Ibrahim took full advantage of holes his teammates created to burst through the line or get to the outside. And when defenders were in Ibrahim's way, he simply lowered his shoulder to run over them. Ibrahim ran for career-high 224 yards and two touchdowns, leading Minnesota to a 34-10 victory over Georgia Tech on Wednesday night in the Quick Lane Bowl. The Golden Gophers (7-6) won three of their last four games, and Ibrahim had a lot to do with that. The 5-foot-10, 205-pound redshirt freshman running back had 121 yards rushing in a win at Wisconsin that made Minnesota bowl eligible and ran for 155 yards last month in a victory over Purdue. The Yellow Jackets (7-6) did not have the speed or strength to slow down Ibrahim, who was so effective Minnesota didn't have to punt once. And their triple-option offense was stunted in Coach Paul Johnson's finale. The Gophers limited Georgia Tech to 206 yards on the ground after it led the nation with 335 yards rushing per game. Minnesota led 13-0 early in the second quarter after Tanner Morgan threw an 18-yard touchdown pass to Tyler Johnson in the first quarter and Emmit Carpenter made two field goals. Ibrahim's 3-yard touchdown run midway through the third quarter made it 20-3. The Yellow Jackets responded with Nathan Cottrell's 20-yard touchdown run, but their defense allowed Ibrahim to score again on the ensuing drive. Morgan connected with Johnson on a 30-yard touchdown strike with 6:19 left, giving the Gophers a 24-point cushion. Minnesota's Ibrahim has the potential to be one of the top players on offense in the Big Ten next season. He runs with a mix of speed and power. Ibrahim had the best day on the ground for a Gopher since 2005 when Laurence Maroney had 258 yards rushing against the Badgers. The Yellow Jackets were in trouble when they fell behind because they don't pass much, making it tough to come back. They averaged fewer than 10 passes during the regular season and it was clear both of their quarterbacks were not comfortable dropping back to throw.

2018 CHEEZ-IT BOWL

The 2018 Cheez-It Bowl was held on December 26, 2018 at Chase Field in Phoenix, Arizona. It was the 30th edition of a bowl game that has gone by various names and was called the Cactus Bowl for its previous four playings. This was the first meeting between the two programs. The Horned Frogs entered the bowl with a 6–6 record (4–5 in conference). The Golden Bears entered the bowl with a 7–5 record (4–5 in conference). Tied 7–7 at the end of regulation, TCU defeated California in the first overtime period, 10–7. The two teams combined for six interceptions in the first half, more than any game during the 2018 season, with a total of nine for the entire game. It became the fourth bowl game in NCAA history with nine or more interceptions, joining the 1942 Orange Bowl, 1968 Sun Bowl, and 1982 Liberty Bowl.

2018 Cheez-It Bowl	Line	1	-	2	-	3	-	4	-	OT	Final
California	(38.0)	7	-	0	-	0	-	0	-	0	7
TCU	(-2.5)	0	-	0	-	7	-	0	-	3	10

Scoring Summary
California – Garbers 4 yard run (Thomas Kick)
TCU – Olonilua 1 yard run (Song Kick)
TCU – Song 27 yard Field Goal

Associated Press Cheez-It Bowl Game Summary - TCU swapped kickers after California called a timeout at the end of regulation — and missed. Faced with a similar decision in overtime, the Horned Frogs stuck with their original kicker. Jonathan Song delivered on his second-chance kick, ending a strange night in the desert. Song kicked a 27-yard field in overtime after being replaced at the end of regulation, lifting TCU to a 10-7 win in an interception-filled Cheez-It Bowl on Wednesday night. TCU and Cal spent the night trading interceptions, turning the Cheez-It Bowl into the Cheez-INT Bowl by combining for nine interceptions, most in the bowl's 30-year history. The Cheez-It Bowl was just the fourth bowl game in NCAA history to feature at least nine interceptions, joining the 1968 Sun Bowl, 1942 Orange Bowl and 1982 Liberty Bowl. TCU's Jawuan Johnson had the final interception of the night to open overtime, nearly returning it for a pick-six. At the end of regulation, the Horned Frogs (7-6) followed a Cal timeout by switching from Song to Cole Bunce, who hooked his 44-yard attempt wide left. TCU sent out Song again in overtime and, after another Cal timeout, opted to leave him. The junior sent the kick straight through the uprights and the Horned Frogs rushing onto the field after a night of survival. TCU's Sewo Olonilua ran for 194 yards and a touchdown — one of the few offensive bright spots outside of Song's kick. Jaylinn Hawkins had three interceptions, breaking the Cheez-It Bowl record while earning defensive player of the game. The Bears (7-6) just couldn't overcome their own miscues. Cal's Chase Garbers threw three interceptions before being replaced by Chase Forrest, who threw two more — including the biggest one by Johnson in overtime. Cal had the first big play after a miscommunication between Muehlstein and Jarrison Stewart led to Hawkins' first interception. Garbers scored two plays later on a 4-yard run. Five more interceptions followed in the first half — one on a failed TCU trick play — and Cal led 7-0. Garbers completed 12 of 19 passes but had three interceptions so Cal's coaches opted to start Forrest in the second half. TCU left Muehlstein in at quarterback despite three first-half interceptions. Hawkins picked up his third interception of the game on the opening drive and Muehlstein was briefly replaced by true freshman Justin

Rogers before returning. The Horned Frogs finally got something going in the third quarter, scoring their only touchdown on Olonilua's 2-yard run — a run initially ruled short before being overturned on review. No team could get much going the rest of the half and the interceptions continued until Song sent his chance kick through the uprights. The Horned Grogs got in their own way all night yet found a way to close out the season with a victory. The Bears also couldn't get out of their own way, suffering a defeat that will sting all offseason. Cal: RB Patrick Laird and top linebacker Jordan Kunaszyk are seniors, but Garbers is a freshman, and the offensive line is relatively young.

2018 INDEPENDENCE BOWL

The 2018 Independence Bowl was played on December 27, 2018. It was the 43rd edition of the Independence Bowl. This was the first meeting between Duke and Temple. The Owls entered the bowl with an 8–4 record, having won 6-of-7 to end their regular season. As Temple head coach Geoff Collins resigned to take the same position at Georgia Tech, the Owls were led in the Independence Bowl by interim head coach Ed Foley. The Blue Devils entered the bowl with a 7–5 record, having lost 4-of-6 to end their regular season.

2018 Independence Bowl	Line	1	-	2	-	3	-	4	-	Final
Temple	(-3.5)	13	-	14	-	0	-	0	-	27
Duke	(56.5)	7	-	14	-	21	-	14	-	56

Scoring Summary
Duke – Harris 2 yard run (Wareham Kick)
Temple – Russo 15 yard run (Mobley Kick)
Temple – Randall 52 yard interception return (Mobley Kick)
Temple – Ritrovato 1 yard run (Mobley Kick)
Duke – Taylor 34 yard pass from Jones (Wareham Kick)
Temple – Yancy 8 yard pass from Russo (Mobley Kick)
Duke – Rahming 22 yard pass from Jones (Wareham Kick)
Duke – Jones 2 yard run (Wareham Kick)
Duke – Rahming 85 yard pass from Jones (Wareham Kick)
Duke – Bobo 7 yard pass from Jones (Wareham Kick)
Duke – Brown 4 yard run (Wareham Kick)
Duke – Koppenhaver 4 yard pass from Jones (Wareham Kick)

Philadelphia Inquirer Independence Bowl Game Summary – It was all going so well for Temple, until the Owls took the field for the second half. Leading 27-21, Temple surrendered touchdowns on Duke's next five possessions and fell, 56-27, to the Blue Devils on Thursday in the 43rd annual Independence Bowl. Duke set the bowl's record for most points scored by a team. The Owls, who entered the game winners of six of their previous seven games, finished 8-5 and are now 3-5 all-time in bowl games. Duke, which lost its last two regular-season games by a 94-13 total, also ended 8-5. Temple running back Ryquell Armstead, and cornerback Rock Ya-Sin sat out. Both will play in the Senior Bowl on Jan. 26, and Ya-Sin will compete in the East-West Shrine game on Jan. 19. Armstead missed two games this season with an ankle injury and tweaked his ankle in the last game of the regular season against UConn. Ya-Sin was sick recently. Neither player was available for comment. Temple could only have wished that Duke quarterback Daniel Jones sat this one out. The 6-foot-5, 220-pound redshirt junior has not declared for the NFL draft, but he could be a potential first-round pick. He can use the tape of this game to boost his reputation. Jones completed 30 of 41 passes for 423 yards and an Independence Bowl-record five touchdowns, with two interceptions. The second interception came when Duke was up, 56-27, and still chucking it in the fourth quarter. For good measure, Jones scored a touchdown and completed a deflected pass to himself. After the game, Jones wouldn't discuss his future, but he was more than happy to talk about why the Blue Devils were successful, especially in the second half. The best matchup involved getting the ball to T.J. Rahming. Getting open all game, the 5-10, 170-pound Rahming had 12 catches for 240 yards and two touchdowns. Temple's Anthony Russo completed 25 of 46 passes for 228 yards and one touchdown, with one interception. The offense that moved so freely in the first half stalled in the second half. The Owls' running game managed only 53 yards on 29 carries, which didn't help. A backbreaker was a short slant to Rahming that the senior turned into an 85-yard touchdown to increase Duke's lead to 35-27 with 7:28 left in the third quarter. And the Blue Devils kept pouring it on. Temple opened the game with a three-and out, and Duke quickly took a 7-0 lead, But the Owls responded with two touchdowns, Russo ran 15 yards for a score, and senior defensive back Delvon Randall, who was named the game's defensive MVP, returned an interception 52 yards for a TD. It was his 12th career interception, moving him to fifth on Temple's list. Twice, the Owls took 13-point leads, on Rob Ritrovato's 1-yard run and Brodrick Yancy's 8-yard touchdown pass from Russo that made it 27-14 with 4:26 left in the first half. After that, it all fell apart in a big way for the Owls. For Temple's coach, this was the end of a devastating week. Last Friday, Foley's younger brother, Cliff, died. Foley wore the initials "CF" for his brother on his hat.

2018 PINSTRIPE BOWL

The 2018 Pinstripe Bowl was played on December 27, 2018. It was the ninth edition of the Pinstripe Bowl and sponsored by the New Era Cap Company. The game was a rematch of the 2017 Orange Bowl, won by Wisconsin, 34–24. This was the second time Miami has played in a New York City bowl game, with their first visit (also in Yankee Stadium) resulting in a 34–36 loss to Nebraska in the 1962 Gotham Bowl. The Badgers entered the bowl with a 7–5 record (5-4 in conference).

2018 Pinstripe Bowl	Line	1	-	2	-	3	-	4	-	Final
Miami	(-2.5)	3	-	0	-	0	-	0	-	3
Wisconsin	(44.0)	14	-	0	-	7	-	14	-	35

Scoring Summary
Wisconsin – Prior 35 yard pass from Coan (Gaglianone Kick)
Wisconsin – Taylor 7 yard run (Gaglianone Kick)
Miami – Baxa 33 yard Field Goal
Wisconsin – Ingold 2 yard run (Gaglianone Kick)
Wisconsin – Coan 7 yard run (Gaglianone Kick)
Wisconsin – Deal 1 yard run (Gaglianone Kick)

Associated Press Pinstripe Bowl Game Summary – Jonathan Taylor played tour guide for his Wisconsin teammates who had never visited New York. They hit the usual landmarks with trips to Lincoln Center and Times Square. Taylor even gave his buds a taste of the luxe life with a window-shopping jaunt along Fifth Avenue. Taylor gave the Badgers one more dazzling sight to see, and the nation's leading rusher heads home with his own sweet souvenir -- an MVP trophy. Taylor ran for 205 yards and a touchdown and topped the 2,000-yard season mark to help Wisconsin rout Miami 35-3 in a chilly Pinstripe Bowl on Thursday night. There are few in football who would argue that point. Taylor, just a sophomore, ripped off runs of 39 and 41 yards at Yankee Stadium and combined with a defense that forced five turnovers to help a Wisconsin (8-5) team ranked fourth in the first AP Top 25 poll salvage its fifth straight bowl victory. The loss had to seem like a rerun for Miami: Taylor ran for 130 yards in Wisconsin's 34-24 win over the Hurricanes last season in the Orange Bowl. Taylor, who finished with 2,194 yards rushing and 16 TDs, has been a bright spot for a team that failed to come close to lofty expectations. Both teams were ranked inside the top 15 last December. A year later, Wisconsin and Miami (7-6) both showed at times why two teams that opened the season inside the top 10 were stuck playing in a ho-hum bowl game with temperatures in the 30s and a sparse crowd in the Bronx. Miami's Malik Rosier threw three interceptions before he was replaced late in the third quarter; Wisconsin's Rafael Gaglianone whiffed on two field goals. The Badgers, certainly used to the cold, came out swinging for the fences -- they scored two touchdowns just 3 1/2 minutes into the game and seemingly knocked the will out of Miami. Jack Coan made the most of his start for injured Alex Hornibrook (concussion) and hit Kendric Taylor for a 35-yard TD on the first drive. Rosier's first pass of the game was intercepted and Taylor capitalized with a 7-yard score to make it 14-0. Coan is a Long Island native and needed nearly 50 tickets for friends and family. He ran right for a 7-yard touchdown in the fourth for a 28-3 lead that made it worth the trip for the thousands of fans in red -- an unseemly sight in June at Yankee Stadium -- that stuck it out to the end. Coan made his fifth appearance this season and burned his eligibility to take a redshirt year. It sure seemed worth it for Wisconsin. Coan was the home state star, but Taylor put a final exclamation point on a season that made one of college football's top stars. Taylor had 117 yards rushing at halftime and finished with his fifth 200-yard game this season, not bad for a running back that averaged 165.8 yards per game. He joined Ron Dayne and Melvin Gordon as Wisconsin's 2,000-yard rushers. Rosier got the start over N'Kosi Perry, who had a rocky season and faced heat for two questionable Snapchat posts, in a move that was quickly second-guessed. His third interception of the game was turned into Alex Ingold's 2-yard touchdown and a 21-3 lead. Perry eventually checked into the game -- but Taylor and Coan had long turned this one into a rout and the Hurricanes offense again was a sore spot (169 total yards).

2018 TEXAS BOWL

The 2018 Texas Bowl was played on December 27, 2018, with kickoff at 9:00 p.m. EST. It was the 13th edition of the Texas Bowl. Despite featuring a pair of .500 teams, fans were treated to one of the highest-scoring games of the bowl season that included five touchdown plays of 50 yards or more, and more than 1,200 yards (combined) of total offense. The teams had previously met twice, with Baylor winning both games, played in 1953 and 1954.

2018 Texas Bowl	Line	1	-	2	-	3	-	4	-	Final
Baylor	(56.5)	10	-	7	-	14	-	14	-	45
Vanderbilt	(-4.5)	14	-	7	-	7	-	10	-	38

Scoring Summary
Vanderbilt – Blasingame 65 yard pass from Shurmur (Guay Kick)
Baylor – Martin 23 yard Field Goal
Baylor – Lovett 12 yard run (Martin Kick)
Vanderbilt – Vaughn 68 yard run (Guay Kick)
Baylor – Hasty 18 yard run (Martin Kick)
Vanderbilt – Vaughn 69 yard run (Guay Kick)
Baylor – Ebner 34 yard run (Martin Kick)
Baylor – Brewer 1 yard run (Mayers Kick)
Vanderbilt – Blasingame 2 yard run (Guay Kick)
Vanderbilt – Blasingame 1 yard run (Guay Kick)
Baylor – Ebner 75 yard pass from Brewer (Mayers Kick)
Vanderbilt – Guay 33 yard Field Goal
Baylor – Jones 52 yard pass from Brewer (Mayers Kick)

Associated Press Texas Bowl Game Summary – Before Baylor faced Vanderbilt in the Texas Bowl on Thursday night, Coach Matt Rhule asked his players to think about where they were a year ago after the team finished 1-11. After taking a moment to reflect on that, the Bears returned their focus to 2018 and finished an impressive turnaround with a huge performance from quarterback Charlie Brewer in a 45-38 win. Brewer threw for 384 yards and two touchdowns, the second a tiebreaking 52-yarder in the fourth quarter, and ran for 109 yards and another score. Brewer, who was selected MVP, connected with Marques Jones for the 52-yard stroke that that made it 45-38 with less than two minutes left. The Bears then stopped Vanderbilt on fourth-and-5 to secure the win. Brewer's other touchdown pass was a 75-yarder earlier in the fourth quarter, and he scored on a 1-yard run in the third. The Bears finished 7-6 a year after losing all but one game in Rhule's first season. Brewer compared his first two seasons at Baylor. Vanderbilt (6-7) was led by Kyle Shurmur, who threw for 286 yards and a touchdown, and Ke'Shawn Vaughn, who ran for two touchdowns and set a Texas Bowl record with 243 yards rushing -- which ranks second in school history. Shurmur moved past Jay Cutler (8,697) for most career yards passing in school history with 8,865. Vanderbilt coach Derek Mason raved about Brewer and was disappointed his team couldn't contain him. Baylor led by three with about 10 1/2 minutes left when a pass intended for Denzel Mims bounced off him as he fell in the end zone and was intercepted by Randall Haynie, who grabbed the ball and stood on tiptoes before falling backward out of the end zone. Two plays later, Vaughn ran 66 yards to get Vanderbilt to the 1, and Khari Blasingame ran it in on the next play to put the Commodores up 35-31. The Bears regained the lead when Trestan Ebner scored on a 75-yard catch and run on the first play of the next drive. Vanderbilt tied it on a 33-yard field goal with 3 1/2 minutes remaining. Ebner's 34-yard touchdown run gave Baylor a 24-21 lead early in the third quarter. The Bears padded the lead when Brewer scrambled for a 1-yard score with about five minutes left in the third. Vanderbilt had a chance to cut the lead to three after that, but Jared Pinkney fumbled after a 32-yard reception and the Bears recovered it at their own 2. But Baylor couldn't move the ball and had to punt. Shurmur threw a 52-yard pass to Amir Abdur-Rahman to get the Commodores to the 2-yard line, and Blasingame scored on the next play to get to 31-28 near the end of the third quarter. The Commodores took a 7-0 lead when Shurmur connected with Blasingame on a short pass and dashed down the field for a career-long 65-yard touchdown reception on the third play of the game. The Bears settled for a 23-yard field goal on their first drive before taking a 10-7 lead when John Lovett ran 12 yards for a touchdown with about two minutes left in the first quarter. Vanderbilt went back on top 14-10 when Vaughn ran 68 yards for a touchdown late in the first. JaMycal Hasty gave Baylor a 17-14 lead when he scored on an 18-yard run early in the second quarter. But Vaughn's second long run came not long after that to make it 21-17. Vaughn broke a couple of tackles and then outran the rest of the defense for a 69-yard score. Jameson Houston dove at his feet near the 20-yard line, but barely clipped one of his legs and Vaughn didn't break his stride on the way to the end zone.

2018 MUSIC CITY BOWL

The 2018 Music City Bowl was played on December 28, 2018 at Nissan Stadium in Nashville, Tennessee. It was the 21st edition of the Music City Bowl. The Boilermakers entered the bowl with a 6–6 record (5–4 in conference). This game was the last attended by Purdue Superfan Tyler Trent, who had become a national inspiration during his battle with terminal osteosarcoma. He and his family traveled to Nashville on an airplane normally used by the Indianapolis Colts, courtesy of team owner Jim Irsay. Trent, who served as an honorary Purdue captain for the game, died four days later on New Year's Day. The Tigers entered the bowl with a 7–5 record (3–5 in conference).

2018 Music City Bowl	Line	1	-	2	-	3	-	4	-	Final
Purdue	(58.0)	7	-	0	-	7	-	0	-	14
Auburn	(-3.5)	28	-	28	-	7	-	0	-	63

Scoring Summary
Auburn – Whitlow 66 yard pass from Stidham (Carlson Kick)
Auburn – Whitlow 2 yard run (Carlson Kick)
Auburn – Whitlow 1 yard run (Carlson Kick)
Purdue – Moore 7 yard run (Evans Kick)
Auburn – Slayton 74 yard pass from Stidham (Carlson Kick)
Auburn – Slayton 52 yard pass from Stidham (Carlson Kick)
Auburn – Bryant 20 yard interception return (Carlson Kick)
Auburn – Schwartz 6 yard run (Carlson Kick)
Auburn – Slayton 34 yard pass from Stidham (Carlson Kick)
Auburn – Davis 5 yard pass from Stidham (Carlson Kick)
Purdue – Blough 22 yard run (Evans Kick)

Associated Press Music City Bowl Game Summary – Jarrett Stidham threw for 373 yards and five touchdowns in his final college game, and Auburn routed Purdue 63-14 in the Franklin American Mortgage Music City Bowl on Friday. Auburn raced out to a 56-7 halftime lead, scoring TDs on its first eight possessions -- spanning only 11 minutes -- to set a record for points in any half of any bowl game, according to ESPN Stats & Information. The Tigers also tied Music City Bowl records for most points and TDs -- set by West Virginia in 2000 -- with 5:36 left in the first half. The 56 points by halftime were the most scored in any half in program history. Auburn (8-5) rolled in the finale of a season in which it opened with a top-10 ranking, stumbled a bit in the middle and concluded with a record-setting performance. It was the Tigers' first postseason victory since beating Memphis in the 2015 Birmingham Bowl. Auburn scored the most points by a Southeastern Conference team in a bowl, topping Alabama's 61-6 win over Syracuse in the Orange Bowl on Jan. 1, 1953. The Tigers had a chance to match the most points ever scored in a bowl (70), most recently reached by Army in the Armed Forces Bowl last week, but they took a knee at the Purdue 1-yard line with 61 seconds left. Stidham, a junior who already has declared his intention to leave school early for the NFL draft, got the Tigers off to a fast start, and they just poured it on from there. Purdue (6-7) dropped three of its last four games in its second season under Coach Jeff Brohm. Auburn started the game with the ball and needed only 63 seconds to set the tone, with Stidham finding JaTarvious Whitlow for a 66-yard TD pass. Whitlow also added a pair of short TD runs as Auburn led 28-7 at the end of the first quarter. The Tigers outgained Purdue 586-263 in total offense and had only one three-and-out late in the third quarter. Purdue was intercepted twice and turned it over on downs twice. Auburn punted once all game. Darius Slayton set a bowl record with three TD catches of 74, 52 and 34 yards. Javaris Davis had a sack and an interception in the first quarter for Auburn, and Big Kat Bryant returned an interception 20 yards for a TD and a 45-7 lead with 12:29 left in the first half. Purdue was without defensive tackle Lorenzo Neal out after tearing an ACL in the regular-season finale against Indiana, the Boilermakers had few answers for anything Auburn tried on offense. For Auburn, It sure looks as if coach Malzahn made the right decision when he took back the play calling duties, he handled his first three seasons at Auburn.

2018 CAMPING WORLD BOWL

The 2018 Camping World Bowl was played on December 28, 2018, between the West Virginia Mountaineers and the Syracuse Orange. It was the 29th edition of the Camping World Bowl. This was the 61st time the two programs had met; Syracuse held a 33–27 series lead in prior games. The Mountaineers Quarterback Will Grier, tackle Yodny Cajuste, and wide receiver Gary Jennings announced that they would sit out the game in order to prepare for the 2019 NFL Draft. Syracuse also entered the game short-handed, as defensive end Alton Robinson, defensive tackle McKinley Williams, and defensive back Antwan Cordy all missed the game for personal reasons.

2018 Camping World Bowl	Line	1	-	2	-	3	-	4	-	Final
#15 West Virginia	(67.0)	3	-	9	-	6	-	0	-	18
#17 Syracuse	(-3.0)	7	-	7	-	3	-	17	-	34

Scoring Summary
West Virginia – Staley 28 yard Field Goal
Syracuse – Adams 4 yard run (Szmyt Kick)
West Virginia – McKoy 3 yard run (Staley Kick)
Syracuse – Adams 1 yard run (Szmyt Kick)
West Virginia – Staley 36 yard Field Goal
West Virginia – Staley 44 yard Field Goal
Syracuse – Szmyt 39 yard Field Goal
West Virginia – Staley 49 yard Field Goal
Syracuse – Jackson 14 yard pass from Dungey (Szmyt Kick)
Syracuse – Szmyt 34 yard Field Goal
Syracuse – Howard 4 yard run (Szymt Kick)

Associated Press Camping World Bowl Game Summary – Syracuse sent Eric Dungey out a winner and got a good look at its future. Dungey capped his record-setting college career by throwing for 303 yards, Abdul Adams and Trishton Jackson combined to score three touchdowns in their Syracuse debuts and the 17th-ranked Orange got their first 10-win season since 2001 by topping No. 15 West Virginia 34-18 in the Camping World Bowl on Friday. The Orange ended with a flourish, too: Down 18-17 going into the final quarter, they scored 17 points in the first 5:01 of the fourth. Adams rushed for two first-half scores, and Jackson hauled in a TD pass from Dungey on the first play of the fourth quarter for Syracuse (10-3), which survived a game that featured eight lead changes. Adams (from Oklahoma) and Jackson (from Michigan State) are transfers who had to sit out a year, which by NCAA rule was satisfied at the end of the first semester. Their touchdowns counted; their year will not. Under the new NCAA rule on redshirting, Adams and Jackson still have two remaining seasons of eligibility, and both are expected to play big roles for the Orange in 2019. Jack Allison, making his first collegiate start because West Virginia star quarterback Will Grier elected to skip the bowl game and focus on preparing for the NFL, completed 17 of 35 passes for 277 yards for the Mountaineers (8-4). Besides Grier, West Virginia was also without two of his three top targets this season -- Gary Jennings was ruled out long ago with an ankle injury, and Marcus Simms was a surprise scratch. He also gave Allison high marks. Allison had thrown 10 passes this season before Friday. Kennedy McCoy had a 3-yard touchdown run for West Virginia on a direct snap, and Evan Staley made four field goals for the Mountaineers. Kendall Coleman had three sacks for the Orange. Andre Szmyt made a pair of field goals for Syracuse, ending his freshman season with 30 -- one shy of the Football Bowl Subdivision record set in 2003 by Georgia's Billy Bennett. Dungey came into the game holding or sharing 18 Syracuse records and got another one in his collegiate finale. He passed Ryan Nassib (9,190) for most passing yards in Syracuse history, finishing his career with 9,340. The Mountaineers fell in a bowl game for the third consecutive season, but probably have a good idea about their starting quarterback in 2019. Allison had nine completions go for more than 15 yards.

2018 ALAMO BOWL

The 2018 Alamo Bowl was held on December 28, 2018. It was the 26th edition of the Alamo Bowl, and sponsored by Valero Energy, the game was officially known as the Valero Alamo Bowl. The game was played between Iowa State from the Big 12 Conference and Washington State from the Pac-12 Conference. This was the first meeting between the two programs. The Cyclones entered the bowl with an 8–4 record (6–3 in the Big 12). The Cougars entered the bowl with a 10–2 record (7–2 in the Pac-12).

2018 Alamo Bowl	Line	1	-	2	-	3	-	4	-	Final
#25 Iowa State	(56.0)	0	-	10	-	10	-	6	-	26
#12 Washington State	(-1.5)	7	-	14	-	0	-	7	-	28

Scoring Summary
Washington State – Bell 22 yard pass from Minshew (Mazza Kick)
Washington State – Minshew 7 yard run (Mazza Kick)
Iowa State – Purdy 9 yard run (Assalley Kick)
Washington State – Patmon 9 yard pass from Minshew (Mazza Kick)
Iowa State – Assalley 50 yard Field Goal
Iowa State – Montgomery 8 yard run (Assalley Kick)
Iowa State – Assalley 23 yard Field Goal
Washington State – Borghi 10 yard run (Mazza Kick)
Iowa State – Purdy 1 yard run (2 point conversion failed)

ESPN News Services Alamo Bowl Game Summary – Gardner Minshew II and that glorious mustache conjured up a final bit of magic in a grand finale for Washington State. Minshew, a graduate transfer quarterback whose whiskered upper lip was loved and mimicked by Cougars fans all season, threw two touchdown passes and ran for another score in sending No. 13 Washington State (No. 12 AP) to a 28-26 win over No. 24 Iowa State (No. 25 AP) in the Valero Alamo Bowl on Friday night. Minshew's passing and scrambling earned the Cougars (11-2) a school record for wins in a season. He also finished with 4,779 passing yards this season, breaking the Pac-12 single-season record previously held by California's Jared Goff (4,719). Minshew passed for 299 yards Friday, none of them bigger than a play made from desperation when Iowa State had all the momentum. After watching a 21-10 lead dwindle to 21-20 by early in the fourth quarter, the Cougars stripped the ball from Iowa State running back David Montgomery at the Cyclones' 30. Minshew, who had been held in check in the third quarter, escaped a third-down pass rush to flip a last-second shovel pass to Tay Martin that went for 20 yards. The play stunned the Cyclones, and Max Borghi scored on a 10-yard run the next play. It was just another big fourth-quarter moment for the transfer from East Carolina whom Coach Mike Leach had lured out West with the promise he could lead the nation in passing. Minshew was the nation's leading passer in yards per game this season and won the Johnny Unitas Award as the nation's top senior quarterback in a season the Cougars fell one game short of playing for the Pac-12 championship. Nearly all his completions this season were more orthodox than the flip to Martin. None were bigger than this one for the season and the legacy it left for the program. The Cyclones did a good job in bottling Minshew up for much of the game. Iowa State's defense held Washington State to 10 points and 135 yards below its season averages, and two of the Cougars' touchdowns came on short drives after turnovers. But after Minshew found a way to get Washington State in the end zone, the Cougars' defense made the one play it had to at the end. Iowa State's last chance came after quarterback Brock Purdy scored from a yard out with 4:02 left. The Cyclones went for two, but a pass to Montgomery was stopped well short of the goal line after a false-start penalty pushed the line of scrimmage back to the 8. Iowa State had seven false-start penalties and had two players ejected for targeting hits on Minshew. Purdy passed for 315 yards, and Cyclones wide receiver Hakeem Butler caught nine passes for 192 yards, 6 yards shy of the Alamo Bowl record. Montgomery rushed for 124 yards. The Cyclones (8-5) had rallied from a 1-3 start to finish third in the Big 12, the program's best conference finish in 40 years. Minshew survived several tough hits in the first half and was excellent when it was time to kill the clock. He completed 9 of 13 passes in the fourth quarter for 78 yards. After Iowa State's final touchdown, he completed three passes, two of them converting third downs, as the Cougars ran out the clock. For Iowa State, turnovers and targeting calls were critical. Purdy threw two first-quarter interceptions, and Montgomery's fumble was a game-changer. Iowa State had two key defenders ejected in the second quarter for targeting hits to Minshew. Senior linebacker Willie Harvey was ejected after smashing Minshew in the face mask on a scramble. Defensive end Eyioma Uwazurike was booted after a sack knocked Minshew's helmet off. Washington State cornerback Marcus Strong had a long touchdown interception return wiped out in the first quarter when he was flagged for taunting on his way into the end zone. Strong stepped in front of a pass intended for Butler and had a clear path to the goal line. He was penalized because he held the ball out and looked back as Purdy made a futile dive for his feet. Instead of the score, the Cougars got the ball on the Iowa State 20 and scored two plays later when Minshew connected with Renard Bell.

2018 CHICK-FIL-A PEACH BOWL

The 2018 Peach Bowl was played on December 29, 2018. It was the 51st edition of the Peach Bowl, and the second Peach Bowl to be played in Mercedes-Benz Stadium. After finishing their regular season with a 10–2 record (8–1 in conference), the Wolverines were selected to their first Peach Bowl appearance. This was their 47th bowl game appearance, tied for 11th-highest total all-time among FBS schools. Several Michigan players, including RB Karan Higdon, DL Rashan Gary, and LB Devin Bush Jr., sat out the game in order to focus on the 2019 NFL Draft. After finishing their regular season with a 9–3 record (5–3 in conference), the Gators were selected to their third Peach Bowl appearance. This was their 44th bowl game appearance.

2018 Chick-Fil-A Peach Bowl	Line	1	-	2	-	3	-	4	-	Final
#10 Florida	(51.0)	3	-	10	-	14	-	14	-	41
#8 Michigan	(-4.0)	7	-	3	-	0	-	5	-	15

Scoring Summary
Florida – McPherson 21 yard Field Goal
Michigan – Peoples-Jones 9 yard pass from Patterson (Moody Kick)
Florida – McPherson 26 yard Field Goal
Michigan – Moody 48 yard Field Goal
Florida – Franks 20 yard run (McPherson Kick)
Florida – Perine 5 yard pass from Franks (McPherson Kick)
Florida – Scarlett 1 yard run (McPherson Kick)
Michigan – Moody 26 yard Field goal
Florida – Perine 53 yard run (McPherson Kick)
Michigan – Safety – Punt blocked through end zone
Florida – Gardner-Johnson 30 yard interception return (McPherson Kick)

Orlando Sentinel Chick-Fil-A Peach Bowl Game Summary – As the confetti fell and flashbulbs pulsated at Mercedes-Benz Stadium, Florida senior pass rusher CeCe Jefferson wished he was coming back for more. The 23-year-old's final game with the Gators showed him what he would be missing. It also left Jefferson to wonder what might have been if Coach Dan Mullen had arrived earlier. Even so, UF's 41-15 win during Saturday's Chick-fil-A Peach Bowl was a nice way for Jefferson to close his college career and the Gators to polish off a promising turnaround during Mullen's first season. Looking for a statement win on a big stage, the No. 10 Gators routed No. 7 Michigan, which held College Football Playoff aspirations back in late November. Florida's fourth consecutive win — and third by more than 25 points — also showed the potential of an attack Mullen was hired to fix following three seasons of offense futility under Jim McElwain. Jefferson can only imagine how good the Gators would have been during his first three years in Gainesville if Mullen had been calling plays. With an announced crowd of 74,006 looking on, the Gators (10-3) dominated the Wolverines (10-3) on both sides of the football and broke open a close game with a 28-point second half. Playing his final college game before leaving for the NFL, defensive back Chauncey Gardner-Johnson ended the Gators' assault with a 30-yard pick-six — the second interception of the day for the game's defensive MVP. Michigan entered the day as the nation's leader in total defense but were without second-team All-America linebacker Devin Bush and top defensive tackle Rashan Gary. Each decided to begin preparing for the NFL. The idea never crossed Gardner-Johnson's mind. A year removed from a 4-7 finish, Gardner-Johnson and the Gators were determined to end 2018 on a high note. With their third win against a ranked team in 2018, the Gators are sure to finish with their highest ranking since the 2009 team ended No. 3 in Tim Tebow's final season. That was the last time Florida won a top-tier bowl game, too. To win one Saturday, the Gators would have beat Michigan for the first time in five meetings, a stretch that included losses by a combined score of 74-24 during the 2016 Citrus Bowl and 2017 season opener. The Wolverines were 5.5-point favorites but also short-handed without Bush, Gary and two starters on offense. The Gators took advantage behind timely play-calling by Mullen and his staff, along with a versatile showing by quarterback Feleipe Franks. Franks finished the day with 247 total yards, including 74 on the ground, to earn offensive MVP honors. He also was 13-of-23 passing for 173 yards and a touchdown to give him 24 passing touchdowns a season after Franks looked lost. Then Mullen arrived. Against Michigan, Franks was confident and in command of the Gators' offense. The redshirt sophomore's biggest play of the day followed an audible he called to catch the Wolverines flat-footed. With UF trailing 10-6 and facing third-and-four from the Wolverines' 20-yard line, the 6-foot-6, 240-pound Franks took the snap and raced up the middle of the field for the go-ahead touchdown. A big play on defense by Gardner-Johnson helped the Gators begin to pull away from the Wolverines. Locked onto his receiver beginning to separate from a UF defender down field, Michigan quarterback Shea Patterson did not see Gardner-Johnson lurking. When Patterson let go of the football, Gardner-Johnson ran it down, came up with the interception and returned it 47 yards to the Michigan 44. Facing a fourth-and-one three plays later, Mullen used a timeout. Eschewing conservatism, the Gators dialed up a jet sweep for Kadarius Toney, who raced 30 yards — a play call Mullen credited to QBs coach Brian Johnson. Two plays later, the Gators scored on a 5-yard tunnel screen to tailback Lamical Perine, who later added a 53-yard touchdown run to ice the game. Known for his play-calling acumen, Mullen deadpanned, "I really didn't do a whole lot today." The line drew laughter in the postgame press conference. But Mullen's players knew better. Mullen's arrival and his magic touch have revived the Gators and give the program a wave of momentum entering 2019. Before the year ended, the 46-year-old gave players like Jefferson, Gardner-Johnson and Franks a lifetime memory.

2018 BELK BOWL

The 2018 Belk Bowl was played on December 29, 2018. It was the 17th edition of the Belk Bowl and was sponsored by the department store chain Belk. In prior games between the two programs, South Carolina held a 21–13–1 lead in the series. The Gamecocks entered the bowl with a 7–5 record (4–4 in conference). The Cavaliers entered the bowl with a 7–5 record (4–4 in conference).

2018 Belk Bowl	Line	1	-	2	-	3	-	4	-	Final
South Carolina	(-3.5)	0	-	0	-	0	-	0	-	0
Virginia	(54.0)	7	-	7	-	7	-	7	-	28

Scoring Summary
Virginia – Zaccheaus 6 yard pass from Perkins (Delaney Kick)
Virginia – Ellis 9 yard run (Delaney Kick)
Virginia – Zaccheaus 10 yard pass from Perkins (Delaney Kick)
Virginia – Zaccheaus 12 yard pass from Perkins (Delaney Kick)

Associated Press Belk Bowl Game Summary – Shortly after winning the Belk Bowl and earning Virginia its first bowl victory since 2005, quarterback Bryce Perkins raised the bar. That would mean knocking off perennial ACC power Clemson, which has won four straight conference titles. For now though, the Cavaliers (8-5) will have to settle for savoring a 28-0 victory over South Carolina in the Belk Bowl, a win that snapped the longest bowl drought in the ACC. Perkins threw three touchdown passes to Olamide Zaccheaus, the game's Most Outstanding Player, and Virginia's 14th-ranked pass defense dominated a South Carolina team that had averaged more than 38 points over its previous five games. Perkins completed 22 of 31 passes for 208 yards and ran for 81 yards. Zaccheaus had 12 catches for 100 yards and Jordan Ellis ran for 106 yards and a touchdown as Virginia held more than a 24-minute edge in time of possession. Perkins said he felt chemistry with Zaccheaus the first day he transferred in last year from Arizona Western Community College -- and his favorite target agreed. Virginia's defense was relentless. It put the clamps on quarterback Jake Bentley, who had thrown for 16 touchdowns over the previous five games, including a 510-yard, five-TD performance against Clemson earlier this month. Bentley was limited to 218 yards on 17-of-39 passing and was intercepted twice. South Carolina (7-6) was 2 of 13 on third down conversions and 2 of 5 on fourth downs. Bentley said he didn't play well at all. The Gamecocks were shut out for the first time since 2006, when they lost 18-0 to Georgia.

2018 ARIZONA BOWL

The 2018 Arizona Bowl was played on December 29, 2018. It was the fourth edition of the Arizona Bowl, and sponsored by the Nova Home Loans mortgage broker company, the game was officially known as the Nova Home Loans Arizona Bowl. In prior games between the two programs, Nevada held a 3–2 lead in the series.

2018 Arizona Bowl	Line	1	-	2	-	3	-	4	-	OT	Final
Arkansas State	(57.0)	0	-	7	-	0	-	3	-	3	13
Nevada	(Pk)	0	-	3	-	0	-	7	-	6	16

Scoring Summary
Nevada – Ahmed 36 yard Field Goal
Arkansas State – Murray 2 yard run (Grupe Kick)
Nevada – Lee 1 yard run (Ahmed Kick)
Arkansas State – Grupe 32 yard Field Goal
Arkansas State – Grupe 24 yard Field Goal
Nevada – Roberson 11 yard pass from Gangi

Arizona Daily Star Arizona Bowl Game Summary — They sat conspicuously on the visitor's sideline at Arizona Stadium: An oversized pair of bright red boxing gloves — the kind your grandfather might have bought your dad to teach him self-defense. An Arkansas State's defensive player receives the gloves every time he forces a ball loose. It's not the only "turnover prop" used by assistant head coach Trooper Taylor, who helped popularize the trend when he was in the Southeastern Conference. A-State players can wear championship belts and bank bags if the plays they make are big enough. Saturday, the Red Wolves' defense came away with every reward imaginable — except for a Nova Home Loans Arizona Bowl trophy. Such is the result when an offense fails in the end zone, two standout defensive players get hurt and the opponent pulls out razzle-dazzle — from a wheel route to a flea-flicker — after lying dormant for three quarters. Arkansas State's defense allowed just 98 yards in the first three quarters, more than enough to bury most teams. Then Nevada gained 197 yards in the fourth quarter and overtime, and the short-handed, exhausted Red Wolves fell. Arkansas State had its chance. Needing one more stop to end the game with 1:44 left in regulation, A-State allowed Nevada to convert on fourth-and-seven. Nevada quarterback Ty Gangi found Dominic Christian for 15 yards to keep the drive going; two plays later, Gangi hit Ben Putnam for 44 yards to the A-State 1-yard line. Devonte Lee's touchdown dive gave Nevada a 10-7 lead with 1:06 left. Though A-State would drive, score and force overtime, the momentum was clearly in Nevada's favor. A-State played conservatively in overtime, opting for three consecutive runs before a field goal by Blake Grupe gave the Red Wolves the lead. The strategy was clear: Anderson was putting the game on his defense's shoulders, with hopes that the unit would make one last stop. A-State had already forced intercepted two passes and sacked Nevada three times. But then Toa Taua rushed four straight times for 14 total yards, moving Nevada to the A-State 11. And then, on third-and-7, Gangi found tight end Reagan Roberson with what he called "a little foot-fire" on the flat. The tight end caught the pass, bolted for the pylon, beat Edmonds and dove in for the win. Gangi said the A-State defense was a tough one to crack. They were also short-handed. Senior defensive end Ronheen Bingham exited the game early with a left knee injury. Defensive back Justin Clifton was hurt on the first play of the second half and did not return. Coach Blake Anderson described Bingham's injury as "not good" and "significant" — bad news for a potential NFL Draft prospect. Even without Bingham and Clifton, A-State rendered Nevada's offense nearly irrelevant for three-plus quarters. Linebacker Tahje Chambers led the team with nine tackles, and Edmonds added eight.

A-State's downfall was offense, and Anderson admitted as much. The Red Wolves were uncharacteristically sloppy. Quarterback Justice Hansen threw his first interception since Oct. 27 — and then threw two more. The Sun Belt Conference's Player of the Year completed just 26 of 46 passes for 275 yards. The Red Wolves and blew a fourth-and-goal from the 4-yard line with an ill-advised pass to an offensive lineman. Arkansas State's players were still grappling with the shocking loss in the minutes after the game ended. Some fell to their knees, sobbing. One ran immediately off the field. Coaches gazed off, wondering how a game that was so in hand for nearly 3 hours came off the rails.

2018 ORANGE BOWL (NATIIONAL SEMIFINAL)

The 2018 Orange Bowl was played on Saturday, December 29, 2018. It was the 85th edition of the Orange Bowl. The Orange Bowl was one of two College Football Playoff semifinal games, with the winner advancing to the 2019 College Football Playoff National Championship. It was sponsored by the Capital One Financial Corporation; the game was officially known as the College Football Playoff Semifinal at the Capital One Orange Bowl. The game featured top-ranked Alabama of the Southeastern Conference (SEC) against fourth-ranked Oklahoma of the Big 12 Conference. The programs had previously met five times, with Oklahoma leading the series, 3–1–1. They first met in the 1963 Orange Bowl, won by Alabama, 17–0. Their most recent meeting was in the 2014 Sugar Bowl, a 45–31 Oklahoma victory.

Alabama Crimson Tide - Alabama defeated Georgia in the 2018 SEC Championship Game on December 1, then received their bid to the Orange Bowl with the release of final CFP rankings on December 2. The Crimson Tide entered the bowl with a 13–0 record (8–0 in conference). On December 25, it was announced that three Alabama players, including starting offensive lineman Deonte Brown, would not play in the game due to an unspecified violation of team rules.

Oklahoma Sooners - Oklahoma defeated Texas in the 2018 Big 12 Championship Game on December 1, then received their bid to the Orange Bowl with the release of final CFP rankings on December 2. The Sooners entered the bowl with a 12–1 record (8–1 in conference); their only loss was to Texas, by a score of 45–48 in the 113th Red River Showdown on October 6.

2018 Orange Bowl	Line	1	-	2	-	3	-	4	-	Final
#4 Oklahoma	(80.5)	0	-	10	-	10	-	14	-	34
#1 Alabama	(-15.0)	21	-	10	-	0	-	14	-	45

Scoring Summary
Alabama – Harris 1 yard run (Bulovas Kick)
Alabama – Ruggs 10 yard pass from Tagovailoa (Bulovas Kick)
Alabama – Harris 1 yard run (Bulovas Kick)
Alabama – Jacobs 27 yard pass from Tagovailoa (Bulovas Kick)
Oklahoma – Sermon 2 yard run (Seibert Kick)
Oklahoma – Seibert 26 yard Field Goal
Alabama – Bulovas 38 yard Field Goal
Oklahoma – Seibert 26 yard Field Goal
Oklahoma – Rambo 49 yard pass from Murray (Seibert Kick)
Alabama – Smith 10 yard pass from Tagovailoa (Bulovas Kick)
Oklahoma – Lamb 10 yard pass from Murray (Seibert Kick)
Alabama – Jeudy 13 yard pass from Tagovailoa (Bulovas Kick)
Oklahoma – Murray 8 yard run (Seibert Kick)

Associated Press Orange Bowl Game Summary – This season's Alabama juggernaut has yet to be stopped, and Oklahoma's shaky defense sure wasn't going to get in the way. Maybe Clemson can. Tua Tagovailoa threw for 318 yards and four touchdowns and No. 1-ranked Alabama beat No. 4 Oklahoma 45-34 on Saturday night in the College Football Playoff semifinal at the Orange Bowl. The high-scoring Sooners reached the semifinal despite a porous defense that was no match for Alabama's diverse attack, and the defending champion Crimson Tide led 28-0 after only 17 minutes. Alabama (14-0) advanced to the national championship game for the fourth consecutive season and will play Jan. 7 in Santa Clara, California against familiar foe Clemson, which beat Notre Dame 30-3 in the Cotton Bowl. The Tigers ranked No. 2, and Alabama will face off in the playoffs for the fourth year in a row and have split two title games. Saban spiked his headset during one of his several sideline tirades. He lobbed oranges during the postgame celebration. Tagovailoa's performance argued for a Florida recount in the Heisman Trophy vote. He finished as the runner-up to Oklahoma's Kyler Murray but won sweet consolation by completing 24 of 27 passes, with scores to four receivers. While Tagovailoa connected on his first nine passes for 184 yards, Murray was sacked twice before he threw a pass, and his first completion came with his team already down 21-0. Murray had one brilliant moment, a perfect deep throw on the move to Charleston Rambo in the end zone for a 49-yard score. He passed for 308 yards and ran for 109 but took several jarring hits, including when All-America nose guard Quinnen Williams dislodged his helmet and forced him from the game for one play in the fourth quarter. The Sooners (12-2) came up short in a bid for their first national title since the 2000 season. His team was bowled over, on one play. When Robert Barnes tried to stop Josh Jacobs in the open field, the Alabama running back lowered his head for the collision and continued to the end zone for a 27-yard score while the Sooners safety spun to the turf, dazed and briefly unable to get up. "When I saw an opportunity to score, I just tried my best to score," Jacobs said with a chuckle. Alabama had the ball for more than 36 minutes and totaled 528 yards. In a matchup between the two highest-scoring offenses in the country, Oklahoma fell too far behind early. On the first snap, DeVonta Smith turned Tagovailoa's short pass into a 50-yard gain. The Crimson Tide went on to score an Orange Bowl-record 21 points in the opening quarter. At one point the disparity in yards was 191-0. The most noise the Sooners mustered in the early going was when linebacker Kenneth Murray talked trash with the Alabama bench -- with his team trailing by three touchdowns. The Sooners rallied and closed to within 11 points three times in the final 18 minutes. But two onside kicks failed, and Alabama ran the final 4:23 off the clock after Oklahoma's last score. Alabama took the opening kickoff and drove 75 yards for a touchdown. Oklahoma was awarded a fumble recovery at the 1, but officials overturned the ruling following a replay review, and Damien Harris scored on the next play. The Sooners' first three plays lost 6 yards, forcing a punt, and eight plays later Tagovailoa hit Henry Ruggs III with a 10-yard touchdown pass. Tagovailoa threw deep to Jerry Jeudy for 40 yards to set up the Crimson Tide's third score, and Jacobs' catch and run for a touchdown made it 28-0. Tide linebacker Christian Miller limped to the locker room in the third quarter with a left hamstring injury. An MRI was planned, and his availability for the title game was uncertain, Saban said. The Crimson Tide need one more win for their sixth national title in the past decade. They have a chance to finish 15-0, which hasn't been done at the top level of college football since Penn went 15-0 in 1897. Saban moved closer to his seventh national title, which would break the record he shares with the Crimson Tide's Bear Bryant.

2018 COTTON BOWL (NATIONAL SEMIFINAL)

The 2018 Cotton Bowl Classic was played on December 29, 2018, at AT&T Stadium in Arlington, Texas. The 83rd Cotton Bowl Classic was a College Football Playoff semifinal with the winner to compete in the 2019 College Football Playoff National Championship. It was sponsored by the Goodyear Tire and Rubber Company; the game was officially known as the College Football Playoff Semifinal at the Goodyear Cotton Bowl Classic. The game featured second-ranked Clemson of the Atlantic Coast Conference against third-ranked Notre Dame, an FBS independent. This was the first time that the two programs met in a bowl game; their more recent regular season meeting had been in 2015, won by Clemson. The only prior Cotton Bowl to feature two undefeated teams had been the 1948 edition, which ended in a 13–13 tie between Penn State and SMU.

Clemson Tigers - Clemson defeated Pitt in the 2018 ACC Championship Game on December 1, then received their bid to the Cotton Bowl with the release of final CFP rankings on December 2. The Tigers entered the bowl with a 13–0 record (8–0 in conference). On December 27, it was confirmed that three Clemson players, including starting defensive lineman Dexter Lawrence, would be suspended from playing in the game by the NCAA, due to drug testing showing "trace amounts of a banned substance", which was identified as ostarine.

Notre Dame Fighting Irish - Notre Dame received their bid to the Cotton Bowl with the release of final CFP rankings on December 2. The independent Fighting Irish entered the bowl with a 12–0 record.

2018 Cotton Bowl	Line	1	-	2	-	3	-	4	-	Final
#3 Notre Dame	(58.0)	3	-	0	-	0	-	0	-	3
#2 Clemson	(-10.0)	3	-	20	-	7	-	0	-	30

Scoring Summary
Clemson – Huegel 40 yard Field Goal
Notre Dame – Yoon 28 yard Field Goal
Clemson – Ross 52 yard pass from Lawrence (Huegel Kick)
Clemson – Ross 42 yard pass from Lawrence (Huegel Kick)
Clemson – Higgins 19 yard pass from Lawrence (Huegel Kick)
Clemson – Etienne 62 yard run (Huegel Kick)

Associated Press Cotton Bowl Game Summary – When Clemson's Dabo Swinney entrusted a team with championship aspirations to freshman quarterback Trevor Lawrence in September, this is what the Tigers' coach had in mind. Lawrence threw for 327 yards and three touchdowns and No. 2 Clemson beat No. 3 Notre Dame 30-3 on Saturday in the Cotton Bowl to reach the College Football Playoff title game. The Tigers (14-0) will play No. 1 Alabama -- a 45-34 winner over No. 4 Oklahoma in the Orange Bowl -- for a fourth straight season in the playoff on Jan. 7 in Santa Clara, California. Clemson's overpowering and experienced defensive line, led by ends Clelin Ferrell and Austin Bryant, smothered Ian Book and the

Fighting Irish (12-1), holding them to 248 yards. On offense, freshmen led the way. Lawrence, making his 10th career start, was 27 for 39 and did not throw an interception against a Notre Dame defense that had been one of the best on the country. Freshman receiver Justyn Ross had six catches for 148 yards and two long touchdowns. The Irish hung around for a quarter, with the teams exchanging field goals. But in the first quarter, Notre Dame All-America cornerback Julian Love went out with what coach Brian Kelly said after the game was a head injury and Lawrence started taking apart the Irish. Lawrence hooked up with Ross deep down the sideline and the big receiver beat Love's backup, Donte Vaughn, for a tackle-breaking, 52-yard score early in the second quarter. The Irish looked as if they might keep it close to halftime, but they couldn't keep Clemson out of their backfield -- even without suspended star tackle Dexter Lawrence. In the final 2 minutes, Trevor Lawrence connected with Ross on a 42-yard score and with Tee Higgins for a one-handed, 19-yard touchdown reception -- again over Vaughn -- with 2 seconds left in the second quarter. Lawrence was 13 for 15 for 229 yards in the quarter. That made it 23-3 at half and once again the Fighting Irish looked outclassed against the best of the best. Not so different from the 42-14 loss to Alabama in the 2012 BCS championship game or the 44-28 loss to Ohio State in the 2016 Fiesta Bowl. In fact, Notre Dame is 0-8 in BCS and New Year's Six games since winning the Cotton Bowl in 1993. Receiver Miles Boykin insisted this Notre Dame team was different. Though to be fair, Clemson has been doing this to everyone since Lawrence settled in. The Tigers haven't had an opponent stay within 20 points since a close call against Syracuse on Sept. 29. That was Lawrence's first game as a starter, one he didn't finish because of a head injury, and Clemson's first after quarterback Kelly Bryant left the team. Bryant, a senior, led the Tigers to the playoff last season and a semifinal loss to Alabama. He was pivotal in an early victory this season at Texas A&M. But Lawrence is a rare talent, a potential first overall NFL draft pick. When Lawrence took over, the ceiling on Clemson's potential rose. Now it is being realized. With his flowing blond hair, Lawrence is positioned to become one of college football's biggest and most recognizable stars. It will help to have receivers such as Ross, Higgins and Amari Rogers, all underclassmen. And a runner like sophomore Travis Etienne, who broke a 62-yard touchdown run in the third quarter. But Lawrence is the leader. In his 11th start, he will try to become the first true freshman quarterback to lead his team to a national championship since Oklahoma's Jamelle Holieway in 1985. Notre Dame, as 12-point underdogs, the Irish needed to play their best and catch a couple breaks. Neither happened. They nearly had a takeaway deep in Clemson territory in the first quarter, but a loose ball was ruled barely out of bounds by replay review. Love's injury left them exposed at corner. And an offensive line, which had been up and down and shifting around much of the season, was no match for Clemson. Clemson's Dexter Lawrence, sidelined by a failed NCAA test for performance-enhancing drugs, was hardly missed. The 340-pound junior was on the sideline, wearing on an orange sweatshirt with a white tiger paw logo. Clemson is working on an appeal for Lawrence and two other players, but it is unlikely the Tigers will have them back for the national title game.

2018 MILITARY BOWL

The 2018 Military Bowl was played on December 31, 2018. It was the 11th edition of the Military Bowl. The game was played between Virginia Tech of the Atlantic Coast Conference (ACC) and Cincinnati of the American Athletic Conference (The American). The two programs had previously met 11 times, with Virginia Tech holding a 6–5 lead in the series. It was their second meeting in the Military Bowl, having previously contested the 2014 edition, with Virginia Tech winning 33–17.

2018 Military Bowl	Line	1	-	2	-	3	-	4	-	Final
Cincinnati	(48.5)	7	-	7	-	7	-	14	-	35
Virginia Tech	(-5.5)	7	-	7	-	10	-	7	-	31

Scoring Summary
Virginia Tech – Kumah 21 yard pass from Willis (Johnson Kick)
Cincinnati – McClelland 38 yard pass from Ridder (Jones Kick)
Cincinnati – Lewis recovered fumble in end zone (Jones Kick)
Virginia Tech – Peoples 1 yard run (Johnson Kick)
Virginia Tech – Johnson 28 Field Goal
Cincinnati – Warren 40 yard run (Jones Kick)
Virginia Tech – Cunningham 2 yard pass from Willis (Johnson Kick)
Cincinnati – Moore 19 yard run (Jones Kick)
Virginia Tech – Willis 5 yard run (Johnson Kick)
Cincinnati – Warren 8 yard run (Jones Kick)

Associated Press Military Bowl Game Summary – Racing back and forth on a drenched field, Cincinnati and Virginia Tech put up some lofty numbers as the rain came down in the Military Bowl. Michael Warren found his footing when it mattered most, scoring the go-ahead touchdown with 1:29 left for the Bearcats, whose 35-31 victory Monday ended Virginia Tech's run of 25 consecutive winning seasons. Warren ran for a career-high 166 yards, including an 8-yard burst up the middle to cap a frantic five-play, 64-yard drive in which he had 54 yards rushing. That was enough to decide a tight game that featured 905 yards in offense and seven lead changes. The Bearcats' offense got a big assist from backup quarterback Hayden Moore, a senior who made 12 starts last year. After throwing only 26 passes in 2018, Moore entered in the first quarter and completed 11 of 25 throws for 120 yards in addition to running for a 19-yard score. The victory gave Cincinnati (11-2) its third 11-win season in the 131-year history of the program following two straight 4-8 finishes. Playing in a bowl game for the 26th successive year -- the longest current run in the nation -- Virginia Tech needed a victory to avoid its first losing season since 1992. Ryan Willis threw two touchdown passes and ran for another score, but it wasn't enough to put an upbeat finish on an unsatisfying season for the Hokies (6-7). A touchdown run by Moore put the Bearcats up 28-24 with 12:44 left, and two minutes later Willis ran it in from the 5 to give Virginia Tech its last lead. The Hokies had a chance to extend the margin with just under nine minutes left but failed on a fourth-and-1 at the Cincinnati 3. Ridder hurt his right leg after being tripped up out of the pocket during the Bearcats' second series. The American Athletic Conference rookie of the year went 4 for 7 for 86 yards and a touchdown before leaving. Moore picked up the slack. After a back-and-forth first half that ended 14-all, Virginia Tech moved 69 yards to open the third quarter before Brian Johnson kicked a field goal for a 17-14 lead. After Warren put the Bearcats in front with a 40-yard touchdown run, Willis threw a 2-yard touchdown pass to Chris Cunningham to make it 24-21 heading into the fourth quarter. The Bearcats fumbled three times and recovered all of them, including a touchdown by Kahlil Lewis on a ball Warren lost at the Virginia Tech 1.

2018 SUN BOWL

The 2018 Sun Bowl was played on Monday, December 31, 2018. It was the 85th edition of the Sun Bowl. The game featured Stanford of the Pac-12 Conference and Pittsburgh of the Atlantic Coast Conference (ACC). The two programs have previously met three times, most recently in 1932, with Pittsburgh holding a 2–1 series lead. The referee for the game, David Smith of the Southeastern Conference (SEC), was the quarterback and MVP for Alabama in the 1988 Sun Bowl.

2018 Sun Bowl	Line	1	-	2	-	3	-	4	-	Final
Stanford	(-3.0)	0	-	7	-	0	-	7	-	14
Pittsburgh	(52.5)	0	-	10	-	3	-	0	-	13

Scoring Summary
Pittsburgh – Kessman 29 yard Field goal
Stanford – Scarlett 1 yard run (Toner Kick)
Pittsburgh – Hall 6 yard run (Kessman Kick)
Pittsburgh – Kessman 28 yard Field Goal
Stanford – Scarlett recovered fumble in end zone (Toner Kick)

Associated Press Sun Bowl Game Summary – With all of the struggles it had on offense, it was a wonder that Stanford was able to hold off Pitt for a 14-13 victory in the Sun Bowl. Pitt had an advantage in nearly every statistical category Monday. The Panthers had more yards (344-208), first downs (18-12), rushes and yards (42-208, 34-103), passing yards (136-105) and third-down conversions (5-1). And Stanford was playing without five starters -- star tailback Bryce Love, receiver Trent Irwin, tight end Kaden Smith, left tackle Walker Little and right guard Nate Herbig. Finally, Pitt's defense was stingy. Stanford quarterback K.J. Costello saw a streak of 16 games with a TD pass end, and the Cardinal was 1 of 10 on third downs. Even the game-winning score was ugly -- the Panthers had stopped Costello on a first-and-goal from the 2-yard line and forced a fumble, which tailback Cameron Scarlett recovered in the end zone. Scarlett carried 22 times for 94 yards, including another score on a 1-yard run, to earn game MVP honors while filling in for Love. Love decided to skip it to rehab an ankle injury ahead of the NFL draft, becoming the second Stanford back to do that in the past three Sun Bowls. In 2016, Christian McCaffrey skipped the game, was drafted eighth overall by Carolina and just finished sixth in the NFL in rushing in his second season. And just as Love kick-started his career with that opportunity, Scarlett gave himself a similar boost. Pitt drove into position for a 55-yard field goal try on the ensuing possession, but Alex Kessman's try was no good. The Panthers still weren't sure how to explain it all afterward. The Cardinal (9-4) finished on a four-game winning streak, much the same way they did two years ago when Stanford won the Sun Bowl for a season-ending six-game streak. The Panthers (7-7) lost their fourth straight bowl game and sixth in the past seven after falling to playoff championship finalist Clemson in the ACC title game. The past three losses have been in four years in under Coach Pat Narduzzi. Pitt, which had a 10-7 halftime lead and was up 13-7 early in the fourth quarter, was led by tailback Darrin Hall, who had 16 carries for 123 yards and a score. Pitt finished the season on a three-game losing skid, in which the offense never scored more than 13 points. That carried over into Monday's game. Pitt got inside Stanford's 10-yard line twice, and each time settled for field goals. Stanford's offense, which had struggled all day, finally got going in the fourth quarter. The Cardinal were 0 for 8 on third downs before Costello hit JJ Arcega-Whiteside for a 12-yard completion. A 49-yard pass to Arcega-Whiteside followed, and Scarlett recovered Costello's fumble for the go-ahead score on the next play with 11:28 left. Stanford's Arcega-Whiteside entered the game needing one touchdown catch to break the school season record of 14 he shared with Hall of Famer James Lofton. But the senior was limited to three catches without a TD. The Cardinal won for the first time this season without forcing a turnover. Stanford had been 0-4 in such games. For Pittsburgh, The game was the final one for the 1-2 rushing punch of Qadree Ollison and Hall, the first duo in program history with at least 1,000 yards apiece in a season. Ollison, who was injured in the first half and didn't return, had 1,213 yards. Hall finished with 1,144 yards.

2018 REDBOX BOWL

The 2018 Redbox Bowl was played on December 31, 2018 at Levi's Stadium in Santa Clara, California, with kickoff at noon PST (3:00 p.m. EST). This was the 17th annual edition the game that was renamed for its new sponsor, the DVD and video game rental company Redbox. The two teams have met six times previously, with each winning three times.

2018 RedBox Bowl	Line	1	-	2	-	3	-	4	-	Final
Michigan State	(-1.5)	0	-	0	-	6	-	0	-	6
Oregon	(47.0)	0	-	0	-	0	-	7	-	7

Scoring Summary
Michigan State – Coghlin 34 yard Field Goal
Michigan State – Coghlin 34 yard Field Goal
Oregon – Mitchell 28 yard pass from Herbert (Stack Kick)

Associated Press RedBox Bowl Game Summary – Justin Herbert did just enough to keep his streak intact for consecutive games with a touchdown pass. Make it an impressive 28 and counting for Oregon's quarterback, the longest active streak in the nation among FBS schools. That it turned out to be the Ducks lone score in their 7-6 win over Michigan State in the Redbox Bowl only emphasized why Coach Mario Cristobal was smiling after Herbert's decision earlier this month to bypass the NFL draft. Herbert shook off a sluggish day and threw a 28-yard touchdown pass to Dillon Mitchell in the fourth quarter, and Oregon held on after Michigan State botched a field goal attempt for a 7-6 victory in the Redbox Bowl on Monday. Herbert passed for 166 yards and extended his streak on a day when the Ducks' offense mostly sputtered. Oregon (9-4) crossed midfield only three times and couldn't get into the end zone until Herbert found Mitchell in the right front of the end zone for the deciding score. The Ducks' defense held up from there but got some help from Michigan State's special teams. The Spartans were lined up for a 50-yard field goal attempt when quarterback Brian Lewerke, who doubles as the holder, bobbled the snap, then attempted to run before hurriedly throwing an incompletion near the sideline. After Michigan State's defense forced a three-and-out on the following possession, the Spartans took over at their own 42, but Lewerke's long pass on 4th-and-12 was knocked down by Oregon cornerback Thomas Graham. Lewerke completed 22 of 40 passes for 172 yards with one interception. It's the third time in four games that Michigan State (7-6) has failed to score a touchdown. Running back LJ Scott ran for 84 yards on 24 carries, ending his injury-riddled season with the Spartans on a high note after being limited to five games. The senior running back declined to redshirt this year and declared for the NFL draft in early December. Matt Goghlin kicked a pair of 34-yard field goals but he also missed one from 50. It was Oregon's first bowl victory since beating Florida State in the 2015 Rose Bowl. The Spartans had more than enough on defense but as has been the case all season, the offense simply couldn't hold up its end of the bargain. Lewerke tried to get the passing game going and took several deep shots, but it was his scrambling that was most effective. The memory of the mistake on the field goal try in the fourth quarter will linger, but the Spartans' inability to get a sustained attack on offense was what ultimately did in Dantonio's team. Getting Cristobal a bowl win in his first season was big and should be a nice lift for the Ducks program. That they won when their offense was held to 25 points below its scoring average is also big. The victory is Oregon's third straight, which should build some momentum heading into the offseason.

2018 LIBERTY BOWL

The 2018 Liberty Bowl was between the #24 Missouri Tigers of the Southeastern Conference and the unranked Oklahoma State Cowboys of the Big 12 Conference. The two programs had previously met 52 times, with Missouri holding a 29–23 series lead. Both programs were members of the Big Eight Conference for many years and met annually from 1960 through 1997; their most recent prior meeting had been the 2014 Cotton Bowl Classic, won by Missouri. The 60th edition of the Liberty Bowl took place on December 31, 2018, at 2:45 p.m. EST and aired on ESPN. Liberty Bowl Memorial Stadium in Memphis, Tennessee, hosted the game for the 54th straight year.

2018 Liberty Bowl	Line	1	-	2	-	3	-	4	-	Final
#24 Missouri	(-9.5)	3	-	13	-	3	-	14	-	33
Oklahoma State	(72.5)	7	-	7	-	21	-	3	-	38

Scoring Summary
Oklahoma State – Stoner 30 yard pass from Cornelius (Ammendola Kick)
Missouri – McCann 24 yard Field goal
Missouri – Gicinto 5 yard pass from Lock (McCann kick)
Oklahoma State – Johnson 7 yard pass from Cornelius (Ammendola Kick)
Missouri – Blanton 16 yard pass from Lock (McCann Kick)
Oklahoma State – Wallace 9 yard pass from Cornelius (Ammendola Kick)
Oklahoma State – Hubbard 4 yard run (Ammendola Kick)
Missouri – McCann 26 yard Field goal
Oklahoma State – Johnson 46 yard pass from Cornelius (Ammendola Kick)
Missouri – Johnson 86 yard pass from Lock (McCann Kick)
Missouri – Rountree 55 yard run (McCann Kick)
Oklahoma State – Ammendola 27 yard Field Goal

Associated Press Liberty Bowl Game Summary – Oklahoma State hung on for dear life to win a Big 12 style Liberty Bowl against its former conference rival. Taylor Cornelius tied a Liberty Bowl record with four touchdown passes and Kolby Peel made a critical fourth-down stop with 1:01 left as the Cowboys upset No. 24 Missouri 38-33 on Monday. The teams combined for 1,139 total yards in the type of game that the Big 12's high-powered offenses produce on most autumn Saturdays. Missouri left the Big 12 for the Southeastern Conference in 2012. Missouri (8-5) faced fourth-and-1 from Oklahoma State's 9-yard line when quarterback Drew Lock attempted a keeper around the right end. Peel, a freshman, made a diving ankle tackle that stopped Lock short of the first-down marker. That allowed Oklahoma State (7-6) to survive a game it had led 35-19 heading into the fourth quarter. The Cowboys snapped Missouri's four-game winning streak and avoided their first losing season since 2005, the first year of Gundy's tenure. Cornelius, a fifth-year senior and former walk-on, went 26 of 44. His four touchdown passes tied a record set four previous times in the Liberty Bowl's 60-year history. Cornelius also threw two interceptions to Cam Hilton that sparked Missouri's comeback try. Both interceptions led to Missouri touchdowns -- an 86-yard completion from Lock to Memphis resident Johnathon Johnson and a 55-yard run by Larry Rountree III. Rountree ran for 204 yards and Johnson caught nine passes for 185 yards. Lock was 23 of 38 for 373 yards with three touchdowns and no interceptions. Chuba Hubbard rushed for 145 yards and a touchdown for Oklahoma State. Tyron Johnson had seven catches for 141 yards and two touchdowns. Missouri wasted two chances to take the lead in the fourth quarter. Oklahoma State was clinging to a 35-33 lead when Mike Scott blocked Tucker McCann's 42-yard field goal attempt with 9:22 left. Matt Ammendola kicked a 27-yard field goal that extended Oklahoma State's lead to 38-33 before Peel's tackle sealed the win. This marks the second straight year that Missouri has lost a bowl game after a late-season surge. Last year, Missouri won its final six regular-season games but followed that up with a 33-16 loss Texas Bowl loss to Texas. The Cowboys entered the game ranked 99th in total defense and tied for 96th in scoring defense, but that beleaguered unit delivered when it mattered most. Oklahoma State is 6-1 in its last seven games against teams in the Top 25, and Gundy owns a 9-4 bowl record. Oklahoma State was clinging to a 35-33 lead when the Cowboys made an unsuccessful fake punt attempt on fourth-and-8 from their own 27. Oklahoma State stayed ahead only after blocking a field-goal attempt. Earlier in the fourth quarter, Missouri made a curious move of its own by calling a timeout after scoring a touchdown to cut Oklahoma State's lead to 35-25. After burning the timeout, Missouri chose to kick an extra point to make it 35-26 rather than attempting a two-point conversion. The four previous Liberty Bowl players to throw four touchdown passes were Purdue's Mark Herrmann (also against Missouri) in 1980, Illinois' Johnny Johnson in 1994, South Carolina's Blake Mitchell in 2006 and Texas A&M's Kyle Allen in 2014. Missouri's 637 total yards also set a Liberty Bowl record. Oklahoma State's offense was missing leading rusher Justice Hill and guard Larry Williams, who sat out the bowl game to prepare for the NFL draft. Its defense lost cornerbacks Rodarius Williams and Kemah Siverand to targeting penalties -- Williams in the first quarter and Siverand early in the fourth period -- and safety Malcolm Rodriguez to a second-quarter injury. Missouri played without injured running back Damarea Crockett and tight end Albert Okwuegbunam. The Tigers also lost receiver Emanuel Hall to an injury after he caught two passes for 72 yards.

2018 HOLIDAY BOWL

The 2018 Holiday Bowl was played on December 31, 2018. It was the 41st edition of the Holiday Bowl. The programs had previously met twice, with Northwestern winning in 1927 and Utah winning in 1981. The Wildcats entered the bowl with an 8–5 record (8–1 in conference). The Utes entered the bowl with a 9–4 record (6–3 in conference).

2018 Holiday Bowl	Line	1	-	2	-	3	-	4	-	Final
#22 Northwestern	(45.0)	0	-	3	-	28	-	0	-	31
#20 Utah	(-6.5)	14	-	6	-	0	-	0	-	20

Scoring Summary
Utah – Dixon 27 yard pass from Shelley (Gay Kick)
Utah – Jackson 4 yard pass from Shelley (Gay Kick)
Northwestern – Kuhbander 21 yard Field Goal
Utah – Gay 32 yard Field Goal
Utah – Gay 20 yard Field Goal
Northwestern – Lees 4 yard pass from Thorson (Kuhbander Kick)
Northwestern – McGee 82 yard fumble return (Kuhbander Kick)
Northwestern – Klock 4 yard pass from Thorson (Kuhbander Kick)
Northwestern – Lees 8 yard run (Kuhbander Kick)

Associated Press Holiday Bowl Game Summary — A cold, hard rain in normally warm, dry San Diego made the Northwestern Wildcats feel right at home, especially as they enjoyed a downpour of Utah turnovers in the Holiday Bowl. In a dizzying nine-minute stretch of the third quarter, the Wildcats turned three turnovers into 21 points to stun the No. 20 Utes 31-20 Monday night. The highlight was Jared McGee's 82-yard fumble return for a touchdown, the middle turnover in the nightmarish stretch for Utah. The Wildcats (9-5) scored 28 points total in the third quarter to win their third straight bowl game under Fitzgerald. The Green Bay Packers reportedly want to interview Fitzgerald for their head coaching job. Fitzgerald credited the seniors for winning 36 games in four seasons and gushed about the program's future. Senior Clayton Thorson became the all-time leading passer for Northwestern, going 21 of 30 for 241 yards for 10,731 career yards. He broke Brett Basanez's school record of 10,580. Thorson threw for two touchdowns and was intercepted once in making his 53rd straight start for the Wildcats, the most by a quarterback in Big Ten history. He is the program's all-time winningest quarterback at 36-17. He was replaced after taking a hard shot midway through the fourth quarter, but came back in. Utah (9-5) cruised to a 20-3 halftime lead behind redshirt freshman quarterback Jason Shelley before it all fell apart in the third quarter. Shelley had two interceptions and a fumble. Utah had four turnovers in the third quarter and five in the second half. On the opening drive of the second half, Shelley threw the ball right to Northwestern's Blake Gallagher. Thorson's 52-yard pass to Ramaud Chiaokhiao-Bowman set up his 4-yard scoring toss to Riley Lees. The Utes had the ball first-and-goal at the 6 when Shelley rolled right, was hit from behind by Joe Gaziano and fumbled. McGee picked it up on the third bounce and ran down the sideline untouched for an 82-yard return that pulled the Wildcats to 20-17. The Utes advanced to the 30 and looked like they had enough for a first down on a catch by Jaylen Dixon, but he was stripped by Trae Williams. JR Pace recovered and returned it 34 yards. Two plays later, Northwestern took a 24-20 lead when Thorson threw a 20-yard touchdown pass to senior offensive lineman Trey Klock, a key player in goal line and short-yardage situations. Northwestern added another touchdown in the third quarter when Lees scored from 8 yards out for a 31-20 lead. Pace had a second interception in the third quarter, on a deflected pass. Shelley was making his fourth start in place of Tyler Huntley, who broke his collarbone against Arizona State on Nov. 3. Also out were leading rusher Zack Moss, leading receiver Britain Covey and leading tackler Chase Hansen, a senior. Shelley threw a 27-yard touchdown pass to Jaylen Dixon and a 4-yarder to tight end Jake Jackson, both in the first quarter. Utah lost for the just the second time in its last 16 bowls dating to 1999. Whittingham's bowl record dropped to 11-2. He was trying to become the first to win the Holiday Bowl as a player and coach. He played in the first four Holiday Bowls with BYU, going 2-2. He was inducted into the Holiday Bowl Hall of Fame in 2009. The Wildcats had minus-6 yards rushing at halftime and didn't get into positive until late in the third quarter. Utah's Shelley was impressive with his passing and his scrambling until running into trouble in the third quarter.

2018 GATOR BOWL

The 2018 Gator Bowl was played on December 31, 2018. It was the 74th edition of the Gator Bowl. This was Texas A&M's second Gator Bowl and NC State's fourth. The Aggies entered the bowl with an 8–4 record (5–3 in conference). The Wolfpack entered the bowl with a 9–3 record (5–3 in conference).

2018 Taxslayer Gator Bowl	Line	1	-	2	-	3	-	4	-	Final
NC State	(58.0)	3	-	10	-	0	-	0	-	13
#21 Texas A&M	(-7.5)	7	-	14	-	14	-	17	-	52

Scoring Summary
Texas A&M – Mond 62 yard run (Small Kick)
NC State – Dunn 43 yard Field Goal
NC State – Riley 9 yard pass from Finley (Dunn Kick)
NC State – Dunn 49 yard Field goal
Texas A&M – Williams 2 yard run (Small Kick)
Texas A&M – Rogers 6 yard pass from Mond (Small Kick)
Texas A&M – Dodson 78 yard interception return (Small Kick)
Texas A&M – Williams 17 yard run (Small Kick)
Texas A&M – Williams 93 yard run (Small Kick)
Texas A&M – Small 35 yard Field goal
Texas A&M – Gillaspia 13 yard run (LaCamera Kick)

Associated Press Gator Bowl Game Summary – Trayveon Williams strolled around the field, his white pants covered in dirt and grass stains, his Gator Bowl hat turned sideways, and his MVP trophy secured tightly in his left hand. He posed for pictures, hugged teammates and friends, and blew kisses to the crowd. It sure looked like a farewell party. Williams ran for 236 yards and three touchdowns, smashing a 30-year-old school record and carrying No. 21 Texas A&M to a 52-13 victory against North Carolina State in the Gator Bowl on Monday night. The Aggies (No. 19 CFP) ended 2018 with a four-game winning streak and broke a three-game postseason skid. It was the first bowl victory for most of Texas A&M's roster, including Williams. It also capped an impressive inaugural season for Coach Jimbo Fisher in Aggieland. Williams earned MVP honors, a potential final curtain call for his college career. The junior is expected to leave school early and enter the NFL draft. He said afterward he's still contemplating his future, but no one could blame him for turning pro after the way he closed out the season. Williams ran for 829 yards and eight scores during Texas A&M's final four games, all wins. His performance against the Wolfpack gave him 1,760 yards for the season, topping Darren Lewis' previous Texas A&M mark of 1,692 set in 1988. Williams had 61 yards rushing in the first half and then got rolling in the third quarter. He carried five times for 82 yards on one drive, including a 17-yard touchdown run. He topped that with a 93-yard scoring run on Texas A&M's ensuing drive. His longest scamper broke the previous Gator Bowl record of 216 yards rushing set by Syracuse's Floyd Little in 1966 against Tennessee. Texas A&M's Kellen Mond completed 14 of 26 passes for 140 yards, with a touchdown and an interception. Mond also ran five times for 85 yards and a score. Kendrick Rogers made a leaping, 6-yard catch in the back of the end zone to help Mond. Little went right for the Wolfpack, which was trying to get to double-digit wins for the second time in school history. North Carolina State finished with 273 yards and went 0 for 13 on third down. Ryan Finley, a senior playing his final game, completed 19 of 32 passes for 139 yards. He threw a touchdown passes and two interceptions. Tyrel Dodson returned one of the picks 78 yards for a score early in the third quarter, a play that turned a close game into a two-touchdown advantage. Finley also was sacked twice before getting pulled in the fourth quarter. Doeren clearly wanted to protect Finley, who's expected to be an early round pick in the NFL draft in April. It certainly didn't help that NC State played without two of its best players, including the team's leading tackler. Receiver Kelvin Harmon and linebacker Germaine Pratt skipped the bowl to protect their NFL draft stocks. It's unlikely Pratt could have done enough to make a difference against Williams, who averaged 12.4 yards on 19 carries against a defense that allowed 109.1 yards a game all season. The Wolfpack failed to get a third straight postseason win. It was a disappointing finale after ending the regular season with three consecutive wins, but still proof that Doeren has the program headed in the right direction. The Aggies have one of the youngest rosters in the Southeastern Conference and have enough talent to challenge Alabama in the coming years. The game drew 38,206, the bowl's smallest crowd since 1952.

2019 OUTBACK BOWL

The 2019 Outback Bowl was played on January 1, 2019. It was the 33rd edition of the Outback Bowl, and played at Raymond James Stadium in Tampa, Florida. The game featured the Iowa Hawkeyes of the Big Ten Conference and the Mississippi State Bulldogs of the Southeastern Conference. It was the first meeting between the two teams. It was Iowa's sixth time playing in the Outback Bowl, and Mississippi State's first.

The Hawkeyes entered the bowl with an 8–4 record (5–4 in conference). The Bulldogs entered the bowl with an 8–4 record (4–4 in conference).

2019 Outback Bowl	Line	1	-	2	-	3	-	4	-	Final
#18 Mississippi State	(-7.0)	6	-	0	-	13	-	3	-	22
Iowa	(40.0)	0	-	17	-	7	-	3	-	27

Scoring Summary
Mississippi State – Christmann 44 yard Field Goal
Mississippi State – Christmann 42 yard Field Goal
Iowa – Recinos 44 yard Field goal
Iowa – Easley 75 yard pass from Stanley (Recinos Kick)
Iowa – Smith-Marsette 15 yard pass from Stanley (Recinos Kick)
Mississippi State – Hill 1 yard pass from Fitzgerald (2 point pass failed)
Mississippi State – Fitzgerald 33 yard run (Christmann Kick)
Iowa – Easley 8 yard pass from Stanley (Recinos Kick)
Mississippi State – Christmann 20 yard Field Goal
Iowa – Recinos 40 yard Field Goal

Associated Press Outback Bowl Game Summary – The Iowa Hawkeyes lost a yard on the last play of the Outback Bowl, pushing their final rushing total to minus 15 yards, and didn't mind a bit. They ran the play from victory formation. Safety Jake Gervase's interception in the end zone helped preserve a late lead, and a ball-hawking defense compensated for a sputtering offense as Iowa beat No. 18 Mississippi State 27-22 on Tuesday. Gervase also batted down an errant fourth-down pass to end the Bulldogs' final drive at the Iowa 32 with 25 seconds left. Two earlier Mississippi State threats in the fourth quarter led to only three points. The Hawkeyes totaled just 199 yards, with 75 coming on a touchdown pass from Nathan Stanley to Nick Easley, but they converted three takeaways into 17 points. The Hawkeyes won despite losing 27 inches per rush. Their three running backs totaled 4 yards in 15 carries. Iowa (9-4) earned its biggest postseason victory since an Orange Bowl win over Georgia Tech to cap the 2009 season. Mississippi State (8-5) lost to a team outside the top 15 for the first time. Trailing 24-19, the Bulldogs had a first down at the Iowa 1 early in the fourth quarter, but three quarterback draws lost 2 yards and they settled for a field goal. They were again on the verge of taking the lead with nine minutes left, but receiver Stephen Guidry bobbled a tipped pass in the end zone, and Gervase snatched it away. The Hawkeyes then drove 50 yards for a field goal, the game's final score. Iowa had no penalties, while Mississippi State was penalized 90 yards, including a holding call that negated a 51-yard completion. Mississippi State receiver Osirus Mitchell put it another way. A takeaway helped Iowa score two touchdowns in 97 seconds for a 17-6 lead -- especially impressive against a team that allowed only 12 TDs during the regular season. Mississippi State rallied with two touchdowns in 18 seconds to go up 19-17. Quarterback Nick Fitzgerald gave the Bulldogs the advantage on a nifty 33-yard touchdown run, his 100th career score rushing or passing. But on their next possession, Fitzgerald's tipped pass was intercepted by defensive lineman Chauncey Golston. Stanley then scrambled to convert a fourth and 1, and on the next play he hit Easley with an 8-yard score to put Iowa ahead to stay, 24-19. Easley had a career-high 104 yards receiving on eight catches and was chosen the most valuable player. He nearly ran out from under his helmet on his long touchdown. Easley and Gervase played their final game as seniors who walked on. Running back Kylin Hill left the game when he took a hit to the helmet in the fourth quarter, but he was back in the lineup on the Bulldogs' final possession. Moorhead said Hill cleared the concussion protocol. Iowa will likely finish in the Top 25 for only the second time in the past nine seasons. Ferentz concluded his 20th season at Iowa and improved to 152-101, including 8-8 in bowl games. The down-to-the-wire finish was a rarity for the Bulldogs, who had only one other game decided by fewer than 14 points.

2019 CITRUS BOWL

The 2019 Citrus Bowl was played on January 1, 2019. It was the 73rd edition of what is now the Citrus Bowl. The teams had previously met five times, with Penn State holding a 3–2 edge; their most recent meeting was the 1999 Outback Bowl, won by Penn State.

2019 Citrus Bowl	Line	1	-	2	-	3	-	4	-	Final
#16 Kentucky	(47.5)	10	-	0	-	17	-	0	-	27
#13 Penn State	(-4.5)	0	-	7	-	0	-	17	-	24

Scoring Summary
Kentucky – Butler 28 yard Field Goal
Kentucky – Bowden 58 yard punt return (Butler Kick)
Penn State – Bowers 1 yard pass from McSorley (Pinegar Kick)
Kentucky – Snell 2 yard run (Butler Kick)
Kentucky – Butler 28 yard Field Goal

Kentucky – Snell 12 yard run (Butler Kick)
Penn State – McCsorley 1 yard run (Pinegar Kick)
Penn State – Freiermuth 18 yard pass from McSorley (Pinegar Kick)
Penn State – Pinegar 32 yard Field Goal

Associated Press Citrus Bowl Game Summary – Winning 10 games, beating Penn State on New Year's Day, and finishing in the Top 20 is no small deal for the Kentucky Wildcats. So, when Mark Stoops took a seat on the podium flanked by linebacker Josh Allen and running back Benny Snell Jr. after Tuesday's 27-24 victory in the Citrus Bowl, the coach understandably was beyond excited. Snell ran for 144 yards and two touchdowns to become Kentucky's career rushing leader and helped the 16th-ranked Wildcats end their best season in more than four decades on a winning note. Snell scored on runs of 2 and 12 yards in the second half, then carried for a couple of crucial first downs to help Kentucky (10-3) run out the clock after Penn State's Trace McSorley trimmed a 27-7 deficit to three points despite playing with a foot injury. McSorley threw for 246 yards and two touchdowns, and the Nittany Lions' career passing and wins leader also rushed for a team-high 75 yards and one TD. Lynn Bowden Jr. scored on a 58-yard punt return for Kentucky. Allen, the Southeastern Conference defensive player of the year, had three of the Wildcats' six sacks. Penn State (9-4) trailed 27-7 entering the fourth quarter, but McSorley's wasn't finished. His 1-yard TD run capped a 75-yard drive, and he followed with an 18-yard TD pass to Pat Friermuth to cut Kentucky's lead to six. The Nittany Lions marched to the Kentucky 14 on their next possession and pulled within 27-24 with 4:12 left. Thanks to Snell, a junior who already has declared for the NFL draft, McSorley didn't get the ball back until just one second was left on the clock. Franklin declined to discuss specifics of McSorley's injury. McSorley, who was to undergo further evaluation, said he hadn't received "definitive information" on whether his foot was broken. Kentucky finished with its first 10-win season since 1977 -- when the Wildcats went 10-1 -- and just the third time in program history. The school also did it in 1950. Snell, meanwhile, broke Sonny Collins' career rushing record on his 12-yard TD run that made it 27-7 late in the third quarter. Collins rushed for 3,835 yards from 1972-75. Facing a tradition-rich opponent in a New Year's bowl was significant for the Wildcats, who made the most of the opportunity. Along with the three sacks, Allen blocked a field goal to key a strong defensive effort, while the offense shrugged off a slow start to help the Wildcats pull away in the second half.

2019 FIESTA BOWL

The 2019 Fiesta Bowl (January) was held on January 1, 2019. It was the 48th edition of the Fiesta Bowl. The game featured LSU of the Southeastern Conference (SEC) and UCF of the American Athletic Conference (The American). This was the first meeting between the two programs. The LSU Tigers defeated the UCF Knights by the score of 40–32, snapping UCF's 25-game winning streak, the longest in the nation at the time. The Tigers dominated time of possession (44:31) and racked up 555 yards of offense. The Knights offense was held to a season-low 250 total yards but scored a Fiesta Bowl record 93-yard interception return for a touchdown. Despite the loss, the Knights extended their NCAA Division I FBS record with their 26th consecutive game scoring 30 or more points, and the FBS-leading 32nd consecutive game forcing a turnover. It was LSU's 26th bowl victory, and first Fiesta Bowl victory. In a game that was described as "chippy", three players were ejected in the first half alone, two for LSU and one for UCF. Tigers defensive back Terrence Alexander was ejected for throwing a punch, while safety Grant Delpit was ejected for targeting. Golden Knights defender Kyle Gibson was ejected for targeting, while linebacker Nate Evans and defensive lineman Randy Charlton each committed costly unsportsmanlike conduct penalties. With the two participating schools from the southeast, the announced attendance for the game was 57,246, the lowest since 1979.

2019 Fiesta Bowl	Line	1	-	2	-	3	-	4	-	Final
#11 LSU	(-7.0)	10	-	14	-	10	-	6	-	40
#7 Central Florida	(58.5)	14	-	7	-	3	-	8	-	32

Scoring Summary
LSU – Tracy 24 yard Field goal
Central Florida – McCrae 25 yard run (Wright Kick)
Central Florida – Moore 93 yard interception return (Wright Kick)
LSU – Jefferson 22 yard pass from Burrow (Tracy Kick)
LSU – Dillon 49 yard pass from Burrow (Tracy Kick)
LSU – Jefferson 33 yard pass from Burrow (Tracy Kick)
Central Florida – Davis 32 yard pass from Mack (Wright Kick)
LSU – Chase 32 yard pass from Burrow (Tracy Kick)
LSU – Tracy 28 yard Field Goal
Central Florida – Wright 37 yard Field Goal
LSU – Tracy 28 yard Field goal
LSU – Tracy 26 yard Field Goal
Central Florida – McGowan 2 yard run (2 point pass good)

Associated Press Fiesta Bowl Game Summary – Joe Burrow watched the ball land in an opposing player's hands and immediately gave chase. Locked in on preventing a pick six, LSU's quarterback didn't see Joey Connors, Central Florida's 313-pound defensive lineman, bearing down on him. With a thunderous, blindside collision, Burrow found himself flat on his back, woozy and wondering what happened. Minutes later, after being helped to his feet, Burrow was back on the field, hitting receivers all over the field. The nation's longest winning streak was over. So was a second self-proclaimed national championship. The LSU Tigers were Fiesta Bowl champions, thanks to their gritty junior quarterback. Burrow shook off the big early hit to throw for 394 yards and four touchdowns, helping No. 11 LSU end No. 7 UCF's 25-game winning streak with a 40-32 victory in the Fiesta Bowl on Tuesday. LSU (10-3, No. 11 CFP) started its first Fiesta Bowl without several key players on defense and fell into an early 11-point hole against the high-scoring Knights (12-1, No. 8 CFP). The Tigers clawed back behind Burrow and a defensive front that made life difficult for UCF quarterback Darriel Mack Jr. Burrow returned from the early blindside hit to pick apart UCF's secondary, hitting 21 of 34 of passes, including two touchdowns to Justin Jefferson. LSU sacked Mack five times and made him rush numerous throws, holding the nation's third-best offense to 250 total yards -- 295 below its average -- while spoiling the Knights' bid for a second straight self-proclaimed national title. Taj McGowan scored on a 2-yard run and the Knights converted a 2-point conversion to pull UCF to within 40-32. After LSU recovered the onside kick, the Knights' last-ditch attempt finished with a tipped interception, ending a run that started after a loss in the 2016 Cure Bowl. UCF declared itself national champions after finishing as the only undefeated FBS team a year ago. The Knights earned another shot at an undefeated season by staging a massive rally to beat Memphis in the American Athletic Conference title game. But just like last year, UCF was on the outside looking in when the College Football Playoff final four was announced, adding to the boulder-sized chip on its shoulder and only a self-awarded national title in its reach. The Speedy Knights got the Fiesta Bowl off to a fast start, going up 14-3 on Greg McCrae's 25-yard TD run and Brandon Moore's 93-yard interception return. The Tigers roared back behind Burrow and their disruptive defensive front. Burrow shook off the big hit on the pick six, finding Jefferson on a pair of scoring passes and a 49-yard TD to Derrick Dillon. UCF sputtered offensively after its opening drive, but Mack hit Gabriel Davis on a 32-yard pass in the closing seconds to pull UCF to within 24-21 at halftime. Burrow opened the second half with a 32-yard TD pass to Ja'Marr Chase, and Cole Tracy hit three field goals to put LSU up 40-24. Tracy's final kick, the 97th of his career, broke the NCAA all-division record and ended the nation's fourth-longest winning streak since 2000. Even depleted, LSU's defense proved to still be formidable, and Burrow showed his grit after the big hit, giving LSU its first 10-win season since 2013. UCF missed injured two-time AAC player of the year McKenzie Milton and had no answer for LSU's passing game to lose for the first time in two years. The first meeting between UCF and LSU was chippy from the start, including three first-half ejections. LSU consensus All-America safety Grant Delpit was among those ejected after being called for targeting in the second quarter. UCF had a key penalty in the second quarter, when Randy Charlton was hit with an unsportsmanlike conduct penalty after the Knights stopped LSU on a third-and-6. That kept the Tigers' drive alive, and Burrow hit Justice for a TD that pulled LSU to within 14-10. LSU had 14 penalties for 145 yards, LSU had 12 for 104 yards.

2019 ROSE BOWL

The 2019 Rose Bowl was played on January 1, 2019 at the Rose Bowl Stadium in Pasadena, California. It was the 105th edition of the Rose Bowl Game. This game marks the first time those two programs met in a bowl game. This was the schools' 12th meeting; Ohio State led the all-time series, 8–3. Ohio State won the game, 28–23, to capture its eighth Rose Bowl championship in program history. Ohio State head coach Urban Meyer announced retirement from coaching the month before, making the 2019 Rose Bowl his final game. "The Melody of Life" was the theme chosen by Pasadena Tournament of Roses president Gerald Freeny. George Halas (Great Lakes Navy), Randall McDaniel (Arizona State), Pop Warner (Stanford), and Vince Young (Texas) were inducted into the Rose Bowl Hall of Fame prior to the game. The 130th Rose Parade was held in downtown Pasadena the morning of the game, with floats from both conferences. The bands and cheerleaders from both schools also participated.

2019 Rose Bowl	Line	1	-	2	-	3	-	4	-	Final
#9 Washington	(55.0)	3	-	0	-	0	-	20	-	23
#5 Ohio State	(-5.5)	7	-	14	-	7	-	0	-	28

Scoring Summary
Ohio State – Campbell 12 yard pass from Haskins (Haubeil Kick)
Washington – Henry 38 yard Field Goal
Ohio State – Dixon 19 yard pass from Haskins (Haubeil Kick)
Ohio State – Berry 1 yard pass from Haskins (Haubeil Kick)
Ohio State – Dobbins 3 yard run (Haubeil Kick)
Washington – Sample 2 yard pass from Gaskin (Henry Kick)
Washington – Gaskin 1 yard run (Henry Kick)
Washington – Gaskin 2 yard run (2 point pass failed)

Associated Press Rose Bowl Game Summary — Urban Meyer says he decided to end his remarkable coaching career at Ohio State partly because of the stress inherent in this high-intensity job. After his Buckeyes blew most of a 25-point lead in the fourth quarter and had to recover a last-minute onside kick to win the Rose Bowl, anybody could understand why this 54-year-old coach can't wait to retire. But the stress is over. Meyer is going out at the top of his profession. And for the first time, he is a Rose Bowl champion. Dwayne Haskins passed for 251 yards and three touchdowns, and Meyer headed into retirement with a 28-23 victory after the fifth-ranked Buckeyes held off No. 9 Washington's thrilling comeback in the 105th Rose Bowl on Tuesday. After the confetti flew in the north end zone, the Buckeyes gathered around Meyer for one last celebration of their coach. He is walking away after going 83-9 at Ohio State with one national championship, three Big Ten titles and this Rose Bowl victory, the Buckeyes' eighth overall in the Granddaddy of Them All. Parris Campbell, Johnnie Dixon and Rashod Berry caught TD passes in the first half for the Buckeyes (13-1), who took a 28-3 lead into the fourth and seemed to be cruising to a blowout. But star running back Myles Gaskin threw a touchdown pass and rushed for two more scores for the Huskies (10-4), scoring from 2 yards out with 42 seconds left. The Huskies got no closer, however. Defensive player of the game Brendon White intercepted Jake Browning's pass on the 2-point conversion attempt, and Dixon recovered Washington's onside kick. Meyer cited his health last month in his decision to step down. A cyst in Meyer's brain causes severe headaches that are even worse for a man who says he gets not just nervous, but "deathly ill" before big games. Meyer largely refused to reflect publicly on his career during the month since he announced his plans. After he shook Washington coach Chris Petersen's hand, raised the trophy and walked off the Rose Bowl turf, Meyer finally thought about the journey that brought him back to his home state for a stellar seven-year tenure capped by this late-breaking thriller. After Southern California's epic win over Penn State and Georgia's double-overtime thriller with Oklahoma over the past two years in Pasadena, the Rose Bowl got another matchup packed with late-game fireworks. Browning passed for 313 yards and Gaskin rushed for 121 in the final game of the four-year starters' landmark careers at Washington, which has lost three straight New Year's Six bowl games. But after three poor offensive quarters, the Pac-12 champions made it awfully interesting late. The Huskies racked up 170 yards of offense while making three strong drives in the fourth, but they had fallen too far behind in their first Rose Bowl game appearance in 18 years. Petersen dropped to 1-4 in bowls during his otherwise remarkable tenure at Washington, including consecutive defeats in the Peach, Fiesta and Rose. While Petersen likely will get more chances for his first Rose Bowl win, Meyer insists his three-decade collegiate coaching career is over. After starting out as a graduate assistant at Ohio State, he has been a head coach since 2001, achieving huge success at Bowling Green, Utah and Florida before his stellar run in Columbus. These Buckeyes are Meyer's eighth team to finish with one loss or fewer in his 17 seasons as a head coach. "He's a really tough guy," said Ohio State running back Mike Weber, who rushed for 96 yards. Although Meyer's final season began with an embarrassing three-game suspension over his mismanagement of domestic abuse accusations against former assistant Zach Smith, he propelled the Buckeyes to another dominant regular season despite missing out on the College Football Playoff. This game could be Haskins' farewell to Ohio State as well, if the sophomore goes pro. The offensive player of the game and Heisman Trophy finalist became the sixth FBS quarterback to throw 50 touchdown passes in a season while picking away at the vaunted Washington secondary minus injured Taylor Rapp, the second-team All-American safety. Gaskin became the fourth running back in NCAA history with four 1,200-yard seasons during the third quarter, but Ohio State increased its lead with J.K. Dobbins' TD run. The Huskies finally scored their first offensive touchdown since the Apple Cup when Gaskin threw a TD pass to Drew Sample with 12:17 to play. Ohio State's offense did enough to win despite punting on five straight late drives. Fans can only wonder whether this bunch of Buckeyes would have done better than overmatched Notre Dame or Oklahoma in the playoff semifinals. Washington's defeat wrapped up an unimpressive Pac-12 football season. The Huskies were the class of the conference, and they showed tremendous heart in the fourth -- but they'll be frustrated with a campaign bookended by losses to national powers Auburn and Ohio State.

2019 SUGAR BOWL

The 2019 Sugar Bowl was played on January 1, 2019.[5] It was the 85th edition of the Sugar Bowl. The Sugar Bowl matches the champions of the Big 12 Conference and Southeastern Conference (SEC), unless a champion team is selected for the College Football Playoff, in which case another team from the same conference is invited. Per that criteria, a matchup of Texas and Georgia was announced on December 2. The two programs had previously met four times, with Texas having won three times (including the 1949 Orange Bowl) and Georgia winning once (the 1984 Cotton Bowl Classic). Texas lost the 2018 Big 12 Championship Game to Oklahoma, then became the Big 12 representative in the Sugar Bowl when Oklahoma was selected for the College Football Playoff. Texas entered the bowl with a 9–4 record (7–2 in conference). Georgia lost the 2018 SEC Championship Game to Alabama, then became the SEC representative in the Sugar Bowl when Alabama was selected for the College Football Playoff. Georgia entered the bowl with an 11–2 record (7–1 in conference).

2019 Sugar Bowl	Line	1	-	2	-	3	-	4	-	Final
#14 Texas	(60.5)	10	-	10	-	0	-	8	-	28
#5 Georgia	(-13.5)	0	-	7	-	0	-	14	-	21

Scoring Summary
Texas – Ehlinger 2 yard run (Dicker Kick)
Texas – Dicker 37 yard Field Goal
Texas – Ehlinger 9 yard run (Dicker Kick)
Georgia – Herrien 17 yard pass from Fromm (Blankenship Kick)
Texas – Dicker 30 yard Field Goal
Texas – Ehlinger 1 yard run (2 point pass good)
Georgia – Hardman 3 yard pass from Fromm (Blankenship Kick)
Georgia – Swift 5 yard pass from Fromm (Blankenship Kick)

Associated Press Sugar Bowl Game Summary – Bevo's pregame strategy was to run right at the Bulldogs. Once the football started, Texas quarterback Sam Ehlinger took the same approach with outstanding results. Ehlinger ran for three touchdowns, the Texas defense largely held Georgia's offense in check, and the Longhorns earned their first 10-win season since 2009 by beating the Bulldogs 28-21 in the Sugar Bowl on Tuesday night. Ehlinger was the star of a gritty win, running for a 2-yard touchdown in the first quarter, a 9-yard score in the second, and a 1-yard TD in the fourth. The 6-foot-3, 230-pound sophomore finished with 64 yards rushing on 21 carries and threw for 169 yards. The quarterback's impressive performance came after a startling pregame display from Bevo, the team's huge longhorn steer mascot. About an hour before kickoff, he charged through a barricade and toward Georgia's red sweater-clad bulldog mascot Uga X. A few people, including photographers, were knocked to the ground, but there were no reported injuries and Bevo was quickly restrained. No. 14 Texas (10-4) continued its quick rise under Coach Tom Herman, capping his second season with a Sugar Bowl win that will surely send expectations soaring after nearly a decade of mostly mediocrity. During the postgame celebration, some Texas players were making snow angels in the confetti on the field. The different position groups -- like receivers and linebackers -- stayed on the field to take pictures together as the Longhorns obviously relished every moment. Texas stretched its lead to 28-7 with 11:49 left in the fourth quarter on Ehlinger's 1-yard run, finally scoring on fourth down after his first three attempts at running for the score fell just short of the end zone. No. 6 Georgia (11-3) was a 12 1/2-point favorite and claimed it would be ready for the Sugar Bowl despite just missing a spot in the College Football Playoff after a loss in the Southeastern Conference championship game. But a sloppy opening sequence indicated otherwise. Texas jumped out to a 17-0 lead by early in the second quarter, largely because of Georgia's mistakes on special teams and offense. The costliest was when D'Andre Swift fumbled deep in Georgia's own territory, giving Texas possession at the 12. Three plays later, Ehlinger deftly escaped trouble in the pocket and scored on a 9-yard run to give the Longhorns a 17-point advantage with 14:53 left in the second quarter. Georgia got back into the game with a methodical 12-play drive that ended with Jake Fromm finding Brian Herrien for a 17-yard touchdown, but Texas still took a 20-7 advantage into halftime. Fromm completed 20 of 34 passes for 212 yards, three touchdowns and one interception. The Bulldogs scored a touchdown with 14 seconds left to pull within 28-21 but Texas recovered the ensuing onside kick. Ehlinger's "We're back!" comment on the Sugar Bowl stage certainly revved up Texas fans. His coach wasn't as big of a fan. The coach was asked if his heart dropped when Ehlinger made the statement, the coach responded with a good-natured "Yes," while Ehrlinger, who was seated next to him, tried to stifle a grin. It's a validating win for Texas, which was the physically dominant team while playing one of the SEC's best programs. It's fair to say the Longhorns are ahead of schedule under Herman and expectations will skyrocket going forward. A very good Bulldogs' season ended with a huge thud after back-to-back losses to Alabama and Texas. Georgia made far too many mistakes against the Longhorns and Fromm didn't have one of his best games.

2019 CFP CHAMPIONSHIP GAME

The 2019 College Football Playoff National Championship was played at Levi's Stadium in Santa Clara, California. The Clemson Tigers defeated the Alabama Crimson Tide by a score of 44–16 to win the championship with an undefeated 15–0 record. Clemson became the first such undefeated team in the CFP era to win the title, and the first to win 15 games in a single season since the 1897 Penn Quakers. The 28-point loss was the largest margin of defeat for Alabama during the Nick Saban era (since 2007) and since Alabama's 31-point loss in the 1998 Music City Bowl. Alabama held a 14–4 series lead over Clemson in prior meetings between the two teams. They had met in the postseason in each of the prior three seasons: the 2016 College Football Playoff National Championship, won by Alabama (45–40); the 2017 College Football Playoff National Championship, won by Clemson (35–31); and the 2018 Sugar Bowl playoff semifinal game, won by Alabama (24–6). This was the first time under the College Football Playoff format (initiated in 2014) that an undefeated team won the championship, as both teams came into the game 14–0. The most recent prior matchup of undefeated teams in a championship game had been the 2011 BCS National Championship Game, which saw 13–0 Auburn defeat 12–0 Oregon. The most recent undefeated winner of a national championship game had been Florida State, who won the 2014 BCS National Championship Game and finished their season with a 14–0 record.

Clemson defeated the Pittsburgh Panthers in the 2018 ACC Championship Game on December 1, then received their bid to the Cotton Bowl with the release of final CFP rankings on December 2. Clemson defeated the Notre Dame Fighting Irish in the Cotton Bowl Classic on December 29 to advance to the championship game. The Tigers entered the championship game with a 14–0 record.

Alabama defeated the Georgia Bulldogs in the 2018 SEC Championship Game on December 1, then received their bid to the Orange Bowl with the release of final CFP rankings on December 2. Alabama defeated the Oklahoma Sooners in the Orange Bowl on December 29 to advance to the championship game. The Crimson Tide also entered the championship game with a 14–0 record.

2019 CFP Championship Game	Line	1	-	2	-	3	-	4	-	Final
#2 Clemson	(57.5)	17	-	14	-	13	-	0	-	44
#1 Alabama	(-5.5)	13	-	3	-	0	-	0	-	16

Scoring Summary
Clemson – Terrell 44 yard interception return (Huegel Kick)
Alabama – Jeudy 62 yard pass from Tagovailoa (Bulovas Kick)
Clemson – Etienne 17 yard run (Huegel Kick)
Alabama – Hentges 1 yard pass from Tagovailoa (Kick failed)
Alabama – Bulovas 25 yard Field Goal
Clemson – Etienne 1 yard run (Huegel Kick)
Clemson – Etienne 5 yard run (Huegel Kick)
Clemson – Huegel 36 yard Field Goal
Clemson – Ross 74 yard pass from Lawrence (Kick failed)
Clemson – Higgins 5 yard pass from Lawrence (Huegel Kick)

CFP Game Summary — After winning the coin toss, Alabama elected to defer, giving Clemson the ball to start the game. The Tigers' opening drive resulted in a three-and-out, and Alabama took over on their own 21-yard-line following a punt. However, three plays later the scoring was opened by Clemson cornerback A. J. Terrell, who intercepted a Tua Tagovailoa pass and returned it 44 yards for a touchdown. Alabama responded quickly, as Tagovailoa made up for the interception three plays later by finding Jerry Jeudy downfield for a 62-yard score. On their ensuing drive, Clemson continued the offensive trend of the first quarter with a 62-yard pass of their own, from Trevor Lawrence to Tee Higgins, which set up a 17-yard touchdown rush by Travis Etienne on the next play. Now trailing 14–7, Alabama marched downfield on their next drive, covering 75 yards in ten plays, to score a touchdown with opportunity to tie the game. However, Alabama freshman placekicker Joseph Bulovas missed the extra point, hitting the right upright; this was his sixth missed extra point of the season and left Clemson ahead by one, 14–13. Clemson's ensuing drive resulted in another three-and-out; they punted to Alabama, who made it to the Clemson 3-yard-line when the first quarter ended. The second quarter began with Clemson holding a one-point lead, although this would not last for long. Two plays into the quarter, Bulovas converted a 25-yard field goal to put Alabama in front by two points, 16–14. Clemson would soon recapture the lead, as Lawrence led the Tigers' offense down the field in six plays; the drive was capped by a one-yard touchdown rush by Travis Etienne. With the Clemson lead at 21–16, Alabama began their next drive. The Clemson defense would make another important play, as Tagovailoa threw his second interception of the game and only his sixth all season. Clemson then capitalized with a five-yard pass from Lawrence to Etienne to make push the lead to 12 points, 28–16. On what would be their last drive of the half, Alabama punted on 4th-and-17, giving Clemson the ball on their own 21-yard-line. With just over two minutes on the clock, Clemson drove down the field and converted a 36-yard field goal that put the lead at 31–16 and gave the Tide the ball back with 45 seconds. After an incomplete pass and a six-yard rush, Alabama head coach Nick Saban elected to let the clock expire and head to halftime trailing by fifteen. On Alabama's first drive of the second half, they gained 53 yards on 12 plays before losing two yards on a fake field goal, turning the ball over on downs and giving the Tigers the football on their own 24-yard-line. Clemson took advantage of the Tide's mistake, scoring on a 74-yard Trevor Lawrence pass to Justyn Ross. Greg Huegel's extra point attempt hit the left upright, leaving the score at 37–16; it was only his second missed extra point of the season. Alabama's next drive spanned 59 yards before they failed to convert a 4th-and-4 on Clemson's 14-yard-line, giving the Tigers the ball with just under six minutes to play in the third quarter. Clemson took advantage, driving 89 yards for a touchdown with a five-yard touchdown catch by Tee Higgins; the successful extra point pushing their lead to 44–16. Alabama's 28-point deficit was the largest in any game under Saban, their coach since 2007. The Tide began their third drive of the second half on their 25-yard-line following a touchback. Following a 48-yard pass from Tagovailoa to Jeudy on the final play of the third quarter, Alabama started the fourth quarter with a first down on Clemson's 27-yard-line. However, Alabama's offense stalled again, losing seven yards on 4th-and-goal from Clemson's 2-yard-line; this was the Tide's third straight turnover on downs, with all three coming in Clemson territory. Clemson was then unable to take advantage of their possession and punted for the first time since the first quarter; the punt was downed at Alabama's 48-yard-line. Alabama began their fourth second-half drive with just over eleven minutes on the clock and Jalen Hurts at quarterback; it ended in a three-and-out, and Mike Bernier's punt was downed at the Clemson one-yard-line. After draining more than seven minutes on the clock and with the ball on Alabama's 17-yard-line, most Clemson's offensive starters were removed from the game and Chase Brice was put in at quarterback. Clemson used up the remaining two minutes off the clock and took a knee on the final play ending the longest drive (10:02) in Clemson history and winning the National Championship, their second title in three years.

2019 BAHAMAS BOWL

The 2019 Bahamas Bowl was played on December 20, 2019. It was the 6th edition of the Bahamas Bowl. The game was played between the Charlotte 49ers from Conference USA (C–USA) and the Buffalo Bulls from the Mid-American Conference (MAC). This was the first time the Bulls and 49ers have ever played against each other. The Bulls entered the bowl with a 7–5 record (5–3 in conference). This is Buffalo's fourth appearance in a bowl game; they are 0–3 in prior bowls, most recently appearing in the 2018 Dollar General Bowl. The 49ers entered the bowl with a 7–5 record (5–3 in conference). This is Charlotte's first postseason game in school history.

2019 BAHAMAS BOWL	Line	1	-	2	-	3	-	4	-	Final
Charlotte	(51.5)	0	-	0	-	6	-	3	-	9
Buffalo	(-7.0)	7	-	10	-	7	-	7	-	31

Scoring Summary
Buffalo – Nunn 12 yard paas from Vantrease (McNulty kick)
Buffalo – Vantrease 1 yard run (McNulty kick)
Buffalo – McNulty 31 yard Field goal
Buffalo – Patterson 6 yard run (McNulty kick)
Charlotte – Tucker 51 yard pass from Reynolds (Pass failed)
Charlotte – Cruz 32 yard Field goal
Buffalo – Patterson 10 yard run (McNulty Kick)

Bahamas Bowl Game Summary – Buffalo running back Jaret Patterson rushed 32 times for 173 yards and two touchdowns to help secure the program's first-ever bowl victory, as the Bulls defeated the Charlotte 49ers 31-9 in the 2019 Makers Wanted Bahamas Bowl. Patterson was also named Offensive Player of the Game and punctuated the victory with his second touchdown run with 1:43 left in the contest. The Bulls' final drive went for 16 plays and spanned 9:07. Patterson accounted for 81 rushing yards on 13 attempts during the drive, as he was handed the ball on the first nine plays of the possession to ice the game. Buffalo defensive end Malcolm Koonce was awarded Defensive Player of the Game thanks to his five tackles, two sacks and one forced fumble. Koonce's strip sack of Charlotte quarterback Chris Reynolds was recovered by Ledarius Mack with 0:06 remaining in the second quarter and helped the Bulls preserve a 17-0 lead heading into halftime. Buffalo finishes the season with an 8-5 record, while Charlotte falls to 7-6 in the team's first bowl appearance in school history. Aside from Patterson's performance on the ground, both defenses turned in solid performances. Buffalo held a slight 282 to 278 advantage in total offense. The combined 560 yards were the fewest in Makers Wanted Bahamas Bowl history, which was a distinction previously held by the 2017 game between Ohio and UAB (812 combined yards). Charlotte's Markees Watts led all players with 11 tackles, while Marquavis Gibbs tallied an interception for the 49ers. Buffalo's James Patterson (Jaret's twin brother) also had an interception for the Bulls. After forcing a 3-and-out on Charlotte's first drive of the game, Buffalo marched 61 yards in seven plays to go up 7-0 at the 9:12 mark of the first quarter. Patterson ran the ball five times for 46 yards on the drive, while Antonio Nunn caught two passes from Kyle Vantrease for 15 yards, including a 12-yard touchdown reception along the right sideline of the endzone. Nunn ended the game with five catches, 53 yards and the touchdown. The Bulls went up 14-0 with 3:33 left in the first half on a sneak by Vantrease from the one. Buffalo moved the ball deliberately down the field for the score, running 15 plays (11 rush) and taking 8:26 off the clock. Vantrease gained five yards on the ground, while Patterson and Kevin Marks had 20 and 12 rushing yards on the drive, respectively. James Patterson intercepted Chris Reynolds on the 49ers' next play from scrimmage and returned it 20 yards to the Charlotte 12, setting up the short field. The 49ers defense held strong, though, holding the Bulls to a 31-yard field goal by Alex McNulty that put Buffalo up 17-0 with 1:25 remaining in the half. Jaret Patterson added to the Bulls' lead at 5:22 in the third with a six-yard touchdown run. Buffalo took over on downs to start the drive at the Charlotte 43-yard line with 9:07 on the clock, and it was a healthy dose of Patterson from there. He rushed the ball on five of the seven plays, including the score to put the Bulls up 24-0. Charlotte got on the scoreboard with 2:20 left in the third on a 51-yard touchdown strike from quarterback Chris Reynolds to Victor Tucker. Tucker caught a short crossing route and did the rest with his feet, alluding several Bulls defenders en route to the end zone. The 49ers two-point attempt came up short, keeping the score at 24-6. On the next Buffalo drive, Charlotte forced a quick 3-and-out. After taking over via punt on their own 31-yard line, the 49ers went 54 yards on 10 plays to set up a successful 32-yard field goal by Jonathan Cruz. That score cut the deficit to 24-9 with 10:50 to go in the game before Patterson and the Bulls put the game away with their final drive.

2019 FRISCO BOWL

The 2019 Frisco Bowl was played on December 20, 2019. It was the 3rd edition of the Frisco Bowl. The game was played between Utah State and Kent State. It was the third time that the teams have played each other; the all-time series is tied at 1–1. The most recent meeting between them saw Utah
State defeating Kent State by a score of 27–24 on October 19, 1974, at Kent State. Utah State finished their regular season with a 7–5 record, finishing in third place in the Mountain Division of the Mountain West Conference. This is the Aggies' 13th bowl game in program history, and eighth bowl appearance in nine seasons. This was Kent State's fourth bowl game in school history, as the Golden Flashes will be seeking their first-ever bowl win after losing the previous three. It is also Kent State's first bowl game since the 2013 GoDaddy.com Bowl, where they lost to Arkansas State, 17–13.

2019 FRISCO BOWL	Line	1	-	2	-	3	-	4	-	Final
Utah State	(-7.0)	10	-	7	-	10	-	14	-	41
Kent State	(71.5)	17	-	6	-	3	-	25	-	51

Scoring Summary
Utah State – Bright 4 yard run (Eberle Kick)
Kent State – McCoy 78 yard pass from Crum (Trickett Kick)
Kent State – Williams 2 yard run (Trickett Kick)
Kent State – Trickett 40 yard Field goal
Utah State – Eberle 41 yard Field goal
Utah State – Mariner 25 yard pass from Love (Eberle kick)
Kent State – Trickett 22 yard Field goal
Kent State – Trickett 36 yard Field goal
Kent State – Trickett 29 yard Field goal
Utah State – Thompkins 17 yard pass from Love (Eberle kick)
Utah State – Eberle 45 yard Field goal
Kent State – Williams 4 yard run (Run good)
Utah State – Thompkins 57 yard run (Eberle kick)
Kent State – Dixon 1 yard pass from Crum (Trickett kick)
Kent State – Trickett 37 yard Field goal
Utah State – Mariner 11 yard pass from Love (Eberle kick)
Kent State – Crum 4 yard run (Trickett kick)

Frisco Bowl Game Summary – The Kent State Golden Flashes (7-6, 5-3 MAC) won its first bowl game in school history with a 51-41 shootout victory over Utah State (7-6, 6-2 MWC) in the Tropical Smoothie Café Frisco Bowl. The Flashes gained gained 550 total yards – the third most in a game this season – and scored 50 points for just the second time all year. The Aggies flew down the field on their opening drive, as Gerold Bright scored a four-yard touchdown give Utah State the early 7-0 advantage. After two plays resulting in -3 yards on Kent State's first drive, Dustin Crum launched a 78-yard touchdown pass to Isaiah McKoy to even the score. The Golden Flashes kept their foot on the gas as Xavier Williams scored from two yards out to extend their lead over the Aggies. Mandela Lawrence-Burke picked off Utah State quarterback Jordan Love on the next possession and Matthew Trickett drilled a 40-yard field goal to give the Flashes a 17-7 advantage. The Flashes scored 17 unanswered points in the opening quarter. Utah State answered with 10 unanswered points capped off by a Dominik Eberle 25-yard touchdown from Love. Kent State's Derek Adams lined up to punt for the first time midway through the second quarter. His kick took a hop into the Utah State returner and Elvis Hines recovered at the Aggies' 10-yard line. Trickett hit a field goal to pull the Flashes back in front. Another field goal from the Mid-American Conference Special Teams Player of the Year gave Kent State a 23-17 lead at the break. On the first possession of the second half, the Flashes went 41 yards in eight plays for Trickett's fourth field goal of the game. The Aggies scored the next 10 points and took a 27-26 lead into the fourth quarter. Utah State punted early in the fourth quarter and the Flashes took full advantage. Crum hit Antwan Dixon on a 53-yard pass that put Kent State inside the five-yard line. Will Matthews ran it in from four yards out and then converted the two-point conversion to give the Flashes a 34-27 lead with 13:31 left to play. After a Utah State touchdown, Crum hit Dixon on a one-yard touchdown pass to give the Flashes a 41-34 lead. Zayin West forced a fumble on the ensuing Aggies' possession and Alex Hoag recovered to put Kent State in Aggie territory. Trickett drilled a 37-yard field goal to put the Flashes ahead, 44-34. His field goal broke the Kent State record for most field goals in a single game, broke the record for most field goals in Frisco Bowl history and tied the NCAA bowl record for most field goals in a single game. Utah State drove the field and Love connected with Mariner on his third touchdown of the day to cut the lead to three, 44-41. The Flashes iced the game away and capped off their first ever bowl victory with a four-yard rushing touchdown by Crum. Crum was named the offensive MVP, totaling 436 total yards including a career-high 147 on the ground while scoring three touchdowns. Qwuantrezz Knight was named the game's defensive MVP, racking up a nine tackles, a career-high 2.5 tackles for loss and a career-high 1.5 sacks. McKoy led the Flashes with six receptions for 103 yards and a touchdown. Dixon snagged five passes for a season-high 99 yards and a touchdown. Matthews posted 56 yards on the ground with a score, while Williams scored for the fourth-consecutive game. Lawrence-Burke tied for the team lead with 10 tackles. It was his fifth double-digit tackle game of the season. Keith Sherald Jr. also posted 10 tackles, a tackle for loss and a pass breakup. The Flashes totaled a nine tackles for loss, their second most in a single game this season. It was the first game all year that Kent State recorded nine tackles for loss, four sacks, a fumble recovery and an interception. The Golden Flashes finished with seven wins on the season for the first time since 2012. **{KentStateSports.com}**

2019 AIR FORCE RESERVE CELEBRATION BOWL

The 2019 Celebration Bowl was played on December 21, 2019. It was the 5th edition of the Celebration Bowl. Alcorn State of the SWAC played North Carolina A&T of the MEAC. Alcorn State earned their berth in the Celebration Bowl via a win over the Southern Jaguars in the SWAC Championship Game on December 7. The Braves enter the Celebration Bowl with a 9–3 overall record (6–1 in conference). This will be their third appearance in the Celebration Bowl, having lost their prior two appearances (2015 and 2018); both losses were to North Carolina A&T. North Carolina A&T, led by second-year head coach Sam Washington, clinched their spot in the Celebration bowl on November 23 with their win over North Carolina Central. They finished runner-up in the MEAC, with a 6–2 conference record, but will appear in the Celebration Bowl instead of Florida A&M's due to postseason ban despite Florida A&M having the best HBCU record in the FCS. This will be the Aggies' fourth appearance in the Celebration Bowl, having won all of the previous three (2015, 2017, 2018).

2019 CELEBRATION BOWL	Line	1	-	2	-	3	-	4	-	Final
Alcorn State		3	-	7	-	21	-	13	-	44
North Carolina A&T		0	-	24	-	28	-	12	-	64

Scoring Summary
Alcorn State – McCullough 28 yard Field goal
North Carolina A&T – Bell 53 yard pass from Carter (Ruiz kick)
Alcorn State – Blair 36 yard pass from Harper (McCullough kick)
North Carolina A&T – Leslie 59 yard pass from Carter (Ruiz kick)
Alcorn State – Ruiz 26 yard Field goal
North Carolina A&T – Banks 4 yard pass from Carter (Ruiz kick)
North Carolina A&T – Martin 75 yard run (Ruiz kick)
Alcorn State – Harper 6 yard run (McCullough kick)
North Carolina A&T – Hunt 43 yard pass from Carter (Ruiz kick)
Alcorn State – Walter 23 yard run (McCullough kick)
North Carolina A&T – Bell 20 yard pass from Carter (Ruiz kick)
Alcorn State – Anderson 35 yard pass from Harper (McCullough kick)
North Carolina A&T – Banks 73 yard pass from Carter (Ruiz kick)

Alcorn State – Wood 13 yard pass from Harper (McCullough kick)
North Carolina A&T – Ruiz 38 yard Field goal
Alcorn State – Harper 1 yard run (Kick blocked)
North Carolina A&T – McNeil blocked PAT return for 2 point conversion
North Carolina A&T – Martin 4 yard run (Ruiz kick)

Associated Press Celebration Bowl Game Summary – North Carolina A&T had a good idea that Alcorn State would try to slow down the running game. However, the Aggies couldn't have predicted that Kylil Carter would have so much success throwing the ball. Carter passed for six touchdowns and North Carolina A&T racked up enormous offensive totals to beat Alcorn State 64-44 in the Celebration Bowl on Saturday for its third consecutive HBCU national championship title and fourth in five years. Carter completed 18 of 30 passes for 364 yards and added 96 on the ground. Korey Banks and Elijah Bell each caught a pair of scoring passes for NC A&T, which has beaten Alcorn State in three of the five Celebration Bowls – including two straight. The Braves led 3-0 after one quarter, and then the scoring started. Alcorn State quarterback Felix Harper passed for 341 yards and three scores, but the Braves trailed 24-10 at halftime and NC A&T steadily stacked points from there. The teams combined for 49 points in the third quarter, when NC A&T scored touchdowns on its first four possessions of the period and Alcorn State banked touchdowns on its first three drives. The Aggies rolled to 290 yards in the quarter, and Alcorn State added 238. NCA&T scored eight touchdowns, two field goals and added two points when Amir McNeil picked up a poorly snapped PAT by Alcorn State and raced nearly 90 yards with less than five minutes to go in the game. The Aggies lost two fumbles and punted three times yet still put up 574 of the game's combined 1,034 yards. NC A&T took the lead when senior Bell ran past the Alcorn State secondary and pulled in a 53-yard touchdown pass with 13:03 left in the second quarter. That was good for a 7-3 edge and extended Bell's school record to 32 career touchdowns receiving. Alcorn State moved ahead briefly when Harper found wide receiver Chris Blair wide open for a 59-yard scoring pass with 7:55 left. That 10-7 advantage didn't last long, as NC A&T scored the final 17 points of the second quarter. The Aggies had a 59-yard touchdown pass to Zachary Leslie and a 4-yard scoring pass to Korey Banks around a 28-yard field goal from Noel Ruiz to take a 24-10 lead at halftime. The field goal came shortly after freshman linebacker Jacob Roberts intercepted Harper's pass and returned it 28 yards to Alcorn State's 5-yard-line. NC A&T receivers repeatedly got open behind Alcorn State defenders for big plays with the Braves gearing up against Aggies running back Jah-Maine Martin. Both quarterbacks grew up outside of Atlanta, and Carter most enjoyed his reunion. Martin helped NC A&T put the game away in the third quarter. He rushed seven times in othe first half for one yard, but he took the first play of the second half 75 yards off right tackle to score. Martin gained 117 yards rushing in the period. He finished with 110 yards on the ground. Although Alcorn State countered quickly when Harper scored on a six-yard run to cap a 10-play, 75-yard drive, NC A&T was quicker to answer when another long pass by Carter found Aggies wide receiver Ron Hunt wide open deep for a 43-yard score and a 38-17 lead early in the third. Alcorn State coach Fred McNair said the Braves were too often too aggressive on defense. The Braves entered the game No. 1 in the nation among FCS schools with 34 takeaways, and they stripped NC A&T's Banks on a punt return to set up possession at the Aggies' 23-yard line. Four plays later, Corey McCullough kicked a 28-yard field goal for the early lead with 3:17 left in the first quarter.

2019 NEW MEXICO BOWL

The 2019 New Mexico Bowl was played on December 21, 2019 at Dreamstyle Stadium on the campus of the University of New Mexico in Albuquerque, NM. It was the 14th edition of the New Mexico Bowl. Central Michigan (MAC) and San Diego State (MWC) faced each other for the first time. Central Michigan entered the game with an 8-5 record. San Diego State entered the game with a 9-3 record.

2019 NEW MEXICO BOWL	Line	1	-	2	-	3	-	4	-	Final
Central Michigan	{40.5}	3	-	0	-	8	-	0	-	11
San Diego State	{-4.0}	7	-	13	-	21	-	7	-	48

Scoring Summary
San Diego State – Matthews 22 yard pass from Agnew (Araiza kick)
Central Michigan – Tice 33 yard Field goal
San Diego State – Araiza 48 yard Field goal
San Diego State – Araiza 31 yard Field goal
San Diego State – Matthews 74 yard pass from Agnew (Araiza kick)
San Diego State – Byrd 2 yard run (Araiza kick)
San Diego State – Sullivan 29 yard pass from Agnew (Araiza kick)
Central Michigan – Lewis 66 yard run (Pass good)
San Diego State – Jasmin 2 yard run (Araiza kick)
San Diego State – Hall 20 yard fumble return (Araiza kick)

Associated Press New Mexico Bowl Game Summary - Coming into the New Mexico Bowl, San Diego State's defense was the focus. The Aztecs ranked second in the nation in rushing defense and second in rushing yards allowed per carry. But San Diego State's offense, with only an average of 19 points-per game, ranked among the nation's worst. Something had to give against Central Michigan and its strong defense. So, the Aztecs offense stepped it up Saturday. Ryan Agnew passed for 287 yards and three touchdowns, Jesse Matthews caught three passes for 111 yards and two touchdowns and San Diego State won a bowl game for the first time since 2016, beating Central Michigan 48-11 on Saturday in the New Mexico Bowl. Jordan Byrd ran for a career-high 139 yards and a touchdown to help the Aztecs (10-3) cap their 10th straight bowl appearance with a victory. San Diego State opened 7-1 record, then dropped two of its last three conference games to fall out of contention for a Mountain West title game berth. San Diego State prevented Central Michigan (8-6) from sustaining consistent, with quarterback Quinten Dormady under pressure and forced to throw into tight coverage. He passed for 164 and threw three interception. Central Michigan's Jonathan Ward, who came into the game with 1,082 yards and 15 touchdowns, was held to 7 rushing yards and 26 yards receiving. Kobe Lewis ran for 97 rushing yards, with a 66-yard rushing touchdown in the third quarter. Despite the loss, Lewis credited Chippewas coach Jim McElwain for changing the culture of the program that went from 1-11 to 8-6 in one year. McElwain said he still felt Central Michigan had a successful season even through the team finished with losses in the Mid-American Conference Championship and New Mexico Bowl. McElwain said he was returning next season as head coach despite talk linking him to over jobs. The victory served as homecoming for Long. He last won the New Mexico Bowl in 2007 as New Mexico's coach. Long is 4-9 in bowl games and used to look at the field from his office.

2019 AUTO NATION CURE BOWL

The 2019 Cure Bowl was played on December 21, 2019, in Orlando, Florida. The game was televised on CBS Sports Network. It was the fifth edition of the Cure Bowl. This was the first Cure Bowl played at Exploria Stadium, as all prior editions were held at nearby Camping World Stadium. Georgia Southern faced Liberty. Both teams entered the game with 7-5 records. This will be Georgia Southern's third bowl game. This will be Liberty's first bowl game since joining the FBS, which they have accomplished in their first season of being eligible to qualify for a bowl game.

2019 CURE BOWL	Line	1	-	2	-	3	-	4	-	Final
Liberty	{58.5}	7	-	9	-	7	-	0	-	23
Georgia Southern	{-5.0}	0	-	7	-	6	-	3	-	16

Scoring Summary
Liberty – Huntley 57 yard pass from Calvert (Probert kick)
Georgia Southern – Kennedy 10 yard run (Bass kick)
Liberty – Mack 3 yard run (Kick failed)
Liberty – Probert 46 yard Field goal
Liberty – Gandy-Golden 14 yard pass from Calvert (Probert kick)
Georgia Southern – Bass 28 yard Field goal
Georgia Southern – Bass 30 yard Field goal
Georgia Southern – Bass 35 yard Field goal

Cure Bowl Game Summary - In just its second year as a member of the FBS, Liberty has already notched its first bowl win after taking down Georgia Southern 23-16 in the Cure Bowl. The win moves head coach Hugh Freeze to 4-1 in bowl games, capping an eight-win campaign for his first season as the Flames' coach. The season started with Freeze leading the team from a hospital bed in the coaches' box because of complications from a herniated disc in his back, but it ended with the former Ole Miss Coach celebrating a breakthrough season for the program that brought him back to the sidelines. Liberty quarterback Buckshot Calvert totaled 270 yards on 16-of-35 passing for two touchdowns, the first breaking the game open in the first quarter on this toss to a wide open Johnny Huntley for a long catch-and-wrong score. As the weather began to have somewhat of an impact -- and would continue to throughout the game -- Georgia Southern was able to keep pace early with it's reliable option attack ground game. A key moment came from Calvert early in the third quarter as the game was still very much in doubt at 16-7. Liberty got the ball to start the second half and drove right down the field, 75 yards in six plays, with Calvert's touchdown toss to Antonio Gandy-Golden ending the scoring drive. The one downside to Calvert's game was the two interceptions that helped keep the Eagles close, but it was otherwise a productive and successful day for the Flames offense. Georgia Southern racked up 194 rushing yards but failed frequently to win on third down and in other scoring opportunities. Liberty capitalizing on this bowl appearance with a win was key for its future scheduling opportunities. The Flames entered the game as underdogs -- albeit by less than a touchdown with a closing line around five points -- but competed as favorites, scoring first and never trailing in the win. That kind of performance is evidence of Liberty's strength after a season where it went 1-3 against bowl teams, defeating Buffalo at home on Sept. 14.

2019 BOCA RATON BOWL

The 2019 Boca Raton Bowl was played on December 21, 2019. It was the 6th edition of the Boca Raton Bowl and played at FAU Stadium in Boca Raton, FL. SMU (AAC) faced Florida Atlantic (C-USA) for the first time. Florida Atlantic won the C-USA championship and entered the Bowl game with a 10-3 record. SMU entered the Boca Raton Bowl with a 10-2 record.

2019 BOCA RATON BOWL	Line	1	-	2	-	3	-	4	-	Final
SMU	-7.0	0	-	14	-	0	-	14	-	28
Florida Atlantic	63.5	7	-	21	-	14	-	10	-	52

Scoring Summary
Florida Atlantic – Emmons 1 yard run (Rivas Kick)
SMU – Jones 1 yard run (Robledo kick)
Florida Atlantic – Charles 1 yard run (Rivas kick)
SMU – Jones 1 yard run (Robledo kick)
Florida Atlantic – Charles 15 yard run (Rivas kick)
Florida Atlantic – Robinson 13 yard pass from Robison (Rivas kick)
Florida Atlantic – Raine 18 yard pass from Robison (Rivas kick)
Florida Atlantic – Smith 34 yard fumble return (Rivas kick)
Florida Atlantic – Rivas 38 yard Field goal
SMU – Becker 2 yard pass from Freeman (Robledo kick)
Florida Atlantic – Posey 23 yard pass from Tronti (Rivas kick)
SMU – Proche 22 yard pass from Buechele (Robledo kick)

Boca Raton Game Summary – Florida Atlantic scored twice in the final minute of the first half to take a 28-14 lead. It never relinquished en route to a 52-28 victory over SMU in the 6th annual Cheribundi Boca Raton Bowl. After SMU (10-3) tied the game at 14 on Xavier Jones' one-yard run with 2:12 remaining in the half, FAU swiftly moved 75 yards in seven plays, capped off by a James Charles 15-yard touchdown run at the one-minute mark. On the first play after the ensuing kickoff, Shane Buechele's pass was intercepted by defensive MVP Rashad Smith (11 tackles, and a fumble recovery to go with the interception) at the SMU 35 and returned to the 13-yard line. Offensive MVP Chris Robison's 13-yard pass to Brandon Robinson on the next play gave the Owls the two-score lead heading into the locker room. FAU added two touchdowns in the third quarter, while holding SMU scoreless and entered the final quarter with an insurmountable 42-14 lead. Robison set a Cheribundi Boca Raton Bowl record with 27 completions (in 37 attempts) for 305 yards and two touchdowns. Charles added two scores on the ground. FAU tied the bowl record with its 52 points and the combined 80 points were the second most in the bowl's history. FAU punter Matt Hayball, the game's special teams MVP, set a bowl record with a 48-yard average on five punts. SMU quarterback Shane Buechele also completed 27 passes and threw for over 300 yards (27-47 for 303) while wide receiver James Proche caught nine passes for 86 yards and a touchdown. FAU was led by defensive coordinator Glenn Spencer, who was named interim coach after Lane Kiffin became the head coach at Ole Miss. The Owls finished the season 11-3, matching the best record in school history, achieved previously in 2017 when they also ended the season with a Boca Raton Bowl victory.

2019 CAMELLIA BOWL

The 2019 Camellia Bowl was played on December 21, 2019. It was the 6th edition of the Camellia Bowl and played at the historic Cramton Bowl in Montgomery, AL. Florida International (C-USA 6-6) played Arkansas State (Sun Belt 7-5). This was the ninth time that FIU and Arkansas State have played each other; Arkansas State leads the all-time series, 6–2. From 2005 to 2012, FIU and Arkansas State were both members of the Sun Belt Conference; their previous meetings spanned that era. This will be Arkansas State's second Camellia Bowl, making them the second team (after Appalachian State) to appear in multiple Camellia Bowls. Their 2017 team had previously appeared in the 2017 Camellia Bowl, losing to Middle Tennessee, 35–30.

2019 CAMELLIA BOWL	Line	1	-	2	-	3	-	4	-	Final
Florida International	-1.0	0	-	13	-	10	-	3	-	26
Arkansas State	58.5	14	-	6	-	7	-	7	-	34

Scoring Summary
Arkansas State – Bayless 4 yard pass from Hatcher (Grupe kick)
Arkansas State – Merritt 9 yard pass from Hatcher (Grupe kick)
Florida International – Maxwell 3 yard run (Borregales kick)
Arkansas State – Grupe 46 yard Field goal
Florida International – Borregales 25 yard Field goal
Arkansas State – Grupe 37 yard Field goal
Florida International – Borregales 25 yard Field goal

Arkansas State – Tyler 15 yard pass from Hatcher (Grupe kick)
Florida International – Maloney 19 yard pass from Morgan (Borregales kick)
Florida International – Borregales 48 yard Field goal
Florida International – Borregales 52 yard Field goal
Arkansas State – Adams 13 yard pass from Hatcher (Grupe kick)

Camellia Bowl Game Summary – Arkansas State had lost four of its last five bowl games, including its last visit to the Camellia Bowl in 2017. After a season of filled with emotions and injuries, the Red Wolves were determined to turn those bowl fortunes. On a soggy night at the historic Cramton Bowl, Arkansas State literally passed that test with fly colors. Redshirt freshman quarterback Layne Hatcher set Camellia Bowl records with 393 passing yards and four touchdowns, and senior wide receiver Omar Bayless set the Camellia Bowl record with 180 receiving yards leading the Red Wolves to a 34-26 win over FIU in the sixth annual Camellia Bowl in Montgomery. Arkansas State (8-5) led by 14 points on two separate occasions but the game was not decided until a pair of late interceptions by the A-State defense sealed the win. Bayless caught nine passes for 180 yards and one touchdown to earn the Bart Starr Most Valuable Player Trophy. He caught a 4-yard touchdown pass on the game's opening drive and added two long receptions to set two more A-State scores. Bayless hauled in a 51-yard pass that led to a second quarter field goal. His 52-yard catch in the fourth quarter set up the final touchdown for the Red Wolves. Arkansas State set Camellia Bowl records for total yards (525), passing yards (393), first downs (31) and touchdown passes (4). The Red Wolves scored on two of their first three possessions to take a 14-0 lead. A-State capped a 15-play opening drive when Hatcher threw a 4-yard pass to Bayless to put the Red Wolves up 7-0 with 9:25 left in the first quarter. Hatcher threw his second touchdown pass of the first quarter when he found Kirk Merritt on a 9-yarder to make it 14-0. The pass to Merritt capped a 13-play, 90-yard drive. FIU (6-7) found its rhythm in the second quarter, outscored the ASU 13-6 over the next 15 minutes to make to 20-13 at halftime. Senior running back Napoleon Maxwell put the Panthers on the board with a 3-yard run to cut the deficit to 14-7 with 12:50 left in the half. The teams then traded field goals the remained of the half. ASU kicker Blake Grupe stretched the lead to 17-7 with a 46-yard field goal with 9:31 left. FIU kicker Jose Borregales followed with a 25-yard field goal to make it 17-10 on the next possession. Grupe added a 37-yard field goal for the Red Wolves to make to 20-10 and Borregales capped the scoring with a 25-yard field goal with 25 seconds left in the half. A-State led 20-13 at halftime. Arkansas State stretched the lead back to 14 points with a touchdown on its opening drive of the third quarter. Hatcher found Reed Tyler on a 15-yard pass to give ASU a 27-13 lead with 12:22 left in the third quarter. Like the first half, FIU answered. FIU took advantage of a Hatcher fumble and turned into a quick touchdown. FIU quarterback James Morgan fired a 15-yard touchdown pass to senior wide receiver Austin Maloney to cut the deficit to 27-20 last in the third quarter. FIU made it 27-23 on Borregales 48-yard field goal with 38 seconds left in the third quarter. Maloney finished with a Camellia Bowl-record 10 receptions for 178 yards and one touchdown. Borregales capped a 13-0 run by the Panthers with a 52-yard field goal in the fourth quarter to trim the lead to 27-26. The 52-yard field goal was the longest in Camellia Bowl history. He also set the Camellia Bowl record with his fourth field goal of the game. FIU was posted to take the lead after another turnover in the fourth quarter, but Borregales pulled a 29-yard field goal to the left with 5:10 left in the game. ASU took advantage of the missed kick and drove 80 yards in five plays for the game-clinching score. Hatcher capped the scoring with a 13-yard touchdown pass to Jonathan Adams. The Arkansas State defense did it part, too. The Red Wolves forced two turnovers on FIU's final two possessions to seal the win. Senior cornerback Jeremy Smith thwarted the first drive with an interception at the A-State 38-yard line. Senior nickel back Darreon Jackson sealed the win with an interception at the A-State 47-yard line in the final 30 seconds.

2019 LAS VEGAS BOWL

The 2019 Las Vegas Bowl was played on December 21, 2019. It was the 28th edition of the Las Vegas Bowl. The 2019 Las Vegas Bowl will be the last edition played at Sam Boyd Stadium, the host of the game since its inception in 1992, as the 2020 game will be played at the new Allegiant Stadium in Paradise. Additionally, the game will receive new conference affiliations, as games starting in 2020 will feature a Pac-12 team against either a Big Ten team or SEC team. The game was played between the Washington Huskies (7-5) of the Pac-12 Conference and the Mountain West Conference (MWC) champions Boise State Broncos (12-1). It was a rematch of the 2012 Maaco Bowl Las Vegas, which saw Boise State defeat Washington, 28–26. It was the fifth overall meeting between Washington and Boise State; currently, the all-time series is tied at 2–2.

2019 LAS VEGAS BOWL	Line	1	-	2	-	3	-	4	-	Final
Washington	-4.0	7	-	10	-	7	-	14	-	38
#18 Boise State	48.0	0	-	0	-	7	-	0	-	7

Scoring Summary
Washington – Baccellia 17 yard pass from Eason (Henry kick)
Washington – Ahmed 8 yard run (Henry kick)
Washington – Henry 32 yard Field goal
Washington – Newton 2 yard run (Henry kick)
Boise State – Holani 10 yard pass from Henderson (Sachse kick)
Washington – Bynum 13 yard pass from Newton (Henry kick)
Washington – Ahmed 12 yard run (Henry kick)

Las Vegas Bowl Game Summary – In what may have been the most hyped Las Vegas Bowl of all time, the Washington Huskies and their spectacular defensive secondary completely smothered Boise State 38-7. The Huskies set the tone early in the first half emphasizing defense and special teams in order to gain field position advantages and to put maximum pressure - both physically and mentally - on Boise State true freshman QB Hank Bachmeier. The strategy worked well as the Dawgs were able to play their very best bend-don't-break style of defense with an optimal amount of quality tackling. Quarterback pressure was present as Bachmeier had to deal with blitzes coming from just about everywhere on the field as well as directly from pass rushers such as Ryan Bowman and Joe Tryon. The net effect was an offense that produced zero points, just 91 yards and a paltry 2.1 yards per rush in the first half. Jacob Eason and the Huskies offense were able to take advantage with some gritty first half offense. With big plays nowhere to be found in the first 30 minutes of game clock, the Dawgs emphasized a heavy rotation of running backs and a short passing game complemented by solid pass protection to move the ball down the field with efficiency. Demonstrating abilities to convert on third downs and in the red zone - areas that had been suspect all season - the Huskies strung together three first half scoring drives including two TD drives that were made up of 12 plays and 13 plays, respectively. Eason was the catalyst in both those TD drives making good decisions with his passes and completing 16 of 22 for 124 yards. Washington ended the first half with a 17-0 advantage. The second half got off to a more explosive start for the Huskies. After an Elijah Molden interception early in the half, Eason came out throwing haymakers. A 22 yard strike to Terrell Bynum led to a subsequent 2 yard TD run for human flame thrower Richard Newton and a commanding 24-0 lead early in the third quarter. Things just got better for the Huskies from there. A trick play called by Boise State head coach and former Chris Petersen protégé Bryan Harsin got the Broncos on the board, but that was about all that the Broncos could muster. The Washington secondary just continued to wreak havoc against a physically overmatched Boise secondary and frustrated not just Bachmeier but Boise backup Jaylon Henderson once he was inserted into the game. On the flip side, Eason and the Washington offense continued to roll. By the time it was over, the numbers told the story of the physical and tactical advantages that UW exploited all game long. Washington finished 50% on third down conversions (7 of 14), 6 for 6 on red zone conversions and +2 in the turnover margin category. The Huskies also enjoyed a +17 yard starting field position average throughout the game. The Coach Pete bowl marks the end of the Chris Petersen era at Montlake and, perhaps, the end of the line for a wildly successful college football coach who has posted an absurd 146-38 record over a decorated career. Petersen leaves a UW legacy that includes two PAC 12 championships, a Rose Bowl, one of just two PAC 12 College Football Playoff appearances and three straight New Year's Six bowl appearances.

2019 NEW ORLEANS BOWL

The 2019 New Orleans Bowl was played on December 21, 2019. It was the 19th edition of the New Orleans Bowl. The game was played between the Alabama-Birmingham Blazers of Conference USA (C–USA) and the Sun Belt Conference champions Appalachian State Mountaineers. It was the first New Orleans Bowl to feature a ranked team, as Appalachian State was ranked #20 in the AP Poll, Coaches Poll, and CFP rankings entering the game. It will also mark the first time that Alabama-Birmingham and Appalachian State have ever played each other. Appalachian State enters the New Orleans Bowl with an overall 12–1 record (7–1 in conference), having won the Sun Belt Championship Game over Louisiana. This will be Appalachian State's second New Orleans Bowl, both consecutively and overall; the Mountaineers are the defending New Orleans Bowl champions, having won the 2018 edition over Middle Tennessee, 45–13. Appalachian State has won all 4 Bowl Games since moving up to FBS. Alabama-Birmingham finished second in Conference USA with a 9-4 record, losing in the Conference Championship game to Florida Atlantic.

2019 NEW ORLEANS BOWL	Line	1	-	2	-	3	-	4	-	Final
Alabama-Birmingham	47.5	14	-	0	-	3	-	0	-	17
#20 Appalachian State	-17.0	0	-	10	-	21	-	0	-	31

Scoring Summary
Alabama-Birmingham – Pittman 25 yard pass from Johnston (Vogel kick)
Alabama-Birmingham – Watkins 25 yard pass from Johnston (Vogel kick)
Appalachian State – Staton 34 yard Field goal
Appalachian State – Hennigan 17 yard pass from Thomas (Staton kick)
Appalachian State – Evans 31 yard run (Staton kick)
Alabama-Birmingham – Vogel
Appalachian State – Cobb 24 yard fumble return (Staton kick)
Appalachian State – Hennigan 27 yard pass from Thomas (Staton kick)

New Orleans Bowl Game Summary - Darrynton Evans ran for 161 yards, including a 31-yard touchdown after he scooped up a fourth-down fumble, and No. 20 Appalachian State defeated UAB 31-17 in the New Orleans Bowl on Saturday night. The Mountaineers (13-1) scored twice in the third quarter on quarterback fumbles. Evans' go-ahead score came first when Zac Thomas lost the ball on a fourth-and-1 sneak. Later, outside linebacker Nick Hampton stripped UAB quarterback Tyler Johnston, and inside linebacker Trey Cobb picked it up and returned the ball 24 yards to put Appalachian State in front 24-17. Johntson, making his first start since injuring his knee Nov. 2 at Tennessee, passed for 298 yards and two touchdowns for UAB (9-5). Listed by odds makers as 17-point underdogs, the Blazers raced to a 14-0 lead in the first five minutes, only to be outscored 31-3 after that. The game marked the head coaching debut for Appalachian State's Shawn Clark, who took over after Eli Drinkwitz was hired by Missouri earlier this month. Clark is a former Appalachian State offensive lineman who'd been coaching the offensive line at his alma mater since 2016. Now, he's running a program that has a good chance to end the season ranked inside the top 20. Thomas Hennigan caught two touchdown passes for Appalachian State. The first came after UAB linebacker Jordan Smith was assessed a personal foul for leaping toward the line of scrimmage on Chandler Staton's missed 48-yard field goal attempt in the second quarter. Just two plays after the penalty, Thomas found Hennigan for a 17-yard TD that cut UAB's lead to 14-10. Hennigan scored his second touchdown when he wrestled an under-thrown, 27-yard pass away from cornerback Starling Thomas as both fell to the turf in the third quarter, widening Appalachian State's lead to 31-17. Zac Thomas finished with 142 yards and two TDs passing for the Mountaineers, who were the Sun Belt Conference champions and finished the season on a six-game winning streak. Austin Watkins caught 10 passes for 159 yards and a touchdown for the Blazers, but most of that came on UAB's first two possessions. Watkins made a 35-yard catch on the first play of the game and followed up with a 12-yard gain on a receiver screen. That set up Johnston's 25-yard pass to Hayden Pittman, who made a diving catch in the end zone to make it 7-0 a mere 1:14 after the opening kickoff. Watkins, who entered the game needing 67 yards receiving to reach 1,000 for the season, surpassed that on his fourth catch, a 41-yard grab down the left side early in the Blazers' second possession. Two plays later, Watkins had a 25-yard catch-and run for a touchdown to make it 14-0.

2019 GASPARILLA BOWL

The 2019 Gasparilla Bowl was played on December 23, 2019. It was the 12th edition of the Gasparilla Bowl, though only the third under that name. It was previously known as the St. Petersburg Bowl and Beef 'O' Brady Bowl. The game was played between the Marshall Thundering Herd (8-4) of Conference USA and the Central Florida Golden Knights (9-3) of the American Athletic Conference. Both Marshall and UCF were making their fourth appearance in the Gasparilla Bowl (though their first against each other); the two teams are tied for the most appearances in the bowl. It will also be the twelfth overall meeting between Marshall and UCF, with UCF leading the all-time series, 8–3. From 2002 to 2012, Marshall and UCF were in the same conference, playing together in the Mid-American Conference from 2002 to 2004, with both teams joining Conference USA together in 2005, playing in that conference until UCF left to join The American in 2013. The Thundering Herd are the defending Gasparilla Bowl champions, their 2018 team having won the 2018 Gasparilla Bowl over South Florida, 38–20.

2019 GASPARILLA BOWL	Line	1	-	2	-	3	-	4	-	Final
Marshall	59.5	0	-	7	-	18	-	0	-	25
Central Florida	-15.5	21	-	3	-	21	-	3	-	48

Scoring Summary
Central Florida – Grant 39 yard interception return (Barnas Kick)
Central Florida – McCrae 26 yard run (Barnas kick)
Central Florida – Morris-Brash 45 yard fumble return (Barnas kick)
Marshall – Abraham 75 yard interception return (Rohrwasser kick)
Central Florida – Barnas 36 yard Field goal
Central Florida – Anderson 35 yard pass from Gabriel (Barnas kick)
Marshall – Green 3 yard run (Rohrwasser kick)
Central Florida – Gabriel 3 yard run (Barnas kick)
Marshall – Johnson 70 yard pass from Green (2 point pass good)

Central Florida – Williams 75 yard pass from Gabriel (Barnas kick)
Marshall – Rohrwasser 50 yard Field goal
Central Florida – Barnas 30 yard Field goal

Associated Press Gasparilla Bowl Game Summary – Central Florida is best known for a high-powered offense, but the Knights are capable of big plays on defense, too. Richie Grant and Tre'mon Morris-Brash had first-quarter defensive touchdowns, Dillon Gabriel led three third-quarter scoring drives and UCF beat Marshall 48-25 in the Gasparilla Bowl on Monday. Grant had a 39-yard interception return on Marshall's third play from scrimmage 56 seconds into the game, and Morris-Brash recovered a fumble and ran it 55 yards for a score that helped UCF go up 21-0 with 7 minutes left in the first quarter. Gabriel threw a 35-yard touchdown pass to Otis Anderson, connected on a 75-yard score with Marlon Williams, and added a 3-yard TD run as UCF went ahead 45-22 with 6:39 remaining in the third. Gabriel completed 14 of 24 passes for 260 yards as the Knights (10-3) reached 10 or more wins in a school-record third consecutive season. Williams caught seven passes for 132 yards and Greg McCrae had 80 rushing yards on 14 carries. Isaiah Green went 9 of 23 for 173 yards with a TD and had a rushing touchdown for Marshall (8-5). Brenden Knox, the Conference USA MVP, had 103 yards on 26 carries. Green had a 3-yard rushing touchdown and hit Willie Johnson on a 70-yard TD pass, and Justin Rohrwasser made a 50-yard field goal during the third quarter. Marshall got within 21-7 with 12:28 to go in the second when Micah Abraham picked off backup quarterback Darriel Mack Jr.'s pass and returned it 75 yards for a touchdown. Abraham's father, Donnie, played his home games with the Tampa Bay Buccaneers (1996-01) at Raymond James Stadium, the site of the Gasparilla Bowl. McCrae had a 26-yard TD run early in the first and Dylan Barnas made a 36-yard field goal as time expired as UCF took a 24-7 halftime advantage.

2019 HAWAII BOWL

The 2019 Hawaii Bowl was played on Christmas Eve, December 24, 2019. It was the 18th edition of the Hawaii Bowl. The game will be played between BYU, an FBS independent, and Hawaii of the Mountain West Conference. This was the 32nd meeting in this rivalry that dates to 1930, but first in the postseason. BYU led the rivalry series, 23–8.

The BYU Cougars (7-5), led by head coach Kalani Sitake, accepted an invitation to the Hawaii Bowl on November 16. This was BYU's first Hawaii Bowl appearance, and their second postseason game in Honolulu; they played in the 1992 Aloha Bowl, where they fell to Kansas by three points.

This was Hawaii's (9-5) ninth appearance in the Hawaii Bowl. They accepted their formal invitation following their loss to Boise State in the Mountain West Conference Football Championship Game. This will be their third Hawaii Bowl appearance under head coach Nick Rolovich, having won in 2016 and lost in 2018. Overall, this was Hawaii's 13th bowl game, with a record of 6–6, including a 4–4 record in the Hawaii Bowl.

2019 HAWAII BOWL	Line	1	-	2	-	3	-	4	-	Final
BYU	-2.5	7	-	17	-	7	-	3	-	34
Hawaii	64.5	14	-	17	-	0	-	7	-	38

Scoring Summary
Hawaii – Smart 7 yard pass from McDonald (Meskell kick)
Hawaii – Smart 40 yard pass from McDonald (Meskell kick)
BYU – Katoa 1 yard run (Oldroyd kick)
Hawaii – McDonald 1 yard run (Meskell kick)
BYU – Wilson 1 yard run (Oldroyd kick)
Hawaii – Meskell 46 yard Field goal
BYU – Simon 11 yard run (Oldroyd kick)
Hawaii – Sharsh 18 yard pass from McDonald (Meskell kick)
BYU – Oldroyd 37 yard Field goal
BYU – Wilson 2 yard run (Oldroyd kick)
BYU – Oldroyd 20 yard Field goal
Hawaii – Mardner 24 yard Field goal (Meskell kick)

Associated Press Hawaii Bowl Game Summary – Hawai'i coach Nick Rolovich had this SoFi Hawai'i Bowl all figured out, except for the details. He told his players there would be times when beating BYU seemed out of reach, but he wanted them to expect to win the game in the fourth quarter. And that's what happened Tuesday at Aloha Stadium in a 38-34 victory for the Rainbow Warriors' first win over the Cougars since 2001. Rolovich just couldn't have scripted how it would happen. Hawai'i scored 31 points by halftime against a BYU defense that had given up more than 30 points in a game once this season, on the road against Washington. The Warriors were blanked so badly in the second half they didn't even get into the red zone until their final possession. And then, Cole McDonald took them 71 yards in three plays, capping off a magnificent Christmas Eve with a 24-yard touchdown pass to Nick Mardner with 1 minute, 17 seconds remaining. Khoury Bethley grabbed his second interception of the game -- and the season -- to stop BYU's final chance and give Hawai'i only its sixth 10-win season in school history and the first since 2010. McDonald finished with 493 yards passing and four touchdowns, taking him over 4,000 yards for the season. He constantly burned the BYU secondary with the deep ball, and he was at his best at the end. BYU (7-6) took its only lead of the game on a 20-yard field goal early in the fourth quarter. The Cougars had a chance to run out the clock until Zach Wilson was hurried and threw incomplete on third-and-2. That gave Hawai'i one final opportunity, all it needed. McDonald had an idea about what the defense was trying to do, and he manipulated the safety by looking right before coming back to the left to find Mardner alone for a 38-yard gain down the left sideline. On the next play, he found Mardner on a post and led him perfectly. Those were the only two catches Mardner had for the game. Rolovich played for Hawai'i in 2001 when it most recently beat BYU, back when both were in the Western Athletic Conference. This was the first time they had met in a bowl game, with Hawai'i (10-5) designated the visiting team on its home field. BYU wasted a solid game by Wilson, whose father grew up in Hawai'i. Wilson threw for 274 yards and ran for 72 yards and two short TDs to help the Cougars rally in the first half. BYU's last chance ended when Bethley picked off Wilson for the second time, and the celebration was on. McDonald finished 28-of-46, and he did most of his damage in the first half by throwing for 331 yards and three scores. Of the four touchdown drives, the shortest was 40 yards. That one followed Bethley's first interception. Two plays later, McDonald found Jared Smart on a post route with a perfectly thrown pass that made it 14-0. Wilson brought the Cougars back, leading them on touchdown drives of 73, 75 and 75 yards, the last one ending on Micah Simon scoring on an 11-yard reverse. BYU still leads the series 23-9.

2019 INDEPENDENCE BOWL

The 2019 Independence Bowl was played on December 26, 2019. It was the 44th edition of the Independence Bowl. This game featured the Louisiana Tech Bulldogs (9-3) of Conference USA (C-USA) against the Miami Hurricanes (6-6) of the Atlantic Coast Conference (ACC). It was the fifth meeting between the two schoools and the first bowl game between them; Miami had won all of their previous four meetings. This was Louisiana Tech's fifth Independence Bowl, tying them with Ole Miss for the most appearances in the game. The Bulldogs have a record of 2–1–1 in the game, most recently with their 2008 team winning the 2008 Independence Bowl over Northern Illinois, 17–10. This was Miami's 2nd appearance in the Independence Bowl, losing to South Carolina in their first appearance.

2019 INDEPENDENCE BOWL	Line	1	-	2	-	3	-	4	-	Final
Miami	-7.0	0	-	0	-	0	-	0	-	0
Louisiana Tech	51.0	0	-	7	-	0	-	7	-	14

Scoring Summary
Louisiana Tech – Tucker 26 yard pass from Smith (Hale kick)
Louisiana Tech – Smith 8 yard run (Hale kick)

Associated Press Independence Bowl Game Summary – J'Mar Smith threw a touchdown pass and had a late scoring run to help Louisiana Tech beat Miami 14-0 on Thursday night in the only shutout in the Independence Bowl's 44-game history. Louisiana Tech (10-3) reached double-digit victories for the first time since 1984 and ran its postseason winning streak to six -- the longest current streak in the country. Miami (6-7) completed its second losing season in 12 years. The Hurricanes have lost nine of 10 bowl games. According to Stats Inc., the Bulldogs became the first Group of 5 program to shut out a Power 5 school in a bowl game since the beginning of the BCS/College Football Playoff era in 1998. Smith connected with Israel Tucker on a 26-yard touchdown strike on a screen pass in the second quarter, capping a 13-play, 91-yard drive. Smith added an 8-yard scoring run with 1:15 left. Bulldogs running back Justin Henderson was selected the Most Outstanding Offensive Player after rushing for 95 yards on 22 carries. Smith completed 13 of 28 passes for 163 yards with one interception. Miami entered the game with the nation's worst third-down conversion percentage and going 5 for 14 on Thursday won't help that much. The Hurricanes finished the year with three straight losses and averaging only 25.7 points per game. It raises more questions about the future of offensive coordinator Dan Enos, whose lone season with the Hurricanes saw the offense perform well below expectations. The teams set the game record for punts at 18, with both tying the single-club record of nine.

2019 QUICK LANE BOWL

The 2019 Quick Lane Bowl was played on December 26, 2019. It was the 6th edition of the Quick Lane Bowl. The game featured the Eastern Michigan Eagles (6-6) from the Mid-American Conference (MAC) playing against the Pittsburgh Panthers (7-5) from the Atlantic Coast Conference (ACC). It will be the third meeting between Eastern Michigan and Pittsburgh; the Panthers have won both of their prior meetings.

2019 QUICK LANE BOWL	Line	1	-	2	-	3	-	4	-	Final
Pittsburgh	-12.5	0	-	17	-	3	-	14	-	34
Eastern Michigan	51.0	10	-	10	-	0	-	10	-	30

Scoring Summary
Eastern Michigan – Ryland 35 yard Field goal
Eastern Michigan – Glass 3 yard run (Ryland kick)
Pittsburgh – Kessman 44 yard Field goal
Pittsburgh – Ffrench 96 yard pass from Pickett (Kessman kick)
Eastern Michigan – Williams 50 yard pass from Glass (Ryland kick)
Pittsburgh – Davis 8 yard run (Kessman kick)
Eastern Michigan – Ryland 45 yard Field goal
Pittsburgh – Kessman 51 yard Field goal
Eastern Michigan – Jackson 10 yard pass from Glass (Ryland kick)
Pittsburgh – Wayne 19 yard pass from Pickett (Kessman kick)
Eastern Michigan – Ryland 48 yard Field goal
Pittsburgh – Mack 25 yard pass from Pickett (Kessman kick)

Associated Press Quick Lane Bowl Game Summary – Pittsburgh players took punches, and one was hit with spit, and the Panthers still kept their cool in critical moments to win a bowl game for the first time in five appearances under coach Pat Narduzzi. Kenny Pickett threw a 25-yard touchdown pass to Taysir Mack with 47 seconds left and the Panthers held on to beat Eastern Michigan 34-30 in the Quick Lane Bowl on Thursday night. After taking its first lead of the game in the final minute, Pittsburgh (8-5) forced Eastern Michigan to turn it over on downs from its 40 to seal its first bowl victory since winning in Detroit six years ago with former coach Paul Chryst. The Eagles (6-7) came up just short in a closely contested game just as they did in three previous bowls with Coach Chris Creighton and the usually disciplined team unraveled at times. Eastern Michigan quarterback Mike Glass was ejected with 10 seconds left after throwing punches at two players and inadvertently grazing an official, who was trying keep players separated. Eagles cornerback Kevin McGill was ejected earlier for unsportsmanlike conduct. Creighton said officials told him McGill spit on an opponent. Glass was 28 of 50 for 311 yards with two touchdowns and an interception. The senior also ran for 83 yards and a score. Pickett completed 27 of 39 passes for 361 yards and three scores, including a school-record, 96-yard TD pass to Maurice Ffrench that tied the game in the second quarter. Ffrench finished with 12 catches for 165 yards.

2019 MILITARY BOWL

The 2019 Military Bowl was played on December 27, 2019. It was the 12th edition of the Military Bowl and played at Navy-Marine Corps Memorial Stadium in Annapolis, MD. The game was played between the North Carolina Tar Heels (6-6) from the Atlantic Coast Conference and the Temple Owls (8-4) from the American Athletic Conference. It will be the first time that North Carolina and Temple have played against each other.

2019 MILITARY BOWL	Line	1	-	2	-	3	-	4	-	Final
Temple	56.5	0	-	6	-	7	-	0	-	13
North Carolina	-6.5	7	-	13	-	21	-	14	-	55

Scoring Summary
North Carolina – Brown 39 yard pass from Howell (Ruggles kick)
North Carolina – Ruggles 26 yard Field goal
Temple – Davis 4 yard run (Kick blocked)
North Carolina – Newsome 16 yard pass from Howell (Ruggles kick)
North Carolina – Ruggles 36 yard Field goal
North Carolina – Williams 1 yard run (Ruggles kick)
North Carolina – Duck 20 yard interception return (Ruggles kick)
North Carolina – Howell 2 yard pass from Groves (Ruggles kick)
Temple – Davis 45 yard pass from Centeio (LaFree kick)
North Carolina – Newsome 29 yard pass from Howell (Ruggles kick)
North Carolina – Williams 2 yard run (Ruggles kick)

Associated Press Military Bowl Game Summary – Freshman Sam Howell threw for 294 yards and three touchdowns in addition to catching a TD pass, and North Carolina blew out Temple 55-13 in the Military Bowl on Friday to cap a satisfying return season for Coach Mack Brown. Howell completed 25 of 34 passes and ran for 53 yards on three carries to help the Tar Heels (7-6) secure their first bowl victory since 2013. North Carolina was 4-6 before winning its last two regular-season games to qualify for a bowl bid. Temple (8-5) has gone to a bowl game five years in a row -- and lost four of them. This was the Owls' first trip under coach Rod Carey, who came to Temple after a run of six-plus seasons at Northern Illinois in which he was 0-6 in the postseason. North Carolina went 3-9 in 2017 and 2-9 last year before hiring Brown, who coached the Tar Heels from 1988-97 prior to heading to Texas for a 16-year stay. Coming off a five-year absence from coaching, the 68-year-old Brown can attribute a portion of his success to securing Howell, a high school star in North Carolina who initially committed to Florida State. Closing out a sensational debut season at the college level, Howell threw a pair of touchdown passes before halftime to stake the Tar Heels to a 20-6 lead. UNC pulled away early in the third quarter by scoring two touchdowns in a 12-second span, the last on a 20-yard interception return by Storm Duck. Howell completed the third-quarter blitz by catching a 2-yard TD pass from wide receiver Rontavius Groves at the end of a razzle-dazzle reverse to make it 41-6. Howell threw 38 touchdown passes this season, most by a true freshman in FBS history. His 3,641 yards passing are an Atlantic Coast Conference record for a freshman who has not redshirted. North Carolina missed a 50-yard field goal on its first possession, then covered 63 yards on two plays for a 7-0 lead. Howell ran for 24 yards before connecting with Dyami Brown in the left corner for a 39-yard score. It was 10-0 before the Owls used a 60-yard pass from Anthony Russo to Jadan Blue to set up a short touchdown run. The conversion was blocked. The Tar Heels then moved 75 yards on eight plays, going up 17-6 when Dazz Newsome got behind safety Amir Tyler on a 16-yard touchdown catch. Officials initially ruled Newsome made the catch out of bounds, but a replay determined he had his right foot in the end zone while gaining possession of the ball. Newsome made an even better catch early in the fourth quarter, snaring the ball in the left back corner of the end zone behind two defenders and getting one foot in before tumbling backward at the end of a 29-yard score.

2019 PINSTRIPE BOWL

The 2019 Pinstripe Bowl was played on December 27, 2019. It was the 10th edition of the Pinstripe Bowl and played at Yankee Stadium in Bronx, NY. The game was played between the Michigan State Spartans (6-6) from the Big Ten Conference and the Wake Forest Demon Deacons (8-4) from the Atlantic Coast Conference (ACC). This was the first time that Michigan State and Wake Forest have played against each other.

2019 PINSTRIPE BOWL	Line	1	-	2	-	3	-	4	-	Final
Wake Forest	51.5	7	-	14	-	0	-	0	-	21
Michigan State	-4.0	10	-	10	-	7	-	0	-	27

Scoring Summary
Wake Forest – Hinton 29 yard pass from Newman (Sciba kick)
Michigan State – Coghlin 23 yard Field goal
Michigan State – Panasiuk 15 yard interception return (Coghlin kick)
Wake Forest – Greene 16 yard pass from Newman (Sciba kick)
Michigan State – Lewerke 8 yard run (Coghlin kick)
Wake Forest – Freudenthal 45 yard pass from Newman (Sciba kick)
Michigan State – Coghlin 44 yard Field goal
Michigan State – White 10 yard pass from Lewerke (Coghlin kick)

Associated Prest Pinstripe Bowl Game Summary – Mike Panasiuk ripped off his Michigan State helmet and hoisted it in the air, unleashing the hidden part of his scruffy beard that's normally a no-no at Yankee Stadium. Facial hair is banned for all Yankees, and so, for the Spartans, are the kind of acts of unsportsmanlike conduct that get a big guy like Panasiuk penalized. The penalty was worth it for the burly Spartans defensive tackle, who rumbled 14 yards on an interception for his first career touchdown. His brother, Jacub, triggered the pick when he swatted the ball at the line. It took a bounce off a fallen player, and into Panasiuk's hands. Brian Lewerke took it from there in his final game. Lewerke threw for 320 yards and a touchdown and ran for a score in Michigan State's 27-21 victory over Wake Forest on Friday night in the Pinstripe Bowl at Yankee Stadium. Lewerke threw a 10-yard pass to wide receiver Cody White in the third quarter to put the Spartans (7-6) ahead 27-21 and they survived down the stretch to give Dantonio his sixth bowl victory. Attitude, sure. But a defense that gave up 250 yards of offense and 21 points to the up-tempo Demon Deacons in the first half pitched a shutout in the second and surrendered just 101 yards. Panasiuk had the ball in his hands for an early contender for wildest play of the bowl season. Wake Forest's Jamie Newman failed to get enough lift on an early pass attempt that turned into a bit of a 4-6-3 touchdown on the Yankee Stadium field. Panasiuk's measurements look a little like this: height, 6-foot-4; weight, 300 pounds; unkempt beard length, oh, let's say 4 to 6 inches. Michigan State got the go-ahead score and not much else, allowing Wake Forest (8-5) chances to win nine games for just the third time in program history. Michigan State tried to give away the game twice in the fourth, the first time on Lewerke's shovel pass to tight end Trenton Gillison inside the 10 that was stripped and recovered by linebacker Ja'Cquez Williams at the 6. The Demon Deacons failed to score on the drive and handed Michigan State another chance to seal the victory. Again, the Spartans couldn't put it away when Matt Coghlin was wide left on a 28-yard field goal attempt with 3:03 left. Wake Forest's last chance ended on an incomplete pass on its own 16. White finished with 97 yards receiving and Elijah Collins had 96 yards rushing. Dantonio said he would play multiple QBs to give the program a better feel for what it had on the depth chart to work with next season. But Michigan State stuck with Lewerke, in his fifth year and making his 38th career start, and he responded in the clutch when he connected with White and was named the bowl MVP. Newman did all his damage for the Demon Deacons in the first half, throwing three touchdown passes for a 21-20 halftime lead. Newman, the MVP of last season's Birmingham Bowl, hit Kendall Hinton with a 29-yard scoring strike on Wake Forest's opening drive and wide receiver Donavon Greene made a sensational one-handed scoring catch early in the second quarter for a 14-10 lead. Newman connected with Jack Fruedenthal on a 44-yard play that again gave Wake Forest the lead, 21-17. Lewerke had an 8-yard TD run and Coghlin kicked 23- and 44-yard field goals for the Spartans in the first half.

2019 TEXAS BOWL

The 2019 Texas Bowl was played on December 27, 2019. It was the 14th edition of the Texas Bowl and played at NRG Stadium in Houston, Texas. The game was played between the #25 ranked Oklahoma State Cowboys (8-4) from the Big 12 Conference and the Texas A&M Aggies (7-5) from the Southeastern Conference (SEC). This was the 28th overall meeting between Oklahoma State and Texas A&M; Texas A&M leads the all-time series, 17–10. Both Oklahoma State and Texas A&M were charter members of the Big 12, playing in the conference from 1996 until 2012, when Texas A&M left the Big 12 to join the SEC. Oklahoma State enters the bowl with a four-game win streak against Texas A&M. This was Texas A&M's third Texas Bowl, the most appearances of any team. Their 2011 team had previously won the 2011 Meineke Car Care Bowl of Texas over Northwestern, 33–22, and their 2016 team lost the 2016 Texas Bowl to Kansas State, 33–28.

2019 TEXAS BOWL	Line	1	-	2	-	3	-	4	-	Final
#25 Oklahoma State	55.5	14	-	0	-	0	-	7	-	21
Texas A&M	-5.0	0	-	7	-	7	-	10	-	24

Scoring Summary
Oklahoma State – Johnson 42 yard pass from Brown (Ammendola Kick)
Oklahoma State – Brown 9 yard run (Ammendola kick)
Texas A&M – Spiller 1 yard run (Small kick)
Texas A&M – Ausbon 10 yard pass from Mond (Small kick)
Texas A&M – Mond 67 yard run (Small kick)
Texas A&M – Small 24 yard field goal
Oklahoma State – Johnson 5 yard pass from Brown (Ammendola kick)

Associated Press Texas Bowl Game Summary – Kellen Mond ran for a career-high 117 yards and threw a touchdown pass as Texas A&M scored 24 straight points to overcome an early deficit and beat Oklahoma State 24-21 in the Texas Bowl on Friday night. Mond ran 67 yards to give the Aggies (8-5) a 21-14 lead early in the fourth quarter. Mond cut to the right to avoid a couple of defenders and outran everyone else. Tre Sterling had a shot to tackle him around the 25, but Mond ran away from his diving attempt. The Cowboys (8-5) went for it on fourth-and-1 from the Texas A&M 34 on their next possession, but Spencer Sanders was stopped for no gain. The Aggies added a 24-yard field goal to make it 24-14 with about three minutes to go. Oklahoma State cut the lead to three on a touchdown reception by Braydon Johnson with about a minute left. The Cowboys attempted an onside kick, but A&M recovered it to secure the victory. Chuba Hubbard, who finished the regular season as the nation's leading rusher, ran for 158 yards, and Johnson had 124 yards receiving and two touchdowns for the Cowboys. Hubbard finished the season with 2,094 yards rushing to become the second player in school history to reach 2,000, joining Barry Sanders, who did it in 1988 when he won the Heisman Trophy. Mond, who threw for 95 yards, fumbled twice early and the Aggies trailed 14-0 after the first quarter and were down by seven at halftime. He had just 35 yards passing in the first half but got going on Texas A&M's first possession of the second half. He had a 28-yard completion on a drive that ended with a 10-yard touchdown pass to Jhamon Ausbon which tied it at 14-14 early in the third. Mond fumbled on A&M's first drive, and it was recovered by Oklahoma State. But the Cowboys came away empty when Matt Ammendola missed a 53-yard field goal. The Cowboys took a 7-0 lead in the first quarter when they capped a 97-yard drive with a 42-yard touchdown reception by Johnson. Hubbard had a 37-yard run to power that drive. Dru Brown connected with Johnson on a 57-yard pass later in the first quarter to give Oklahoma State a first down at the 9. The Cowboys pushed the lead to 14-0 when Brown dashed into the end zone on the next play. Brown threw for 184 yards and two touchdowns. Mond fumbled again early in the second quarter, but once again the Cowboys couldn't turn the mistake into points, and they had to punt it away. The Aggies cut the lead to 14-7 on the next drive on a 1-yard touchdown run by Isaiah Spiller. Oklahoma State had a chance to pad the lead just before halftime, but Ammendola's 46-yard field goal attempt sailed wide left.

2019 HOLIDAY BOWL

The 2019 Holiday Bowl was played on December 27, 2019 as SDCCU Stadium in San Diego, California. It was the 42nd edition of the Holiday Bowl. The game featured the USC Trojans of the Pac-12 Conference and Iowa Hawkeyes of the Big Ten Conference. It was the 10th meeting between the two teams. USC will be playing in its third Holiday Bowl (2014, 2015), and Iowa will be playing in its fourth (1986, 1987, 1991). The Trojans enter the game with an 8–4 record (7–2 in conference). The Hawkeyes enter the game with a 9–3 record (6–3 in conference).

2019 HOLIDAY BOWL	Line	1	-	2	-	3	-	4	-	Final
#19 Iowa	54.5	7	-	21	-	7	-	14	-	49
#22 USC	-1.5	7	-	10	-	7	-	0	-	24

Scoring Summary
Iowa – Tracy 23 yard run (Duncan kick)
USC – London 5 yard pass from Slovis (McGrath kick)
Iowa – Smith-Marsette 6 yard run (Duncan kick)
USC – Malepeai 16 yard pass from Slovis (McGrath kick)
Iowa – Smith-Marsette 98 yard kickoff return (Duncan kick)
Iowa – Smith-Marsette 12 yard pass from Stanley (Duncan kick)
USC – McGrath 22 yard Field goal
USC – Carr 3 yard run (McGrath kick)
Iowa – Goodson 1 yaard run (Duncan kick)
Iowa – Smith 6 yard pass from Stanley (Duncan kick)
Iowa – Niemann 25 yard interception return (Duncan kick)

Associated Press Holiday Bowl Game Summary – A tough month for the Iowa Hawkeyes ended with a rousing Holiday Bowl victory over Southern California that would have made Hayden Fry and Bump Elliott proud. Ihmir Smith-Marsette scored on a 6-yard run, a 98-yard kickoff return and a 12-yard reception -- all in the second quarter -- to lead No. 19 Iowa to a 49-24 rout of No. 22 USC on Friday night. Senior Nate Stanley threw two touchdown passes and the Hawkeyes (10-3) won their fourth straight game for their sixth 10-win season in coach Kirk Ferentz's 21 years. The Hawkeyes honored both Fry, the former coach who died Dec. 17 at age 90, and Elliott, a former athletic director who died Dec. 7 at 94. The Hawkeyes even did the Hokey Pokey during a locker room celebration, continuing one of many traditions Fry started during his tenure from 1979-98. Smith-Marsette, the offensive player of the game, was late getting into the locker room because of the trophy presentation. USC freshman quarterback Kedon Slovis, who threw two touchdown passes, was knocked out of the game with an injured right elbow in the third quarter. The Trojans (8-5) fell apart after Slovis left and had their three-game winning streak snapped. Smith-Marsette helped the Hawkeyes to a 28-17 halftime lead. Smith-Marsette scored on a 6-yard sweep for a 14-7 lead. After USC tied it on Slovis' 16-yard pass to Vavae Malepeai, Smith-Marsette returned the kickoff 98 yards to give the Hawkeyes the lead for good. Smith-Marsette, a junior wide receiver, also had a 95-yard kickoff return for a score in the regular-season finale, a 27-24 victory over Nebraska. Stanley found Smith-Marsette on a 12-yard scoring pass on Iowa's next possession for a 28-14 lead. Chase McGrath kicked a 32-yard field goal as the clock expired to pull USC to 28-17 at halftime. The Trojans pulled to 28-24 on Stephen Carr's 2-yard run to cap the opening drive of the second half. It followed a 55-yard pass from Slovis to Amon-Ra St. Brown to the Iowa 5. Jack Koerner was called for roughing the passer when he slammed down Slovis, whose head hit the turf. Kicker Michael Brown then recovered his own onside kick. Slovis was hurt two plays later when he was sacked and fumbled, which was recovered by USC. Slovis came out and was replaced by Matt Fink. Slovis took over after JT Daniels suffered a season-ending knee injury in the opener and threw for 3,242 yards and 28 touchdowns, against nine interceptions in the regular season. He threw for a school-record 515 yards as well as four touchdowns in a 52-35 victory over UCLA. Iowa put it away with a 90-yard drive capped by Tyler Goodson's 1-yard run for a 35-24 lead late in the third quarter. Stanley had a 34-yard pass to Smith-Marsette and gained 8 yards on a sneak to the USC 3. USC lost two fumbles late in the second half, including when a high shotgun snap went off Fink's hands, with Iowa's Kristian Welch recovering at the Trojans' 6. Iowa converted on Stanley's 6-yard TD pass to Brandon Smith to make it 42-24. Iowa's Nick Niemann intercepted Fink and returned it 25 yards for a TD with 1:43 left. Iowa's Tyrone Tracy Jr. scored on a 23-yard run on the game's first drive and USC answered with Slovis' 4-yard scoring pass to Drake London. Slovis completed 22 of 30 passes for 260 yards.

2019 CHEEZ-IT BOWL

The 2019 Cheez-It Bowl was played on December 27, 2019 at Chase Field in Phoenix, Arizona. It was the 31st edition of the Cheez-It Bowl, though only the second under the current name. It was previously known as the Insight Bowl and Copper Bowl. The game was played between the Washington State Cougars from the Pac-12 Conference and the Air Force Falcons from the Mountain West Conference (MWC). This will be the first meeting between the two programs. This was Washington State's second Cheez-It Bowl; their 1992 team won the then-Copper Bowl over Utah, 31–28. This was Air Force's second Cheez-It Bowl; their 1995 team appeared in the then-Copper Bowl, losing to Texas Tech, 55–41.

2019 CHEEZ-IT BOWL	Line	1	-	2	-	3	-	4	-	Final
#24 Air Force	-2.5	0	-	17	-	7	-	7	-	31
Washington State	71.5	0	-	14	-	0	-	7	-	21

Scoring Summary
Air Force – Hammond 1 yard run (Koehnke kick)
Washington State – Patmon 2 yard pass from Gordon (Mazza kick)
Air Force – Koehnke 28 yard Field goal
Air Force – Birdow 3 yard run (Koehnke kick)
Washington State – Borghi 5 yard pass from Gordon (Mazza kick)
Air Force – Hammond 7 yard run (Koehnke kick)
Washington State – Arconado 13 yard pass from Gordon (Mazza kick)
Air Force – Remsburg 3 yard run (Koehnke kick)

Associated Press Cheez-It Bowl Game Summary — Air Force clung to a three-point lead, the clock showing plenty of time left for one of the nation's most prolific offenses. A field goal was not going to be good enough. The Falcons needed a touchdown to leave Washington State no chance. Going for it on fourth down was the only option -- and it worked. Kadin Remsberg ran for 178 yards and stretched to the pylon for a 3-yard touchdown on a late fourth down, lifting No. 24 Air Force to a 31-21 victory over Washington State in the Cheez-It Bowl on Friday night. The Falcons (11-2) had their triple option working to near perfection, grinding out 371 yards rushing while setting a Cheez-It Bowl time of possession record of 43:24. Donald Hammond III scored two touchdowns and Air Force carried a 10-point lead into the fourth quarter, yet couldn't shake the high-scoring Cougars. Anthony Gordon, the FBS passing leader, kept Washington State within reach, throwing for 351 yards and three touchdowns. He hit Brandon Arconado on a 13-yard TD to pull Washington State (6-7) within 24-21 late in the fourth quarter, giving the Cougars a shot at the comeback finish. Air Force methodically worked the ball down to Washington State's 4-yard line but failed to punch the ball into the end zone on three tries. After a timeout, Hammond ran an option left and pitched the ball to Remsberg, who got the edge and reached the ball to the pylon with a defender draping him. The touchdown was upheld on review. The 2018 game was dubbed the Cheez-INT Bowl after TCU and California combined for nine interceptions. A year later, Air Force and Washington State brought philosophical differences to the desert. The Falcons like to stay grounded, running 57 times a game while finishing third in the FBS at 292.5 yards per game. The Cougars love to fly, putting it up 56 times a game to lead the nation with nearly 450 yards a game. Washington State started the Cheez-It Bowl quickly, racing down the field with a series of completions, only to get stuffed by an Air Force goal-line stand. The Falcons' opening drive was a yard-churning, clock-winding grind, covering 98 yards in 20 plays and 12:23. Hammond capped it with a 1-yard TD run. Air Force's next two drives took less time combined than the first, ending in Jake Koehnke's 28-yard field goal and Taven Birdow's 3-yard run after Gordon lost a fumble at Washington State's 23. The Cougars had two more quick-hitting drives to pull within 17-14 at halftime on Gordon's two TD passes. Air Force went right back to the ground to open the second half; 13 plays, 75 yards, capped by Hammond's 7-yard TD run. Washington State had another fourth-down failure, this one at Air Force's 5-yard line, but bounced back quickly with Gordon's TD pass to Arconado. The Cougars just couldn't stop Air Force and Remsberg's diving TD run capped another long scoring drive to seal it.

2019 CAMPING WORLD BOWL

The 2019 Camping World Bowl was played on December 28, 2019 at Camping World Stadium in Orlando, Florida. It was the 30th edition of the Camping World Bowl. The game was played between the Iowa State Cyclones from the Big 12 Conference and the Notre Dame Fighting Irish, an FBS independent. This was the first meeting between the two programs. This was Notre Dame's second Camping World Bowl; their 2011 team appeared in the then-Champs Sports Bowl, losing to Florida State, 18–14.

2019 CAMPING WORLD BOWL	Line	1	-	2	-	3	-	4	-	Final
Iowa State	54.0	0	-	6	-	3	-	0	-	9
#14 Notre Dame	-3.5	10	-	10	-	10	-	3	-	33

Scoring Summary
Notre Dame – Doerer 39 yard Field goal
Notre Dame – Claypool 24 yard pass from Book (Doerer kick)
Iowa State – Assalley 41 yard Field goal
Notre Dame – Doerer 51 yard Field goal
Notre Dame – Armstrong 1 yard run (Doerer kick)
Iowa State – Assalley 26 yard Field goal
Notre Dame – Jones 84 yard run (Doerer kick)
Iowa State – Assalley 42 yard Field goal
Notre Dame – Doerer 19 yard Field goal
Notre Dame – Doerer 39 yard Field goal

Associated Press Camping World Bowl Game Summary – So much for the notion that No. 14 Notre Dame didn't have anything to play for in the Camping World Bowl. A year removed from an appearance in the CFP national semifinals, the Fighting Irish closed out another double-digit win season with arguably their best all-around performance in a 33-9 victory over Iowa State on Saturday. Ian Book threw for 247 yards and a touchdown, Tony Jones Jr. scored on an 84-yard run and game MVP Chase Claypool had seven receptions for 146 yards and a TD for the Irish (11-2, No. 15 CFP), who finished on a six-game winning streak after losing to Michigan to tumble out of contention for a playoff berth in late October. Notre Dame also lost to Georgia in September; however, Kelly said the team remained focused and continued to focus and get better. Book completed 20 of 28 passes without an interception, including a 27-yard TD throw to Claypool, who went over 1,000 yards receiving for the season and recovered a fumble on special teams to set up an early field goal. Iowa State (7-6) lost to four ranked teams -- Iowa, Oklahoma, Baylor and Oklahoma State -- by a combined 11 points this season and was hoping to end its fourth season under Matt Campbell with a signature win for a once-downtrodden program. Brock Purdy was 17 of 30 for 222 yards and no interceptions for the Cyclones, but he was unable to get his team into the end zone after throwing for a school single season record 27 TDs during the regular season. The sophomore quarterback left the game in the closing minutes with what Campbell described as a high ankle sprain. Connor Assalley kicked field goals of 41, 26 and 42 yards.

2019 COTTON BOWL

The 2019 Cotton Bowl Classic was played on December 28, 2019. It was the 84th edition of the Cotton Bowl Classic. The participants were selected by the College Football Playoff selection committee on December 8, 2019. This was the first time that Memphis and Penn State have ever played against each other.

Memphis was selected to the Cotton Bowl as the highest-ranked team from the Group of Five conferences, a spot they secured by winning the American Athletic Conference championship. This was Memphis' first Cotton Bowl Classic, as well as their first New Year's Six game overall. On December 9, Head Coach Mike Norvell announced that he would not coach Memphis in the bowl, after accepting the Head Coaching position at Florida State, allowing interim head coach Ryan Silverfield to do so. On December 13, it was announced that the interim tag would be removed and that Silverfield would be promoted to head coach in time for the bowl game.

Penn State was selected to the Cotton Bowl as the highest-ranked team to already be selected to a New Year's Six bowl. This was Penn State's fourth Cotton Bowl Classic; the Nittany Lions have a 2–0–1 record in the game, most recently their 1974 team winning the 1975 Cotton Bowl Classic over Baylor, 41–20.

2019 COTTON BOWL	Line	1	-	2	-	3	-	4	-	Final
#13 Penn State	-6.5	7	-	28	-	10	-	8	-	53
#15 Memphis	59.0	13	-	10	-	13	-	3	-	39

Scoring Summary
Memphis – Patterson 48 yard Field goal
Penn State – Brown 32 yard run (Pinegar kick)
Memphis – Taylor 3 yard run (Patterson kick)
Memphis – Patterson 37 yard Field goal
Penn State – Cain 1 yard run (Pinegar kick)
Penn State – Ford 2 yard run (Pinegar kick)
Penn State – Brown 56 yard run (Pinegar kick)
Memphis – Gainwell 2 yard run (Patterson kick)
Penn State – Dotson 4 yard pass from Clifford (Pinegar kick)
Memphis – Patterson 44 yard Field goal
Memphis – White 1 yard run (Patterson kick)
Memphis – Patterson 51 yard Field goal
Penn State – Pinegar 45 yard Field goal
Memphis – Patterson 41 yard Field goal
Penn State – Taylor 15 yard interception return (Pinegar kick)
Memphis – Patterson 42 yard Field goal
Penn State – Cain 1 yard run (2 point pass good)

Associated Press Cotton Bowl Game Summary – All-America linebacker Micah Parsons led the big blitz for Penn State, and he had Brady White all wrapped up when the Memphis quarterback suddenly flipped away the ball -- right into the hands of Garrett Taylor. On a day when the Nittany Lions' defense gave up its most points and yards all season, Taylor turned that gift into a 15-yard interception return for a touchdown in a 53-39 victory over the Group of Five Tigers on Saturday in the highest-scoring Cotton Bowl ever. Journey Brown ran for 202 yards with two long touchdowns, but the Parsons-created pick-six came three plays after Brown was stopped short on a fourth-and-1. Taylor put the No. 13 Nittany Lions up 45-36 going into the fourth quarter of the 84th Cotton Bowl. Brown was the offensive MVP and Parsons, with 14 tackles and two sacks, was the game's top defensive player. Both had gone back and forth about that possibility during practice this week. American Athletic Conference champion and No. 15 Memphis (12-2, No. 17 CFP) played its first game under Coach Ryan Silverfield. The offensive line coach was promoted when Mike Norvell left after four seasons to become Florida State's coach earlier this month. White was 32-of-51 passing for 454 yards with two interceptions. He had a rushing touchdown, as did Patrick Taylor Jr. and Kenneth Gainwell. The rest of the Tigers' points came on a Cotton Bowl-record six field goals by Riley Patterson, including a record-long 51-yarder. The Tigers, who set a school record for victories while winning their first outright conference title since 1969, finished with 542 total yards. But White was sacked a season-high six times and didn't throw a touchdown for the first time since the season opener. Freshman running back Noah Cain added 92 yards and two touchdowns rushing for Penn State, which won for the 30th time in its 50 bowl appearances. The Nittany Lions had 529 total yards. Brown got his 202 rushing yards on 16 carries, including a tackle-shredding 32-yard touchdown early and a 56-yard score when he went up the middle virtually untouched.

2019 CHICK-FIL-A PEACH BOWL (NATIONAL SEMIFINAL)

The 2019 Chick-Fil-A Peach Bowl was played on December 28, 2019. It was the 52nd edition of the Peach Bowl and played at Mercedes-Benz Stadium in Atlanta, Georgia. The Chick-Fil-A Peach Bowl was one of two College Football Playoff semifinal games, with the winner advancing to the 2020 College Football Playoff National Championship. This was the third meeting between LSU and Oklahoma. The series is tied 1-1, with the most recent meeting being an LSU victory in the 2004 Sugar Bowl.

LSU defeated Georgia in the 2019 SEC Championship Game on December 7th, then received their bid to the Peach Bowl with the release of final CFP rankings on December 8th. The Tigers enter the bowl with a 13–0 record (8–0 in conference). This was LSU's seventh appearance in the Peach Bowl; the Tigers' only loss came in their last appearance, when they were defeated by Clemson in the 2012 Chick-fil-A Bowl. This is LSU's first College Football Playoff semifinal appearance. **Oklahoma** defeated Baylor in the 2019 Big 12 Championship Game on December 7, then received their bid to the Peach Bowl with the release of final CFP rankings on December 8. The Sooners enter the bowl with a 12–1 record (8–1 in conference); their only loss was to Kansas State by a score of 41–48. This was Oklahoma's first appearance in the Peach Bowl. This is Oklahoma's fourth College Football Playoff appearance. Oklahoma is 0-3 in CFP semifinals, with the most recent game being a loss to Alabama in the 2018 Orange Bowl.

2019 PEACH BOWL	Line	1	-	2	-	3	-	4	-	Final
#4 Oklahoma	75.0	7	-	7	-	7	-	7	-	28
#1 LSU	-12.0	21	-	28	-	7	-	7	-	63

Scoring Summary
LSU – Jefferson 19 yard pass from Burrow (York kick)
Oklahoma – Brooks 3 yard run (Brkic kick)
LSU – Marshall 8 yard pass from Burrow (York kick)
LSU – Jefferson 35 yard pass from Burrow (York kick)
LSU – Jefferson 42 yard pass from Burrow (York kick)
LSU – Jefferson 30 yard pass from Burrow (York kick)
Oklahoma – Hurts 2 yard run (Brkic kick)
LSU – Moss 62 yard pass from Burrow (York kick)
LSU – Marshall 2 yard pass from Burrow (York kick)
LSU – Burrow 3 yard run (York kick)
Oklahoma – Hurts 12 yard run (Brkic kick)
Oklahoma – Pledger 1 yard run (Brkic kick)
LSU – Emery 6 yard run (Brkic kick)

Associated Press Chick-Fil-A Peach Bowl Game Summary – Joe Burrow and the LSU Tigers turned in a first half for the ages, a breathtaking offensive display even as their coordinator grieved a horrific tragedy from his box high above the field. This team from the bayou is truly something special. With one more victory, it will be a national champion. In his first game as a Heisman Trophy winner, Burrow threw for seven touchdowns and 493 yards as No. 1 LSU romped to a stunning 63-28 victory over No. 4 Oklahoma in the Peach Bowl semifinal game Saturday. The Tigers (14-0) are headed to the title game against No. 3 Clemson -- a 29-23 winner over No. 2 Ohio State in the second semifinal in Arizona -- clicking on all cylinders, having dismantled the Sooners (12-2) with a 30-minute outburst that will long be remembered in Cajun country. Certainly, the Sooners couldn't. Burrow tied the record for any college bowl game with his seven TD passes -- which all came before the bands hit the field for the halftime show at Mercedes-Benz Stadium. Justin Jefferson was on the receiving end for four of those scoring plays, also tying a bowl record. As if that wasn't enough, Burrow scored an eighth TD himself on a 3-yard run in the third quarter, thoroughly dominating his expected duel with Oklahoma quarterback Jalen Hurts, the Heisman runner-up. Yet, the postgame celebration was weighed down by heavy hearts. LSU offensive coordinator Steve Ensminger learned shortly before kickoff that his daughter-in-law, broadcaster Carley McCord, was among five people killed in a plane crash in Louisiana. The small plane went down shortly after takeoff for what was supposed to be a flight to Atlanta for the game. Head coach Ed Orgeron delivered the news to Ensminger, who was seen with tears running down his cheeks but stuck to the task at hand. Then the coordinator headed to his usual spot in the box, calling plays alongside passing game coordinator Joe Brady. It was a brilliant, poignant performance in the face of such grief. The players didn't learn until afterward what Ensminger was going through. LSU needed only three plays to race 42 yards for its first score -- a perfectly thrown ball over Jefferson's shoulder for a 19-yard TD less than 3 minutes into the game. Oklahoma briefly put up a fight. Hurts' 51-yard pass to CeeDee Lamb set up a 3-yard touchdown run by Kennedy Brooks that tied the score at 7. After that, the rout was on. It was 49-14 by halftime. The Tigers' potent spread offense made this one look much like the Harlem Globetrotters carving up the Washington Generals, only it was the Sooners playing the hapless victim. Jefferson hauled in a 35-yard pass for touchdown No. 2. Then a 42-yarder for No. 3. And, finally, a 30-yard scoring strike that left him counting off four fingers for the crowd -- all before the midway point of the second quarter. Terrace Marshall Jr. contributed to the onslaught with TD catches of 8 and 2 yards. Tight end Thaddeus Moss -- the son of NFL Hall of Fame receiver Randy Moss -- made his daddy proud by getting free behind the secondary, hauling in a pass and shoving off a fast-closing defender to complete the 62-yard scoring play. It was a miserable finale for Hurts, who closed out a nomadic college career that began with him leading Alabama to a pair of national championship games before losing his starting job to Tua Tagovailoa. After graduating, Hurts transferred to Oklahoma for a one-and-done season that produced some dazzling numbers but ended short of the ultimate goal. Running for his life most of the game, Hurts was largely stymied on the ground and through the air. He ran for a pair of touchdowns but gained just 43 yards with his legs. He was held to 15 of 31 for 217 yards passing, giving up a brilliant, leaping interception to Kary Vincent Jr. that quickly brought the LSU offense back on the field as the Tigers were blowing the game open. Oklahoma defensive back Brendan Radley-Hiles was ejected early in the second quarter for a brutal hit on LSU's Clyde Edwards-Helaire. With Burrow scrambling toward the sideline, Radley-Hiles delivered the blindside shot to Edwards-Helaire coming out of the backfield. The officials did not throw a flag, but a video review showed that Radley-Hiles leaped into the defenseless player with a shoulder to the helmet. Three plays later, Burrow went deep to Jefferson for a TD that extended LSU's lead to 28-7.

2019 FIESTA BOWL (NATIONAL SEMIFINAL)

The 2019 Fiesta Bowl was played on December 28, 2019. It was the 49th edition of the Fiesta Bowl and played at State Farm Stadium in Glendale, Arizona. The Fiesta Bowl was one of two College Football Playoff semifinal games, with the winner advancing to the 2020 College Football Playoff National Championship. This was the fourth meeting between Clemson and Ohio State. The Tigers have won all three games, with the most recent win occurring in the 2016 Fiesta Bowl.

This was Ohio State's ninth appearance in the Fiesta Bowl. The Buckeyes are 5-3 in Fiesta Bowl games, with the most recent game being a loss to Clemson in the 2016 Fiesta Bowl. This is Ohio State's third College Football Playoff semifinal game. The Buckeyes are 1-1 in CFP semifinals, with the most recent game being a loss to Clemson in the 2016 Fiesta Bowl. This is Ohio State's fourth CFP game overall, when the win over Oregon in the 2014 College Football Playoff National Championship is included. The Buckeyes are 2-1 in CFP games.

This was Clemson's second appearance in the Fiesta Bowl, with the first game being a win over Ohio State in the 2016 Fiesta Bowl. This is Clemson's fifth College Football Playoff semifinal game. The Tigers are 3-1 in CFP semifinal games, with the most recent game being a win over Notre Dame in the 2018 Cotton Bowl. This is Clemsons' eighth CFP game overall, including national championship games. The Tigers are 5-2 in CFP games, with the most recent game being a win over Alabama in the 2019 College Football Playoff National Championship.

2019 FIESTA BOWL	Line	1	-	2	-	3	-	4	-	Final
#2 Ohio State	62.0	10	-	6	-	0	-	7	-	23
#3 Clemson	-2.5	0	-	14	-	7	-	8	-	29

Scoring Summary
Ohio State – Haubeil 21 yard Field goal
Ohio State – Dobbins 68 yard run (Haubeil kick)
Ohio State – Haubeil 22 yard Field goal
Ohio State – Haubeil 33 yard Field goal
Clemson – Etienne 8 yard run (Potter kick)
Clemson – Lawrence 67 yard run (Potter kick)
Clemson – Etienne 53 yard pass from Lawrence (Potter kick)
Ohio State – Olave 23 yard pass from Fields (Haubeil kick)
Clemson – Etienne 34 yard pass from Lawrence (2 point pass good)

Associated Press Fiesta Bowl Game Summary – Blaring from the Clemson locker room after yet another playoff victory was Aretha Franklin's classic "Respect." The Tigers have won two of the last three national titles and become college football's gold standard program, yet still often feel overlooked. Doubted. Disrespected. Sure, Clemson ran roughshod through the Atlantic Coast Conference. But was it too easy? Facing a serious challenger for the first time in months, No. 3 Clemson and its perfect quarterback had to tap into their championship DNA to advance to the College Football Playoff title game for the fourth time in five years. Trevor Lawrence connected with Travis Etienne on a 34-yard, go-ahead touchdown with 1:49 left in the fourth quarter, capping a 94-yard march, and the defending national champions beat No. 2 Ohio State 29-23 Saturday night in the Fiesta Bowl. The Tigers (14-0) will play No. 1 LSU on Jan. 13 in New Orleans, looking for their third national title in the last four seasons. Clemson played only one close game this season, a one-pointer way back in September against North Carolina. Otherwise, the Tigers rarely needed to play a starter in the fourth quarter. Ohio State (13-1) proved to be every bit Clemson's match, though the Buckeyes walked away frustrated by several close officiating calls. Especially two video reviews that could have gone either way and did not go theirs. The Buckeyes had their 19-game winning streak snapped, losing for the first time under Day. Ohio State jumped out to a 16-0 lead in the first half and then responded to a Clemson rally to retake the lead, 23-21 in the fourth quarter. The Tigers got the ball down two at their own 6 with 3:07 left in the fourth quarter. Lawrence, after being up and down for much of the night, suddenly found the Golden Boy form that he used to lead Clemson to a national title as a freshman last year. The Tigers needed four plays and 1:18, with Lawrence completing all three of his passes and mixing in an 11-yard run. The sophomore quarterback who has never lost a college start passed for 259 yards and two scores and ran for a career-high 107 yards, including a 67-yard touchdown late in the first half. Lawrence added a 2-point conversion pass to Higgins but left plenty of time for Ohio State and Justin Fields to respond. The Buckeyes drove to the Clemson 23, but on second-and-7, Fields fired to the end zone and was picked off by Nolan Turner with 37 seconds left. Ohio State receiver Chris Olave had broken off his route thinking Fields was going to scramble. The pick secured Clemson's 29th straight victory and the Tigers improved to 6-2 in playoff games. Ohio State went into the fourth quarter trailing 21-16, and with everything seemingly going Clemson's way. Buckeyes star J.K. Dobbins ran for 174 yards, including two 60-plus yarders in the first half, but was slowed by a twisted left ankle late in the second quarter. Fields heated up and orchestrated an 84-yard drive, capped by a fourth-and-short, 23-yard touchdown pass to Olave to give make it 23-21 with 11:46 left in the fourth. Fields, who went to high school 20 miles from Lawrence in the northwest suburbs of Atlanta, passed for 320 yards and a touchdown. But he was picked off twice after throwing just one interception in the regular season. It was the first matchup between the two former five-star recruit quarterbacks from the class of 2018. They were far from perfect, but both delivered in crunch time. If this is the start of a long rivalry, bring it on.

2019 FIRST RESPONDER BOWL

The 2019 First Responder Bowl was played on December 30, 2019. It was the 10th edition of the First Responder Bowl. The 2019 First Responder Bowl will be played in Gerald J. Ford Stadium on the campus of Southern Methodist University in University Park, Texas. The move was necessitated by the National Hockey League's announcement that the league's annual New Year's Day outdoor game would be played in the bowl's normal host stadium, Dallas' Cotton Bowl, which created a scheduling conflict.

The game featured the Western Michigan Broncos of the Mid-American Conference (MAC) going up against the Western Kentucky Hilltoppers of Conference USA (C-USA). It will be the 16th meeting between the two programs, and the first since 1947; Western Michigan leads the all-time series, 11–3–1

2019 FIRST RESPONDER BOWL	Line	1	-	2	-	3	-	4	-	Final
Western Kentucky	-3.0	0	-	10	-	0	-	13	-	23
Western Michigan	55.5	3	-	7	-	7	-	3	-	20

Scoring Summary
Western Michigan – Kapps 30 yard Field goal
Western Kentucky – Pearson 17 yard pass from Storey (Munson kick)
Western Kentucky – Munson 26 yard Field goal
Western Michigan – Ali 88 yard interception return (Kapps kick)
Western Michigan – Bussell 6 yard pass from Wassink (Kapps kick)
Western Kentucky – Jackson 5 yard pass from Storey (Munson kick)
Western Michigan – Kapss 20 yard Field goal
Western Kentucky – Munson 31 yard Field goal
Western Kentucky – Munson 52 yard Field goal

Associated Press First Responder Bowl Game Summary – Western Kentucky freshman kicker Cory Munson ran onto the field, then off and then back on. All of that before kicking a career-long 52-yard field goal with no time left after a rules review moved him five yards closer to the goal posts. And Munson, who'd sliced a 29-yarder wide right on the final play of the first half, closed the game with the kick that gave the Hilltoppers a 23-20 victory over Western Michigan in the First Responder Bowl on Monday. The Hilltoppers (9-4) drove 36 yards in 27 seconds before Munson kicked his third field goal in four tries. The game appeared headed to overtime when Ty Storey's desperation heave was knocked down by the Broncos. But the Broncos were hit with a five-yard defensive substitution penalty and Munson was awarded an untimed down after a video review determined that Western Michigan had 12 players on the field as it switched between its field-goal unit and regular defense. Munson had tied the score at 20 on a 31-yarder with 1:36 to play. He also kicked a 26-yarder. Thiago Kapps' 20-yard field goal with 4:58 to play gave Western Michigan (7-6) a 20-17 lead. Kapps' field goal, his second of the game, capped a 62-yard drive that took 5:35 after Western Kentucky had tied the score on a 15-yard touchdown pass from Storey to Lucky Jackson with 10:40 to go. Jackson had 17 catches for 148 yards and was named the game's most valuable player. Western Michigan's other touchdowns came on a 6-yard pass from Jon Wassink to DaShon Bussell midway through the third quarter and an 88-yard interception return by Kareem Ali in the first half's closing minutes. Storey, a graduate transfer from Arkansas, threw a 17-yard pass to Jahcour Pearson in the second quarter for the Hilltoppers' other touchdown.

2019 MUSIC CITY BOWL

The 2019 Music City Bowl was played on December 30, 2019. The 22nd edition of the Music City Bowl, will feature Atlantic Coast Conference member Louisville and Southeastern Conference member Mississippi State. The teams have met five times previously, with Mississippi State winning all five games. The teams last met in the 2017 TaxSlayer Bowl, won by the Bulldogs, 31–27.

The Bulldogs enter the bowl with a 6–6 record (3–5 in SEC). This was Mississippi State's second Music City Bowl; their 2011 team won the 2011 Music City Bowl over Wake Forest, 23–17. This bowl will continue the streak of being bowl eligible for the Bulldogs, making it ten straight bowl apperances since the program's 2010 season. This will be Mississippi State's 23rd overall bowl game in the program.

Louisville enters the bowl with a 7–5 record (5–3 in ACC), including an upset win against No. 19 Wake Forest by three points on October 12, 2019. This was Louisville's second Music City Bowl; their 2015 team won the 2015 Music City Bowl over Texas A&M, 27–21. This bowl will be the first bowl game for the Cardinals since 2017 and will be the 23rd bowl game overall in the program.

2019 MUSIC CITY BOWL	Line	1	-	2	-	3	-	4	-	Final
Louisville	63.5	0	-	10	-	14	-	14	-	38
Mississippi State	-4.5	7	-	7	-	0	-	14	-	28

Scoring Summary
Mississippi State – Stevens 3 yard run (Christman kick)
Mississippi State – Gibson 3 yard run (Christman kick)
Louisville – Atwell 33 yard pass from Ford (Chalifoux kick)
Louisville – Chalifoux 31 yard Field goal
Louisville – Peete 24 yard pass from Cunningham (Chalifoux kick)
Louisville – Pass 31 yard fumble return (Chalifoux kick)
Louisville – Ford 8 yard pass from Cunningham (Chalifoux kick)
Mississippi State – Guidry 18 yard pass from Stevens (Christman kick)
Louisville – Hawkins 5 yard run (Chalifoux kick)
Mississippi State – Mitchell 24 yard pass from Stevens (Christman kick)

Associated Press Music City Bowl Game Summary – Consider the Louisville Cardinals' turnaround in Coach Scott Satterfield's debut a smashing success. Micale Cunningham threw for 279 yards and two touchdowns and ran for 81 more, and Louisville beat Mississippi State 38-28 Monday in the Music City Bowl. The Cardinals (8-5) rallied from a 14-point deficit by scoring 31 straight to finish their big turnaround from 2-10 last season. Louisville also finally beat Mississippi State on the field for the first time in six tries, though the series now is tied 3-3 thanks to a pair of forfeits by the Bulldogs in the 1970s. Satterfield noted Louisville lost 22 scholarship players from last season. Mississippi State (6-7) had been trying to finish the season with a three-game winning streak for the first time since 2013 and only the third time since the end of World War II. Instead, the Bulldogs go home having lost a bowl game in each of Coach Joe Moorhead's two seasons. The Cardinals had four sacks and recovered two fumbles, one returned 31 yards for a TD by safety Khane Pass. Javian Hawkins led Louisville with 105 yards rushing, and he ran for a TD late. The Cardinals outgained Mississippi State 510-366. Louisville was poised to take control on its opening drive, going from the Cardinals 3 down the field. Cunningham hit Dez Fitzpatrick on a 19-yard pass only to be stripped of the ball by linebacker Willie Gay Jr., with linebacker Tim Washington recovering for the Bulldogs just short of the end zone. Tommy Stevens led Mississippi State on a 99-yard drive, and he put the Bulldogs up 7-0 with a 3-yard TD run. Mississippi State added an 80-yard drive and went up 14-0 on a 3-yard TD run by Nick Gibson with 10:19 left in the second quarter. Louisville finally got on the board with a bit of trickery. Micale Cunningham lateraled left to wide receiver Tutu Atwell, who threw back across the field to a wide-open Marshon Ford, who then ran in for a 33-yard TD midway through the second. Ryan Chalifoux added a 31-yard field goal as the first half expired to pull Louisville within 14-10. Cunningham put Louisville ahead to stay with a 24-yard TD pass to Devante Peete with 5:01 left in the third. Pass scored when he recovered the ball after Gary McCrae chopped it out of Stevens' arms. Cunningham added an 8-yard TD pass to Ford early in the fourth for a 31-14 lead.

2019 REDBOX BOWL

The 2019 Redbox Bowl was played on December 30, 2019. It was the 18th edition of the Redbox Bowl, which was previously known as the Foster Farms Bowl and Kraft Hunger Bowl. The Redbox Bowl was played at Levi Stadium in Santa Clara, California. The game was played between the Illinois Fighting Illini (6-6) from the Big Ten Conference and the California Golden Bears (7-5) from the Pac-12 Conference. This was the 11th meeting between the programs; Illinois leads the all-time series, 7–3. This was Illinois' second Redbox Bowl; their 2011 team won the then-Kraft Fight Hunger Bowl over UCLA, 20–14. This was California's second Redbox Bowl; their 2008 team won the then-Emerald Bowl over Miami, 24–17.

2019 REDBOX BOWL	Line	1	-	2	-	3	-	4	-	Final
Illinois	48.0	10	-	3	-	0	-	7	-	20
California	-6.0	7	-	14	-	7	-	7	-	35

Scoring Summary
Illinois – McCourt 25 yard Field goal
California – Moore 4 yard pass from Garbers (Thomas kick)
Illinois – Barker 5 yard pass from Peters (McCourt kick)
California – Garbers 1 yard run (Thomas kick)
California – Brown 3 yard pass from Garbers (Thomas kick)
Illinois – McCourt 30 yard Field goal
California – Reinwald 2 yard pass from Garbers (Thomas kick)
California – Remigio 6 yard pass from Garbers (Thomas kick)
Illinois – Corbin 6 yard run (McCourt kick)

Associated Press Redbox Bowl Game Summary – As a freshman a year ago, Chase Garbers was benched at halftime for ineffectiveness during his first trip to a bowl game. The California quarterback made his second appearance in the postseason much more memorable for both himself and the Golden Bears. Garbers threw four touchdown passes and ran for another score, leading California to a 35-20 win over Illinois on Monday in the Redbox Bowl. Garbers, who had been in and out of the lineup all season because of a shoulder injury, got going after being sacked on the first play from scrimmage and throwing an incomplete pass on the second. The offensive MVP of the game, Garbers completed 22 of 31 passes for 272 yards with TD passes of 4, 3, 2 and 6 yards. He also scored on quarterback sneak from the 1 early in the second quarter while helping the Bears set a season-high for scoring. The Bears won all seven games this season when the oft-injured Garbers played more than one half. Christopher Brown Jr. ran for 120 yards on 20 carries, and Makai Polk caught five passes for a season-high 105 yards as Cal (8-5) won its first bowl game since 2015. Brandon Peters passed for 273 yards and one touchdown for Illinois (6-7) in his return after sitting out the regular-season finale with a concussion. Peters, who was shaken up again after diving out of bounds following a scramble late in the fourth quarter, completed 22 of 37 passes and added a team-high 68 rushing yards. The Illini lost despite outgaining the Bears in total yards 450-395. The strong showing by Garbers offset an uneven day by California's defense. The Bears allowed a field goal and touchdown on the Fighting Illini's first two drives, then surrendered a late field goal before halftime. Illinois' offense was mostly stagnant after that, while California pulled away. The Bears had lost three of their previous four bowl games. California led 14-10 late in the second quarter before the teams combined for 10 points in the final 25 seconds. After Wilcox made the decision to go for it on a 4th-and-goal, Garbers threw a short swing pass to Brown, who stiff-armed Illinois linebacker Tolson Khalan before reaching the end zone. Peters helped the Illini answer quickly. He completed three consecutive passes for 58 yards, setting up a 30-yard field goal by James McCourt.

2019 ORANGE BOWL

The 2019 Orange Bowl was played on December 30, 2019. It was the 86th edition of the Orange Bowl and played at Hard Rock Stadium in Miami Gardens, Florida. The game was played between the Virginia Cavaliers and the Florida Gators. This was the second meeting of these schools, with the Gators having won the first meeting, 55–10, in 1959.

Florida entered the Orange Bowl with an overall 10–2 record (6–2 in conference). They finished their regular season second in the East Division of the Southeastern Conference (SEC), behind Georgia.

Virginia entered the Orange bowl with an overall 9–4 record (6–2 in conference), having lost the ACC Championship Game to Clemson. Unranked in the AP Poll at the time they received their bowl invitation, they become the first AP-unranked participant in the Orange Bowl since Florida in the 1967 edition. The Cavaliers were ranked #25 in the Coaches Poll.

2019 ORANGE BOWL	Line	1	-	2	-	3	-	4	-	Final
#6 Florida	-165	14	-	10	-	3	-	9	-	36
#25 Virginia	55.0	7	-	7	-	0	-	14	-	28

Scoring Summary
Florida – Perine 61 yard run (McPherson kick)
Virginia – Jana 34 yard pass from Perkins (Delaney kick)
Florida – Perine 16 yard pass from Trask (McPherson kick)
Virginia – Dubois 9 yard pass from Perkins (Delaney kick)
Florida – McPherson 23 yard Field goal
Florida – Perine 10 yard run (McPherson kick)
Florida – McPherson 49 yard Field goal
Virginia – Reed 7 yard pass from Perkins (Delaney kick)
Florida – Trask 1 yard run (2 point pass failed)
Florida – McPherson 42 yard Field goal
Virginia – Dubois 2 yard pass from Perkins (Delaney kick)

Orange Bowl Game Summary – Lamical Perine made the most of his opportunities, scoring three first-half touchdowns to lead the Florida Gators past the Virginia Cavaliers 36-28 in the Capital One Orange Bowl in front of 65,157 on Monday night. Perine finished with 181 all-purpose yards, racking up 138 yards rushing on 13 carries and two touchdowns, while also compiling 43 yards receiving on five receptions, including a touchdown to earn Orange Bowl MVP honors. Down 36-21 with 2:32 remaining, Virginia (9-5) did its best to tie the game behind the play of quarterback Bryce Perkins, who finished with 323 yards passing and four touchdowns. Perkins connected with Hasise Dubois for his second touchdown of the night with 38 seconds left to cut Florida's lead to eight, but Freddie Swain recovered the onside kick to preserve the victory for the Gators. Florida (11-2) also got a solid game from quarterback Kyle Trask, who finished with 305 yards on 24-of-39 passing and a touchdown, while also scoring on a 1-yard run. With the win, Florida improves to 4-0 all time at the Orange Bowl, beating Georgia Tech 27-12 in 1967, Syracuse 31-10 in 1999 and Maryland 56-23 in 2002. The Gators also won the 2009 BCS National Championship in Miami, defeating Oklahoma 24-14. With Florida leading 27-21 earlier in the fourth quarter, Perine came up with a huge first-down run on 4th-and-1 to keep the drive alive. Trask then found Tyrie Cleveland across the middle for a 30-yard gain and a first down at the Cavaliers 24. Perine looked like he was headed fourth his fourth touchdown of the night as he raced into the end zone for a 24-yard run but was called out at the 1. On the next play, Trask kept it and scored from 1-yard out, giving the Gators a 33-21 lead after a failed two-point conversion. Perine got the show going on the Gators first series of the game as he took the first handoff of the game for a 61-yard touchdown run just 40 seconds into the game. On the Gators next series, Trask was intercepted by Nick Grant, to give the Cavaliers the ball at the Florida 34. Perkins found Terrell Jana in the back of the end zone for a 34-yard score to tie the game at 7. Florida marched right down the field as Perine scored his second touchdown of the game on a short pass from Trask, turning it up field for a 16-yard score, with just over five minutes to go in the first quarter. Virginia answered again as Perkins did his magic, scrambling on 3rd-and-8, before finding Hasise Dubois in the back of the end zone, who made a leaping grab for a 9-yard touchdown. Dubois had a game-high 10 catches for 83 yards and two scores to finish the season with 1,062 receiving yards. After a 23-yard field goal from Evan McPherson put the Gators up three, Florida got one more shot to score before halftime. Mullen decided to go for it on fourth-and-8 at the Virginia 35 as Freddie Swain caught an 11-yard reception to keep the drive alive. Four plays later, Perine scored his third touchdown, this time from 10 yards out, giving the Gators a 24-14 lead with 2:13 left before halftime. Perkins kept Virginia fighting, throwing his third touchdown or the game, hooking up with Joe Reed for a 7-yard score to cap a 75-yard, 6-play drive, cutting the lead to 27-21 with 13:05 remaining. But after Trask's 1-yard run, Florida freshman Kaiir Elam intercepted Perkins at the 3-yard line with just over five minutes to play.

2019 BELK BOWL

The 2019 Belk Bowl was played on December 31, 2019. It was the 18th edition of the Belk Bowl and played at Bank of America Stadium in Charlotte, North Carolina. The game was played between the Kentucky Wildcats from the Southeastern Conference (SEC) and the Virginia Tech Hokies from the Atlantic Coast Conference (ACC). This was the 20th meeting between the programs; Kentucky leads the all-time series, 11–6–2. This was Kentucky's first appearance in the Belk Bowl. This was Virginia Tech's second Belk Bowl; their 2016 team won the 2016 Belk Bowl over Arkansas, 35–24.

2019 BELK BOWL	Line	1	-	2	-	3	-	4	-	Final
Virginia Tech	-2.0	10	-	7	-	10	-	3	-	30
Kentucky	46.0	7	-	7	-	10	-	13	-	37

Scoring Summary
Virginia Tech – Johnson 54 yard Field goal
Kentucky – Bowden 25 yard run (Ruffolo kick)
Virginia Tech – Hazelton 18 yard pass from Hooker (Johnson kick)
Virginia Tech – Keene 6 yard pass from Hooker (Johnson kick)
Kentucky – Rodruiguez 2 yard run (Ruffolo kick)
Kentucky – Ruffolo 40 yard Field goal
Virginia Tech – McLease 43 yard run (Johnson kick)
Kentucky – Bowden 61 yard run (Ruffolo kick)
Virginia Tech – Johnson 40 yard Field goal
Virginia Tech – Johnson 27 yard Field goal
Kentucky – Ali 13 yard pass from Bowden (Ruffolo kick)
Kentucky – Hayes 28 yard fumble return

Associated Press Belk Bowl Game Summary – Lynn Bowden Jr. outplayed Virginia Tech all day with his feet. Then he closed them out with his arm. Bowden ran for 233 yards on 34 carries, and then tossed a 13-yard touchdown pass to Josh Ali with 15 seconds left as Kentucky rallied behind its remarkable receiver-turned-quarterback to beat Virginia Tech 37-30 on Tuesday in the Belk Bowl. Bowden ran for two touchdowns before leading an 18-play, 85-yard game-winning drive that took more than eight minutes off the clock. It ended with Ali getting open down the middle of the end zone. Bowden, who took over as Kentucky's quarterback after five games because of injuries, passed for 73 yards on 12 attempts. His rushing day was the biggest in a bowl game since Texas A&M's Johnny Manziel ran for 219 yards vs. Oklahoma in 2013. Bowden said he never would have believed his final play as a college player would be a touchdown pass to win a bowl game. But a pregame scuffle with Virginia Tech players -- in which TV footage showed Bowden apparently throwing a punch -- could have written a very different story for the dynamic quarterback. For two programs that hadn't met since 1987 -- long before anyone on either roster was born -- this one got testy before kickoff. Tussles broke out between players during pregame warmups, but officials didn't levy penalties or warnings for the actions. Wildcats coach Mark Stoops said if Bowden had been the starting quarterback since the beginning of the season, he would have been a Heisman Trophy candidate. Hendon Hooker threw for 110 yards and two touchdowns and Deshawn McClease ran for 126 yards and a score to lead the Hokies (8-5). Kentucky overcame two second-half turnovers by holding Virginia Tech to two field goals and a punt on its final three possessions. Bowden, the game's MVP, carried 13 times on the winning drive, converting a fourth down along the way to take a 31-30 lead. The Wildcats (8-5) added a final touchdown as time expired when Jordan Wright returned a failed lateral attempt by the Hokies 28 yards for a score. With both Western Kentucky and Louisville winning their bowl games, the state of Kentucky improved to 3-0 on the season.

2019 SUN BOWL

The 2019 Sun Bowl was played on December 31, 2019. It was the 86th edition of the Sun Bowl and played at Sun Bowl Stadium in El Paso, Texas. The game was played between the Arizona State Sun Devils (7-5) from the Pac-12 Conference and the Florida State Seminoles (6-6) from Atlantic Coast Conference (ACC). This was the fifth meeting between the programs; Florida State leads the all-time series, 3–1. The Sun Bowl is the 4th oldest Bowl Game, having started in 1935.

This was Arizona State's seventh Sun Bowl; the Sun Devils are 3–2–1 in prior appearances. This was Florida State's third Sun Bowl; in their previous two appearances, their 1954 team lost the 1955 Sun Bowl to Texas Western (now UTEP), 37–14, and their 1966 team lost the 1966 Sun Bowl to Wyoming, 28–20.

2019 SUN BOWL	Line	1	-	2	-	3	-	4	-	Final
Florida State	51.5	0	-	0	-	14	-	0	-	14
Arizona State	-3.0	3	-	6	-	0	-	11	-	20

Scoring Summary
Arizona State – Zendejas 40 yard Field goal
Arizona State – Zendejas 26 yard Field goal
Arizona State – Zendejas 24 yard Field goal
Florida State – Wilson 3 yard run (Aguayo kick)
Florida State – Terry 91 yard pass from Blackman (Aguayo kick)
Arizona State – Zendejas 34 yard Field goal
Arizona State – Harts 25 yard interception return (Zendejas kick)

El Paso Times Sun Bowl Game Summary – The most probable result of the 86th Tony the Tiger Sun Bowl is that it produced an improbable hero. In a strange and entertaining 20-14 Arizona State victory against Florida State in front of 42,412 fans on New Year's Eve, freshman safety Willie Harts, making his fourth start of the year, his Sun Devil defensive teammates and kicker Christian Zendejas filled that role. Harts' 25-yard interception return with 10:06 remaining in the game was Arizona State's lone touchdown and one of five turnovers they forced from FSU quarterback James Blackman. The Sun Devils, playing their first game under newly promoted defensive coordinator and El Pasoan Tony White, held the Seminoles to 2-of-15 on third-down conversions as they won in the postseason for the first time since the 2014 Sun Bowl. They did it without an offensive touchdown, as Zendejas was four-of-four on field goals. The biggest play was made by Harts, who had the fourth of the six turnovers forced by the defense. On third-and-4 from Florida State's 20, he jumped a route and took his clear path to the end zone. That was a fitting way for ASU to win, as they dominated for all but two possessions, a pair of 91-yard Seminole drives back-to-back late in the third quarter that in a span of 2:13 turned a 9-0 Sun Devil lead into a 14-9 hole. The second of those touchdowns was a 91-yard pass from Blackman to Tamorrion Terry that was the longest play in Sun Bowl history. ASU answered with its fourth Zendejas field goal on its next possession, then Harts' pick-6 and a two-point conversion to make it 20-14. From there the defense got a fourth-down stop on its own 34, a fourth interception of Blackman, this one by Khaylan Kearse-Thomas with 3:51 left. Arizona State forced a sixth turnover with 1:18 remaining on a Tyler Johnson fumble recovery. Johnson, an injury-plagued sophomore, announced his retirement immediately following the game, so the recovery that ended the game was also the end of his career. Florida State gained 470 yards, but the four interceptions and two fumbles rendered that moot. The turnovers, though, didn't quit coming and that proved too much for Florida State to overcome. Arizona State did on this Tuesday.

2019 LIBERTY BOWL

The 2019 Liberty Bowl was played on December 31, 2019. It was the 61st edition of the Liberty Bowl and played at Liberty Bowl Stadium in Memphis, Tennessee. The Liberty Bowl is the 8th oldest of all the Bowl Games having started in 1959. The game featured the Navy Midshipmen (10-2) of the American Athletic Conference going up against the Kansas State Wildcats (8-4) of the Big 12 Conference. This was the first time the two programs have met.

This was Navy's second Liberty Bowl; their 1981 team appeared in the 1981 Liberty Bowl, losing to Ohio State, 31–28. The Midshipmen improved from 3–10 in their prior season to 10–2 during the regular season, including their December 14 win in the Army–Navy Game. Their two losses were to Notre Dame and Memphis. Navy averages 360.82 yards rushing per game—49 yards more than any other FBS team.

This was Kansas State's second Liberty Bowl; their 2015 team appeared in the 2016 Liberty Bowl, losing to Arkansas, 45–23. The Wildcats improved from 5–7 in their prior season to 8–4, including handing No. 4 Oklahoma its only loss of the regular season. Kansas State is coached by Chris Klieman, who came to Kansas State after leading North Dakota State to four FCS titles. Kansas State ended the regular season ranked second in the Big 12, allowing only 21.5 points per game and had the third-best passing defense based on passing yardage. Jordan Brown led the offense with 698 yards in only 10 games; as a team, they averaged 189 rushing yards per game.

2019 LIBERTY BOWL	Line	1	-	2	-	3	-	4	-	Final
#21 Navy	-1.5	3	-	7	-	7	-	3	-	20
Kansas State	52.5	0	-	10	-	0	-	7	-	17

Scoring Summary
Navy – Nichols 21 yard Field goal
Kansas State – Brooks 66 yard punt return (Lynch kick)
Navy – Makekau 27 yard pass from Perry (Nichols kick)
Kansas State – Lynch 39 yard Field goal
Navy – Warren 20 yard run (Nichols kick)
Kansas State – Thompson 1 yard run (Lynch kick)
Navy – Nichols 23 yard Field goal

Associated Press Liberty Bowl Game Summary – Navy built the biggest turnaround of any team in college football this season by relying on the nation's most prolific rushing attack. So, naturally, the 21st-ranked Midshipmen won the AutoZone Liberty Bowl on Tuesday by completing a fourth-down halfback option pass in the final minute. CJ Williams' 41-yard completion to Chance Warren on fourth-and-3 gave Navy first-and-goal from the 5-yard line. After quarterback Malcolm Perry spiked the ball, Bijan Nichols kicked a 23-yard field goal with two seconds remaining to give Navy a 20-17 victory over Kansas State. Perry was named the Liberty Bowl most valuable player after rushing for 213 yards and throwing a touchdown pass. Perry ran for 2,017 yards this year to set a Football Bowl Subdivision record by a quarterback. The mark had been owned by Jordan Lynch, who ran for 1,920 yards for Northern Illinois in 2013. But the ball was only briefly in Perry's hands on the play that mattered most of all. Twenty-nine seconds remained when Navy (11-2) snapped the ball at the Kansas State 46. Perry pitched right to Williams, who found Warren racing wide open down the right side of the field. That big play left things up to Nichols, who missed a 38-yard field goal earlier in the fourth quarter. This time, Nichols stayed poised and made the kick even after Kansas State (8-5) called three straight timeouts to ice him. A most fitting way to end a bounce-back season. After going 3-10 last year, Navy matched the second-biggest season-to-season improvement in win-loss record of any team in Football Bowl Subdivision history. Hawaii went 9-4 in 1999 after finishing 0-12 in 1998. Navy tied a program record for wins. The Mids also went 11-2 in 2015. Navy outgained Kansas State 421-170 but wasted a couple of opportunities to put the game away. The Mids led 17-10 late in the third quarter when a holding penalty wiped out a 31-yard run by Perry that would have given them first-and-goal at the 2. Navy ended up punting. Nichols then sent his 38-yard field goal attempt wide left with 8:26 left in the game. Kansas State finally got its offense going at that point, as Skylar Thompson connected with Wykeen Gill on a 15-yard completion and a 42-yard pass on back-to-back plays. Those long gains set up Thompson's 1-yard sneak that tied the game with 5:14 left. Then came Navy's dramatic winning drive.

2019 ARIZONA BOWL

The 2019 Arizona Bowl was played on December 31, 2019. It was the 5th edition of the Arizona Bowl and played at Arizona Stadium in Tucson, Arizona. The game was played between the Wyoming Cowboys (7-5) from the Mountain West Conference (MWC) and the Georgia State Panthers (7-5) from the Sun Belt Conference. This was the first time that the two programs have met.

2019 ARIZONA BOWL	Line	1	-	2	-	3	-	4	-	Final
Georgia State	49.0	7	-	3	-	7	-	0	-	17
Wyoming	-7.0	17	-	7	-	14	-	0	-	38

Scoring Summary
Georgia State – Ellington 4 yard run (Wright kick)
Wyoming – Rothe 53 yard Field goal
Wyoming – Conway 18 yard pass from Williams (Rothe kick)
Wyoming – Valladay 8 yard pass from Williams (Rothe kick)
Georgia State – Wright 25 yard Field goal
Wyoming – Eberhardt 51 yard pass from Williams (Rothe kick)
Wyoming – Valladay 1 yard run (Rothe kick)
Georgia State – McCoy 44 yard pass from Ellington (Wright kick)
Wyoming – Williams 6 yard run (Rothe kick)

Associated Press Arizona Bowl Game Summary – Wyoming wanted to make the most of its bowl game after being passed over in the postseason last year. Giving a freshman quarterback his first career start didn't seem like the best approach to accomplishing that goal. Levi Williams handled it just fine and the Cowboys are riding off from the 2019 season with a bowl victory. Williams accounted for four scores, Xazavian Valladay ran for 204 yards and scored two touchdowns, and Wyoming rolled over Georgia State 38-17 in the Arizona Bowl on Saturday. The Cowboys won six games to become bowl eligible in 2018 yet found themselves at home watching TV after they weren't among the 78 teams to get bowl invites. Once at the 2019 Arizona Bowl, the Cowboys turned to Williams over Tyler Vander Waal, who entered the transfer portal but remained with the team for bowl practices. Williams did not shy away from the spotlight, hurting the Panthers with his arm and legs. He threw for 234 yards and three touchdowns, with 53 yards and a score on the ground for the Cowboys (8-5), who racked up 524 yards to end the season on a high note. Georgia State (7-6) jumped to a 10-0 lead in the first quarter but had a hard time stopping the big-play Cowboys. The Panthers also turned the ball over twice on downs deep in Wyoming's end in the second half and had a crucial roughing the punter penalty that led to Wyoming touchdown just before halftime. The miscues spoiled a gritty performance by Dan Ellington. Georgia State's senior quarterback accounted for 236 yards and two touchdowns despite playing with a torn right ACL. The Panthers got off to a fast start, marching quickly for Ellington's 4-yard TD run and going up 10-0 after a field goal. The Cowboys took over from there, scoring two touchdowns in less than two minutes. Williams threw an 18-yard TD to Austin Conway and, following an interception thrown by Ellington, he found Valladay on an 8-yard score to put Wyoming up 17-7. Early in the second quarter, Williams had an interception deep in Georgia State's end on an ill-advised back-foot throw. He made a similar throw just before halftime, but that one turned into a 51-yard touchdown when Ayden Eberhardt broke two tackles, weaved through Georgia State's secondary and broke another tackle diving into the end zone. The touchdown came after Georgia State was called for roughing the punter on a fourth and 16. Williams and Valladay connected on a 63-yard pass to open the second half and Valladay scored on a 1-yard run the next play. Georgia State responded quickly, pulling within 31-17 when Ellington hit Cornelius McCoy on a 44-yard TD. Wyoming kept gouging the Panthers' defense, though. Valladay broke two tackles on a 62-yard run, setting up Williams' 6-yard TD run around the right end.

2019 ALAMO BOWL

The 2019 Alamo Bowl was played on December 31, 2019. It was the 27th edition of the Alamo Bowl and played at the Alamodome in San Antonio, Texas. The game was played between the Texas Longhorns (7-5) of the Big 12 Conference and the Utah Utes (11-2) of the Pac-12 Conference. This was the second time the two programs have met; their prior meeting was in 1982, won by Texas. This was Texas' fourth Alamo Bowl, tying the Longhorns with Iowa and Oklahoma State for most Alamo Bowl appearances. Texas is 2–1 in prior Alamo Bowl appearances.

2019 ALAMO BOWL	Line	1	-	2	-	3	-	4	-	Final
#12 Utah	-7.0	0	-	0	-	3	-	7	-	10
Texas	56.0	3	-	7	-	14	-	14	-	38

Scoring Summary
Texas – Dicker 29 yard Field goal
Texas – Johnson 5 yard pass from Ehlinger (Dicker kick)
Texas – Ingram 11 yard pass from Ehlinger (Dicker kick)
Utah – Redding 32 yard Field goal
Texas – Ehlinger 6 yard run (Dicker kick)
Utah – Simpkins 4 yard pass from Huntley (Redding kick)
Texas – Duvernay 15 yard pass from Ehlinger (Dicker kick)
Texas – Ingram 49 yard run (Dicker kick)

Associated Press Alamo Bowl Game Summary – Sam Ehlinger passed for three touchdowns and ran for another, and Texas excised the frustrations of a disappointing regular season with a dominant 38-10 win over No. 12 Utah in the Valero Alamo Bowl on Tuesday night. After a 10-win season in 2018 set up a top-10 ranking to start 2019, Texas underwhelmed in a season the Longhorns expected to contend for the Big 12 title. Instead, they ended the year with both the offensive and defensive coordinators getting replaced. For one game at least, Texas (8-5) wiped all that away with a bruising and convincing win over a Utah team that only a month ago was on the verge of making the College Football Playoff. The Utes (11-3) didn't get there after they were swamped in the Pac-12 title game by Oregon and perhaps struggled to shake off the heartbreak of what could have been. Texas physically handled the Utes at the line of scrimmage. Longhorns linebacker Joseph Ossai had three sacks of quarterback Tyler Huntley and six total tackles for a loss. Texas also pounded out 231 yards on the ground against the nation's No. 1 rush defense, which had held 10 opponents under 70 yards. Texas' most important run came on a 31-yard burst by Ehlinger on third down on the drive that led to his 6-yard touchdown that made it 24-3 late in the third quarter. Keaontay Ingram later had a 49-yard TD burst on the sideline late in the fourth. Ehlinger finished with 201 yards passing. His first touchdown went to Collin Johnson, who missed six games this season because of a nagging hamstring injury. His last was to Devin Duvernay, who caught three passes for 92 yards.

2020 CITRUS BOWL

The 2020 Citrus Bowl was played on January 1, 2020. It was the 74th edition of the Citrus Bowl and played at Camping World Stadium in Orlando, Florida. The game featured the Michigan Wolverines from the Big Ten Conference and the Alabama Crimson Tide from the Southeastern Conference (SEC). This was their fifth meeting against each other, with the all-time series tied at 2–2. Alabama won the most recent meeting against Michigan 41–14 in the 2012 Cowboys Classic in Arlington, Texas.

After finishing the regular season 9–3 (6–3 in conference), the Wolverines were selected to their sixth Citrus Bowl appearance. The Wolverines are 4-1 in previous Citrus Bowl games. This will be their 48th bowl game appearance (21-26), the 11th highest total all-time among FBS schools. After finishing the regular season 10–2 (6–2 in conference), the Crimson Tide were selected to their third Citrus Bowl appearance. Alabama won their previous two appearances in the Citrus Bowl. This was Alabama's 71st Bowl Game appearance (41-26-3), the highest total among FBS schools.

2020 CITRUS BOWL	Line	1	-	2	-	3	-	4	-	Final
#17 Michigan	60.0	10	-	6	-	0	-	0	-	16
#9 Alabama	-8.0	7	-	7	-	7	-	14	-	35

Scoring Summary
Alabama – Jeudy 85 yard pass from Jones (Bulovas kick)
Michigan – Eubanks 7 yard pass from Patterson (Turner kick)
Michigan – Nordin 36 yard Field goal
Michigan – Nordin 42 yard Field goal
Alabama – Harris 9 yard run (Bulovas kick)
Michigan – Nordin 57 yard Field goal
Alabama – Smith 42 yard pass from Jones (Bulovas kick)
Alabama – Forristall 20 yard pass from Jones (Bulovas kick)
Alabama – Harris 2 yard run (Bulovas kick)

Associated Press Citrus Bowl Game Summary – Jerry Jeudy could have sat out Alabama's bowl game and still almost certainly would have been a first-round draft pick. He played instead -- and if this was his finale, his stock likely soared. Mac Jones threw three touchdown passes, Jeudy became the first Alabama player to top 200 receiving yards in a bowl game and the ninth-ranked Crimson Tide topped No. 17 Michigan 35-16 on Wednesday in the Citrus Bowl. Jones connected with Jeudy for an 85-yard score on Alabama's first snap, DeVonta Smith and Miller Forristall added touchdown grabs in the second half for the Crimson Tide (11-2), which trailed 16-14 at the break. Najee Harris ran for 136 yards and two touchdowns for Alabama. Jeudy finished with six catches for 204 yards. His previous career-high for yards was 147 set last season against Missouri, and the Alabama bowl record had stood for more than a half-century -- Ray Perkins had 178 yards against Nebraska in the 1967 Sugar Bowl. Jones -- who took over as Alabama's starter when Tua Tagovailoa was lost for the season with an injury in November -- completed 16 of 25 passes for 327 yards. Shea Patterson completed 17 of 37 passes for 233 yards and a touchdown for Michigan (9-4), which dropped its fourth consecutive bowl game. Quinn Nordin kicked three field goals for the Wolverines, including a school-record-tying 57-yarder to end the first half and give Michigan the lead. The Crimson Tide had two touchdown drives of 90 seconds or less -- Jeudy's score on Alabama's first play and a long go-ahead touchdown grab by Smith early in the third quarter. They were quick strike all season long, with 22 TD drives taking 1:30 or less and 38 TDs coming in 2:00 or less. And the last of those was the one that put this game away for Alabama with 10:01 remaining. Facing 3rd-and-11 from its own 8, Jones connected with Jeudy for 14 yards. On the next snap, Jones and Jeudy hooked up for 58 more yards. And the next snap was a 20-yard scoring pass to a wide-open Forristall.

2020 OUTBACK BOWL

The 2020 Outback Bowl was played on January 1, 2020. It was the 34th edition of the Outback Bowl and played at Raymond James Stadium in Tampa, Florida. The game was played between the Minnesota Golden Gophers (10-2) from the Big Ten Conference and the Auburn Tigers (9-3) from the Southeastern Conference (SEC). This will be the first meeting between the programs. This will be Auburn's fifth Outback Bowl; the Tigers are 2–2 in their previous appearances. This was the Golden Gophers first Outback Bowl appearance.

2020 OUTBACK BOWL	Line	1	-	2	-	3	-	4	-	Final
#16 Minnesota	53.5	10	-	14	-	0	-	7	-	31
#9 Auburn	-7.0	10	-	7	-	7	-	0	-	24

Scoring Summary
Auburn – Carlson 24 yard Field goal
Minnesota – Lantz 40 yard Field goal
Auburn – Igbinoghene 96 yard kickoff return (Carlson kick)
Minnesota – Ibrahim 16 yard run (Lantz kick)
Minnesota – Witham 1 yard pass from Green (Lantz kick)
Auburn – Cannella 37 yard pass from Nix (Carslon kick)
Minnesota – Johnson 2 yard pass from Morgan (Lantz kick)
Auburn – Whitlow 3 yard run (Carlson kick)
Minnesota – Johnson 73 yard pass from Morgan (Lantz kick)

Associated Press Outback Bowl Game Summary – With the clock winding down on a dominating performance in the Outback Bowl, Minnesota fans broke into a chant of "Row The Boat, Row The Boat, Row The Boat." The never-give-up mantra coach P.J. Fleck used to help change the culture of Golden Gophers football continues to inspire a program determined to recapture its glory days. Tyler Johnson had 12 receptions for 204 yards and two touchdowns to become the Gophers' career receiving leader and Minnesota outrushed the Tigers 215 yards to 56 while dominating time of possession to limit Auburn's ability to keep pace. Johnson broke Eric Decker's school record for receiving yards on his second catch of the day and became Minnesota's all-time leader for scoring receptions on a one-handed, 2-yard TD catch that put the Gophers (11-2) up 24-17 at halftime. The senior's 73-yard catch-and-run put his team ahead for good early in the fourth quarter. Minnesota, which began the season with nine straight victories before losing two of its last three to Big Ten rivals Iowa and Wisconsin, finished with more than 10 wins for the first time since 1904. Auburn (9-4) concluded a season in which all four of its losses came against opponents ranked in the Top 25. Tanner Morgan completed 19 of 29 passes for 278 yards, one interception and both TDs to Johnson, who finished with 3,305 receiving yards and 33 TD catches in his career. Receiver Seth Green tossed a 1-yard touchdown pass to Bryce Witham on fourth-and-inches midway through the second quarter. Noah Igbinoghene, whose mother and father were Olympic track and field athletes in Nigeria, returned a kickoff 96 yards for Auburn's first touchdown. Bo Nix threw a 37-yard TD pass to Sal Cannella and JaTarvious Whitlow scored 3-yard run that made it 24-24 heading into the fourth quarter. Morgan broke the tie with his second TD throw to Johnson, who posted the 16th 100-yard game of his career and caught at least one TD pass for the seventh straight game, tying another school record. The Gophers dominated on the ground, too, with Mohamed Ibrahim running for 140 yards on 20 carries. Nix was 17 of 26 for 176 yards, one TD and no interceptions.

2020 ROSE BOWL

The 2020 Rose Bowl Game was played on January 1, 2020, with kickoff scheduled for 5:00 p.m. EST (2:00 p.m. local PST) on ESPN. It was the 106th edition of the Rose Bowl Game. The game was played between Big Ten Conference runner-up Wisconsin and Pac-12 Conference champion Oregon.

Oregon secured a spot in the Rose Bowl with their win over the Utah Utes in the Pac-12 Championship Game. The Ducks enter the Rose Bowl with an 11–2 record (8–1 in conference). This will be Oregon's eighth appearance in the Rose Bowl, with a record of 3–4 in prior appearances; they last played in the 2015 edition against the Florida State Seminoles. **Wisconsin** finished their regular season schedule with an overall 10–2 record (7–2 in conference), then were defeated by Ohio State in the Big Ten Championship Game. The Badgers received an invitation to the Rose Bowl on December 8, 2019 and enter the game with an overall 10–3 record. Wisconsin is 3–6 in prior Rose Bowl appearances, most recently playing in the 2013 edition against the Stanford Cardinal.

2020 ROSE BOWL	Line	1	-	2	-	3	-	4	-	Final
#11 Wisconsin	-3.0	10	-	7	-	7	-	3	-	27
#7 Oregon	52.5	7	-	7	-	7	-	7	-	28

Scoring Summary
Oregon – Herbert 4 yard run (Lewis kick)
Wisconsin – Cruickshank 95 yard kickoff return (Larsh kick)
Wisconsin – Larsh 44 yard Field goal
Oregon – Herbert 5 yard run (Lewis kick)
Wisconsin – Cephus 11 yard pass from Coan (Larsh kick)
Oregon – Breeze 31 yard fumble return (Lewis kick)
Wisconsin – Stokke 2 yard run (Larsh kick)
Wisconsin – Larsh 27 yard Field goal
Oregon – Herbert 30 yard run (Lewis kick)

Associated Press Rose Bowl Game Summary – Justin Herbert faked a handoff and went on the run of his life in the fourth quarter of the Rose Bowl. Oregon's 6-foot-6 quarterback gracefully stiff-armed Wisconsin linebacker Jack Sanborn at the line of scrimmage. He surged downfield, found his blockers and sprinted to the green-painted end zone, even absorbing a very late hit from the frustrated Badgers as a reward. The Eugene kid who took over his beloved hometown team during its worst season of this century had just scored the decisive touchdown of the biggest win of his career. A few minutes and a couple of big passes later, the Ducks all celebrated amid confetti and roses at midfield after Herbert's final college game. Herbert scored his third rushing touchdown of the 106th Rose Bowl on that thrilling 30-yard run with 7:41 to play Wednesday night, and No. 7 Oregon held off No. 11 Wisconsin 28-27 to win its third straight trip to the Granddaddy of Them All. Herbert passed for just 138 yards without a touchdown, and Oregon (12-2) managed just 204 yards of offense -- the fewest by any Rose Bowl team in 40 years. The Ducks still managed to win yet another frenetic edition of this venerated bowl game, surviving six lead changes and big special-teams mistakes by both schools. While the offense sputtered, the Ducks scored 21 points off the Badgers' four turnovers, including Brady Breeze's early 31-yard fumble return for a TD off a botched punt. And on the next snap after Breeze forced another fumble in the fourth quarter, Herbert rambled through the Wisconsin defense for that 30-yard score in what's sure to be the signature moment of the four-year starter's career. Winston's praise aside, Herbert had only 10 rushing touchdowns in the first 41 starts of his career. He turned into a big-play ball-carrier on Arroyo Seco's hallowed ground, and Oregon improbably relied on its quarterback's long legs to grind out a landmark victory under second-year head coach Mario Cristobal, Herbert's third coach in four years. Herbert scored on runs of 4 and 5 yards in the first half, stiff-arming Wisconsin defenders on both runs. After his go-ahead TD, Herbert got back to what he normally does best: He made a key 12-yard throw to Mycah Pittman for a first down with 1:51 to play, and his 28-yard throw to Juwan Johnson with 1:03 left allowed the Ducks to run out the clock. Three years after coach Mark Helfrich was fired when the Ducks went 4-8 in Herbert's freshman season, Oregon held on to cap a Pac-12 championship campaign with its 12th win in 13 games and the fourth Rose Bowl victory in school history. Aron Cruickshank returned an early kickoff 95 yards for a touchdown for the Big Ten runner-up Badgers (10-4), but they lost in their fourth consecutive trip to Pasadena over the last 10 years, including two losses to Oregon. Jonathan Taylor rushed for 94 yards and Quintez Cephus caught seven passes for 59 yards and a score, but Wisconsin quarterback Jack Coan's offense couldn't capitalize on its whopping advantages in time of possession (38:03-21:57) and total yards (322-204). Herbert scored his first TD on the Ducks' drive from the kickoff in 68-degree temperatures on another postcard-perfect New Year's Day in Pasadena, but Cruickshank took the ensuing kick straight down the Oregon sideline for an electrifying score and a rarity in the Rose Bowl. The kickoff return was just the second for a touchdown in Wisconsin's lengthy bowl history, but just the third in 106 Rose Bowls -- and the first in 17 years. Oregon got a break right after halftime when Wisconsin punter Anthony Lotti caught the snap but dropped the ball on the ground instead of kicking it under pressure. Breeze alertly picked it up and sprinted for the go-ahead score. The Badgers responded with a drive capped by Mason Stokke's 2-yard scoring run, and they went up 27-21 on a field goal with 12:09 to play. But Breeze forced another fumble by Wisconsin's Danny Davis with a big hit, and Herbert took the next snap on his 30-yard TD run.

2020 SUGAR BOWL

The 2020 Sugar Bowl was played on January 1, 2020 between the Georgia Bulldogs (11-2) and Baylor Bears (11-2). It was the 86th edition of the Sugar Bowl and played at the Mercedes-Benz Superdome in New Orleans, Louisiana.

Georgia earned the SEC spot in the game when conference champion LSU was selected for the College Football Playoff. Similarly, Baylor earned the Big 12 spot as a result of Oklahoma's selection to the playoff. This was the fifth all-time meeting between Baylor and Georgia; the Bulldogs won each of the prior four meetings, most recently winning in 1989, 15–3. **Baylor** secured their berth as the Big 12 runners-up, since the conference champion, Oklahoma, was selected as one of the four teams in the College Football Playoff. This was Baylor's second Sugar Bowl, and their first since their 1956 team won the 1957 edition over Tennessee, 13–7. Georgia secured their berth as the SEC runners-up, since the conference champion, LSU, was selected as one of the four teams in the College Football Playoff. This was Georgia's eleventh Sugar Bowl (the third-most of any team); the Bulldogs have a 4–6 record in prior editions of the bowl. It will also be Georgia's second consecutive Sugar Bowl, following their 2018 team's loss to Texas in the 2019 edition, 28–21.

2020 SUGAR BOWL	Line	1	-	2	-	3	-	4	-	Final
#8 Baylor	44.0	0	-	0	-	14	-	0	-	14
#5 Georgia	-3.5	3	-	16	-	7	-	0	-	26

Scoring Summary
Georgia – Blankenship 24 yard Field goal
Georgia – Pickens 27 yard pass from Fromm (Blankenship kick)
Georgia – Blankenship 31 yard Field goal
Georgia – Landers 16 yard pass from Fromm (2 point pass failed)
Baylor – Mims 12 yard pass from Brewer (Mayers kick)
Georgia – White 13 yard run (Blankenship kick)
Baylor – Brewer 1 yard run (Mayers kick)

Associated Press Sugar Bowl Game Summary – Georgia freshman receiver George Pickens left behind his regrettable ending to the regular season and put the rest of college football on notice that he will be an exceedingly tough cover in 2020. Pickens caught 12 passes for 175 yards and a touchdown, and No. 5 Georgia defeated eighth-ranked Baylor 26-14 in the Sugar Bowl on Wednesday night. Baylor quarterback Charlie Brewer, coming back from a concussion in the Big 12 title game on Dec. 7, was sidelined again in the fourth quarter when the back of his head appeared to hit the turf hard as he was taken down by two defenders while going out of bounds. Baylor coach Matt Rhule said Brewer did not appear concussed this time. Medical staff was concerned about possible spinal and neck injuries. Rhule expected Brewer to be monitored overnight but added that early indications were the injuries were not career threatening. Travon Walker was penalized for a late hit, giving Baylor a first down, but the drive stalled on a sack of backup Jacob Zeno on fourth down with five minutes to go and Baylor down 12. Jake Fromm completed 20 of 30 passes for 250 yards and two touchdowns without an interception for Georgia (12-2), which lost the Sugar Bowl to Texas last season. Zamir White carried 18 times for 92 yards and a touchdown, and Matt Landers caught his first career TD on a 16-yard pass. Georgia defensive back Richard LeCounte intercepted two passes, the second sealing the victory in the final minutes. Pickens was selected the game's most outstanding player. Brewer completed 21 of 41 passes for 211 yards and one touchdown to Denzel Mims. After Georgia led 19-0 at halftime, Baylor (11-3) showed signs of mounting a comeback on the opening series of the second half with a scoring drive dominated by Mims. He had catches of 40 and 8 yards before his 12-yard touchdown grab trimmed the Bulldogs' lead to 19-7. Mims also surpassed 1,000 yards receiving for the season on the drive. The Bears quickly forced a Georgia punt and moved back across midfield when momentum suddenly changed. Linebacker Azeez Ojulari sacked and stripped Brewer on fourth-and-4 and Walker recovered on the Baylor 47. The Bulldogs capitalized with a touchdown drive extended by a fake field goal in which holder Jake Camarda ran off tackle for 6 yards on fourth-and-2. White finished the series with a tackle-breaking 13-yard run to the pylon to make it 26-7. Brewer's short, second-effort TD run late in the third quarter trimmed Georgia's lead, but Baylor got no closer. Pickens' 46-yard catch deep down the middle on a flea flicker set up the first points of the game on Rodrigo Blankenship's field goal. The Bulldogs widened the lead on Fromm's 27-yard fade pass to the Pickens in the left side of the end zone. Georgia was without about a dozen regulars, including three starting offensive linemen. Some players were hurt while others sat out to preserve their health for the NFL draft. Meanwhile, top running back D'Andre Swift saw only limited action because of an ailing shoulder.

2020 BIRMINGHAM BOWL

The 2020 Birmingham Bowl was held on January 2, 2020. It was the 14th edition of the Birmingham Bowl and played at historic Legion Field in Birmingham, Alabama.

The game featured the Boston College Eagles (6-6) of the Atlantic Coast Conference (ACC) going up against the Cincinnati Bearcats (10-3) of the American Athletic Conference (American). This will be the eighth overall meeting between the two programs; the Eagles lead the all-time series, 4–3. This was Cincinnati's second Birmingham Bowl; their 2007 team won the then-PapaJohns.com Bowl over Southern Miss, 31–21.

2020 BIRMINGHAM BOWL	Line	1	-	2	-	3	-	4	-	Final
Boston College	54.0	0	-	0	-	6	-	0	-	6
#23 Cincinnati	-7.0	7	-	10	-	7	-	14	-	38

Scoring Summary
Cincinnati – Ridder 13 yard run (Crosa kick)
Cincinnati – Crosa 32 yard Field goal
Cincinnati – Ridder 14 yard run (Crosa kick)
Cincinnati – Mbodj 8 yard pass from Ridder (Crosa kick)
Boston College – Sebastian 67 yard Blcoked Field goal return (2 point pass failed)
Cincinnati – Ridder 13 yard run (Crosa kick)
Cincinnati – Montgomery 1 yard run (Crosa kick)

Associated Press Birmingham Bowl Game Summary – Desmond Ridder and No. 23 Cincinnati wrote a much happier ending to their season. Ridder ran for 105 yards and three touchdowns and threw a scoring pass to lead No. 23 Cincinnati to a 38-6 victory over Boston College on Thursday in the lightning-delayed Birmingham Bowl. It was a cathartic win for a team coming off back-to-back losses to No. 15 Memphis, including in the American Athletic Conference championship game. They didn't have to worry about that possibility for long, dominating after the delay of about 1 1/2 hours midway through the first quarter. The Bearcats (11-3) reached 11 wins for the second straight season and fourth in program history. The Eagles (6-7) were outgained 459-164 in total yards to finish a turbulent postseason. Coach Steve Addazio was fired after seven seasons and star tailback A.J. Dillon declared for the NFL draft and skipped the bowl game. Dillon was clearly missed. Wide receivers coach Rich Gunnell led the team through the bowl game, while newly hired Jeff Hafley was on hand as a spectator after finishing his duties as Ohio State's co-defensive coordinator. Boston College got its only points on special teams. Mike Palmer blocked a field goal and Brandon Sebastian scooped it up and returned it 67 yards in the third quarter. Ridder had two 13-yard scoring runs and a 14-yarder, setting a Cincinnati bowl record for rushing and total TDs. He had 21 carries and passed for 95 yards with an 8-yard score to Malick Mbodj before leaving the game early in the fourth quarter. Michael Warren Jr. also had 105 yards on 21 carries. Boston College couldn't generate any consistent offense and clearly missed Dillon. Other than two big plays in the first half, the Eagles produced just 32 yards on 27 plays. David Bailey gained 28 yards on eight carries in Dillon's place. Cincinnati was dominant on both sides of the ball. The programs only other 11-win seasons came under Brian Kelly in 2008 and 2009. The defense set up a touchdown with Ethan Tucky's forced fumble.

2020 TAXSLAYER GATOR BOWL

The 2020 Gator Bowl was played on January 2, 2020. It was the 75th edition of the Gator Bowl and played at TIAA Bank Field in Jacksonville, Florida. The game was played between the Tennessee Volunteers (7-5) from the Southeastern Conference (SEC) and the Indiana Hoosiers (8-4) from the Big Ten Conference. This was the second meeting between the programs; they met in the 1988 Peach Bowl (January), won by Tennessee, 27–22. This was Tennessee's seventh Gator Bowl; the Volunteers have a record of 4–2 in their previous appearances.

2020 GATOR BOWL	Line	1	-	2	-	3	-	4	-	Final
Indiana	56.0	0	-	3	-	16	-	3	-	22
Tennessee	-3.5	0	-	6	-	3	-	14	-	23

Scoring Summary
Tennessee – Cimaglia 23 yard Field goal
Tennessee – Cimaglia 32 yard Field goal
Indiana – Justus 24 yard Field goal
Indiana – Ramsey 1 yard run (Justus kick)
Indiana – Johnson 63 yard interception return (Kick failed)
Tennessee – Cimaglia 43 yard Field goal
Indiana – Justus 49 yard Field goal
Indiana – Justus 30 yard Field goal
Tennessee – Crouch 1 yard run (Cimaglia kick)
Tennessee – Gray 16 ayrd run (Cimaglia kick)

Associated Press Gator Bowl Game Summary – Tennessee sure knows how to get out of a huge hole. The Volunteers scored twice in a 30-second span late, using an onside kick to help escape a 13-point deficit, and then held on to stun Indiana 23-22 in the Gator Bowl on Thursday night. The rally was indicative of Tennessee's season, which started 1-4 and ended with six consecutive wins. Pruitt was talking about the season. He could have been talking about the game. The Hoosiers (8-5) looked to be in control in the second half after scoring two touchdowns in a 1:03 span, the second one coming on Jamar Johnson's 63-yard interception return, and later adding a pair of field goals. Indiana was up 22-9 before Tennessee shocked most of the nearly 62,000 fans on hand. Quavaris Crouch scored on a 1-yard plunge and then fellow running back Eric Gray recovered a surprise onside kick that barely went the mandatory 10 yards. Gray scored from 16 yards out a few plays later to put the Vols on top for good. Gray was named the game's Most Valuable Player. Logan Justus missed an extra point in the third quarter that turned out to be costly and was wide right on a 52-yard field goal attempt with 2:12 remaining. Justus' kick had the distance but sailed just outside the right upright. Tennessee punted with 1:02 remaining, but Indiana failed to get back into field goal range. Tennessee receiver Jauan Jennings, who was suspended for the first half for stepping on an opponent in the regular-season finale, had to wait until the fourth quarter to touch the ball. Jennings had receptions of 22 and 5 yards, setting up the first of the two late touchdowns. Indiana Coach Tom Allen had a game-management issue that might have cost his team points. The Hoosiers moved the ball to the 6-

yard line in the waning seconds of the first half, but instead of calling timeout, Allen had Peyton Ramsey line up and spike the ball with 3 seconds remaining. They could have used their final timeout much earlier, taken a shot into the end zone and still had time for a field goal.

2020 FAMOUS IDAHO POTATO BOWL

The 2020 Famous Idaho Potato Bowl was played on January 3, 2020. It was the 23rd edition of the Famous Idaho Potato Bowl and played at Albertsons Stadium in Boise, Idaho. The game was played between the Ohio Bobcats (6-6) from the Mid-American Conference (MAC) and the Nevada Wolf Pack (7-5) from the Mountain West Conference (MWC). This was the first meeting between the two programs. This was Ohio's second Famous Idaho Potato Bowl; their 2011 team won the 2011 Famous Idaho Potato Bowl over Utah State, 24–23. This was Nevada's third Famous Idaho Potato Bowl; the Wolf Pack are seeking their first victory in the bowl after losses in the 2006 MPC Computers Bowl (to Miami (FL)) and the 2008 Humanitarian Bowl (to Maryland), when the bowl operated under different names.

2020 Famous Idaho Potato BOWL	Line	1	-	2	-	3	-	4	-	Final
Ohio	-10.0	3	-	17	-	10	-	0	-	30
Nevada	62.0	3	-	6	-	0	-	12	-	21

Scoring Summary
Nevada – Talton 51 yard Field goal
Ohio – Zervos 29 yard Field goal
Ohio – Ross 12 yard run (Zervos kick)
Nevada – Talton 38 yard Field goal
Ohio – Rourke 35 yard run (Zervos kick)
Ohio – Zervos 33 yard Field goal
Nevada – Talton 33 yard Field goal
Ohio – Zervos 26 yard Field goal
Ohio – Tuggle 2 yard run (Zervos kick)
Nevada – Cooks 8 yard pass from Strong (Kick blocked)
Nevada – Lee 1 yard run (2 point pass failed)

Assocaited Press Famous Idaho Potato Bowl Game Summary – Ohio quarterback Nathan Rourke is projected to be the top quarterback taken in the Canadian Football League draft this spring. He's pretty good at the American collegiate version, too. Rourke, from Oakville, Ontario, accounted for 231 yards of offense and ran for a touchdown to help Ohio beat Nevada 30-21 on Friday in the Famous Idaho Potato Bowl. Ohio (7-6) rebounded from a 1/3 start for its fifth straight winning season under Coach Frank Solich. The 75-year-old former Nebraska coach received a two-year contract extension this week. Nevada (7-6), which dismissed defensive coordinator Jeff Casteel and two other defensive position coaches at the end of the regular season, didn't find much of an answer for Ohio's high-powered offense until the fourth quarter. The Wolfpack also were missing three key defensive starters, suspended for their participation in a fight in a loss to rival UNLV in the regular-season finale. Rourke, who finished with 144 yards passing and 87 yards rushing along with one touchdown, garnered MVP honors, but was uninterested in talking about it. When asked about his award, he quickly pivoted to talk about the defense and their stand at the end of the game. Later, Rourke apologized for never winning a MAC championship during his three years at the school. Rourke is also thinking beyond the CFL, hoping to fulfill his dream of playing in the NFL, even if it's not a traditional route. Rourke might be overlooked in the NFL draft, but he finished just one touchdown shy of joining an elite trio of college quarterbacks who threw for 50 or more touchdowns and rushed for 50 or more in their career-Lamar Jackson, Tim Tebow, and Colin Kaepernick, all of whom made it to the NFL. And Rourke, unlike Tebow and Kapernick, achieved his stats in only three seasons. Ohio raced to a 20-9 lead and scored the first 10 points of the third quarter before holding off Nevada's late rally. The Bobcats lost leading rusher O'Shaan Allison late in the first quarter with an undisclosed injury. De'Montre Tuggle took over, rushing for 97 yards and a touchdown to spark a ground attack that finished with 285 yards on 50 carries spread among five players. Rourke tied Kareem Wilson's school record for career rushing touchdowns of 49. Wilson played from 1995-98.

2020 ARMED FORCES BOWL

The 2020 Armed Forces Bowl was played on January 4, 2020. It was the 17th edition of the Armed Forces Bowl and played at Amon G. Carter Stadium in Fort Worth, Texas. The game featured the Tulane Green Wave (6-6) of the American Athletic Conference (American) against the Southern Miss Golden Eagles (7-5) of Conference USA (C-USA). It was the 31st all-time meeting between the two programs, with the Golden Eagles leading the all-time series, 23–7. From 1996 to 2013, Southern Miss and Tulane were both in Conference USA as charter members, before Tulane left to join the American Athletic Conference in

2014. Since 1999, a bell trophy began has been awarded to the winner of their rivalry game, making it the Battle for the Bell. The regular season rivalry is set to resume in 2022; it is currently unclear whether possession of the Bell will be on the line in this bowl game.

2020 ARMED FORCES BOWL	Line	1	-	2	-	3	-	4	-	Final
Southern Mississippi	57.5	13	-	0	-	0	-	0	-	13
Tulane	-7.5	0	-	6	-	24	-	0	-	30

Scoring Summary
Southern Mississippi – Watkins 44 yard pass from Abraham (Kick failed)
Southern Mississippi – Abraham 3 yard run (Stein kick)
Tulane – Glover 31 yard Field goal
Tulane – Glover 31 yard Field goal
Tulane – McClesky 52 yard pass from McMillan (Glover kick)
Tulane – Glover 36 yard Field goal
Tulane – Robertson 7 yard pass from McMillan (Glover kick)
Tulane – Jones 20 yard pass from McMillan (Glover kick)

Associated Press Armed Forces Bowl Game Summary – Justin McMillan won two Texas state championships playing for a high school only about 35 miles away from where he played his last game for Tulane. Both of his parents served in the Army. The Armed Forces Bowl provided a storybook finish for his college career. McMillan, who started for the Green Wave for two seasons after transferring from LSU, threw three touchdown passes in the third quarter as Tulane rallied for a 30-13 win while renewing a rivalry against Southern Mississippi on Saturday. Tulane (7-6) finished consecutive seasons with bowl wins for the first time in school history. The Golden Eagles (7-6) took a 13-0 lead after Jack Abraham threw a touchdown pass and ran for a score on their first drives, but the quarterback took a hard shot on his last snap before halftime and didn't play again. They also lost top running back De'Michael Harris to a hamstring injury in the first half. Tulane tied the game at 13-all on its first possession after halftime, when McMillan threw a 52-yard TD pass to Jalen McCleskey. The Green Wave certainly did after halftime, when Southern Miss struggled without two of its offensive threats. McMillan had a high-stepping 18-yard run to set up Merek Glover's third field goal, a tiebreaking 36-yarder, before TD passes to Jacob Robertson (7 yards) and a wide-open Amare Jones (20 yards) on the next two drives. After only 22 yards passing at halftime, McMillan was 9-of-10 for 193 yards in the second half. Abraham, only the third Golden Eagles quarterback with a 3,000-yard passing season, threw 44-yard touchdown pass to Quez Watkins and ran 3 yards for another score for the 13-0 lead. But Abraham took a shot on a blitz by linebacker Lawrence Graham and fell hard on his shoulder on a third-down incompletion in the final minute of the first half. Abraham never returned, though he was still in uniform on the sideline after halftime. The Green Wave not only got the Armed Forces Bowl trophy, but they also won the "Battle for the Bell" and took home that trophy. While their campuses are only about 115 miles apart, both teams traveled more than 500 miles for their first meeting since 2010.

2020 LENDING TREE BOWL

The 2020 LendingTree Bowl was played on January 6, 2020. It was the 21st edition of the LendingTree Bowl and played at Ladd-Peebles Stadium in Mobile, Alabama. The game was played between the Mid-American Conference (MAC) champions Miami RedHawks (8-5) and the Louisiana Ragin' Cajuns (10-3) from the Sun Belt Conference. This was the third meeting between the two programs; the RedHawks have won both previous meetings.

This was Miami's third LendingTree Bowl. The RedHawks have won both of their previous appearances; the 2003 GMAC Bowl (over Louisville) and the 2011 GoDaddy.com Bowl (over Middle Tennessee), when the bowl operated under different names. The Cajuns come off a record-breaking year at 10-3 and Sun Belt West Champions, losing to Appalachian State 45-38. This was the Ragin' Cajuns' seventh bowl game in ten years and just nine overall, but their first in the LendingTree Bowl. The Cajuns, with new head coach Mark Hudspeth, competed in four consecutive New Orleans Bowls. In 2011 New Orleans Bowl, the 8-4 Cajuns beat San Diego State 32-30 on a game-winning field goal. In the 2012 New Orleans Bowl, the 8-4 Cajuns defeated East Carolina 43-34. In the 2013 edition, the 8-4 Cajuns competed against the hometown Tulane Green Wave, winning 24-21. In the 2014, the last consecutive year, the 8-4 Cajuns would defeat Nevada 16-3. Ultimately, the Cajuns would have to vacate the 2011 and 2013 wins due to NCAA violations. In 2016, the 6-6 Cajuns would once again play in the New Orleans Bowl, losing to Southern Miss 21-28, one of the closes games in rivalry history. In 2018, the Cajuns hired a new head coach, Billy Napier, who would lead the 7-6 Cajuns to the Sun Belt West Divisional Championship and the 2018 Cure Bowl, losing to Tulane 24-41.

2020 MOBILE ALABAMA BOWL	Line	1	-	2	-	3	-	4	-	Final
Miami-Ohio	55.0	0	-	7	-	3	-	7	-	17
Louisiana-Lafayette	-16.0	0	-	10	-	14	-	3	-	27

Scoring Summary
Miami-Ohio – Bester 5 yard run (Sloman kick)
UL-Lafayette – Artigue 33 yard Field goal
UL-Lafayette – Mitchell 2 yard run (Artigue kick)
UL-Lafayette – Bradley 9 ayrd pass from Lewis (Artigue kick)
Miami-Ohio – Sloman 39 yard Field goal
UL-Lafayette – Bradley 12 ayrd pass from Lewis (Artigue kick)
Miami-Ohio – Bester 1 yard run (Sloman kick)
UL-Lafayette – Artigue 38 yard Field goal

Associated Press Lending Tree Bowl Game Summary – Levi Lewis and Louisiana-Lafayette added one more win to the most successful season in school history. Lewis threw two touchdown passes to Ja'Marcus Bradley, and the Ragin' Cajuns beat Miami of Ohio 27-17 in the LendingTree Bowl on Monday night. Louisiana-Lafayette earned its first bowl win since 2014. It finished with a school-record 11 victories, two more than the previous mark. Lewis was 19 for 26 for 246 yards for the Ragin' Cajuns (11-3), and Bradley finished with seven receptions for 88 yards. Lewis also had eight carries for a game-high 62 yards. Lewis found Bradley for a 9-yard score with 10:51 left in the third quarter. They connected for a 12-yard TD with 2:26 left in the third, lifting Louisiana-Lafayette to a 24-10 lead. Elijah Mitchell also had a 2-yard touchdown run for the Ragin' Cajuns, who earned their first bowl win outside their home state since 1944. Miami (8-6) pulled within seven on Jaylon Bester's 1-yard touchdown run with 11:35 left, but Stevie Artigue kicked a 38-yard field goal to help Louisiana-Lafayette close out the victory. The Ragin' Cajuns also had a big goal-line stand, stopping the RedHawks four times from inside the 2-yard line. Brett Gabbert was 22 for 31 for 248 yards for Miami, and Jack Sorenson had 10 receptions for 107 yards. Gabbert is the younger brother of NFL quarterback Blaine Gabbert.

2020 CFP CHAMPIONSHIP GAME

The 2020 College Football Playoff National Championship was played at Mercedes-Benz Superdome in New Orleans, Louisiana, on January 13, 2020. The game was between the LSU Tigers of the Southeastern Conference (SEC) and the Clemson Tigers of the Atlantic Coast Conference (ACC). With both teams entering the bowl with 14–0 records, the winning team's 15–0 record will equal that of the 2018 Clemson Tigers, and the champion will become only the second team to finish 15–0 in a single season since the 1897 Penn Quakers. LSU defeated Georgia in the SEC Championship Game on December 7 and received a bid to the Peach Bowl with the release of final CFP rankings on December 8. The Tigers defeated Oklahoma, 63–28, in the CFP semifinal Peach Bowl on December 28, which was LSU's first CFP semifinal appearance. The Tigers enter the championship game with a 14–0 record (8–0 in conference). LSU's most recent loss was to Texas A&M on November 24, 2018; a seven overtime contest. This is LSU's first appearance in a CFP National Championship game; their last national championship game appearance was a loss to Alabama in the 2012 BCS National Championship Game.

Clemson defeated Virginia in the ACC Championship Game on December 7 and received a bid to the Fiesta Bowl with the release of final CFP rankings on December 8. On December 28, the Tigers defeated Ohio State in the CFP semifinal Fiesta Bowl, 29–23. Clemson also enters the championship game with a 14–0 record (8–0 in conference). The Tigers' most recent loss was to Alabama in the CFP semifinal Sugar Bowl on January 1, 2018. Including national championship contests, this is Clemson's ninth overall CFP game; they have a 6–2 record in prior CFP games, and are the defending champions, having defeated Alabama in the 2019 CFP National Championship.

2020 CFP CHAMPIONSHIP	Line	1	-	2	-	3	-	4	-	Final
#3 Clemson	66.5	7	-	10	-	8	-	0	-	25
#1 LSU	-4.0	7	-	21	-	7	-	7	-	42

Scoring Summary
Clemson – Lawrence 1 yard run (Potter kick)
LSU – Chase 52 yard pass from Burrow (Cade kick)
Clemson – Potter 52 yard Field goal
Clemson – Higgins 35 yard run (Potter kick)
LSU – Burrow 3 yard run (Cade kick)
LSU – Chase 14 yard pass from Burrow (Cade kick)
LSU – Moss 6 yard pass from Burrow (Cade kick)
Clemson – Etienne 3 yard run (2 point pass good)
LSU – Moss 4 yard pass from Burrow (Cade kick)
LSU – Marshall 24 yard pass from Burrow (Cade kick)

Game Summary – LSU won the coin toss, and deferred possession to the second half, giving Clemson the opening kickoff. After a promising start to their opening drive, Clemson was forced to punt on 4th-and-23, giving LSU the ball on their own 7-yard-line. LSU's opening drive was far less productive, as they punted after three plays totaling a net loss of four yards. Clemson opened their ensuing drive on the LSU 45. A three-and-out followed, but the Clemson punt coverage team again came up big, downing the ball at the 4-yard-line. While the next LSU drive resulted in positive yards, a punt was the result, and Clemson took over at their own 33 and scored in five plays, opening the scoring with a Trevor Lawrence rushing touchdown 8:26 into the game. LSU opened their next drive with a touchback, and recorded a first down for the first time, but again punted, giving Clemson the ball at their own 25; Clemson punted right back, and LSU took over at their own 29. On this drive, the LSU offense showed up to drive seventy yards in just 4 plays, capped by a long Joe Burrow pass to wide receiver Ja'Marr Chase, tying the game at seven with 2:20 remaining in the opening quarter. Clemson had possession for the remainder of the quarter and made it to the LSU 42 before time expired.

Clemson ran three additional plays in the second quarter before settling for a 52 yard field goal, converted by kicker B.T. Potter, giving them a 10–7 edge. Following LSU's fourth punt of the evening, Clemson started with their worst field position yet, as they got the ball at their own 4. This did not deter the Clemson offense, as they covered the ninety-six yards ahead of them in only four plays, capping the touchdown drive with a long run by Tee Higgins; this extended Clemson's lead to ten. LSU responded with a quick drive of their own, scoring in five plays to narrow the lead to three. Clemson's next drive ended in a punt, and LSU capitalized with another long touchdown drive to take their first lead of the contest, by four, with just over five minutes until halftime. Clemson was unable to respond on offense; they punted, and LSU got the ball on their own 5-yard-line. Joe Burrow and the LSU offense continued to build their momentum with their third consecutive touchdown drive of 75-plus yards to increase the lead to 11 heading into halftime.

LSU opened the second half by receiving the kickoff; their ensuing drive resulted in a three-and-out, and Clemson took over on the 50-yard-line. For the first time in nearly an entire quarter, the Clemson offense found the end zone, as Travis Etienne capped a 6 play drive with his first touchdown of the day. Trevor Lawrence completed a pass to Amari Rodgers for the two-point conversion, cutting the LSU lead to three points. Joe Burrow's offense was again unable to produce on offense, and the second half (as did the first half) began with two three-and-outs for LSU. Clemson's next drive finished similarly, as a punt followed four plays totaling 14 yards. LSU took over on their own 32. On the fifth play of LSU's ensuing drive, Clemson starting MLB James Skalski was ejected from the game for a targeting penalty; LSU scored on the next play on a touchdown pass from Burrow to Thaddeus Moss (one that gave Burrow sole possession of the FBS record for touchdown passes in a season with 59) to increase their lead to ten. Clemson couldn't produce on their next drive and punted for the seventh time; LSU got the ball on their own 32. They drove to the Clemson 27 before attempting a 45-yard field goal, which Cade York missed wide right. Lawrence and the Clemson offense were unable to capitalize on the mistake, however; they went three-and-out and punted to the LSU 43. The quarter expired several plays later; LSU entered the fourth quarter leading 35–25.

LSU came out firing in the fourth quarter; they scored for just the second time this half on a Joe Burrow pass to Terrace Marshall Jr., his first receiving touchdown of the contest. For the fourth drive in a row, Clemson punted; the ball was downed at the LSU 10. After taking 5:24 off the clock, LSU punted the ball back, and Clemson took over with just under five minutes left, on their own 15. However, three plays later, Trevor Lawrence fumbled at the end of his rush; it was recovered by LSU's Derek Stingley Jr. with 3:53 to go. LSU was able to run the remaining time off the clock and finish the season as undefeated national champions

Other Paperback Books available from Steve's Football Bible LLC

www.stevesfootballbible.com

www.ingramcontent.com/pod-product-compliance
Lightning Source LLC
Chambersburg PA
CBHW082144230426
43672CB00015B/2840